ISBN 978-0-265-69200-4
PIBN 10457590

The Descendants

OF

OF YARMOUTH, MASS.

1638-1888.

WITH AN

APPENDIX

CONTAINING SOME NOTICES OF

By SAMUEL P. MAY,

Mem. N. E. Hist. Gen. Society.

ALBANY, N. Y.:

JOEL MUNSELL'S SONS, PUBLISHERS.
1890.

4156

In Memoriam Majorum.

"There be of those that have left a name behind them,
That their praises may be reported;
And some there be which have no memorial,
Who are perished as though they had never been,
And are become as though they had never been born,
And their children after them."

[Ecclesiasticus, xliv : 8, 9.]

PREFACE.

In the arrangement of the genealogical record, I have mainly followed the plan adopted in the New England Historical Genealogical Register.

Each person by the name of Sears has his, or her, serial number in Arabic figures, and family number in Roman numerals.

The column of figures on the left margin of the page is, from beginning to end, the general enumeration, and when any such number is *starred*, the asterisk denotes reference to a distinct paragraph or chapter further on, where a more full account of the individual and his family may be found. This applies to all in the male line who are known to have married, and whose issue I have recorded.

By the plan adopted, the different branches of a family of the same generation are grouped together, so that their connection may be readily seen, and individuals are placed as by right of primogeniture.

To trace the ancestry of any individual Sears, you have only to take the number at the head of the chapter or paragraph, and turn back to the same number in the margin, and you will there find his parentage, etc., and the same process continued will take you back to the first generation.

The double-dating, which occurs in the mention of early generations, is in conformity with the general practice of the period.

In public records previous to A. D. 1752, the *old-style* system of dating prevailed ; March was the first month, the year beginning March 25.

The *new style*, adopted by Pope Gregory XIII in 1582, became that of Great Britain and her American Colonies in 1752, from which time January became the first month.

To correct dates of the *old style*, or Julian manner of computation, to conform to the *new style* or Gregorian calendar, ten days should be added to all dates to the close of 1699, and eleven days thereafter. But even this does not exactly conform to the solar year.

Some apparent discrepancies in dates of marriages, birth of children, etc., are accounted for by the early mode of dating.

To condense the record as far as possible, I have reluctantly been obliged to omit many anecdotes, which, though characteristic of the parties concerned, are yet of but local interest — and have included but three generations in the female lines ;— I have also generally made use of the customary and well-known abbreviations ; and towns once named in an article are thereafter designated by first syllables — *e. g.*, Barns. for Barnstable, Br. for Brewster, Den. for Dennis, etc., and b. for born, adm. for admitted, bap. for baptized, d. for died, d. s. p. (*decessit sine prole*,) for died without issue, m. for married, gr.-st. for grave-stone, Ch. Rec. for Church Records, T. C. for Town Clerk, T. Rec. for Town Records, and others which, in their connection, will suggest their own meaning. Wherever (?) occurs, it will be understood to indicate uncertainty. Where a date is placed in brackets, [   ] it is because I have found different dates given for the same event, and have not certainly ascertained which is the correct one, or I have desired to call attention to the fact that authorities differ.

It should be borne in mind that many changes have taken place in boundaries and town names.

Plymouth Colony was merged in the Province of Massachusetts in 1692. The east precinct of Yarmouth was incorporated as the town of Dennis, June 19, 1793, and part of Harwich was set off as Brewster, Feb. 19, 1803.

In giving birth-places, etc., I have generally followed the original records, which do not usually take note of the popular names for localities or district subdivisions; for instance, a child born in South Yarmouth is entered as of Yarmouth; or if in East Dennis, as of Dennis, etc.

I have been taken to task for writing that a person was of Yarmouth, his descendant gravely affirming that his " grandfather lived and died in Dennis," when in point of fact there was not then any such town.

In Colonial and Provincial times the title of Captain was given only to officers of that rank in the army, militia and navy; commanders of vessels in the merchant service were styled Master or Skipper.

The early Searses called " Capt. " in records were, therefore, of the militia, though some of them may also have been seafaring men.

Some persons may feel aggrieved that fuller mention is not made of themselves and their families.

It has been my aim to treat all alike, but while many, and I am pleased to say most, of the persons to whom I have applied for information have cheerfully interested themselves to procure for me required data, others have made no response, or such as was little better than none; if, therefore, some families are left out entirely, or imperfect, perhaps erroneous data given, it is not my fault.

No genealogist can expect absolute correctness, but I have been at great pains to make the record reliable as far as it goes, and to reduce errors to the minimum, and I will esteem it a favor if any of my readers will inform me of any errors that may come to their notice, and send me any additions to family records for use when occasion may offer.

During the seven or eight years that I have been engaged in collecting material for this work, I have had much pleasant correspondence with persons connected with the family, and many kind words of encouragement ; and now that my book is submitted for their approval, I shall hope to again hear from them, and will cordially receive any friendly criticism.

I will only add, that while I have deemed it my duty to expose errors in the heretofore published accounts of the family history, etc., I have not *" set down aught in malice,"* and I have not cared to record individual peculiarities or frailties.

272 Centre St.,   }   S. P. M.
   Newton, Mass., Apr., 1890. }

ERRATA.

p. 24. 7th line from top, for *Sesreit*, read, Sesuit.

p. 34. 4th line from top, insert, *he m.*, before 2d, July 8, 1691.

p. 55. 12th line from top, for *wife*, read, wife's.

p. 58. *dele* * after No. 55.

p. 71. 6th line from bottom, for *say she*, read, says he.

p. 75. 6th line from top, for *child*, read, children.

p. 92. 13th line from bottom, insert *m.*, before 2d, Feb. 22.

p. 93. 26th line from top, *dele* his.

p. 97. 6th line from top, *now Tremont St.*, should be in parenthesis.

p. 99. 3d line from top, for *Jonas*, read, Jones.

p. 106. 10th line from bottom, for *1793*, read, 1763.

p. 123. last line, insert [5], after Richard Sears.

p. 135. 8th line from bottom, for *Robert*, read, Roberts.

p. 144. 8th line from bottom,—Lydia E. m. Asa S. Edgerly, and lives in Fresno City, Cal.

p. 145. 8th line from top, substitute [12.] Zenas, b. May 20, 1819; d. Stockton, Cal., Mar. 12, 1876; m. Sep. 17, 1843, Susan Heath, who d. there May 22, 1854; 2d, June 2, 1857, Mrs. Mary E. McLaud, who d. Mar. 19, 1872; children, i. Adelaide Ella Ruth, b. Aug. 1, 1845; d. Mar. 12, 1851. ii. Alfred De Bois, b. Mar. 22, 1848; m. Sep. 17, 1879, Olga Gibbs. iii. Emma Delaina, b. Oct. 29, 1850; d. June 27, 1852. iv. Susan Ella, b. Jan. 2, 1854; m. Jan. 2, 1873, B. F. Wellington.

p. 160. 16th line from bottom, for *Ebenezer*, read, Eben.

p. 181. 22d line from top, for *not of Thomas*, read, not grandson of Thomas.

p. 188. 867. Silas Sears, b. Feb. 10, 1781; d. Orwell, Bradford co., Pa., Apr. 1, 1830; m. Sally Dietrich, who d. Orwell, 1845. Children: i. Mary Ann, m. Silas Washburn, who d. She lives in Camptown, Pa. ii. Betsy, b. Schoharie, N. Y., Nov. 22, 1805, m. there 1825, John Gray; rem. to Dimock, Pa., and d. Feb. 4, 1874, had Jonas A., lives in Dimock, m. and has 10 children. Silas, d. 1886. iii. Ella, m. O. J. Ross, and died a year after. iv. Emeline, m. O. J. Ross, had, George L., a grocer in Towanda, Pa.

Errata.

Silas Sears removed from Schoharie, N. Y., to Orwell, Pa., his residence was near the Presbyterian Church, and he was buried close by. His will dated Feb. 20, 1830, was proved April 30, 1830, and mentions wife Sally, and daus. Mary Ann, Betsy Gray, Elly and Emeline.

p. 221.   insert ix, after No. 1163.

p. 223.   17th line from top, for *Jllson*, read Jillson.

p. 250.   8th line from top, strike out, *in recognition of services to the Queen, and was the next year advanced a grade*, and read, — and a year later that of Kalakaua, both for services to the King and Queen, and as tokens of personal friendship.

p. 250.   10th line from bottom, insert, from plans of **Dr.** Jacob Bigelow.

p. 251.   14th line from top, for 9, read, 12.

p. 257.   19th line from bottom,— it was not Ossawattomie (John) Brown, who was trustee of Oberlin College, but perhaps a brother.

p. 257.   Strike out 20th line from bottom.

p. 271.   7th line from bottom, after *b.'England*, insert d.

p. 292.   5th line from top, insert,   ii. Frank M., b. Sep. 12, 1886.

CONTENTS.

ENGLISH ANCESTRY.

Some years since, at the earnest solicitation of members of the family, I undertook the task of revising the "Sears Genealogy" and bringing it down to date.

I did so in the belief, common to the family and public generally, that the English Ancestry of Richard Sares, of Yarmouth, as published, was entirely authentic, and that little more was to be learned on that head.

Soon after commencing my labors however, my attention was drawn to discrepancies in the pedigree, seemingly irreconcilable, and an investigation was found necessary.

The result of my researches proves beyond question that not one step of the pedigree can be substantiated by existing records, and on the contrary some portions are impossible, and others in conflict with known authorities.

I have been desired to give the facts publicity, *in order that the pedigree may no longer be copied, and quoted as authority*, as has been done in numerous local histories and family genealogies, *and in the hope that, attention being drawn to the subject, renewed searches may discover the true origin of Richard Sares.*

In the proper places I have alluded to many errors, and will here therefore only refer to those most vital to the pedigree, as printed in "Pictures of the Olden Time," etc., edn. 1857, Crosby, Nichols & Co., Boston, and edited by the late Rev. Edmund H. Sears, D. D.

Part II, p. 10. "John Sayer of Colchester, Alderman, etc., d. 1509, leaving by Elizabeth his wife, three sons, viz., John, Robert and George.

"The eldest of these, John, d. in 1562, leaving two sons, viz.,
Richard and George.

"The eldest of these, Richard, is the subject of the first of
the sketches in 'Pictures of the Olden Time.' He was born
in Colchester in 1508, married Ann Bourchier, dau. of Edmd.
Knyvet, * * * , of Ashwellthorpe, co. Norf., second son
of Sir Edwd. Knyvet, * * *. Richard became a fugitive to
Holland in 1537, and d. Amsterdam, 1540, * * *. His wife,
the Lady Anne, clung faithfully to her husband in his adver-
sity, and incurred the lasting displeasure of the Knyvets. It is
inferred that her father became so bitterly estranged from her,
as to erase her name from all his family records, that she
might be forgotten forever, for he gave to a younger daughter
the name of Anne, while she was yet living. * * * George
Sayer in consequence of Richard's flight, secured for himself
possession of the patrimonial inheritance. This George d.
1577, * * * ' His descendant, and eventual heiress, married Sir John Marsham."

There is much confusion in the various printed accounts of
the Sayer family of Colchester. Morant in his Hist. of Col.,
Book 2, p. 43, says, "John Sayer, Alderman of this town d.
Feb. 14, 1509. John Sayer, his son, d. 1563.

"George Sayer son of the last, was an Alderman of this
Corporation, and one of the Bailiffs. * * * Richard his
eldest son, d. Sep. 1610. * * * George the second son,
who departed this life the 3 July, 1596, married Rose Cardi-
nall."

Wright in his Hist. of Essex, Book 2, p. 409, says, "John
Sayer, Alderman, d. 1509, and his son John in 1563.

"George his son was an Alderman," etc.

Whether he means that George was son of the first, or of
the second John, is not clear.

Morant errs in stating that the Richard Sayer who died in
1610, was the son of George. It is true he, (George,) did have
a son Richard, but as he is not mentioned in his father's will
dated 1573, and proved in 1577, it is probable he was then
dead without issue.

But George does give £20 to his "*nephew* Richard," doubtless the son of his brother John, and the same Richard who

died in 1610, "aged full four score," as inscribed on his brass in St. Peter's Ch. Col. The arms on that brass, quarter Sayer and Wesden. George Sayer, and John, his younger brother, married sisters, co-heiresses of Wesden of Lincolnshire, and as George's son Richard was dead before 1573, it follows that the Richard quartering the maternal arms of Wesden, must have been the son of John, and it is so stated in the Heralds Visitation of Essex, for the year 1612, pub. Har. So., 1878, Part I, p. 286.

If, as Morant says, the Richard who died in 1610, was the elder son of George, why did his younger brother, George, Jr., who died in 1596, succeed to the paternal estates in 1577?

Here we have an apparent case of *a Richard Sayer the eldest son*, being *supplanted by his younger brother George*, and I have no doubt that the person who constructed the pedigree of Richard Sares of Yarmouth, had in mind this erroneous statement of Morant. It is in the highest degree improbable that two elder brothers Richard were disinherited, and supplanted by two younger brothers George, in succeeding generations.

The Heralds Visitation of Essex, for 1612, says that " George Sayer of Col. in com. Essex, gentle, sonne & heire," and " John Sayer of Col. 2d sonne," were the sons of " . . . Sayer of Col. in Ess. Gentleman," which leaves it an open question whether George was the son of John Sayer the Alderman, or, as Morant says, his grandson.

That John, (bro. of George,) was a second son, is confirmed by his brass in St. Peter's Ch. Col., whereon his coat of arms is differenced by a crescent, the distinguishing heraldic mark of a second son.

The late John Sayer, Esq're., Barrister, of Pett Hall, Charing, and Lord of the Manor of Smarden in Kent, who died in 1886, was the representative head of the elder line of George Sayer of Colchester.

He was at great pains in compiling a pedigree of the family, entered in " The College of Arms," London, to eliminate the errors in the published accounts of the family, and to supply the omissions. An abridged extract from this pedigree was printed in the "Memorials of Smarden," pub. 1886, just before his death, and the proof carefully revised by him.

In this pedigree he gives as the children of John Sayer the Alderman, "1· George, d. 1577, 2. John, d. 1563, 3. Robert, living 1573," and I have no doubt correctly. Admitting this then Richard Sayer "The Exile," who is said to have died in Amsterdam in 1540, if he was the brother of George as claimed, must have been the son, not the grand-son, of the Alderman. The brass to the latter in St. Peter's Ch. Col., represents him kneeling with his wife, *four* sons and a daughter, but does not give his children's names. The question arises, what was the name of the fourth son, and what became of him? Most probably he died young, and perhaps the question may be answered in his father's will, or in the *inquisition post-mortem*, taken in those days to show who were the heirs to an estate, and liable to pay *entry fine* to the crown.

Up to the year 1570, the borough of Colchester enjoyed the privilege of Probate, and upon application to the town clerk, I was informed that the court-rolls were still preserved in his office, and were in his custody.

He further said that they were written in the ancient court-hand and would require the services of an expert, (which he was not,) to decipher. I thereupon wrote to an antiquarian in Colchester, who I knew to be an expert in such matters, to see if he could find the wills of John Sayer and his sons, and make certain extracts for me.

Upon application to the town clerk he was informed that permission to examine the court-rolls, and make extracts, could not be granted. My friend expressed great dissatisfaction at this decision, claiming that as a rate payer for many years in Colchester, he should have the right to search the archives, etc., and declared his intention of applying to the General Probate Office in London for the desired permission. And so the matter rests at present.

A special, but not exhaustive search in London, made by Mr. H. F. Waters, at my request, resulted in finding many Sayers wills, but none certainly identified with the Colchester

family, except that of George Sayer, "the elder," who died
1577. He mentions therein, his children and grand-children
then living, "nephew Richard Sayer," and "brother Robert's
children."

The middle names of Bourchier, given to Anne Knyvet, and
later to John Sayer, father and son, in the pedigree, are clearly
anachronisms; as is also that of Jane Knyvet Sayer, born 1596,
and tend to discredit it.

Middle names did not come in vogue with the *gentry* till
long after, viz., *temps* Charles I. according to various writers
in "Notes and Queries," London.

Rev. Augustus Jessopp, D. D. of East Dereham, co. Norf.,
Eng., has for years made the history of the Knyvet family an
especial study with a view to publication.

Some time since he kindly drew up for me a pedigree of
Edmund Knyvet, of Ashwellthorpe, and his descendants,
which he informed me could be relied upon, as it was compiled
from the original documents.

He found that Edmd. Knyvet had four married daughters,
but none named Anne, much less two of the name; that he
died *insolvent*, and in his will mentions *none* of his children
by name;—if therefore, he did have a daughter Anne, she
does not seem to have been treated differently from her sisters,
in respect to inheritance.

It appears however, that Edmund Knyvet's son William,
did have two daughters named Anne, one baptized at Funden-
hall, 30 May, 1562, the other 2 Mar., 1566. I do not know if
they were both living at the same time, but if they were, the
circumstance would not be without precedent; instances of
two children bearing the same name not being uncommon in
those days, even three of a name being on record.

But do we find in this coincidence the basis for the "two
daughters named Anne"?

It is a fact that Edmund Knyvet's daughter Alice, married
one Oliver Sheres, of Wreningham, a village some five miles
from Ashwellthorpe, and the name may have easily become
changed to Seres, Sares and Sears, at a later date. Jane,

"daughter & sole heyer of John Bourchier, Knyght, late Lord Berners," made her will 8 April, 1560, and leaves to "Alice, my daughter, now wife to Oliver Sheres," £60, on condition that he shall settle lands in Wreningham, Ashwell-thorpe and other towns, on himself and Alice. 1 May, 1565, Oliver Sheres of Wreningham, co. Norf., gent., and Alice his wife, demised to Anthony Grey of Shelton, gent., the manor house of Wreningham, "wherein said Oliver and Alice now dwelleth." "I suspect Alice died early, for I find in a Will of Mrs. Downes who lived in the parish of St. Martins-in-the-Fields, London, (whose husband was almost certainly a member of a good Norfolk family,) who made her will 1601, that she left to a daughter, Elizabeth Mawdit, "the £100, which my son-in-law Oliver Sheres owes me." Query, did Oliver Sheres remove to London?

As yet I have not learned what children, if any, he had, but may succeed in doing so later.

Did this marriage of Oliver Sheres and Alice Knyvet originate another step in the Sears pedigree?

The Registers of St. Peter's Ch. Col., of which John Sayer the Alderman and his sons were parishioners, commence only about 1653, more than one hundred years after the alleged flight of Richard Sayers to Holland, and from them therefore, we can learn nothing of the family previous to that date.

Briefly;—I conclude that John Sayer, Ald., who d. 1509, had four sons, viz.: George, d. 1577; John, d. 1563; Robert living in 1573; and another, name and date of death unknown, but who may have been a Richard;—that George had a son Richard who died *vita patris;* and that John, Jr., had also a son Richard, who d. Col., 1610, aged 80, leaving an heiress, Jane by name; and that neither of these Richards, sons of George and John, Jr., could have been the husband of Ann Knyvet in 1528.

The children of John Sayer, Ald., must have been born not long before his death in 1509; his wife survived him 21 years, and he was probably but a middle aged man at his decease, although attaining to the Aldermanic dignity.

P. 12. "John Bourchier Sayer, was born, say the family papers, in 1528. I suspect, however, that this is a mistake, and that the date is too early, for it would make his father but little more than 19 years of age at his marriage. * * * Another date has it in 1535. * * * He married Elizabeth, daughter of Sir John Hawkins, * * * and died in Holland, leaving by Elizabeth, his wife, four sons, viz.: John Bourchier, Henry, William and Richard. Of the last three we have no facts, except that they were born in Plymouth, Engd., and that they settled in Kent. Plymouth was probably the temporary residence of their mother, while their father was with Hawkins as a navigator. Of John Bourchier, I have given some account in the 'Pictures.'

" The date of his birth is given in the family papers as 1561.
"I have put it a little later for several reasons. He married Marie L., daughter of Philip Lamoral van Egmond, and acquired with her a large fortune, principally in money."

The biographers of Sir John Hawkins, generally state that he was born in 1520, but they are wrong, and probably follow some one erroneous authority.

He died Nov. 12, 1595, and his widow, (his 2d wife,) erected a monument to his memory in St. Dunstans-in-the-East, London, (of which he had been a parishioner many years,) with a Latin inscription setting forth his *forty-three* years of service by sea and land; and a wooden mural tablet with English verses, a copy of which may be found in Stow's London, edn. Strype, 1720, Vol. I, Book II, pp. 44, '5. It ends thus:

"Ending his life with his experience,
By deep decree of God's high Providence,
His years to six times ten, & three amounting,
The ninth, the seventh climacterick by counting.
Dame Katherine, his first religious wife,
Saw years, thrice ten, & two of mortal life." * * *

We see therefore, that he was but 63 years of age in 1595, and so born about 1532, and this is confirmed by reckoning his "43 years of service," back from 1595, which brings us to 1552, when he would have been about 21; — also by the fact that he was admitted a freeman of Plymouth in 1555-6, a step altogether necessary at that period to a man in his position, and one that would not have been unnecessarily delayed after he attained his majority.

He removed to London before 1573, and succeeded his father-in-law, Gunson, as Treasurer of the Navy.

His wife was then living, and as she died at the age of 32, she could not have been born earlier than 1541.

John Bourchier Sayer, Jr., is said to have been born in 1561, (although Rev. E. H. Sears thinks the date too early.)

At that time John Hawkins was but 29, and his wife 20 years of age.

Neither could have had a daughter of marriageable age at that date, nor for many years after.

These dates and conclusions, are confirmed by R. N. Worth, F. G. S., author of Histories of Plymouth, and of Devonshire, and of an address on "Sir John Hawkins, Sailor, Statesman and Hero," reprinted from Transactions of the "Devon Association for the Advancement of Science, Lit. and Art," 1883, pp. 40.

The Registers of St. Andrew's Church, Plymouth, to which parish the Hawkins family belonged, only go back to 1573, at which date John Hawkins was a resident of London.

As to the marriage with Marie L. von Egmond. The late Mr. S. Alofsen of Jersey City, a well-known and esteemed Antiquarian, (who came to this Country in connection with the Embassy from the Netherlands,) wrote to the late S. G. Drake, then Editor of the N. E. Hist. Gen. Register, a letter which is on file.

In it he states that "the Egmond family never had a residence in Amsterdam;" — that "the family genealogy brought down to the latter part of the last century, has been printed;" — that "it contains the name of but one Philip v. Egmond, viz., the son of Count Egmond;" and that, "if John Bourchier Sayer did marry one of the family, his wife must have been of an obscure and unknown branch;" — a fact that seems to me somewhat inconsistent with the "large fortune," even in money, which she is said to have brought her husband.

P. 13. "John Bourchier Sayer, married Marie L. von Egmond, Amsterdam, 1585, and had Marie L., b. 1587, Richard, 1590; John, 1592; and Jane Knyvet, 1596.

"These dates are copied from the family papers of the Searses of Chatham, and I think they are correct.

"Such a series depending upon each other would not be all wrong. John Bourchier Sayer purchased with his wife's fortune, property in England, adjoining the lands which he hoped soon to recover. Among the estates thus bought were Bourchier *and* Little Fordham Manors, *both* of which had in former times belonged to his ancestors."

There formerly hung in the parlor of Mrs. Richard Sears of Chatham, a chart pedigree of the family, given to her by her husband's nephew, which is now in possession of a descendant in Framingham.

According to this chart, Richard Sares was born in Amsterdam in 1613,—twenty-three years later than the date given by Rev. E. H. Sears.

While I think 1613, to be nearer the correct date of Richard Sares' birth, there is no evidence that it is the true one.

Both Morant and Wright, in their Histories of Essex, state that Bourchier Hall *or* Little Fordham in Aldham, derives its name from its ancient owners, the Earls of Essex. "Sir Robert Bourchier died possessed of Bourchiers Hall in 1328, and it remained in the family until confiscated. Queen Elizabeth regranted it to William, Marquis of Northampton, who sold it to *George Sayer* in 1574. It continued in his descendants, finally passing to the Marsham family by marriage, fell into decay, was divided and sold."

A part is now used as a farm-house. I find no mention that it ever belonged to the Sayers, previous to 1574.

The "Notices of the Sears Family," page 4, says "In 1577, George Seares of Colchester died in possession of 'The Abbots' in Stanway, *under trust for Richard Sayers in Holland;*" — and confuses it with Bourchier Hall, or Little Fordham, an entirely different estate in Aldham, a neighboring parish.

George Sayer bought Bourchier Hall, paying *ingress fine* in 1574, and died 1577; yet he is said to have held the estate under trust for Richard Sayer in Holland, who, the "Pictures" say, had died 37 years previous, viz.: 1540. The author of the "Notices" probably got his data from Morant's Hist. Col.,

2

Book II, p. 111, which gives a list of Geo. Sayer's estates as found by *inq. p. m.*, but not a word is said therein of any Richard Sayers, and the words "under trust," etc., are undoubtedly an interpolation.

P. 14. Here Rev. E. H. Sears prints his only piece of documentary evidence, viz.: a letter from J. Hawes, dated Yarmouth, June 20, 1798, to Daniel Sears of Chatham, in which he signs himself

"Your affectionate relative, and friend, J. Hawes."

In it Mr. Hawes refers to sundry "curious and important documents," * * * "I have heard from your brother Richard, that Knyvet Sares, or Sears, before he went to London, and some years before his death, collected and arranged these valuable papers with the intention of using them. They had long remained neglected and uncared for. Among them was a list of marriages, births and deaths, similar to that which I now send, and many original deeds and letters, with a long correspondence between the Sayers, the Knyvets and others in England. It seemed to be closed by a letter from John Bourchier Sares, dated Leyden, 1614.

"Your brother always speaks highly of this letter. * * *

"A highly interesting manuscript was compiled from these papers, and came into possession of Daniel Sears, your father.

"The original letters were taken to England, by Knyvet, and are possibly still there in the hands of some of the family.

"The manuscript was last seen and read so late as 1760, but neither the one, nor the other, are now to be found.

"It may be the originals are not lost, but the copy, your brother thinks, was either burnt, or carried away when the family mansion was nearly destroyed in 1763. * * *

"I send such facts as I have been able to collect, assisted by Richard and Mr. Colman."

I have been quite unable to identify the writer of this letter, or ascertain his relationship to the family.

The signature attracts attention by its variance from the common custom of the period, of writing the name in full.

The only male persons of the name of Hawes that I find residing in Yarmouth in 1798, and bearing the initial J., are John Hawes, Dea. Joseph Hawes the school-master, and his son, Joseph, Jr.

The latter is out of the question, by reason of his youth,

etc., and a comparison of the letter with an article by the worthy deacon, printed in Swift's "Old Yarmouth," 1884, p. 223, shows such a difference in style of composition, that I feel certain they were not by the same author.

John Hawes was 31 years old in 1798, but not likely to be the writer of the letter.

The only marriage recorded between the Sears and Hawes families, during the last century, is that of Jonathan Sears and Elizabeth, dau. of Dea. Joseph Hawes of Yarmouth, in 1721. This Jonathan was a second cousin, once removed, of Daniel Sears.

I am aware that the Sears Genealogy says that Daniel Sears of Chatham, married in 1708, Sarah Hawes, daughter of J. Hawes of Yarmouth, (another mysterious J.,) and this error, for such it is, has been perpetuated on the Sears monuments in Chatham, Yarmouth and Colchester. On the Yarmouth town records, the name is clearly written *Howes*, and the will of Samuel Howes, of Yar., recorded Barns. Prob. Rec., IV, 90, mentions "daughters Sarah Sears, and Hope Sears," who married the brothers, Daniel and Richard Sears, and "Mercy Sears," who married their cousin, Josiah Sears.

The only Sarah Hawes living in 1708, and on record in Yarmouth, was the dau. of Dea. Joseph Hawes, she born 1696, married in 1719 to Thos. Hallet.

There is no tradition, or record found in Chatham, of the family mansion having been "nearly destroyed in 1763."

Benj. Bangs a merchant of Harwich, who chronicled in his diary more trivial events happening in Chatham at that time, makes no mention of the occurrence, and when the old building was taken down in 1863, the original timbers were found in place, with the bark still on, and there were no marks of its having ever passed through the fiery ordeal.

Daniel Sears though born in Chatham, was in business in Boston in 1798, having removed to that place with his mother, at her second marriage in 1763.

But why should he apply to J. Hawes for particulars of his family, instead as would have been natural, to his brothers,

Richard or David? His bro.-in-law Mr. Colman, was also his neighbor.

We may admire the vivid recollection attributed to Richard Sears, after the lapse of thirty-eight years, of the letters, etc., read last when he was a boy of eleven.

P. 16. "John Bourchier Sayer, died 1629. By Marie L. Egmond, his wife, he left two sons, and two daughters, viz., Richard, John, Marie and Jane. The three latter, went to England, and settled in Kent.

"Richard Sayer or Sears. * * * His birth is variously given, but 1590, we think is the true date.

"He married Dorothy Thacher, at Plymouth, in 1632.

"The likeness of him was taken from a painting in Holland, in possession of the Egmont family, and is supposed to be correct. * * * He died 1676, and his wife in 1680. By her he had the following children, viz., Knyvet, Paul, Silas and Deborah. * * * Knyvet was born in 1635, married Elizabeth' Dymoke, * * * went to England on a second voyage, and died 1686, at the residence of his relative, Catharine (subsequently Baroness Berners,) dau. of Sir John Knyvet, and wife of John Harris Esq. The evidences he carried with him were never recovered. He left two children, Daniel and Richard."

I have already alluded to the doubtful date assigned for Richard's birth. If born 1590, he would have been 42 years old in 1632, an unusual age to remain single, in those days of early marriages, and the statement that he married Dorothy Thacher at Plymouth in 1632, requires confirmation. His name is found there, only in the tax list of 25 March, 1633.

No record of his marriage is now to be found, and no Dorothy is known to the Thacher genealogists, except as found in the "Sears Genealogy." It is claimed that she was a sister of Antony Thacher of Yarmouth, and Richard Sares in his will calls him, "bro. Thacher," and Antony's son John, in an affidavit appended thereto calls him "my uncle Sares." Several other explanations of the terms of relationship may however be given.

Antony Thacher was twice married; — the name of his first wife was Mary ———, and she may have been a sister of

Richard Sares; or Antony's second wife, Elizabeth Jones, may have been a sister of Richard's wife.

It is possible that Richard Sares married Dorothy Batts, at Marblehead in 1638–9.

She came over in the "Bevis" which sailed from Southampton, before May 2, 1638, with her brother, Christopher Batts of Salisbury, and his wife Anne, who was a sister of Antony Thacher. Antony Thacher's brother Peter, married as his second wife, Alice Batts, sister of Dorothy, so the families were doubly connected. The connection of Dorothy Batts and Antony Thacher, fully justified the terms of relationship in Richard Sares' will; see an almost parallel case quoted by the late Col. J. L. Chester, in N. E. Hist. Gen. Reg., XXI, 365; and the family connection perhaps influenced Richard Sares to join the party led by Antony Thacher, in the spring of 1639, which settled Yarmouth.

If however Richard Sares did marry Dorothy Batts, she must, I think, have been his second wife, for his eldest son was born in 1637–8, which would be before she came over, or at the latest, a few months after her arrival.

Thomas Thacher, of Beckington, co. Somerset, in his will proved 1611, mentions "bro. Antony," and Clement Thacher of Marston Bigot, in his will dated 1629, and proved 1639, names "bro. Antony" and others. Rev. Peter Thacher of Sarum, made his will in 1640, and mentions "bro. Antony," and "sister Ann, wife of Chris. Batts," and other relatives, among them his "wife's sister Dorothy."

It is natural to suppose that one of the brothers whose wills are here referred to, would have made some mention of their sister Dorothy, if they had such; and, we may ask, how did she, a single woman, happen to be in Plymouth in 1632, three years before her brother and his family came over?

In a note to the first edition of the "Pictures," the portrait of Richard "The Pilgrim," is said to be from the Egmont gallery in *Amsterdam*, which more definitely locates it.

There once hung in the west parlor of Madame Richard Sears of Chatham, a painting which Mrs. Sears, was wont to

call "Sir Richard," and which has been said by some persons
to have been the original of the engraved portrait.   This is an
error.   The portrait was given after the Squire's death to his
widow, by his nephew, and was a copy from a painting in possession of the latter.   It resembles some of the family, but
when, or where the original was painted, is a mystery.

There is no reason for believing that Richard Sares was ever
in Holland, but some descendants from the Colchester Sayers
took service, and married in the Netherlands, and portraits of
some of that family may have been preserved there; —— the
picture bears also some likeness to an engraving of the Rev.
Samuel Seyer, the historian of Bristol, Engd., in my possession.

It is evident that Rev. E. H. Sears did not know of Richard
Sares' will recorded in Plymouth, or he would not have written
that he had an *eldest* son Knyvet, born in 1635, died 1686.

In his will dated 10. 3 mo. 1667, Richard Sares names "my
elder son Paule Sares," and in the codicil dated 3 Feb., 1676,
he again mentions " my *eldest* son Paule Sares."

Paul made oath to the inventory, 15 Nov., 1676, before
John Freeman, Assistant, who calls him "Paule Sares *eldest*
son of Richard Sares, deceased."   John Freeman lived in a
neighboring town, and probably personally knew the family.

There is no allusion to Knyvet in the will, or codicil,
although he is said to have been living twenty years after the
former, and ten years after the latter was written, nor is there
any reference to property in England.

Neither the name of Knyvet Sares, or Elizabeth Dymoke
his wife, is to be found in colony, town, church or court
records, nor any gravestone to either.

There is no record of administration upon their estates, nor
of appointment of a guardian for their children.

The late Amos Otis, whose knowledge of Barnstable history
and families was unrivalled, in his "Hist. of Barns.," gives
from church records the names of three children of Elder
Thomas Dimmock, the first settler of the name, but neither
named Elizabeth, adding, "he may have had other children
before he came to Barnstable, but it is not probable."

I believe that Richard Sares never had a son named Knyvet. The name was unknown upon the Cape until about 1845, the period of Mr. Somerby's researches; and it has never been adopted as a family name except in one instance.

Although "the family papers taken to England by Knyvet were never recovered," and the copies in Chatham were "lost or destroyed," a tablet was erected to his memory in Colchester in 1858, which states that it was "Inscribed by Catharine Harris in 1687"!

It did not, as may well be supposed, take the place of an older, and perhaps dilapidated one, nor has any original been found elsewhere to my knowledge.

An unfortunate fatality appears to have attended all the family papers. We are told in the J. Hawes letter that the originals taken to London by Knyvet Sears, were never recovered, and that the copies remaining in Chatham were lost or destroyed in 1763.

I have been informed that after the death of Mrs. Richard Sears of Chatham in 1852, the house was ransacked by persons having no right there, and many articles of value carried away, including family papers. This is partly accounted for by the fact that Mrs. Sears, like many other very old ladies, had a habit of promising articles to various persons, "when she had no further use for them," forgetting that she had already disposed of them, and there were thus several claimants for the same things. When she died some of these people, knowing her foible, and believing "possession nine points of the law," were unwilling to take their chances in the settlement of the estate, and so helped themselves.

Why any papers should be taken, I cannot imagine.

None of Richard Sears' descendants now living, ever heard of his having made any "genealogical collection," nor of his having a family Bible containing the record of the marriage of Richard Sares and Dorothy Thacher, and the birth of Knyvet Sears.

The Bible in which he kept his own family record is carefully preserved, but contains no others.

The "family papers" of Hon. David Sears of Boston, from which Rev. E. H. Sears derived the material for his account of the family, are believed to be no longer in existence. After his death in 1871, his house in Beacon Street, with much of its contents, passed to his eldest son, the late David Sears, Jr., who is understood to have found in it an extraordinary accumulation of correspondence and memoranda preserved by his father in the course of his exceptionally long life. David Sears, Jr., a popular and exemplary member of Society, did not inherit his father's tastes, and was more devoted to field-sports and yachting than to family history. Not being himself in the habit of keeping letters, and having to sell this house, he is stated to have caused masses of the above-mentioned manuscript to be destroyed after a very cursory examination. It is not unlikely that some genealogical material was included in this holocaust, and if so, whatever value it may have once possessed as *evidence*, is now *nil*.

At the same time the library of Hon. D. Sears was divided and scattered, and the old Bible containing the records of Richard Sares, which was once in Mr. Sears' possession, has not since been seen.

As he at one time expressed the intention of depositing it with some institution, it may yet be recovered, but so far, enquiries for it have been in vain.

The genealogical papers of Rev. E. H. Sears are not now to be found, and are supposed to have been given or loaned by him to some member of the Sears family, but were perhaps destroyed after using.

P. 19. "Paul Sears, b. 1637. He inherited most of his father's property. * * * He adopted the children of his bro. Knyvet after the death of their father in England, and they were brought up in his family. His will is on Old Colony records, in which his brother's children are named as his own sons. * * * The names of his sons were, Samuel, Paul and John."

Paul Sears died Feb. 20, 1707–8, in his 70th year, according to his gravestone in the old cemetery in Yarmouth, and was therefore born *after* Feb. 20, 1637–8. His will is recorded in *Barnstable* county, not in *Old Colony* (*i. e.* Plymouth,) records.

The names of his children on the Yarmouth town records have been obliterated, but the births of seven remain.

From other sources we have been enabled to learn the names of his five sons and five daughters. His last two children were his sons, Richard, born 1680, and Daniel, born 1682. In the "Sears Genealogy" these names are given in reverse order, Richard being called the youngest, and born 1684·

Their gravestones in Chatham prove the contrary, and copies of the epitaphs are given in the appropriate places.

In his will Paul Sears gives his real estate to his sons, Samuel, Paul and John, charged with payments to "*their brothers*," Richard and Daniel, towards their purchase of land in Monamoy.

Until positive evidence to the contrary is produced, we hold the probate records to be the highest authority, and cannot doubt that Richard and Daniel were the true sons, and not merely "adopted sons" of Paul Sears.

To sum up briefly: — There is no evidence that Richard Sares of Yarmouth was descended from the Colchester family of Sayer. It is true that John Sayer, Jr., of Col., who died in 1563, had a son Richard, but it is no less certain that the said Richard was not disinherited and exiled to Holland, nor did he marry a Knyvet; on the contrary he was his father's heir, and married first, Alice Spooner, and second, widow Ellen Lawrence, and died in Colchester, Sep., 1610, leaving a daughter, Jane, his sole heir. He was then aged "full fourscore," so born only about 1530, while according to the "Pictures," "Richard the Exile," *son of John Sayer, Jr.*, was married, and in Holland in 1537.

John Sayer the Alderman *may* have had a son named Richard, but it remains to be proved, and is not claimed in the "Pictures."

There can be little doubt that George, ob. 1577;—John, ob. 1563;—and Robert, living in 1573, were his sons, and born in the order named.

3

Sir John Hawkins, Adm., could not have had a daughter of marriageable age in 1560, nor for years after, and John Bourchier Sayer if born in 1561, or thereabouts, was not his grandson.

The Egmont connection is alike mythical, and unsupported by proofs.

It is doubtful if Richard Sares was ever in Holland, or that he married a Thacher; and there is no evidence that he ever had a son Knyvet.

According to Probate records, Richard and Daniel Sears who settled in Chatham, were the sons of Paul Sears, and they must have been his youngest sons, so that the claim put forth by Burke in his "Visitations of Seats & Arms," that the Chatham branch is the "Head of the American Family of Sears in America," has no foundation in fact.

The claim to Ancestral Estates in England, is apparently unfounded, and all documents upon which the "English Ancestry" was based, have been destroyed.

———

For the benefit of future investigators, I will note the genesis of the Pedigree, etc., so far as can now be ascertained.

About the year 1845, the late Mr. H. G. Somerby was employed to collect data regarding the Sears family, and a pamphlet was issued, entitled "Notices of the Sears Family, from Sir Bernard Burke's works, and Somerby's Collections in England," etc. The manuscript of his collection is in the library of the Mass. Hist. So., Boston.

It consists of a mass of extracts from English local works, relative to the families of Sayer and Sears there, but showing not the slightest connection with the American family; and of "Extracts from parish registers, and family papers in possession of Hon. David Sears, Boston."

I do not understand Mr. Somerby's reference to "Extracts from parish registers," for as I have already said, the register of St. Peter's Ch., Colchester, does not commence until more than 100 years after the alleged exile of Richard Sayer, and that of St. Andrew's Ch., Plymouth, until after the removal of Sir John Hawkins to London; it is evident therefore that nothing pertinent to the American Ancestry could have been found in them.

Certainly Mr. Somerby in his researches found nothing to connect the English and American families, or he would have given the data, with reference to authorities, as he has done in other genealogies.

Not long before his death, in conversation with gentlemen well known in genealogical circles, he gave them clearly to understand that he did not wish to be held accountable for many of the statements in the Sears pedigree.

But this it must be borne in mind, is an *ex parte* statement.

Somerby did in fact furnish Sir Bernard Burke with the material for his articles on the Sears family, and the "Notices of the Sears family" was published with his approval, if not written by him, for my copy bears his autograph, "with compliments of H. G. Somerby," and he also was the agent in putting up the objectionable tablets in St. Peter's Church, Colehester. In view of these undeniable facts, I do not see how he could avoid responsibility for the errors contained therein. It was certainly disingenuous to quote Burke as authority, when the reverse was the case.

In 1852, Sir Bernard Burke published the first volume of "Visitations of Seats & Arms," which contains at page 52, of Part II, an account of the family, claiming that by right of primogeniture, the Chatham branch is the "Head of the American Sears Family." This was followed in 1863, in the 3rd series of "Vicissitudes of Families," by a sketch entitled "A Pilgrim Father."

Burke now repudiates these articles, and they are left out of later editions. In 1884, he wrote me that he *received the material from Mr. Somerby*, but had since made investigation, and found "that the details were not only *not proven*, but also *incapable of proof, if not altogether wrong, and opposed to fact.*"

In 1857, Rev. E. H. Sears published "Pictures of the Olden Time," to which was added in a later edition for private distribution, a Genealogy of the family.

In his preface he states that he derived his facts mainly from Burke's " Visitations of Seats & Arms," and from " family papers," etc.

He doubtless simply acted as editor, and did not apparently deem it his duty to verify his authorities.

In the letter of J. Hawes, before quoted, he says he was "assisted in his collections by Mr. Colman and Richard."

This is confirmed by a manuscript in the handwriting of Hon. D. Sears of Boston, dated Feb. 10, 1845, in possession of Gen. C. W. Sears of the University of Mississippi, entitled " Memoranda of the Sears, from Minutes collected by J. Hawes and Wm. Colman to 1800, and continued by Richard Sears of Chatham to 1840," — " Copied from the original in possession of Mrs. Richard Sears of Chatham."

The manuscript contains many important errors, and varies from the records, and from the published genealogy. It was evidently written from memory.

I cannot now determine the share of either of the trio in the production of these " Minutes," but one fact will show how little Richard Sears could have had to do with them.

In this document his mother, Fear Freeman, is said to have been the daughter of *John* Freeman of *Sandwich*, and the printed genealogy makes a similar statement.

She was in fact, the daughter of *Benjamin* Freeman of *Harwich*, by his wife Temperance Dimmick, as is shown by his will recorded in Barnstable.

Richard Sears was nine years old when his grand-father died, and twenty-four when his grand-mother died. They lived in adjoining towns, and it is absurd to suppose that he did not know his grand-parents' names and residence, or that such a gross error could have escaped his notice and correction.

Mr. Colman was his bro.-in-law, and resided in Boston ; his part in the matter is not evident.

Of J. Hawes I have already written ; if his letter be accepted as evidence, then the story is apparently traced back to Daniel Sears who died in Chatham, in 1761, aged 49.

It appears by the records of the Probate Court in Barnstable, that on Feb. 10, 1758, "Upon inquisition of the Selectmen of Chatham, Daniel Sears was adjudged *non compos*, and his wife Fear Sears was appointed his guardian."

Swift's "Hist. of Old Yarmouth," pub. 1885, states that "the marriage of Richard Sears and Dorothy Thacher, and the birth of Knyvet Sears, are recorded in a Bible left by Richard Sears of Chatham, kept in the family for several generations."

A Bible answering this description was once in possession of Hon. David Sears, but has long since disappeared, and may have been deposited with some institution for safe-keeping. All that I have been able to learn in regard to it is, "it measured perhaps six inches by four, and the entries in it were in a small, fine hand."

Enquiries have been made of all the immediate descendants of Richard Sears of Chatham now living, who say "they have never seen, or before heard of such a Bible."

They would be very grateful for any information as to its present whereabouts.

In conclusion:—It is now evident that Hon. David Sears was most grievously deceived relative to the early history and genealogy of the family, and there is not one particle of evidence to show who Richard Sares' parents were, or where he was born.

There is little hope of tracing him except through the records of wills, etc., in England;—the names Sares, Sears, etc., are very common there in different counties, and that of Richard is of frequent occurrence in the early part of the seventeenth century.

It is possible there may have been ancient alliances of the Sayer, Knyvet and Hawkins families, and the family genealogist may have erred in placing "the flesh on the wrong bones."

About 1500, a family of Knyvets was settled in Stanway, a parish adjoining Colchester, and about that date one Edmund Knyvet died there, leaving his second sister, Lady Thomasine Clopton, his heir; and a family of Hawkinses was at the same period settled in Braintree, only twelve miles distant, of which one John Hawkins, a wealthy clothier, purchased estates in Colchester, and settled at Alresford Hall hard by, *circa* 1600.

I have already referred to the marriage of Oliver Sheres with Alice Knyvet, dau. of the sergeant-porter to Henry VIII; their descendants should be traced to the third generation.

There was more than one family of Hawkins in Plymouth, and another John Hawkins was made a freeman there, the very same year as the Admiral.

In another place I refer to the fact that Marblehead, (where we find Richard Sares resident in 1638,) was largely settled by people from the islands of Guernsey and Jersey; — the names of Sarres and Serres have been represented in Guernsey for several centuries, and are found there to-day.

There is a popular belief that the family of Sears is of Norman origin, and it is noticeable that in the eastern parishes of London, and adjacent villages, which contained many Huguenot, Flemish and Walloon emigrants, the name of Sears or Sares is common about 1600.

"*Magna est veritas, et prevalebit.*"

FIRST GENERATION.

The parentage, place and date of birth of Richard Sares are alike unknown.

His name is first found upon the records of Plymouth Colony, in the tax-list of March 25, 1633, when he was one of forty-four, in a list of eighty-six persons, who were assessed nine shillings in corn, at six shillings per bushel.

He soon after crossed over to Marblehead, in Massachusetts Colony, and was taxed as a resident of that place, in the Salem rate-list for Jannary 1, 1637–8, and on October 14, 1638, was granted four acres of land "*where he had formerly planted.*" This would seem to indicate that he had then some family.

What his reasons were for removing can now only be conjectured. It has been suggested that he sympathized with Roger Williams and followed him in his removal, but this is improbable.

It may be that he wished to be near friends, former townsmen, or perhaps relatives.

Antony Thacher, who in his will he calls "brother," was then living in Marblehead, and this fact offers the best reason for his removal.

The early settlers of Marblehead were many of them from the channel islands, Guernsey and Jersey, and in these places the family of Sarres has been established for several centuries, and is still represented in Guernsey under the names of Sarres and Serres.

It may be that Richard Sares was from one of these islands, and a thorough search of the records there might produce satisfactory results, otherwise there seems to be no clue, not even the slightest indication to the place of his nativity, and only a fortunate chance may enable us to trace his ancestry.

Early in the year 1639, a party under the leadership of Antony Thacher crossed over to Cape Cod and settled upon a tract of land called by the Indians Mattakeese, to which they gave the name of Yarmouth.

With them went Richard Sares, accompanied probably by his wife and infant son, Paul. He took up a residence on Quivet Neck, between Quivet and Sesreit creeks, where in September of the same year their daughter Deborah was born, perhaps the second white child, and first girl born there; Zachary Rider being supposed to have been the first boy.

His first house was built upon the southerly side of the bluff near the sea shore, where the cellar, a mere hole for vegetables some ten feet square, was pointed out to my informant early in this century.

At a later date he built again a short distance north-west from the ancient house built by Captain John Sears, *circa* 1704, which is still standing, and the site of this later residence is still recognizable.

His first house was, perhaps, what was called " a palisade house; " " such houses were built by placing sills directly upon the ground, in these, two parallel rows of holes were bored, some six inches apart, for the insertion of poles, the space between being filled in with stones and clay, openings being left for a door and windows.

" The roof was thatched with the long sedge-grass found in the meadows, and as a substitute for glass in the windows, oiled paper was used.

" The chimney was built of sticks, laid up cob-house fashion, and well daubed with clay, or mortar made from shells.

" A southerly slope for the house was preferred, and the back of the chimney was then hollowed out of the hill-side, thus saving some labor in building.

" The fire-place was of stone, some eight feet wide and four feet deep, and the mantel laid so high that a tall person could walk under it by stooping a little.

" The oven was often built upon the outside of the house with the mouth opening in one corner, on the back side of the fire-place. The fire was built in the center, and on a cold winter evening a seat in the chimney-corner was a luxury unknown in modern times.

"Straw or sedge-grass served for a floor and carpet.

"Some of the palisade houses built by the early settlers were the most comfortable and durable houses built.

"That of Mr. John Crow stood for nearly two centuries, seldom needing repairs, and in fact the last owners did not know the peculiarities of its construction until it was taken down. The walls of this house were plastered inside and outside with shell mortar, and at some later period, it had been clap-boarded, thus concealing the original construction."

Tea was unknown, and china and porcelain are not found in inventories before 1660.

Forks were not in use in England when the Pilgrims left, and chairs were articles of luxury, the use of stools being almost universal.

An idea of the household furniture may be obtained from the inventories printed later on.

In early colonial times a large family was considered a great blessing in a pecuniary point of view. The boys assisted the father on the farm, and at seventeen were able to do the work of a man. The girls were also brought up to more than earn their own living. They assisted the mother, spun and wove the flax and the wool, and made their own and their brothers' garments, and in hay-time and harvest assisted with their brothers in the fields.

A man with a large and healthy family of children was then the most independent of men. From his farm and his household he obtained an abundance of the prime necessaries of life. The surplus which he sold was more than sufficient to pay the bills of the mechanic, and to buy the few articles of foreign merchandise then required.

Taxes were paid in agricultural products, at a rate fixed by law; and if land or other property was sold, unless it was expressly stipulated in the contract that payment should be made in silver money, it was a barter trade, payable in produce at "the prices current with the merchants."

Aged people were wont to remark that their ancestors estimated that every son born to them added £100 to their wealth and every daughter £50.

However heterodox this theory may now appear to parents or to political economists, it was undoubtedly true in early times.

The Searses with but few exceptions all married in early life, had large families, acquired good estates, lived comfortably and were respected and honored members of society.

The early settlers were engaged principally in agricultural pursuits, stock-raising and fishing.

Many whales were cast upon the coast, and the shore was divided in sections, under the charge of whaling squads chosen by the town.

Capt. Paul Sears and Lt. Silas Sears belonged to one of these gangs, and some of Paul's whaling gear is enumerated in his will and inventory. Capt. John Sears was also engaged in whaling.

Oil, fish and tar were exchanged with the traders visiting the coast for goods which were needed, and which they did not themselves produce.

They traded in their own vessels with the West Indies, bringing home molasses and spirits, and built vessels which they themselves manned.

The Cape seamen have always been famed for their skill and daring.

At a later date John Sears invented the method of making salt by solar evaporation, and was the pioneer in an industry that added much to the wealth of the Cape, until superseded by the salt-springs of Syracuse, etc.;— and Elkanah Sears of Dennis was the first to set out cranberries at Flax Pond in 1819.

The Cape farms produced good crops of Indian corn, rye, barley and some wheat, and all sorts of vegetables; berries were plenty, and cranberries were indigenous.

Game was plenty, and with fish abundantly supplied the table; cows and goats were kept for milk, and bees for honey.

Beer was regarded a necessity, and each family brewed at

regular intervals. Spirits were consumed in considerable quantities, and the names of many of the best citizens are upon record as "licensed to draw wine," etc.

The mothers of the town were expert in the use of the loom and made most of the cloth used in their families.

In the summer they wore home-spun linen, and in winter flannel.

The sails of a vessel built at Hockanum at the close of the Revolutionary war were made of cloth woven by them.

Clocks were at first unknown, a sun-dial cut upon the sill of a southern window gave them the time of day, and it was long customary to face the house due south.

In 1745, but one clock and one watch were taxed in the town of Harwich.

The observance of the Lord's day was rigidly enforced, and no one was allowed to labor, engage in any game or recreation, or travel upon that day, under penalties proportioned to the offense.

The tithing men appointed in each town had with other duties, that of keeping order among the boys in church, and were armed with long rods, tipped at one end with a squirrel tail or rabbit's foot, for the purpose of awaking sleeping women, and at the other with brass or a deer's hoof, which they brought down with emphasis on the heads of male offenders.

The journey to and from meeting was, to many, long and tedious.

Those who had horses were wont to "ride and tie," i. e., one would ride a specified distance, and then alight and fasten the animal, and proceed on foot, leaving the coming pedestrian to mount and ride for the next stage.

The women and small children rode on pillions behind their lords and masters, but the young people of either sex were expected to make the journey on foot, and no doubt with congenial company they found the miles short enough.

In winter the only mode of keeping themselves warm in meeting was by the use of foot stoves, or a hot brick or stone.

In the intervals between morning and afternoon service, the

men and boys assembled outside to discuss town affairs, the
prospect of crops, or fishing; while the women over their
luncheon, in the meeting-house, or at some convenient neighbors, had their gossip.

But to return to my narrative.

In 1643, the name of Richard *Seeres* appears in the list of
"inhabitants of Yarmouth. between the ages of 16 and 60,
liable to bear arms." June 3, 1652, Richard *Seeres* was "propounded to take up Freedom," and Richard *Sares* "took
oath of Fidellyte at Plimouth," June 7, 1653. Richard *Sares*
was chosen Grand Juryman, June 7, 1652, and Constable, June
6, 1660.

June 3, 1662, Richard *Saeres* was chosen Representative to
the General Court at Plymouth.

These are some of the early spellings of the name on the
records, but in his will, and in the deed to him of Sesuit, his
name is written *Sares,* and such I assume to have been the correct form of spelling and pronunciation in those days.

Why Richard Sares did not sooner apply to be made a freeman does not appear.

To become a freeman each person was legally required to
be a respectable member of some Congregational church, and
none but freemen could hold office or vote for rulers. Many
people avoided citizenship to escape petty offices and court
duties which a freeman might not decline without suffering a
fine, and the Government found it necessary to use persuasion
and something like compulsion to lead desirable men to accept
these duties and privileges.

It does not appear that Richard Sares was at first a member
of the church in Yarmouth, and from the fact that he chose to
settle upon the extreme verge of the town, near what was
afterward known as the " Wing neighborhood," where Quaker
meetings were sometimes held, it has been inferred that he
perhaps had a leaning that way; — be this as it may, we find
the name of Richard *Seares* as one of the Committee appointed
Mar. 1, 1658, to levy church tax, and 30. 4 mo. (June) 1667,
the name of Richard Sares is signed with fourteen others to a

complaint against Nicholas Nickerson for slander of Rev. Thomas Thornton.

The original document is now in possession of Mr. H. C. Thacher of Boston, and a reduced fac-simile of it may be seen in Swift's " Hist. of Old Yarmouth," 1884.

The name of Richard Sares is well and plainly written, but it is not certain that it is his autograph, (and no other is known,) as it and several others may have been written by one hand, such is their resemblance, one to the other.

The document is not a legal one, and it was not unusual for parties then, as now, to allow their names to be appended by others to such papers.

His will dated 10. 3 mo. (May) 1667, and the codicil thereto, dated ten years later, viz., 3 Feb., 1676, are both signed with his mark, a by no means unusual circumstance in those days.

It will be noticed that he made his mark to his will a month previous to the date of the Thacher document, to which a full signature is affixed.

Mr. H. G. Somerby in his manuscript collections in the library of Mass. Hist. So. Boston, mentions a *tradition* that he held a commission in the militia, and lost his right arm by a gun-shot wound in a fight with Indians in 1650, but neither fact is recorded, nor is any such tradition known to Cape antiquarians. The mark appended to his will and codicil is apparently the letters R. S., one over the other. I infer that he had been able to write his name, but was then prevented by disability, perhaps rheumatism.

Oct. 26, 1647, he entered a complaint against Nepoytam, Sachamus, and Felix, Indians ; and Oct. 2, 1650, he with sixteen others complained of Wm. Nickarson for slander, damage £100, and at same term of court we find his name with seventeen others against Mr. John Crow, Wm. Nickarson and Lieut. Wm. Palmer for trespass, damage £60.

In 1664, Richard Sares, "husbandman," purchased a tract of land at Sesuit, from Allis Bradford, widow of Gov. Wm. Bradford, for the sum of £20. A copy of the deed, and of a quit-claim from her son, Major Wm. Bradford, to Paul Sears, will be found farther on.

On 10. 3 mo. (May) 1667, he made his will, to which he added 3 Feb., 1676–7, a codicil which with the inventory are recorded in Ply. Rec., Book 3, Part 2, pp. 53–55.

Therein he mentions "wife Dorothy," "*elder*" and "*eldest* son Paule Sares," "youngest son Sylas Sares," "daughter Deborah," "son-in-law Zachery Padduck," and "Ichabod Padduck, son of Zachery Padduck," and requests "*brother* Thacher with his two sons as friends in trust," etc.

His inventory in the original record is footed up £169.06.06, · a manifest error, the real estate alone being valued at £220, and the amount of the last item not being carried out.

Nor would the corrected sum represent his worldly condition fairly, as he had no doubt previously given to his children such portions of his property as he could conveniently spare.

In the proper places I give copies of the wills and inventories of Richard Sares and his sons, by a careful examination of which, the location of the original estates may be traced in part, and some idea be formed of the relative wealth and personal belongings of each.

It is to be regretted that no plan is now known to be in existence showing the bounds of the original estates in Yarmouth and Harwich, and recent attempts to construct such have not met with much success.

No gravestones remain to mark the burial places of Richard Sares and his wife, though they are supposed to rest in the ancient cemetery in Yarmouth, and they probably never had any inscribed stones; upright gravestones did not come in use in England until the time of Queen Elizabeth, and the early graves in Plymouth Colony were generally marked with a boulder.

Some years since a granite monument was erected in Yarmouth cemetery by the late Hon. David Sears of Boston, which is popularly supposed to mark the spot of their interment, but I am informed by aged members of the family that it was really placed over the grave of Paul Sears, his gravestone being removed for the purpose, although it is highly probable that Paul was buried by the side of his parents.

There is no stone to his (Paul's) wife Deborah, nor to his brother Silas, whose burial-place is unknown.

The stone to Paul Sears records his death in 1707–8, and it is the oldest inscribed memorial in the cemetery, although Swift in his " Hist. Old Yarmouth," accords that credit to the grave-stone of Col. John Thacher, who died in 1713.

There are no reliable traditions extant of Richard Sares and his family, and our only sources of information relative to them are the public records to which I have referred.

In Plymouth Colony, the governor, deputy-governor, and magistrates and assistants, the ministers of the gospel and elders of the church, schoolmasters, commissioned officers in the militia, men of wealth, or men connected with the families of the nobility or gentry, were alone entitled to the prefix, Mr., pronounced Master, and their wives, Mrs., Mistress.

This rule was rigidly enforced in early Colonial times, and in lists of names it was almost the invariable custom to com mence with those who stood highest in rank, and follow that order to the end. Our forefathers claimed, and were cheerfully accorded the title due to their birth and position, and it is un-wise to claim for them any title which they did not themselves assume.

I do not find that Richard Sares was given the prefix of re-spect, and in the town records it is written that his wife, " Goody Sares was buried Mar. 19, 1678–9."

He was a farmer, hard-working and industrious, an affection-ate husband and kind parent, a God-fearing man, and respected by his neighbors.

His descendants showed good breeding, and many of them were prominent in church and town affairs, and in the militia.

Their names may be found in the records of the Indian and French wars, the Revolutionary war, and that of 1812. Num-bers served during the late Civil war, and shed their blood freely for their country.

The family has always been very religious in its tendency, in latter years leaning to the Methodist and Baptist persuasions, and rather given to *isms;* some of its members have been fore-most in the temperance and anti-slavery movements, but it has never given rise to any prominent politicians, and while holding many local offices, not aspiring beyond the State Legislature.

Of good stature, and comely appearance, they are healthy and long-lived, enterprising and esteemed citizens wherever found.

> " Worth is better than Wealth,
>   Goodness greater than Nobility,
>   Excellence brighter than Distinction."
>
>   [Sears' Monument.]

1.

RICHARD SARES[1], parentage, place and date of birth unknown, d. in Yarmouth, P. C., and was buried Aug. 26, 1676. His widow, *Dorothy* ——, was buried there Mar. 19, 1678–9. It is not certain that she was his only wife, or the mother of all, if any, of his children. Children :

2.* i. Paul, b. (? Marblehead,) 1637–8 ; d. Yar., Feb. 20, 1707–8, in his 70th year ; gr.-st., Yar.

3.* ii. Silas, d. Yar., Jan. 13, 1697–8 ; a memorandum on Town Rec. by Amos Otis, says he was æ. 60, but gives no authority for the statement, and it is doubtful. If correct he would appear to be born same year as Paul, and was, perhaps, a twin.

4. iii. Deborah, b. Yar., Sep., 1639 ; adm. 2d Ch. from 1st Ch., Yar., Aug. 6, 1727 ; d. there Aug. 17, 1732, " within about one month of 93 years of age ; " m. 1659, *Zachary Paddock*, son of Robert and Mary P., he b. Plymouth, Mar. 20, 1636 ; (his obit. says beginning of 1640, d. Yar., May 1, 1727, æ. 88.) If he was born Mar. 20, 1636, as stated in Ply. Rec., he would have been aged 91, but perhaps there were two Zacharys, the first dying in infancy.

"Yarmouth, co. Barnstable, May 1, 1727.

"This day died here Mr. Zachariah Paddock, in the 88th year of his age, was born in Plymouth in the beginning of the year 1640. He retained his reason to an uncommon degree, until his last illness, which lasted but a few days. He was married in 1659, to Mrs. Deborah Sears, *born in this town*, and now survives him, having lived together about 68 years, and by her, God blest him with a numerous offspring, especially in the third and fourth generations, having left behind him of his own posterity, 48 grand-children and 38 great grand-children, and of this latter sort no less than 30 descendants from his second son. The old gentleman, his wife, one of his sons and his wife lived for a considerable time in a house by themselves, without any other person, when their ages computed together, amounted to over 300 years. Mr. Paddock had obtained the character of a righteous man, and his widow, now near fourscore and eight years old, is well reputed for good works." ["N. E. Weekly News Letter."]

Children, PADDOCK: [1.] Ichabod, b. Yar., Feb. 2, 1661–2; "went to Nantucket to teach whaling." [2.] Zachariah, b. Yar., Apr. 14, 1664; d. Apr. 8, 1717–18, æ. 54, gr.-st., Den.; m. Bethia ——, who d. Mar. 8, 1708, æ. 41, gr.-st.; 2d, July 29, 1708, Mary Thacher, dau. of Elisha Hedge, and widow of Dea. Josiah T., (who d. May 12, 1702,) she b. Mar., 1671; adm. 2d Ch., Yar., from 1st Ch., Aug. 6, 1727; children, i. Ichabod, b. June 1, 1687; adm. 2d Ch., July 12, 1741; d. July 17, 1748; [Ichabod Paddock et al. brought suit against town of Boston, May 28, 1735,] m. Joanna Faunce, dau. Elder Thomas and Jean (Nelson) F., she b. 1689; removed to Middleboro. ii. Deborah, b. Apr. 2, 1689; m. Oct., 1709, Benjamin Bunker. iii. Elizabeth, b. Feb. 11, 1690–1; m. Nov. 2, 1710, Joseph Howes. iv. Zachariah, b. Nov. 10, 1692; adm. 2d Ch., Yar., Sep. 15, 1728; m. June 15, 1718, Eliz'h Howes, dau. Joseph H., she b. Feb. 28, 1694; adm. 2d Ch., May 5, 1728. v. James, b. Dec. 24, 1694; adm. 2d Ch., May 13, 1739; m. Nov. 5, 1719, Rebecca Chapman, dau. of Isaac and Rebecca (Leonard) C., she b. June 10, 1697; adm. 2d Ch., May 5, 1728. vi. Peter, b. May 27, 1697; m. Mar. 16, 1720–21, Sarah Howes, dau. of Jona. H., she b. June 30, 1695; adm. 2d Ch., Aug. 4, 1728. vii. Bethia, b. May 25, 1699; d. Oct. 16, 1728; m. Oct., 1718, Lot Gray. viii. Mary, b. July 10, 1721. ix. John, b. May 21, 1703; m. Feb. 13, 1728, Martha Hopkins, dau. Judah H., of Harwich, she b. Mar. 25, 1705. x. David, b. Aug. 12, 1705; m. Oct. 12, 1727, Mary Foster, dau. Chillingsworth and Mercy (Freeman) F., she b. Jan. 1, 1709–10. xi. Priscilla, b. Feb. 29, 1707; and by wife Mary, xii. Hannah, b. mid. Aug., 1709; m. Feb. 23,

5

1728–9, David Howes, who d. Feb. 3, 1781. xiii. Anthony, b. Feb. 5, 1710–11. [3.] Elizabeth, b. Aug. 1, 1666; m. Nov. 28, 1689, John Howes, son of Matthew H., d. s. p.; 2d, July 8, 1691, Mary Matthews, and d. Apr. 30, 1736. [4.] Capt. John, b. May 5, 1669; d. Feb. 18, 1717–18, in 49 yr., gr.-st.; — m. (pub'd 1694,) Priscilla Hall, dau. of John and Priscilla (Bearse) H., she b. Feb., 1671; d. Jan. 2, 1724–5, in 57 yr., gr.-st.; and had, i. John, b. June 4, 1695; adm. 2d Ch., Aug. 6, 1727; d. Sep. 30, 1732, in 38 yr., gr.-st.; m. 1716, Rebecca Thacher, dau. of Josiah T., she adm. 2d Ch., Aug. 6, 1727; 2d, Hannah ——, adm. 2d Ch., Dec. 3, 1738. ii. son, Feb. 1, 1696–7; d. Feb. 3, 1696–7. iii. Elizabeth, b. Apr. 14, 1698; d. June, 1772, æ. 75; m. Har., Apr. 17, 1718, Joseph Sears, No. 28, and d. s. p. iv. Joseph, b. Mar. 8, 1700; adm. 2d Ch., Mar. 31, 1728; m. Mar. 17, 1725–6, Reliance Stone, dau. Rev. Nathan and Reliance (Hinckley) S., she b. Apr. 26, 1703; adm. 2d Ch., Mar. 31, 1728; d. Mar. 26, 1734, æ. 31; 2d, Nov., 1735, Margaret Crosby, who d. Nov. 27, 1738; 3d, Nov., 1739, Elizabeth Mayo of Eastham. v. Priscilla, b. Jan. 30, 1701–2; m. Feb. 22, 1721–2, Thomas Clark, Jr. vi. Dea. Ebenezer, b. Mar. 18, 1703–4; adm. 2d Ch., Aug. 4, 1728; d. Oct. 18, 1767, in 64 yr., gr.-st.; m. Oct. 21, 1725, Mary Sears, No. 50; adm. 2d Ch., May 5, 1728. vii. child, b. Feb. 25, 1705–6; d. Mar. 6. viii. Thankful, b. June 26, 1710; d. Nov. 26, 1730, in 21 yr., gr.-st. ix. Dr. Josiah, b. Apr. 9, 1712; m. Feb. 17, 1736–7, Mercy Sears, No. 97. [5.] Robert, b. Jan. 17, 1670–1; m. Mar. 6, 1701–2, Martha Hall, dau. John and Priscilla (Bearse) H., she b. May 24, 1676; and had, i. son, b. Feb. 2, 1702–3; d. 7 weeks after. ii. Seth, b. Mar. 13, 1704–5; m. Apr. 13, 1727, Mercy Nickerson. [6.] Joseph, b. Sep. 12, 1674; had, i. Seth, b. Nantucket, July 9, 1699. [7.] Nathaniel, b. Sep. 22, 1677; m. Nantucket, Dec. 15, 1706, by William Worth, Esq., to Ann Bunker. [8.] Capt. Judah, b. Sep. 15, 1681; adm. 2d Ch., Aug. 23, 1761; d. Mar. 31, 1770, in 89 yr., gr.-st.; m. Dec. 5, 1706, Alice (or Else) Alden, dau. David and Mary (Southworth) A., and gr.-dau. John and Priscilla (Mullens) A., she adm. 2d Ch., June 23, 1728; d. July 12, 1774, in 89 yr., gr.-st.; had, i. Reuben, b. Dec. 27, 1707. ii. Judah, b. Mar. 27, 1709–10. iii. Samuel, b. Oct. 12, 1711; d. July 27, 1757, in 46 yr., gr.-st.; m. Dec. 2, 1744, Thankful Howes; adm. 2d Ch., May 21, 1775;

d. June 27, 1789, in 78 yr., gr.-st. iv. Mary, b. Mar. 5, 1714–15 ; m. Nov., 1731, Judah Sears, No. 30. v. Grace, b. Jan. 27, 1715–16 ; d. Sep. 17, 1780, æ. 65 ; m. Nov., 1731, John Sears, No. 31. vi. Rebecca, b. May 12, 1718. vii. Nathaniel, b. Feb. 27, 1723–4.

1664. Prence, Govr.:

A deed appointed to be recorded.

" Witnesseth these p^{r}sents, that I, Allis Bradford the widow of William Bradford, late of Plymouth in America, Esqre, deceased, have the day and year aforesaid, for and in consideration of the sum of twenty pounds to me the said Allis Bradford in hand payed before the ensealing and delivery of these p^{r}sents, by Richard Sares of the town of Yarmouth, in the colony of New Plymouth, aforesaid, husbandman, whereof and of every p'te and p'cell thereof, I the said Allis Bradford do fully acquit and discharge him the said Richard Sares, his heirs and assigns forever, bargained and sold, enfeoffed, assigned and confirmed, and by these presents do bargain, sell, enfeoffe, assign and confirm unto him the said Richard Sares, his heirs and assigns, two allotments of land containing forty acres, be they more, or be they less, lying and being at a place commonly called and known by the name of Sasnett, between a brook commonly called and known by the name of bound brook, and a brook called Saquahuckett brook,—twenty acres whereof was the first lot, (so-called) of upland with a small neck of land next the said bound brook, on the Easter side the said brook, and was the lot of the aforesaid William Bradford, deceased ; the other twenty acres of land lying and being the next adjoining hereunto on the Easter side called the 2cond lott, and was late an allotment of land of Experience Michels ; both which allotments of land are bounded on the Wester side with bound brook aforesaid, and on the Easter side with an allotment of land late Nicholas Snowes, now in the tenure and possession of Peter Worden, as also a certain tract of meadow to the aforesaid lots appertaining, of seven acres and one half be it more or less, lying, being and abutting, between the norther side of the said nook of upland bound brook and small creeke, as from the Easter corner of the said nook, from a spring which runs through the meadows into the said bound brook ; together with all the perquisites, profits, ways, easements, emoluments and appurtenances thereunto belonging ; with all my right, title, claim and interest unto the said lots of upland and meadow or any part or parcel thereof.

To have and to hold the said two lots of upland, nook and

meadow with every p'te and p'eell thereof, together with all the perquisites, profits, emoluments, ways, easements and appurtenances thereunto or to any part or parcel thereof any ways belonging.

To him the said Richard Sares, his heirs and assigns forever, I say to the only use and behoof of him the said Richard Sares, his heirs and assigns forever.

In witness whereof the said Allis Bradford have heerto these presents set my hand and seal even the twenty third day of November, Anno dom. 1664.

ALLIS BRADFORD,

Signed, sealed and delivered ⎱   her + mark,
  in the presence of   ⎰   and a seale.   ×

THOMAS SOUTHWORTH,
MARY CARPENTER, her + mark.

Plymouth, ss. June 2, 1885. The foregoing is a true copy from Plymouth Colony Record of Deeds, Vol. 3, Part 1, Page 18. Attest, Wm. S. Danforth, Reg. of Deeds, and having charge of the Plymouth Colony Records.

1667.

The last Will and Testament of Richard Sares, of Yarmouth, late deceased, as followeth ; —

In the name of God, Amen. I, Richard Sares of Yarmouth, in the Colony of New Plymouth, in New England, do this 10th day of the third month, Anno Dom. 1667, make and ordain this my last Will and Testament, in manner and form following :—

First,— I give and surrender up my soul to God that gave it, and my body to the earth, from whence it was, in comely and decent manner to be buried, &c.; and all my lands and goods as God hath given me, I give and bequeath as followeth :

First.— I give and bequeath, and my Will is, that Silas Sares, my younger son, shall have all my land, that is, all the upland upon the neck where his house stands in which he now dwells, thus bonded and lying between the cart pathway as runs through the swamp into the said neck unto the land of Peter Werden, and so all along by the lands of the said Peter Werden unto the meadows as are betwixt the said upland and the sea, and so as it is surrounded by the meadows unto the aforesaid cartpath as runs through the swamp aforesaid, after mine and my wifes deccase.

To him, the said Sylas Sares, to him, and his heirs and assigns forever, (provided, and my will is, that whereas my son-in-law Zachery Padduck is possessed of, and now lives in an house that is his own proper right within the aforesaid tract of land, that he the said Zachery shall have and enjoy two acres of the aforesaid lands about his said house for and during the life of Deborah, his now wife; together with all ways, easements, and emoluments, to the same appertaining, without any molestation, and eviction or denial of him the said Silas, his heirs or assigns:) And my will is, and I do hereby give unto the said Silas Sares, all that tract of meadow land, as is, and lyeth between the aforesaid neck of upland, and the river, commonly called and known by the name of Sasuett harbor, river bound: also thus from the Great Pine tree as bounds the meadows between the meadows of the aforesaid Peter Werden, and my meadows, unto a knoll of upland called the Island, towards the said harbour's mouth, to the said Sylas and his heirs and assigns forever, after mine and my wifes decease.

Further,— I do give and bequeath to my son Sylas, after mine and my wifes decease, as aforesaid, one half moiety of all that my land called Robins, as is unfenced.

I mean only one half moiety, and part of the upland.

To him the said Sylas, his heirs and assigns forever.

And my Will is, and I do give and bequeath unto my elder son Paul Sares, all the rest and remain of my lands, whatsoever, and every part and parcel of them whatsoever, after mine and my wifes decease, both upland and meadow lands, which I have not in this my last Will, disposed of.

To him, the said Paul Sares, his heirs and assigns forever.

And my Will is, and I do give unto Dorethy my wife, all my lands whatsoever to be at her dispose during her natural life, and I do give unto her all my other goods and cattle whatsoever during her life, and at or before her death, to give and bequeath them amongst my children, at her pleasure, who also I do make sole executrix of this my last Will and testament: and do intreat my brother Thacher, with his two sons as friends in trust, to see this my last will performed:

Furthermore my Will is, that whereas I have bequeathed to my two sons Paul and Silas all that tract of upland called Robins, as is unfenced, by an equal proportion between them, my Will is, I say, that my son-in-law Zachery Padduck shall have two acres of the said upland before it be divided as aforesaid during his said wifes life: and after the decease of his said now wife, my will is, and I do give unto Ichabod Padduck, the

said two acres of Robins, and also the aforesaid two acres of
land adjoining to the house of his father, Zachery Padduck
during his natural life.

In witness whereof, I have to this my last Will and Testament set my hand.

In the presence of   The marke of
    ANTHONY THACHER   RICHARD (RS) SARES.
    ANTHONY FREY

Anthony Frey testifieth to the former part of this Will that
he saw Richard Sares sign it as his Last Will and Testament,
this second day of March, 1676.

             Before me, JOHN FREEMAN, *Assistant.*

Be it known to all to whom these presents shall come, that
I, Richard Sares of Yarmouth, in the Colony of New Plymouth,
as in this my will before mentioned, being now weak in body,
but of perfect sense and memory, do by these presents ratify
and confirm my Will, as it has been made on the other side,
bearing date the 10th of the third month 1667.

And I do add hereto as followeth, that at my wifes decease
my eldest son Paul Sares shall have and enjoy to his own
proper use, the house which I now live in, and my bed and the
bedding thereto belonging, and my clothing, and the cattle that
shall be left at my wifes decease, and also my warming pan, and
the earthen pott with the cover that belongs to it, and the iron
pot and the table: and in witness hereof I have hereunto set
my hand and seale, this third day of February Anno Dom.
1675.76.

In the presence of   The mark of (RS) RICHARD SARES.
    JOHN THACHER
    JUDAH THACHER

I, John Thacher do testify, that myself and my brother did
set our hands as Witnesses to this Will, as being his last Will
and Testament, and when my Uncle signed this Appendix to
the Will, he delivered the Will to me, and desired me to new
draw the whole Will, and to leave out of the new draft, the
legacy of land that is given to Ichabod Paddock, for saith he,
I have anseized it in another way, but if I die before you have

done it, then it must go as it is; and trouble took me off so
that I did not redraw the will.

I having thus explained myself, do testify that this Will is
the last Will and Testament of my Uncle Sares, so far as I
know.

This fift of March 1676.

Mr. John Thacher attested to this Will before me,

JOHN FREEMAN, *Assistant.*

October the Eighth day in the year of our Lord, one thousand, six hundred and seventy six,

This being a true Inventory of the Estate of Richard Sares,
lately deceased, according to our best information and judgment, taken by us whose names are under written, as followeth:

	£	s.	d.
Imp. his house and land......................	220	00	00
Item, five cows...............................	10	00	00
Item, 1 bull, 1 heifer of three years and vantage.	03	10	00
Item, 1 heifer of two years and vantage.......	01	10	00
Item, 5 year olds.............................	05	00	00
Item, 2 calves...............................	01	00	00
Item, his bed and the furniture thereto belonging.	08	07	00
Item, more, 2 pairs of sheets.................	02	15	00
Item, 2 sheets, and 2 pairs of drawers........	01	01	00
Item, 1 table cloth, 1 pillow beare, 1 napkin, 3 towels.....................................	00	08	00
Item, britches and hat.......................	02	03	00
Item, his coat and cloak......................	02	00	00
Item, 1 pair of stockings and shoes...........	00	05	00
Item, 1 great Bible and other books...........	01	03	00
Item, pewter and tin	01	03	00
Item, brass.................................	00	06	00
Item, 1 pair of stilliyards....................	00	15	00
Item, iron furniture for the fire..............	00	12	00
Item, more on rugg..........................	00	04	00
Item, 2 chests...............................	00	16	00
Item, 1 beer barrell & one earthen pott.......	00	04	00
Item, 3 chairs..............................	00	07	00
Item, his bees	01	00	00
Item, other householdments..................	00	08	00
Item, more, two waistcoats	00	12	00

	£	s.	d.
Item, 1 mare and colt...............	00	10	00
Item, debts in cash........	0!	19	00
Item, more, 2 Indian trays.............			
	169	06	06

       Thomas Boardman
       Lancher Winslow
       Samuel Worden
       This 15th day of November 1676.
           Dorothy Sares the relict of
           Richard Sares, and Paul Sares
           his eldest son, made their appearance
           and gave oath to the truth of this
           Inventory above written
           before me,   JOHN FREEMAN, *Assistant.*

Plymouth, ss. Apl. 24, 1883.   The foregoing is a true copy from Plymouth Colony Records, Vol. III of Wills, folios 53, 54, 55.

Attest, WM. S. DANFORTH, *Reg.*

SECOND GENERATION.

2.

Capt. PAUL SEARS[2] [*Richard*[1]], b. (prob. in Marblehead, Mass.), after Feb. 20, 1637–8; d. Yarmouth, Mass., Feb.
20, 1707–8, in 70 yr., gr.-st.; m. Yar., 1658, *Deborah Willard,*
dau. of George W.; she bap. Scituate, P. C., by Rev. Wm.
Witherell, Sep. 14, 1645; d. Yar., May 13, 1721; (her mother
was, perhaps, Dorothy Dunster, see *post.*)   Children:

5. i. MERCY, b. Yar., July 3, 1659; "13 yrs. old, 3 July,
       1672."
6. ii. BETHIA, b. Yar., Jan. 3, 1661–2; "11 yrs. old 3 Jan.,
       1672;" d. Chatham, Mass., July 5, 1724, æ. 63, gr.-st.;
       m. May 27, 1684, *John Crowell, Jr.,* of Nobscussett, he b.
       1662; d. Oct. 11, 1728; children, CROWELL: [1.] Joseph,
       b. Mar. 20, 1685; m. Oct. 27, 1709, Bathsheba Hall; 2d,
       Sep. 4, 1723, Sarah Howes; and had, i. Joseph, b. Aug.
       20, 1713. ii. Stephen, b. Apr. 28, 1727. [2.] Paul, b.
       Apr. 20, 1687; m. Oct. 21, 1714, Eliz'h Hallet; 2d, Feb. 25,
       1724–5, Margery Hall of Yar.; lived in Chatham, and had,
       i. Abigail, m. —— Collins. ii. Paul, m. Rebecca ——,
       who d. Dec. 30, 1746; 2d, Reliance ——; 3d, Mehitable
       ——. iii. Jonathan, m. July 13, 1738, Ann Nickerson.
       iv. Eliz'h, m. —— Doane. v. Daniel. [3.] Bethia, b.
       Apr. 13, 1689; m. Oct. 12, 1710, Joseph Atwood, and had,
       i. Joseph, b. Feb. 19, 1720–1; m. Deborah Sears, No. 66.
       [4.] Mehitable, b. Sep. 3, 1691; m. May 20, 1713, John
       Ryder. [5.] John, b. July, 1693; m. Oct. 23, 1718, Ke-
       zia Eldridge; rem. to Falmouth, Mass., and had, i. Debo-
       rah, b. Sep. 21, 1719; m. Aug. 24, 1738, John Sears, No.
       47. ii. Mehitable, b. Aug. 14, 1721; m. Mar. 31, 1743,
       Zech. Sears, No. 83. iii. John, b. Jan. 9, 1723–4; m.
       Mar. 11, 1747, Mary Howes. iv. Bethia, b. Mar. 4, 1726–
       7. v. Kezia, b. July 13, 1729; d. July 29. vi. Kezia, b.
       May 18, 1730; d. May 29. vii. Samuel, b. Mar. 21, 1733–4;

d. June 28.   viii. Kezia, b. May 17, 1734.   ix. Samuel,
b. Dec. 29, 1735; d. Mar. 7, 1735-6.   x. Anna, b. Mar.
29, 1738.   xi. Mary, b. Dec. 13, 1739; m. 1759, Judah
Sears, No. 130.   [6.] Deborah, b. July 1, 1695; d. Jan.
11, 1705-6.   [7.] Christopher, b. July 24, 1698; d. Jan.
12, 1781; m. Sep. 23, 1724, Sarah Matthews, she b. 1702;
and had, i. Hannah, b. Sep. 9, 1725; m. Apr. 9, 1742,
Edmund Sears, No. 44. ii. Eliz'h, b. July 3, 1728; d. Dec.
3, 1744.   iii. Sarah, b. July 14, 1729; m. Dec. 11, 1745,
Seled (or Sealed) Sanders.   iv. Mary, b. Mar. 19, 1731.
v. Temperance, b. Apr. 19, 1733; m. Jan. 3, 1760, Isaac
Howes.   vi. William, b. Mar. 25, 1734; m. Jan. 21, 1773,
Hannah Sears, No. 317.   vii. Christopher, b. Apr. 7,
1737; m. Dec. 24, 1761, Deborah Sears, No. 236.   viii.
Enoch, b. May 25, 1739; m. Dec. 9, 1763, Bathsheba Pad-
dock. ix. Bethia, b. Aug. 28, 1741. x. John, b. Feb. 2, 1744;
d. Apr. 6, 1825.   [8.] Elizabeth, b. Oct. 8, 1700; m. Dec.
22, 1721, Benj. Homer of Boston, son of Capt. John and
Margery (Stephens) H.; he b. May 8, 1698; d. Yar., Feb.
24, 1776, æ. 78; had, i. Bethia, b. Mar. 18, 1722; m. Benj.
Cobb of Boston.   ii. John, b. Sep. 28, 1724; m. Sep.
28, 1749, Abigail Osborn of Nantucket.   iii. Margery, b.
June 13, 1727; m. Jan. 3, 1765, Willard Sears of Har.,
No. 49; 2d, Benj. Higgins of Eastham; she d. Aug. 6,
1787, æ. 60, gr.-st. iv. William, b. July 14, 1729; a loyalist,
rem. to Barrington, N. S.   v. Benjamin, b. Aug. 15, 1731;
rem. to Boston; m. Oct. 23, 1759, Mary Parrott, dau. of
Bryant and Ruth (Wadsworth) P.; d. Oct. 24, 1776; from
them derives Albertina Homer Shelton, who m. Fred. R.
Sears, No. 1494. vi. Stephen, b. Apr. 15, 1734; m.
Eliz'h Chapman of Yar.   vii. Thomas, b. Mar. 21, 1736;
m. Nov. 21, 1765, Eliz'h Sears, dau. of Capt. Edm'd
and Hannah (Crowell) S.; she b. Oct. 16, 1745; d. 1819;
rem. to Vermont.   viii. Elizabeth, b. Nov. 18, 1738; m.
David Knowles of Eastham.   ix. Robert, b. Jan. 28,
1742; m. Jan. 7, 1768, Jerusha Sears, dau. of Dan'l and
Mercy (Snow) S.; she b. June 28, 1740; d. soon; 2d,
widow of John Thacher.   [9.] Mercy, b. Dec. 25, 1704;
m. Sep. 4, 1723, Thos. Bray.

7.* iii. Samuel, b. Yar., last of Jan., 1663-4; "9 yrs. old last
Jan., 1672."

8. iv. *Dau.*, b. Yar., Oct. 24, 1666; "6 yrs. old 24 Oct., 1672;"
perhaps Lydia; m. *Eleazer Hamblen,* son of Jas. H.,
2d, of Har.; he b. Apr. 12, 1668; d. about 1697; 2d,

Thomas Snow, son of Mark and Jane (Prence) S. Children, HAMBLEN: [1.] Elisha, b. Jan. 26, 1697–8; m. Eliz'h Mayo of Eastham. SNOW: [2.] Lydia, b. 1707. [3] Thomas, b. June 15, 1709. [4.] Aaron, b. Feb. 15, 1710–11. [5.] Ruth, b. 1713.

  9.* v. PAUL, b. Yar., June 15, 1669; " 3 yrs. old 15 June, 1672."

10. vi. ——RY (Mary or Margery), b. Yar., Oct. 24, 1672; is thought to have been MARY, wife of Col. John Knowles of Eastham, who d. 1745, æ. 77, (if my copy of the epitaph on her gravestone be correct,) but the age does not agree with that of her birth as recorded; children, KNOWLES: [1.] Willard, (Col.,) m. Bethia Atwood, dau. of Joseph A. [2.] Joshua, b. 1696. [3.] John, b. 1698. [4.] Seth, b. 1700. [5.] Paul, b. 1702; m. Feb. 28, 1729, Phebe Paine, dau. of Thos. P. [6.] James, b. 1704. [7.] Jesse, b. 1707. [8.] Mary, b. 1709.

11. vii. ANN, b. Yar., Mar. 27, 1675; d. Nov. 14, 1745, in 71 yr., gr.-st., Truro; m. *John Merrick* of Harwich, Jan. 28, 1703.

12.* viii: JOHN, b. Yar., 1677–8; d. Apr. 9, 1738, in 61 yr., gr.-st.

13.* ix. RICHARD, b. Yar., 1680–1; d. May 24, 1718, in 38 yr., gr.-st.

14.* x. DANIEL, b. Yar., 1682–3; d. Aug. 10, 1756, in 74 yr., gr.-st.

Paul Sears took the oath of "Fidellyte" in 1657, held a commission as captain in the militia, and made claim for a horse lost in the Narragansett war, but I find no record of his services. October 30, 1667, he was one of the grand jury, in an inquest held on the child of Nicholas Nickerson. He was one of the original proprietors of lands in Harwich, between Bound and Stony brooks, known as "Wing's Purchase," as appears by deed of John Wing et als., to Paul Seers et als., dated Apr. 16, 1677, recorded at Plymouth.

The early town records of Yarmouth were destroyed by fire at the burning of the town clerk's house in 1674, and from the succeeding volume the first twenty-six pages are gone, and others mutilated and worn.

The names and dates of birth of his children have been supplied from various sources, and are believed to be correct.

I annex copies of the will and inventory of Paul Sears;— the will is signed with his mark, as is also the inventory of John Burge's estate, rendered by him, and recorded Barns. Rec. II, 1701, p. 130.

He left property valued at £467 03 03, to his "loving wife Deborah," and to his sons, "Samuel, Paul and John;" that to his sons being charged with a payment to "*their brothers*, Richard and Daniel, towards their purchase of lands at Manamoy;" having given to his daughters, (whose names are unfortunately omitted,) "such parts or portions as I was able or thought fitt."

In the ancient cemetery in Yarmouth lies a stone slab, removed from its place to make room for the granite monument to the Searses, which bears the following inscription, surmounted by a cherub's head and scroll work:

HERE LYES THE
BODY OF PAUL
SEARS, WHO
DEPARTED THIS
LIFE FEBRUARY Y^E
20TH 1707, in Y^E 70TH
YEAR OF HIS AGE."

It is the oldest dated memorial in the cemetery.

His wife was doubtless laid by his side, but there is no stone to her memory.

George Willard, the father of Paul Sears' wife, was the son of Richard and Joane (Morebread) W., of Horsmonden, Kent, Eng., where he was bap. Dec., 1641; he settled at Scituate for a time, removing thence it is said to Maryland. There is some reason to believe that his wife was Dorothy Dunster, dau. of Henry D., of Baleholt, near Bury, Lanc., sister to Eliz'h D., who m. his bro. Simon Willard; and to Rev. Henry D., Pres. of Harvard College. [See Willard Mem., 1858, p. 339.]

Paul Sears was the first to adopt the present spelling *Sears.*

In the name of God, Amen, the Twentieth Day of February, 1707-8.

I, Paul Sears, Senr. of Yarmouth, in ye County of Barnstable, in New England, being at this time ill and weak in body, but of Disposing mind and memory, Praised be God, Do make, Constitute, ordain and Declare this my Last Will and Testament, in manner and form following:

First, and principally. I Comitt my soul to God, most humbly depending upon the gracious Death and merits of Jesus Christ my only Lord and Saviour for Salvation, and to the free pardon of all my sins. And my Body to the Earth to be buryed in such Decent Christian manner as to my Executors hereafter named shall be thought fitt.

And as for my outward Estate, as Lands, Chattels and Goods, I do order Give and Dispose in manner and form following;

First,— I will that all those Debts and Duties that I owe in Right or Conscience To any person whatsoever shall be truly paid in convenient time, after my Decease by my Executors hereafter named, out of my movable Estate.

Item,— I do give and bequeath to my eldest son Samuel Sears, all that my land and meadow in the township of Harwich upon part whereof his house now stands as is comprehended within and between the boundaries now following: (that is to say,) bounded on the east by Kenelm Winslows Land at ye known and accustomed bounds; and on the west side beginning at a remarkable rock, (lying about four Rods eastward from Yarmouth bound Rock at bound brook,) and from the s^d Remarkable Rock the line runs Southerly over the Swamp and up ye hill to a great Pine tree marked in s^d Yarmouth line: and thence up ye same straight line Southerly to the highway: and thence eastward as the way runs to ye said Winslows Land, (the s^d highway being the bounds on ye south side) And the beginning again att ye sd Remarkable Rock the line runs northerly to a stone sett in ye ground: and thence easterly to the edge of ye marsh by a straight line to another stone sett in to the ground, and so bounded by the marsh to another stone sett in the ground northerly on a straight line to a bend of ye main Creek at a stone sett in the Marsh, and on the north side tis bounded by the known and accustomed bounds: and of my interest in the undivided lands in sd Harwich, viz.: that is my sd son Saml. shall have sixteen acres to himself in ye next Division (ye proprietors make of the undivided Lands) and the one half of all the rest of my interest there. All which sd Lands and Meadows shall be to my sd son Samuel Sears, and to his heirs and assigns forever, he yielding to his mother, my wife, one third part of ye proffits thereof during her natural life, and also paying to his two brothers Richard and Daniel, forty and two pounds in money towards the paying their purchase at Manamoy. I do give him my Try pott and Kettle.

It.— I do give and bequeath to my son Paul Sears and to his heirs and assigns forever, one peice of fresh meadow called the Green Meadow which lyeth on the north side of my old house and is bounded eastward at ye Well or Spring, then

westward taking in all ye Marsh or ground to ye old cartway
(which leads into ye neck) on Joseph Sears fence: thence
northeastward as the sd old cartway and fence runs to Zachariah Paddocks fence or line which is ye bounds on ye north
side to bound brook, the s^d bound brook and well or spring
being the bounds on the east side, and also one quarter part of
my interest of the undivided Lands in sd Harwich (besides the
above sd Sixteen acres given to my son Samuel,) and for the
rest of my son Pauls land is in ye neck where he now dwells,
and by me confirmed by Deed of Gift formerly, and my Will
is that he shall yield to his mother, my wife, one third of the
proffits or income of all I have given him, during her natural
life, and that he shall pay to his two brothers Richard and
Daniel, forty and four pounds in money towards the paying
their purchases att Manamoy.

My will further is that the Ditch which hath been the
accustomed bounds in the marsh betwixt my son Paul, and my
kinsman Josiah Sears shall remain forever; beginning southerly
att ye upland and running straight northerly to the Creek
which did run on ye north side of ye island, which creek shall
be the north bounds:

And my Will is, and I do give all that slip of meadow on
the West side of ye sd ditch unto the said Josiah Sears, his
heirs and assigns forever.

It.—I do give and bequeath unto my son John Sears, and
to his heirs and assigns forever, all the rest of my Homestead,
both housings, lands and meadows, also one quarter part of all
my interest in the undivided lands in ye sd Harwich, excepting
the sixteen acres before given to my son Saml— he my sd son
John allowing and yielding to his mother, my wife, the one
third part of my Housing, and the third of the proffits of ye
lands during her natural life, and he paying to his two brothers
Richard and Daniel, forty and four pounds in money towards
their purchase att Manamoy.

It.—I do give and bequeath all my movable Estate as Cattle, sheep, horses, swine and household stuff &c, unto my loving wife Deborah, (my Debts and Funerall charges being first
paid.) She shall have the rest for her comfort while she lives:
and what she leaves at her death to be equally divided amongst
my daughters to whom I have to each of them given such
parts or portions as I was able or thought fitt.

Lastly,—I do nominate and appoint my sd son Saml Sears
and my Loving Wife Deborah executors to this my last will
and testament.

In witness whereof, I have hereunto sett my hand and seal ye day and year in ye other side first above written.

Signed, sealed & declared in   The mark and seal of
presence of   Paul (=) Sears, Senr. (seal)
     JOHN THACHER
     ZACHARIAH PADDOCK
     SAMUEL HOWES.

Barnstable, ss. April 14, 1883. A true copy of the record, Attest, FREEMAN H. LOTHROP, *Register of Probate Court.*

A true inventory of all and Singular ye Goods, Chattels, Housing, Lands and Credits of Paul Sears, yeoman, deceased, prised at Yarmouth, ye 19th day of March 1708: By Peter Thacher & Kenelm Winslow, as followeth :

	£	s.	d.
Imp^r.— his money 1 17 6 his apparell of all sorts 10 9 0.....................	11	18	6
It.— Two feather beds, two other beds, bedstead, curtains and valance with bolsters, pillows, and all ye coverlids and sheets....................	21	13	6

£ s. d.

	£	s.	d.
It.—Table and chairs 1 4 0 andirons, trammels iron potts & pot hooks........................	03	08	06
Tongs, & fire flue, iron kettles, skillets, frying pans.	03	02	06
It.— Brass kettle, warming pan, hitchell, stillyards chests and boxes...........................	02	06	00
It.— Spinning wheels 10^s pewter platter, plates cups & potts..............................	01	17	00
It.— Koolers, pails, trays, trenches & spoons, table linen & towels.....	01	02	00
It.— his saddle, bridle, pilyon, & cloth, flax & linen yarn..................................	02	00	00
It.— Cash, candlestick, lamp, draving knife axes, sickle & hoes..............................	00	17	00
a sifting trough, wool, five washing tubs knife, scissors, Looking glass................	00	09	00
It.— Salt & feathers, and iron wedge, ye iron belonging to ye cart, and plows and spade a staple and cap ring, & caps & ring..................	02	19	06
It.— 4 bushels Rye, 24 of Indian, 3 of Wheat and ½ his books.................................	05	00	00

	£	s.	d.
Tobacco, 10ˢ pitchforks, powder horn, bullets, and sword...................	00	17	00
Grindstone, and tin ware, 2 oxen, 5 cows, 2 steers.	23	05	00
It.— 2 yearlings, a bull and one horse, 3 swine, 25 sheep...................	11	05	06
It.— his housing, lands, and meadows at 350.....	350	00	00

more about 3 acres of English corn upon ye ground not prised.

	£	s.	d.
The total............	445	07	09
now due to ye Estate about.................	21	15	06

April 8th, 1708.

Samuel Sears Executor to the last Will and Testament of Paul Sears of Yarmouth his deceased father, before Barnabas Lothrop, Esq., Judge of Probate and granting letters of Administration, within this County of Barnstable, made oath that the above written is a true Inventory of ye Estate of ye sd Paul Sears so far as he knows, and that if any thing else that is material shall yt farther come to his knowledge he will bring it to this Inventory.

Attest WM. BASSETT, *Reg.*   PETER THACHER,
                                    KENELM WINSLOW, Jun.

Barnstable, ss. April 14, 1883.   A true copy of the record.
Attest, FREEMAN H. LOTHROP, *Register of Probate Court.*

3.

Lieut. SILAS SEARS² [*Richard* ¹], died Yarmouth, Mass., Jan. 13, 1697–8; m. *Anna* ——, (perhaps *Bursell*, dau. of James B., of Yar.,) who died a widow Yar., Mar. 4, 1725–6. Children :

15.* i. SILAS, b. Yar., 1661.
16.* ii. RICHARD, b. Yar.
17.   iii. HANNAH, b. Eastham, Dec., 1672; adm. Ch. Harwich, 1701; m. Feb. 8, 1692–3, *Thomas Snow*, son of Mark and Jane (Prence) S., he b. Aug. 6, 1668; (m. 2d, Sep. 30, 1706, Mrs. Lydia (Sears) Hamblen, widow of Eleazar H., of Har., and dau. of Paul Sears, by whom he had Lydia, b. 1707. Thomas, b. June 15, 1709. Aaron, b. Feb. 15, 1710–11, and Ruth, b. 1713.) Children, SNOW: [1.] Elizabeth, b. Oct. 25, 1693. [2.] Mary, b. 1696. [3.] Josiah,

b. Jan. 27, 1699. [4.] Ebenezer, b. Feb. 14, 1700–1 ; the first child baptized in Har., Mar. 30, 1701. [5.] Hannah, b. 1703.

18.* iv. JOSEPH, b. Yar., about 1675.

19.* v. JOSIAH, b. Yar., 1675.

20. vi. ELIZABETH, b. Yar., m. there Nov. 22, 1705, *John Cooke.*

21. vii. DORRITY, b. Yar., about 1687 ; m. Yar., Feb. 8, 1715–16, *Joseph Staples ;* was adm. 2d Ch. Yar., June 30, 1728 ; and d. Feb. 28, 1753, æ. 65, gr.-st., No. Dennis. (Joseph Staples was adm. 2d Ch. Yar., July 6, 1766 ; perhaps a son.)

Lieut. Silas Sears lived in that part of Yarmouth known as the East precinct, now East Dennis ; was "propounded to take up Freedom," June 6, 1682 ; com^d Ensign, Oct. 28, 1681 ; Lieut. July 7, 1682 ; chosen Representative to the General Court at Plymouth, 1685–91 ; Selectman, 1680–94 ; Juryman, 1680–82.

25 Dec., 1689, "Silace Sears and others fined 20^s for not appearing and attending at Court, or disorderly departing therefrom ;"—fines remitted later, "it being first offense of the kind."

1694, "Lt Silas Sears on Com. to seat men, women and others in the meeting house ;" an onerous duty in those days.

1 Nov., 1676, Emott Bursell and Silas Sears appointed administrators of the Estate of James Bursell of Yarmouth.

It has been suggested that his wife may have been a daughter of the above James Bursell, but I find nothing whatever to confirm the supposition, which is based, so far as I know, simply upon his being chosen one of the administrators.

He left no will, and letters of administration were granted to his widow Anna, May 1, 1698. The "settlement" of his estate made May 5, 1698, a copy of which is annexed, mentions sons Silas, Richard, Joseph and Josiah ; and daughters, Hannah, Elizabeth and Dorrity.

Rev. E. H. Sears states in the "Sears Genealogy," that Lieut. Silas Sears had a son Thomas, born Yar., 1664, who removed to Newport, R. I., and died there 1707, leaving issue.

About 1860, a gravestone was erected by Hon. David Sears in the old burying ground on Thames street, Newport, which bears the following inscription. [Copy of epitaph in N. E Hist. Reg., communicated by Hon. D. S.]

"HERE LYETH THE BODY OF
THOMAS SEARES,
SON OF L^T. SYLAS SEARES,
OF YARMOUTH, P. C.,
AND GRANDSON OF RICHARD
THE PILGRIM.
BORN IN 1664, AND DIED
AUGUST YE 16TH 1707,
AGED 43 YEARS.

"Beneath this stone the empty casket lies,
The polished jewel brightens in the skies."

P. Stevens & Sons.

This stone is surmounted by the arms of " Sears of Chatham."

The name of Thomas Sears is not found in town or church records of Yarmouth or Newport, nor in the Probate records of Barnstable county, or Newport, R. I.; and the fact that he is not mentioned in the settlement of the estate of Lient. Silas Sears, nine years previous to his alleged death, should be considered good evidence that Silas Sears had no son of that name then living, if he ever had such.

Silas Sears, Jun., did have a son Thomas, born in 1702–3, named for his maternal grand-father, Rev. Thomas Crosby.

SETTLEMENT OF ESTATE OF L^T. SILAS SEARS.

May ye 15th, 1698, by Barnabas Lothrop, Judg of Probate and granting administration in ye county of Barnstable, a settlement of ye Estate of Liu^t. Silas Sears late of Yarmouth deceased Intestate: and to be devided as hereafter exprest.

The widow Anna Sears shall have when debts are paid, one third of ye personal Estate to herself forever: to be at her dispose. And for her dower she shall have one third of ye housing and Land that was her Late husbands sd Silas Sears or ye Improvement thereof During her Natural Life.

The Rest of ye Estate shall be equally divided amongst ye sd deceaseds children, only his eldest son to have a dubble part, at ye Death of ye widow her Dower to be a like divided as aforesaid.

There is to be added to ye Inventory of ye sd personal estate fifty four pounds which sum of sd deceaseds children own that they have allRedy Received of their father as portion, so that ye widows thirds of ye personal Estate when debts are paid coms to thirty three pounds, ye childrens part of ye personal and Real Estate beside ye widows Dower with what they have allRedy had is as followeth:

The eldest son Silas Sears hath as he owned, had alredy, two pounds, and must have more nine pounds.

(The word "thirty" before "two" was doubtless omitted by mistake of the Register in 1698.)

Richard Sears hath had allRedy four pounds and seven shillings, and must have more, sixteen pounds and three shillings.

Hannah Sears hath had allRedy fifteen pounds, and is to have more five pounds and ten shillings.

Joseph Sears hath had allRedy three pounds and is to have more seventeen pounds and ten shillings.

Josiah Sears is to have twenty pounds and ten Shillings.

Elizabeth Sears is to have Twenty pounds and ten shillings.

Dorrity Sears is to have twenty pounds and ten shillings. only if debts should appear more than yet doth due from sd Estate, then widow and children according to what they have or shuld Receive must pay their proportions thereof.

BARNABAS LOTHROP, *Judg of Probate.* (Seale)

Barnstable, ss. Oct. 8, 1885. A true copy of the record, Attest, FREEMAN H. LOTHROP, *Register of Probate Court.*

The Inventory of Liut. Silas Sears of Yarmouth, Lately deceased and his estate prized and ye prise of each particeler set down as followeth:

	£	s.	d.
To houses lands and meadow.	130	00	00
To swine.	01	05	00
To one bed and furniture belonging to it	07	00	00
To another bed and furniture belonging to it	06	00	00
To pewter.	01	05	00
To two Brass Kittles.	01	10	00
To two skillets, a warming pan, spice mortar, box iron	1	00	00
To two tubbs and trays and a earthern pot	00	10	00
To Bookes	00	08	00
To two pailes and to earthern pots	00	02	00
To Barrels	00	07	00

	£	s.	d.
To two wheels and a pair of cards..............	00	05	00
To three old chests..........................	00	07	00
To four chairs...............................	00	03	00
To two tables	00	02	00
To one Gun...............................	01	10	00
To another Gun	00	18	00
To Linnen cloths	00	15	00
To a bed.....	01	00	00
To Flax and Linnen Yarn.....................	00	13	00
To Sheeps wool .....,.....................	00	04	00
To a piece of cloth	00	06	00
To wearing cloaths...........................	08	00	00
To a sett of coopers tools	01	10	00
To 3 axes, and 2 wedges 2 sithes..............	00	10	00
To one carte	00	16	00
To youks, and a chain, and hows, a spade........	01	00	00
To plow irons and a chaine.......	00	06	00
To one grinding stone....................	00	05	00
To 3 sickles, a sourd a candlestick a Tramel Tonges,	00	14	00
To 20 sheepe..............................	05	00	00
To 4 oxen	16	00	00
To 5 cowes and other young cattle..............	20	00	00
To one iron pott and a Looking Glass at.........	00	09	06
To money	00	07	00
To some od small things.....................	00	04	00
To powder and Bulletts........	00	06	00
To account of Debts which is to be paid out of ye Estate			
To Mr John Sloos	02	12	00
To Mr Isaac Chapman	00	10	00
To Nathaniel Cole	10	00	00
To Thankful Boarman.........................	05	15	00
To Samuel Taylor............................	01	10	00
To Seth Taylor James Sturgis..... ....,.....	00	11	06
To Mr Jonathan White........................	00	06	04
To John Paddock	01	12	04
To Mr. Barnabas Lothrop	00	18	06

Anna Sears wid Relict of Lieu[t]. Silas Sears late of Yarmouth deceas'd made oath to ye truth of this Invintory before Barnabas Lothrop Esq Judg of Probate and granting administration May ye 2[d]. 1698.

Examined and entered May ye fourth 1698.

Attest, JOSEPH LOTHROP, *Regist.*

Barnstable, ss. Oct. 8, 1885. A true copy of the records.

Attest, FREEMAN H. LOTHROP, *Register of Probate Court.*

THIRD GENERATION.

7.

Capt. SAMUEL SEARS³ [*Paul²*, *Richard¹*], b. Yarmouth, P. C., the last of Jan., 1663–4; d. Jan. 8, 1741–2, in 78 yr., gr.-st., West Brewster; m. *Mercy Mayo*, dau. of Dea. Samuel and Tamzin (Lumpkin) M., and gr.-dau. of Rev. John Mayo, she b. 1664; d. Jan. 20, 1748–9, in 84 yr., gr.-st., W. Br. Children:

23. i. HANNAH, b. Harwich, July 1, 1685; m. Har., Nov. 2, 1710, *John Vincent*, adm. 2d Ch., Yar., Mar. 10, 1728; children, VINCENT: [1.] Samuel, mentᵈ in will of his uncle Joseph Sears, 1765. [2.] Hannah, bap. 2d Ch., Yar., Feb. 8, 1729–30; adm. Aug. 8, 1742. [3.] David, bap. Apr. 30, 1732; m. Mehitable ——. [4.] John; m. Hannah ——. [5.] Isaac, adm. 2d Ch., Yar., Oct. 16, 1742–3.
24.* ii. SAMUEL, b. Har., Sep. 15, 1687.
25.* iii. NATHANIEL, b. Har., Sep. 23, 1689.
26. iv. TAMSEN, b. Har., Nov. 13, 1691; d. July 17, 1761, æ. 69; m. Mar. 19, 1718–19, *John Freeman*, son of Nath¹ and Mary (Howland) F.; he b. June 15, 1695; d. Eastham, June 9, 1772, æ. 76, (having m. 2d, Oct. 26, 1761, Eliz'h Merrick, who survived him); children, FREEMAN: [1.] John, b. Jan. 30, 1719–20; d. Apr. 1, 1753, æ. 34. [2.] Mary, b. Mar. 27, 1721; m. Joshua Doane of E. [3.] Mercy, b. May 8, 1722; m. Jan. 9, 1739–40, Daniel Freeman. [4.] Abigail, b. June 6, 1723; m. 1751, Elisha Atwood. [5.] Joseph, b. Jan. 6, 1724–5; m. Feb. 16 1748–9, Phebe Paine; and d. 1778. [6.] Gideon (Major), b. May 3, 1726; m. Feb. 25, 1747–8, Hannah Freeman, dau. Capt. Sam¹ F.; and d. Nov. 4, 1807. [7.] Hannah, b. July 12, 1728. [8.] Joshua, b. May 1, 1730; d. young. [9.] Eunice, b. May 1, 1730, *gem.;* m. June 10, 1762, Isaac Foster of Har. [10.] Joshua, b. Nov. 29, 1731.

[11.] Tamsen, b. July 3, 1734; m. John Freeman of Har., his 2d wife; and d. Nov. 23, 1824, æ. 89.

27.* v. JONATHAN, b. Har., Sep. 3, 1693.

28. vi. JOSEPH (Capt.), b. Har., July 15, 1695; d. s. p. Aug. 25, 1765, gr.-st., W. Br.; m. Har., Apr. 17, 1718, *Elizabeth Paddock*, dau. of John P. (see his will, 1723, Barns. Rec. IV, 152), who d. June, 1772, æ. 75, gr.-st., W. Br. He was a Capt. in Militia, and called in Record, "Secundus." "His illness was short, he had scarcely ever a day's sickness; he lived nearly fifty years with his wife, but had no children."

His will dated Aug. 7, 1765, was proved Sep. 24, 1765, by his wife Elizabeth, Exec^x.; names Samuel, son of Bro. Samuel; Seth, son of Bro. Seth; Prince, son of Bro. Jonathan, deceased; Samuel Vincent, son of sister Hannah, and other near relatives.

"Elizabeth, wife of Joseph Sears, Secundus," was adm. 2d Ch., Yar., from Ch., Har., Aug. 3, 1735. Her estate was adm^d upon by Thos. Clarke, Aug. 5, 1772, and was valued at £50 18 11.

29.* vii. JOSHUA, b. Har., May 3, 1697.

30.* viii. JUDAH, b. Har., Oct. 29, 1699.

31.* ix. JOHN, b. Har., July 18, 1701; bap. Aug. 24.

32.* x. SETH, b. Har., May 27, 1703; bap. July 18.

33.* xi. BENJAMIN, b. Har., June 16, 1706; bap. Aug. 18.

Capt. Samuel Sears was one of the earliest inhabitants of Harwich. His first house was just over the line that separates that part of Har., now West Brewster, and East Dennis, formerly a part of Yarmouth, and stood until after 1800, and was occupied by his sons.

The house of the late Capt. Constant Sears was built upon its site. He built again where Samuel Ripley Sears lived, and this house was demolished a few years since.

The will of Samuel Sears of Harwich, dated Apr. 7, 1740, was filed Mar. 6, 1741-2, by Judah and Seth Sears, Exrs., and names surviving sons, Joseph, Joshua, Judah, John, Seth and Benjamin; Jonathan, Joseph and Prince, sons of Jonathan, deceased; Samuel and Seth, sons of Samuel, deceased; and daus. Hannah Vincent and Tamsin Freeman; also grand-daus. Abigail Hall, Mercy Hawes, Ruth Sears, Desire Freeman, Mary Snow, Hannah Foster and Sarah Sears.

He was Constable in 1702; com^d Lieut. 1706, and later Capt.; 1715, "Capt. Sears granted liberty to build a pew in the meeting-house;" 1723, "Capt. Sears pew No. 3, £40."

1722, "Provision made to refund Capt. Samuel Sears money which he paid to the soldiers the last time they went out on King's service."

His wife was admᵈ to the Ch. in Har., June 15, 1701.

She was familiarly called "Marcy Sam," to distinguish her from Paul Sears' wife, known as "Marcy Paul."

She was the daughter of Tamsen Lumpkin, who m. 1st, Dea. Samˡ Mayo, who d. 1663, estate settled Apr. 26, 1664 ; 2d, John Sunderland, whose first wife had died Jan. 29, 1664-5.

Freeman in Hist. Cape Cod, says she was born 1665, probably an error for 1663, as John Sunderland's will mentions, "wife, daus. Mary Bangs, Sarah Freeman, and Mercy Sears," and she was doubtless the dau. of Dea. Mayo.

John Sunderland had been a parchment maker in Boston, and agent for John Scottoway before his removal to Eastham.

Feb. 9, 1651-2, Letters of Admⁿ were granted to John Sunderland, on estate of Mary Sears of Boston, "her husband Daniel being at sea."

Who was this Daniel Sears, and was his wife Mary a connection of John Sunderland?

9.

PAUL SEARS³ [*Paul²*, *Richard¹*], b. Yarmouth, P. C., June 15, 1669 ; d. Feb. 14, [17] 1739-40, in 71 yr., gr.-st., W. Br. ; m. Harwich, 1693, *Mercy Freeman*, dau. of Dea. Thomas and Rebecca (Sparrow) F., she b. Har., Oct. 30, 1674 ; d. Aug. 30, 1747, in 74 yr., gr-st., W. Br.   Children:

34.* i. EBENEZER, b. Yar., Aug. 15, 1694.
35.* ii. PAUL, b. Yar., Dec. 21, 1695.
36.   iii. ELIZABETH, b. Yar., Aug. 27, 1697; d. Feb. 28, 1728-9 ; m. Feb. 10, 1725-6, *Nathaniel Crosby* of Har.; (who m. 2d, 1732, Esther Young ;) had one child, CROSBY : [1] Moses, 1727.
37.* iv. THOMÁS, b. Yar., June 6, 1699.
38.   v. REBECCA, b. Yar., Apr. 2, 1701; d. 1791; m. Oct. 15, 1719, *Joseph Hall, Jr.*, he b. Aug. 6, 1697; d. Feb. 22, 1772; children, HALL: [1.] Joseph, Jan. 7, 1723-4. [2.] Edmund, Jan. 22, 1724-5. [3.] Stephen, Jan. 9, 1735-6. [4.] Nathaniel, June 1, 1740. [5.] Barnabas, Apr. 20, 1742. [6.] Betsy, m. 1758, Prince Sears, No. 119.
39. vi. MERCY, b. Yar., Feb. 7, 1702-3 ; m. Rochester, Jan. 9, (7) 1724-5, by Rev. Peter Thacher, to *Joseph Blackmore* of R.

40. vii. DEBORAH, b. Yar., Mar. 11, 1705–6; adm. 2d Ch.
    May 5, 1728; m. *Thomas Howes* of E. Yar., son of Eben[r]
    and Sarah (Joyce) H., he b. Jan. 22, 1699; children,
    HOWES: [1.] Moody, b. July 18, 1724; m. 1748, Hannah
    Snow. [2.] Desire, b. Jan. 8, 1726–7; m. Mar. 7, 1748–9,
    Samuel Sears, No. 107. [3.] Deborah, b. Dec. 1, 1727;
    m. Mar. 16, 1748–9, Nathaniel Sears, No. 53. [4.] Betty,
    b. Jan. 2, 1730–1; m. Dec. 28, 1749, Ebenr. Fish.
    [5.] Mercy, b. May 25, 1732. [6.] Jerusha, b. Jan. 7,
    1735–6; m. Nov. 4, 1772, Daniel Hall. [7.] Daniel, b.
    Oct. 14, 1738; m. 1765, Sarah Collins. [8.] Edmund, b.
    Apr. 10, 1742. [9.] Reuben, b. Aug. 29, 1745; m. July
    8, 1773, Bethia Sears, No. 314. [10.] Sarah, b. Oct. 18,
    1749; m. Dec. 12, 1771, George Howes.
41. viii. ANN, b. Yar., Dec. 27, 1706; baptd. Harwich, "by
    communion of churches," Feb. 16, 1707–8; m. Yar., Dec.
    18, 1727, *Ebenezer Bangs*, son of Capt. Edward B., of
    Har.; and perhaps removed to Gorham, Me.; children,
    BANGS: [1.] Barnabas, b. Mar. 11, 1727–8. [2.] Ebenezer,
    b. Oct. 28, 1729. [3.] Ruth, b. Sep. 28, 1731. [4.] Sylvanus,
    b. Feb. 10, 1735–6. [5.] Willard; and four others.
42.* ix. JOSHUA, b. Yar., Nov. 20, 1708.
43.* x. DANIEL, b. Yar., July 16, 1710.
44.* xi. EDMUND, b. Yar., Aug. 6, 1712.
45. xii. HANNAH, b. Yar., Mar. 6, 1714–15; m. there July
    4, 1734, *Thomas Howes*, son of Prince and Dorcas (Joyce)
    H., he b. June 27, 1706; (m. 2d Bethia Sears, No. 89);
    children, HOWES: [1.] Sarah, b. June 8, 1735; m. Feb.
    12, 1756, James Matthews. [2.] Thomas, b. July 17,
    1737; m. Bathsheba Sears, No. 233.

"Mr. Paul Sears" lived on Quivet Neck, and was prominent in the church of the East precinct of Yarmouth, to which
he was adm. June 23, 1728, and his wife Aug. 6, 1727.

"Aug. 4, 1724, Paul Sears was one of Committee to inform
Mr. Taylor of call to ministry;" Oct. 5, 1725, one of Com. "to
lay out meeting-house floor for pews;" June 24, 1726, "to
receive Mr. Dennis answer;" Mar. 16, 1727, on Com. "on
ordination of Mr. Dennis."

I find no record of adm[n]. upon the estate of Paul Sears, and
he perhaps divided his property before his death, but all early
records in Reg. Deeds Barns., have been destroyed by fire.

He is buried by the side of his wife in the old family burying-ground at Bound Brook in West Brewster.

His wife, known as " Marcy Paul," was a grand-dau. of Maj.
John and Mercy (Prence) Freeman, and great gr.-dau. of Ed-
mund Freeman, "The Proprietor." Her mother, Rebecca
Sparrow, was dau. of Jon[a]. and Rebecca (Bangs) S., and her
grand-mother, Mercy Prence, was dau. of Gov. Tho[s]. and
Patience (Brewster) P., and gr.-dau. of Elder Wm. Brewster.

Her will dated Dec. 13, 1746, was filed Sep. 9, 1747, by
Daniel and Edmund Sears, Ex[rs].; and names, children, Ebenezer,
Paul, Thomas, Joshua, Daniel, Edmund, Rebecca Hall,
Deborah Howes, Mercy Blackmore and Ann Bangs. The
estate was appraised at £562 04 02.

12.

Capt. JOHN SEARS[3] [*Paul[2], Richard[1]*], b. Yarmouth,
1677–8; d. Sabbath morning, Apr. 9, 1738, in 61 yr., gr-st.,
W. Br.; m. Eastham, June 1, [5] 1704, *Priscilla Freeman*,
dau. of Capt. Samuel and Elizabeth (Sparrow) F., she b. Oct.
27, 1686; d. May 8, 1764, in 78 yr., gr-st., W. Br. Children:
46.* i. ELISHA, b. Yar., ab't 1706.
47.* ii. JOHN, b. Yar., ab't 1712.
48. iii. BATHSHEBA, b. Yar., ab't 1712; d. Apr. 19, 1735, in
        24 yr., gr-st.
49.* iv. WILLARD, b. Yar., 1714.
50. v. MARY, m. Yar., Oct. 21, 1725, *Ebenezer Paddock*,
        son of John and Priscilla (Hall) P., he b. Mar. 18, 1703–4;
        children, PADDOCK: [1.] Ebenezer, b. July 12, 1727; d.
        Mar. 10, 1728–9. [2.] Priscilla, b. Oct. 10, 1728; bap.
        Oct. 13; m. May 16, 1746; David Hall. [3.] Thankful,
        b. Nov. 23, 1730; bap. Dec. 13; m. Mar. 9, 1748–9,
        Thomas Blossom. [4.] Ebenezer, b. Feb. 15, 1732–3;
        bap. Mar. 19, 1733–4, "like to dye." [5.] Seth, b. Mar.
        22, 1733–4; d. Apr. 10, 1734. [6.] Mary, b. Apr. 15,
        1736; d. Apr. 29. [7.] Mary, b. Apr. 24, 1737; d. June
        7. [8.] Josiah, b. May 9, 1738. [9.] Mary, b. Aug. 23
        1739; m. Aug., 1760, Kimbal Clark, son of Seth C., he
        b. July 20, 1734, and had, i. Isaac, 1761; m. Temperance
        Sears, No. 224. ii. Lot, 1763; d. young. iii. Mary,
        1765; m. Dr. Josiah Myrick. iv. Phebe, 1771; m. Luke
        Baker. v. Kimbal, 1777; m. Mercy Snow. vi. Isaiah,
        1779; m. Deborah Sears, No. 608, and vii. Charlotte,
        1781; m. Rev. Simeon Crowell.
51. vi. PRISCILLA, styled "Junior," adm. 2d Ch., Yar., June
        23, 1728; m. Yar., Mar. 6, 1728–9, *John Howes*, son of

John and Mary (Matthews) H., he b. Oct. 31, 1699; d.
1750; will dated, July 16, 1750; wife Priscilla and bro.-
in-law John Sears, Exrs.; children, HOWES: [1.] Mary, b.
Feb. 19, 1729–30; m., 1756, Wm. Howes. [2.] Sarah, b.
Mar. 16, 1731–2; m. July 26, 1750, Saml. Eldred. [3.] Heman, b. Sep. 7, 1734; m. Dec. 12, 1755, Mary Howes.
[4.] John, b. Mar. 4, 1736–7, d. July 4, 1737. [5.] Bathsheba, b. Feb. 24, 1738–9; m. Nov. 17, 1761, Saml.
Howes. [6.] Priscilla, b. July, 29, 1742; m. Nov. 4,
1765, Eben'r Howes. [7.] James, b. June 25, 1746.
52.   vii. BETTY, b. about 1719; adm. 2d Ch., Sep. 17, 1738;
        m. Yar., Aug. 23, 1739, *John Webb;* and d. Sep., 1755, in
        36 yr., gr.-st., W. Br.; children, WEBB: [1.] George,
        (Capt.), b. 1740; m. Ann Sears. [2.] Ann. [3.] John,
        1746.
53.*   viii. NATHANIEL, b. Yar., about 1720.
54.   ix. HEMAN, b. Yar., Jan. 28, 1724–5; bap. Apr. 10,
        1726; d. Aug. 1, 1726, gr.-st., W. Br.
55.*   x. BETHIA, b. Yar., Oct. 15, 1726; bap. Nov. 19, 1727;
        d. Sep. 8, 1736, gr.-st., W. Br.

Capt. John Sears lived in the East precinct of Yarmouth,
now East Dennis, and his house is still standing a short distance
south-westerly from the family burying-ground at Bound Brook,
and was until recently occupied by Capt. Constant Sears.

He was admitted to the 2d Ch., June 23, 1728; was a
wealthy and prominent man, active in church and town affairs,
and in the militia. For 15 years his name is annually found
upon the precinct records as moderator, assessor and prudential
committee. He was chosen Surveyor, 1711–14–18; Juror,
1712; Fence Viewer, 1720; Selectman, 1734–5; Ensign, 1722;
Lieut., 1726; and Captain, 1736.

March 7, 1721–2, " Mr. John Sears " was appointed one of
the committee to receive from the Treasury, the town's portion
of £50,000.

In his will dated April 1, 1738, he calls himself " Yeoman,"
but in the Inventory is styled " Gentleman." Names wife
Priscilla; sons, Elisha, John, Willard, and Nathaniel; daughters,
Mary Paddock, Priscilla Howes, and Betty Sears. We note
therein, an Indian Girl, at £3 10 0. Real Estate, £2380 02 01.
Personal, £593.

His gravestone in the family burying-ground says he " died
Apr. 9, 1739; " a manifest error for 1738, as his Inventory was
filed June 12, 1738.

His wife was a grand-daughter of Dea. Samuel and Mercy

(Southworth) Freeman of Eastham, and great gr.-dau. of
Samuel and Apphia F., of Watertown, Mass. She was adm.
to 2d Ch. from 1st Ch., Yar., Aug. 6, 1727.

13.

RICHARD SEARS³ [*Paul²*, *Richard¹*], b. Yarmouth,
1680; d. May 24, 1718, in 38 yr., gr.-st., Chatham; m. May
15, 1706, *Hopé Howes*, dau. of Samuel H. of Yar.; (she m. 2d,
John Rich of Eastham, who d. there in summer of 1747, of
small-pox, leaving issue by her.)   Children:

56. i. THANKFUL, b. Yar., Mar. 18, 1706–7; m. 1727, *John
Rich, Jr.*, of E.
57.* ii. PAUL, b. Chat., 1710.
58. iii. SAMUEL, b. Chat., 1712; d. Dec. 21, 1738, æ. 26 yr.,
gr.-st.   Paul Sears rendered an account of his estate, Oct.
22, 1742.
59. iv. HANNAH, b. Chat., m. Feb. 23, 1737-8, *Zoheth Smith*
of E., he b. Dec. 11, 1716; children, SMITH: [1.] Zoheth, b. Oct. 12, 1739. [2.] Richard, b. Mar. 18, 1741–2.
[3.] Elizabeth, b. Feb. 6, 1745–6. [4.] Hannah, b. Mar.
9, 1746–7. [5.] Joshua Mayo.

Richard Sears purchased land in Manamoy, now Chatham,
in 1707.   30 Mar. 1708, "the inhabitants gave Richard Sears
leave to fence across the highway in two places, said Sears to
make and maintain convenient gates on the highways, for those
who wish to pass," etc.

He was on the grand jury, 1710; Town Treasurer, 1713;
Constable, 1714–15; Selectman, 1717.

His estate was settled Sep. 19, 1723, and Daniel Sears and
Hope Sears, adm⁸. discharged.   "Hope Rich, formerly widow
of the deceased was allowed £70 6 2, being her full part of
the moveable estate, and right of dower;" Thankful Sears,
£70 6 3; Hannah Sears the other third part of the personal estate; Paul, eldest son, two-thirds of the real estate, his guardian
to pay to Thankful, £57 16 3, and to Hannah, £19 5 5.   Samuel, youngest son, one-third of real estate, his guardian to pay
Hannah, £38 10 0.

Daniel Sears of Chatham was appᵈ guardian of Samuel, æ.
10; Thankful, æ. 17, and Hannah, æ. ——; and John Rich of
Eastham, guardian to Paul, æ. 13.

The real estate was appraised at £500, and the personal at
£280 18 11.

In the ."Sears Gen'y," by Rev. E. H. Sears, Richard Sears is made the junior by two years of his brother Daniel, and born 1684. On the contrary it appears by their gravestones in Chatham old burying-ground, that Daniel was the younger; being born in 1682, and Richard in 1680.

On a half sunken gravestone in a south-easterly direction from the Sears monument, may still be read the following inscription :

"Here lyes ye Body of Richard Sears, who died May ye 24th 1718 in ye 38th year of his age."

Samuel Howes of Yarmouth, in his Will, June 8, 1722, gives to his "dau. Hope Sears, 40^s in addition to what she has already had."

14.

Capt. DANIEL SEARS^3 [*Paul^2, Richard^1*], b. Yarmouth, 1682; d. Chatham, Aug 10, 1756, in 74 yr., gr.-st., Chat.; m. Yar., Feb. 12, 1708–9, *Sarah Howes*, dau. of Samuel H., of Yar., she b. there 1685; d. Chat., Nov. 9, 1748, æ. 63, gr.-st. Children :

60. i. REBECCA, b. Chat., Mar. 19, 1710–11; d. of small-pox Dec. 9, 1765, æ. 55; m. *Thomas Howes* (who m. 2d, Mrs. Hope (Sears) Doane, No. 267); children, HOWES : [1.] David, b. May 9, 1732; d. Jan. 17, 1751-2, æ. 19. [2.] Thomas, b. Oct. 31, 1738; not ment^d in Danl Sears' will, 1753. [3.] Richard, b. Apr. 19, 1742. Thos Howes and Rebecca, his wife, made their marks to receipt for portion of her father's estate, June 10, 1758.

61.* ii. DANIEL, b. Chat., June 1, 1712.

62. iii. SARAH, b. Chat., Apr. 11, 1714; d. Apr. 30, 1751; m. Aug. 1, 1734, by Rev. Mr. Lord to *Joshua Atkins* (who was pub^d in 1751, to Mary Doane); children, ATKINS : [1.] Desire, b. Mar. 10, 1734–5; d. Jan. 6, 1766. [2.] John, b. Mar. 7, 1736–7. [3.] Susanna, b. Mar. 6, 1738–9; m. Oct. 8, 1775, Edmund Snow of E. [4.] Sarah, b. June 28, 1742. [5.] Rebecca, b. Oct. 6, 1744; m. Apr. 7, 1762, Moses Nickerson, and had, i. Moses, m. Patience Bassett. ii. Zoeth, m. Mercy Godfrey. iii. Joshua, m. Sarah Morse. iv. Atkins, m. Zilpha Harding. v. Ezra, 1770; m. Eliz'h Crowell. vi. Anna, m. Joseph Young. vii. Fear, m. David Nickerson. viii. Sarah, m. Benj. Smith. ix. Desire, m. Dean Smith. x. Rebecca, m. Thacher Ryder. [6.] Fear, b. Mar. 15, 1746–7. [7.] Ann, b. June 11, 1750; d. Sep. 16, 1750.

63. iv. MERCY, b. Chat., July 17, 1716; d. Dec. 23, 1765; m.
Stephen Ryder, who d. Jan. 18, 1766; children, RYDER:
[1.] Jerusha, b. Oct 3, 1740. [2.] Mary, b. Feb. 4, 1742–3.
[3.] Stephen, b. Apr. 20, 1745. [4.] Experience, b. July
23, 1747. [5.] Richard, b. Nov. 26, 1749. [6.] David,
b. Mar. 31, 1752. [7.] Simeon, b. Mar. 16, 1758, and
three other children. All of the ten except Simeon died in
1765–6, of small-pox, imported in a package of clothing,
sent from the West Indies, and washed in the house. Another account says the disease originated in the family of
Dea. Paul Crowell, a wealthy citizen who lived near Ryder's mill; in all 65 persons took the infection; the town
expended £901 7 0, besides individual contributions. Mr.
Ryder, his wife and ten children were stricken down with
the disease at once. At that early day the science of
medicine was comparatively in its infancy: but few of the
doctors knew any thing practically about the malady. The
two resident doctors died of the disease; finally a physician
was brought from Boston to see the family, who pronounced the disease to be small-pox, of the most virulent
and malignant type. The father, mother and nine children died of the foul disease. Simeon, a child of eleven
years, was the only survivor, and the only heir of a large
landed property. The bodies were buried on the farm, in
a row of eleven mounds, where they remain to this day,
an object of sad curiosity to the passer by. There were
buried in this spot, in all about twenty, connected with the
family. A sister of Mrs. Ryder, Rebecca Howes, died of
the disease; also Nehemiah Doane, who m. Hope Sears.
Simeon Ryder, the surviving child, was born in 1755; he
lived and died on the place he inherited. He married
1st, Mercy Godfrey; 2d, in 1788, Patience Crowell, and
had several children, of whom were Stephen and Simeon;
the latter a noted shipmaster, and for many years a prominent railroad man and citizen of Alton, Ill., where he died
in 1877, aged 82 years.

64. v. RICHARD, b. Chat., Apr. 26, 1718; d. 1746.
65. vi. DAVID, b. Chat., Apr. 20, 1720; d. 1746. Daniel
Sears was app^d adm^r upon the estates of these two
brothers, May 13, 1747. They were styled "mariners,"
and probably died, or were lost while on a voyage, as 12
months were allowed to elapse before taking out letters of
administration. David was probably the one mentioned
by Benj. Bangs of Harwich, in his diary in 1744, as having

"got home from the Spaniards." They perhaps went on the Louisburg Expedition in 1745, in Col. Gorham's Regt, or as sailors, and never returned.

In the "Sears Gen'y" it is stated that "these two brothers went to England, possibly to recover the family estates, were officers in the Pretender's army, and both fell at the battle of Culloden, Apr. 16, 1746." In the "GEN. REGISTER," IX, 134, we read, "Capt. Peter Sears," of Revolutionary army, "son of Col. Sears of Chatham, killed at Culloden." There is no truth in either statement. Benj. Bangs, a merchant of Harwich, was in Boston, June 7, 1746, and on that date enters in his diary that he had "lately heard of the death of Richard and David Sears of Chatham." The news of the battle of Culloden was not received in Boston until nearly a month later, viz.: July 2, and was first published in the "Boston News Letter," for Thursday, July 3, 1746. "A letter from Belfast, April 25, gives undoubted intelligence of the entire defeat of the rebels on Culloden muire, on the 16th." Unless Mr. Bangs had a spiritual communication, he could not have heard of the brothers' death at Culloden, at the date of the entry in his diary, and I need say nothing of the improbability of two common seamen brought up in a Puritan family joining the Catholic Army, and being commissioned as officers. The Capt. Peter Sears referred to above was of Scituate, and son of Jonathan Sears of Halifax, Mass., of the line of Silas, and only distantly connected with the Chatham branch. Gen. Duvall, from whose "Minutes" the Register article is quoted, was a pension agent in Tallahassee, Fla., and would not be likely to know any thing of the family history. I have a copy of the letter which he addressed to Mr. Orin Sears of Hingham (probably the identical copy referred to in the Register article), and in which he gave the lists of Sears in Rev. army, quoted in REG., and it contains not a word about "Col. Sears of Chatham killed at Culloden."

66. vii. DEBORAH, b. Chat., Oct. 13, 1722; d. Jan. 6, 1796, æ. 74, gr.-st.; m. 1742, *Joseph Atwood*, son of Joseph and Bethia (Crowell) A., and gr.-son of John and Bethia (Sears) C., who d. Feb. 18, 1794, æ. 73, gr.-st.; children, ATWOOD: [1.] Bethia, b. Feb. 3, 1743–4; m. July 27, 1762, Benj. Godfrey; (who m. 2d, Sarah ——, who d. Jan. 23, 1815, æ. 75, gr.-st.) [2.] David, b. Feb. 3, 1745–6; d. June 25, 1751. [3.] Deborah, b. Sep. 3, 1748. [4.] Joseph, b. May

25, 1752; d. May 30, 1774. [5.] Sarah Sears, b. May 15, 1754; d. Apr. 3, 1828, æ. 74, unm. [6.] Salome, b. Aug. 31, 1758; m. March 8, 1783, Weal Cushman of New Bedford. [7.] Sears, b. July 25, 1761; d. Mar. 1, 1832; m. Oct. 31, 1782, Azubah Collins, and had, i. Joseph, b. Sep. 25, 1783. ii. Solomon, b. Aug. 5, 1785; m. Lucy Smith, and had Levi. iii. David, b. Aug. 29, 1787. iv. John, b. Aug. 20, 1789. v. Sears, b. Mar. 21, 1792. vi. James, b. Feb. 4, 1801. vii. Azubah C., b. Oct. 18, 1806. Of this family is Levi Atwood, town clerk of Chatham; and editor of the "Chatham Monitor."

Capt. Daniel Sears purchased land in Manamoy, now Chatham, in 1707; was Town Clerk, 1714-21, 1725; Selectman, 1719–1730; Ensign, 1722, and later Captain. 1722, "School to be kept at quarter of Ensign Daniel Sears, he to select the school master."

His will, dated "20 Jan., 1753, new stile," was proved July 27, 1756, by Daniel Sears, Exec^r, and mentions Daniel, Rebecca, Sarah, Mercy and Deborah. Paul Sears, James Covel and Wm. Nickerson appraised the estate Sep. 14, 1756. R. Est. £300, and personal £70 10 8.

In the "Sears Gen'y" it is stated that Daniel Sears married Sarah, dau. of *J. Hawes* of Yarmouth, and in a manuscript of Hon. D. Sears, referred to in the chapter on English Ancestry, see *ante*, she is called "dau. of *Jere.* Hawes."

The error has been perpetuated on the Sears monuments in Yarmouth, Chatham and Colchester.

She was the daughter of *Samuel Howes* of Yarmouth, gr.-dau. of Joseph Howes, and gt.-gr.-dau. of Thomas Howes.

The will of Samuel Howes, dated 1722, recorded in Barns. Prob. Rec., IV, 90, names daughters Sarah Sears, and gives her 20^s with what she has already had; Hope Sears and Mercy Sears (who had married respectively, Daniel and Richard Sears, brothers, and Josiah Sears, their cousin).

On the Yarmouth records the name is clearly written Sarah *Howes*. The first Sarah Hawes in Yarmouth, was the dau. of Dea. Joseph H., and born Apr., 1696, therefore but thirteen years of age in 1709, when Daniel Sears married. The first Jeremiah Hawes was born in 1711.

The old family mansion was taken down in 1863, having after the death of Madame Richard Sears been occupied by divers families, and allowed to become dilapidated. It was originally, perhaps, a one story, or one and a half story building with gambril roof, and added to until it occupied much ground.

In a letter from J. Hawes to Daniel Sears of Chatham, printed in the "Sears Gen'y," reference is made to its "partial destruction by fire in 1763," at which time the ever to be lamented loss of the "family papers," is said to have taken place. The old building, when taken down, bore no marks of having ever passed through the fiery ordeal; the original timbers were in place, with the bark still on, nor does "the oldest inhabitant" remember any tradition of such an event. Benjamin Bangs of Harwich, to whose diary I have before referred, makes no allusion to any fire in Chatham at that time, though chronicling more trivial events happening there.

An amusing anecdote is related in connection with the old house, and the marriage of Deborah Sears in 1741.

The ceremony was performed at home, and the guests remained for the evening, as there was to be a dance in honor of the occasion.

The "long chamber" had been cleared, and made ready, and in due time they were "tripping it on the light fantastic toe."

The bride, a buxom lass, and not sylph-like in form, enjoyed dancing immensely.

In the course of the evening her animation became excessive, and while dancing vigorously her foot broke through the floor, causing some confusion, and slight injury.

This tradition being remembered by some of the neighbors when the old house was torn down, an examination was made to see if there was any evidence of the disaster, and in confirmation of the story, they found a square of board had been let into the center of the flooring.

The gravestones of Daniel Sears and his wife may still be seen in the Chatham burying-ground, laid face down; one of them bears this inscription,

"Here lyes ye body of Capt. Daniel Sears, who departed this life, August ye 10, 1756, in ye 74th year of his age."

15.

SILAS SEARS^3 [*Silas^2, Richard^1*], b. Yarmouth, 1661; d. 1732; m. 1692, *Sarah Crosby*, dau. of Rev. Thomas and Sarah C., she b. Mar. 24, 1667; d. Mar. 20, 1705–6; and he m. Yar., May 1, 1707, *Elizabeth O. Killey*, dau. of David and Jane O. K., of Yar. Children, by *Sarah:*

67. i. PHEBE, b. Yar., June 26, 1694; m. Mar. 10, 1719–20, *John Buck*, and lived in Harwich; children, BUCK: [1] Deborah, m. Silas Sears, No. 90; and others.

68.* ii. SILAS, b. Yar., Dec., 1695.
69. iii. SARAH, b. Yar., Apr. 3, 1697; m. 1718, *Eleazar Hamlin*, son of Isaac H., of Barns.; who m. 2d, Alice Phinney, had [1.] Barnabas, b. Mar. 30, 1719. [2.] Sarah, b. Mar. 16, 1720-1. [3.] Eleazar, b. May 24, 1723, prob. ancestor of Vice Pres. H.
70. iv. DEBORAH, b. Yar., Jan., 1699-1700; m. Oct. 8, 1719, *William Gray*, and remᵈ to vicinity of Haddam, Ct.; children, GRAY: [1.] William, b. Feb. 13, 1720-1. [2.] Rebecca, b. 1723; m. 1744, Jabez Berry; and remᵈ to Putnam co., N. Y. [3.] Thankful, b. 1725. [4.] Sarah, b. 1726. [5.] Thomas, b. Nov. 19, 1728. [6.] Anna, b. 1730. [7.] Mary, b. 1732. [8.] Deborah, b. 1734. [9.] John. [10.] Silas.
71. v. HANNAH, b. Yar., Jan. 1701-2; d. Mar. 18, 1705-6.
72.* vi. THOMAS, b. Yar., Mar. 3, 1702-3.
73.* vii. JAMES, b. Yar., Mar. 30, 1704; bap. Har., Sep. 17, 1704, "by Communion of churches."
74. viii. ELEAZAR, b. Yar., Jan. 1, 1705-6; d. s. p., July 4, 1796, in 92 yr., gr-st., Yar.; m. there Feb., 1729, *Mary Nickerson*, dau. of John N., of Yar.; who d. Nov. 10, 1765, in 65 yr., gr.-st.; and he m. 2d, Yar., Dec. 4, 1766, *Lydia Gray*, who d. Feb. 9, 1795, in 67 yr., gr.-st.

Silas Sears, Yeoman, resided in the East precinct of Yarmouth, now Dennis, and was a prominent man there.

His will dated July 28, 1727, "in ill health," was proved Nov. 29, 1732, by Judah Paddock and Eleazar Sears, Execᵗˢ, and was witnessed by Peter Thacher, Joseph Hall and Edward Sturges.

It mentions "wife Elizabeth; sons Silas, Thomas, Eleazar, and James; and daus. Sarah Hamlin, Phebe Buck, and Deborah Gray." The old homestead fell to Eleazar.

He left R. Estate valued at £1200, and personal do. £299 3 7.

16.

RICHARD SEARS³ [*Silas²*, *Richard¹*], b. Yarmouth, about 1665; m. Plymouth, Mass., Oct. 21, 1696, *Bashua Harlow*, dau. of William and Mary (Shelley) H., of Ply., she b. Apr. 21, 1667; and 2d, Lyme, Conn., after 1711, Mrs. *Sarah (Graham) Marvin*, dau. of Henry and Mary G. of Hartford, Ct., who d.

9

Lyme, Dec. 14, 1760, æ. 91, "relict of Richard Sears." (Her
first husband was John Marvin of Old Lyme, who d. Dec. 11,
1711, æ. 47.) Children:

By *Bashua:*

75. i. SILAS, b. Ply., Aug. 23, 1697; bought land of John Alger of Lyme, by deed Nov. 8, 1727.

76.* ii. SETH, b. Ply., Mar. 18, 1699–1700.

77. iii. MARY, b. Ply., Feb. 3, 1702–3; d. Lyme, May 20, 1731,
æ. 28. 4.

78. iv. JAMES, b. Ply., June 22, 1705; bought land of Sam¹
Mott of Lyme, deed Apr. 5, 1728. He may have been the
James Sears who was chosen pathmaster at Kent, N. Y.,
Apr. 7, 1747, and "of Rev. Mʳ. Knibloe's old Gilead Ch.
Carmel."

79.* v. JOHN, b. Ply., middle Nov., 1707.

80. vi. ANNA, b. Lyme; m. *Richard Smith* of Smithtown,
L. I., of the "Bull Smiths;" child, SMITH: [1.] Sarah,
b. 1728; m. Rev. Napthali Daggett of Yale Coll., he b. Attleboro, Mass., Sep. 8, 1727; d. New Haven, Nov. 25, 1780;
Yale, 1748; N. J. Coll., 1774; scholar and divine; minister of Smithtown, L. I., Sep. 18, 1751, to Nov., 1755;
Prof. Div. Yale, Mar. 4, 1756, till his death; and acting
Prest. 1766–77; D.D. from Yale and N. J. He fought
in defense of New Haven, was wounded and taken prisoner; children: i. Mary, m. Robert Platt, no iss. ii.
Sarah. iii. Grace, lived in New Haven. iv. Henry, an
officer in Revⁿ, grad. Yale; d. New Haven, June 20, 1843,
æ. 85. [Richard Smith m. 2d, Martha Howell, and had 8
children, viz.: Martha, b. 1731; m. John Adams of Plattsburg, N. Y. Hannah, b. 1732. Charity, b. 1737. Elisha, b.
1739; accidentally shot while gunning, æ. 15. Sabrana, b.
1741; m. Jos. Bryant, who was lost at sea. Nancy, m.
Abner Smith. Isaac, b. 1745; m. Margaret Field. Phebe,
b. 1746; m. Capt. Nathaniel Platt, of Smithtown, he b.
1741; d. Plattsburg, N. Y. (which place was settled and
named by him) in 1816.]

Richard Sears bought land in Plymouth, of Sam¹ Lucas in
1697, which he sold in 1699 to Eleazer Rogers, buying of him
part of the Elder Brewster lot, which he sold in 1708 to Jonᵃ
Barnes.

In what year he settled in Old Lyme is not known, but Dec.
6, 1719, Joseph Southwick of that place sold land to " Richard
Sears of Hingham, Suffolk co., Province of Massᵗˢ." He had

probably lived in Hingham, between 1708 and 1719, but his name is not found in the church or town records there.

I find no further reference to him in town or church records, of Lyme. As his sons Silas and James bought land there in 1727-8, they were probably married at that date, but their names do not appear again in the records.

I have been unable, after repeated applications, to obtain a search of Probate Records in New London, altho' offering to pay the usual fees therefor. I am told the files are in utter confusion and unindexed.

The old cemeteries in Lyme may perhaps furnish some data.

I have assumed that the Anna Sears of Old Lyme, who married Richard Smith, was the daughter of Richard Sears, as I find no other family of Sears on the records; and his mother's name was Anna, which adds to the probability, but it needs confirmation.

18.

Capt. JOSEPH SEARS[3] [*Silas*[2], *Richard*[1]], b. Yarmouth, about 1675; d. May 7, 1750, in 75 yr., gr.-st., N° Dennis; m. Yar., Sep. 19, 1700, *Hannah Hall* of Yar., who d. July 28, 1753, in 73 yr., gr.-st.; she was adm. Ch., Har., Mar. 21, 1708, and to 2d Ch., Yar., Aug. 6, 1727. Children:

81. i. PRISCILLA, b. Yar., July 1, 1701; bap. Har., May 2, 1708; adm. 2d Ch., Yar., Aug. 6, 1727; m. Yar., Mar. 15, 1721-2, *Josiah Gorham;* his 2d w., son of Joseph and Sarah G., he b. Sep. 7, 1692, d. Apr. 3, 1775; children, GORHAM: [1.] Samuel, bap. Aug. 20, 1727. [2.] Isaac, bap. Aug. 20, 1727. [3.] Joseph, bap. July 14, 1728.

82. ii. HANNAH, b. Yar., Dec. 10, 1703; bap. Har., May 2, 1708; m. Yar., Nov. 3, 1725, *Peter Blackmore.*

83.* iii. ZACHARIAH, b. Yar., Apr. 22, 1706; bap. Har., May 2, 1708.

84.* iv. JOSEPH, b. Yar., Mar. 27, 1708; bap. Har., May 2, 1708.

85.* v. STEPHEN, b. Yar., July 22, 1710.

86.* vi. ROLAND, b. Yar., May 17, 1711.

87.* vii. BARNABAS, b. Yar., Apr. 5, 1714.

88. viii. PETER, b. Yar., May 20, 1716; prob. d. in 1746, perhaps on Louisburg Exp[n].

89. ix. BETHIA, b. Yar., Mar. 20, 1718-19; adm. 2d Ch., June 29, 1742; m. Yar., Oct. 15, 1741, *Thomas Howes,* son of Prince and Dorcas (Joyce) H., he b. June 27, 1706; d.

1764 ; (his 1st wife was Hannah Sears, No. 45;) children,
Howes: [1.] Ebenezer, b. Feb. 1, 1743; m. Apr. 4, 1765,
Priscilla Howes. [2.] Solomon, b. Aug. 18, 1744; m.
Dec. 30, 1773, Abigail Howes. [3.] Hannah, b. June 12,
1748 ; m. Nov. 14, 1765, Isaac Howes.
90.* x. Silas, b. Yar., Feb. 11, 1719–20.
91. xi. Thankful, b. Yar., Apr. 11, 1723; m. Yar., Sep. 20,
1744, *Jasher Taylor;* children, Taylor: [1.] Hannah,
bap. May 25, 1755. [2.] Jasher, bap. May 17, 1761.

The will of Joseph Sears of Yar., Yeoman, dated Dec. 9,
1746, names, wife Hannah ; sons, Zachariah, Joseph, Peter,
"*if still alive,*" and Rowland ; and daus. of son Stephen, dec^d,
and Stephen, Hannah and Mary, children of Barnabas, dec^d,
also son Silas, and daus. Priscilla Gorham, Hannah Blackmore,
Bethia Howes, and Thankful Taylor. Inv'y £320 08 08.
Styles him " Gent."
He lived in East precinct Yarmouth, now East Dennis, and
was also styled " Captain."

19.

JOSIAH SEARS[3] [*Silas[2], Richard[1]*], b. Yarmouth, P. C.,
about 1675; d. Provincetown, Mass., 1727; m. Yar., Apr. 3,
1702, *Mercy Howes,* dau. of Samuel H., of Yar., who d. 1720 ;
and 2d, Aug. 18, 1720, *Judith Gilbert* of East Bridgewater,
Mass. Children :
By *Mercy :*
92.* i. Edward, b. Yar., June 23, 1704.
93.* ii. Samuel, b. Yar., July 6, 1706.
94.* iii. Josiah, b. Yar., Aug. 25, 1708.
95.* iv. David, b. Yar., Oct. 2, 1710.
96.* v. Jonathan, b. Bridgewater, Jan. 13, 1713–14.
97. vi. Mercy, b. Bridge., Aug. 17, 1717 ; m. Yar., Feb. 17,
1736–7, Dr. *Josiah Paddock,* son of John and Priscilla
(Hall) P., he b. Apr. 9, 1712.
98. vii. Hannah, b. Bridge., May 20, 1720 ; adm. 2d Ch.,
Yar., Oct. 16, 1744 ; m. Yar., Nov. 19, 1741, *John Vincent;* child, Vincent: [1.] Mary, bap. July 18, 1756.
By *Judith:*
99. viii. Nathaniel, b. Bridge., July 12, 1721.
100. ix. Elizabeth, b. 1725, perhaps on the Cape.

Josiah Sears removed to East Bridgewater, Mass., about
1711, and lived in the old house afterward owned by Capt.

John Bass, in rear of Samuel B. Allen's, returning to the Cape about 1725.

The estate of Josiah Sears of Provincetown was settled in 1727, his widow Judith being app^d adm^x, Aug. 23, in that year.

The inventory amounted to £122 7 0, and dower was set off Apr. 25, 1728. The estate proved to be insolvent.

The will of Samuel Howes of Yarmouth, dated June 8, 1722, names "Samuel, Mercy and Hannah Sears, children of my daughter Mercy Sears, deceased," and "grand-son Samuel Sears, son of Josiah Sears, now living with me."

FOURTH GENERATION.

24.

SAMUEL SEARS[4] [*Samuel*[3], *Paul*[2], *Richard*[1]], b. Harwich, P. C., Sep. 15, 1687; d. there Nov. 22, 1726, in 40 yr., gr.-st., W. Br.; m. Har., Nov. 2, 1710, *Ruth Merrick*, dau. of Wm. M., of Har., who d. Feb. 13, 1766, æ. 82; (having m. 2d, Dec. 7, 1731, Chillingsworth Foster, his 3d wife, who d. Dec. 22, 1764, æ. 84.) Children:

101. i. ABIGAIL, b. Har., Nov. 23, 1711; bap. Oct. 15, 1715; m. Yar., Sep. 28, 1738, *Peter Hall*, son of Dea. Joseph and Mary H.; he b. May 19, 1715; children, HALL: [1.] Morton, b. Apr. 6, 1743, and four daughters.

102. ii. MERCY, b. Har., Oct. 21, 1713; m. Oct. 10, 1734, *Philip Howes*, son of Joseph and Mary (Vincent) H., he b. May 25, 1705; children, HOWES: [1.] Mary, b. July 10, 1735; m. Dec. 12, 1755, Heman Howes. [2.] Seth, b. Feb. 3, 1737-8. [3.] Mercy, b. Dec. 28, 1740; m. Dec. 2, 1762, Joshua Howes. [4.] Dau., b. July 8, 1743; d. Aug. 29. [5.] Ruth, b. Apr., 1744; m. Feb. 2, 1769, Edward Howes, Jr. [6.] Desire, b. Mar., 1747; m. Dec. 10, 1772, Joseph Clark of Har.

103. iii. RUTH, b. Har., July 4, 1715; bap. Oct. 15; m. May 21, 1733, *Joseph Sears*, No. 84.

104. iv. DESIRE, b. Har., Mar. 9, 1716-17; bap. Apr. 21; m. Mar. 4, 1735-6, *Lemuel Freeman* of Har., son of Nathl and Mary (Watson) F., he b. Apr. 18, 1717; d. 1790; she d. 1790; children, FREEMAN: [1.] Desire, b. Oct. 3, 1736; m. Jan. 13, 1757, Benj. Thacher, Jr.; 2d, Nathl Stone. [2.] Ruth, b. Apr. 3, 1739; adm. Ch., Har., 1767; d. Oct. 3, 1812, æ. 73, unm. [3.] Mary, b. July 4, 1741; m. —— Hall; bap. "in private, being in ill health," Apr. 2, 1767; d. soon after. [4.] Grace, b. Jan. 22, 1743; m. Dec. 6, 1770, Judah Berry. [5.] Lemuel, b. Sep. 22, 1746; m. Polly Doane; d. Feb. 4, 1825. [6.] Seth, m. Oct. 14,

1773, Temperance Bangs; d. June 12, 1825. [7.] Cyrenius, b. 1758; m. May 30, 1781, Thankful Hopkins, and
was drowned, Apr. 4, 1785, æ. 27 ; for account of which,
see Jonathan Sears, No. 384. [8.] Isaac, b. Aug. 28,
1759; m. Nov. 28, 1779, Jane Clark, dau. of Edward C.;
d. Jan. 12, 1823, æ. 64.

105. v. MARY, b. Har., Aug. 9, 1718; m. Nov. 30, 1738,
      Joseph Snow, son of Samuel and Eliz^h (Freeman) S.;
      children, SNOW : [1.] Martha, b. Mar. 27, 1739. [2.]
      Joseph, b. Sep. 27, 1740; d. Apr. 19, 1793. [3.] Isaac,
      b. Dec. 31, 1741. [4.] Nathan, b. Nov. 11, 1743. [5.]
      Mary, b. Apr. 24, 1745. [6.] Hannah, b. July 3, 1746.
      [7.] Desire, b. Sep. 7, 1748. [8.] Sarah, b. Aug. 10,
      1750. [9.] Mercy, b. Aug. 26, 1752.

106. vi. HANNAH, b. Har., June 3, 1720 ; bap. June 12 ; m.
      Nov. 2, 1738, *Isaac Foster*, son of Dea. Chillingsworth F.,
      he b. June 17, 1718; d. Sep. 10, 1777; was a blacksmith,
      and lived on the old homestead ; children, FOSTER : [1.]
      Isaac, b. May 29, 1739; m. 1764, Sarah Thacher, she b.
      Dec. 1, 1741; d. Oct. 3, 1777. [2.] Samuel, b. May 31,
      1741. [3.] David, b. Mar. 24, 1743. [4.] Lemuel, b.
      Feb. 24, 1744. [5.] Seth, b. Mar., 1747. [6.] Hannah,
      b. Mar. 4, 1749 ; m. Zoeth Snow. [7.] Nathaniel, b. Apr.
      8, 1751. [8.] Thomas. [9.] Nathaniel.

107.* vii. SAMUEL, b. Har., Dec. 5, 1721; bap. Feb. 23, 1721--2.

108. viii. ISAAC, b. Har., Oct. 5, 1723 ; bap. Oct. 13; d. Jan.
      13, 1724–5, gr.-st.

109. ix. SETH, b. Har., Apr. 9, 1725 ; bap. Apr. 18; m. May
      16, 1765, *Kezia Wing,* who adm. upon his estate ; Inv'y
      filed May 28, 1770, £68 12 6.   The estate was insolvent,
      and paid Mar. 9, 1773, 12-10 in the pound.   He is styled
      mariner, and owned ½ of a vessel then in charge of John
      Webb in Boston.   His adm^x received for vessel and earn-
      ings £122 8 0.

Samuel Sears lived in that part of Harwich, now known as
West Brewster, and his house stood on the site of that recently
built and occupied by Capt. Constant Sears.

His will is dated Nov. 25, 1726, and was proved Jan. 20, 1726–7
(though his gravestone say she died 22 Nov. ;) names, wife and
8 children then living. Inv'y by John Paddock, John Sears and
Peter Paddock, foots R. Est. £230.   Personal, £245 12 3.

His father's will 1740 mentions Samuel, Seth, Abigail
Hall, Mercy Howes, Ruth Sears, Desire Freeman, Mary Snow,
and Hannah Foster.

25.

NATHANIEL SEARS[4] [*Samuel[3], Paul[2], Richard[1]*], b. Harwich, P. C., Sep. 23, 1689; d. July 19, 1720; m. Har., Oct. 10, 1712, *Susannah Gray*, dau. of John and Susannah (Clark) G., of Har.; who was adm. Ch. Har., Sep. 11, 1720; she d. Dec. 7, 1730; (having m. 2d, Har., Aug. 10, 1721, Dea. Chillingsworth Foster, his 2d wife.)   Child:

110.   i. THANKFUL, b. Har., ab't 1718; m. Jan. 15, 1735-6, *Seth Winslow*, son of Kenelm W., he b. 1715; and d. Mar. 7, 1736-7, æ. 18. (He m. 2d, 1737, Priscilla Freeman;) child, WINSLOW: [1.] Nathaniel, b. June 29, 1736; d. inf.

Susannah Sears, widow, was app. adm[x], Aug. 16, 1720; and John Gray of Har., app. guardian to Thankful, she " aged about 4 years," Feb. 21, 1721-2; on which date £24 were "allowed to Hannah Foster, late widow of Nath[l] Sears, for her support and child."

27.

JONATHAN SEARS[4] [*Samuel[3], Paul[2], Richard[1]*], b. Harwich, Mass., Sep. 3, 1693; d. Sep. 3, 1738, in 45 yr., gr.-st., W. Br.; m. Yar., June 29, 1721, *Elizabeth Howes*, dau. Dea. Joseph H. of Yar., she b. Nov. 7, 1697; adm. Ch. Har., Oct. 20, 1723; d. Jan. 8, 1748-9, in 52 yr., gr.-st.   Children:

111.   i. DAVID, b. Har., Sep. 2, 1722; d. inf.
112.   ii. DAVID, b. Har., Mar. 26, 1724; d. young.
113.* iii. JONATHAN, b. Har., Sep. 9, 1725 ; bap. Sep. 12.
114.   iv. JOSEPH, b. Har., May, 1728; d. Mar. 14, 1758, in 30 yr., gr-st., W. Br., unm.   Joseph Sears and Tabithy Kendrick, were pub. Jan. 19, 1754, but she m. Theo. Hopkins. The will of Joseph Sears of Yar., late of Rochester, dated Feb. 5, 1758-9, makes his bro. Prince, sole heir and exec[r]; — mentions Jonathan and Elizabeth, children of deceased bro. Jonathan.
115.   v. MARY, bap. Har., July 12, 1730; d. young.
116.   vi. SARAH, b. Har., July 28, 1731; d. Dec. 16, 1749, æ. 19, gr.-st.
117. vii. PRINCE, bap. Har., July 30, 1732; d. Oct. 31, 1732.
118. viii. NATHAN, b. Har., Sep. 25, 1733; bap. Sep. 30; d. young.
119.* ix. PRINCE, bap. Har., Apr. 13, 1735.

John Sears was app. Adm^r of the estate of Jonathan Sears, deceased; and Daniel Hall, Judah Sears and Eben^r Paddock, rendered an Inventory Oct. 26, 1738; R. Est., £575. Personal, £374 18 0.

He "left widow and four children." His widow Eliz^h was app. Guardian to Jon^a., Joseph and Sarah, Mar. 12, 1742.

She died Jan. 8, 1748, and Joseph Sears of Har., adm. on her estate Mar. 10, 1748, and was app. guardian of Prince and Sarah. Jan. 28, 1757, the estate of Jonathan Sears was divided by Danl Hall, Elisha Bassett, Theo. Crosby and Joseph Howes, Jr., who set off to the eldest son Jonathan, deceased; to Joseph, and to Prince; the widow and other children being then all deceased.

Joseph Howes in his will 1752, names "Jonathan, Joseph and Prince Sears, sons of my daughter Elizabeth Sears."

In the "Sears Gen'y," her name is erroneously given as Sarah.

29.

JOSHUA SEARS^4 [*Samuel^3, Paul^2, Richard^1*], b. Harwich, Mass., May 3, 1697; d. Norwalk, Ct., July 21, 1754, in 58 yr., gr.-st.; m. Yarmouth, Mass., Sep. 17, 1719, *Mary Thacher*, dau. of Dea. Josiah and Mary (Hedge) T., who was adm. to Ch. Har., Mar. 14, 1721; and dism. to Mr. Dennis' Ch., Dec. 8, 1734; but her name is not recorded there, and she was dismissed from Ch. Har., to Ch. at Norwalk, Mar. 28, 1736. Children:

120.   i. JOSIAH, b. Har., June 14, 1720; bap. May 21, 1721; rem. to Norwalk, Ct., with his parents; m. *Sarah* ——, who adm. on his estate, July 6, 1761.

121.   ii. NATHANIEL, b. Har., July 21, 1722; bap. Aug. 19; d. Jan. 4, 1724-5, gr.-st., W. Br.

122.* iii. JOSHUA, b. Har., May 15, 1724.

123.* iv. NATHANIEL, bap. Har., Apr. 20, 1725 or 6.

124.   v. MARY, bap. Har., Apr. 25, 1728; m. —— *Ketchum*.

125.* vi. ISAAC, bap. Har., July 12, 1730.

126. vii. PHEBE, bap. Har., Apr. 8, 1733; m. *Antony Squire* of Weston, Ct., who died; and she m. 2d, *Thaddeus Hubbell* of Wilton, Ct., a widower with a large family of children.

Her home with each husband was in Wilton. Left again a widow, she returned to Norwalk, and lived with

10

her son Selah Squires until her death, Dec. 8, 1807. She was buried in St. Paul's church-yard, in the rear of the church, a white stone marking her grave. Family tradition tells of her strong character, her ability and kindness, her tact in managing three sets of children, and every trait that endeared her as a wife, mother and friend. Her children by 1st marriage were, SQUIRE: [1.] Elizabeth, b. 1759; m. Seth Raymond of Wilton; he b. 1757; d. Aug. 1, 1812; she d. Mar. 17, 1812; both of an epidemical fever, and were buried in the Cong. Ch. yard, No. Salem. They had: i. Sarah, b. July 27, 1778; m. James Seymour of Norwalk, he b. Mar. 16, 1775; d. Apr. 17, 1853; she d. Apr. 11, 1866. ii. Samuel, b. May 12, 1784; m. June, 1804, Clarissa Davenport, of New Canaan, Ct., she b. Apr. 25, 1782; d. Wilton, Ct., Jan. 19, 1887, at the great age of 104 8 25; her husband d. 1816. iii. Anne, d. young. iv. Polly, m. Jas. Ashby of Fishkill, N. Y., and d. Jan. 8, 1867, æ. 82. v. Phebe, b. Nov. 14, 1786; m. 1808, Eric Northrop of No. Salem, who d. 1812; 2d, 1817, Joseph Platt Hanford of Norwalk; he b. Apr. 17, 1782; d. Aug. 10, 1870; she d. May 26, 1860. vi. Harriet, b. Dec. 13, 1788; m. Apr. 13, 1814, Daniel Aymar, (at Bridgeport, Ct., by Rev. Elijah Waterman;) he d. Newry, Ireland, Dec. 3, 1825, æ. 35; and she d. May 20, 1870. Children: Jane Eliz[h], b. Jan. 18, 1815; d. Aug. 9, 1822; Harriet, b. May 2, 1816; lives in So. Norwalk, Ct., unm.; John David, b. Sep. 19, 1817; m. Harriet A. Doane, dau. of John Jay, and Sarah (Wentworth) D., of New Hampshire, and had a son, John Wentworth; Charles Raymond, b. May 24, 1820; d. May 11, 1874. vii. Abigail, m. Sam[l] Clark of Fishkill, N. Y. viii. Betty, m. Benj. Sherwood of Ridgefield, Ct.; — the old Raymond Bible containing the family records was burnt in their house. ix. Eunice, d. young. x. John, b. Apr. 20, 1795; d. Jan. 26, 1875; m. Betsy Picket of Danbury, Ct., who d. Mar. 20, 1858; 2d, Sarah (Picket) McCord. xi. Anne, b. Apr. 2, 1799; m. Sep. 12, 1824, Gilbert Allen; he b. Dec. 28, 1794; d. June 29, 1858; she d. Mar. 22, 1858. [2.] Phebe, m. Mordecai Homan of Fishkill, N. Y. [3.] Anne, m. Oct. 18, 1767, Thos. Keeler, and settled in Binghamton, N. Y.; had, i. Lewis, b. Aug. 14, 1768. ii. Henry, b. Sep. 2, 1770. iii. James, b. Feb. 18, 1773. iv. Isaac, b. Nov. 15, 1775. v. Thomas, b. Oct. 4, 1778. vi. Jasper Sears, b. May 8,

1781; m. 1799, Mary Plumb; and d. Albany, 1866. vii.
Anna, b. Jan. 5, 1784. viii. Erastus, b. Mar. 2, 1787. ix.
Caroline, b. Mar. 20, 1789. x. George, b. Feb. 1, 1791.
xi. Sally Sears, b. Oct. 21, 1793. [4.] Isaac. [5.] An-
thouy. [6.] Selah ; m. Hannah Abbot, and lived in Norwalk; —— by her 2d marriage Phebe had, child: HUBBELL.
[7] Polly, m. Rev. Joseph Mix, of New Haven, Ct.
[8.] Sears, m. a Southern lady, and settled in Charleston,
S. C.

127. viii. JOHN, b. Norwalk, is mentioned in his father's
will in 1754. Stephen Sayre, the American banker, and
sometime sheriff of London (of the Southampton, L. I.,
family of Sayre), writing to Isaac Sears, Feb. 17, 1764, de-
sires " to be remembered to bro. John."

A John Sears was married in Trinity Ch., N. Y., Oct.
24, 1780, to Sarah Halstead, who may be this John, but
was more probably a son of Col. Isaac Sears, who had long
been a member of that church. Some of the name are
found settled in Virginia *circa* 1750.

128. ix. ANTHONY, b. Norwalk; is mentioned in his father's
will in 1754.

Joshua Sears built and lived in the old house in West Brewster, at Bound Brook, nearly opposite the ancient Sears burying
ground; and here the first seven of his children, including
Isaac Sears, the famous " Liberty Boy " of the Revolutionary
period, were born.

He removed to Norwalk, Ct., about the year 1734, (not
1724, as stated in " Sears Genealogy,") and was dismissed
from the church in Har., to Ch. Norwalk, Mar. 28, 1736.

His estate in Har., was sold to Willard Sears of Yarmouth,
and is still in possession of some of his descendants. It was occupied until 1880, by Miss Vienna Sears, and has since been
renovated, and additions made thereto.

In 1732, Joshua Sears purchased of his brother-in-law, Josiah
Thacher, Jr., one acre of the so-called " Home Lot," situated
on Washington avenue, South Norwalk, and marked on the
plan in Hall's " Norwalk " with the names of C. Raymond and
W. Raymond; and in the house which he built upon this spot
he lived until his death in 1752.

The house of Mrs. Charles Raymond, his great-gr.-dau., had
for foundation stones those taken from the old homestead.

The Thacher house stood where the Pottery is marked on
Hall's map.

Joshua Sears possessed other lands in Norwalk, which at various times he deeded to his children ; amongst which was land at " Old Well," now South Norwalk, to his sons Nathaniel and Joshua.

Family tradition relates that he was an excellent man, a prominent citizen, occupying various positions in the gift of the town, a good husband and a generous father.

He was buried in Pine Island Cemetery, a blue stone marking his grave; — near by is a similar memorial to his son Nathaniel, and a nameless mound between father and son, is probably the grave of the wife and mother.

His will, dated June 11, 1754, was proved October 15, 1754, and mentions wife Mary ; and children, Josiah, Mary Ketchum, Phebe Squires, Joshua, Isaac, John and Anthony ; and grandsons, Nathaniel and Thacher. The estate was appraised at £1640.

In the "Sears Gen'y," his wife is erroneously stated to have been Mercy, dau. of John Thacher.

I find no record of her death, but her estate was adm. upon by her son Isaac, July 25, 1761.

30.

JUDAH SEARS[4] [*Samuel[3], Paul[2], Richard[1]*], b. Harwich, Mass., Oct. 29, 1699; d. Rochester, Mass., about 1776; m. Yarmouth, Nov., 1731, *Mary Paddock*, dau. of Judah and Alice (Alden) P., she b. 1714, was adm. to Ch. Har., May 23, 1726; and dismissed to Ch. Roch., Aug. 12, 1770. Children:

129.   i.   ANN, b. Har., Mar. 31, 1733 ; bap. June 6, 1736 ; m. *Anthony Gage.*

130.* ii. JUDAH, b. Har., Nov. 19, 1734 ; bap. June 6, 1736.

131.   iii. MARY, bap. Har., Nov. 7, 1736 ; d. young.

132.* iv. ALDEN, b. Har., Feb. 24, 1738-9 ; bap. Apr. 1, 1739.

133.* v. NATHAN, b. Har., June 18, 1741.

134.* vi. DAVID, b. Har., May 10, 1744 ; bap. June 17.

135.* vii. RICHARD, b. Har., June 8, 1746.

136.   viii. MARY, b. Har., Apr. 15, 1750 ; bap. June 24 ; m. Rochester, Nov. 13, 1766, by Rev. Ivory Hovey to *Jonathan Hatch* of Falmouth.

137.   ix. ELIZABETH, bap. Har., July 8, 1752.

138.   x. ALICE, m. Roch., Mar. 29, 1769, *Chas. Church.*

139.   xi. SARAH, bap. E. Yar., Mar. 30, 1755.

Judah Sears' house at "Punkhorn," Harwich, now West

Brewster, was standing recently, a very ancient structure, now much dilapidated, and has been said to be the oldest house in Brewster. It is two stories in front, and one in the rear, and was occupied about 1863, by Capt. David Sears, No. 1812, the Swivel maker.

It is probable that the house of Capt. John Sears in Dennis, is the oldest of the Sears houses now remaining, and that of Joshua Sears in Brewster, the next; Judah Sears' being the third in point of age.

In the locality known as " Punkhorn," the manufacture of lampblack was carried on to some extent formerly, and a cart drawn by one ox, used for transporting the lampblack, was known as " the Punkhorn stage."

In the allotment of pews in the 2d Ch., Yar., Aug. 24, 1761, Mr. Judah Sears had ¼ right hand door, at £53 10 0 old tenor.

He removed to Rochester, Mass., with his family, and joined the church there in 1769, being then "near 70 years old." He was chosen Tything man in Roch., in 1764-7.

His will dated Feb. 5, 1773, was proved Sep. 2, 1776, and mentions wife Mary; sons, Alden, Nathan, Judah, David and Richard; and daus. Ann Gage, wife of Anthony Gage; Mary Hatch, wife of Jon[a] Hatch; Alice Church, wife of Charles Church, and Sarah Sears. Judah Sears was Exec[r].

31.

JOHN SEARS[4] [*Samuel[3]*, *Paul[2]*, *Richard[1]*], b. Harwich, Mass., July 18, 1701; d. 1774, æ. 74; m. Yarmouth, Nov., 1734, *Grace Paddock*, dau. of Judah and Alice (Alden) P., she b. 1716; adm. 2d Ch., Yar., May 16, 1735, and to full communion, Har., Apr. 10, 1774; d. Sep. 17, 1780, æ. 65. She and her sister, Mary, who m. Judah Sears, were gr.-daus. of David, and gt.-gr.-daus. of John and Priscilla (Mullens) Alden, who came over in the " Mayflower." Children:

140.   i. DAU., b. Yar., Nov. 13, 1735; d. Dec. 15, 1735.
141.*   ii. JOHN, b. Yar., June 5, 1737.
142.   iii. REBECCA, bap. Har., May 3, 1741.
143.   iv. NATHAN, bap. Har., July 5, 1741; d. young.
144.   v. PHEBE, bap. Har., Dec. 4, 1743; m. —— *Atwood*.
145.*   vi. DAVID, bap. Har., Apr. 27, 1746.
146.   vii. SAMUEL, bap. Har., Apr. 27, 1746; d. young.
147.   viii. RHODA, bap. Har., Oct. 16, 1748; pub. Har., Feb. 29, 1772, to *Stephen Atwood* of Boston; prob. d. in 1779.

148.	ix. GRACE, bap. Har., Aug. 12, 1752; d. 1771.
149.	x. ENOCH, bap. Har., May 11, 1755. He was a prisoner
	at R. I., and sent to Boston, Aug. 6, 1777, in Sch[r] " Speed-
	well," Capt. Josiah Godfrey, in exchange; prob. d. in 1779.
150.	xi. EZRA, bap. Har., June 12, 1755; was Doctor on the
	privateer brig "Gen. Arnold," Capt. Magee, owned by
	Col. Isaac Sears and others, and with nearly all the crew
	was frozen to death in Plymouth harbor, Dec. 25, 1778.

John Sears of Har., made his will, Oct. 12, 1770; wife
Grace Sears, Exec[x]; names children, John, David, Rebecca,
Rhoda, Enoch, Grace and Ezra.

Grace Sears, widow, made her will July 20, 1779, which was
proved Oct. 10, 1780. She mentions son John, gr.-daus. Rebecca and Catherine, heirs to son David, deceased; and daus.
Rebecca Sears and Phebe Atwood; dau. Rebecca, Exec[x].

32.

SETH SEARS[4] [Samuel[5] Paul[2], Richard[1]], b. Harwich,
Mass., May 27, 1703; adm. 2d Ch., Yar., June 23, 1728; d.
Mar. 5, 1750, in 48[t]yr., gr.-st., W. Br.; m. Yar., Oct. 14, 1725,
Priscilla Ryder, she b. 1712; received into 2d Ch., Yar., May
5, 1728; d. Jan. 18, 1747, in 36 yr., gr.-st., W. Br. Children:
151.*	i. ROLAND, b. Har., Sep. 18, 1726.
152.	ii. TAMSEN, b. Har., Sep. 5, 1727; bap. E. Yar., Sep. 22;
	m. Har., July 27 (24), 1746, *David Hall*, son of Daniel
	H., he b. Mar. 6, 1724–5; (he m. 2d, Ruth Atkins, adm.
	to 2d Ch., Yar., Aug. 17, 1760; and 3d, Rebecca
	Crosby); children, HALL: [1.] Roland, bap. July 15,
	1753. [2.] Tamsen, bap. June 15, 1755.
153.	iii. PRISCILLA, b. Har., Dec. 31, 1730; bap. E. Yar.,
	Jan. 3, 1730–1; m. June 29, 1749, *Jonathan Sears*, No.
	113; 2d, Apr. 11, 1754, Dea. *John Sears*, No. 47; she
	died of old age, Apr. 12, 1819, æ. 89.
154.	iv. SETH, b. Har., Nov. 2, 1732; d. May 31, 1733, in
	2 yr., gr.-st.
155.	v. LYDIA, b. Har., Apr. 17, 1734; m. Nov. 24, 1757,
	Stephen Sears, No. 332.
156.	vi. SETH, b. Har., Apr. 25, 1737; m. there Dec. 19,
	1757, *Sarah Lincoln*, and removed to Ashfield, she being
	dism. from Ch. Har., May 25, 1777. He d. s. p. about
	1810 or 12, his wife having died some years previous. He
	was mentioned in Uncle Joseph's will 1765.
157.	vii. REUBEN, b. Har., May 24, 1739; d. young.

The estate of Seth Sears, Yeoman of Harwich, was adm·
upon by Jonᵃ Sears and David Hall. Inventory was filed
Mar. 5, 1750, foots £177 07 11, of which £91 06 08 was
in real estate. David Hall of Yar., was app. guardian to
Lydia Sears.

33.

BENJAMIN SEARS⁴ [*Samuel³*, *Paul²*, *Richard¹*], b.
Harwich, Mass., June 16, 1706; m. Yar., Mar. 16, 1731–2,
Lydia Ryder of Yar., who was adm. to Ch. Har., from Ch.
Yar., June 3, 1733; and d. Mar. 24, 1733–4, in 23 yr., gr·st.,
W. Br.; 2d, (pub. July 16, 1735,) to *Mercy Snow*, dau.
Prince and Hannah S., she b. Har., Nov. 18, 1705; d. there
June 29, 1736, in 31 yr., gr.-st., W. Br. ; (her father was son of
Mark and grand-son of Nicholas Snow;) 3d, Har., June 30,
1737, *Abigail (Burgess) Sears*, widow of Stephen Sears, No.
85. Children:

By *Lydia*:
158. i. Daughter, b. Har., Feb. 8, 1732–3; d. Feb. 11.
159. ii. HEMAN, b. Har., Mar. 13, 1733–4; bap. 17; and d. June
2, 1734.

By *Mercy*:
160. iii. HEMAN, b. Har., June 18, 1736; bap. 20; and d. Aug.
15, 1737.

By *Abigail*:
161.* iv. BENJAMIN, b. Har., May 2, 1738; bap. 7.
162.* v. STEPHEN, b. Har., May 2, 1738; bap. 7;* *gemini*.
163.* vi. ENOCH, b. Har., Sep. 5, 1741; bap. 27; "went west."
164. vii. REUBEN, bap. Har., Feb. 19, 1743–4; may be the
Reuben Sears who m. in 1790, *Hannah Benedict*, she b.
Dec. 23, 1772, and rem. to Wayne co., N. Y.; but more
probably his son; and *Daniel Sears*, who m. *Lydia Burt*
of Ridgefield, Ct., was perhaps another.
165.* viii. SUNDERLAND, b. (prob. in South East,) Dec. 14, 1749.
166.* ix. SETH, b. South East, N. Y.
167.* x. SAMUEL, b. South East.

Benjamin Sears removed to New York, and located on " Joe's
Hill" in South East, then known as part of " Oblong," and
was one of the earliest settlers there.

He was adm. to Ch. Har., July 14, 1734–5, and " dismissed
to church in Oblong, whereof Mʳ Kent is pastor," May 20, 1749.

34.

EBENEZER SEARS[4] [*Paul*₃ *Paul*², *Richard*¹], b. Yarmouth, Mass., Aug. 15, 1694; d. E. Hampton, Ct.; m. Yar., May 26, 1720, *Sarah Howes*, dau. of Ebenezer and Sarah (Gorham) H., she b. Jan. 20 (22), 1699; was adm. 2d Ch., Yar., from 1st Ch., Aug. 6, 1727. Children:

168. i. SARAH, b. Yar., Mar. 10 (6), 1720-1; m. there, Oct. 6, 1742, *James Higgins*.

169. ii. DESIRE, b. Yar., Apr. 23, 1722; d. July 6, 1722 (1723).

170.* iii. EBENEZER, b. Yar., June 13, 1723.

171. iv. DESIRE, b. Yar., Aug. 15, 1725; bap. Har., Feb. 16, 1725-6; m. Nov. 3, 1748, *John Markham*, who d. Mar. 3, 1788, æ. 83; she d. Nov. 19, 1786, æ. 63. They lived at Pocatopag Lake, in Chatham, Ct., and were the ancestors of all of the name there; children, MARKHAM: [1.] Elizabeth, b. July 30, 1749. [2.] Desire, b. Mar. 10, 1750-1; m. Lemuel West. [3.] Nathaniel, b. May 5, 1754. [4.] John, b. May 9, 1756. [5.] Dinah, b. Apr. 2, 1761. [6.] Jane, or James, b. May 25, 1763. [7.] Abigail, b. Mar. 23, 1766. [8.] Margery, b. Apr. 16, 1768.

172. v. HEZEKIAH, b. Yar., May, 1727; bap. E. Yar., June 25; d. Dec., 1727.

173.* vi. HEZEKIAH, b. Yar., Dec. 30, 1728; bap. Jan. 26, 1728-9.

174. vii. THOMAS, b. Yar., Sep. 22, 1731; bap. Oct. 2.·

175. viii. BETSY, b. Yar., Aug. 27, 1733; m. Middletown, Ct., Oct. 5, 1753, *Wm. Norcutt;* children, NORCUTT: [1.] Reuben, b. July 20, 1754. [2.] Ruth, b. June 21, 1756. [3.] Sarah, b. Sep. 9, 1758. [4.] Abner, b. Feb. 27, 1761. [5.] Hannah, b. Feb. 23, 1763. [6.] Ephraim, b. July 20, 1765.

176. ix. DINAH, b. Yar., Dec. 1, 1735.

177. x. MERCY, b. Yar., Feb. 11, 1738-9; m. Jan. 10, 1760, *Thomas Shepard;* children, SHEPARD: [1.] Hannah, b. Nov. 10, 1760. [2.] Edward, b. Feb. 7, 1763. [3.] Alden, b. Dec. 9, 1773. [4.] Paul, b. May 2, 1775. [5.] Elijah, b. Mar. 18, 1782. [6.] Mercy, b. Aug. 12, 1784.

178. xi. HANNAH, b. Yar., Nov. 23, 1739; d. Apr. 26, 1742.

179. xii. ANN, b. Yar., Feb. 5, 1741; d. Apr. 18, 1741.

180. xiii. SON, b. Yar., Mar., 1742-3; d. Apr., 1743.

181.* xiv. PAUL, b. Yar., Nov. 29, 1744.

Ebenezer Sears removed with his family to Middletown,

Ct., where, in 1748, he made a purchase of land on the east side of the Connecticut river, in that part afterward set off as Chatham.

Eben[r] Howes of Yarmouth, in his will dated Dec. 3, 1760, mentions his daughter, Sarah Sears.

35.

PAUL SEARS[4] [*Paul*[3] *Paul*[2], *Richard*[1]], b. Yarmouth, Mass., Dec. 21, 1695; d. Rochester, Mass., early in 1771; m. there, May 30, 1721, by Rev. Tim° Ruggles, to *Charity Whittredge*, dau. of William and Mary W., she b. about 1702; d. between 1760 and 1767. Children:

182.   i. MERCY, b. Roch., Apr. 28, 1724.

183.* ii. WILLIAM, b. Roch., Jan. 14, 1725-6.

184.* iii. PAUL, b. Roch., 1728, or perhaps 1722.

185. iv. MARY, b. Roch., Apr. 20, 1730. *Mary Sears* and *Ezekiel Clarke*, both of Roch., were pub. Aug. 13, 1748; *Mary Sears* of Roch., and *William White* of Dartmouth were pub. Nov. 17, 1751.

186.* v. NATHANIEL, b. Roch., Sep. 1 (5), 1738.

187.   vi. ELIZABETH, b. Roch., Mar. 17, 1741, (Mar. 26, 1743, T. Clk.) *Elizabeth Sears and Joshua Clapp* were m. May 7, 1761.

188. vii. HANNAH, b. Roch., was pub. Oct. 1, 1752, to *Mark Snow*, son of Jon[a] and Thankful (Freeman) S., of Harwich; he b. Aug. 6, 1731; she d. 1768; (and he m. 2d, [pub. July 18, 1774], Mrs. Susannah Whelden of Tisbury;) children, SNOW: [1.] Edmund, b. Dec. 25, 1753. [2.] Paul, b. Dec. 7, 1755; d. young. [3.] Thankful, b. Jan. 30, 1758. [4.] Mark, b. Mar. 6, 1760; d. young. [5.] Hannah, b. Feb. 27, 1762. [6.] Ebenezer, b. July 16, 1764; d. young. [7.] Charity, b. July 21, 1766; m. —— Hoar of Middleboro. [8.] Jonathan, b. July 12, 1768; d. Mar. 31, 1846; m. Feb. 11, 1790, Lydia Hammett, dau. of Barnabas and Hannah (Braley) H., of Long Plains, Mass., and rem. in 1789 to East Montpelier, Vt., had, i. Hannah, b. Oct. 28, 1791; m. Isaac Alden; d. Nov. 23, 1869, in Calais, Vt.; had Ruby H., Emily D., Charles L., of Troy, N. Y., Alonzo, and Avis E. ii. Polly, b. Apr. 8, 1793; m. Zenas Johnson; d. Oct. 2, 1861. iii. Charity, b. Jan. 29, 1795; d. Aug. 24, 1858; m. Henry Simmons; 2d, Asaph Kendall. iv. Barnabas H., b. Oct. 28, 1796; d. May 31, 1873; m. Lucy

11

Bancroft.   v. Abner H., b. July 13, 1798 ; m. Eliz[h] Misc.
vi. Mark, b. Jan. 13, 1800 ; d. Oct. 26, 1848.   vii. Avis H.,
b. Nov. 25,1801 ; m. Asa Alden.   viii. Horace, b. Sep. 30,
1803 ; d. May 29, 1849 ; m. Lucy Taber.   ix. Elias S.,
b. July 16, 1805 ; d. Aug. 22, 1882 ; m. Irene Cummings.
x. Nancy, b. July 22, 1807 ; d. Mar. 28, 1833; m. Wm.
Scott. xi. Jonathan M., b. Oct. 30, 1809 ; d. Apr. 30, 1862;
m. Hannah Vincent.   xii. Alonzo, b. Sep. 2, 1811 ; m.
Ruby Bassett ; 2d, Sarah Short.   (Mark Snow by his 2d
wife had, Susanna, b. Sep. 3, 1775, Lydia, b. Aug. 17, 1777 ;
Loammi, b. Sep. 15, 1779, m. Nancy Swift ; West, b. Jan.
1, 1782 ; d. young ; Abner, b. May 21, 1785 ; d. unm.   In
his will dated June 27, 1799, he mentions sons, Edmund,
Jonathan, Loammi and Abner ; and daus. Thankful,
Hannah, Charity, Susanna and Lydia.   He derived through
Jonathan[4], Nicholas[3], Mark[2], from Nicholas Snow[1].)

Paul Sears removed to Rochester, Mass., in 1721, where he
purchased land of the Winslows, which was partly in Dartmouth, the site of the old homestead being now in Acushnet.
The original deed is in possession of his descendant, Nathaniel
Sears of Hyannis, who has also many other old family documents, Bibles, etc.

His deed of gift giving his property to his children was
dated Dec. 28, 1770, and filed Mar. 27, 1771.   He was then
too feeble to write his name, and died soon after.

37.

THOMAS SEARS[4] [*Paul₃ Paul², Richard¹*], b. Yarmouth, Mass., June 6, 1699 ; d. Plymouth, Mass., 1755 ; m.
there in 1734, *Elizabeth Bartlett*, dau. of Robert and Sarah
(Bartlett) B., she b. Ply., 1707.   He m. 2d, 1752, (pub. Mar.
21, 1751–2,) *Mehitable Fish*, of Sandwich, who survived him.
Children :

By *Elizabeth :*

189.* i. THOMAS, b. Ply.
190.* ii. WILLARD, b. Ply.
191. iii. BETTY, b. Ply.; m. 1761, *Samuel Sherman*, his 2d
     wife ; children, SHERMAN : [1.] Thomas, b. 1762. [2.]
     William, b. 1764. [3.] Andrew, b. 1767. [4.] Betsy ;
     m. Lewis Holmes.
192. iv. REBECCA, b. Ply.; perhaps m. *Joshua Bramhall* of
     Ply.; he b. 1736.

193. v. CHLOE, b. Ply.
194. vi. SARAH, b. Ply.; m. 1767, *Seth Paine* from Eastham;
    he b. there June 12, 1740; d. Apr. 29, 1775; she d. Bel-
    grade, Me., a widow, about 1811–12; children, PAINE:
    [1.] Bartlett, b. Sep. 13, 1769. [2.] Betsy, b. Dec. 12,
    1771. [3.] Mercy. [4.] Seth, b. Feb. 24, 1775; d. Rut-
    land, Meigs co., Ohio, May 6, 1865, æ. 90.
By *Mehitable:*
195. vii. MARY, b. Ply.; d. young.
196. viii. MARY, b. Ply., May 3, 1755; m. Oct. 24, 1773, Capt.
    Samuel Smith, son of Dr. Thos. S.; he b. Nov. 11, 1746;
    d. June 17, 1809; children, SMITH: [1.] Mehitable, b.
    July 22, 1774; m. Jireh Phinney of Machias. [2.]
    Deborah, b. Apr. 10, 1777. [3.] Bethia, b. July 10, 1781;
    d. 1856. [4.] Mercy, b. Sep. 23, 1783. [5.] Samuel, b.
    July 31, 1786.

The will of Thomas Sears of Plymouth, dated July 2, 1755,
was allowed July 17; Jeremiah Howes, Exec[r]; it names wife
Mehitable, sons Thomas and Willard, and daus. Bettye, Rebecca, Chloa, Sarah and Mary Sears.

The inventory of widow Mehitable Sears, late of Sandwich,
was filed Feb. 6, 1769, by Prince Tupper, Adm[r], and foots up
£26 13 8.

The children's names are perhaps not placed in the order of
their birth; the town records are very imperfect, but the old
church records, which I have not examined, may give further
data.

42.

JOSHUA SEARS[4] [*Paul[3], Paul[2], Richard[1]*], b. Yarmouth,
Mass., Nov. 20, 1708; d. Middletown, Ct., Sep. 27, 1753; m.
Eastham, Mass., Feb 10, 1731–2, *Rebecca Mayo*, dau. of John
and Susannah (Freeman) M., of E.; she b. Oct. 10, 1713; was
adm. to Ch. Har., May 27, 1739, and with her husband dismissed to East Ch., Middletown, Ct., Feb. 5, 1748. Children:

197.   i. REBECCA, b. Yar., Nov. 14, 1732; bap. Har., June
    24, 1739; was in Sheffield, Mass., Oct. 20, 1773; unm.
198.* ii. ELKANAH, b. Har., Apr. 12, 1734; bap. June 24,
    1739.
199.* iii. JOSHUA, b. Har., Feb. 14, 1735–6; bap. June 24,
    1739.

200.   iv. BETSY, b. Har., June 19, 1738; bap. June 24,
        1739; m. *Samuel Hitchcock* of New Marlboro, Mass., Oct.
        20, 1773, and June 14, 1798, Eliz[h] Hitchcock et ux.,
        signed deeds to Elkanah Sears of Middletown, Ct.
201.*   v. PAUL, b. Har., Oct. 18, 1740; bap. Nov. 2, 1743.
202.*   vi. SIMEON, b. Har., Jan. 14, 1742-3; bap. Jan. 16.
203.   vii. THOMAS, b. Har., rem. to Sheffield, Mass., and was
        killed by the fall of a tree.   He with others signed deed
        to Elkanah Sears of Midd[n], Ct., Oct. 20, 1773, and was
        then resident of Sheffield.   Served in Capt. Enoch Noble's
        Co , Col. John Brown's Reg[t], June 29 to July 28, 1777;
        in Capt. John King's Co., Col. A. Shelley's Reg[t], July
        21 to Aug. 15, 1777, 25 days, 74 miles, wages, 16[s] 8[d], and
        in Capt. Mat. Goodwin's Co., Col. Theo. Cotton's Reg[t],
        "secret expedition against Newport, R. I."; wages, £1 4 0.
204.   viii. SARAH, m. —— *Hitchcock* of Sheffield.
205.   ix. HANNAH, bap. Har., Oct. 26, 1746; m. *Elisha Shel-
        don* of New Marlboro, Mass.; he b. 1736; father of the
        late Hon. Benj. Sheldon, and grand-father of Judge Shel-
        don of Illinois, also father of Elisha Sheldon, b. 1778,
        who settled in Newark Valley, N. Y., and has descendants
        still living there. [Isaac Sheldon, b. 1629; rem. 1654, from
        Windsor, and d. 1708; by his wife, Mary Woodford, who
        d. 1684, he had Samuel, b. 1675, who m. Mary ——, and
        had Samuel, b. 1700, who lived in Marlboro, and by his
        wife, Mehitable Strong, had Elisha, b. 1736; m. Hannah
        Sears as above.]
206.   x. WILLARD, bap. Har., Mar. 24, 1774-5; d. Aug. 24,
        1754.
207.   xi. THEOPHILUS, b. Midd[n], Ct., Apr. 2, 1749; was in
        Sandisfield, Mass., Nov. 8, 1770, at which date he signed
        a deed to his brother Elkanah; but I do not find his name
        upon the town records there.
208.   xii. BENJAMIN, b. Midd[n], Nov. 3, 1751.

Joshua Sears was Constable of Harwich in 1745.

He was a man of large stature, and of great strength and
hardihood.

In 1746, he removed to Middletown, Ct., and purchased
land on the east side of the Connecticut river, in that part of
the town afterward set off as Chatham.

In Col. Rec. Ct., vol. X, we find the memorial of Rebecca
Sears, adm[x], to the Assembly, setting forth that debts exceeded
personal estate by £135 16 10, and asking liberty to sell real
estate.

Mar. 9, 1732, Eben[r] Nickerson deeded to Joshua Sears, for the consideration of £532, "about 36 acres of land with the buildings, &c., eastward of Point of Rocks, Harwich, 3 Lots: First, the eastern-most originally laid out to Capt. Jon[a] Bangs; ——. Second, to successors Mark Snow; ——. Third, the westward to Thos. Clark, bounded on Dea. Chillingsworth Foster, Nathaniel Hopkins, John Freeman, and Clark & Cole lot."

I have found no record of marriage of Theophilus, or Benjamin Sears; but think Dr. Willard Leonard Sears, b. Glastenbury, Ct., Sep. 16, 1816, derived from one of them, perhaps Benjamin, as he named his eldest son Benjamin Willard Sears.

43.

DANIEL SEARS[4] [*Paul[3], Paul[2], Richard[1]*], b. Yarmouth, Mass., July 16, 1710; d. Nov. 28, 1771, in 61 yr., gr.-st., W. Br.; m. Eastham, Jan. 13, 1736-7, *Mercy Snow*, dau. of Micajah S., of E.; she b. Sep. 16, 1713; d. May 8, 1790, æ. 76, gr.-st. Children:

209.* i. MICAJAH, b. Yar., Apr. 25, 1738.
210. ii. JERUSHA, b. Yar., June 28, 1740; m. Jan. 7, 1768, *Robt. Homer*, son of Benj. and Eliz[h] (Crowell) H., he b. Jan. 28, 1742; she d. soon, and he m. 2d, widow of John Thacher.
211. iii. HANNAH, b. Yar., Aug. 17, 1742; not ment[d] 1771 in father's will, and probably d. young and unm.
212.* iv. DANIEL, b. Yar., June 17, 1744.
213. v. PHEBE, b. Yar., Mar. 31, 1747; m. Dec. 26, 1771, John Sears, No. 237.
214.* vi. PAUL, b. Yar., June 2, 1750.
215.* vii. ENOS, b. Yar., June 11, 1752; bap. 2d Ch., Aug. 30, 1752.

Daniel Sears lived in the East precinct of Yarmouth, now East Dennis, and with his wife was admitted to the church there, May 16, 1742. Mar. 7, 1749, Daniel Sears on committee "to keep boys in order on the Sabbath day," and again Mar. 22, 1750-1. Dec. 16, 1760, app[d] on committee to locate school. Oct. 23, 1762, on com. "to procure wood for Mr. Dennis." Oct. 3, 1765, on com. "to see Mr. Dennis." Dec. 14, 1767, "remitted 1 poll for Mr. Daniel Sears."

His will, dated Nov. 29, 1771, was proved Dec. 5, 1771, by Daniel Sears and Paul Sears, Exec[rs], and mentions Phebe

Sears, Micajah, Daniel, Paul and Enos. R. Est. £578. Personal, £179 13 2.

Paul and Enos sold out their rights to Micajah.

Mrs. Mercy Sears is mentioned in the will of her father, Micajah Snow, of Eastham.

44.

Capt. EDMUND SEARS⁴ [*Paul₃ Paul², Richard¹*], b. Yarmouth, Mass., Aug. 6, 1712; d. Aug. 12, 1796, in 85 yr., gr.-st., W. Br.; m. Yar., Apr. 7, 1743, *Hannah Crowell*, dau. of Christopher and Sarah (*Matthews*) C., she b. Sep. 9, 1725; d. June 22, 1802, in 77 yr., gr.-st. Children:

216.* i. EDMUND, b. Yar., Jan. 3, 1743–4.
217. ii. ELIZABETH, b. Yar., Oct. 16, 1745; d. 1819; m. there Nov. 21, 1765, *Thomas Homer*, son of Benj. and Eliz. (Crowell) H., he b. Mar. 21, 1736; rem. to Vermont.
218. iii. JANE, b. Yar., Nov. 17, 1748; m. there Nov. 12, 1772, *Roland Hallet* of Barnstable; and d. July, 1799; lived in Hyannis, and had Roland, *inter alios*.
219. iv. JOSHUA, b. Yar., July 25, (21), 1751; d. 1751.
220.* v. JOSHUA, b. Yar., July 1, 1753; bap. 2d Ch., Yar., July 22.
221.* vi. CHRISTOPHER, b. Yar., Aug. 16, 1756; bap. Aug. 22.
222.* vii. ELKANAH, b. Yar., Oct. 22, 1758.
223. viii. MERCY, b. Yar., Mar. 7, 1761; bap. May 3; adm. 2d Ch., Sep. 14, 1800; d. unm., Jan. 27, 1849, æ. 89, gr.-st., W. Br.
224. ix. TEMPERANCE, b. Yar., Aug. 9, 1764; bap. Nov. 18, 1764; m. Yar., Apr. 28, 1789, Capt. *Isaac Clark*, son of Kimbal and Mary (Paddock) C., he b. Oct. 10, 1761; was a shipmaster in the Russian trade, and at the close of the Rev'y war, achieved the distinction of commanding the first mercantile vessel to display the United States flag in the White Sea, having been obliged to wait six months at St. Petersburg, for the arrival of the American Minister, before he was permitted to discharge his cargo. He was Representative to the General Court from Brewster 1803–12, and died on coast of Africa, Feb. 11, 1819; children, CLARK: [1.] Mary Paddock, b. May 27, 1791; d. Apr. 11, 1877; m. Jere. Mayo of Br., his 2d wife; he b. Jan. 29, 1786; d. June 20, 1867; had, i. Mary Catherine, b. Apr. 1, 1826; d. Aug. 7, 1845; m. Nov. 27, 1844, Wm. H. Bangs of Boston; he b. Nov. 19, 1813. ii. Charles Edwin, b.

Oct. 26, 1827; m. May 7, 1861, Eliza Caroline Fitch; she
b. Westfield, N. Y., Apr. 16, 1832; lives in St. Paul,
Minn. iii. Sarah Augusta, b. Aug. 24, 1830; d. unm.,
Apr. 7, 1886. [2.] Hannah, b. June 29, 1792; d. Nov.
3, 1841; m. Nov. 4, 1813, Winslow Hall; he b. Sep. 2,
1792; d. Aug. 13, 1875; lived in Sandwich, Mass., and
had, i. Winslow C., b. Sep. 9, 1814; d. Feb. 9, 1815. ii.
Eunice, b. Dec. 9, 1815; d. Aug. 30, 1852. iii. Joshua, b.
Feb. 9, 1818; m. Feb. 18, 1847, Abby Jones Holway; she
b. Sandwich, Apr. 4, 1827; he is a farmer at Spring Hill,
Mass. iv. Isaac C., b. Oct. 7, 1820; m. Jan. 16, 1843,
Susannah G. Ryder; she b. Chatham, Mass., May 1, 1822;
lived in Winthrop, Mass., and Grand Rapids, Dakota. v
Temperance C., b. Dec. 30, 1823; d. May 1, 1848. vi.
Winslow, b. Aug. 22, 1836; m. Hannah Ryder of
Chatham; who d.; 2d, Ellen Page of Stockton, Cal.;
and lives in San Francisco, Cal. vii. Hannah, b. Mar. 23,
1829; d. Mar. 27, 1860; m. Feb. 24, 1853, Isaac Swift
Lawrence of Falmouth, Mass., a farmer. viii. Caroline,
b. Apr. 5, 1832; d. July 16, 1862; m. Feb. 9, 1861, Isaac
S. Lawrence; his 2d wife. ix. Mary Clark, b. Apr. 7,
1836; m. Sep. 7, 1859, Wm. S. Chadwick; he b. Falmouth, May 15, 1824; d. Dorchester, Mass., Jan. 26,
1862; she lives in Grand Rapids, Dakota. [3.] Isaac, b.
May 18, 1794; d. unm. [4.] Lot, b. July 25, 1796; went
to Boston in 1815, was in store of R. M. Barnard, and in
1818, of firm Means & Clark; d. Feb. 24, 1880; m. Aug.
26, 1826, Mary Barnard Eaton, dau. of R. S. E., of Boston; she b. Oct. 19, 1803; d. Dorchester, May 26, 1889;
had, i. Mary E., b. May 12, 1827; m. Fred. Pierce
Moseley, iron merchant; he b. Dorchester, Sep. 20, 1826;
d. Jan. 8, 1881. ii. Eliza, b. Feb. 22, 1829; m. June 29,
1860, Henry Hurd Darrah, ; he b. Chester, Vt., Oct. 4,
1825; d. Jan. 24, 1883; she lives in Boston. iii. Sarah,
b. May 27, 1831; unm. iv. Caroline, b. July 12, 1834;
m. Chas. Henry Little, cash[r] Water Board, Boston; he b.
New Gloucester, Me. v. Charles H., b. Oct. 22, 1836;
m. Oct. 11, 1866, Martha Cooper Pierce; was of firm Mayo
& Clark, St. Paul, Minn. vi. George Albert, b. July 12,
1839; unm. vii. Anna A., b. Jan. 9, 1842; m. Aug. 17,
1864, Abraham W. Sears, No. 2001. viii. Grace, b. Dec.
26, 1844; unm. ix. Lot, b. Jan. 9, 1850; unm. [5.]
Strabo, b. 1798; d. 1799. [6.] Strabo, b. June 9, 1801;
m. 1838, Adeline Dunbar, who d. Aug. 2, 1860; he d.

Brewster, Nov. 23, 1869; had, i. Strabo Franklin, b. Nov. 22, 1839; d. at sea, Sep., 1862. ii. Adeline, b. Mar. 20, 1842; d. Oct. 26, 1870. iii. Mary Burr, b. Apr. 21, 1844; d. July 24, 1871. iv. Georgianna, b. Mar. 13, 1847; d. Nov. 25, 1870. v. John Henry, b. Aug. 21, 1850; m. June 8, 1882, Celia A. Parker of Brewster. [7.] Temperance, b. Oct. 21, 1802; d. W. Br., Mar. 24, 1887; m. Dec., 1840, Benj. Baker of Yar., he b. Apr. 27, 1800; children: i. Benj. Clark, b. Sep. 29, 1841; m. Sep., 1869, Mary E. Tucker of Middléboro; was a shipmaster, and now coal dealer in Auburndale, Mass. ii. Edmund Freeman, b. May 22, 1845; d. Nov. 5, 1875. [8.] Edmund Sears, b. Apr. 5, 1804; unm. [9.] Albert Paddock, b. Nov. 24, 1807; m. Feb. 23, 1849, Sarah Freeman, dau. of John and Bethia (Crowell) F., of Brewster; she b. Aug. 12, 1818; he d. Dorchester, Mass., July 24, 1882. He was well known in commercial circles, having been in the salt trade many years. He went to Pernambuco in early life, where he remained several years, and on his return started in the fish business on Cape Cod. He subsequently was located at the West, but after a short stay came back to Boston, to engage in the salt trade, which he followed until about 1872, when he retired with a competency. He was among the first of the natives of Cape Cod to cultivate with success the cranberry, which has since ranked among the prominent products of that region. His children were: i. Ella, b. Sep. 20, 1850; d. Sep. 15, 1852. ii. Albert, b. Aug. 8, 1852; d. Aug. 23, 1854. iii. Frederick A., b. May 19, 1855; d. Sep. 24, 1864. iv. Henry F., b. Apr. 20, 1857; d. June 20, 1860. v. Sarah Maria, b. Feb. 10, 1760; d. Sep. 16, 1861. [10.] Eliza Jane, b. Apr. 22, 1810; m. July 29, 1830, Nathl Winslow; he b. Apr. 14, 1804; d. Jan. 4, 1880; lived in Brewster; children: i. Mary Francis, b. Feb. 13, 1832. ii. Eliza, b. Mar. 18, 1835; d. Jan. 29, 1844. iii. Emma, b. Apr. 13, 1839; d. Feb. 24, 1840. iv. Albert, b. Jan. 23, 1841. v. Eliza Emma, b. Dec. 15, 1844; m. July 6, 1868, Capt. Francis B. Foster, who d. at sea in 1886. vi. Ida Maria, b. Jan. 8, 1848; d. July 19, 1878.

225. x. HANNAH, b. Yar., Dec. 8, 1766; bap. E. Yar., Mar. 22, 1767; m. Sep. 19, (21 T. C.,) 1786, *Willard Sears*, No. 257.

Edmund Sears and wife were admitted to the church in E. Yar., May 12, 1745.

He was a sea captain during many years.

It is related of him that at the time of the " Boston Tea Party," he was unloading his vessel in the vicinity.

He went on board the vessels and participated in throwing the tea overboard.

Upon his return to the Cape soon after, though he had been long absent from home, on entering the house he went straight to the " *bowfat*," and without saying a word to any one, seized the teapot and caddy, and threw them into the garden with a crash.

His astonished wife whispered to the children, " your poor father has come home crazy."

He then proclaimed that from that time henceforth none of his family were to drink tea, or wear upon their persons any articles of British manufacture.

His four sons were in the Revolutionary Army, but nevertheless, when a landing was threatened on the Cape, he mounted his horse and galloped to the spot to offer his services. He set up the first chaise, and owned the first ingrain carpet in the town.

His will, dated June 20, 1796, was witnessed by John Chapman, Peter Sears and Joseph Sears ; a codicil bears no date. He mentions wife Hannah ; daus. Mary Sears, Eliz[h] Homer, Jane Hallet, Temperance Clark and Hannah Sears ; and sons Christopher, Elkanah, Edmund and Joshua.

46.

ELISHA SEARS[4] [*John[3], Paul[2], Richard[1]*], b. Yarmouth, Mass., 1706 ; d. Mar. 7, 1790, in 84 yr., gr.-st., W. Br. ; m. Yar., Mar. 11, 1735–6, *Sarah Vincent*, dau. of Philip V., she b. 1709 ; d. Apr. 12, 1783, in 75 yr., gr.-st. Children :

226. i. SAMUEL, b. Yar., Dec. 10, 1736 ; d. Mar. 18, 1792, in 56 yr., gr.-st.

227. ii. BETHIA, b. Yar., Mar. 29, 1739 ; d. Apr. 26, 1759, in 21 yr., gr.-st.

228.* iii. ELISHA, b. Yar., Sep. 26, 1741.

229.* iv. JOHN, b. Yar., May 30, 1743.

230. v. ENOCH, b. Yar., July 17, 1746 ; d. Mar. 29, 1767, in 21 yr., gr.-st.

231. vi. CONSTANT, b. Yar., June 17, 1749 ; d. June 27, 1768, in 19 yr., gr.-st.

232.* vii. NOAH, b. Yar., Apr. 11, 1751.

Elisha Sears was adm. to 2d Ch., Yar., Sep. 17, 1738.

He lived on the old homestead, and with his wife and children lies buried in the family cemetery in West Brewster.

47.

Dea. JOHN SEARS[4] [*John*[3], *Paul*[2], *Richard*[1]], b. Yarmouth, Mass., 1712; d. Dec. 5, 1791, in 79 yr., gr.-st., W. Br.; m. Yar., Aug. 24, 1738, *Deborah Crowell*, dau. of John and Kezia (Eldredge) C.; she b. 1720; d. Sep. 18, 1753, æ. 53, gr.-st., W. Br.; 2d, Yar., Apr. 11, 1754, *Priscilla Sears*, dau of Seth and Priscilla (Ryder) S., and widow of Jon[a] Sears, No. 113; she b. Dec. 31, 1730; d. of old age, Apr. 12, 1819, in 89 yr., gr.-st.   Children :

By *Deborah :*

233.   i. BATHSHEBA, b. Yar., Sep. 13, 1739; m. there Jan. 29, 1760, *Thos. Howes*, 4th son of Thos. and Hannah (Sears) H., he b. July 17, 1737; his 2d wife; dism. to Ch. Ashfield, Apr. 24, 1791; children, HOWES: [1.] Deborah, b. Nov. 15, 1761; m. Jan. 31, 1782, Lot Bassett. [2.] Ezekiel, b. Dec. 3, 1763; m. Apr. 21, 1791, Rose Vincent. [3.] Mark, b. July 28, 1765; m. Jan. 7, 1790, Abigail Gorham. [4.] Azubah, b. Aug. 5, 1767. [5.] Joseph, b. Jan. 5, 1771. [6.] Bathsheba, b. Jan. 22, 1773. [7.] Kezia, b. Jan. 2, 1775. [8.] Tamsen, b. Mar. 18, 1779. [9.] Sarah, b. Aug. 28, 1781. [10.] Sylvanus, b. Jan. 16, 1785.

234.   ii. KEZIA, b. Yar., Oct. 26, 1740; m. Dec. 24, 1761, *Isaac Hamblen ;* and d. before 1772; children, HAMBLEN: [1.] Betsy. [2.] Kezia. [3.] Isaac.

235.   iii. JOHN, b. Yar., Jan. 13, (17) 1741-2; d. Jan. 31.

236.   iv. DEBORAH, b. Yar., Jan. 27, 1742-3; m. there Dec. 24, 1761, *Christopher Crowell*, son of Chris. and Sarah (Matthews) C., he b. 1737; children, CROWELL: [1.] Sarah, b. Nov. 22, 1762. [2.] Levi, b. May 16, 1764; m. Jan. 29, 1789, Susanna Sears, No. 258. [3.] Nathan, b. May 29, 1766; m. Mar. 10, 1790, Hannah Hall. [4.] Heman, b. July 19, 1768; d. Nov. 6, 1769. [5.] Deborah, b. Aug. 26, 1770. [6.] Bethia, b. Oct. 18, 1772; m. Dec. 26, 1793, John Freeman. [7.] Eliza, b. Nov. 10, 1774. [8.] Joshua, b. Feb. 7, 1777. [9.] Isaiah, b. Mar. 10, 1779; d. Jan. 2, 1864; m. Hannah Howes; 2d, 1807, Abigail Kelly. [10.] Priscilla, b. Mar. 20, 1781. [11.]

Christopher, b. Sep. 21, 1783. [12.] David, b. Jan. 11,
1786. [13.] Barzillai, b. Aug. 14, 1789.
237.* v. JOHN, b. Yar., July 20, 1744.
238. vi. HEMAN, b. Yar., Apr. 11, 1746; not ment^d in
father's will, 1789.
239. vii. FREEMAN, b. Yar., Sep. 25, 1747; d. Jan. 6, 1748-9.
240. viii. PRISCILLA, b. Yar., Apr. 5, 1749; m. Dec. 3, 1767,
Daniel Sears, No. 212.
241. ix. BETTY, b. Yar., Dec. 3, 1750; m. Nov. 3, 1767, *Benjamin Howes*, son of Amos and Rebecca (Matthews) H.;
he b. June 1, 1748; and perhaps, 2d, —— *Tobey;* children,
HOWES: [1.] Reuben, b. June 15, 1768; m. Dec. 8, 1791,
Betsey Howes. [2.] Tamsen, b. Dec. 8, 1769. [3.] Elizabeth, b. June 18, 1773.
242. x. FREEMAN, b. Yar., June 16, 1752; bap. Aug. 9; d.
Aug. 21, 1753.
By *Priscilla :*
243. xi. FREEMAN, b. Yar., July 5, 1755; bap. Aug. 3; is not
mentioned in father's will in 1789; he perhaps rem. to
Nova Scotia.
244. xii. TAMSEN, b. Yar., Jan. 31, 1757; bap. May 8; d. inf.
245. xiii. TAMSEN, b. Yar., Dec. 13, 1758; bap. Mar. 11, 1759;
m. Feb. 12, 1777, *Levi Eldridge.*
246. xiv. BETHIA, b. Yar., Mar. 10, 1761; bap. May 3; m.
Jan. 4, 1789, *Edward Sears*, No. 251.
247. xv. LUCY, b. Yar., July 15, 1763; bap. Aug. 21; m. Yar.,
Sep. 13, 1781, *Joseph Hall, Jr.;* he b. May 15, 1757; d.
Dec. 24, 1831; she d. Nov. 29, 1844, Ashfield, Mass.;
children, HALL: [1.] Hephsibeth, b. July 21, 1782. [2.]
Hannah, b. May 28, 1785. [3.] Joseph, b. Dec. 25, 1786.
[4.] Levi, b. Dec. 9, 1790. [5.] Lot, b. Oct. 19, 1792.
[6.] George, b. Feb. 4, 1795. [7.] Barnabas, b. July 26,
1797. [8.] Seth, b. Nov. 7, 1799. [9.] Lucy, b. Jan.
29, 1803.
248. xvi. SETH, b. Yar., Mar. 6, 1765; bap. June 9; d. Aug.
4, 1766.
249.* xvii. SETH, b. Yar., Dec. 8, 1767; bap. Mar. 27, 1768.
250. xviii. KEZIA, b. Yar., Aug. 9, 1772; bap. Aug. 16.

John Sears and wife were adm. to 2d Ch., Yar., Aug. 5,
1739; he was chosen deacon, Feb. 29, 1768, which office he
held until his death; was a prominent man in church, and precinct affairs, for many years chosen moderator, assessor, and on
prudential committee.
His will, dated Mar. 10, 1789, mentions wife, Priscilla, and

children, John, Seth, Bashua Howes, Deborah Crowell, Betsy Tobey, Bethia Sears, Lucy Hall and Kezia Sears. Wife Priscilla and son Seth, Ex^{rs}.

Widow Priscilla Sears made her will, Jan. 7, 1815, naming daus. Eliz^h Hall, Bethia Sears, Lucy Hall, and Kezia Sears (some of them by her first marriage), and grand-children, sons and daus. of Jonathan Sears, deceased, Jonathan, Asarelah, Abigail and Clarinda; and Lydia Sears, dau. of Rev. Freeman Sears, deceased; and daus. of Seth Sears, Hephsibeth Gibson, Priscilla and Belinda Sears, Herdphebah (*sic*) Sears, and sons, Luther and Mark.

49.

WILLARD SEARS⁴ [*John*³, *Paul*², *Richard*¹], b. Yarmouth, Mass., 1714; d. Aug. 19, 1765, in 51 yr., gr.-st., W. Br.; m. Yar., Nov. 17, 1745, *Susannah Howes*, dau. of Capt. Ebenezer and Lydia (Joyce) H.; she b. Oct. 10, 1720; d. Apr. 9, 1763, in 42 yr., gr.-st.; 2d, Yar., Jan. 3, 1765, *Margery Homer*, dau. of Benj. and Eliz'h (Crowell) H., and gr.-dau. of John and Bethia (Sears) C., she b. June 13, 1727; d. Aug. 1, 1795, in 69 yr., gr.-st., W. Br., (having m. 2d, Yar., Mar. 19, 1774, Benj. Higgins of Eastham).   Children:

By *Susannah :*

251.* i. EDWARD, b. Har., Oct. 22, 1746; bap. E. Yar., Feb. 17, 1765.

252. ii. WILLARD, b. Har., Nov. 8, 1748; d. Dec. 18, 1748.

253. iii. MARY, b. Har., Apr. 1, 1750; d. Dec. 1, 1774; bap. E. Yar., Feb. 17, 1765; m. Yar., Nov. 21, 1771, *Joshua Howes*, son of David and Hannah (Paddock) H.; he b. Sep. 17, 1746; 2d, Feb. 22, 1776, Mary Paddock; children, HOWES: [1.] Susanna, b. Feb. 11, 1773. [2.] Mary, b. Nov. 24, 1774.

254. iv. WILLARD, b. Har., Jan. 7, 1751–2; d. July 4, 1752.

255.* v. REUBEN, b. Har., Sep. 27, 1753; bap. E. Yar., Feb. 17, 1765.

256.* vi. EBENEZER, b. Har., Oct. 11, 1755; bap. E. Yar., Feb. 17, 1765.

257.* vii. WILLARD, b. Har., May 26, 1759; bap. E. Yar., Feb. 17, 1765.

By *Margery :*

258. viii. SUSANNAH, b. Har., Oct. 19, 1765; bap. E. Yar., Dec. 1, 1765; m. Yar., Jan. 29, 1789, *Levi Crowell*, son

of Chris. and Deborah (Sears) C.; he b. May 16, 1764; rem. to Barre, Vt.; children, CROWELL: [1.] Zerviah, b. Oct. 23, 1791, and others.

(After his marriage, Willard Sears purchased the house belonging to Joshua Sears, in Harwich, on the opposite side of the road from the old family burying-ground at Bound Brook, which had been previously occupied by several families.)

At his death it remained some time unoccupied, and was said to be bewitched. Every pane of glass in the house was broken by mischievous boys.

It was occupied by Miss Vienna Sears until her death in 1880, since which it has been repaired, and some additions made, and bids fair to stand for many years.

⸎ It was built about 1719, and is worthy of note as the birthplace of "King Sears," the "Liberty Boy.")

Willard Sears was adm. to the Ch. in E. Yar., Dec. 16, 1764; a few months later he was taken sick with a fever, and died after a short illness.

His first wife, Susannah Howes, was a descendant of Elder John Chipman, John Howland, Gov. Thos. Prence, and Elder William Brewster.

The inventory of his estate taken Oct. 18, 1765, was filed Oct. 22. He is styled "Yeoman of Harwich;" the estate was valued at £425 0 10.

Nath¹ Sears of Yar., was app. guardian to Mary, Ebenezer, Reuben, Edmund and Willard; and his widow Margery, guardian to her daughter Susannah. John Sears of Yar., Admʳ.

53.

NATHANIEL SEARS⁴ [*John³, Paul², Richard¹*], b. Yarmouth, Mass., 1720; d. ab't 1802; m. Yar., Mar. 16, 1748-9, *Deborah Howes*, dau. of Thos. and Deborah (Sears) H., she b. Dec. 1, 1727; adm. 2d Ch., Yar., July 3, 1757. Children:

259.   i. DEBORAH, b. Yar., Feb. 16, 1749-50; bap. July 10, 1757; m. Yar., Sep. 17, 1767, *David Collins, Jr.*, of Chatham; he b. Sep. 12, 1747.

260.   ii. ANNA, b. Yar., July 10, 1751; d. June 10, 1753.

261.   iii. ANNA, b. Yar., Oct. 16, 1753; not mentᵈ in father's will, 1802.

262.   iv. JERUSHA, b. Yar., July 28, 1756; bap. July 10, 1757; m. 1773, *Lemuel Howes*, son of Samˡ and Mary (Howes) H.; he b. Mar. 26, 1752; children, HOWES: [1.] Alvin,

b. Jan. 24, 1775. [2.] Kimbal, b. Mar. 2, 1777. [3.] Sears, b. Feb. 5, 1779. [4.] Deby, b. Feb. 15, 1781. [5.] Lot, b. Dec. 25, 1785.

263.* v. NATHANIEL, b. Yar., Feb. 15, 1758.

264. vi. LOT, b. Yar., Nov. 25, 1761; bap. Apr. 25, 1762; served in Capt. Sam¹ King's Co. in Col. Josiah Whitney's Regt., from June 1 to Dec., 1776; and charged for 85 miles travel; is not mentioned in father's will, 1802.

265. vii. ACHSAH, b. Yar., Apr. 25, 1767; bap. May 24; d. May 25, 1768.

266. viii. SARAH, bap. Yar., Jan. 25, 1768, *" in his house ; "* prob. d. soon.

Nathaniel Sears lived in East Yarmouth. Oct. 28, 1765, he was appointed guardian to the minor children of Willard Sears of Harwich (by his first wife), viz.: Mary, Ebenezer, Reuben, Edmund and Willard.

His will, Mar. 31, 1802, names wife Deborah; son Nathaniel, and daus. Jerusha Howes, wife of Samuel Howes; and Deborah Collins, wife of David C.

57.

PAUL SEARS⁴ [*Richard³, Paul², Richard¹*], b. Chatham, Mass., 1710; m. 1730, *Anna Atkins*, dau. of Joseph Atkins; she b. 1713; d. Chat., Oct. 17, 1783, æ. 70. Children:

267. i. HOPE, b. Chat., Feb. 11, 1730-1; m. 1749, by Rev. Stephen Emery to *Nehemiah Doane* of C., who d. of small-pox, Jan. 17, 1766; and she m. 2d, Aug. 22, 1767, *Thomas Howes*, who d.; and 3d, *Job Chase* of Harwich; children, DOANE: [1.] Samuel, b. Jan. 11, 1750-1. [2.] Reuben, b. Nov. 29, 1752. [3.] Paul, b. Jan. 21, 175-. [4.] Sarah, d. Oct. 1, 1821. [5.] Mercy, d. May 11, 1824.

268. ii. MARTHA, b. Chat., Nov. 14, 1732; m. Mar. 22, 1750, *Joseph Eldredge* of Yar.; child, ELDREDGE: [1.] Seth, b. Mar. 9, 1752.

269. iii. HANNAH, b. Chat., Nov. 27, 1734; m. Har., Nov. 17, 1755, *Samuel Wing* of Har.; children, WING: [1.] Ruth, b. June 20, 1759. [2.] Paul, b. Feb. 1, 1760. [3.] Daniel, b. Feb. 1, 1762. [4.] Tabitha, b. Apr. 5, 1765. [5.] William, b. May 25, 1767. All b. Har.

270. . THANKFUL, b. Chat., July 26, 1736; d. Mar. 17, 1747.

271.   v. ANNA, b. Chat., Feb. 27, 1737–8; d. Apr. 4, 1747.
272.   vi. RUTH, b. Chat., Oct. 12, 1740; d. Apr. 11, 1747.
273.   vii. EXPERIENCE, b. Chat., Oct. 20, 1743; pub. Oct. 26, 1765, to *James Eldredge*, who d. 1804, æ. 70.
274.   viii. ELIZABETH, b. Chat., July 11, 1745; d. May 26, 1766.
275.   ix. THANKFUL, b. Chat., Mar. 2, 1747–8.
276.   x. ANNA, b. Chat., July 10, 1753; m. Nov. 10, 1774, *Hezekiah Higgins* of Eastham.

Paul Sears was chosen Surveyor of Highways, 1733; Tything-man and pound-keeper, 1739; Sealer of Weights and Measures, 1739; Selectman, 1742; and Town Clerk, 1752–3.

Rev. E. H. Sears, in his Gen'y of the family, says he removed to Maine. I find nothing to confirm the statement, and his wife died in Chatham, but she may have returned.

61.

DANIEL SEARS[4] [*Daniel[3], Paul[2], Richard[1]*], b. Chatham, Mass., June 1, 1712; d. Jan. 10, 1761, æ. 49, gr.-st., Chat.; m. Harwich, Oct. 31, 1745, *Fear Freeman*, dau. of Benjamin and Temperance (Dimmick) F., of Har.; she b. Mar. 23, 1721–2; (m. 2d, by Rev. Stephen Emery, Nov. 1, 1763, to Samuel Ballard of Boston; his 2d wife); d. Boston, 1808, æ. 86. Children:

277.   i. SARAH, b. Chat., Feb. 13, 1747; m. Boston, Apr. 4, 1765, by Rev. Andrew Elliot, to *William Ballard*, son of above-named Samuel and —— (Pickering) B. of B.; he b. June 13, 1741; d. June 13, 1818, æ. 77; she d. Aug. 4, 1773, æ. 26, gr.-st., Chat.; children, BALLARD: [1.] Betsy, b. 1767; d. 1785, æ. 18. [2.] Sarah, d. young. [3.] William, d. young. [4.] dau., d. inf. (He m. 2d, Ann Marshall of Framingham, elder sister of Mehitable M., wife of Richard Sears of Chatham. By his 2d wife, who d. Mar. 29, 1807, æ. 58, he had nine children, viz.: William, Mehitable, Ebenezer Marshall, Samuel, John, Joseph, Sally Sears, Mary Cotton, and Eliza.)
278.* ii. RICHARD, b. Chat., Jan. 30, 1749.
279.* iii. DAVID, b. Chat., Nov. 29, 1752, (Aug. 12.)
280.   iv. FEAR, b. Chat., 1754; m. *William Colman* of Boston; d. 1797; child, COLMAN: [1.] William, ("trader," Boston, 1815.)
281.   v. DANIEL, b. Chat., 1757; d. unm., Watertown, Mass., Nov., 1814. In 1798, he was a merchant on Sears' wharf,

Purchase street, Boston, residing on Common street, probably with his mother, who lived at what is now the corner of Tremont street and Temple place. At the time of his death he kept bachelor's hall in Watertown, and had apparently given up business. His death is recorded in Boston, but not in Watertown, and his estate was adm. upon in Mid. co., by his brother David; succeeded by David, Jr., and Wm. P. Mason. He left a house and ⅞ acre of land in Dedham, appraised at $1,000, and household goods, etc., $511; was styled "Husbandman" and "Yeoman." Mary and Penelope Aspinwall kept house for him, as appears by court records.

Daniel Sears lived in Chatham, in the house built by his father, and taken down in 1863.

He was Coroner, 1751; Town Treasurer and Clerk from 1733 to 1754; Selectman, 1756, 1757; and was a Lieut. in the Militia.

It appears by the records of the Prob. Court, Barnstable, Feb. 10, 1758, "Upon inquisition of the Selectmen of Chatham, Daniel Sears was adjudged '*Non Compos*,' and Fear Sears, his wife, was app[d] his guardian." Letters of adm. were granted to his widow in 1761, and she was app. guardian to the children, viz.: Richard, David, Sarah and Fear. Inventory foots up R. Est., £689 6 8. Personal, £716 4 3. Mar. 11, 1772, ⅖ was set off to Richard, he to pay David, Daniel, Sarah Ballard and Fear Sears in money; he also had land in Dartmouth, bought by his father of Joseph Ellis, set off to him, he paying his bros. and sisters their part.

The "Sears Genealogy" says, "Fear Sears was the daughter of John Freeman of Sandwich;" but she was the daughter of Benj. F., of Harwich; as is abundantly proved by his will dated Nov. 25, 1757, and proved Apr. 4, 1758; and by the town records.

The "Freeman Genealogy" says "she m. 2d, Samuel Ballard, a wealthy merchant of Boston, who brought up her son David in his counting-house, and dying childless, left him the chief of his large property," and adds, (apparently copying some gravestone, which I have not found,) "Madame Fear Freeman Sears, d. 1808, æ. 86, a *widow Ballard*."

Mr. Freeman is quite wrong in his statement.

Samuel Ballard had by his 1st wife four children, who survived him, and had numerous descendants. He died in Boston about 1793, and his will recorded there, names: wife Fear; sons William, Samuel, Ebenezer, and grand-dau. Betsy Pope. The

Sears children are none of them mentioned. He gives to his wife his house near the Common, with the furniture, and his chaise, while she remains unmarried; also certain claims against persons in Barnstable county, due to her late husband.

In the Directory for 1789, he is called "hay-weigher," Common st. now Tremont st.; he lived in the third house south of Winter st., between Mr. Cole's and Mrs. Swan's houses, about half way to West st., or at the corner of Temple Place, then known as "Turnagain Lane."

Mrs. Sears, on her second marriage, took her children to Boston, but Richard soon returned to the Cape, and was brought up and received his education there.

In a letter from one J. Hawes, printed in the "Sears Genealogy," Daniel Sears is said to have possessed a manuscript history of the family, and other interesting family papers and documents now lost, a statement that needs confirmation.

68.

SILAS SEARS[4] [*Silas[3], Silas[2], Richard[1]*], b. Yarmouth, Mass., Dec., 1695; d. Apr. 10, 1760; m. *Elizabeth Nickerson*, dau. of John N., of Yar. Children:

282. i. JAMES, b. Yar., June 24, 1722; was living in 1755.
283. ii. MARY, b. Yar., Sep. 4, 1724; m. Yar., Jan. 15, 1746, *Seth Crowell*.
284.* iii. SILAS, b. Yar., Feb. 2, 1726–7.
285.* iv. EDWARD, b. Yar., Oct. 21, 1729.
286. v. HANNAH, b. Yar., Jan. 19, 1732–3; m. Jan. 16, 1755, *Wm. Kent* of Eastham.
287.* vi. MOODY, b. Yar., May 6, 1734; called *Mercy* in "Sears Genealogy."
288.* vii. ELEAZAR.
289. viii. RACHEL, not ment[d] in father's will, 1755.
290. ix. ELIZABETH, perh. m. Nov. 12, 1758, *Stephen Sears*, No. 320.
291. x. TABATHY, m. Yar., May 12, 1763, *Moses Godfrey* of Chatham; he b. Jan. 8, 1740–1.

Silas Sears was a member of the West Church in Yarmouth, in 1729. His will, dated July 11, 1755, was filed May 6, 1760; names wife Elizabeth, and children James, Silas, Moody, Eleazar, Mary Crowell, Hannah Kent, Elizabeth Sears, and Tabathy Sears.

Wife Elizabeth and son Edward, Ex[rs]. Eleazar had the homestead.

13

John Nickerson of Yar., in his will, July 2, 1744, names daus. Elizabeth Sears, Mary Sears, and Patience Sears, three sisters married to three brothers.

72.

THOMAS SEARS[4] [*Silas*[3], *Silas*,[2] *Richard*[1]], b. Yarmouth, Mass., Mar. 3, 1702–3; d. May 29, 1785, in 85 yr., (? 83,) gr.-st., Yar.; m. there July 26, 1732, *Patience Nickerson*, dau. of John N., of Yar.; she d. Jan. 22, 1783, in 79 yr., gr.-st. Children:

292.* i. Thomas, b. Yar., Nov. 6, 1733.
293.* ii. Eleazar, b. Yar., May 9, 1739.

The will of Thomas Sears of Yarmouth, dated July 4, 1777, was filed June 30, 1785, and names grand-children, Samuel and Allen Sears and Sarah Hatch. Eleazar Sears, Exec[r], who was living with his father, to have the estate after the death of wife Patience.

73.

JAMES SEARS[4] [*Silas*[3], *Silas*[2], *Richard*[1]], b. Yarmouth, Mass., Mar. 30, 1704; d. Ridgefield, Ct., Mar. 17, 1791, æ. "near 87;" m. Yar., May 28, 1730, *Desire Tobey;* she b. 1707; d. July 28, 1781, "æ. about 74." Children:

294.* i. David, b. Yar., Aug. 25, 1731.
295. ii. Sarah, b. Yar., Nov. 21, 1732; m. *Reuben Crosby*, and settled in Patterson, N. Y., where he was many years church trustee; children, Crosby: [1.] Abial; had, i. Charles; ii. Reuben; iii. Horace. [2.] James. [3.] Tertullus.
296. iii. Thankful, b. Yar., Nov. 26, 1734; m. *James Foster;* lived in South East, N. Y., and d. July 27, 1772, æ. 37, gr.-st., Milltown, N. Y.; he d. Aug. 18, 1819, æ. 81, gr.-st.; child, Foster: [1.] James, d. 1855, "æ. almost 84."
297.* iv. Seth, b. Yar., Oct. 31, 1736.
298.* v. Knowles, b. 1738.
299.* vi. Thomas, b. Apr. 30, 1745.
300. vii. Desire, m. *Timo. Foster* and removed to Western N. Y.
301.* viii. James, b. 1747.

302. ix. REBECCA, b. about 1750; m. *Eli' Crosby* of So. East, N. Y., and d. Mar. 20, 1842, æ. 91, gr.-st.; he d. Nov. 22, 1827, æ. 78, gr.-st., in old Cem'y, one mile north of Milltown, N. Y.

303.* x. COMFORT, b. Mar. 20, 1751.

Oscar Weed, who lives in the old Sears homestead at Mill Plains, Ct., has a deed dated July 10, 1739, from Robt. Hebard, Jr., and Ruth, his wife, of the town and county of Windham, Ct., to James Sears, late of Yarmouth, county Barnstable, Province of Mass. Bay, of a tract of land in Windham, near the Shautucket river, containing 52 acres, the consideration being £275.

How long James Sears remained in Windham, if he lived there at all, is not known, but he probably removed to Mill Plains, then a part of Ridgefield, about 1740–45, although his name does not appear in "listable estates" of Ridgefield for 1746.

There was a James Sears, pathmaster, Kent, N. Y., (which is near by,) Apr. 7, 1747, and in 1756, of the Old Gilead Church in Carmel; but this may have been his nephew James, son of his brother Silas; or perhaps the son of Richard Sears of Old Lyme.

He was one of the organizers of the Congregational Church in Ridgebury, (the northern society of Ridgefield) in 1769.

After the death of his wife, Desire, he lived with his son Comfort, and tradition tells of his orderly habits and rigid religious observances.

When he first settled in Ridgefield wild turkeys and other game abounded.

It is related that one Sabbath morning a flock of wild turkeys alighted in his corn-field.

Taking his gun, he started to shoot them, but remembering that it was the Lord's Day, he returned, remarking, "you did not get me that time, Mr. Devil."

76.

SETH SEARS[4] [*Richard[3], Silas[2], Richard[1]*], b. Plymouth, Mass., Mar. 18, 1699–1700; m. Newport, R. I., Dec. 2, 1733, *Ann Jones*. Perhaps dau. of Richard and Edith Higgins, of Newport, R I.; she b. Sep. 6, 169-, and widow of —— Jonas. Child:

304.* i. GEORGE, b. Newport, 1735.

I have *assumed* that Seth Sears, son of Richard S., of Old
Lyme, Ct., was the Seth who married Ann Jones, in Newport
in 1733, as recorded in register of Trinity Church there; and
that they were the parents of George Sears, whose gravestone
says he was born there in 1735, but this needs confirmation.

The lineage of above-named George Sears as given in the
"Sears Genealogy" is erroneous. Lieut. Silas Sears of Yarmouth, had no son Thomas, as I have shown in the proper place.

The name of Sears does not occur in Newport Probate Records till Dec. 10, 1801, when adm. was granted on the estate
of George Sears; — there is no account of distribution of his
property, nor mention of his children, of whom there were
probably more than one.

The following names may belong to this family, viz.:

MARY SEARS m. *Joseph Rider*, Aug. 28, 1748. [Trin. Ch.
Rec.]

MARTHA SEARS m. *Isaac Chapman*, Dec. 23, 1754. [Cong.
Ch. Rec.]

79.

Capt. JOHN SEARS[4] [*Richard*[3], *Silas*[2], *Richard*[1]], b. Plymouth, Mass., middle Nov., 1707; d. Lyme, Ct.; m. there June
13, 1734, *Elizabeth Watrous*, dau. of Isaac W.   Children:

305.* i. JOHN, b. Lyme, Mar. 4, 1735–6.
306. ii. RICHARD, b. Lyme, July 30, 1738; bap. Aug. 6;
          d. ab't 1776, Horton, Kings co., Nova Scotia; as appears
          by a deed of gift dated Feb. 26, 1776, from his brother
          Seth to Judith Sears.
307. iii. ELIZABETH, b. Lyme, Oct. 9, 1741; bap. Oct. 11.
308. iv. MARY, b. Lyme, Aug. 24, 1744; bap. Sep. 30.
309.   v. SETH, b. Lyme, Oct. 16, 1748; bap. Oct. 30; was in
          Hartford, Ct., Feb. 26, 1776, at which date he deeded to
          Judith Sears, certain land in Lyme, "except that which
          fell to me by my brother, Richard Sears, late of Horton,
          in Nova Scotia, lately deceased."
310. vi. CORNELIUS, b. Lyme, Nov. 11, 1755.

Capt. John Sears was a large land-owner. In 1737, Isaac
Watrous deeded to John Sears and wife Elizabeth a piece of
land, said Elizabeth being his daughter.

In 1760, he bought of Dr. Mather, a tract of 500 acres in
Lyme. Numerous other deeds are on record.

John Sears, mariner, sold Henry J. Corwin of Newport,

R. I., a certain lot which was the estate of John Sears, Senior, and was given to his children in common, on condition that John Sears will obtain a good title, some of the heirs not being of age. Mention is made of bro. Richard, and other bros. and sisters.

In the Col. Rec., we find the memorial of Joseph Wade of Lyme, showing that he "borrowed of Capt. John Sears, late of Lyme, deceased, the sum of £800, old tenor, and to secure the payment, executed to said Sears an absolute deed of the house in which said memorialist lives, with lot adjoining, deceased to reconvey said house and lot on repayment. Deceased died before redemption."

83.

Lieut. ZACHARIAH SEARS[4] [*Joseph*[3], *Silas*[2], *Richard*[1]], b. Yarmouth, Mass., Apr. 22, 1706; d. Yar., Jan. 13, 1796, in 90 yr., gr.-st., No. Den.; m. Yar., Mar. 31, 1743, *Mehitable Crowell*, dau. of John and Keziah (Eldridge) C.; she b. Aug. 14, 1721; adm. 2d Ch., Aug. 5, 1750; d. Feb. 8, 1760, in 39 yr., gr.-st.; 2d, Yar., June 28, 1761, *Mary Oakes*, who d. July 20, 1765, in 58 yr., gr.-st.; 3d, Chatham, Dec. 14, 1768, *Mary Howes*, who d. Oct. 2, 1789, in 75 yr., gr.-st.; she was adm. 2d Ch., Oct. 14, 1770. Children:

By *Mehitable:*

311. i. PETER (Capt.), b. Yar., July 29, 1743; m. there Jan. 12, 1769, *Thankful Howes*, dau. of Thomas and Mary (Hedge) H.; she b. Nov. 1, 1743; who made her will in 1810. He d. July 22, 1802, æ. 58; will dated Apr. 4, 1802. Having no children of their own, they adopted Peter Sears, son of Roland S., of Ashfield, who was Ex[r] and heir to each. "Thankful, wife to Peter Sears, was dismissed from Ch., Dennis, to Ch., Ashfield, Dec. 16, 179—" (between 1795 and 1799). Capt. Peter Sears lived in East Yarmouth, now Dennis, and after he retired from the sea, kept store there, dealing in rum, salt, sulphur, molasses, tea, sugar, etc., "and a little more rum." He also manufactured salt. Mar. 20, 1794, he was on com. to repair the meeting-house, and to provide Mr. Stone's wood and hay. He appears to have removed to Ashfield, Mass, and probably lived with his adopted son Peter until his death.

312.* ii. ROLAND, b. Yar., Feb. 3, 1744–5.

313.   iii. ZACHARIAH, b. Yar., Feb. 13, 1746-7; d. Apr. 7,
       1747.
314.   iv. BETHIA, b. Yar., Aug. 28, 1748; dism. to Ch., Wil-
       liamsburg, June 29, 1777; m. Yar., July 8, 1773, *Reuben
       Howes*, son of Thomas and Deborah H.; he b. Aug. 29,
       1745; dism. to Ch., Williamsburg, June 29, 1777; chil-
       dren, HOWES: [1.] Mehitable, bap. Sep. 11, 1774. [2.]
       Mary, bap. June 23, 1776.
315.   v. MEHITABLE, b. Yar., Sep. 2, 1750; m. Dec. 14, 1780,
       John Sears, No. 229.
316.   vi. ZACHARIAH (Capt.), b. Yar., July 8, 1752; bap. 2d
       Ch., Aug. 9, 1752; m. (pub. Boston, Aug. 19, 1779,)
       Sally Freeman; d. s. p., Boston, Sep. 13, 1783, æ. 30.
       His brother Peter adm. upon his estate; moiety to widow
       Sally, and moiety to father. Under date of Apr. 17, 177–,
       his wife wrote that he had been captured on a transport,
       and taken into New Providence, and expresses great anx-
       iety for him, etc. He was styled Capt. He was brought
       in first cartel from R. I., Jan. 18, 1777, for exchange.
       Signed by John Ayres, Providence. Mass. Arch., IX, 69.
317.   vii. HANNAH, b. Yar., June 25, 1754; bap. July 28; d.
       July 28, 1818; m. Yar., Nov. 16, 1780, *Josiah Crowell*,
       son of Aaron and Priscilla (Smith) C., he b. Oct. 25, 1753;
       children, CROWELL: [1.] Zachariah, b. Mar. 28, 1782.
       [2.] Oliver, b. Apr. 28, 1785. [3.] Hittie, b. June 25, 1787.
       [4.] Priscilla, b. Jan. 3, 1791.
318.* viii. JOSEPH, b. Yar., July 20, 1756; bap. Aug. 29,
       1756.

Zachariah Sears, and wife Mehitable, were adm. to 2d Ch.,
Yar., Aug. 5, 1750.

He was a Lieut. in the Militia, and active in town and
church affairs; was Constable, 1755; and Surveyor of Highways, 1765.

Rev. E. H. Sears says he removed to Windham, Ct., but I
find nothing to confirm the statement, and his descendants are
quite sure he never lived there. He died and was buried in
North Dennis, Mass.

In 1778, he writes from Yarmouth, to his son Roland, at
Ashfield, intimating that he was an old man; that his wife was
living; that he had sons Zachariah and Roland, and several
daughters; that his son, Zachariah, was a sea-faring man, and
on a voyage to the West Indies with " Capt. Tailor of hianus; "
addressed, " Mr. Roland Sears living at Ashfield, Yrs. to the
Lord."

Gen. C. W. Sears of Univ., Miss., and Sol⁰. F. Sears of Ann
Arbor, Mich., have old family letters and papers from 1770.

He made his will Oct. 26, 1786, and mentions his wife, (but
does not give her name), and children, Peter, Roland, Joseph,
Bethia Howes, Mehitable Sears, and Hannah Crowell; gave the
homestead to son Joseph. Peter and Joseph, Exʳˢ.

Oct. 3, 1755, Lᵗ Zachary Sears on com. "to see Mr. Dennis."

Oct. 16, 1760, Mr. Zachary Sears to procure wood for Mr.
Dennis.

Aug. 24, 1761, allotted pew next to men's alley for £170,
old tenor.

Feb. 9, 1763, "Mr. Zachary Sears paid £170 for his pue."

84.

JOSEPH SEARS⁴ [*Joseph³, Silas², Richard¹*], b. Yarmouth, Mass., Mar. 27, 1708; d. Aug. 6, 1779, in 72 yr., gr.-
st., W. Br.; m. Harwich, May 21, 1733, *Ruth Sears*, dau. of
Samuel and Ruth (Merrick) S., No. 103; she b. July 4, 1715;
adm. 2d Ch., Aug. 3, 1735; d. Mar. 27, 1761, in 46 yr., gr.-st.,
he m. 2d, Har., Oct. 28, 1761, *Thankful Snow;* 3d, Har., Dec.
4, 1766, *Bashua (Nickerson) Chase*, née Smalley; (her 1st
husband was a Nickerson, and her 2d, Gowel Chase.) Children:

By *Ruth:*

319. i. ISAAC, b. Har., Oct. 28, 1734; d. Mar. 24, 1759, in 25
yr., gr.-st.
320.* ii. STEPHEN, b. Yar., Sep. 5, 1736.
321. iii. LARNED, b. Yar., Oct. 22, 1738; m. Har., July 20,
1760, *Ann Bangs;* and d. s. p., Oct. 11, 1760, in 22 yr.,
gr.-st.
322. iv. RUTH, b. Yar., Dec. 10, 1740; m. Har., July 17,
1760, *James Wing;* and d. before 1776, leaving issue.
323. v. JOSEPH, b. Yar., May 25, 1746; not mentioned in
father's will, 1776.

Joseph Sears, styled in the records, *3rd* and *junʳ*, lived in that
part of Harwich now West Brewster, though all but his first
child are recorded in Yarmouth.

He was admitted to 2d Ch., E. Yar., June 29, 1742.

His will, dated July 12, 1776, and proved Sep. 9, 1779, mentions children of dau. Ruth Wing; and son Stephen, Exʳ.

Inventory £5,364 14 6. Dower was set off to Bashua Sears,
widow, Sep. 28, 1779.

85.

STEPHEN SEARS[4] [*Joseph*[3], *Silas*[2], *Richard*[1]], b. Yarmouth, Mass., July 22, 1710 ; m. Yar., Apr., 1733, *Abigail Burgess*, who was adm. Ch., E. Yar., Aug. 8, 1736 ; he died soon after marriage ; (she m. 2d, Har., June 30, 1737, Benjamin Sears, No. 33.)   Child :

324. i. SARAH, b. Yar., Mar. 31, 1734 ; m. *Seth Sears*, No. 297

86.

ROLAND SEARS[4] [*Joseph*[3], *Silas*[2], *Richard*[1]], b. Yarmouth, Mass., May 14, 1711 ; d. Greenwich, Mass., Mar., 1784 ; m. (pub. Rochester, Mass., Nov. 11, 1738,) *Mary Freeman*, dau. of John and Mercy (Watson) F., of Roch. ; she b. Har., Oct. 13, 1719 ; d. Greenwich, Apr. 22, 1784, æ. 65.   Children :

325.*   i. FREEMAN, b. Hardwick, July 29, 1740.
326.*   ii. BARNABAS, b. Hard., Nov. 20, 1743.
327.   iii. THANKFUL, b. Hard., July 15, 1745 ; d. Apr. 12, 1766, æ. 21 ; m. July 19, 1764, *John Cobb*, son of Elisha C. ; child, COBB : [1.] Molly, b. Mar. 18, 1765.
328.*   iv. ELISHA, b. Hard., June 6, 1748.
329   v. MERCY, b. Hard., Apr. 11, 1751 ; m. May 11, 1769, *Reuben Snow ;* children, SNOW : [1.] Samuel, b. May 28, 1770.   [2.] Stephen, b. May 16, 1772.   [3.] Barnabas, b. Aug. 22, 1774 ; d. Oct. 31, 1775.   [4.] Barnabas, b. May 11, 1778 ; bap. June 8.
330.   vi. HANNAH, b. Hard., Feb. 20, 1754 ; d. Jan. 8, 1756.
331.   vii. MARY, bap. Hard., June 4, 1758 ; d. Apr. 11, 1770, æ. 13.

"Roland Sears of Upton," was pub. Rochester, Mass., Nov. 11, 1738, to Mary Freeman, and soon after removed to Hardwick, Mass., where he purchased land on Moose brook, near Barre, in 1742.

He was a "bloomer," or iron forger, and his forge was probably on the site of the one long-called "Taylor's Mills."

He was chosen Selectman, 1767–71, after which he removed to Greenwich, Mass.   In Hist. Hardwick, he is confused with his grand-son Roland Sears, No. 831.

His wife was dismissed from Ch. Hardwick to Ch. Greenwich, Sep. 13, 1779.

In 1776, he was rated on 1 poll, 9[s] 7[d].

His residence was on north side of Old County road from Furnace Village to Greenwich.

87.

BARNABAS SEARS[4] [*Joseph*[3], *Silas*[2], *Richard*[1]], b. Yarmouth, Mass., Apr. 5, 1714; d. 1740-1; m. Rochester, Mass., Sep. 25, 1732, by Rev. Tim°. Ruggles, to *Thankful Freeman*, dau. of John and Mercy (Watson) F., of Roch.; she b. Harwich, Oct. 6, 1714; bap. Oct. 10. Children:

332.*   i. STEPHEN.
333.   ii. HANNAH is mentioned in her grand-father, Joseph Sears' will, in 1746, and was, perhaps, brought up in Yar.; she may be the Hannah who m. Jan. 21, 1773, *William Crowell*, son of Chris. and Sarah (Matthews) C.; he b. Mar. 25, 1734; children, CROWELL: [1.] William, b. Dec. 6, 1774. [2.] Molly, b. Mar. 26, 1776. [3.] Paul, b. Mar. 27, 1778; m. May 4, 1797, Sally Sears. [4.] Temperance, b. Feb. 28, 1780.
334   iii. MARY, b. Hardwick, Apr. 27, 1738; bap. Sep. 11, 1743, m. May 1, 1760, Capt. *Jonathan Fletcher* of Rutland dist., now Barre, Mass.

Barnabas Sears was a " bloomer," or iron forger, and probably an associate in business with his bro. Roland.

He removed from Rochester to Hardwick before the birth of his dau. Mary in 1738, and his dau. Hannah was born there. From thence he removed to Brookfield, where he purchased one-eighth part of certain iron-works, Jan. 5, 1740, and died soon, as his inventory was rendered Oct. 28, 1741, £220.

His bro. Roland settled the estate, and appears to have adopted the dau. Mary, who was bap. Hard., Sep. 11, 1743, being styled in the record " *nephew* of Rolon Sears." Stephen was brought up in Yarmouth, as also was probably his sister Hannah.

Rev. E. H. Sears says there was an elder son " Barnabas, who was in the Rev'y war, was wounded and died in consequence."

This is an error; it was a *grand-son*, No. 856, son of Stephen Sears.

90.

SILAS SEARS[4] [*Joseph*[3], *Silas*[2], *Richard*[1]], b. Yarmouth, Mass., Feb. 11, 1719-20; d. Greenwich, Mass., Feb. 29, 1780, "*an old man;*" m. Harwich, June 9, 1743, *Deborah Buck*, dau. of John and Phebe (Sears) B., of Har. Children :

335.   i. PHEBE, m. —— *Partridge.*
336.* ii. RICHARD.
337. iii. HANNAH, b. 1756 ; m. *Elisha Sears*, No. 328.
338. iv. DEBORAH, m. —— *Wheeler.*
339.* v. BARNABAS, b. Hardwick, Mar. 21, 1765.

Rev. E. H. Sears says Silas Sears removed to Rochester, Mass., but his name is not found in town or church records there, (prob. means No. 501.)

He was in Hardwick in 1765, and with his wife was admitted to church there, May 6, 1770 ; he died in the adjoining town of Greenwich in 1780 ; was in Capt. Joseph Hooker's Co., Col. Ruggles Woodbury's Reg^t, Aug. 19 to Nov. 30, 1777, 175 miles travel, wages £3 8 7 ; called "of Greenwich."

His will, dated Feb. 22, 1780, was filed June 6 following by wife Deborah, Exec^x, and mentions children in above order, which is not, perhaps, that of their births.

92.

EDWARD SEARS^4 [*Josiah^3, Silas^2, Richard^1*], b. Yarmouth, Mass., June 23, 1704 ; m. *Desire* ——. Children :

340.* i. EDWARD.
341. ii. SARAH, b. Halifax, Mar. 24, 1735 ; d. Oct. 19, 1825, æ. 90 ; m. there, Jan. 17, 1754, *Sylvanus Bryant* of Plympton, son of Dea. Saml and Tabitha (Ford) B. ; he b. Mar. 20, 1729–30 ; 2d, Capt. *James Harlow* of Plymp. ; his 2d wife ; he b. Pl., Apr. 20, 1730 ; d. Sept. 23, 1802,
342. iii. MERCY, b. Hal., Sep. 14, 1736 ; m. Dec. 25, 1752. *Ephraim Tillson;* children, TILLSON : [1.] Polly, b. Oct. 28, 1772 ; d. Apr. 12, 1850 ; m. Mar. 5, 1794, Wm. Hooper of Bridgewater ; he b. Oct. 12, 1793 ; d. Mar. 27, 1825.
343. iv. BETSY, b, Hal., June 17, 1739 ; m. Feb. 24, 1766, *Benj. Carter* of Hal.
344.* v. JOSIAH, b. Hal., Nov. 17, 1740.
345. vi. DESIRE, b. Hal., Mar. 15, 1742–3 ; bap. Mar. 20 ; m. Apr. 29, 1762, *Benj. Washburn, 3d*, of Bridgewater.

Edward Sears removed to Halifax, Mass., and in 1747 was chosen to represent the Church in Council.

93.

SAMUEL SEARS^4 [*Josiah^3, Silas^2, Richard^1*], b. Yarmouth, Mass., July 6, 1706; d. Oct. 24, 1764, in 59 yr., gr.-st,. No. Dennis; m. Yar., Aug. 13, 1730, *Hannah Howes*, dau. of Nathaniel and Esther (Rider) H., of Yar.   Children :

346.* i. NATHANIEL, b. Yar., Feb. 21, 1731–2; bap. E. Yar., Feb. 27.

347. ii. HANNAH, b. Yar., Sep. 14, 1735; d. Nov. 16, 1780; prob. m. Jan. 7, 1768, *Barnabas Howes ;* his 2d wife; children, HOWES: [1.] Lois, bap. Jan. 12, 1772. [2.] Hannah, bap. May 8, 1774; (he had a large family by his 1st wife Lois, who were bap. Oct. 19, 1766, viz. : Kimbal, Sparrow, Barnabas, Enos, Phebe and Betsy.)

348. iii. SAMUEL, b. Yar., Apr. 28, 1738; was living in 1764.

Samuel Sears was admitted to 2d Ch., Yar., Mar. 31, 1745.

He made his will Sep. 1, 1764, and calls himself "first of Yar.;" mentions wife Hannah, sons Nathaniel and Samuel, and dau. Hannah.

His son Nathaniel and Seth Tobey were Exec[rs].   Inventory £352 13 0.

Samuel Howes of Yar., in his will, dated 1722, names "Samuel Sears, son of Josiah Sears," then living with him ; and Nathaniel Howes of Yar., in his will, June 10, 1745, gave "to grand-son, Nathaniel Sears, a new Bible," and "to beloved dau., Hannah Sears, £15, old. tenor."

94.

JOSIAH SEARS[4] [*Josiah[3], Silas[2], Richard[1]*], b. Yarmouth, Mass., Aug. 25, 1708; d. Eastham, Mass., Jan., 1772; m. E., Sep. 30, 1736, *Azubah Knowles*, dau. of Samuel K., of E. ; she d. Mar., 1762; he m. 2d, May 26, 1763, *Mercy Hopkins*, who survived him.   Children :

By *Azubah :*

349. i. MERCY, b. East., Aug. 23, 1737 ; m. —— *Harding.*

350. ii. MARTHA, b. East. ; m. —— *Harding.*

351. iii. JERUSHA, b. East., Feb. 25, 1742 ; d. before 1772.

352. iv. JOSIAH, b. East., Feb. 1, 1744 ; d. young.

353. v. AZUBAH, b. East., Nov. 5, 1747 ; m. Oct. 29, 1765, *Anson Kenrick* of Orleans, Mass. ; he b. about 1743 ; removed to Barrington, N. S.

354. vi. BETHIA, b. East., July 15, 1750 ; m. Dec. 26, 1776, by Rev. Mr. Bascom, to *Theophilus Baker ;* children, BAKER: [1.] Sally, bap. E. Yar., Apr. 19, 1778. [2.] Ab-

ner, bap. Apr. 5, 1779. [3.] Josiah, bap. May 28, 1780.
355.* vii. DAVID, b. East., Apr. 14, 1753.
356. viii. SAMUEL, b. East., Apr. 18, 1755; d. So. East, N. Y.,
1778; was in Capt. Solo. Higgins' Co., July 13 to Dec.
31, 1775.
357. ix. JOSIAH, b. East., a minor in 1772; m. Apr. 6, 1797,
Anna Crowell of Chatham, and was the first to settle in
Barrington, N. S.

Josiah Sears was a cordwainer. His will, dated Jan. 2, 1772,
names wife Mercy, and children Mercy Harding, Azubah
Knowles, Bethia Sears, Martha Harding, David, Samuel; and
Josiah, *not of age*. Gideon Freeman was Ex[r], and proved
will Feb. 11, 1772.

95.

Lt. DAVID SEARS[4] [*Josiah³, Silas², Richard¹*], b. Yarmouth, Mass., Oct. 2, 1710; d. Middleboro, Mass., Aug. 20,
1788, æ. 78; m. Phebe ——, who d. Midd., Oct. 9, 1779, æ.
67; 2d, Midd., Dec. 20, 1781, by Joseph Barker to Hannah
Weston of Midd.; she b. Apr. 21, 1723; d. Apr. 14, 1802, " æ.
79, lacking 7 days." Children:
By *Phebe*:
358.* i. ZEBEDEE, b. Midd., June 16, 1734.
359. ii. HULDAH, b. Midd., Aug. 10, 1737.
360.* iii. ABNER, b. Midd., Feb. 19, 1738-9.
361. iv. DAVID, b. Midd., June 25, 1741; pub. Bridgewater,
July 30, 1765, to *Eliz'h Snow* of B.

Second Lt. David Sears was at Oneida Station, N. Y., Sep.
23, 1758; and his son Zebedee a private.

96.

JONATHAN SEARS[4] [*Josiah³, Silas²· Richard¹*], b.
Bridgewater, Mass., 1714; m. Halifax, Mass., Apr. 18, 1738,
Hannah Briggs of H. Children:
362.   i. DEBORAH, b. Hal., May 16, 1739.
363.   ii. JONATHAN, b. Hal., Dec. 25, 1740.
364.   iii. DORATHA, b. Hal., Oct. 2, 1743; d. Sep. 8, 1747.
365.   iv. HANNAH, b. Hal., Jan. 29, 1745-6; bap. Feb. 2; d.
Sep. 7, 1747.
366.   v. DORATHY, b. Hal., June 8, 1748; bap. June 12.

367. vi.   ISAAC, b. Hal., July 15, 1750; bap. July 29; was in
    Capt. Fred. Pope's Co., Col. Paul D. Sargent's Reg$_t$, 177–.
368.   vii. HANNAH, b. Hal., June 6, 1752; bap. June 7.
369.* viii. PETER, b. Hal., Nov. 29, 1753; bap. Dec. 2.
370.   ix. JOHN, b. Hal., Mar. 22, 1756; was in Capt. John
    Bradford's Co., Col. Theoph. Cotton's Reg^t.
371.   x. SARAH, b. Hal., June 16, 1757.

Jonathan Sears removed to Halifax, Mass., and was in full
communion with the church there in 1737, and his wife in 1741.

I find nothing further of the family in town or church records, and they may have removed.

FIFTH GENERATION.

107.

SAMUEL SEARS[5] [*Samuel*[4], *Samuel*[3], *Paul*[2], *Richard*[1]], b. Harwich, Mass., Dec. 5, 1721; d. Aug. 13, 1774, in 53 yr., gr.-st., W. Br.; m. Yar., Mar. 7, 1747–8, *Desire Howes*, dau. of Thomas and Deborah (Sears) H.; she b. Jan. 8, 1726–7; d. Jan. 6, 1804, in 78 yr., gr.-st.   Children :

372. i. THOMAS, b. Har., Jan. 5, 1748–9; bap. July 4, 1756; was a mariner, and at sea in 1774.

373. ii. SAMUEL, b. Har., Dec. 31, 1751; d. Nov. 5, 1754.

374. iii. ABIGAIL, b. Har., Nov. 15, 1753; d. Feb. 17, 1756.

375. iv. ELIZABETH, b. Har., Sep. 12, 1755; d. young.

376. v. ABIGAIL, b. Har., May 2, 1757; bap. June 5; d. Dec. 13, 1828, æ. 72, gr.-st., W. Br.; m. Har., May 15, 1777, *Freeman Remick*, who d. Nov. 30, 1826, æ. 71; children, REMICK: [1.] Freeman, d. Guadaloupe, Mar. 10, 1804, in 18 yr. [2.] Thomas, lost at sea, 1810. [3.] Abraham, lost at sea, 1810.

377. vi.   , b. Har., Aug. 20, 1759; bap. Aug. 23; d. July 8, 1MARY

378. vii. HANNAH, b. Har., Apr. 4, 1761; bap. May 10; d. Jan. 15, 1835, æ. 74, gr.-st.

379. viii. SAMUEL, b. Har., Sep. 2, 1763; bap. Oct. 2; d. July 31, 1783, in 20 yr., gr.-st.

380. ix. ELIZABETH, b. Har., Apr. 3, 1765; bap. May 26; d. unm. Oct. 23, 1798, in 34 yr., gr.-st.

381. x. MARY, b. Har., Apr. 3, 1765; *gem.;* bap. May 26; d. unm. Apr. 11, 1794, in 30 yr., gr.-st.

382. xi. DESIRE.

Samuel Sears and wife were admitted to full communion in Ch., Har., June 13, 1756.

He made his will Apr. 25, 1774, and mentions " wife Desire," "son Thomas gone to sea," Samuel, Abigail, Hannah, Elizabeth, Mary, and Desire. Inventory £359 15 11, of which £224 11 1 was Real Estate.

113.

JONATHAN SEARS[5] [*Jonathan[4], Samuel[3], Paul[2] Richard[1]*], b. Harwich, Mass., Sep. 9, 1725; d. Dec. 16, 1752, in 28 yr., gr.-st., W. Br.; m. Har., June 29, 1749, *Priscilla Sears*, No. 153, dau. of Seth and Priscilla (Ryder) S.; she b. Har., Dec. 31, 1730; adm. 2d Ch., Yar., May 19, 1751; (she m. 2d, Yar., Apr. 11, 1754, Dea. John Sears, No. 47,) and died of old age, Apr. 12, 1819, æ. 89, gr.-st. Children:

383.* i. JONATHAN, b. Har., May 7, 1750.
384. ii. ELIZABETH, b. Har., Jan. 4, 1752; bap. E. Yar., Apr. 5; m. Yar., Apr. 13, 1773, *Samuel Hall*, son of Danl H.; he b. Mar. 7, 1752; rem. to Ashfield; she dism. to Ash., Oct. 25, 1795; is mentioned in mother's will, Jan. 7, 1815; children, HALL : [1.] Jonathan, b. Mar. 29, 1774; bap. June 26. [2.] Lot, bap. Nov. 10, 1776. [3.] Elizabeth. [4.] Samuel, bap. Sep. 6, 1778. [5.] Atherton. [6.] Mehitable.

Jonathan Sears of Harwich, mariner, made his will Mar. 28, 1752, "being then very sick;" wife Priscilla and bro. Joseph, Ex[rs]; mentions his children, but not by name.

The inventory was filed Feb. 6, 1753, and amounts to £128 12 0.

Nov. 23, 1757, John Sears was appointed guardian of Jon[a] and Eliz[h]. For mention of his wife's will, see No. 47.

119.

PRINCE SEARS[5] [*Jonathan[4], Samuel[3], Paul[2], Richard[1]*], b. Harwich, Mass., 1735; d. Feb. 25, 1829, æ. 94, gr.-st., W. Br.; m. (pub. June 17, 1758,) *Betsy Hall*, dau. of Joseph and Rebecca H., of Yar.; she b. May 16, 1738; d. July 1, 1818, æ. 81, gr.-st. Children:

385. i. SARAH, b. Har., Dec., 1759; bap. Aug. 2, 1760; m. May 28, 1778, *Joshua Sears*, No. 220; and d. Jan. 15, 1792, æ. 32, gr.-st.
386.* ii. JOSEPH, b. Har., Apr. 21, 1764; bap. June 17.

Eliz[h], wife of Prince Sears, was admitted to full communion in Ch., Har., July 12, 1760. Mar. 21, 1786, Prince Sears, Pound-keeper.

His will, dated Brewster, 1829, names wife Betsy, son Joseph, and grand-children, Ezra Sears and Rebecca Gray.

Joseph was appointed Exec[r].

122.

JOSHUA SEARS[5] [*Joshua[4], Samuel[3], Paul[2], Richard[1]*], b. Harwich, Mass., May 15, 1724 ; m. —— *Marvin*. Children :

387.   i. ENOCH, (Sergeant N. Y. Mil.)
388. ii. ISAAC M.
389. iii. HANNAH.
390.* iv. JOSHUA, b. Jan. 8, 1757 ; (Ensign N. Y. Mil.)

The names of the first three children are given upon the authority of H. G. Somerby's manuscript collections, *re.* Sears. The fourth is ascribed by family tradition to a bro. of Col. Isaac Sears, and was probably a son of Joshua, and I have so placed him subject to correction.

Joshua Sears removed to North Salem, N. Y., and some data of his family may be found in the records or churchyards of that place. I find nothing in the County Surrogate's office relative to his estate.

John Marvin, son of Matthew M., of Norwalk, Ct., m. Apr. 27, 1721, Rachel St. John ; had daus. Hannah, b. Dec. 4, 1722 ; Rachel, b. Mar. 27, 1728-9 ; Ann, b. Sep. 7, 1741 ; one of these may have m. Joshua Sears.

123.

NATHANIEL SEARS[5] [*Joshua[4], Samuel[3], Paul[2], Richard[1]*], bap. Harwich, Mass., Apr. 20, 1725-6 ; d. Norwalk, Ct., Dec. 19, 1752, in 27 yr., gr.-st. ; m. Nor., *Ruth Raymond*, (who m. 2d, Ebenezer Church, his 2d wife.) Children :

391. i. NATHANIEL, a minor in 1765 ; d. about 1785, in West Indies. His estate was adm. upon Dec. 20, 1785 ; Ruth Church, Eben[r] Church, Sarah Perry, Thatcher Sears, Josiah Church, John Church, Isaac Church, Esther Church, Betsy Church and Ruth Betts were interested therein. It appears by a deed that he was living in the W. I. in 1774.
392.* ii. THATCHER, b. 1752.

Nathaniel Sears removed to Norwalk, Ct., with his parents; married and died there.

He was buried in Pine Island Cemetery, near his father's grave, a nameless mound between them, being probably that of his mother.

Jan. 23, 1753, Ruth Sears and Josiah Sears were appointed Adm[rs]; and Ruth Sears, guardian to Nathaniel and Thatcher Sears, minors.

The inventory, dated Jan. 8, 1753, was approved Apr. 3, 1753, above £2,000. Apr. 1, 1765, Nathaniel Sears made choice of Ebenezer Church as guardian.

The estates of Thatcher Sears, confiscated during the Rev[n], passed into the Church family.

(Ebenezer Church's first wife was Susannah Fitch, to whom he m. Jan., 1746; she d. Oct. 7, 1747, leaving 2 chil., viz.: Daniel and Richard. By his marriage with widow Ruth Sears, he had, Sarah, b. Oct. 15, 1756; m. —— Perry; Ebenezer, b. July 31, 1758; Ruth, b. Jan. 29, 1760; m. —— Betts; Esther, b. Mar. 23, 1762; Samuel, b. Nov. 25, 1763; Grace, b. Aug. 7, 1765; Josiah, b. Jan. 10, 1767; John, b. Jan. 12, 1769; Elizabeth, b. Oct. 10, 1770, and Isaac, b. May 3, 1772.)

125.

Col. ISAAC SEARS[5] [*Joshua*[4], *Samuel*[3], *Paul*[2], *Richard*[1]], b. Harwich, Mass., 1729; d. Canton, China, Oct. 28, 1786, in his 57 year; m. Trinity Ch., N. Y., *Sarah Drake*, dau. of Jasper D., of N. Y., (who kept the Tavern on Beekman street, which was the rendezvous of the "Liberty Boys.") Children:

393.   i. SON, b. 1759; drowned at Beekman Slip, Sunday, July 20, 1766, æ. 7 yrs.

394.   ii. ISAAC, b. 1770; was at Phillips Academy, Andover, Mass., "from Boston in 1779, æ. 9;" d. Washington, D. C., Feb., 1795.

395. iii. JASPER, b. 1772; was at Phillips Acad., with his bro. Isaac, in 1779, æ. 7; but neither continued but one term.

396.   iv. HESTER, m. (Lic., N. Y., Feb. 14, 1774,) *Paschal Nelson Smith*, son of William Henry and Margaret (Lloyd) S., of St. George's Manor, L. I., who was a partner in business with his father-in-law, and later one of the first directors in the Manhattan Bank, organized in 1799 by Aaron Burr. He died of yellow fever at his summer residence at Bloomingdale, N. Y., in 1805-6; children,

15

SMITH: [1.] Harriet, d. about 1801, unm. [2.] Augusta, d. about 1801, unm. [3.] William. [4.] Georgianna, m. —— Bryan, a lawyer of N. Y. city; and had, i. Isaac Sears; ii. Frederic H. — perh. others. Both sons were of their father's profession, and in his office *circa* 1856, but neither name is now found in the Directory. They lived at Fort Hamilton.

[Paschal N. Smith was of the "*Tangier Smiths*" of Setauket, L. I., so called to distinguish them from the "*Bull Smiths*," who lived in the next township, now known as Smithtown. Col. Wm. Smith, his great-gr.-father was born at Newton, near Higham Ferrers, North-amptonshire, Eng., Feb. 22, 1654–5; and died at the Manor of St. George, Setauket, L. I., Feb. 18, 1704–5. In the reign of Charles II, Col. Smith was the English Governor of Tangier, Africa, and m. there, Nov. 6, 1675, Martha Tunstall of Putney, co. Surrey, who d. Sep. 1, 1709. He was app. Chief Justice and Pres^t of the Council of the Province of New York, by Gov. Fletcher, and his lands erected into the "Manor of St. George." Col. Henry Smith, his 3d son, b. Tangier, m. Charlestown, Mass., Jan. 9, 1704, Anna Shepard, of C.; 2d, Fairfield, Ct., Oct. 7, 1737, Mrs. Francis Carver; 3d, Brookhaven, L. I., Nov. 6, 1742, Margaret Biggs; and d. May 3, 1747. Wm. Henry Smith, his 3d son, b. Oct. 29, 1708, m. Margaret Lloyd at Queen's village, and d. Brookhaven, 1776. Their children were, i. Henry, m. Widow Eliz^h Draver, who d. 1797; he was in business in Boston with his Uncle Henry Lloyd, under the British Gov^t, rem. to Halifax at the evacuation, but returned at the peace, was a commission merchant, and lived next his bro. Oliver on Pearl st.; he d. Apr. 11, 1801, greatly honored. ii. Paschal Nelson, see *ante*. iii. William, known as "*Dollar Smith*," d. Halifax, N. S., 1778, was Treasurer of the Province. iv. Gilbert, d. in West Indies. v. Oliver, an apothecary, came to Boston under the patronage of his uncle, Dr. Jas. Lloyd. He was a religious man and a philanthropist, one of the founders of the Boston Medical Dispensary, and an active agent in ornamenting the Common, commencing with Tremont Street Mall, for which the town gave him a *unique* china service, portions of which are still preserved in the family. He d. s. p. Feb. 6, 1797. vi. Rebecca, m. Capt. Wm. Aspinwall of Flushing, L. I. vii. Anna, m. Judge Selah Strong of New York, and lived at the

Manor house on L. I.; — in 1852, Geo. Strong, a lawyer of New York, was their only descendant. viii. Catherine, m. John Grinnell of N. Y., and left two children. ix. Margaret, d. inf. x. Shepard, d. young. xi. Child, d. inf.]

397. v. MARY, m. Trinity Ch., N. Y., by license, June 15, 1778, *Thos. Hamilton.*

398. vi. JOHN, m. Trinity Ch., N. Y., by license, Oct. 24, 1780, *Sarah Halstead.*

399. vii. MARIA, m. Trinity Ch., N. Y., by license, June 21, 1785, *Peregrine Bourdieu;* (son of James B., a respectable merchant of London, of a Huguenot family;) who came to this country with intention of establishing a mercantile house here, bringing letters of introduction from Henry Laurens, London, to James Lovell, Boston. In 1792, he was in business at Dominica, W. I.

(One Bourdieu was bearer of dispatches from Silas Deane, Paris, to Benjamin Franklin, London.)

400. viii.
401. ix.
402. x.
403. xi.

It is singular that so little is now known of the family of a man so prominent during a long period as was Col. Isaac Sears.

He had eleven children; his son-in-law, Paschal N. Smith, was also one of a family of eleven; and Hester Sears, his wife, it is said was the last survivor of the twenty-two.

The first seven children are, I think, correctly given, though the order, perhaps, should be changed.

Many of the records of New York and Trinity Church were destroyed by fire, and I find no will or administration recorded in the Surrogate's office.

Papers of the day speak of the daughters of " King Sears " as " beautiful and accomplished, and dispensing the hospitalities of their father's house like princesses."

John Q. Adams writes to his sister, Mrs. Wm. S. Smith, in 1785, giving an account of a dinner with Gen. Knox, Sec. of War, and mentions as among the guests, " Miss Sears," and says: " Miss Sears has been ill, and looks pale; but she is very pretty, and has the reputation of being witty and sharp. I am sure she does not look *mechante.*"

Among the distinguished names in Mrs. John Jay's invitation lists, we find " Mr. Sears and family."

In reply to an inquiry of mine, Mr. Stevens, then editor of the " Magazine of American History," printed the following account, derived from papers in the archives of the Chamber of Commerce, N. Y.:

" Isaac Sears was one of the most prominent figures in the stirring scenes enacted in America during the latter half of the last century.

" His profession as the captain of a peaceful trader being broken up by the French war, he entered at once into privateering.

" In 1757, he took out the dogger ' Decoy,' of 6 guns, and later the sloop of war ' Catherine ;' but his most daring exploits were while in charge of the sloop ' Belle Isle,' of 14 guns, owned by John Schermerhorn & Co., New York merchants, which put to sea in 1759.

" In September he fell in with a large French sloop of 24 guns and 80 men, and attacked her without hesitation.

" He was twice disabled, and forced to withdraw to refit, the third time he grappled the Frenchman, and a long contest took place, but the grapplings giving way, the Frenchman sheered off, with 9 men killed and 20 wounded. A gale springing up, separated the vessels.

" In 1761, he was shipwrecked on Sable Island, and with difficulty saved the lives of himself and crew.

" The prestige of these exploits gave him a great moral ascendancy over his fellow-citizens, and he seems to have fairly won the title of ' King,' which was given to him.

" In the resistance to the Stamp Act, and the daily struggles which took place about the Liberty Pole, Sears was always in the front ranks, and exposed himself without hesitation.

" A complete sketch of his life would make a history of this stormy period, for there is hardly an event connected with it, in which he does not appear.

" Fresneau, in his political squib against Gaines, the trimming editor of the ' New York Mercury,' gives an amusing account of him :

> ' At this time there arose, a certain ' KING SEARS,'
> Who made it his duty, to banish our fears,
> He was, without doubt, a person of merit,
> Great knowledge, some wit, and abundance of spirit,
> Could talk like a lawyer, and that without fee,
> And threaten'd perdition, to all that drank Tea.'

" He was one of the Com. of Correspondence of Fifty-one in 1774, and clung steadfastly to his old friend McDougal, in the division of that body. He was also one of the Com. of One

Hundred, chosen by the citizens in 1775, and with four others, was appointed to superintend the fortifying of West Point.

" Was member of the New York Provincial Congress, and of the Assembly in 1783, and in 1776, was appointed by Gen. Charles Lee, Dep. Adj.-Gen., with rank of Lieut.-Col.

" He was known from one end of America to the other as a daring ' Son of Liberty.'

" When John Hancock passed through New York in May, 1775, he lodged with Mr. Sears at his residence, No. 1 Broadway, afterward Sir Henry Clinton's Head-quarters.

" In a letter to Dorothy Quincy, dated New York, May 17, 1775, he writes ' sat down to supper of fried oysters, and at 11 o'clock went to Capt. Sears (the *King* here), and lodged.'

" In the autumn of that year, Sears entered the city at noonday, with a company of Ct. Light Horse, and destroyed the Tory press of Rivington, which had made itself obnoxious to the Whigs.

" Before the war he was engaged in a small European and West India importing business, which does not appear to have been very successful, as he accepted the office of Inspector of Pot and Pearl Ashes, which he held until 1772, when he was removed upon the false charge of neglecting duty, which was made to punish him for his prominence in the public censure of the Assembly, although warmly espoused by George Clinton, Philip Schuyler and Nath. Woodhull.

" During the war he was engaged in some business in Boston, and made a partnership with his son-in-law, Paschal N. Smith, who appears at an earlier time as captain of an eastern trader. (In New York Directory for 1786, we find ' Sears & Smith, Merchants, 62 Water street.')

" This business was not successful, the firm failing in 1784-5, and Mr. Sears resumed his voyages. Feb. 4, 1786, he sailed with one of his sons for Batavia and Canton, in ship ' Hope,' Capt. James Magee (who had commanded the privateer ' Gen. Arnold,' belonging to Col. Isaac Sears and others, which was wrecked in Plymouth bay, Christmas, 1778, when most of the crew were frozen to death), in company with Mr. Samuel Shaw, First American Consul at Canton, and Capt. Thomas Randall, Vice-Consul, Canton, was taken with a fever at Batavia, from which he was recovering, when a flux set in, from which he died Oct. 28, 1786, and was buried on French Island, Canton harbor; a monument with a suitable inscription was erected over his grave. His son returned to the United States, and was living at St. Eustatius, W. I., in 1792.

" His son Isaac died at Washington, D. C., Feb., 1795.

" Capt. Sears was a member of the Corporation of Trinity Church, N. Y., and was chosen vestryman, Apr. 17, 1784, serving until Apr. 6, 1786, when he resigned and sailed for China."

Isaac Sears was at Cambridge with Washington, and at the evacuation of Boston took up his residence on Tremont street, opposite the north end of the chapel burying-ground, in the mansion of Gov. Phillips.

He purchased the Com. Loring house, now known as the " Greenough Place," at Jamaica Plain, near Boston, upon its confiscation by the State, and Drake says lived there for a time.

During his residence in Boston he engaged in fitting out privateers.

Isaac Sears was " a thorn in the flesh " of the Tories of New York and their sympathizers, and no man of the period was more vilified.

Various historians of New York have followed the example, and no epithet was too strong to apply to him by some of them.

He was no doubt a rough and uncultured seaman by education, but of sterling character and honesty.

His manners acquired on the quarter-deck, and prompt methods of action, did not at all suit the timid and wavering, any more than they did the pronounced Tories or Loyalists.

Maj. Samuel Shaw, our first American Consul to China, in his diary, which has been published, speaks in terms of praise of Col. Sears, his fellow passenger on the outward voyage. " To give his character in few words, he was an honest man, an agreeable acquaintance and a warm friend," and there is nothing like a long sea-voyage to bring out the idiosyncrasies of a man.

Many of his letters are preserved in the archives of New York and Connecticut, and they give a very good insight into his character and principles.

130.

Lt. JUDAH SEARS[5] [*Judah*[4], *Samuel*[3], *Paul*[2], *Richard*[1]], b. Harwich, Mass., Nov. 19, 1734; d. Rochester, Mass., 1782; m. Yarmouth, Sept. 21, 1760, *Molly Crowell*, dau. of John and Kezia (Eldredge) C., she b. Dec. 13, 1739. Children:

404. i. TEMPERANCE, b. Roch., Apr. 2, 1763; bap. Sep. 3, 1770; possibly lived in the family of Benj. Sears, Jr., of South East, N. Y.; m. —— Paddock.

405.   ii. OBED, b. Roch., Aug. 10, (30,) 1764; bap. Sep. 3, .1770.
406.   iii. HANNAH, b. Roch., Dec. 25, 1765; bap. Sep. 3, 1770.
407.   iv. NATHAN, b. Roch., June 28, 1767; bap. Sep. 3, 1770.
408.   v. WILLIAM, b. Roch., Nov. 13, 1768; bap. Sep. 3, 1770.
409.   vi. JUDAH, b. Roch., 1772; bap. Apr. 26, 1772.
410.   vii. MARY, bap. Roch., Oct. 10, 1773.
411.   viii. REBECCA, bap. Roch., Sep. 24, 1775.

Judah Sears removed to Rochester, Mass., with his parents, previous to 1764. Was a Minute Man in Capt. Seth Briggs' Co., and on alarm at Lexington marched eighty miles, —— four days service, expense and wages, 12^s and 4^s 3^d was Com. 2d Lt. in Col. Cary's Reg., Cap. Stephen Wing's Co., 177—.

On the occasion of the Convention at Barnstable in Sep., 1774, Judah Sears, Jr., was on Com. "to hear and determine all offenses against morality, decency and good manners, that shall be complained of during the time of our present enterprise," etc.

His estate was settled in 1782, and found insolvent; his wife Mary is mentioned, but no children; and the family perhaps removed, as they are not again found in town or church records.

132.

Capt. ALDEN SEARS[5] [*Judah[4], Samuel[3], Paul[2], Richard[1]*] b. Harwich, Mass., Feb. 24, 1738-9; d. Bristol, N. Y., Mar. 25, 1803, æ. 64; m. *Hannah Bassett*, who d. s. p., Liverpool, N. S.; 2d, Dighton, Mass., Dec. 29, 1769, *Phebe Walker*, dau. of Col. Elnathan W.; she b. 1748; d. Bristol, N. Y., Oct. 23, 1830, æ. 92. Children:

By *Phebe*:
412.* i. ALDEN, b. 1770.
413.   ii. PHEBE, b. 1771; m. Maj. *Sylvanus Jones;* and d. Oct. 22, 1841, æ. 71; children, JONES: [1.] Sylvanus. [2.] Jason. [3.] Eleanor. [4.] Asael. [5.] Phebe. [6.] Roxanna. [7.] Sabra. [8.] Martha. [9.] Mary.
414.   iii. HANNAH, b. 1773; m. *Stephen Sisson;* and d. Mar., 1849, æ. 76; children, SISSON: [1.] Phebe, b. Oct., 1794. [2.] Rebecca, b. Sep. 7, 1796. [3.] Stephen, b. Mar. 19, 1798. [4.] Horace, b. Jan. 1, 1800; d. Feb., 1867.

[5.] Judah, b. Dec., 1802; d. Aug., 1870. [6.] Charles, b. Mar., 1804. [7.] Hannah, b. Mar. 9, 1806.

415.   iv. ABIGAIL, m. *John Kent;* and d. Mar., 1813 ; children, KENT: [1.] John, b. Dec. 30, 1799. [2.] Walker, b. May 27, 1801. [3.] Phineas, b. Oct. 4, 1804. [4.] Charity, b. Feb. 10, 1806. [5.] Alford, b. Jan. 12, 1811. [6.] Calvin, b. Mar. 28, 1813.

416.*   v. EDWARD, b. Apr. 25, 1778.

417.   vi. ELEANOR, m. *Richmond Simmons* from Dighton, 1790 ; and d. 1866; children, SIMMONS: [1.] Maria, b. May 10, 1802; d. Oct. 4, 1874. [2.] Sardis, b. July 22, 1804; d. Mar. 13, 1879. [3.] Richmond, b. June 11, 1806 ; d. Feb. 11, 1862. [4.] Elnathan W., b. June 2, 1811 ; is a physician in Canandaigua, N. Y. [5.] Eleanor, b. June 1812; d. July. [6.] George W., b. Feb. 27, 1813 ; d. 1877. [7.] Abigail, b. Feb. 4, 1815 ; m. Richmond Simmons of Victor, N. Y., her cousin. [8.] Aroc L., b. Feb. 8, 1816; d. May 31, 1857. [9.] Mary J., b. Feb. 16, 1818.

418.* vii. JOHN.

Alden Sears, " yeoman," of Rochester, resided for a time in Nova Scotia, and was one of the grantees of the town of Liverpool in 1761.

His wife dying, he returned to the States, living for a time in Pawtucket and Providence, engaged in boat-building and distilling.

He had been previously a seaman, and is said to have commanded a whaling vessel before he was of age.

Marrying again, he settled in Dighton, Mass., on the old Walker homestead, which, on the death of her father, fell to his wife. The old house is still standing, near 200 years old, and is a good specimen of early colonial times.

About the commencement of the Revolutionary War he resumed his voyages, and in returning from the West Indies with a cargo of molasses was captured by the British, lost his vessel and cargo, and was held prisoner several years.

An English officer, with whom he made friends, finally procured his release and supplied him with funds for his return.

His wife is said to have had full faith during all the years of his absence that he would return, although others had given him up as dead.

According to the superstitions of the times, there were many *signs* convincing to her that he would return.

One evening in turning her tea-cup, the peculiar position of the leaves was proof that he was *then* on his way home.

She rose hastily, saying : "Alden will be home to-night, and I must put the house in order, and dress and go to meet him."

Upon opening the door, she really saw him in the distance approaching the house.

They removed to Bristol, N. Y., in 1792, with others from the vicinity of Dighton. For his land he paid six cents an acre.

He was in Capt. Elijah Walker's Co., in Col. John Hathaway's Regt, and marched on "ye alarm of Aug. 2, 1780, to Tiverton, 18 miles' travel, 7 days' service, wages £1 8 0."

133.

Ensign NATHAN SEARS[5] [*Judah*[4], *Samuel*[3], *Paul*[2], *Richard*[1]], b. Harwich, Mass., June 18, 1741; d. Rochester, Mass., Feb. 27, 1825, (Feb. 6, Ch. Rec.); m. Chatham, Mass., Dec., 1764, by Rev. Stephen Emery to *Rebecca Crowell*, dau. of Paul and Rebecca C. of Chat.; she b. Oct. 18, 1742; 2d, Roch., Sep. 18, 1779 (1777, T. Clk.), by Rev. Jonathan Moore to *Thankful Bassett* of Roch.; she b. May 29, 1752; d. Mar. 4, 1818, æ. 65 yrs. 9 m. 6 da. (in the entry of death of her son, Stephen, she is called Thankful *Handy*.) Nathan Sears may have m. about 1770, to a —— *Sherman*, but the tradition is vague, and not supported by records.   Children :

By *Rebecca :*
419.*   i. PAUL, b. Roch., Nov. 11, 1765.
420.   ii. BETTY, b. Roch., Aug. 21, 1768; d. Woodstock, Vt., 1851; m. Aug. 20, 1797, Thomas Barrows; he b. June 19, 1768; he absconded, was supposed to have been murdered, but turned up in New Orleans, married to another woman; had [1.] Jane, b. Aug. 9, 1798; d. May 29, 1824. [2.] Thomas, b. Dec. 21, 1799; d. inf.
421.   iii. ELEAZAR, b. Roch., Aug. 20, 1770; bap. Nov. 4.
By *Thankful :*
422.   iv. STEPHEN B., b. Roch., about 1780; m. Oct., 1802, *Azubah Mendall*; and d. s. p. Roch., Mar. 14, 1847, æ. 66.
423.   v. REBECCA, b. Roch., Sep. 20, 1782; m. *Presbury Clark;* and d. Mar. 24, 1819; children, CLARK : [1.] Leonard. [2.] Nathan. [3.] Susan. [4.] Dorcas. [5.] Rebecca. [6.] Presbury. [7.] Rufus. [8.] Warren, and twins who d. Mar. 24, 1819.
424.* vi. NATHAN, b. Roch., Sep. 27, 1785.
       16

425. vii. SUKEY, b. Roch.; m. July 2, 1820, by Rev. Oliver
Cobb of Roch., to *Presbury Clark*, his 2d wife; children, CLARK: [1.] Eleanor. [2.] Eunice. [3.] Elvira.
[4.] Susan. [5.] Lunas.

Family tradition says, Nathan Sears was Captain of a company at the battle of Bunker Hill. He was an Ensign in
Capt. Edward Hammond's Co., which marched Apr. 20, 1775,
on alarm at Lexington; 7 days' service; 80 miles' travel,
16ˢ 8ᵈ.

134.

DAVID SEARS⁵ [*Judah⁴, Samuel³, Paul², Richard¹*], b.
Harwich, Mass., May 10, 1744; d. Rochester, Mass.; m. there,
Aug. 26, 1762, *Abigail Gerry;* 2d, Roch., Feb. 13, 1766,
by Rev. Ivory Hovey, to *Susannah Handy*, dau. of Zaccheus
and Susannah H.; she b. Sep. 27, 1746; adm. Ch., Roch., Aug.
23, 1770. (Zaccheus Handy, b. Jan. 16, 1708, was son of
John H., of Sandwich, he b. 1677; m. Nov. 14, 1704, Kezia
Wing.) Children:

By *Susannah:*
426.* i. LOT, b. Roch., July 2, 1767; bap. Sep. 6, 1772.
427.* ii. PRINCE, b. Roch., Oct. 15, 1768; bap. Sep. 6, 1772.
428. iii. SUSANNAH, b. Roch., Dec. 29, 1770; bap. Sep. 6,
1772.
429. iv. ALICE, b. Roch., Sep. 1, 1773; bap. Oct. 10; m. Dec.
12, 1792, *Ebenezer Clarke* of Roch.
430. v. ACHSAH, b. Roch., Apr. 9, 1776; bap. May 19; m.
Oct. 23, 1796, *Daniel Belden Stow* of Claverack on the
Hudson; he b. Aug. 10, 1771; d. Mar. 20, 1859. He
was one of the rare ones of the earth, a grand and noble
Christian gentleman, by profession a lawyer. His wife
died, after a long illness of consumption, Feb. 15, 1815.
She was a woman of superior mind and judgment, and
one of faith and prayer, and each of her children were
strong Christian characters; children, STOW: [1.] William
Sears, b. Oct. 6, 1797; m. Sep. 12, 1825, Maria Augusta
De Burg, dau. of Frederic Augusta De B., (Baron von
Zing,) by his wife, Mary Lawrence; she b. Apr. 6, 1799;
d. Dec. 25, 1873; had, i. Wm. De Burg, b. Mar. 2, 1827;
d. May 18. ii. John Barber, b. Dec. 25, 1829; d. Nov.
15, 1885. iii. Marie Antoinette, b. June 8, 1834; m.
Dec. 10, 1856, Charles C. Cady. iv. De Lancey, b. Sep.

4, 1841; m. Sep. 27, 1863, Eunice Sophia Scott. [2.] Dennis, b. Conway, Mass., July 29, 1799; d. Beloit, Wis., Nov. 25, 1883; m. Claverack, N. Y., Jan. 14, 1821, Sarah Ann Van Deusen, who d. Niles, Mich., Aug. 9, 1866; had, i. Wm. Augustus, b. Nov. 6, 1821; d. May 1, 1824. ii. Frederie Edmonds, b. Mar. 18, 1823; killed at Nicaragua with Col. Walker, Nov., 1854. He served under Gen. Scott in the Mexican War, and was body-guard to Gen. Worth during one or two important battles. iii. Wm. Augustus, b. Mar. 4, 1831; m. Niles, Mich., Oct. 15, 1855, Kate C. Seymour; and lives Greensboro, N. C. iv. Mary Frances, b. May 8, 1833; m. Niles, Mich., Sep. 29, 1852, Charles F. Bentley, and lives St. Anthony's Park, St. Paul, Minn. [3.] Jonathan, b. Oct. 25, 1802; d. Sep. 18, 1860, leaving issue. [4.] Frederic, b. Sep. 14, 1805; d. Oct. 18, 1805. [5.] Daniel Belden, b. Nov. 14, 1806; m. Ghent, N. Y., Sep. 29, 1829, —— ——; was b. Apr. 25, 1811; he d. Dec. 2, 1852; had, i. John Adams, b. Apr. 24, 1831. ii. Margaret Achsah, b. Oct. 3, 1834; d. ——. iii. Margaret A., b. June 9, 1836. iv. Mary E., b. July 11, 1838. v. Helen Augusta, b. Dec. 16, 1840. vi. Mary Livingston, b. Feb. 3, 1844. vii. Theodore H. C., b. Jan. 11, 1845. viii. Son, b. and d. Aug. 3, 1847. ix. Emma Amelia, b. July 10, 1848. [6.] Jane Matilda, b. May 10, 1810; m. Peter V. Hermance; d. Sep. 20, 1850; had *inter alios*, Achsah, who m. —— Richardson, and lives in Brooklyn, N. Y. [7.] Julia Ann, b. Nov. 19, 1813; d. Sep. 28, 1814.

431. vi. DAVID, b. Roch., July 19, 1778; bap. same day; m. Hudson, N. Y., *Phebe Pease*, and had issue. He removed to N. Y. with his brother in 1793, and settled in Hudson, where he engaged in business; but, being unsucessful, went to Canada, and later to Charleston, S. C. Some of his children lived in Hudson or Claverack.

The estate of David Sears was settled in 1782.

David Sears marched in Capt. Seth Briggs' Co. on the alarm at Lexington, leaving home Apr. 19; 80 miles; 4 days' service; wages and expense, 12ˢ and 4ˢ 3ᵈ; and on alarm at Dartmouth, in 2d Foot Co., Lieut. John Doty, Sep. 5 to Sep. 11, 1778, 6 days; wages, £1 12 0. He was also called on alarm at Dartmouth, May 6 and 7, 1776.

135.

RICHARD SEARS [*Judah*[4], *Samuel*[3], *Paul*[2], *Richard*[1]],

b. Harwich, Mass., June 8, 1746; was pub. Rochester, Mass., Mar. 26, 1769, to *Sarah Bumpus* of Wareham, Mass.   Children:

432.* i. (?) RICHARD.

Richard Sears "was a non-com[d] officer in militia," and marched on alarm, Apr. 19, 1775, from Wareham to Marshfield, "71 miles' travel, 4 days' service"; served 3 days at Elizabeth Island, alarm Dec. 7, 1776; was in Capt. Isaac Woods' Co., Col. Thos. Carpenter's Regt., July 20 to Aug. 27, 1777, in R. I., 1 mo. 7 days' service; on alarm Sep. 12, 1778, served 7 days; 50 miles "out and in;" was drummer in 2d Foot Co., Capt. David Nye, to Falmouth, Sep. 10, 1779; 32 miles, 4 days' service; and served in Capt. David Noyes' Co., Lt.-Col. White's Regt., in R. I., July 30 to Aug. 8, 1780; 9 days' service.

He may have removed later to Hyannis, Mass.

141.

JOHN SEARS[5] [*John[4], Samuel[3], Paul[2], Richard[1]*], b. Yarmouth, Mass., June 5, 1737; m. Harwich, Mass., Oct. 13, 1763, *Elizabeth Sillew*, dau. of Philip S.; she b. 1741; d. Nov. 1, 1764, æ. 23, gr.-st., Chatham; 2d, pub. Chat., Apr. 4, 1767, to —— *Sisson* of Tiverton, R. I.   Child:

By *Elizabeth :*
433. i. *Child*, b. Chatham, Nov. 1, 1764; d. Nov. 13.

John Sears lived in Chatham for a time, and is said to have occupied the old Richard Sears house; he removed to Rochester, Mass., and thence to Rhode Island, perhaps to Tiverton or Bristol.   He was in 2d Foot Co., called out on alarm at Dartmouth and Falmouth, May 6 and 7, 1776, and again Sep. 5 to Sep. 11, 1778, under Lt. John Doty, in Col. Eben Sproul's Regt.; served 6 days; also Sep. 13 to Sep. 17, 1778.

I find in records of Middleboro, Mass., "Dec. 17, 1805, by Rev. Dan[l] Gurney, John Sears of Bristol, R. I., to Melinda Keith of Bridgewater."   This may be a son.

145.

DAVID SEARS[5] [*John[4], Samuel[3], Paul[2], Richard[1]*], bap. Harwich, Mass., Apr. 27, 1746; m. Harwich, Oct. 27, 1765, *Katharine Sillew*, dau. of Philip S.; 2d, by Rev. Mr. Bascom,

Apr. 8, 1773, to *Phebe Taylor*, dau. of John T., (she m. 2d, Rev. Jon^a Bascom, his 2d wife, who m. 3d, Betsy Freeman.) Children:

434. i. REBECCA, bap. Sep., 1782 ; m. Oct. 2, 1797, *Robt. Wheeler* of Camden, Me.
435. ii. KATHARINE, bap. Sep. 29, 1782.

Rebecca and Katharine are mentioned in will of Grace Sears, widow, July 20, 1779 ; see No. 31.

151.

ROLAND SEARS[5] [*Seth*[4], *Samuel*[3], *Paul*[2], *Richard*[1]], b. Harwich, Mass., Sep. 18, 1726 ; d. May 1, 1750, in 24 yr., gr.-st., W. Br.; m. Har., Nov. 2, 1789, *Elizabeth Crosby* of Yar. Child:

436.* i. ROLAND, b. Har., Aug. 23, 1750. (Aug. 12, T. C.)

Lived in that part of Harwich, now Brewster.

161.

BENJAMIN SEARS[5] [*Benjamin*[4], *Samuel*[3], *Paul*[2], *Richard*[1]], b. Harwich, Mass., May 2, 1738 ; d. Mar. 12, 1827, æ. 90, gr.-st., Milltown, N. Y.; m. *Mary Hall* of South East, N. Y., who d. May 26, 1814, æ. 78 (? 73), and is buried beside her husband. Children:

437.* i. PETER, b. So. East, Dec. 20, 1763.
438.* ii. HEMAN, b. So. East., Jan. 7, 1767.
439. iii. DELIVERANCE, b. So. East, Dec. 19, 1769 , d. Apr. 17, 1791; m. *Noah Smith ;* child, SMITH: [1.] Benjamin, 1791.
440.* iv. ISAAC, b. So. East, Mar. 2, 1772.
441.* v. SAMUEL, b. So. East, July 17, 1774.

Benjamin Sears is said to have lived for a time in Richfield, or Litchfield, N. Y. (the record is not clear, but as the towns adjoin, his farm may have been in both); he is also said to have lived in Sardinia, but his children were all born in South East, and he and his wife are buried there.

"Benjamin Sears, pound-keeper," So. East, Apr. 6, 1793 ; and taxed there, 1777. A Temperance Sears lived in his family, and m. —— Paddock ; she was perhaps a dau. of Lt. Judah Sears, No. 130.

162.

Capt. STEPHEN SEARS[5] [*Benjamin[4], Samuel[3], Paul[2], Richard[1]*], b. Harwich, Mass., May 20, 1738; d. New York city, 1791; m. Sharon, Ct., *Eliz'h Hyde* [Ch. Rec.]; 2d, *Sarah Hunter;* 3d, Mar. 9, 1769, *Mrs. Sybil (Hunt) Pardee;* d. Feb. 8, 1834, æ. 94. (By her 1st marriage, Mrs. P. had a dau. Sybil, who m. Dr. Simeon Blackmore; and d. Sharon, Aug. 15, 1844, æ. 82.)   Children:

By *Sarah:*

442.   i. ABIGAIL, m. Feb. 15, 1781, *Alpheus Jewitt* of Sharon and Skaneateles; child, JEWITT: [1.] Freedom G., of Skaneateles, whose son, "Bill Jewitt," left a widow, now (1883) Mrs. Judge Marvin of S.

443.   ii. ANNA, b. June 30, 1760; m. 1783, *Isaac Crane* of So. East, N. Y.; son of Judge Joseph C., Jr.; he b. June 26, 1753; d. Mar. 6, 1810; she d. 1857, æ. 97; children, CRANE: [1.] Henry, b. Jan. 21, 1784; m. Jan. 15, 1808, Amarilla H. Moses, dau. of Elijah and Hannah (Merrill) M., she b. Aug. 1, 1789; d. Apr. 17, 1866; he d. Mar. 6, 1875. [2.] Sarah, m. Wm. Plumb. [3.] Charles, m. Huldah Bronson. [4.] Ralph. [5.] Hunter, m. Maria McMullany, and settled near Sackett's Harbor, N. Y., and at Oswego. [6.] Della. [7.] Albert, m. Margaret Oliver; 2d, Abigail Maynard. [8.] Isaac.

They lived at Crane's Corners, 4 miles from Litchfield, and 10 miles from Herkimer, N. Y. (Judge Joseph Crane, Jr., of So. East, m. Esther Belden, dau. of Dan[l] B. He was son of Joseph C., by his wife Mary Couch dau. of Sam[l] C.; — gr.-son of Jon[a] C., and wife Deborah; gt.-gr.-son of John Crane from England, and I suppose gt.-gt.-gr.-son of Jasper Crane, who settled in New Haven Colony, E. Haven and Branford, a magistrate in Newark, N. J., in 1673, where he died aged.

444.   iii. SARAH, m. *Elisha Wright*, and settled in West Bloomfield, N. Y.

By *Sybil:*

445.* iv. STEPHEN, b. May, 1770.

446.   v. TAMSEN, b. Dec., 1775; m. after Oct., 1798, *Allen Pease*, a clothier of Sharon, his 2d wife; who d. Apr. 8, 1843; children, PEASE: [1.] Eunice, b. Mar. 13, 1806; m. Philo C. Howland. [2.] John S., b. July 17, 1807; m. Emily Ingram.

447.* vi. JOHN.

448. vii. DELIA, b. July 10, 1771; m. June 7, 1795, *Joel Benton* of Amenia, N. Y.; he b. May 13, 1771; d. Apr. 13, 1850. Joel Benton, editor and antiquarian, of Amenia, is a grand-son.

449. viii. AZENATH, m. *David Skidmore* of Newtown, Ct.

450. ix. ALMA, m. —— *Hitchcock*, and lived in Amenia, N. Y.

Capt. Stephen Sears removed with his parents to South East, Putnam co., (then Dutchess co.,) N. Y., and about 1760, to Sharon, Ct., where, at a later date, he purchased the Dea. Hunter (his wife's father's) place of 150 acres, where Benjamin Sears, No. 1032, lately lived.

He was a carpenter by trade, and in that capacity superintended the erection of the meeting-house built in 1768, which was taken down when the brick church was built.

He died of yellow fever at New York in 1791, while at work upon a contract there. He held the office of Sheriff, and during the Revolution, was a Captain and Commissary.

163.

ENOCH SEARS[5] [*Benjamin[4], Samuel[3], Paul[2], Richard[1]*], b. Harwich, Mass., Sep. 5, 1741; was lost at sea, in winter of 1773–4; m. Kingston, N. Y., —— *Underhill;* who died soon after the birth of her only child:

451.* i. IRA, b. Dutchess county, N. Y., Mar. 7, 1774.

Enoch Sears removed with his parents about 1749, to South-East, then a part of Oblong, N. Y.; "went west," and was lost on Long Island Sound, three months before the birth of his son. His wife died of grief eight months after Ira's birth, and the child was brought up by an uncle's wife, who cared for him as her own babe.

The Underhills were Quakers.

165.

SUNDERLAND SEARS[5] [*Benjamin[4], Samuel[3], Paul[2], Richard[1]*], b. (probably in Oblong, N. Y.), Dec. 3, 1749; d. Ballston Centre, N. Y., Mar. 20, 1827, æ. 78; m. Ballston, N. Y., Jan. 2, 1776, *Mary Andrus;* she b. May 22, 1755; d. Balls., Nov. 5, 1844, æ. 89. Children:

452. i. LYDIA, b. Oct., 1776; m. Jan. 1, 1798, *Ezra Hollister* of Tompkins county, N. Y., and had seven children.

453.* ii. ISAAC, b. Nov. 22, 1778.

454.* iii. REUBEN, b. Nov. 22, 1778, *gemini*.

455.* iv. WILLIAM, b. June 11, 1781.

456.* v. ABRAM, b. Oct. 27, 1783.

457. vi. MARY, b. Feb. 26, 1786; m. Jan. 13, 1813, *James Comstock*.

458. vii. ASENATH, b. Sep. 27, 1788; m. June 14, 1817, *Salmon Wakeman*, and d. Sep. 18, 1871.

459. viii. LEVI, b. Nov. 1, 1790.

460.* ix. JAMES, b. Nov. 1, 1790, *gemini;* d. 1871.

461.   x. CHARLOTTE, b. July 25, 1793; m. Balls., N. Y., Dec. 18, 1817, Rev. *Halsey A. Wood;* he b. there Sep. 7, 1793; d. Nov. 27, 1825, æ. 32; was pastor of the church at Amsterdam, N. Y.; children, WOOD: [1.] Martha Staunton, b. Amst., Jan. 18, 1818; m. Union Village, N. Y., Aug. 31, 1843, Rev. D. H. Hamilton, D. D., of Kingsboro, N. Y. [2.] Morgan LeRoy, b. Amst., May 8, 1820; m. Lockport, N. Y., 1846, Eliz^h Wakeman; she b. Saratoga, 1825; d. 1857, æ. 32; 2d, Mary Wakeman, b. Balls., 1828; d. Oxford, Ohio, 1868. He lives in Marion, Kansas; children; i. Alice Martha, b. Bristol, Ind., 1847; d. at Western Female Sem'y. ii. Lillian Elizabeth, b. 1850; m. 1872, J. M. Brown, and lives Marion, Kans. iii. Maggie Reynolds, b. Peoria, Ill., 1860. iv. Linda Curtis, b. Peoria, 1862. v. Willard Hamilton, b. Carrolltown, Ill., 1864. vi. Mary Lyon, b. Carr., 1867. [3.] Howard, b. Amst., Apr. 27, 1823; d. Oct. 26, 1825. [4.] Margaret Terhune, b. Amst., Jan. 1, 1826; m. Kingsboro, N. Y., July 26, 1849, Joseph Steele; he b. there Dec. 14, 1824; and had, i. Charlotte Wood, b. Mar. 24, 1851; m. Mar. 23, 1876, —— ——. ii. Frederika, b. Nov. 28, 1854. iii. James Green, b. Nov. 6, 1857; m. Apr. 10, 1879, —— ——. iv. D. H. Hamilton, b. May 24, 1861; address, 64 Livingston street, Brooklyn, N. Y. v. Minerva, b. Nov. 29, 1867.

462. xi. CHARLES, b. July 25, 1793, *gemini*.

463. xii. MELINDA, b. June 25, 1797; m. Mar. 23, 1833, *Curtis Taylor* of Ballston Centre, N. Y., and was living in 1883.

Sunderland Sears removed to Ballston Centre shortly after 1776, a pioneer settler in the wilderness, moving his worldly goods with the help of oxen. Was a farmer.

During the Revolutionary War he lived in Schenectady.

166.

SETH SEARS[5] [*Benjamin[4], Samuel[3], Paul[2], Richard[1]*], b. Oblong, N. Y.; m. —— ——. Children :

464.* i. WILLIAM, b. Oct. 19, 1775.
465. ii. LYDIA, b. Jan., 1780 ; m. *Stephen Crosby* of So. East; had a large family; d. July 3, 1867, æ. 87-6.
466. iii. SALLY, m. —— *Hubbell.*
467. iv. BETSY, m. —— *Green.*

167.

SAMUEL SEARS[5] [*Benjamin[4], Samuel[3], Paul[2], Richard[1]*], b. South East, N. Y.; d. Cortland county, N. Y.; m. —— ——. Children :

468. i. LEWIS.
469. ii. (?) SAMUEL, b. about 1793; d. So. East, Oct. 10, 1830, æ. 37.

170.

EBENEZER SEARS[5] [*Ebenezer[4], Paul[3], Paul[2], Richard[1]*]; b. Yarmouth, Mass., June 13, 1723; d. Chatham, Ct., 1814; m. there, Jan. 25, 1753, *Elizabeth Cooke*, who d. July 4, 1797, æ. 63; 2d, Apr. 25, 1798, *Dorcas Beebe.* Children :

By *Elizabeth :*
470. i. ANNA, b. Chat. Feb. 17, 1755; m. July 12, 1781, *Amos Clarke*, son of Jabez and Sarah (Judd) C., he b. Oct. 12, 1754; d. Mar. 20, 1843; she d. July 8, 1835; children, CLARKE: [1.] Anna, b. Apr. 20, 1782; d. Jan. 5, 1786. [2.] Philena, b. Sep. 28, 1784. [3.] Anna, b. Jan. 21, 1787. [4.] Abner Nelson, b. Apr. 12, 1789. [5.] Sarah, b. Apr. 22, 1791. [6.] Amos, b. Dec. 26, 1794.
471.* ii. DAVID, b. Chat., Nov. 27, 1757.
472. iii. SARAH, b. Chat.; m. Sep. 5, 1793, (July 3, Hist. Mid. Co., Ct.) *Seth Alvord*, son of Seth and Eliza (Spencer) A., his 2d wife, he b. July 18, 1754; d. July 14, 1836; she d. Feb. 2, 1819; children, ALVORD: [1.] Otis, b. May 26, 1794. [2.] BEULAH, b. June 27, 1796. [3.] Elizabeth, b. Mar. 14, 1802. [4.] Chauncey Hart, b. Dec. 16, 1803.
473. iv. HANNAH, b. Chat., June 3, 1760; m. Capt. *Timo. Ruggles*, from Cape Cod, a Revolutionary soldier; he taught school in Middletown; was Rep. 1793-4 in Gen-

17

eral Assembly from Chatham; d. Sep. 27, 1796, æ. 39;
child, Ruggles: [1.] Nancy, b. Jan. 12, 1793. She m.
2d, Dec. 7, 1803, *Nathaniel Markham,* son of John and
Desire (Sears) M., his 3d wife. (He had m. Sep. 2, 1780,
Margaret Hall; 2d, Mary Strong, who d. Oct. 25, 1802;)
children, Markham: [1.] Timothy, b. Oct. 11, 1806.
[2.] John, d. æ. 98.

474. v. Betsy, b. Chat.; m. Aug. 5, 1794, *John Willey, Jr.,*
of Chat. ; rem. to Granby, Ct., and d. s. p.

173.

HEZEKIAH SEARS[5] [*Ebenezer[4], Paul[3], Paul[2], Richard[1]*], b. Yarmouth, Mass., Dec. 30, 1728; d. Haddam, Ct.;
m. Middletown, Ct., Dec. 25, 1755, *Deborah Spencer,* dau. of
Nath[1] and Abigail (Hurlburt) S., of M., she b. Apr. 9, 1736.
Children :

475.   i. Annis, b. June 3, 1758; m. Dec. 7, 1780, *Nathl.
        Cooke,* who d. Oct. 18, 1816, æ. 61; she d. Haddam, Sep.
        8, 1850.
476.   ii. Tamsen, bap. Dec. 25, 1763.
477. iii. Tamsen, bap. Sep. 1, 1765; m. *Samuel Arnold* of
        Haddam.
478.   iv. Lucy, b. Mar. 14, 1768 : d. Dec. 26, 1773.
479.   v. Deborah, b. Aug. 31, 1772 ; m. *Elisha Day.*
480.   vi. Lucy, bap. July 9, 1775; m. Jan. 14, 1795, *Joseph
        Smith,* son of David S.; he b. Mar. 10, 1774 ; children,
        Smith: [1.] Anna, b. Nov. 13, 1795.   [2.] Anson, b. Feb.
        27, 1797.   [3.] Polly, b. Dec. 4, 1798.
481. vii. Sarah, b. Sep. 19, 1777; m. Oct. 25, 1795, *David
        Brainard,* son of Dea. Ezra B., he b. Jan. 17, 1775; d.
        Nov. 26, 1809 ; 2d, *Wm. Kelley ;* and d. Aug. 8, 1855 ;
        children, Brainard : [1.] Harriet, b. Feb. 4, 1796.
        [2.] Narcissa, b. Apr. 25, 1797.   [3.] Cyrus, b. Dec. 15,
        1798. [4.] David Artemas, b. Oct. 16, 1809.

Hezekiah Sears lived in East Haddam, Ct.
In 1780 he was of committee appointed to provide necessities for the Continental Army.

181.

PAUL SEARS[5] [*Ebenezer[4], Paul[3], Paul[2], Richard[1]*], b.
Yarmouth, Mass., Nov. 29, 1744; d. Winthrop, Me., Jan.

30, 1810, æ. 67 ; m. —— ——, who d. ; 2d, Winth., Jan. 27, 1778, *Mercy Stevens*, dau. of James S., 1st, of W., who d. Jan. 27, 1829, æ. 76.   Children :

By —— —— :
482.   i. *Child*, d. inf.
483.   ii. *Child*, d. inf., *gemini*.
By *Mercy* :
484.* iii. JOHN, b. Winth., Sep. 3, 1778.
485.   iv. MOSES, b. Winth., Dec. 3, 1779.
486.*   v. PAUL STICKNEY, b. Winth., July 5, 1781.
487.   vi. MERCY, b. Winth., July 5, 1781, *gemini;* m. ab't 1831, *John R. White*, asst. Surg. U. S. N., and d. s. p., Freedom, Me.
488.* vii. SILAS, b. Winth., Mar. 17, 1783.
489. viii. ALICE, b. Winth., Oct. 22, 1785 ; m. *Nathl. Whittier* of Farmington, Me.; children. WHITTIER ; [1.] Hiram. [2.] Caroline, and 2 other boys, and twin girls.
490.   ix. THOMAS, b. Winth., Feb. 15, 1788 ; d. Oct. 4, 1790.
491.   x. CHARLOTTE, b. Winth., Nov. 27, 1791 ; d. Sep. 13, 1814, æ. 22 yr. 11 mo.
492.   xi. TRYPHENA, b. Winth., Oct. 21, 1793 ; m. *Tillottson Chandler*, son of John C., Jr., lived in Monmouth, Me.; and d. Apr. 12, 1864.   He d. some years since ; children, CHANDLER : [1.] John. [2.] Emily. [3.] Malvina. [4.] Augustus.   [5.] Son.

Rev. E. H. Sears says: "Paul Sears married a worthy lady of Marblehead, who died in giving birth to twins, in the absence of her husband.   On his return, finding his wife and babes all dead, he left the country broken-hearted, went to Nova Scotia, and was not heard of afterward."

I have been unable to verify the statement, but presume it to be correct.

In the Hist. of Winthrop, he is called "a cooper from Cape Cod."

The soldiers' monument there was placed over his grave, but his grave-stone, (if he had one,) is missing.

183.

WILLIAM SEARS[5] [*Paul[4], Paul[3], Paul[2], Richard[1]*], b. Rochester, Mass., Jan. 14, 1725–6 ; d. Dover, Vt. ; m. Roch., Sep., 1753, *Patience Parker*, 3d child of Ebenezer and Thank-

ful P., of Roch., she b. July 4, 1726; d. Mar. 28, 1768; and
2d, Roch., Jan. 29, 1770, *Betty Wood*.   Children :

By *Patience:*
493.*   i. EBENEZER, b. Roch., Dec. 15, 1754.
494.   ii. MARY, b. Roch., July 8, 1756.
495. iii. SAMUEL, bap. Roch., Aug. 18, 1762.
496.* iv. WILLIAM, b. Roch., May 9, 1762; bap. Aug. 18.
By *Betty:*
497.   v. PRISCILLA, b. Roch., Sep. 21, 1771; bap. June 29,
       1774.
498. vi. HATSULD, b. Roch., Jan. 23, 1773; bap. June 29,
       1774.
499. vii. HANNAH, bap. Roch., Sep. 24, 1780.
    William Sears, and Patience, his wife, were baptized at
Rochester, Aug. 17, 1758.
    In 1780, he removed to Douglass, formerly New Sherburne,
Mass., and thence to Dover, Vt., where he died.

184.

    PAUL SEARS[5] [*Paul[4], Paul[3], Paul[2], Richard[1]*], b. 1728;
d. Egg Harbor, N. J.; pub. Rochester, Mass., Nov. 30, 1755,
(Nov. 15, T. C.,) *Parnell Hammond* of Roch.   Child :

500. i. WILLIAM, is said to have left issue.

    Paul Sears was a seaman.   I do not understand that he lived
at Egg Harbor, but probably died there while on a voyage.
There may have been other children.

186.

    NATHANIEL SEARS[5] [*Paul[4], Paul[3], Paul[2], Richard[1]*],
b. Rochester, Mass., Sep. 1, 1738; d. Apr. 28, 1816; (Apr. 20,
T. C.), æ. 77; m. Roch., Nov. 26, 1761, by Rev. Tim° Ruggles to *Elizabeth Winslow* (a gt.-gt.-gr.-dau. of Gov. Edward
W.); she b. Roch., 1741; adm. to Ch. there, 1771; d. Sep. 24,
1828, æ. 87.   Children :

501.*   i. SILAS, b. Roch., Nov. 26, 1762; bap. July 28, 1771.
·502·   ii. JESSE, b. Roch., July 28, 1771; d. Charleston, S. C.,
       of yellow fever, before 1816.
503.* iii. NATHANIEL, b. Roch., 1766; bap. July 28, 1771.
504.* iv. PRINCE, bap. Roch., July 28, 1771.

505. v. ELIZABETH, b. Roch., Jan. 3, 1767; bap. July 28,
1771; m. Jan. 23, 1791, *Martin Bryant* of Chesterfield,
Mass., son of Nath¹ B.; he b. Plympton, Mass., Dec. 27,
1765; d. Weathersfield, Vt., Jan. 13, 1833; she d. Warsaw,
N. Y., Feb. 20, 1850; children, BRYANT: [1.] Betsey, b.
June 24, 1792; d. Nov. 23, 1813. [2.] Martin, b. Mar.
20, 1794; d. Oct. 30, 1834. [3.] Asa, b. Feb. 22, 1796;
d. in Wisconsin, June, 1850. [4.] Harvey, b. Feb. 13,
1798; d. Oct. 10, 1828. [5.] Spencer, b. Apr. 16, 1799;
d. Apr. 27, 1877. [6.] Mary, b. Mar. 14, 1801; m. Feb.
9, 1826, Linus Thayer; and after his death a Rev. Mr. Hill,
who was killed in Iowa, 1871. [7.] Susan, b. Apr. 21,
1803; d. 1861. [8.] Deborah, b. Feb. 23, 1805; d. Nov.
10, 1866. [9.] Eunice, b. Sep. 13, 1807; d. Mar. 30,
1847. [10.] Patrick, b. Mar. 13, 1810; d. June 15, 1862.
506. vi. PAUL, bap. Roch., Apr. 4, 1773; d. at sea before
1816.
507. vii. SUSANNA, m. Dea. *Ebenezer Keene* of Fair Haven,
Mass. (bro. to Hannah Keene, who m. Nath¹ Sears, Jr.);
and d. in Amherst, Mass., leaving issue. " She was tall and
erect, lively and cheerful."
508. viii. DEBORAH, bap. Roch., July 13, 1777; m. 1795,
Abiel Pierce, Jr.; he b. May 30, 1770; she d. Middleboro, Mass., Apr. 23, 1810; children, PIERCE: [1.] Abiel,
b. Mar. 6, 1796; m. abt. 1820, Eliza Cushman; was com.
Ensign, Roch., July 25, 1821, and Capt. 1824; was a carpenter, and d. Macon, Ga., abt. 1855. [2.] Nathan, b.
Apr. 23, 1799; unm. [3.] Betsy, b. Mar. 2, 1802; d.
July 25, 1806. [4.] Nathaniel S., b. Sep. 20, 1804; m. abt.
1825, Mary Simmons, and removed to Illinois. [5.] Samuel N., b. Sep. 15, 1808; d. New York, 1834; unm.
[6.] John S., m. abt. 1828, Mary Wilbur; d. Peoria, Ill.,
1859.
509. ix. MARY, bap. Roch., Aug. 12, 1781; d. before 1816, of
consumption.
510.* x. JOHN, bap. Roch., Sep. 11, 1785.

Nathaniel Sears was in Capt. Josiah Thacher's Co. in Col.
Thomas' Regt., which landed at Halifax, N. S., May 11, 1759,
and like many others, is marked as " *absconded.*"

He was also a member of 2d Co. Foot, Capt Nath'l Hammond, from Rochester, called after the battle of Lexington;
marched as far as Marshfield; 80 miles' travel; 4 days' service;
12ˢ, and 4ˢ 2ᵈ; served in Capt. Barnabas Doty's Co., alarm at
Dartmouth, Sep. 5 to 11, 1778; also Sep. 13 to 17, at £8 per

mo.; and did duty at R. I., Mar. 9 to 31, in Capt. Stephen Churchill's Co., and from Aug. 5 to Dec. 1, 1781, in Capt. Elijah Baker's Co.; wages, £7 17 4.

He was a farmer, and an active man in his day.

His will, dated Apr. 1, 1816, was allowed May 25, 1816; John Sears, Ex^r; and names wife Elizabeth, sons Nathaniel, Prince, Silas and John, and daus. Susanna Keene and Elizabeth Bryant.

189.

THOMAS SEARS⁵ [*Thomas⁴*, *Paul³*, *Paul²*, *Richard¹*], b. Plymouth, Mass.; m. Ply., Oct. 28, 1770, *Rebecca Rider*, dau. of Charles and Rebecca R., of Ply.; she b. 1750. Children:

511.* i. THOMAS, b. Ply., 1771.
512. ii. BARTLETT, b. Ply.; m. Nov. 16, 1798, *Bathsheba ——— vens* of P., and d. s. p. His will, dated Dec. 13, 1805, was allowed Aug. 20, 1821; and names wife Bathsheba, Ex^x, brother Thomas, and a sister, name not given.
513. iii. REBECCA, m. 1808, *Nicholas Smith.*
514. iv. DANIEL, was lost at sea.
515. v. AZUBAH, m. *John Murdock* of Carver; children, MURDOCK: [1.] Philip, b. 1798. [2.] Bartlett, b. 1799. [3.] Chloe, b. 1801; m. Blaney Phillips. [4.] Sally, b. 1802. [5.] Azubah Sears, b. 1804. [6.] Deborah, b. 1806.

The children's names may not be in the order of their birth, and there may have been others.

The town records are very imperfect, but church records may give further data.

190.

WILLARD SEARS⁵ [*Thomas⁴*, *Paul³*, *Paul²*, *Richard¹*], b. Plymouth, Mass.; m. *Sarah Robbins*, dau. of Eleazar and Rebecca (Jackson) R., of Plympton, Mass. Children:

516.* i. ELEAZAR, b. Ply., May, 1778.
517.* ii. DAVID, b. Ply., Aug. 1, 1786.
518.* iii. EDMUND.
519. iv. WILLARD, d. inf.; his bro. Eleazar, a chair-maker,‧ was boiling varnish, when it took fire; he threw the pot of varnish out of the window on to his bro. Willard as he was passing unseen by him, and he died from the injuries.
520.* v. JOSEPH.
521.* vi. THOMAS, b. Ply., 1799.

522. vii. MERCY, m. 1819, *Samuel Lewis*, his 2d wife; children, LEWIS: [1.] Edwin, b. 1821. [2.] Christiania White, b. 1823. [3.] Wealthy Sampson, b. 1825. [4.] William, b. 1827.

523. viii. BETSY, m. *Thomas Sherman*, he b. 1791; 2d, *Eliab Wood*.

524. ix. SALLY, m. 1793, *Bezaliel Lucas* of Carver; children, LUCAS: [1.] Oliver, b. 1794. [2.] Willard Sears, b. 1796. [3.] George, b. 1798.

The children are perhaps not in order of birth.

Willard Sears enlisted in Capt. Moses Soule's Co., in Col. John Fellows' Regt., Apr. 21, 1775, and went to Quebec, Sep. 9; was in Col. Whitcomb's Regt. at Boston, May, 1776.

198.

Capt. ELKANAH SEARS[5] [*Joshua[4], Paul[3], Paul[2], Rich.[1]*], b. Harwich, Mass., Apr. 12, 1734; d. East Hampton Ct., Sunday, Nov. 24, 1816, æ. 83; m. Middletown, Ct., Jan. 6, 1757, *Ruth White*, dau. of Joseph W., of M., who d. Mar. 9, 1823, æ. 90. Children:

525.* i. ISAAC, b. E. Hamp., Nov. 3, 1757.

526.* ii. WILLARD, b. E. H., Sep. 8, 1760.

527. iii. RUTH, b. E. H., Mar. 13, 1763; d. July 29, 1764.

528. iv. RUTH, b. E. H., Mar. 21, 1765; d. Meredith, N. Y., 1830; m. Nov. 5, 1784, *Joshua Bailey;* children. BAILEY: [1.] Lucy, bap. May, 1794. [2.] Timothy, bap. May, 1794. [3.] Anna, bap. Apr. 9, 1797. [4.] Joshua, bap. Oct. 26, 1800. One of the sons was the inventor of the machine for weaving under-wear, and d. in Cohoes or vicinity.

529. v. RACHEL, b. E. H., Sep. 9, 1768; d. Sep. 19, 1850, æ. 82; m. Nov. 20, 1791, *Nathl. Bailey*, (bro. of Joshua,) who was drowned in his mill-pond, Sep. 1, 1817, æ. 49; children, BAILEY: [1.] Henry, m. and d. s. p. [2.] Rhoda, m. Henry Robert of Middle Haddam, Ct., and had 5 or 6 children, who mostly live there. [3.] Clarissa, b. Apr. 19, 1800; d. Oct. 26, 1834; m. Wm. Wadsworth Richmond of E. Hamp., he b. Oct. 27, 1797, 2d son of Dr. John and Prudence (Wadsworth) R., (who had formerly lived in E. Hartford, Ct., and previously in Brookline, Mass.;) they had, i. William H., b. Marlboro, Ct., Oct. 23, 1821; m. 1849, Lois R. Morss of Windham, N. Y.,

and had Mary R., b. Jan. 30, 1855 ; m. Oct. 6, 1881, Fred K. Tracy of Mansfield, Ohio. Emeline K., b. Nov. 7, 1858.   Clara Morss, b. Sep. 16, 1860, and 2 daus., d. inf. He resides at Scranton, Pa., and is Pres^t Elk Hill Coal and Iron Co., and Treas. Richmond Hill Farm, etc. ii. Harriet K., b. Dec. 31, 1823 ; m. Geo. W. Cheney, and lives So. Manchester, Ct.; has Wells W., Louis R., and Geo. Herbert.   iii. Emily F., b. Nov. 17, 1826 ; d. Jan., 1858 ; m. Wm. Jones of Marlboro, Ct., and had 1 son.   iv. Frances A., b. May 1, 1828; d. July 6, 1857 ; m. Aug. S. Smith ; no chil. living.   v. Albert Wadsworth, b. June 30, 1831; d. Nov. 25, 1868 ; m. Laura ——, and had 1 dau.   They lived at Carbondale, Pa.   [4.] Harriet, m. Alfred Williams of E. Hamp., and had 5 children, of whom 2 are living.

530.* vi. Benjamin, b. E. H., Feb. 21, 1773.

Capt. Elkanah Sears removed with his parents to Middletown, Ct., in 1746, and after his marriage in 1757, lived on a farm just west of Pocotapaug lake in E. Hampton.

In 1780 he was of committee appointed to provide necessities for the Continental army.

In 1794 he purchased land in Freehold, Albany co., N. Y., being part of the township sold to Benj. Spees *et al.*, of Chatham, called "Lothania, of Maitland claim," the consideration therefor being £60.

May 9, 1778, he deeded land in E. Hampton to his son Isaac, and in 1795, another parcel to his son Willard.

"Many personal anecdotes are related of him. He was a man of large frame, tall and muscular, with a mind fitted for the body it inhabited, filled with a spirit of enterprise, and reckless of danger.

" After the War of the Revolution broke out, he equipped a vessel which he commanded himself, and which preyed on the British convoys.

" His vessel was captured by a British ship, and he, with one of his men, were made prisoners and confined on board.

" From what he heard and saw, he suspected that preparations were making for their summary execution in the morning.

" He expressed his suspicions to his man, and prepared to escape and swim ashore.

" His man thought the attempt desperate, but Sears replied : ' I would rather trust my neck in the water than the rope.'

" About midnight they eluded the sleepy guard, and let them

selves down into the water, but were soon discovered, and fired upon from the ship.

"Sears reached the shore, but his man gave out. He took a boat, went out and picked him up, and both escaped in safety.

"Nothing daunted by his hair-breadth escape, he went to work immediately to fit out another vessel.

"After the war he became actively engaged in mechanical and agricultural pursuits."

He died of apoplexy on Sunday morning, Nov. 24, 1816, æ. 83. He was greatly beloved, and his funeral was largely attended,— his body was borne to the grave, on a bier carried by four of his old neighbors.

In his will he devised to his children some $15,000.

His house stood till 1848, when it was taken down.

199.

JOSHUA SEARS[5] [*Joshua*[4], *Paul*[3], *Paul*[2], *Rich.*[1]], b. Harwich, Mass., Feb. 14, 1735-6; d. Sandisfield, Mass.; m. there Nov. 28, 1760, *Sarah Blackmore* of Newburyport, Mass., she b. 1744; d. Sand., Aug. 21, 1824, æ. 80. Children:

531.   i. RHODA, b. Sand., Oct. 1, 1761; d. Nov. 19.
532.* ii. DAVID, b. Sand., Oct. 2, 1762.
533. iii. CALEB, b. Sand., Nov. 4, 1764; d. young; was in Capt. Jere. Hickok's Co., Lt. Col. Sears' Regt., Aug. 6, 1781, to Nov. 8, 1781; 3 mos., 7 days, £12 bounty.
534.* iv. JOSHUA, b. Sand., Nov. 7, 1766.
535.* v. DANIEL, b. Sand., Feb. 2, 1769.
536.· vi. AMOS, b. Sand., Jan. 12, 1771; m. *Susanna Daland*, who d. Oct. 11, 1828, æ. 44; 2d, *Betsy Daland*, who d. Dec. 23, 1866, æ. 74, in a fit. He d. Dec. 25, 1861, æ. 91.
537.   vii. SARAH, b. Sand., Apr. 1, 1774.
538. viii. MARY, b. Sand., Oct. 3, 1776.
539.* ix. JOSEPH, b. Sand., 1778.

Joshua Sears removed to Middletown, Ct., with his parents in 1746, and later to Sandisfield, Mass., where he was one of the earliest settlers.

"He enlisted in the old French war, and joined the expedition commanded by Abercrombie, against Ticonderoga and Crown Point, then in possession of the French under Montcalm.

"Abercrombie without waiting for his artillery, made a

18

brave, but imprudent assault upon the fortress of the former place.

"The result was disastrous. His troops were mowed down in ranks before the guns of the fort.

"Sears used to describe the horrors of the carnage, and his own wonderful preservation.

"Three times we were marched up in front of those guns, and each time, the men on my right, and my left, were cut down, and I was left standing alone.

"The hardships of the campaign were great, but he survived them, and returned to Sandisfield, but died in middle life in consequence of them."

201.

PAUL SEARS[5] [*Joshua*[4], *Paul*[3], *Paul*[2], *Rich.*[1]], b. Harwich, Mass., Oct. 18, 1740; (Nov. 7, 1739, Fam. Rec.;) d. Sandisfield, Mass., Aug. 19, 1832; m. *Elizabeth Slawter* of Simsbury, Ct., who d. July 18, 1800; 2d, Mrs. *Lydia (Lyon) Knight;* she b. 1754; d. Mar. 28, 1850, æ. 96. Children: By *Elizabeth*:

540.   i. ELIZABETH, b. Sand., Feb. 16, 1763.
541.   ii. NANCY, b. Sand., Nov. 12, 1766; m. —— *Handy.*
542.*   iii. PAUL, b. Sand., Feb. 2, 1769.
543.   iv. HULDAH, b. Sand., Oct. 22, 1773.
544.*   v. SIMEON, b. Sand., Oct. 7, 1776.
545.   vi. JOHN, b. Sand., Nov. 9, 1779.
546.   vii. ESTHER, b. Sand., June 23, 1782; m. —— *Hawley.*

Paul Sears removed with his parents to Middletown, Ct., and was one of the earliest settlers of Sandisfield, Mass.

202.

SIMEON SEARS[5] [*Joshua*[4], *Paul*[3], *Paul*[2], *Rich.*[1]], b. Harwich, Mass., Jan. 14, 1742; m. —— ——. Children:

547.*   i. SIMEON.
548.   ii. ELISHA, removed to Bennington, Vt.; was a horse dealer; left large family, mostly sons, some of whom are *said* to have "removed to Boston, and became wealthy."
549.   iii. DANIEL, "*went to Canada.*"
550.*   iv. JOSEPH.
551.   v. RHODA, b. Bennington, Vt., 1776; m. Pawlet, Vt., *Ephraim Fitch* of P.; and d. Jan., 1854; children, FITCH:

[1.] Nancy, m. Dr." James Willard of P., who d. 1858; she d. New York State in 1864. [2.] Ferris, m. Sally Porter, and d.; his widow lives in Fremont, Ohio. [3.] Catharine, d. young. [4.] Catharine. [5.] George, d. unm. [6.] Moses Porter, b. P., 1811; m. Granville, N. Y., June 16, 1840, Chloe Atwater Cook, a descendant of Francis Cook, " The Pilgrim ;" and d. Traverse City, Mich., Dec. 2, 1883; had, i. Martha, b. Sep. 10, 1841; m. Laramie City, Wyoming, Apr. 19, 1872, Albert J. Barry, and was divorced in 1882. ii Mary Chloe, b. Oct. 17, 1843; m. Chicago, Ill., Oct. 2, 1872, Charles M. Smith; he b. Providence, R. I.; lives in Longwood, Mass.

552.   vi. LAURA, m. Capt. *Wm. Curtis* of Avon, N. Y.
553.   vii. BETSY.
554.   viii. MARY, m. —— *Gregory,* and had a dau., who m. Jacob Edgerton of Rutland, Vt.

Simeon Sears removed to Sandisfield, Mass., and thence to Bennington, N. Y., (now Vt.), where his name appears in list of original members at the organization of the 1st Ch., Dec. 3, 1762. He perhaps returned to Sandisfield, as a deed to his bro. Elkanah is dated there in Oct., 1765. Oct. 20, 1773, in deed to Elkanah, he calls himself of " Rheuport," (Rupert, Vt.,) and his name is found there on town records, Dec. 12, 1768. Dec. 24, 1773, he gives his residence as Suffield, Hartford county, Ct. Oct. 17, 1780, he hails from Bennington, N. Y., (now Vt.)

He was in Capt. (afterward Col.) Robinson's company at the battle of Bennington, Aug. 16, 1777.

He bought a section of land in northern Vermont, with the intention of removing, but died without carrying out his purpose.

His sons, Simeon and Elisha, were large dealers in horses, buying colts in Canada, keeping them in Vermont till maturity, and then shipping them to the West Indies.

209.

Lt. MICAJAH SEARS[5] [*Dan'l*[4], *Paul*[3], *Paul*[2], *Rich.*[1]], b. Yarmouth, Mass., Apr. 25, 1738; d. Feb., 1823, of mortification; m. (pub. Yar., Jan. 6, 1759,) *Anna Crowell* of Windham, Ct., who was adm. 2d Ch., Yar., Sep. 28, 1760; d. May 26, 1785, in 47 yr., gr.-st., W. Br.; he m. 2d, Harwich, Dec. 6, 1785, *Huldah (Clark) Bangs,* dau. of Seth and Huldah

(Doane) C., she b. Mar. 8, 1738 ; d. 1828. (She had m. 1st, Tully Clark ; 2d, Edward Bangs ; by the latter she had Anne and Huldah ; bap. 2d Ch., Yar., May 8, 1786.) Children :

By *Anna :*

555.   i. LAVINIA, b. Yar., Nov. 26, 1760; bap. Apr. 12, 1761; m. Yar., Feb. 23, 1779, *Zachary Howes*, son of Joseph and Ann (Vincent) H., he b. May 23, 1753.

556.   ii. KEZIA, b. Yar., May 4, 1762 ; d. June 4.

557.   iii. MOLLY, b. Yar., Sep. 27, 1763 ; bap. Aug., 1764 ; m. Nov. 14, 1787, *Amaziah Tobey* of Conway.

558.   iv. NATHAN, b. Yar., June 24, 1766 ; bap. Sep. 28 ; d. at sea.

559.   v. ANN, b. Yar., June 27, 1773 ; bap. July 4.

560.* vi. HENRY, b. Yar., Aug. 8, 1775 ; bap. Oct. 22.

Micajah Sears was a Lieut. in the Militia, and for twenty-five years prominent in church and town affairs, holding numerous offices. Was Rep. 1794, 1795, 1798. " Micajah Sears, Lt. in Capt. Micah Chapman's Co. march toward Marshfield at the time of the Lexington battle — 2 days' service ; 14 miles' travel." Lt. in Capt. Elisha Hedges' Co., Sep., 1777 ; and Lt. in Capt. Micah Chapman's Co., at alarm Dartmouth and Falmouth, Sep. 6, 1778 ; 13 days' service.

212.

DANIEL SEARS[5] [*Dan'l*[4], *Paul*[3], *Paul*[2], *Rich.*[1]], b. Yarmouth, Mass., June 17, 1744; d. Sep. 25, (23 T. C.) 1776, in 31 yr., gr.-st., W. Br. ; m. Yar., Dec. 3, 1767, *Priscilla Sears*, No. 240, dau. of Dea. John and Deborah (Crowell) S., she b. Apr. 5, 1749 ; adm. 2d Ch., Yar., Sep. 1, 1776 ; d. Mar. 11, 1777, æ. 28, gr.-st., W. Br. Children :

561.   i. KEZIA, b. Yar., Oct. 25, 1769 ; bap. Oct. 27, 1776 ; d. July 29, 1787, æ. 18, gr.-st.

562.   ii. RHODA, (or JEHODAH,) b. Yar., May 1, 1771 ; bap. Oct. 27, 1776.

563.   iii. DINAH, b. Yar., July 25, 1773 ; bap. Oct. 27, 1776 ; m. Yar., June 27, 1793, *Nehemiah Howes*, son of Wm. and Mary (Howes) H., he b. Jan. 6, 1770.

564.   iv. PRISCILLA, b. Yar., Feb. 27, 1775 ; bap. Nov. 10, 1776 ; m. Ashfield, Mass., ab't 1793, *Rufus Sears*, No. 887, and d. Hawley, Mass., Nov., 1802, æ. 28, of scarlet fever. She was early left an orphan, and was brought up by her uncle, Paul Sears of Ashfield.

565. v. MERCY, b. Yar., Feb. 17, 1777; bap. Mar. 16; d. June 9, 1855.

The inventory of Daniel Sears was filed Mar. 21, 1777.

The last four children are mentioned in the will of their grand-father, Dea. John Sears Mar. 10, 1789.

214.

Capt. PAUL SEARS[5] [*Dan'l[4], Paul[3], Paul[2], Rich.[1]*], b. Yarmouth, Mass., June 20 (or June 2), 1750; d. Ashfield, Mass., Sep. 3, 1808, æ. 58; m. (probably in Buckland, Mass.,) Oct. 25, 1782, *Eleanor Smith* of Ct., she b. July 23, 1760; d. Ashfield, Aug. 3, 1824, æ. 64. Children:

566. i. LYDIA, b. Ash., July 29, 1783; m. —— *Gray;* and d. Mar., 1815.

567. ii. JERUSHA, b. Ash., Oct. 7, 1784; d. Apr., 1864, unm.

568.* iii. LEMUEL, b. Ash., Dec. 30, 1785.

569. iv. FANNY, b. Ash., Aug. 27, 1787; d. Apr. 12, 1790.

570. v. ACHSAH, b. Ash., Apr. 11, 1789; m. *George Ranney*, and d. Apr. 7, 1869; had *inter alios*, Henry S., for many years Town Clerk of Ashfield.

571.* vi. NATHAN, b. Ash., Feb. 14, 1791.

572. vii. FANNY, b. Ash., Oct. 21, 1793; m. there June 8, 1815, *Thomas Bassett*, son of Lot B., he b. Ash., Apr. 10, 1789; d. Plainfield, Mass., Jan. 22, 1869, æ. 79; she d. Mar. 13, 1847, æ. 53; children, BASSETT: [1.] Deborah, b. Aug. 14, 1816; m. Dec. 27, 1842, Thos. P. Howes; and d. July 7, 1860. [2.] Elisha, b. June 6, 1818; m. Plainfield, Sep. 5, 1843, Mary Ann Porter Joy, she b. there June 23, 1819; d. Boston, Mar. 26, 1859, æ. 39; 2d, Boston, Oct. 4, 1860, Mary Elizabeth Cox, she b. Holderness, N. H., Oct. 12, 1833; he has been for many years Clerk of U. S. Dist. Court in Boston, and lives Newton Centre, Mass.; had, i. Mary Joy, b. Oct. 13, 1845. ii. Francis, b. Oct. 23, 1849, grad. Har., 1871. iii. Fanny Adelaide, b. Jan. 25, 1859; d. Feb. 26, 1864. iv. Anna Rogers, b. Mar. 31, 1867. v. Isabel Sears, b. Oct. 2, 1868. [3.] Lydia Sears, b. Oct. 19, 1820; m. Dec. 5, 1838, Wm. F. Longley of Cobden, Ill. [4.] William, b. May 31, 1822; m. Apr. 2, 1845, Antoinette A. Joy, and lives in Heath, Mass. [5.] Thomas, b. Feb. 13, 1826; m. Oct. 23, 1850, Betsy Vilas, and d. June 20, 1878. [6.] Dwight, b. Apr. 13, 1828; m. Jan. 18, 1853, Lucette Wood, and d. Apr. 18,

1861. [7.] Ellen, b. Oct. 9, 1830; m. Nov. 3, 1859, Chas. M. Clark; and d. Dec. 30, 1864. [8.] Fanny S., b. May 15, 1835; m. May 14, 1856, Noah J. Carter; and d. May 17, 1867. [9.] Lot, b. May 31, 1833; d. unm., Apr. 22, 1853. The first seven were born in Ashfield, the last two in Plainfield.

573. viii. CLARISSA, b. Ash., Nov. 26, 1795; m. Sep. 15, 1814, *Sanford Boice;* and d. Mar., 1864.

574. ix. BETSY, b. Ash., June 20, 1798; m. Apr. 5, 1826, *Ansel Taylor;* and d. Dec. 6, 1882, æ. 84.

575. x. PAUL, b. Ash., Apr. 4, 1800; d. unm., New Orleans, La. He dealt largely in real estate, buying and locating soldiers' claims in Texas, about Houston, and is reputed to have been very wealthy.

576. xi. HENRY, b. Ash., May 25, 1802; was twice married, and had several daughters. Was Judge of Circuit Court in Arkansas, during many years, and removed to Texas about 1843. Was a prominent man there.

577. xii. PRISCILLA, b. Ash., Dec. 31, 1805; m. *Emmons Pratt;* and d. June 7, 1866.

Paul Sears at one time owned and sailed whaling vessels; removed to Ashfield, and lived on Cape street till his death in 1808. "Paul Sears, from Hampshire co.," was in Capt. Benj. Phillips' Co., Col. Elisha Porter's Regt., July 10 to Aug. 12, 1777, and corporal in Capt. Sam'l Westcott's Co., Col. Jos. Ashley's Regt., Sep. 19 to Oct. 18, 1777, in Northern army.

215.

ENOS SEARS[5] [*Dan'l[4], Paul[3], Paul[2], Rich.[1]*], b. Yarmouth, Mass., June 11, 1752; d. July 17, 1822, æ. 69; m. Yar., Feb. 11, 1777, *Rebecca Kelley,* dau. of Sylvanus K. Children:

578.* i. DANIEL, b. Ash., Oct. 6, 1779.

579.* ii. WILLIAM, b. Ash., about 1785.

580. iii. HANNAH, m. *Barnabas Eldredge;* he b. Ash., July, 1780; d. Aug., 1857, æ. 77; she d. May, 1862, æ. 82; children, ELDREDGE: [1.] Thankful, m. Mark Howes of Ash., who d. Sep., 1884, æ. 82; she d. June, 1876. [2.] Rebecca, b. Oct., 1810; d. May 7, 1879, æ. 69. [3.] Allen, b. Aug. 6, 1812; m. Ash., Sep. 7, 1834, Mary Hall; she b. Dec. 8, 1814. [4.] Barnabas, b. Apr. 20, 1822.

581. iv. TAMSEN, m. *Joseph Hall;* he b. Yar., Dec. 25, 1786; d. Apr. 16, 1869; was a farmer; children, HALL: [1.] Han-

nah, m. David Jenkins. [2.] Enos. [3.] Alvan. [4.] Hepsibah, m. Luther Howes. [5.] Freeman. [6.] Dinah, m. Philander Bates of East Cummington, Mass. [7.] Tamsen. [8.] Charles.

582. v. DINAH, m. —— *Baldwin ;* a grand-son, H. L. Phelps, lives in South Hampton, Mass.

583. vi. MERCY, d. Dec. 16, 1821, æ. 22.

Enos Sears was deranged for many years previous to his death.

216.

EDMUND SEARS[5] [*Edm'd*[4], *Paul*[3], *Paul*[2], *Rich.*[1]], b. Yarmouth, Mass., Jan. 3, 1743-4; d. Mar. 16, 1832, æ. 88, gr.-st., W. Br.; m. Yar., Jan. 24, 1771, *Hannah Taylor*, dau. of Jacob T., of Yar.; she b. Hyannis, Mass , 1753, (another account says in Plymouth, 1752); was adm. to Ch., E. Yar., Apr. 23, 1775; d. July 7, 1828, æ. 76, gr.-st. Children :

584.* i. JACOB, b. Yar., Oct. 9, 1771; bap. May 14, 1775.

585.* ii. JUDAH, b. Yar., Oct. 6, 1773; bap. May 14, 1775.

586. iii. MARY, b. Yar., Feb. 13, 1776 ; bap. Mar. 24, 1776; d. May 15, 1785, æ. 9, gr.-st.

587.* iv. PAUL, b. Yar., Nov. 20, 1777; bap. Jan. 4, 1778.

588. v. SALLY, b. Yar., June 26, 1780; bap. July 30; d. West Sandwich, Mass., Aug. 14, 1861, æ. 81; m. Dennis, May 4, 1797, *Paul Crowell*, son of William and Hannah (Sears) C.; he b. Mar. 27, 1778; d. West Sand., Aug. 25, 1866, æ. 87; they removed to West Sand., in 1818, settling on a farm in that part now known as Sagamore in the town of Bourne, and lived to see their children's children to the fifth generation, for their daughter Mary placed in their arms her gt.-gr.-dau., Mabel Ellis; children, CROWELL: [1.] Olive, b. Dec. 30, 1797 ; bap. Oct. 3, 1802 ; d. 1865 ; m. 1819, Capt. Phineas Swift, who was lost at sea, in sight of home, Nov. 23, 1863, æ. 65 yrs. 9 mo.; they had, i. Elisha, b. ——. ii. Sarah, b. ——; both of whom died young, leaving no descendants. [2.] Mary, b. Nov. 6, 1799 ; bap. Oct. 3, 1802; d. Oct. 12, 1870, æ. 70; she was brought up in the family of her grand-father, Edmund Sears, Jr., with whom she lived till the age of 18; m. Aug. 5, 1820, Capt. Pelham Gibbs of Sand., who d. Oct. 12, 1870, æ. 70 yrs. 11 mo.; had, i. Russel, b. Apr. 14, 1821. ii. Bradford, b. Mar. 15, 1824 ; d. Dec. 23, 1883. iii. Wil-

liam Crowell, b. Feb. 7, 1826. iv. Pelham Savery, b.
June 23, 1829. v. Paul Crowell, b. July 21, 1832.
vi. George Washington, b. Feb. 24, 1835. vii. Lafayette,
b. Nov. 7, 1837. viii. Mary Olive, b. Aug. 22, 1840; m.
L. R. Leavitt of Sagamore. ix. Prince Crowell, b. Apr.
11, 1843. [3.] Temperance, b. June 11, 1801; bap. Oct. 3,
1802; d. Aug. 17, 1868, æ. 67 yrs. 2 mos.; m. Thos. Swift;
had, i. Phebe S., b. May 19, 1818; d. Aug. 17, 1868.
ii. Mary Ann, b. Apr. 16, 1822. iii. Thos. C., b. Feb.
23, 1825; d. Apr. 8, 1883. iv. Seth F., b. Jan. 28, 1828.
v. Tempe C , b. Sep. 24, 1830. vi. Eliza E., b. Aug. 31,
1834. vii. Sarah D., b. Sep. 11, 1836. viii. Geo. W., b.
July 4, 1839. ix. Abbie P., b. Dec. 17, 1841. [4.] Edmund, b. Nov. 26, 1802; bap. Jan. 2, 1803; was lost at sea,
June 4, 1825; unm. [5.] Sally, b. Dec. 26, 1804; bap.
Feb. 15, 1805; d. Jan. 15, 1885; m. 1822, Capt. Wm.
Swift, he b. Sep. 22, 1795; d. Dec. 9, 1868, and had, i. Aurelia Parker, b. Feb. 22, 1823. ii. William, b. Dec. 26,
1824. iii. Noble Parker, b. Sep. 5, 1830. iv. Edmund,
b. June 20, 1826; was lost at sea, with two uncles Crowell, in gale of 1840, æ. 18. v. Adaline Appleton, b.
Sep. 29, 1832. v¹. Caroline Beal, b. Apr. 9, 1835; m.
May 5, 1853, Josiah B. Hallet, son of ——— and Susan
(Blossom) H., he b. Chatham, Mass.; she lives in Bridgeport, Ct., and had, Herbert Francis, b. Mar. 5, 1854; m. Nov.
24, 1885, Anna Ultzler of West Cornwall, Ct. Willard,
b. Jan. 20, 1859. George De Wayne, b. Jan. 5, 1866,
Carrie Adella, b. Sep. 10, 1867; d. May 4, 1871; and
Harrison H., b. July 1, 1873. vii. Nathaniel, b. June 29,
1837. viii. Gustavus Franklin, b. June 24, 1839. ix. Sarah Elizabeth, b. Oct. 17, 1841; d. Nov. 24, 1842. x. Edmund Sears, b. Sep. 26, 1844; d. Sep. 30, 1845. xi. Edwin Carlton, b. Aug. 5, 1847; d. Sep. 14, 1848.
xii. Edwin Carlton, b. Mar. 13, 1849. [6.] Paul, b. Nov. 11,
1806; bap. Dec. 14; d. Oct. 13, 1870, æ. 63 yrs. 10 mos.; m.
June 19, 1833, Lydia Ellis, and had, i. Hannah Rebecca, b.
July 4, 1834. ii. Lydia E., b. June 28, 1837. iii. Hiram
E., b. May 5, 1839. iv. Thomas P., b. May 18, 1845; d.
Nov. 17, 1870. v. Emma H., b. Sep. 7, 1846; d. Feb. 7,
1849. [7.] William, b. Nov. 26, 1808; lost at sea, June
4, 1825; unm. [8.] Hannah, b. Oct. 22, 1810; d.; m.
Wm. Bent, and had, i. Hannah Maria, b. ———. ii. Nathan, b. ———; d. young in California. iii. Phebe, b. ———.
[9.] Prince, b. Dec. 3, 1812; was lost at sea, Mar. 24,

1840; m. Betsy Sears, but had no issue. [10.] Priscilla
S., b. Feb., 1815; d. Aug. 3, 1880; m. Elisha Ellis, and
had, i. Priscilla, b. ——; d. ii. Elisha Winslow, b. ——.
iii. Priscilla, b. ——. iv. Nathan Prince, b. ——; lives
in Lynn, Mass. v. Edmund Crowell, b. ——. vi. Thomas,
b. ——; lives in Sagamore. vii. Sarah, b. ——. viii. Benj.
F., b. ——; lives in Waltham, Mass. [11.] Nathan, b.
Feb. 24, 1817; lost at sea, Mar. 24, 1840; unm. [12.] Zenas, b. May 20, 1819; d. Stockton, Cal., Mar., 1876; m.
Susan Heath, and had, i. Alfred D., b. ——. ii. Susan Adelaide, b. ——; d. in Cal. iii. Susan, b. ——. [13.] Lydia,
b. June 19, 1821; d. June 21, 1821. [14.] Hiram, b. Aug.
7, 1822; m. July 11, 1850, Eliza Ellis; 2d, Dec. 1, 1857,
Hepsibah Harlow; 3d, July 22, 1866, Mrs. Martha Per-
kins; he had a dau., d. inf. [15.] Calvin, b. Aug. 27, 1824;
m. Apr. 23, 1857, Laura A. Swift, and had, i. Walter L., b.
May 31, 1858. ii. Emma F., b. Apr. 12, 1863; d. Jan. 11,
1867. iii. Annie F., b. Feb. 4, 1866. iv. Frank C., b.
Aug. 10, 1869. v. Ada L., b. Oct. 5, 1873. vi. Bertha
M., b. Nov. 22, 1879; d. Mar. 18, 1881. vii. Maybelle
E., b. June 28, 1882.

589. vi. ZERVIAH, b. Yar., Aug. 7, 1782; bap. Sep. 8; d. Dec.
20, 1867, æ. 85 yrs. 5 mos.; m. Den., Oct. 20, 1803, *Reuben Howes*, who d. on board brig "Two Brothers," on the
passage from Charleston to Cadiz, Aug. 10, 1815; children, HOWES: [1.] Daniel, b. June 23, 1804; d. at sea,
June 20, 1843, on schr. "Ontisie;" m. Aug. 19, 1830,
Mercie Lincoln Howes, and had, i. Reuben, b. Feb. 23,
1832; m. Dec. 23, 1857, Margaret Brown. ii. Dan'l
Willis, b. Feb. 23, 1835; m. Dec. 2, 1862, Abbie J. Nye.
iii. Mercie Caroline, b. Aug. 12, 1842; m. Aug. 11, 1863,
Henry Howes. [2.] Paulina, b. Feb. 4, 1809; lives in
Dennis; m. Mar. 13, 1834, Edward Hall, and had, i. Paulina Howes, b. June 22, 1835; d. Feb. 13, 1859; m. Jan.
4, 1856, Henry Howes. ii. Edward Freeman, b. Mar. 29,
1842; m. Feb. 6, 1868, Martha A. Layman. iii. Joel
Brainard, b. Oct. 28, 1846; m. Feb. 8, 1870, Lucy F.
Howes. iv. Zerviah S. H., b. May 9, 1853; d. Feb. 4,
1854. [3.] Reuben, b. Dec. 17, 1810; d. July 14, 1827,
æ. 16 yrs. 7 mos.

590. vii. MOLLY ATWOOD, b. Yar., June 3, 1785; bap. July
3; d. Den., Jan. 26, 1840, æ. 55; m. *Zenas Howes;* children, HOWES: [1.] Mary, b. Mar. 6, 1807; m. Hollis
DeWitt. [2.] Caroline, b. July 4, 1809; d. Apr. 26,

19

1850. [3.] Zenas, b. Aug. 3, 1811; m. Olive Hall. [4.] Seth,
b. June 15, 1814; m. Lydia Howes. [5.] Laban, b. June
18, 1818; m. Persis Howes. [6.] Larosia, b. June 9, 1820;
m. 1st, Paul Earl; 2d, Barnabas Crocker; 3d, Stephen
Atkins; and 4th, Wm. Oliver.

591. viii. HANNAH, b. Yar., June 24, 1787; bap. July 22; d.
Den., Dec. 22, 1877, æ. 90; m. *Abner Howes;* children,
HOWES: [1.] Edmund Sears, b. Dec. 3, 1809; d. Nov. 4,
1812. [2.] Harriet, b. June 7, 1812; m. Heman Howes.
[3.] Hannah Sears, b. Jan. 11, 1815; m. Peter Howes.
[4.] Clarissa, b. Dec. 24, 1818; m. Henry Nickerson.
[5.] Abner, b. June 13, 1821; m. Eliz'h Day. [6.] Priscilla, b. Feb. 22, 1826; m. Joshua C. Howes. [7.] Alfred, b. Feb. 16, 1828; m. Eliza Wright. [8.] Abigail,
b. Sep. 25, 1830; m. Lemuel Hall.

592. ix. PRISCILLA, b. Yar., Apr. 9, 1790; bap. May 23; d.
Feb. 28, 1826, æ. 36; she was adm. to Ch., Den., May 9,
1819; m. *Moses Howes;* children, HOWES: [1.] Albert,
b. Feb. 4, 1811; m. 1st, Huldah Gorham; 2d, Joanna
Howes. [2.] Carlton, b. Sep. 6, 1812; m. Eunice C. Paddock. [3.] Zerviah Sears, b. Jan. 1, 1816; m. John Howes,
2d, Obed Howes. [4.] Moses, b. Sep. 18, 1817; m. Jerusha S. Hall.

593.* x. EDMUND, b. Yar., Apr. 8, 1792; bap. June 10.

594. xi. LYDIA, b. Yar., Nov. 13, 1794; d. Den., Feb. 25,
1848, æ. 53; m. June 2, 1817, *Nathan Howes;* children,
HOWES: [1.] Lydia, b. July 2, 1818; m. Benj. Dillingham. [2.] Nathan, b. May 20, 1820; d. July 9, 1820.
[3.] Nathan, b. Sep. 18, 1821; d. May 10, 1822. [4.] Harriet Newell, b. July 24, 1823; m. 1st, Anson Ellis; 2d,
Lewis Howes; 3d, Nathan Swift. [5.] Silas, b. Dec. 26,
1825; m. Priscilla Lord. [6.] Hannah, b. Jan. 6, 1828;
m. Joseph Sylvan. [7.] Phebe, b. Mar. 14, 1830; m.
Frank N. Parker. [8.] Olive Sears, b. Feb. 26, 1832; d.
Apr. 13, 1832. [9.] Joseph, b. Apr. 3, 1833; m. Abby
Sears Hedge. [10.] Benjamin Perkins, b. Oct. 16, 1835;
m. Lucy Lord. [11.] Charles Wesley, b. May 29, 1839;
d. Jan. 1, 1840.

Edmund Sears was admitted to the Ch., Dennis, July 24,
1809.

He was a soldier in Lieut. Micajah Sears' company, and on
the alarm at Dartmouth and Falmouth, Sep. 6, 1778, marched
and did 13 days' service.

His will, dated 1820, was proved 1832, and mentions wife,

Hannah; children, Sally Crowell, Zerviah Howes, Molly A. Howes, Hannah Howes, Priscilla Howes, Edmund, Jacob, Judah and Paul Sears.

220.

JOSHUA SEARS[5] [*Edm'd*[4], *Paul*[3], *Paul*[2], *Rich.*[1]], b. Yarmouth, Mass., July 1, 1753; d. Mar. 31, 1825, in 73 yr., gr.-st., W. Br.; m. Harwich, May 28, 1778, *Sarah Sears*, No. 385, dau. of Prince Sears; she b. Dec., 1759; adm. to Ch., E. Yar., Aug. 3, 1788; d. Jan. 13, 1792, æ. 32, gr.-st. He m. 2d, (pub. Har., Dec. 1, 1792,) *Olive Clark*, dau. of Reuben and Jerusha (Freeman) C.; she b. Feb. 15, 1765; d. Dec. 14, 1817, in 53 yr., gr.-st. Children:

By *Sarah:*
595.   i. BETSY, b. Har., Dec. 9, 1778; d. Oct. 5, 1787, in 9 yr., gr.-st., W. Br.
596.   ii. JOSHUA, b. Har., May 18, 1781; bap. E. Yar., Aug. 10, 1788; was master of a schooner, and lost at sea, Sep. 3, 1803, on passage from Straits Belle Isle, gr.-st., No. Den.
597.   iii. REBECCA, b. Yar., July 29, 1783; bap. Aug. 10, 1788; m. (pub. Yar., Jan. 11, 1801), *Leverett Gray*, and removed to Thomaston, Me.
598.   iv. LOT, b. Yar., Oct. 15, 1785; bap. Aug. 10, 1788; was mate with his bro. Joshua, and lost at sea, Sep. 3, 1803, gr.-st, No. Den.
599*   v. EZRA, b. Yar., Mar. 31, 1789; bap. May 3.
600.   vi. BETSY, b. Yar., July 15, 1791; bap. Aug. 7; d. inf.
By *Olive:*
601.   vii. SALLY, b. Dennis, Oct. 8, 1793; m. Jan. 1, 1815, *Zoheth Howes*, son of Joseph and Hannah (Hopkins) H., he b. Aug. 1, 1789; d. Feb. 28, 1832; she d. May 28, 1836; children, HOWES: [1.] Calvin A., b. Jan. 28, 1816; lost at sea, Dec. 21, 1831. [2.] Olive Clark, b. Dec. 26, 1817; m. Mar. 3, 1836, Elisha Crowell, he b. Sep. 3, 1813, residences Dennis, and Brooklyn, N. Y.; had, i. Calvin S., b. Jan. 3, 1838. ii. Olive A., b. Mar. 31, 1842. iii. Elisha F., b. Jan. 22, 1849; d. Mar. 2, 1854. iv. Son, b. Feb. 28, 1851; d. Mar. 21. v. Ella F., b. Jan. 22, 1855. vi. Elisha F., b. Sep. 25, 1857. [3.] Abby, b. Nov. 17, 1819; m. Dec. 17, 1839, Calvin Howes; and d. Den., Jan. 5, 1844; had, i. Calvin C., b. Jan., 1840; lives Binney, Montana. [4.] Sarah, b. Oct. 9, 1821; m. Jan. 20, 1844, Wm.

Crowell. [5.] Joel, b. Oct. 15, 1823; m. Jan. 7, 1847, Isabel Hall; and d. Nov., 1847. [6.] Rhòda, b. Nov. 21, 1825; m. June 16, 1846, Isaiah Crowell; and d. Aug. 8, 1850. [7.] Zoheth, b. Dec. 10, 1827; m. Jan., 1851, Mrs. Joan H. Hall, née Crowell, she b. Feb. 26, 1852; had, i. Joan H. C., b. Dec. 21, 1851. [8.] Henry, b. Aug. 17, 1829; m. Jan., 1856, Lucy P. Burgess, she b. Sep. 24, 1835; and had, i. Zoeth, b. Aug. 11, 1861. ii. Mary, b. July 23, 1862. iii. Charles F., b. Mar. 1, 1864; d. Feb., 1866. iv. Lewis J., b. Oct. 26, 1868. v. Olive C., b. Nov. 11, 1870.

602.* viii. GEORGE, b. Den., Sep. 8, 1795; bap. Oct. 18.

603. ix. ABIGAIL, b. Den., Mar. 25, 1797; bap. May 8; m. July 11, 1820, *John Hedge*, school-master, he b. Aug. 16, 1797; d. Nov. 30, 1871; children, HEDGE: [1.] Silas L., b. Sep. 20, 1821; d. July 11, 1834. [2.] Mehitable, b. Aug. 9, 1823; d. Aug. 31, 1825. [3.] Milton P., b. Aug. 15, 1825; m. Aug. 15, 1848, Elizabeth Lowe Sears, No. 1770, dau. of Zachariah and Olive S., she b. Nov. 9, 1828; lives in E. Den.; had, i. Milton Lee, b. Mar. 6, 1855; d. young. ii. John M., b. Aug. 3, 1857; m. Dec. 6, 1879, Hattie Phelps, she b. Dec. 6, 1861; — is a lumber dealer at Clear Creek, Nebraska. iii. Joseph, b. Jan. 27, 1860; m. Aug. 22, 1882, Julia Smalley, she b. Sep., 1861; runs a sheep ranch in Cambridge, Kansas. iv. George Sears, b. July 4, 1865. [4.] Lucy L., b. Jan. 11, 1828; m. Mar. 14, 1850, Sylvanus Sears, No. 1407, of Worcester, Mass. [5.] Mehitable, b. Aug. 22, 1830; d. Nov. 30, 1869. [6.] Susan G., b. Feb. 18, 1833; m. Nov. 29, 1855, Isaiah B. Hall, he b. Oct. 12, 1828; lives in Dennis; had, i. Chloe C., b. Apr. 22, 1858. ii. Susan E., b. Sep. 29, 1861. iii. Emma G., b. July 27, 1868. iv. Child. [7.] Abby S., b. Jan. 23, 1836; m. May 1, 1855, Joseph Howes, a farmer; he b. Apr. 3, 1833; d. Den., Apr. 15, 1878; had, i. Nathan A., b. Apr. 26, 1857. ii. John S., b. Mar. 19, 1859; d. Feb. 18, 1868. iii. Lydia A., b. Sep. 23, 1861. iv. Lizzie L., b. Feb. 9, 1865. v. Lucie J., b. Sep. 2, 1872. vi. Hettie H., b. Nov. 2, 1874. [8.] John S., b. Jan. 10, 1838; lost at sea, 1856. [9.] Daniel, b. Nov. 5, 1839; m. Sep. 8, 1864, Abby M. Crowell, she b. Sep. 10, 1838; he commands str. "Gate City," Boston to Savannah, and lives in Den.; had, i. Anna C., b. Nov. 1, 1868; d. Feb. 13, 1878. ii. Howard C., b. Dec. 22, 1879. iii. Child. [10.] George S., b. Nov. 26, 1842; d. Feb. 28, 1865.

604. x. CLARISSA, b. Den., Apr. 1, 1799; bap. May 5; m. Nov. 30, 1822, *Peter Hall*, a farmer, he b. Feb. 12, 1799; d. July 20, 1861; she d. Sep. 2, 1834; children, HALL: [1.] Achsah H., b. Sep. 17, 1821; m. Apr. 25, 1844, Franklin Nye of Sandwich, Mass., and had, i. Clarissa Sears, b. Aug. 30, 1845. ii. Rebecca, b. July 1, 1848; d. Sep. 3, 1861. [2.] Olive Sears, b. Apr. 8, 1823; d. Aug. 26, 1825. [3.] Elizabeth, b. Dec. 26, 1824; d. Aug. 28, 1851. [4.] Clarissa Sears, b. July 30, 1830; m. Jan. 20, 1853, Capt. Josiah Nickerson, he b. Sep. 8, 1825; ship and insurance broker in Portland, Me.; and had, i. Peter Hall, b. Oct. 28, 1854; d. Aug. 5, 1856. ii. Peter Sears, b. Sep. 15, 1856; m. Ella F. Nash. iii. George Arthur, b. Feb. 18, 1862; d. July 14, 1870.

605. xi. REUBEN CLARKE, b. Den., Oct. 10, 1800; bap. Jan. 11, 1801; d. Jan. 5, 1829, æ. 28, gr.-st., W. Br.

606. xii. CALVIN, b. Den., Jan. 29, 1803; bap. Mar. 20; d. Apr. 12, 1806, gr.-st., No. Den.

607. xiii. OLIVE, b. Den., Sep. 7, 1805; bap. Oct. 20; scalded to death, Nov. 1, 1810, gr.-st., No. Den.

Joshua Sears was, when young, a seaman, and later a farmer; served in Lt. Micajah Sears' Co., Sep. 6, 1778, on alarm at Dartmouth and Falmouth; and shipped in ship "General Putnam," Capt. Daniel Waters, for naval service, July 12, 1779, at £2 per mo.; was taken prisoner and committed to Forton Prison, England, and imprisoned several years, during which he had the small-pox, from which and other hardships he nearly died.

He was an active member of the church in Dennis.

His will, dated Sep. 3, 1824, and proved 1825, names children: Ezra, George, Reuben C., Rebecca Gray, wife of Leverett G.; Sarah, wife of Zoeth Howes; Nabby, wife of John Hedge; and Clarissa, wife of Peter Hall.

221.

CHRISTOPHER SEARS[5] [*Edm'd*[4], *Paul*[3], *Paul*[2], *Rich.*[1]], b. Yarmouth, Mass., Aug. 16, 1756; d. Feb., 1809, æ. 53; m. *Deborah Manter* of Martha's Vineyard; and 2d, Harwich, Mar. 13, 1788, *Mary Snow* of Har., who was adm. to Ch., Dennis, Aug. 2, 1795. Children:

By *Deborah* :

608. i. DEBORAH-MANTER, b. Yar., Aug. 30, 1785; m. Brewster, Jan. 1, 1804, *Isaiah Clark*, son of Kimbal C., he b.

Nov. 30, 1777; d. July 29, 1838; she d. Aug. 27, 1838; children, Clark: [1.] Isaiah, b. Oct. 6, 1805; d. May 28, 1810. [2.] William, b. Feb. 27, 1808; m. July 5, 1831, Lydia F. Crosby, she b. Sep. 25, 1810, and had, i. Deborah M., b. Oct. 9, 1832; m. Barnabas Sears, No. 3257. ii. Wm. Henry, b. July 12, 1839; d. at sea, Jan. 25, 1883. iii. Lydia Francis, b. July 19, 1844; d. July 4, 1847. iv. Henrietta C., b. Oct. 23, 1847; d. July 21, 1856. [3.] Isaiah, b. July 28, 1811; d. July 10, 1835, Indian Key, Fla. [4.] Jeremiah Manter, b. July 6, 1814; m. Oct. 20, 1836, Margaret Thayer, she b. Nov. 14, 1810; he was a farmer, went to California, and on his return died of cholera on board of brig "Wm. Penn," Nov. 5, 1850, and was buried at sea; had, i. Phebe, b. Oct. 20, 1838. ii. Margaret A., b. Mar. 15, 1840. iii. George Albert, b. Aug. 16, 1849. [5.] Isaac, b. Sep. 12, 1818; m. Jan. 12, 1843, Mary Ann Weld, who d. Aug. 18, 1866; 2d, Eliza Jane Brintnall; lives 46 Madison st., Prov., R. I.; had, i. Mary Louisa, b. Mar. 4, 1845; d. Dec. 26, 1863. ii. Rosa Ferrin, b. Apr. 12, 1849; d. Apr. 27, 1867. iii. Isaac Henry, b. Apr. 19, 1852; m. 1873, Lillian E. Cornell. iv. Rosa Etta, b. May 24, 1871.

By *Mary:*

609.   ii. Christopher, b. Yar., Jan. 21, 1789; bap. Den., Oct. 18, 1795; lost at sea, Aug., 1816.

610.   iii. Polly, b. Yar., Feb. 6, 1790; bap. Den., Oct. 18, 1795.

611.*   iv. William, b. Yar., July 9, 1791; bap. Den., Oct. 18, 1795.

612.   v. Nancy, b. Den., Nov. 9, 1794; m. Har., Nov. 6, 1814, *Reuben Sears*, No. 660.

613.   vi. Eunice, b. Den., Aug. 16, 1796; bap. Sep. 25; m. Nov. 28, 1816, *Alexander Robbins.*

614.   vii. Elizabeth, b. Den., Apr. 26, 1799; bap. June 23; joined the Shakers at Harvard.

615.   viii. Lucinda, b. Den., May 10, 1801; bap. Aug. 16.

616.   ix. Lot, b. Den., Aug. 31, 1805; bap. Feb. 23, 1806; d. unm., Dec. 26, 1829, gr.-st., Br.

Was a Revolutionary soldier, and served from Jan. 27 to Nov. 21, 1776, in Capt. Elisha Nye's Co., at Elizabeth Islands; and in Capt. Micah Chapman's Co., Lt. Micajah Sears, on alarm at Dartmouth and Falmouth, Sep., 1778; 3 days' service.

222.

ELKANAH SEARS[5] [*Edm'd*[4], *Paul*[3], *Paul*[2], *Rich.*[1]], b. Yarmouth, Mass., Oct. 22, 1758; d. Dennis, Mass., June 1, 1836, æ. 78, gr.-st., W. Br.; m. Yar., Jan. 10, 1788, Mercy Bray, dau. of William B., she b. Yar., Apr. 7, 1763; bap. Oct. 21, 1792; and d. July 9, 1846, æ. 83, gr.-st.   Children :

617.   i. SARAH, b. Yar., Nov. 20, 1788; bap. Nov. 11, 1792; m. May 10, 1805, *Peter Baker* of So. Den., and d. Apr. 29, 1878.

618.   ii. TEMPERANCE, b. Yar., Nov. 28, 1790; bap. Nov. 11, 1792; m. Oct. 29, 1829, *Ezekiel Hallet* of Yar., and d. Mar. 1, 1859.

619.   iii. SUSAN, b. Den., Apr. 27, 1794; d. unm., June 2, 1857, æ. 63, gr.-st.

620.   iv. LUCY, b. Den., May 29, 1797; bap. July 2; m. Dec., 1816, *Ezekiel Thacher* of Barnstable, and d. Nov. 27, 1852.

621.* v. ELKANAH, b. Den., Feb. 16, 1800; bap. Apr. 3.

622.* vi. THOMAS, b. Den., Feb. 16, 1800, *gemini;* bap. Apr. 3.

623.*vii. WILLIAM, b. Den., Apr. 4, 1808.

Elkanah Sears lived in the east precinct of Yarmouth, now East Dennis.

Was a soldier in Lt. Micajah Sears' Co., and marched on alarm at Dartmouth and Falmouth, Sep. 6, 1778; was on duty 3 days.

In the fall of 1819, Elkanah Sears with his son William, set out some cranberry vines at Flax pond (now called Scargo lake), in E. Dennis, and was the pioneer in the large and profitable business of cranberry raising.

Some years later Henry Hall of Dennis, having a marshy lot which produced some very fine berries, was led to follow the experiment of transplanting some of the vines to another portion of the same swamp, and the experiment proving a success, he and others continued their efforts in the same direction. But it took years of careful study, and laborious and costly experiment to ascertain the processes, soil and conditions necessary to success.

In 1888, the shipments of cranberries from Cape Cod were 80,128 barrels and 13,463 boxes.

In 1677, to appease the wrath of Charles II, who was angry with Massachusetts Colony for coining "pine-tree shillings," the General Court ordered a present to be sent him of "ten barrels of cranberries, two hogsheads of samp, and three thousand codfish," luxuries which it was thought would soften the ire of an angry monarch.

228.

ELISHA SEARS[5] [*Elisha[4], John[3], Paul[2], Rich.[1]*], b. Yarmouth, Mass., Sep. 26, 1741; d. of old age, East Dennis, Mass., Dec. 5, 1822, æ. 81, gr.-st., W. Br.; m. Harwich, Sep. 7, 1794, *Thankful Snow*, dau. of Thos. S., of H., who d. E. Den., Dec. 10, 1811, in 44 yr., gr.-st. (1810, æ. 48, Fam. Rec.) Children:

624.*   i. ELISHA, b. E. Den., Aug. 25, 1795; bap. Oct. 18.
625.   ii. EPHRAIM, bap. E. Den., Mar. 26, 1797.
626.   iii. BETHIA, b. E. Den., Nov. 27, 1799; bap. Jan. 12, 1800; m. *Philander Sears*, No. 662, of Worcester, Mass.
627.* iv. CONSTANT, b. E. Den., July 26, 1802; bap. Aug. 29.
628.   v. THOMAS SNOW, b. E. Den., Dec. 10, 1810; lost at sea, 1834.

229.

Capt. JOHN SEARS[5] [*Elisha[4], John[3], Paul[2], Rich.[1]*], b. Yarmouth, Mass., May 30, 1743; adm. Ch., Den., June 21, 1801; d. East Dennis, Aug. 24, 1812, in 68 yr., gr.-st, W. Br.; m. Yar., Dec. 14, 1780, *Mehitable Sears*, No. 315, dau. of Lieut. Zachariah and Mehitable (Crowell) S.; she b. Sep. 2, 1750; adm. to Ch., Den., May 16, 1798, "in private;" and d. May 19, æ. 48, gr.-st., W. Br.; 2d, Den., Oct. 7, 1800, *Kezia Howes;* she b. Den., 1770; adm. Ch., Den., June 21, 1801; d. Sep. 4, 1827, æ. 57, gr.-st. Child:

By *Kezia:*
629.   i. MEHITABLE, b. Den., Sep. 8, 1801; bap. Nov. 15.

232.

NOAH SEARS[5] [*Elisha[4], John[3], Paul[2], Rich.[1]*], b. Yarmouth, Mass., Apr. 11, 1751; d. Sep. 23, 1835, in 85 yr., gr.-st., W. Br.; m. Yar., 1794 (pub. Feb. 8), *Desire Merrill* of Den., who was adm. to Ch., Den., Sep. 14, 1794; d. Sep. 28, 1828, in 62 yr., gr.-st. Children:

630.   i. SARAH, b. Brewster, Mar. 2, 1806; bap. Den., May 3; d. June 23, 1834, in 29 yr., gr.-st., W. Br.

631.   ii. NOAH, b. Br., Apr. 10, 1808 ; d. Aug. 25, 1828, in
     21 yr., gr.-st.
632.* iii. SAMUEL RIPLEY, b. Br., Nov. 3, 1810.

He was in Lieut. Micajah Sears' company, and served 3 days,
alarm Dartmouth, Sep. 6, 1778.

237.

Capt. JOHN SEARS[5] [*John*[4], *John*[3], *Paul*[2], *Rich.*[1]], b.
Yar., Mass., July 20, 1744; d. Dennis, June 9, 1817, of consumption ; m. Yar., Dec. 26, 1771, *Phebe Sears*, No. 213, dau.
of Daniel S., she b. Yar., Mar. 31, 1747; d. Jan., 1818. Children :

633.   i. OLIVE, b. Yar., Dec. 8, 1772 ; m. Aug. 9, 1794,
     Capt. *Zoeth Berry* of Brewster.
634.   ii. DEBORAH, b. Yar., Sep. 19, 1774.
635.   iii. DANIEL, b. Yar., Apr. 19, 1777; d. at sea, 1797.
636.*   iv. HEMAN, b. Yar., Apr. 10, 1780.
637.   v. JERUSHA, b. Yar., Nov. 27, 1781·
638.*   vi. ENOS, b. Yar., Oct. 10, 1783.
639.   vii. LAVINIA, b. Yar., Sep. 6, 1785.
640.* viii. MOODY, b. Yar., Nov. 19, 1788.
641.   ix. FANNY, b. Yar., Apr. 28, 1791.

Capt. John Sears will long be remembered on Cape Cod in
connection with his invention of the process of making salt by
solar evaporation.

In 1776, he constructed a vat, one hundred feet long, and
ten feet wide. Rafters were fixed over it, and shutters were
contrived to move up and down, that the vat might be covered
when it rained, and exposed to the sun in fair weather. But
the works were leaky, and the first year he obtained but eight
bushels of salt.

He was ridiculed by his neighbors, and his invention was
styled, "Sears' Folly."

Capt. Sears persevered, the works were made tight, and the
second year thirty bushels of salt were obtained.

In this and the third year the salt water was poured into the
vat from buckets ; a tedious and laborious operation.

In the fourth year he rigged a pump, procured from the
wreck of the British man-of-war "Somerset," which had been
cast away upon the Cape ; it was worked by hand, which was
still great labor.

20

In 1785, at the suggestion of Maj. Nathl. Freeman of Harwich, Capt. Sears contrived a pump to be worked by wind, thus greatly abridging the labor.

Covers to move on rollers were invented by Reuben Sears, a carpenter of Harwich ; and Capt. Sears was further assisted in the improvement of the works by Capt. Wm. Crowell, Capt. Christopher Crowell and Capt. Edward Sears of Dennis.

These persons assigning to him their right and title in the invention, he applied for a patent, which he obtained in 1799.

Incidentally to this industry, the manufacture of Glauber Salts, once much used in medicine, became an important branch of the business.

Rev. Ephraim Briggs of Chatham, a skillful chemist, greatly improved the process of manufacture.

The salt business was for many years one of great value and importance to Barnstable county.

In 1832 there were in the county 1,425,000 feet of vats, producing 358,250 bushels, but in 1834 the industry was checked by the reduction of the duty.

The development of the Salt Springs in New York and elsewhere served to make the business unprofitable, and there are now (1887) few works standing and in operation.

Like many other inventive geniuses, Capt. Sears had fits of abstraction, and his neighbors gave him the nickname of "Sleepy John," which he held till the success of his invention caused it to be displaced by that of "Salt John."

He once undertook to build an Orrery, and rigged up an old cart-wheel, to the spokes of which he affixed his planets. This was hung up over the door of his shop, in which he used to fasten himself while at work on his hobbies.

One day his wife wishing to enter the shop forced the door, when the contrivance fell upon her, injuring her severely.

When asked what was the matter with her, a neighbor said: "John Sears' earth fell upon her."

He was in Lt. Micajah Sears' Co., and served 3 days from Sep. 6, 1778, on alarm at Dartmouth and Falmouth ; and as Sergeant in Capt. Elisha Hedges' Co., in Col. Freeman's Regt., Sep. 13 to 18, 1778 ; 52 miles' travel.

249.

SETH SEARS[5] [*John*[4], *John*[3], *Paul*[2], *Rich.*[1]], b. Yarmouth, Mass., Dec. 8, 1767 ; d. East Dennis, Mar. 5, 1806, in 36 yr., gr.-st., W. Br. ; m. Yar., Nov. 29, 1792, *Hephsibah Hall*, who

d. June 9, 1793, in 22 yr., gr.-st.; 2d, Eastham, Jan. 1, 1795, *Sarah Hurd* of Orleans, who d. Sep. 29, 1812, æ. 40, gr.-st. Children:

By *Hephsibah :*

642. i. LUTHER, bap. Oct. 23, 1803; m. Orleans, Oct. 16, 1831, *Ruth G. Hurd*, and rem. to Illinois.

643. ii. MARK, bap. Apr. 7, 1805 ; was lost at sea.

By *Sally :*

644. iii. HEPSIBAH, b. Den., Oct. 6, 1795 ; bap. Nov. 8; m. Nov. 1, 1814, by Rev. Mr. Johnson of Orleans, to *Solomon Hurd ;* and d. Brewster, Apr. 10, 1870, æ. 75. In the will of her gr.-mother, Priscilla Sears, dated Jan. 7, 1815, she is called " Hepsibeth *Gibson*."

645. iv. PHEBE, b. Den., Feb. 14, 1797 ; bap. Mar. 26.

646. v. PRISCILLA, b. Den., Sep. 13, 1798; bap. Oct. 14; a Priscilla Sears m. Capt. *Edward Hall*, Jan. 14, 1819.

647. vi. SETH, b. Den., Apr. 12, 1800 ; bap. May 18 ; d. Mar. 11, 1808, gr.-st.

648. vii. BELINDA, bap. Mar. 28, 1802 ; was living in 1815.

251.

EDWARD SEARS[5] [*Willard[4], John[3], Paul[2], Rich.[1]*], b. Harwich, Mass., Oct. 22, 1746 ; d. Sep. 14, 1807, æ. 61, gr.-st., W. Br. ; m. Har., Jan. 4, 1789, *Bethia Sears*, No. 246, dau. of Dea. John Sears of Yar., she b. Mar. 10, 1761 ; was adm. to Ch., E. Yar., Jan. 10, 1790 ; and d. Nov. 10, 1842, æ. 81, gr.-st.   Children :

649.   i. EDWARD, b. Har., Mar. 30, 1790; bap. E. Yar., May 30; lost at sea in 1804.

650.   ii. SAMUEL, b. Har., Aug. 5, 1791 ; bap. E. Yar., Oct. 2; d. unm., Jan. 29, 1855, æ. 63, gr.-st.

651.   iii. TAMSEN, b. Har. ; bap. E. Yar., Mar. 10, 1793 ; m. *Zebina Howes*, son of Thos. and Jerusha (Howes) H., he b. Mar. 22, 1792, and had, Edward, who lived in Chelsea and Worcester, and others.

652.   iv. BETHIA.

653.* v. JOHN, b. Har., Dec. 31, 1794; bap. Den., May 10, 1795.

654.   vi. SUSANNA, b. Har., 1797; bap. Den., May 14, 1797 ; d. Feb. 8, 1800, æ. 3 yrs., gr.-st.

655. vii. VIENNA, b. Har., May 28, 1799 ; bap. Den., July 7; d. June 27, 1880, æ. 81, gr.-st. ; she never married, but

lived until her death in the old homestead in West Brewster, purchased by her grand-father, Willard Sears, of Joshua Sears, it being then in Harwich.

On alarm at Dartmouth and Falmouth, Sep., 1778, he marched in Lt. Crowell's Co., Col. Nathl. Freeman's Regt., and did 13 days' service.

255.

REUBEN SEARS[5] [*Will'd*[4], *John*[3], *Paul*[2], *Rich.*[1]], b. Harwich, Mass., Sep. 25, 1753; d. Brewster, Nov. 4, 1844, æ. 91, gr.-st., W. Br.; m. Har., Dec. 13, 1781, *Rhoda Mayo*, who d. Apr. 16, 1784, in 28 yr., gr.-st., W. Br.; 2d (pub. Har., Mar. 12, 1785,) *Abigail Vincent*, who d. Apr. 24, 1828, æ. 69, gr.-st. Children:

By *Rhoda*:
656.   i. Mary, b. Har., Nov. 6, 1782; m. Br., Nov. 5, 1805, *Amos Kelley.*
657.   ii. Rhoda, b. Har., Apr. 5, 1784; d. 1820.

By *Abigail*:
658. iii. Willard, b. Har., Jan. 6, 1786; d. at sea, Jan. 25, 1805.
659.   iv. David, b. Har., July 23, 1788; d. Sep., 1806.
660.* v. Reuben, b. Har., July 29, 1791.
661.   vi. Abigail, b. Har., Aug. 9, 1793; m. *Heman Sears*, No. 636.
662.* vii. Philander, b. Har., Dec. 29, 1795; bap. Feb. 16, 1796.
663.* viii. Thomas, b. Har., Dec. 11, 1797; bap. Feb. 4, 1798.
664.   ix. Joanna, b. Har., Oct. 14, 1799; d. Nov. 16, 1800.
665.* x. Orin, b. Har., Sep. 9, 1802.
666.   xi. Rosanna, b. Br., May 15, 1805; bap. June 16; m. Jan. 5, 1829, *Dean Sears*, No. 1317.

Reuben Sears lived in that part of Harwich, now West Brewster.

Was chosen Surveyor of Highways, 1786.

He was a carpenter and salt-works builder, and was of great assistance to Capt. John Sears in carrying out his invention of salt-pans and covers.

He built for ——, the house in Brewster, in which he afterward lived; the thumb-latch on the front door bears the date of 1770.

He is said to have reported at Plymouth, for duty during the Revolutionary war, "walking the distance, 40 miles, in one day, carrying his gun and equipments, and a bushel of corn in a sack;" was in Capt. Benj. Berry's Co. on alarm Bedford and Falmouth, Sep. 7, 1778, 7 days' service, 112 miles' travel.

He was a staunch member of the old church, and when Rev. Mr. Simpkins promulgated his Unitarian doctrines, he demurred, and said, "if that be your doctrine, I worship here no longer," and turning to his children, bade them gather up his books and cushions, and left the church to return no more.

Late in life his daughter Abigail induced him to be baptized by immersion, and he was, with others, admitted into fellowship with the church at the water's edge; not understanding the proceeding, he did not consider himself a member at first, and soon after, not liking the doctrines of close fellowship, etc., left and went to the Methodists.

His death was sudden and unexpected.

He had been working in his garden, on an Easterly day, and in the evening, complaining of feeling unwell, he had his bed removed into the parlor. His daughter went for some hot water to warm his feet, which he said were cold; but before she returned, he was dead.

He was a very estimable man, and his brother Ebenezer was wont to say, "Reuben is a saint on earth."

256.

Capt. EBENEZER SEARS[5] [*Will'd[4], John[3], Paul[2], Rich.[1]*], b. Harwich, Mass., Oct. 11, 1755; d. Yarmouth, Sep. 17 (20 T. Clk.), 1835, æ. 80; m. Yar., Feb. 2, 1786, *Hannah Gray;* she b. Yar.; d. Feb. 18, 1817 (Feb. 19, 1816, T. Clk.). Children:

667. i. EBÉNEZER, b. Yar., June 19, 1787; d. Sep. 13, 1789.
668.* ii. CHARLES, b. Yar., July 31, 1789.
669.* iii. JOSHUA, b. Yar., Aug. 20, 1791.
670.* iv. WILLARD, b. Yar., Apr. 2, 1794.
671. v. SUSANNA.
672. vi. LUCY, b. Yar., Mar. 22, 1798; m. Yar., Mar. 4, 1819, Capt. *Isaac Myrick;* he b. Har., Feb. 23, 1796; d. June 3, 1869; she d. May 24, 1872; children, MYRICK: [1.] George, m. Carrie Whitney, and d. Dec. 26, 1877, æ. 42; was on staff of Gen. Foster during the Rebellion, and later of firm Hitchcock, Myrick & Co., wholesale grocers

in Boston; had, i. Whitney; d. Dec. 1, 1882, æ. 11.
[2.] Isaac. [3.] Mary Jane. [4.] Clara; m. Winthrop
Sears, No. 1568. [5.] Lucy.

673.   vii. Hannah, b. Yar., May 26, 1800; m. Yar., Oct.,
1826, *Benj. Hamblen;* who d. 1837; she d. Feb., 1884;
children, Hamblen: [1.] Deborah. [2.] Joseph E., b.
Jan. 13, 1828; d. July 3, 1870, of disease contracted during the war. Was Adj. of Duryea's Zouaves, 5th N. Y.
Vols.; Col. 65th Reg. N. Y. Vols.; and Brevet
Maj.-Gen.

674.   viii. Sally, b. Yar., May 22, 1803; m. Yar., Nov., 1824,
Edward W. Crocker; he b. Barnstable, July, 1798; d.
Mar. 1, 1865; she d. Mar. 17, 1867.

675.   ix. Mary, b. Yar., Aug. 21, 1807; m. Boston, May 8,
1852, *Nathaniel T. Simpkins* of Brewster.

676.   x. Warren, b. Yar., Mar. 29, 1809; d. Jan. 9, 1811.

677.*   xi. Thomas Warren, b. Yar., May 10, 1812.

Ebenezer Sears was master of a vessel in the coasting trade,
and later a tanner, living in Yarmouth.

He served at various times during 7 years of the Revolutionary war; was a corporal, and one of the guard over the unfortunate Major Andre, the night previous to his execution.

In muster-roll, Mass. Archives, XXXV, 202, he is described as
Ebenezer Sears of Yarmouth, age 18; 5 ft. 8 inches in height;
ruddy complexion. He served from Sep. 1 to Nov. 24, 1776,
in Capt. John Grannis' Co., sea-coast service, at Elizabeth
Islands; also 1 mo. 10 days from June, 1776; Sep. to Dec.,
1776, 3 mos. in Capt. Abijah Bangs' Co.; May 29, 1779, 3 mos.
2 days on brigantine "Active," Capt. Allen Hallet, at £2 14 0
pr. mo.; enlisted July 10, 1780, arriving at Springfield, July
19, 1780, to reinforce Northern Army, and served 6 mos. 22
days; wages £13 9 4; travel, 280 miles.

He is said to have been the first to carry the American flag
to the east of the Cape of Good Hope, and hoist it in the
Indian seas.

He made the voyage in the sloop "Stork," a vessel of 200
tons, with a short lower mast, and carrying a square foresail
and standing royal-yard, a rig that may be frequently seen in
the North Baltic seas at the present day.

Capt. Sears' sea-letter was signed by Gen. Washington.

The "Stork" sailed from a port in the North Sea, home-
ward bound, some years later, under Capt. Gideon Eldredge,
and was never heard of after.

257.

WILLARD SEARS[5] [*Will'd[4]*, *John[3]*, *Paul[2]*, *Rich.[1]*], b.
Harwich, Mass., May 26, 1759; d. W. Newton, Mass., July
27, 1852, æ. 93, gr.-st., Br.; m. Yar., Sep. 19, 1786,—*Hannah Sears*, No. 225, dau. of Edmund and Hannah (Crowell)
S., she b. Dec. 8, 1766; was adm. to full communion in Ch.,
Har., Sep. 2, 1796; and d. Feb. 6, 1843, æ. 76, gr.-st. Children:

678.   i. NANCY, b. Har., May 20, 1788; (Mar., T. C.) bap.
Oct. 24, 1796; m. Feb. 9, 1812, Capt. *Isaiah Howes*, son
of Isaiah and Lydia (Chapman) H., he b. July 10, 1788,
who died from the effects of a fall from a wagon at Worcester.   She was killed by the cars at Grantville Station, Mass.,
June 11, 1852, æ. 64; children, HOWES: [1.] Clinton, b.
May 8, 1813; d. Nov. 15, 1837. [2.] Arlette, b. Mar. 12,
1815; d. July 31, 1816. [3.] Arlette, b. Aug. 17, 1817;
d. Dec. 23, 1819. [4.] Willard Sears, b. Oct. 30, 1819;
d. Nov. 4. [5.] Lorenza, b. May 27, 1821; m. May 6,
1845, Leander Elmer Mann, and d. Apr. 19, 1880; had,
i. Susan Emma, b. Feb. 23, 1847; m. Jan. 1, 1868, Stephen L. Newton.   ii. Willard Clinton, b. July 21, 1849;
m. Nov. 10, 1880, Mattie Winslow of Paris, Me.   iii. Lucius Elmer, b. Mar. 1, 1851; m. Mar. 30, 1880, Emma L.
Bell of Worcester, Mass. [6.] George W., b. Aug. 8,
1823; m. Apr. 20, 1881, Clara M. Howland of Stafford,
Ct. [7.] Martha Custis, b. Jan. 3, 1826; m. Nov. 29,
1855, Rev. Ogden Hall, his 2d wife, and had, i. Mattie
Isa, b. July 16, 1857; m. Sep. 2, 1879, Sextus P. Goddard, "The Petersham Bard," who died Nov. 2, 1885, of
heart disease.   ii. Cecil S., b. June 1, 1859; d. Mar. 11,
1860.   iii. Mary S., b. Mar. 18, 1861; m. Mar. 27, 1879,
Capt. Geo. Otis Trefethen of Taunton, Mass., and had,
Grace Hanscom, b. Feb. 18, 1880. [8.] Mary Burr, b.
Sep. 28, 1828; m. Nov., 1860, Charles R. Brown of Gardner, Mass., and had, i. Charles Eugene, b. Oct. 15, 1861;
m. Oct. 20, 1886, Hattie L. Graves. [9.] Arlette, b. Sep.
9. 1832; unm.; lives in Newton, Mass.

679.   ii. SUKEY, b. Har., June 24, 1790; bap. Oct. 24, 1796;
m. Nov. 16, 1815, *Eben. Higgins*, son of Jacob and Mercy
H. of Brewster, who d. Apr. 7, 1875, æ. 85; she d. July
15, 1874, æ. 84; children, HIGGINS: [1.] Susan Sears, b.
Aug. 28, 1816; unm. [2.] Eben., b. May 12, 1818; m

July 15, 1841, Lydia Ann Tucker of Gloucester, Mass., and d. May 23, 1880; had, i. Lydia Ann, b. Apr. 25, 1843; m. July 9, 1867, Abraham Bigelow, and d. Natick, May 24, 1876. ii. Eben., b. Mar. 31, 1845; m. Sep. 15, 1868, Sarah Goulding. iii. Susan Abby, b. Nov. 29, 1849; m. Sep. 7, 1870, Roger S. Bartlett, and d. Jan. 14, 1872. iv. Willard Sears, b. May 23, 1847; m. Apr. 7, 1870, H. Maria James, and had, Willard Elliot, Roger Winslow and Ralph. v. Howard Holbrook, b. Oct. 6, 1852. [3.] Jacob, b. Feb. 6, 1821; d. Dec. 20, 1838. [4.] Abigail Freeman, b. Mar. 11, 1823; m. Nov. 12, 1844, Asaph Crosby of Br., and had, i. Jacob Higgins, b. Sep. 16, 1845; d. Oct. 6, 1864. ii. Mary Adelaide, b. July 23, 1847; m. Nov. 19, 1868, Moses E. Wiles of Orleans. iii. Alice P., b. Oct. 25, 1853; d. Apr. 1, 1885. [5.] Willard Sears, b. Dec. 12, 1826; m. Aug. 21, 1854, Olive Clark Freeman, she b. June 4, 1827, dau. of Solo. and Huldah (Crosby) F., of Br. He was drowned in going on board of his ship at Queenstown, Ireland, Jan. 9, 1866; left no children, (and his wife m. 2d, Dec. 2, 1869, Elisha D. Winslow of Br., he b. Apr. 25, 1807; d. Sep. 12, 1882; by a previous marriage he had, Walter T., an architect of Boston, who m. Sarah L. Sears, No. 2008, dau. of Capt. Joseph H. S.)

680.   iii. JANE, b. Har., Oct. 17, 1792; bap. Oct. 24, 1796; m. Dec. 14, 1815, *Jonathan Foster*, and d. Sep. 1, 1849, æ. 56; he m. again; children, FOSTER: [1.] Jonathan, b. Aug., 1817; d. July 1, 1849, æ. 31.

681.* iv. EBENEZER, b. Har., Jan. 17 or 24, 1795; bap. Oct. 24, 1796. The entry of birth was not made at once, and it has always been a question which of above dates is correct.

682.   v. HANNAH, b. Har., Feb. 17, 1797; bap. Apr. 2; m. Dec. 31, 1821, *Hopkins Foster*, he b. Nov. 15, 1796; was drowned Apr. 15, 1823, æ. 26; she d. Mar. 27, 1865, æ. 68; children, FOSTER: [1.] Mary Hopkins, b. Sep. 8, 1822; m. May 1, 1844, George E. Sickles, and had, i. George Edward, b. Feb. 14, 1845. ii. William Ambrose, b. Aug. 23, 1847; lives in Chicago, Ill.

683.   vi. MARY, b. Har., Apr. 26, 1799; bap. by name of Polly, May 5, 1799; dism. Mar. 7, 1847, from Ch., Br., to Ch., Brookline, Mass., and now lives, unm., in Brewster.

684.* vii. WILLARD, b. Har., Nov. 29, 1803; bap. Mar. 18, 1804.

685. viii. HARRIET, b. Har., Oct. 30, 1807 ; m. Dec. 8, 1835, (Oct. 25, T. C., *perh. pub.*) *John Crosby*, who d. May 1, 1867, æ. 57 ; she was dism. to Ch. Br., July 20, 1851 ; and d. June 11, 1871, æ. 63; children, CROSBY : [1.] Charles Clinton, d. young. [2.] John H., b. 1838 ; d. July, 1870, æ. 32, of disease contracted in the army. [3.] Charles Clinton, d. young. [4.] Harriet Sears, b. May 14, 1847 ; m. George R. Hall of Chelsea, Mass., and d. Grantville, Mass., Apr. 11, 1876, æ. 28 ; had, i. Mary Sears, b. Aug., 1873. ii. Hattie R., b. Aug., 1875 ; d. Apr. 16, 1876, æ. 8 mos.

Willard Sears lived near the site of the ancient tide-mill at Stony Brook, Har., later Br., on land which he purchased of Major Nathl. Freeman ; the land was known as Sachamus Neck, the residence of the Sachem of the Sauguatucket Indians.

The house which he erected was taken down some years since by Mr. Augustus Paine, (to whom he had sold the place,) and another built in its place.

He was an enterprising housewright, built many salt-works, and engaged also in ship-building and the manufacture of salt.

During the Revolution he was in the Militia, and on alarm at Falmouth and Bedford, Mass., 7 Sep., 1778 ; marched in Capt. Benj. Berry's Co., 112 miles' travel, and 7 days' service.

Previous to his death he divided his property among his children, and left no estate to be administered upon.

The births of some of his children have been incorrectly entered in Harwich town records ; those given here are from the family Bible.

Willard Sears and his wife were buried in the " New Cemetery," at Brewster, the latter being the first interment there.

263.

NATHANIEL SEARS[5] [*Nath'l*[4], *John*[3], *Paul*[2], *Rich.*[1]], b. Yarmouth, Mass., Feb. 15, 1758 ; d. East Dennis, Nov. 26, 1834, æ. 76, of old age ; m. Yar., Jan. 25, 1781, *Rachel Rules*, who d. Oct., 1827. Children :

686.* i. ARNOLD, b. Yar., Dec. 25, 1781.
687. ii. POLLY, b. Yar., Apr. 10, 1783 ; d. Jan., 1820, of dropsy.
688. iii. ACHSAH, b. Yar., Dec. 6, 1784 ; d. Aug. 28, 1836.
689.* iv. NATHANIEL, b. Yar., Aug. 12, 1785.

21

690.   v. RACHEL, b. Yar., Dec. 13, 1788; d. Oct. 10, 1878,
       æ. 90 yr. 10 mos., gr.-st., Br.
691.* vi. LOT, b. Yar., Apr. 11, 1791.
692. vii. DEBORAH, b. Yar., May 4, 1793; m. ——— *Merchant;*
       and d. Brewster, June 2, 1862, of consumption.
693. viii. HOWES, b. Den., Sep. 15, 1795; rem. to Nantucket.
694.* ix. FREEMAN, b. Den., Jan. 24, 1799.

Nathaniel Sears lived in the East precinct of Yarmouth,
and was adm. to the church there "in private," July 7, 1799.

On alarm at Dartmouth, Sep. 6, 1778, he served 13 days in
Lt. Micajah Sears' Co.

278.

Hon. RICHARD SEARS[5] [*Dan'l[4], Dan'l[3], Paul[2], Rich.[1]*],
b. Chatham, Mass., Jan. 30, 1749; d. there May 13, 1839, æ.
90; m. Framingham, Mass., Nov. 25, 1778, *Mehitable Marshall,* dau. of Ebenezer and Mehitable (Haven) M., of F., she
b. Oct. 27, 1758; d. Chatham, July 8, 1852, æ. 94.   Children:
695.   i. SARAH, b. Chat., Oct. 5, 1779; d. Boxford, Mass., Apr.
       29, 1812; m. Chat., Oct. 17, 1799, by Rev. Ephraim
       Briggs of C., to his bro. Rev. *Isaac Briggs;* he b. Hali-
       fax, Mass., May 26, 1775; was son of Rev. Ephraim and
       Rebecca (Waterman) B., of H.; he grad. Brown Univ.,
       1795, and was settled in York, Me., 1797; at Boxford,
       Mass., 1808–33; and at Chatham, 1834–36.   He rem. to
       No. Rochester, Mass., and lived there till 1852, when he
       went to reside with his dau., Mrs. John J. Crane of Mor-
       risania, N. Y., and died there Feb. 22, 1862, æ. 87; "a
       good man, and a faithful minister."   [He m. 2d, Chat.,
       Nov. 16, 1813, Hitty Sears, his sister-in-law, who d. s. p.,
       Boxford, Aug. 1, 1814, æ. 30; and 3d, Feb. 6, 1816, Hen-
       rietta Chester, dau. of Leonard C., of Weathersfield, Ct.,
       by whom he had one daughter.]   Children, BRIGGS:
       [1.] Mary, b. Old York, Me., Feb. 1, 1801; m. Boxford,
       Mass., Apr. 23, 1823, Gilman Prichard, youngest son of
       Lieut. Jere. P., a Revolutionary soldier; he b. Ipswich,
       N. H., Nov. 23, 1795; was a successful merchant in Bos-
       ton, Deacon of Essex St. Ch., and Supt. of the S. S.
       School, and died Feb. 8, 1833.   Mrs. P. rem., in 1834, to
       New Haven, and died there Nov. 23, 1882, esteemed by all
       who knew her; had, i. Sarah Sears, b. Boston, Mar. 3, 1824;
       m. N. Y., Sep. 6, 1854, Rev. Theodore Dwight Woolsey,

(his 2d wife,) he b. N. Y., Oct. 31, 1801. ii. Mary, b. Boston, Mar. 29, 1826; m. New Haven, Apr. 23, 1850, Rev. William H. Goodrich, son of Prof. Chauncey A. G., of Yale Coll., by his wife, Julia (Webster) G.; he b. there Jan. 19, 1823; d. Lauzanne, Switzerland, July 11, 1874; he grad. Yale, 1843; was pastor of Cong. Ch., Bristol, Ct., of Presb. Ch., Binghamton, N. Y.; and of Cleveland, Ohio. iii. Gilman, b. Boston, May 14, 1828; d. Oct. 1, 1831. iv. Ellen Maria, b. Boston, July 19, 1831; unm.; resides with her sister, Mrs. Woolsey, in N. Haven. [2.] Richard Sears, b. Old York, Me., June 24, 1803; entered Phillips Acad., Andover, Mass., Aug. 12, 1817; and left May, 1818; he was a clerk in Boston, but his health becoming impaired, he made a voyage to So. America, and d. Pernambuco, Jan. 9, 1827; unm. The cause of his death was small-pox, contracted from a body that washed ashore on the beach. [3.] Charles Marshall, b. Old York, Aug. 21, 1805; m. Framingham, Nov. 3, 1840, Mary Ann Ballard, a 2d cousin; she b. Apr. 8, 1817; d. Oct. 15, 1881. He was in the carpet business on Washington st., Boston; rem. to Framingham, and died there Aug. 22, 1865; had, i. Richard Sears, b. June 22, 1844; m. June 22, 1875, Eliz'h G. Partridge; she b. Hollister, Mass., Feb. 25, 1842; lives in Fram. ii. Mary Elsie, b. Feb. 5, 1852; unm.; and lives in Fram. [4.] George, b. Portsmouth, N. H., Sep. 24, 1807; m. New York, Nov. 18, 1835, Elsie Schuyler Crane, dau. of Benj. C., of N. Y.; she b. there, Aug. 14, 1811; d. there Dec. 26, 1851; and 2d, Bristol, Ct., Oct. 10, 1854, Julia Elizabeth Brewster, dau. of Noah and Elizabeth (Root) B., of B.; she b. there Mar. 29, 1828. He was a shipmaster during many years, and later Pres. Dry Dock Co., South st., N. Y.; had, i. Gilman Prichard, b. Dec. 13, 1837; m. Canandaigua, N. Y., Feb. 25, 1867, Charlotte Botsford; and d. Albany, Feb. 18, 1872. ii. Benjamin Crane, b. Sep. 30, 1842; m. N. Y., Oct. 1, 1874, Caroline Hains; who d. s. p. Hoboken, N. J., Aug. 11, 1885; he is employed in his father's office. iii. George Isaac, b. May 16, 1845; d. Oct., 1857. iv. Augustus Crane, b. Jan. 28, 1847; m. Albuquerque, N. Mex., Nov. 27, 1883, Mary Phelan, is in a bank there. v. Elsie Schuyler, b. Dec. 16, 1851; d. Feb. 18, 1871; and by 2d wife, vi. Julia Isabella, b. Dec. 12, 1856. vii. Mary, b. Nov. 6, 1858. viii. Sarah, b. Feb. 7, 1864; m. May 27, 1885, Edward W. Kemble, an

artist. ix. George, b. Oct. 25, 1866. [5.] James Freeman,
b. Boxford, Mass., Sep. 4, 1809 ; d. there Oct. 16, 1810.
696.   ii. Richard (Capt.), b. Chat., Oct. 29, 1781 ; m. (pub.
Chat., Mar. 18, 1815,) his cousin, *Alathena Marshall*, dau.
of Gilbert and Jane (Jones) M., of Ashland, Mass.; she b.
Mar. 28, 1792 ; d. 1839 ; (will proved that year ; inventory,
$3,410;) he d. s. p. of consumption, at Chatham, Nov. 28,
1830 ; his will, dated Oct. 5, 1828, and codicil Oct. 5,
1830, were proved Feb. 9, 1831 ; mentions sisters-in-law,
Rebecca and Elizabeth Marshall ; nephew Charles M.
Briggs ; and gives to bro. Daniel his watch and chain.
Charles Scudder of Boston, Exec.

In early life he sailed as supercargo and master, and
after retiring from the sea, kept a store on the beach where
the salt-works were, in partnership with Isaac Hardy, father
of the late Hon. Alpheus H., of Boston.

In connection with his father-in-law he built a foundry,
and also a saw-mill on the Sudbury river.

His residence was next his father, on the old homestead.

He was very fine looking, extremely gentlemanly and
courteous in manner, resembling his father in many ways.

Was appointed Justice of the Peace, 1822 ; chosen Town
Clerk, 1827 ; and represented the town in State Leg.,
1826, 1827.   Was Aid-de-Camp, etc.
697.   iii. Daniel, b. Chat., Dec. 4, 1783 ; d. unm., Oct. 10,
1854 ; æ. 71 ; the last of the line in Chatham.

He was plain in feature, and much deformed, owing to
an accident in childhood.

His mother was driving with friends, when the horse
became frightened, the carriage was overturned, and the
person who held him, fell upon him, causing internal
injuries. It was for a time supposed that he could not
live, and gradually this deformity came upon him.

He died three years after his mother, of heart disease ;
he had driven to Yarmouth on a very cold day, returned
much chilled, and died in two days.
698.   iv. Hetty, b. Chat., Dec. 4, 1783 ; [1784, Briggs' Bible,]
gemini; m. Nov. 4, 1813, by Rev. Ephraim Briggs, to her
brother-in-law, Rev. *Isaac Briggs*, and d. s. p., Boxford,
Mass., Aug. 1, 1814, æ. 30.
699.   v. Ebenezer Marshall, b. Chat., Nov. 24, 1788 ; d.
Havana, Cuba, Aug. 10, 1810, æ. 22, gr.-st., Chat. ; he
was a clerk in Boston, and went to Cuba on his employer's
business.

700.   vi. FEAR, b. Chat., Nov. 24, 1788, *gemini;* d. Boston,
Aug. 8, 1822; m. July 2, 1817, by Rev. Stetson Raymond
to Charles Scudder of Boston, he b. Hyannis, June 5,
1789; d. Boston, Jan. 21, 1863; was son of David and
Desire (Gage) S. of Barnstable.

He was a prominent merchant in Boston, Deacon of Essex St. Ch., and Supt. S. S. School, and during many
years an officer of the A. B. C. F. M. of Cong. Ch.; (he m.
2d, Oct. 27, 1823, his wife's cousin, Jane Marshall, dau.
of Gilbert and Jane (Jones) M., she b. Framingham, Oct.
17, 1796; d. Boston, Mar. 20, 1833; by whom he had,
Elisha, b. 1824.   Jane Marshall, b. 1828.   Eugenie I., b.
1831, and Evarts, b. 1833; 3d, May 8, 1834, Sarah Lathrop Coit, dau. of Elisha and Rebecca (Manwaring) C., of
N. Y.; and had, Horace Elisha, 1838; m. Grace Owen of
Cambridge, Samuel H., and David C.;) children, SCUD-
DER: [1.] Marshall Sears, b. May 31, 1818; d. s. p., Aug.
24, 1875; a merchant; m. July 24, 1839, Rebecca C.
Blatchford, dau. of Rev. Henry and Mary Ann (Coit) B.
[2.] Charles William, b. Jan. 4, 1820; m. Aug. 16, 1841,
Alicia H. Blatchford, (sister to above Rebecca,) a hard-
ware merchant in Boston, and lives Brookline, Mass.; had,
i. Frank H., b. Mar. 30, 1842; m. June 11, 1867, Sarah
Trufant.   ii. Henry Blatchford, b. June 18, 1844; m.
Apr. 21, 1866, Julia R. Perry of Andover, and lives
Longwood, Mass.   iii. Winthrop Salstonstall, b. July 24,
1847; with Houghton, Mifflin & Co., Book Publishers,
Boston.   iv. Mary Windeal, b. May 27, 1851; d. Sep. 14,
1853.   v. Bessie Marshall, b. Oct. 1, 1853.

Richard Sears' father died when he was eleven years of age,
and two years later his mother married Samuel Ballard of Boston, removed with her children to that town, and lived on the
corner of Common st. and Turnagain lane, now known as
Tremont st. and Temple place.

Richard soon returned to Chatham, and was brought up
there, receiving a common school education, and, arriving at
the age of manhood, settled upon the old homestead farm, and
devoted himself to its cultivation.   He spent seven years of
his youth in the family and store of Gen. Joseph Otis of Revolutionary fame.

He became the largest real estate owner in Chatham; carried on his farm on an extensive and liberal scale, having a
farmer to superintend, and a number of farm hands always
employed; kept considerable live stock; a goodly number of
cattle and sheep, which were pastured on the downs.

He kept a variety store next his 'house, which was on the Main street just left of the soldiers' monument; engaged in the manufacture of salt; and to some extent in shipping, in connection with his brother David of Boston.

The old house, supposed to have been built by his grandfather, Daniel Sears, was taken down in 1863, having, after the death of his widow, been occupied by various parties, and allowed to become dilapidated.

He was appointed Coroner in 1781; Session Justice for the county in 1814, and to qualify civil officers; Justice of the Peace, *quorum unus*, 1801; Representative, 1780, 1781, 1783, 1785, 1786, 1792, 1796, 1806, 1809, 1813, 1814; Senator, 1804, and Town Treasurer and Clerk, 1775, 1776.

Was in 1st Co. of Chatham, in 2d Regt. Militia, Revolutionary war, date and service not given.

Mr. Sears was tall, and of great dignity in manner; calm in speech and action; civil and attractive in his intercourse with his fellows.

He was a conscientious Christian man, and a strong supporter of the church.

His dress, up to a very short time before his death, was of the late Revolutionary period; he wore long hose, shoe and knee-buckles, ruffled shirts at all times, and his iron-gray hair brushed over and tied in a cue with a black ribbon.

Mrs. Sears, " Grandma," as she was called by her intimates, was, by nature, a courtly lady, capable of gracing any position, and uniting with her husband in practical religion, she was ever doing good, especially among children, aiming to instill into their minds the lesson: " Remember now thy Creator in the days of thy youth."

The " Squire," as he was called, would frequently invite his city friends to Chatham for fishing and gunning, and many distinguished men, as Webster, Otis, Quincy and others, have enjoyed the comforts and agreeable society of that hospitable roof.

The clergy ever found a home there, and always made it their stopping place when in town.

Most of the traveling, 80 or 90 years ago, from Chatham to Boston, was on horseback.

During the many years that the Squire represented the town in the Legislature, he was in the habit of riding all the way to Boston, where he remained during the session, the guest of his brother David, at his residence on Beacon street, enjoying its luxurious appointments and the cultured society to which he had access, returning to his quiet home in the spring, ready and eager to resume his country life and the duties connected with it.

The day before his death he was engaged in superintending his out-of-door business; but in the afternoon came in from a drive to the shore, complaining of a pain in the region of the heart, walked through the house to his bed-room, and lying down, never rose again; he died the next forenoon, very calmly and peacefully gliding out of existence, aged 90.

At the time of Mrs. Sears' death, a maid in the house was quite ill, and a nurse from the village was in attendance; hearing a movement during the night in Mrs. Sears' bedroom below stairs, she went down and found her sitting up and looking from the window.

In reply to the question, " Are you not feeling well, Grandma ? " she said, " O, yes, only restless and wakeful. I often get up and sit at the window when the moon shines, and think."

She was persuaded to go to bed, and was soon sleeping, but breathing rather strongly; from this sleep she never awoke. She, too, gently departed this life; at 3 o'clock the next afternoon she no longer lived, and the old house was desolate then.

The family were originally buried in the family cemetery on the hill where is now the Methodist church; but after the death of Daniel Sears in 1854, their remains were removed to the Congregational cemetery.

The will of Richard Sears is dated Oct. 15, 1833, and mentions beloved wife, Mehitable Sears, and son Daniel; grandson Charles M. Briggs, and son-in-law Charles Scudder, trustees and executors; gr.-dau. Mary Prichard, widow of Gilman P.; gr.-sons George Briggs, Marshall S. Scudder and Charles W. Scudder, and "*reserving forever* the buryingground as fenced for a family burying place, together with a convenient way to the same for the purpose of a burial place, and my will is that a fence be kept in good repair under the care and direction of my executors."

279.

DAVID SEARS[5] [*Dan'l[4], Dan'l[3], Paul[2], Rich.[1]*], b. Chatham, Mass., Nov. 29, 1752; (another account says Aug. 12,) d. Boston, Oct. 23, 1816, æ. 64; m. Boston, June 6, 1786, *Ann Winthrop*, dau. of John Still and Jane (Borland) W., of New London, Ct., who died Oct. 2, 1789, æ. 33.   Child :

701.* i. DAVID, b. Boston, Oct. 8, 1787.

Mr. Sears removed to Boston with his mother in 1763, and

was brought up by his step-father, Samuel Ballard, who lived on Common st., now Tremont st., between Mr. Cole's and Mrs. Swan's houses, being the third house from Winter st., and corner of Turnagain lane, now Temple place.

He became one of the most successful merchants in Boston, having his counting-room on Central Wharf.

In 1775 he sailed for London in company with Daniel Greene and others, (who desired to avoid the troublous times consequent upon the outbreak of the Revolution,) traveled upon the Continent during several years, and made his business connections useful to his country.

Upon his return, he narrowly escaped capture by an English frigate.

He engaged to some extent in privateering, and in the summer of 1779 fitted out the " Mars," of 22 guns, under command of Capt. Ash.

During the Presidency of the elder Adams, he was chairman of a Com. of the Citizens of Boston for building a frigate, the " Boston," at their private expense, to be presented to the Federal government, himself subscribing $3,000.

He was in favor of Jay's treaty, and suffered considerable loss by French spoliations prior to 1800.

Mr. Sears was an able financier, and Director of the First Bank of the United States from its commencement to its termination ; was often a referee in intricate cases of equity and mercantile usage, and his whole career was marked by incorruptible integrity.

That large tract of land in Maine, known as the "Waldo Patent," having been confiscated by the government, was sold ; three-fourths to Gen. Knox, his wife owning the remaining fourth, and by him mortgaged to his sureties, Gen. Lincoln, and Col. Jackson, who assigned the mortgage to Israel Thorndike, David Sears and William Prescott of Boston, who foreclosed it.

The territory was originally 30 miles square, and included all the islands of Penobscot Bay, the sites of the towns of Searsmont, Prospect, Knox and Searsport.

Our institutions do not readily lend themselves to the maintenance of a great absentee proprietor, in remote parts of the country.

It was not an easy matter to secure a competent agent, and still less to deal with refractory tenants, or with that numerous class of settlers who persuade themselves that they ought to be allowed to occupy, rent free, the soil they have begun by appropriating.

It is therefore not to be wondered at that the heirs availed themselves of opportunities for selling this estate, and the only portion now remaining unalienated is the well-known Brigadier's Island.

Mr. Sears was a benevolent man, and a contributor to many charities.

He was a founder of the "Widow's Fund," in Trinity Church, in which he was a worshipper, and in which he was honored as a benefactor.

A too copious indulgence in that favorite repast of the olden time, a "Saturday salt-fish dinner," brought on serious indigestion, followed by a congestion which proved fatal.

He fell dead as he was getting into his carriage, in front of his residence, on the upper corner of Beacon and Somerset streets, Oct. 23, 1816.

Dr. John Sylvester John Gardiner, then Rector of Trinity Church, preached his funeral sermon from the text: "There is but one *step* between me and death," in allusion to the fact that Mr. Sears had fallen on the step of his carriage in a fit of apoplexy.

His wife, Ann Winthrop, was a dau. of John Still Winthrop, by his first wife Jane Borland, and a lineal descendant in the fifth degree of the old first Governor, and was an elder sister of Lieut.-Gov. Thomas Lindall Winthrop.

284.

SILAS SEARS[5] [*Silas*[4], *Silas*[3], *Silas*[2], *Rich.*[1]], b. Yarmouth, Mass., Feb. 2, 1726-7; m. Yar., Dec. 17, 1756, *Elizabeth Williams.* Children:

702. i. MERCY, b. Yar., May 13, 1757.
703. ii. REUBEN, b. Yar., Aug. 26, 1758; a "Reuben Sears m. 1790, *Hannah Benedict*, she b. Dec. 23, 1772; rem. to Wayne county, N. Y." (Ben. Gen'y.)
704. iii. SILAS, b. Yar., Feb. 22, 1762; d. May 30, 1765.

285.

EDWARD SEARS[5] [*Silas*[4], *Silas*[3], *Silas*[2], *Rich.*[1]], b. Yarmouth, Mass., Oct. 21, 1729; d. before Apr., 1782; m. Yar., Sep. 24, 1750, (14th T. C.) *Mary Bray*, who d. Feb. 6, 1750-1; and he m. 2d, Yar., Nov. 26, 1767, *Priscilla Baker*. (An Ed-

22

ward Sears was pub. to *Mercy Sears*, Yar., June 4, 1764.)
Children :
By *Priscilla :*
705.   i. MARY, b. Yar., Oct. 8, 1771.
706.* ii. EDWARD, b. Yar., Apr. 9, 1779.

Edward Sears of Yarmouth died intestate, and Barnabas
Eldredge of Yar., was appointed admr. of his estate, which
was appraised Apr. 26, 1782, at £102 11 2.
Dower was set off to Priscilla Sears, widow, Dec. 3, 1782.

287.

MOODY SEARS[5] [*Silas[4], Silas[3], Silas[2], Rich.[1]*], b. Yarmouth, Mass., May 6, 1734 ; d. Nov. 24, 1795, æ. 61, gr.-st.,
Yar. ; m. Yar., Dec. 20, 1759, *Elizabeth Lewis*, dau. of Antipas L.   Children :
707.   i. MARY, b. Yar., Jan. 1, 1763 ; m. *Enoch Hallet, Jr.*,
       of Yar., he b. Feb. 19, 1760 ; and 2d, Nov. 9, 1797, *Benj.*
       Parker of Falmouth.
708.   ii. MOODY, b. Yar., Sep. 5, 1764 ; was a mariner ; his
       vessel was seized by the British, and the crew thrown into
       prison ; a family tradition says he died there unmarried ;
       but another account says he was drowned on Nantucket
       shoals, in 1789, in a new schooner belonging to Mr. Evans
       of Prov., R. I., and commanded by Howes Hallett, and
       is doubtless correct.
709.* iii. JAMES, b. Yar., Apr. 12, 1766.
710.   iv. ELIZABETH, b. Yar., Feb. 19, 1768 ; m. Dec. 7, 1797,
       David Crosby of Dennis.
711.* v. PRINCE, b. Yar., Dec. 20, 1769.
712.   vi. DEBORAH, b. Yar., July 7, 1772 ; m. Yar., Feb. 23,
       1792, *John Thacher, Jr.*, a seaman, and rem. to So. Dart-
       mouth, Mass., in 1805 ; he sailed from Dart., Mar. 7, 1820,
       with his sons Sears and John, and are supposed to have
       been lost the same night ; children, THACHER : [1.] Lavi-
       nia, b. Oct. 2, 1792.   [2.] Sears, b. Oct. 3, 1797 ; drowned
       Mar. 7, 1820.   [3.] Rebecca, b. Oct. 3, 1797, *gem. ;* d.
       Apr. 1, 1850.   [4.] Isaiah, b. Sep. 26, 1799 ; d. Jan. 17,
       1801.   [5.] Serena, b. June 28, 1802 ; m. Ebenr. Alden.
       [6.] Sarah, b. Oct. 7, 1803 ; m. —— Parker.   [7.] John,
       b. Nov. 26, 1804 ; drowned Mar. 7, 1820.   [8.] Job, b.
       Jan. 1, 1807 ; d. Jan. 3.   [9.] Isaac, b. Jan. 1, 1807,
       gem. ; d. Jan. 18.   [10.] Deborah, b. July 14, 1808.
       [11.] Charlotte, b. Apr. 3, 1812 ; d. Feb. 12, 1813.

713. vii. MARTHA, b. Yar., Mar. 3, 1775; d. unm.
714.*viii. ISAIAH, b. Yar., Mar. 18, 1777.
715.* ix. ENOCH, b. Yar., June 28, 1779.
716. x. CHARLOTTE, b. Yar., Oct. 31, 1782; m. (pub. Yar., Oct. 1, 1801,) Benj. Baxter of Dennis.

Moody Sears of Yarmouth made his will, but not having three witnesses failed of probate. Mar. 19, 1796, the heirs agreed to a settlement ; they were, Isaiah, Enoch and Charlotte Sears; Enoch and Mary Hallet; John and Deborah Thacher; Elizabeth, Martha, James and Prince Sears.

On alarm at Dartmouth and Falmouth, Sep., 1778, Moody Sears marched in Capt. Lot Crowell's Co.

288.

ELEAZAR SEARS[5] [*Silas*[4], *Silas*[3], *Silas*[2], *Rich.*[1]] b. Yarmouth, Mass., about 1728; d. there Sep., 1810, æ. 82; m. Yar., (pub. Aug. 23, 1760, as "Eleazar, Jr.,") *Ruth Lewis*, dau. of Antipas L.; and 2d, Yar., Feb. 17, 1786, *Jane Baker;* and 3d, Yar., Nov. 9, 1790, *Sarah Young*, who d. Mar. 19, 1831. ᵛ
Children ::

By *Ruth:*
717. i. PHEBE, b. Yar., Mar. 1, 1761; m. there Jan. 26, 1786, *Aaron Crowell*, son of Jona. and Phebe (Snow) C., he b. May 22, 1766; children, CROWELL: [1.] Aaron, b. July 1, 1790. [2.] Gideon, b. May 14, 1791. [3.] Zeno, b. Aug. 5, 1793. [4.] Ebenr., b. June 31, 1796. [5.] Sarah, b. Mar. 4, 1800; m. Barnabas Hallet; and 2d, Jona. Sears. [6.] Ezra, b. Nov. 14, 1803.
718. ii. HANNAH, b. Yar., Nov. 18, 1762; d. Apr. 9, 1765.
719. iii. RUTH, b. Yar., June 21, 1765; d. 1784.
720.* iv. LEWIS, b. Yar., Oct. 26, 1768, (1767, T. C.)
721. v. LYDIA, b. Yar., Aug. 5, 1770; m. Yar., June 23, 1788, *Joseph Crowell*, son of Thos. and Mercy (Stuart) C., he b. Feb. 20, 1761; d. 1825; children, CROWELL: [1.] Lewis, b. Jan. 11, 1789; m. 1817, Betsy Freeman. [2.] Nathan, b. Nov. 27, 1791; m. Hannah ——. [3.] Joseph, b. Apr. 23, 1793; m. 1817, Rebecca Matthews; d. 1824. [4.] Hannah B., b. Aug. 10, 1795; m. 1816, Eleazar Crowell. [5.] Winthrop, b. Feb. 1, 1798; m. 1821, Rebecca Bassett. [6.] Obed, b. June 30, 1800; m. Feb. 20, 1823, Hannah Bessey. [7.] Lydia, b. Oct. 17, 1802; m. Jan. 14, 1821, Ebenr. Crowell. [8.] Calvin, b.

Apr. 28, 1805; d. Apr. 18, 1831. [9.] Diantha T., b. Aug. 21, 1807; m. Sep., 1826, Warren Lewis. [10.] Tabitha, b. Apr. 17, 1810; m. Jan., 1837, Freeman Crowell.

722. vi. TABITHA, b. Yar., July 19, 1773; m. Yar., Nov. 16, 1791, *Samuel Crowell*, son of Thos. and Mercy (Stuart) C., he b. Mar. 18, 1767; children, CROWELL: [1.] Ruth, b. Jan. 19, 1794. [2.] Sears, b. Oct. 14, 1795. [3.] Mercy, b. Nov. 4, 1797. [4.] Samuel, b. Aug. 10, 1800.

723.* vii. EDWARD, b. Yar., July 11, 1777.

By *Sarah :*

724. viii. HANNAH, b. Yar., Sep. 1, 1792.

The will of Eleazar Sears of Yarmouth, dated May 31, 1803, was proved Jan. 8, 1810, and names wife Sarah; and children Lewis, Edward and Hannah Sears; Phebe Crowell, Lydia Crowell and Tabitha Crowell; son Lewis, Exec.

Eleazar Sears was in Lt. Crowell's Co., in Col. Freeman's Regt., and marched on alarm at Dartmouth and Falmouth, Sep. 6, 1778, serving 13 days.

292.

THOMAS SEARS[5] [*Thos.[4], Silas[3], Silas[2], Rich.[1]*], b. Yarmouth, Mass., Nov. 6, 1733; d. Sep. 25, 1761, in 28 yr., gr.-st., Yar.; m. Nov. 28, 1754, *Mercy Gray* of Tisbury. Children :

725. i. SAMUEL, b. Yar., Nov. 5, 1756.

726. ii. SARAH, b. Yar., Sep. 15, 1758; m. Aug. 17, 1775, *Benj. Hatch* of Rochester.

727.* iii. ALLEN, b. Yar., Aug. 5, 1760.

293.

Capt. ELEAZAR SEARS[5] [*Thos.[4], Silas[3], Silas[2], Rich.[1]*], b. Yarmouth, Mass., May 9, 1739; d. Jan. 20, (22) 1824, in 85 yr., gr.-st., Yar.; m. Yar., 1761, (pub. Chat., Nov. 18, 1761, as "Eleazar 3d,") *Bethia Godfrey* of Chatham, she b. 1743; d. June 7, 1800, in 57 yr., gr.-st.; (is called in records "wife of Eleazar, *Jr. ;*) and 2d, Dennis, Jan. 5, 1801, *Thankful Nickerson* of Yar., who died a widow, Feb. 6, 1834. Children :

By *Bethia :*

728. i. PATIENCE, b. Yar., Aug. 23, 1763; m. Yar., Sep. 13, 1783, *Willard Crowell.*

729.   ii. BETHIA, b. Yar., Dec. 17, 1765 ; m. —— *Matthews ;*
       children, MATTHEWS: [1.] Sears, bap. Aug. 11, 1799.
       [2.] Benjamin, bap. Aug. 11, 1799; —— she m. 2d, *Gor-*
       ham Baker ; children, BAKER: [3.] Polly, bap. Aug. 11,
       1799. [4.] Gorham, bap. Aug. 11, 1799. [5.] Judah,
       bap. May 28, 1803. [6.] Winthrop Sears, b. Apr. 27,
       1804; bap. June 10 ; m. Yar., 1824, Sally Hawes; she
       b. Yar , July 22, 1805 ; d. No. Bridgewater, May 3, 1858 ;
       he d. Brockton, Apr. 28, 1878; had, i. Abby, b. Nov. 7,
       1825 ; m. Yar., Aug. 30, 1852, Rufus P. Kingman of
       Brockton. [7.] Eliza, bap. June 21, 1807. [8.] Pauline,
       bap. July 26, 1801, (Apoline, T. C.) [9.] Alexander,
       bap. Aug. 13, 1809.
730.   iii. THOMAS, b. Yar., Jan. 16, 1768; d. Oct. 15, 1780 ;
       (26, T. C.) in 13 yr., gr.-st.
731.* iv. WINTHROP, b. Yar., May 1, 1772.
732.   v. SALLY, b. Yar., May 8, 1775 ; m. Yar., Apr. 23,
       1795, *Isaac Smalley* of Harwich; children, SMALLEY:
       [1.] Leonard, b. Apr. 6, 1796. [2.] Winthrop S., b. May
       23, 1798. [3.] Lydia, m. —— Wheeler of Uxbridge,
       Mass.
733.   vi. SABRA, b. Yar., Dec. 23, 1777; m. Jan. 22, 1799,
       Sam'l Matthews.
734.   vii. THOMAS, b. Yar., Mar. 16, 1781; m. Yar., July 16,
       1805, *Lydia Gray,* and died soon after; lived in Barnsta-
       ble. June 27, 1816, the court made an allowance to his
       widow Lydia.
735.*viii. RICHARD, b. Yar., July 22, 1783.

Eleazar Sears, styled in the records "Third," and later
"Junr.," was a sea captain, and resided in Yarmouth.
   May 9, 1829, the court made an allowance to his widow
Thankful.

294.

DAVID SEARS[5] [*Jas.*[4], *Silas*[3], *Silas*[2], *Rich.*[1]], b. Yarmouth, Mass., Aug. 25, 1731 ; d. Lenox, Mass., July 12, 1827,
æ. 97 ; m. *Mary Paddock,* (doubtless dau. of Zachariah and
Elizh. (Howes) P.), who d. Lenox, July 19, 1826, æ. 92. Children :
736.* i. PHILIP, b. North East, N. Y., 1759.
737.* ii. DAVID.
738.* iii. ISAAC.

739.* iv. LUTHER, b. Lenox, 1772.
740.* v. JAMES, b. Len., May 15, 1776.
741.* vi. ZACHARIAH, b. Len., Apr., 1778.
742.* vii. CALVIN, b. Len., about 1769.(?)
743. viii. ELIJAH.
744. ix. BETHIA, m. *Jacob Goodrich* of Pittsfield, Mass., and
    had, George, who lived in Monroe, Green county, Wis.
745. x. ELIZABETH, m. *Jonathan Root* of Pitts.
746. xi. POLLY, m. *Robert McKnight* of Pitts.

David Sears rem. to North East, south precinct, Dutchess
county, N. Y. (where "David Sears subscribed 10s. for Mr.
Kent's support," in 1754,) and thence previous to the Revolution to north part of Lenox, Mass.

Dec. 3, 1777, at a meeting of the Com. of Safety, it was
"Voted John Whitlock, Ephraim Smith, David Sears, Philip
Sears and Edward Martindale are dangerous to the United
States of America."

"Chose by ballot Major Caleb Hyde to procure evidence
and support an action on behalf of said town against John Whitlock, David Sears, Philip Sears, Ephraim Smith and Edward
Martindale, at a court of general sessions of the peace for the
county of Berkshire, to be held at Gt. Barrington, on Tues-
day, the 9th day of Dec. current, for their being inimically
disposed and dangerous to remain in the States of America."

Mar. 21, 1774, David Sears was appointed Com. to lay out
school money. Mar. 12, 1776, David Sears on School Com.
Mar. 24, 1788, chose David Sears, Tything-man. Mar. 2, 1789,
David Sears, Surveyor of Highways. Apr. 25, 1794, he is
returned as a Baptist.

A hole in the mountain at Lenox was called "the tory-
hole," and was occupied by Gid. Smith of Stockbridge as a
hiding-place, he being supplied with food by David Sears.

I think some of his daus. were born before Luther.

297.

SETH SEARS[5] [*Jas.*[4], *Silas*[3], *Silas*[2], *Rich.*[1]], b. Yarmouth,
Mass., Oct. 31, 1736; d. Milltown, N. Y., Aug. 2, 1809, æ.
73; and was buried beside his bro. Knowles; m. *Sarah Sears*,
No. 324, dau. of Stephen and Abigail (Burgess) S., of Yar.,
she b. Mar. 31, 1734. Children:
747.* i. ENOCH HAMLIN.
748.* ii. SETH, b. about 1771.

749.* iii. ELEAZAR H., b. in So. East, or Danbury, 1771.
750. iv. SARAH.
751. v. THANKFUL, b. So. East, N. Y., June 30, 1775; m. there Dec. 27, 1793, Rev. *Wm. Smith* of Litchfield, Herkimer county, N. Y., and d. July 28, 1808. [Mr. Smith was a son of Richard and Mary (Brush) S., and b. West Farms, L. I., Mar. 20, 1770; lived at one time at Huntington, L. I., and was a dry-goods clerk at Jamaica, and in N. Y. city. In 1793 he rem. to Litchfield, and settled on a farm, selling out in June, 1846, and removing to Bedford, Ohio, with his wife and four youngest children, his sons Seth, Charles and Richard being established on neighboring farms. He m. 2d, Oct. 28, 1809, Rhoda Rockwell, who d. May 25, 1822; and 3d, Sep. 20, 1824, Catharine Kelty, who d. June 10, 1858, at Bedford, O., and he d. there July 29, 1857;] children, SMITH: [1.] Seth, b. Mar. 31, 1795; d. Oct. 28, 1801. [2.] Orrin Gazebe, b. May 6, 1797, d. s. p., July 1, 1880; m. Mary Crawford of Arkwright, Chaut. co., N. Y. He rem. to Chaut. co. with his bro. Nathl., and helped to run the mills erected by them, and also worked at the joiner's and carpenter's trade. Later he was a preacher of the Meth. E. Ch., traveling on horseback through So. Chaut., into Cattaraugus, fording the Allegheny river, at Penn. In 1855 they sold out and moved to Illinois, near Carthage, and stayed three or four years, returning to Hamlet, where he died; he was for years a great sufferer from inflammatory rheumatism, which left him a cripple. [3.] Nathaniel, b. July 3, 1799; m. Feb. 20, 1823, Polly Gordon, she b. May 7, 1796; d. June 11, 1855, had 4 sons and 3 daus., of whom Furilla m. M. C. Jay; 2 sons are dead. He lived on the farm with his parents until 21, studied medicine one year, then went with his bro. Orrin to Chautauqua co., where they located 100 acres of land, and erected a saw-mill on the west branch of the Conowauga creek, being among the first pioneers of that section, then a wilderness without roads, and nothing but marked trees to guide one through the forest from one log cabin to another. A few years later they built a grist-mill. These mills were the first in that section, and a Godsend to the early settlers. He was pretty well versed in the law, a Justice of the Peace, *circa* 1834, and an acting magistrate for 20 years. He played the flute, fife and drum, was often appointed on town committees, was a man of influence and a member of the

M. E. Church. [4.] Silas, b. Oct. 14, 1801 ; m. Apr. 15, 1825, Minerva McCracken, who d. Dec. 10, 1830 ; and 2d, Sep. 15, 1831, Mary Ann Bristol, she b. Cato, N. Y., May 18, 1808 ; he d. Medina, N. Y., Mar. 22, 1880 ; had, i. Frances E., b. Jan. 1, 1828 ; m. Rochester, N. Y., Wm. Sexton, who d. soon ; and 2d, Seymour Sexton, he b. Palmyra, N. Y., Nov. 20, 1820 ; lives Gloversville, N. Y. ii. Charles Bristol, b. Jan. 8, 1833 ; m. Selon, O., 1855, Adelaide Hickox. iii. Wm. McKnight, b. Mar. 1, 1836 ; m. Sep., 1863, Alice Frary. iv. George Albert, b. June 17, 1844 ; m. Feb. 17, 1870, Hattie S. Lewis of Cleveland, O., she b. Burlington, Iowa, Sep. 6, 1851. [5.] Amanda Maria, b. Jan. 12, 1804 ; m. April 22, 1823, Norman Spencer, he b. Sep. 14, 1800 ; d. Oct. 5, 1872, Fowlersville, Mich. ; she d. Apr., 1876 ; had, i. Ery M., b. Dec. 3, 1823. ii. Henry N., b. May 16, 1826. iii. Thankful C., b. Aug. 7, 1829. iv. Julia M., b. Jan. 11, 1832. v. Wm. C., b. Dec. 5, 1834. vi. Sarah Ann, b. Sep. 22, 1837. vii. Jane N., b. Apr. 8, 1840. viii. Charles E., b. Sep. 5, 1842. ix. James P., b. Nov. 18, 1844. [6.] Seth Sears, b. Apr. 10, 1806 ; m. Sep., 1826, Lydia Ann Morgan ; and 2d, Sep. 14, 1848, Mary Richards, who d. May 6, 1853 ; he d. July 5, 1884 ; " an upright man, of grave and modest demeanor ; " had, i. Amanda M., b. July 12, 1827 ; m. Jan. 3, 1848, Edson Irving Wilcox. ii. Amelia Clarissa, b. Oct. 21, 1829 ; m. Nov. 10, 1850, Alfred Stevens at Bedford, O. iii. Albert M., b. Nov. 29, 1831 ; m. July 3, 1853, Minerva Haniford, who d. Oct., 1880 ; and 2d, Dec., 1881, Minnie Haniford. iv. Wm. M., b. Sep. 27, 1836 ; m. May 13, 1862, Josephine L. Parkinson ; —— and by *Mary :* v. Fannie V., b. July 17, 1849. vi. Addie, b. Nov., 1852 ; d. Oct., 1853.

298.

Capt. KNOWLES SEARS[5] [*Jas.*[4], *Silas*[3], *Silas*[2], *Rich.*[1]], b. 1738 ; d. Ridgefield, Ct., June 17, 1817, æ. 79, gr.-st. ; m. *Susanna Townsend*, who d. Apr. 24, 1782, æ. 43, of smallpox ; and 2d, *Charity Haviland*, who d. Danbury, Ct., Sep. 18, 1836, æ. 86. Children :

By *Susanna :*
752.* i. DANIEL, b. Ridge., May 14, 1762.
753. ii. BETTY, b. Ridge., Oct. 31, 1763 ; m. Apr. 14, 1785, *Nathan Hawley*, he b. Sep. 9, 1763 ; d. Feb. 27, 1810 ;

she d. at the house of her son Aaron in Albany, July 28, 1846 ; children, HAWLEY : [1.] Elizabeth, b. July 20, 1786. [2.] Comfort Sears, b. Jan. 27, 1788 ; d. 1874. [3.] Aaron, b. Jan. 25, 1790. [4.] Arza, b. Mar. 14, 1792 ; d. Sep. 16, 1823. [5.] Harvey, b. Feb. 20, 1794. [6.] Samuel, b. Mar. 22, 1796 ; d. Apr. 11, 1852. [7.] Henry. [8.] George, b. July 12, 1800 ; Prest. Bank, Baldwinsville, N. Y. [9.] James, b. June 4, 1803 ; d. Oct. 31, 1872. [10.] Matilda, b. Mar. 26, 1805 ; d. Jan. 2, 1877. [11.] Maria, b. Dec. 26, 1807. [12.] Susanna, b. Mar. 13, 1810.

754. iii. SUSANNA, b. Ridge., July 9, 1766 ; m. *Heman Sears*, No. 438.
755. iv. KNOWLES, b. Ridge., July 29, 1768 ; d. unm., near Danbury, Ct., Oct. 24, 1848, gr.-st.
756. v. MARY, b. Ridge., Aug. 7, 1770 ; m. Nov. 23, 1786, *Isaac Townsend* of Fredericksburg, N. Y. ; and 2d, *Elijah Benedict*, (father of Ezra B., who m. Altha Sears, No. 788, dau. of Comfort S.,) who d. Nov. 23, 1822, æ. 57 yrs. 8 days, gr.-st. ; and 3d, *Forward Stevens*, who d. many years before her, she d. Dec. 16, 1866, æ. 96 yrs. 4 mos. 10 days, gr.-st. They lived in the " Boggs District," Danbury, Ct.
757.* vi. JOHN, b. Ridge., Oct. 15, 1772.
758.* vii. ABIJAH, b. Ridge., Aug. 8, 1774.
759.*viii. ISAAC, b. Ridge., Aug. 7' 1776.
760. ix. DESIRE, b. Ridge., May 25, 1778 ; m. Nov. 13, 1796, *Caleb Curtis Gregory* of Westchester, N. Y., he b. Danbury, Ct., July 18, 1771, d. Dec. 1, 1845, æ. 74 yrs. 4 mos. 23 days, gr.-st. ; she d. Danbury, Feb. 17, 1879, at the great age of 100 yrs. 8 mos. 23 days, and is buried in Cem., 2 miles N. E. of Danbury ; children, GREGORY : [1.] Delos ; lives in Dan. [2.] A dau. ; m. Levi Starr Benedict, and lives in Dan.
761.* x. CHARLES, b. Ridge., Aug. 3, 1780.

By *Charity* :

762. xi. CHARITY, b. Ridge., Aug. 14, 1789 ; m. *Stephen Crosby*.
763. xii. ELIZABETH, b. Ridge., Nov. 26, 1790 ; m. *Nathl. Brush*, and rem. to Huron, N. Y.
764. xiii. DAVID H., b. Ridge., 1794 ; m. *Sally Morris*, and d. s. p. Danbury, Ct., Sep. 26, 1830, æ. 35, gr.-st.
765. xiv. PHEBE, b. Ridge., d. unm.

23

Capt. Knowles Sears, as he is styled in the records, lived and died on the farm adjoining his father's at Ridgefield, Ct., and was buried with his wives in Milltown Cemetery.

299.

Capt. THOMAS SEARS[5] [*Jas.*[4], *Silas*[3], *Silas*[2], *Rich.*[1]], b. Apr. 30, 1745; d. South East, N. Y., Apr. 26, 1804, æ. 59, gr.-st.; m. Sep. 9, 1767, *Deborah Baldwin*, she b. Nov. 23, 1749; d. So. East, Sep. 13, 1828, æ. 79, gr.-st.   Children :

766.* i. ELI, b. So. E., Oct. 16, 1768.
767. ii. THOMAS BALDWIN, b. So. E., Feb. 21, 1773; m. Dec. 2, 1789, *Betsy Lewis*, and d. s. p., Carmel, N. Y., 1855.
768. iii. ELIZABETH, b. So. E., Sep. 3, 1775; d. Sep. 23, 1790.
769.* iv. JAMES, b. So. E., Mar. 24, 1778.
770.* v. ARCHIBALD, b. So. E., Aug. 8, 1780.
771. vi. SOPHIA C., b. So. E., May 12, 1784; m. Apr. 28, 1801, *Archibald Young*, and d. Apr. 12, 1869.   Arch. Young of Bath, L. I., and Benj. and Elkanah Young of Phelps, N. Y., are descendants.
772. vii. ISAAC, b. So. E., July 23, 1786.
773. viii. DEBORAH, b. So. E., Oct. 18, 1789; m. Dec. 25, 1805, —— *Craft ;* and 2d, —— *Ludington.*
774. ix. SALLY B., b. So. E., June 26, 1792; m. Mar. 27, 1810, *Ezra Young*, and had Thomas.

Thomas Sears was a captain in the Revolutionary Army, and after the peace settled in South East, Putnam county, N. Y. on land which he bought of the government, and on which his descendants still live.

He was a prominent church member and trustee during many years.

301.

JAMES SEARS[5] [*Jas.*[4], *Silas*[3], *Silas*[2], *Rich.*[1]], b. 1747; m. (*Abigail ?*) *Sherwood*, dau. of Jehiel S.   Children :

775. i. HEZEKIAH.
776. ii. WILLIAM.
777. iii. LYMAN.
778.* iv. JARED, b. LENOX, MASS., Aug. 12, 1779.
779. v. BETSY, m. *Joseph Montague* of Cambridge, Vt. ; children, MONTAGUE : [1.] Harry. [2.] Dau. m. —— *Porter* of Hadley, Mass.

780. vi. HULDA, perhaps m. *Gideon Bronson* of Sunderland, Vt.
781.* vii. (?) JAMES.

James Sears lived for a time in Lenox, Mass.; was in Capt. Oliver Belding's Co., in Maj. Caleb Hyde's Regt., July 8 to July 26, 1778, in Northern Department.

He removed to the "Lake Region," (Canada).

The last-named son, James, taking all the family traditions together, I think belongs to this family, but needs confirmation.

303.

COMFORT SEARS[5] [*Jas.*[4], *Silas*[3], *Silas*[2], *Rich.*[1]], b. Ridgefield, Ct., Mar. 20, 1751; d. there Dec. 24, 1827, æ. 76, gr.-st., Milltown, N. Y.; m. Dec. 18, 1777, *Eunice Crane*, dau. of Judge Joseph C., of South East, N. Y., she b. Nov. 20, 1754, d. Jan. 23, 1839, æ. 84, gr.-st. Children:

782.   i. THIRZA, b. Ridge., Mar. 22, 1779; m. Oct. 24, 1796; *Wm. Sears*, No. 464.
783.   ii. ESTHER, b. Ridge., July 29, 1780; m. June, 1799, *Jere. Griffiths*, and d. Oct. 10, 1811; had 4 chil.
784.   iii. DESIRE, b. Ridge., May 24, 1782; m. Oct. 1, 1815, *Czar Benedict*, and d. Apr. 22, 1854; had 4 chil.
785.   iv. EUNICE, b. Ridge., Feb. 4, 1784; m. Dec. 18, 1810, *James Weed*, he b. Mar. 31, 1783; d. May 8, 1814, of the malignant fever that raged in So. E., that spring; she d. July 8, 1858; children, WEED: [1.] Oscar, b. Dec. 4, 1812; m. Nov. 6, 1837, Ann Eliza Quintard of Norwalk, Ct., she b. Oct. 23, 1818; had, i. George Elmore, b. Oct. 3, 1839; m. Jan. 5, 1859, in N. Y., C. L. Salladee; he was foreman of John Roach, ship-builder, Phila., and later his assignee. ii. Mary Francis, b. Oct. 7, 1842; m. Dec. 19, 1872, Daniel R. Sears, No. 2179. [2.] James Orville, b. Sep. 4, 1814; m. Apr. 12, 1843, Sarah E. Crane of So. East, she b. Oct. 23, 1818; no chil.; they live on the old homestead of Comfort Sears, his grandfather.
786.   v. CAMILLA, b. Ridge., Apr. 26, 1786; m. July 4, 1810, *Elijah Crosby*, a bro. of James Sears' 1st wife; and d. Jan. 9, 1815; had 2 chil.
787.* vi. JAMES, b. Ridge., Nov. 10, 1788.
788.   vii. ALTHA, or *Atha*, b. Ridge., Dec. 18, 1790; m. Jan. 22, 1811, *Ezra P. Benedict*, and d. Sep. 17, 1827, gr.-st.,

- "Bogg's Dist." Cem.; he d. Jan. 19, 1852, æ. 59 yrs. 4 mos. 19 days, gr.-st.; had 3 chil.
789.* viii. JOSEPH CRANE, b. Ridge., Dec. 18, 1792.
790.* ix. LEWIS, b. Ridge., June 26, 1795.
791. x. POLLY M., b. Ridge., July 26, 1800; m. Oct. 22, 1831, *Nehemiah Perry*, who d. 1872; she d. Apr. 12, 1873; had, *inter alios:* [1.] Mary, m. Hawley Hayt, and d. 1833; she had 5 children, one of whom is Carrie Hayt of Towners, N. Y.

Comfort Sears, like his father, was strict in the observance of the Sabbath, and required the same of his children, though he never united with the church.

In February, 1793, his house took fire in the night, and was entirely destroyed. He turned out with only his shirt on, and got out the things; first of all a barrel of pork; in some way he injured his great toe, either by freezing or a bruise, and it was the cause of his death many years after.

He built another house on the same site, which is now occupied by James O. Weed, his grandson, and a very good house it still is.

It stands on "Joe's Hill," now called "Federal Hill," Millplain, Fairfield county, Ct.

Judge Joseph Crane, his wife's father, was descended from one of the first settlers, and owned a large tract of land in South East, N. Y., and "Joe's Hill" was named for him.

The line now runs over the range of hills, and that in South East is still called Joe's Hill, while that in Ridgefield is now called Federal Hill.

Eunice Crane was a sister of James Weed's wife Sarah, and of Darius Crane's, (of Hillsdale, Mich.) grand-father. See *ante*, No. 445.

304.

GEORGE SEARS[5] [*Seth[4], Rich.[3], Silas[2], Rich.[1]*], b. 1735; d. Newport, R. I., 1801, æ. 66, gr.-st.; m. Newport, Jan. 2, 1765, *Abigail Hall*, b. 1737; d. 1821, æ. 84, gr.-st. Children:
792.* i. GEORGE, b. 1765.
793. ii. RUTH, b. 1770; m. *Joseph Rogers*, and d. 1802, æ. 32, gr.-st.; leaving a dau. and son William.
794. iii. *Dau.;* m. —— *Rathbone*, and died at an advanced age in Newport, leaving a son George, who lived in Providence, R. I.

795. iv. *Dau.*; d. at her bro's. house in Baltimore, Md., of confluent small-pox, and was buried in his lot, cor. Fayette and Green streets, with a marble gr.-st.

796.* v. (?) JOHN T.

George Sears lived in Newport, R. I., and was one of the Committee of Council on adoption of the Federal Constitution, appointed in 1784.

He died intestate, and letters of admn. were granted to his widow Abigail, Dec. 10, 1801, but I find no record of distribution of his estate.

In the old burying-ground on Thames street in Newport are grave-stones with these inscriptions, viz. :

"George Seares, Esquire, (grandson of Thomas) born 1735, and died 1801, æ. 66 years. Common Council, 1784.

"Abigail his wife, born 1737, died 1821, æ. 84 years."

"Ruth Sears, wife of Joseph Rogers, Esquire, and daughter of George Sears, born 1770, and died 1802, æ. 32 yrs."

These stones were erected at the same time as that to Thomas Seares, see *ante* No. 3.

I have no reason to doubt the accuracy of the dates given, and have adopted them in foregoing records; but George Sears, not *Seares*, was probably son of Seth, certainly not of *Thomas*, as the epitaph asserts, for the very good reason that there was no Thomas Sears at that time of adult age.

In the proper place, I give my reasons for including John T. Sears in this family.

The account of this family in each generation is imperfect, and needs revision.

305.

Capt. JOHN SEARS[5] [*John[4], Rich.[3], Silas[2], Rich.[1]*], b. Lyme, Ct., Mar. 4, 1735–6; d. Dec. 28, 1766; m. Lyme, Jan. 24, 1760, by Rev. Stephen Johnson, pastor of 1st church, to *Judith Peck*, dau. of Jasper and Sarah (Clark) P., she b. Lyme, Jan. 22, 1740; (m. 2d, Nov. 20, 1777, Capt. Gates of Colchester, Ct., by whom she had i. Judith Marvin, bap. Aug. 8, 1779, and ii. Sarah Clark, bap. Oct. 30, 1785). Children :

797. i. RICHARD, b. Lyme, Aug. 28, 1761 ; bap. Aug. 4, 1771.

798.* ii. JASPER PECK, b. Lyme, July 7, 1763 ; bap. Aug. 4, 1771.

799. iii. Betsy, b. Lyme, Nov. 22, 1765 ; bap. Aug. 4, 1771 ;
m. *Elijah Ransom* of Montville, Ct.

Capt. John Sears was received into the church in Lyme,
Nov., 1755, and widow Judith Sears, July, 1771.

He was a large land-owner, as appears by records of Old
Lyme.

312.

ROLAND SEARS[5] [*Zach.*[4], *Jos.*[3], *Silas*[2], *Rich.*[1]], b. Yarmouth, Mass., Feb. 3, 1744–5 ; m. Apr. 9, 1777, *Jedidah Conant*, dau. of Zilphah C., of Bridgewater, Mass., she b. 1752.
Children :

800.   i. Lois, b. Ashfield, Mass, June 6, 1777.
801.   ii. Mehitable, b. Ash., Dec. 21, 1778.
802.   iii. Mary, b. Ash., July 26, 1780.
803.* iv. Zachariah, b. Ash., Mar. 19, 1782.
804.* v. Ahirah, b. Ash., Dec. 12, 1783.
805.* vi. Peter, b. Ash., Aug. 23, 1787.
806.* vii. Roland, b. Ash., Feb. 3, 1789.
807.* viii. Thomas, b. Ash., Jan. 29, 1791.
808.   ix. Roxanna, b. Ash., Oct. 14, 1792.
809.   x. Abner, b. Ash., Apr. 2, 1796, was a Dr. and lived
in Shiawassee co., Mich.

Roland Sears removed to Ashfield, Mass., and bought a farm,
May, 1773 ; was in Lt. Bartlett's Co., which marched on Lex-
ington Alarm, 22d Apr., 1775 ; and was credited with 5 days'
service and mileage, £7. 1. 2 ; he subsequently enlisted in Capt.
Eben Webber's Co., Col. John Fellows' Regt. A dau. m. ——
Fuller of Ann Arbor, Mich., and another m. —— Thayer of
Williamsburg, Mass.

318.

JOSEPH SEARS[5] [*Zach.*[4], *Jos.*[3], *Silas*[2], *Rich.*[1]], b. Yarmouth, Mass., July 20, 1756, d. May 30, 1836, æ. 79, gr.-st.,
Brewster ; m. (pub. Dec. 7, 1782,) *Thankful (Clark) Howes*,
widow of Henry Howes, and dau. of Scotto and Thankful
(Crosby) C., she b. Oct. 22, 1759 ; was adm. 2d ch. Yar., June
9, 1793 ; and d. Dennis, Apr. 22, 1842, æ. 83, gr.-st., (she had
a dau. Rebecca Howes, bap. E. Yar., June 16, 1793). Children :
810.* ·i. Zachariah, b. Yar., Dec. 29, 1783 ; bap. June 16,
1793.

811.* ii. HENRY, b. Yar., May 5, 1785, bap. June 16, 1793.
812. iii. HITTY, b. Yar., Oct. 21, 1788; bap. June 16, 1793;
    d. Aug. 4, 1806, in 18 yr., gr.-st., No. Den.
813.* iv. ZEBINA, b. Yar., Mar. 11, 1790; bap. June 16, 1793.
814.* v. JOSEPH, b. Yar., June 24, 1792; bap. June 16, 1793.
815. vi. THANKFUL, b. Dennis, May 8, 1794; m. Mar. 20,
    1817, *Isaiah Howes*, who d. Oct. 24, 1849; she d. Sep.
    29, 1878; children, HOWES: [1.] Myra, b. Jan. 1, 1818;
    m. Capt. Levi Howes, and d. May, 1851. [2.] Harry, b.
    Jan. 20, 1820; d. Sep. 24, 1832. [3.] Sarah Clark, b.
    Feb. 20, 1823; m. Nathan Sears, No. 1324. [4.] Roland,
    b. Oct. 27, 1827; m. Harriet M. Chapman.
816.* vii. PETER, b. Den., May 9, 1796; bap. June 19.
817.* viii. ROLAND, b. Den., Nov. 23, 1798; bap. Jan. 10, 1802.

Joseph Sears had the old homestead in East Yarmouth, now
Dennis, at his father's decease in 1796.

He took a prominent part in town affairs, was Selectman for
11 years from 1794, and was Rep. in 1800.

He was in Capt. Elisha Hedge's Co., in Col. Nat. Freeman's
Regt., and served in R. I., 1 mo. 4 days; and in Lt. Micajah
Sears' Co., at alarm Dartmouth and Falmouth, Sep. 6, 1778,
serving 3 days.

320.

STEPHEN SEARS[5] [*Jos.[4], Jos.[3], Silas[2], Rich.[1]*], b. Yar-
mouth, Mass., Sep. 5, 1736; m. Nov. 12, 1758, *Elizabeth
Sears*, No. 290, dau. of Silas and Elizabeth (Nickerson) S.
Children :

818. i. MARY, bap. Har., Oct. 19, 1766.
819. ii. RUTH, bap. Har., Oct. 19, 1766; pub. Har., Dec.
    15, 1792, to Jona. Covil of Yar.
820.* iii. ISAAC, bap. Har., Oct. 19, 1766.
821. iv. DAVID, bap. Har., May 3, 1767. (Was David
    Sears of Br., who m. Esther ——, before 1828, his son ?)
822.* v. LARNED, bap. Har., May 3, 1767.
823.* vi. LEVI, bap. Har., Jan. 22, 1769.
824. vii. MARY, bap. Har., May 17, 1772.
825.* viii. STEPHEN.
826. ix. ELIZABETH, bap. Har., June 12, 1774.
827.* x. JOSEPH, bap. Har., Oct. 12, 1776.
828. xi. LAVINIA, bap. Har., May 23, 1779.
829.* xii. WASHINGTON, b. Har., Oct. 26, 1781; bap. Nov. 25.

830. xiii. GREENE, b. Har., Oct. 26, 1781; *gemini;* bap. Nov. 25.

Stephen Sears lived in the ancient Judah Sears' house at " Punkhorn," West Brewster.

On alarm Bedford and Falmouth, Sep. 7, 1778, he turned out in Capt. Samuel Berry's Co., doing 7 days' service, and marching 112 miles.

325.

FREEMAN SEARS[5] [*Roland*[4]*, Jos.*[3]*, Silas*[2]*, Rich.*[1]], b. Hardwick, Mass., July 29, 1740; d. June 30, 1807; m. Oct. 22, 1761, *Mehitable Haskell*, dau. of Andrew and Jane (Clark) H., she b. July 9, 1744; d. Apr. 6, 1845, at the great age of 100 yrs. 8 mos. 29 days. " She was the mother of 9 children, 60 grand-children, 138 great-grand-children, and 14 great-great-grand-children, making a posterity of 223." Children:

831.* i. ROLAND, b. Hard., Dec. 24, 1762.
832.* ii. ANDREW HASKELL, b. Hard., Mar. 29, 1765.
833. iii. MILLICENT, b. Hard., Sep. 20, 1767; m. —— *Field*, and d. Erving, Mass., Mar. 6, 1853, æ. 85.
834. iv. MARY, b. Hard., Mar. 17, 1771.
835. v. MERCY, b. Hard., Jan. 23, 1773.
836. vi. CHARLES DOOLITTLE, b. Hard., Oct. 7, 1775, (?) bap. Aug. 8.
837. vii. SUSANNA, b. Greenwich, Aug. 23, 1780.
838. viii. JOHN, b. Green., Oct. 13, 1781, was a Deacon.

Freeman Sears was in Capt. Timo. Paige's Co., and marched to Bennington, Vt., on alarm — 90 miles' travel, and served Aug. 21 to Aug. 31, 1777.

He had probably removed to Greenwich previous to Feb. 2, 1779, when his wife was dismissed from Ch., Hard., to Ch., Green.

326.

Lt. Col. BARNABAS SEARS[5] [*Roland*[4], *Jos.*[3], *Silas*[2], *Rich.*[1]], b. Hardwick, Mass., Nov. 20, 1743; m. Barre, Mass., Nov. 1, 1764, *Rachel Bullard,* who d. June 30, 1811, æ. 65. Children:

839. i. JOHN, b. Hard., Aug. 2, 1765; d. s. p. April 14, 1825, Scipio, N. Y.

840.   ii. HANNAH, b. Hard., Mar. 4, 1767; m. Oct. 25, 1785, *Ezekiel Baker ;* rem. to Marcellus, N. Y., and d. Aug. 15, 1841 ; children, BAKER : [1.] Joshua, b. Oct. 8, 1786 ; d. 1849–50. [2.] Isaac, b. June 17, 1788 ; d. July 23, 1813. [3.] Ezekiel, b. Feb. 20, 1790; d. Dec. 30, 1879. [4.] Joseph, b. Feb. 8, 1792; d. Jan. 30, 1884. [5.] Rachel, b. May 29, 1794 ; d. July 1, 1822. [6.] Moses, b. Aug. 17, 1796 ; d. Dec. 30, 1879; rem. to Ohio. [7.] John, b. June 25, 1799 ; d. Nov. 1. [8.] Anson, b. Aug. 7, 1801 ; d. Dec., 1881. [9.] Dau., b. July 6, 1803 ; d. July 7. [10.] Benjamin, b. June 23, 1804; d. Oct., 1848. [11.] Hannah, b. Aug. 15, 1807 ; d. Aug., 1865. [12.] Mary, b. Sep. 23, 1809 ; d.

841.*   iii. JOSEPH, b. Hard., April 12, 1769.

842.*   iv. MOSES, b. Hard., Apr. 22, 1771.

843.   v. BARNABAS, b. Hard., May 18, 1773 ; bap. June (? May) 23 ; d. June 2, (?) 1773.

844.   vi. FREEMAN, bap. Hard., May 15, 1774; d. June 18, 1774.

845.   vii. MARY, b. Hard., June 10, 1775 ; bap. June 11; d. Northampton, Mass.

846.   viii. ROLAND, b. Greenwich, Feb. 14, 1792; d. s. p. Dec. 6, 1839 ; m. Nov. 2, 1837, Mary Avery Smith, dau. of Maj. Sim. Smith of New London, Ct., she b. Oct. 15, 1794 ; he was a Dr. in Whitesboro, N. Y.

847.*   ix. BARNABAS, b. Greenwich, May 1, 1782.

848.   x. *Dau.* m. —— *Lewis,* and d. in Ohio, leaving a dau.

Barnabas Sears was a farmer, and lived on part of the old homestead in Hardwick.

The farm was sold in 1777 to Rev. Samuel Dennis, and he removed to the adjoining town of Greenwich, his wife being dismissed to the church there Sep. 13, 1779.

He taught school in 1772, — was on " Committee of Correspondence " in 1777, and a member of Constitutional Convention, 1779–80.

His military service during the Revolution was abundant and conspicuous. He was sergeant of the Minute Men, marched in Capt. Simon Hazeltine's Co. on the Lexington alarm, April 19, 1775, and was allowed for 150 miles travel, and 16 days service £1. 19. 11.

He returned and assisted Capt. Samuel Billings in organizing a company for the regular service, of which he was com. Lt. May 23, 1775, and was captain of a company in the camp at

24

Dorchester Heights, Feb. 15, 1776. He was elected Major of Col. Holman's Regt., June 26, 1776, and served as Lt. Col. in the three months' service, Aug. 12 to Nov. 15, 1781, 3 mos., 10 days' service, and 140 miles travel.

In the troublous times which followed the Revolution, like many other officers and privates, he was concerned in the unlawful effort of relief, styled " Shay's Rebellion."

His offense was pardoned by the government, and he subscribed the oath of allegiance in 1787.

328.

Sergt. ELISHA SEARS⁵ [*Roland⁴, Jos.³, Silas², Rich.¹*], b. Hardwick, Mass., June 6, 1748; d. Barre, Mass., 1820–21; m. Hard., Oct. 31, 1771, *Hannah Sears*, No. 337, dau. of Silas and Deborah (Buck) S., she b. 1756; d. Barre, Oct. 20, 1842, æ. 86. Children:

849.   i. POLLY, b. Barre, 1774; d. unm., Jan. 29, 1844, æ. 70.

850.*   ii. BARNABAS, b. Barre, June 11, 1777.

851.   iii. THANKFUL, b. Barre; m. —— *Winslow*, and had 5 children.

852.   iv. LYDIA, b. Barre; m. —— *Smith;* and 2d, Aug. 15, 1806, *Asher Witherell,* a farmer in Ashtabula, Mich.; children, WITHERELL : [1.] Franklin ; lives in Mich. [2.] William; lives in Penna. [3.] Lyman ; lives in Olean, N. Y. [4.] Mary, m. —— *Stone*, and lives in Chatsworth, Ill.

853.   v. MERCY, b. Barre; m. *Robert Shadders*, and d. s. p. Albion, N. Y.

854.   vi. HANNAH, b. Barre; m. *John Cassiday,* and d. Tuscarora, N. Y., leaving 3 sons.

855.*   vii. FRANKLIN, b. Barre, Oct. 3, 1785.

Elisha Sears of Hutchinson, now Barre, Mass., marched on Lexington alarm, in Capt. John Black's Co., Apr. 20, 1775, 180 miles, and 11 days' service, £1 6 6½; served in Capt. Benj. Nye's Co. for assistance to Northern army, Sep. 26, 1777; 29 days' service and 128 miles' travel; Mar. 27 to July 29, 1778, he was in Capt. Marean's Co., in Col. Sternes' Regt. of Guards at Cambridge, "*guarding troops of the Convention,*" and was Sergeant in Lt. Wm. Muzzy's Co., Col. Nathan Sparhawk's Regt., from July 5 to July 15, 1778, at the barracks in Rutland; 10 miles travel.

He was blind for many years previous to his death.

His widow resided with her daughter Polly, and her name appears as a U. S. pensioner in 1840, then of Barre, æ. 84.

They were worthy, industrious people.

The children are perhaps not placed in order of birth.

332.

STEPHEN SEARS[5] [*Barnabas*[4], *Jos.*[3], *Silas*[2], *Rich.*[1]], b. about 1736; d. May 24, 1815, in 79 yr., gr.-st., No. Den.; m. Yar., Nov. 24, 1757, *Lydia Sears*, No. 155, who d. Mar. 8, 1792, in 57 yr., gr.-st.; and 2d, (pub. Dennis, Nov. 30, 1794,) *Martha Hale* of Sandwich, Mass., who d. Jan. 25, 1838, æ. 79. Children:

By *Lydia* :

856. i. BARNABAS, b. Yar., Oct. 7, 1758; bap. Mar. 20, 1774; d. Jan. 18, 1777, being killed by an accidental shot from a British man-of-war while on board of a transport in the harbor of Newport, R. I.; he served Feb. 5 to June 1, 1776, in Capt. John Grannis' Co., at Tarpaulin Cove.

857. ii. THANKFUL, b. Yar., Oct. 15, 1760; bap. Mar. 20, 1774; m. Yar., June 3, 1779, *Levi Eldredge* of Ashfield, Mass.

858. iii. KEZIA, b. Yar., Aug. 14, 1763; bap. Mar. 20, 1774; adm. Ch., July 21, 1792; m. *Enoch Hall*, he b. June 15, 1759; d. Aug. 1, 1833; children, HALL: [1.] William, b. Sep. 17, 1785. [2.] Enoch, b. June 15, 1787. [3.] Stephen, b. Sep. 3, 1792; d. at sea. [4.] Hannah; all bap. July 21, 1793. [5.] Kezia, bap. Nov. 10, 1799. [6.] Dinah, bap. Nov. 29, 1801. [7.] Francis, bap. July 3, 1803. [8.] John Young, bap. Oct. 27, 1805.

859.* iv. STEPHEN, b. Yar., Oct. 2, 1765; bap. Mar. 20, 1774.

860. v. PRISCILLA, b. Yar., Aug. 13, 1768; bap. Mar. 20, 1774; m. Yar., Dec. 10, 1789, *James Howes*, son of Josiah and Lydia (Howes) H., he b. May 13, 1739.

861. vi. LYDIA, b. Yar., July 24, 1771; bap. Mar. 20, 1774; m. Mar. 3, 1791, *Stephen Sears, Jr.*, No. 825.

By *Martha* :

862. vii. SOPHRONIA, bap. Yar., June 11, 1797; m. Jan. 31, 1819, *Parker Miller* of Yar.

Stephen Sears and wife Lydia were admitted to full communion in the 2d Ch., Yar., Mar. 20, 1774, and he was chosen Deacon, Mar. 9, 1789.

He was active in town and church affairs.

Stephen Sears of Dennis, "*gentleman*," made his will Dec. 15, 1815 (? 1814,) and mentions wife Martha, daus. Sophronia Sears, Thankful Eldredge, Keziah Hall, Priscilla Howes, Lydia Sears and son Stephen.

336.

Sergt. RICHARD SEARS[5] [*Silas[4], Jos.[3], Silas[2], Rich.[1]*], perhaps born in Hardwick, Mass., prob. d. Hoosick, N. Y., after June 1, 1814; m. Hard., Dec. 29, 1771, *Mary Lee*, dau. of Abner and Sarah (Merrick) L., of H., (of the Ipswich, Concord and Worcester family of Lees, and Harwich Merricks). He m. 2d —— *Edgecumb*, who became insane, and d. s. p. Children:

By *Mary:*
863.*   i. John, b. Feb. 22, 1773.
864.*   ii. Richard, b. Oct. 9, 1775, perhaps in Ashfield.
865.*   iii. Orange, b. Amherst, Mass., Dec. 4, 1776.
866.   iv. Polly, m. *Daniel Harrington*, and rem. to Albany, N. Y.; had a son, Charles, a tinner, who lived in Canandaigna, N. Y.
867.   v. Silas, rem. with his parents to Hoosick, was a wagonmaker by trade, and a preacher in the Baptist Church. He is said to have rem. to South-western Ohio, married and had family, but it is believed no sons.
868.   vi. Sally, d. unm.
869.* vii. Abner, b. June 15, 1787.

The children may have been born in different order.

Richard Sears was probably born in Hardwick, or in the adjoining town of Greenwich, Mass., but I do not find his name on record in either place prior to his marriage in 1771.

Richard Sears, *from Ashfield*, was a Corporal in Capt. Isaac Gray's Co. in Col. Jon. Brewer's Regt., 1775, which fought at Bunker's Hill; and Sergeant in Capt. Abner Pomroy's Co. in Col. Ezra Wood's Regt.; marched into N. Y. State, 160 miles travel, 7 mos., 27 days' service, wages £15 16 0.

Family tradition says he was at battle of Bunker's Hill, and his grandson, Walter S. Sears, of Adrian, Mich., possesses the powder-horn which he carried on that memorable occasion.

After the Revolution he removed to Hoosick, N. Y., and is supposed to have died there.

He was a member of Federal Lodge No. 33 of Mark Masons, at Hoosick, June 1, 1814.

His grandson, Rev. Hiram Sears of Effingham, Ill., and of the Seamen's Bethel Home, Cleveland, Ohio, earnestly requests any person having knowledge of Richard Sears or of either of his children to communicate with him.

339.

BARNABAS SEARS[5] [*Silas*[4], *Jos.*[3], *Silas*[2], *Rich.*[1]], b. Hardwick, Mass., Mar. 21, 1765; d. Amherst, Mass., Feb. 20, 1850, æ. 85; m. *Thankful Sears.* (Whose dau. was she?) Children :

870.*   i. BARNABAS, b. Hard., 1787.
871.   ii. RHODA, b. Hard., 1793; d. unm., Aug. 17, 1871, æ. 78.
872.   iii. THANKFUL, b. Hard., 1796; d. unm., Oct. 9, 1879, æ. 83.
873.   iv. RUTH, b. Hard., 1797; d. unm., Oct. 5, 1848, æ. 51.
874.   v. ELI, b. Hard., 1799; d. unm., Oct. 6, 1841, æ. 42.
875.   vi. SIMEON, b. Hard.; m. *Hannah Hinds*, and rem. to Batavia, N. Y.
876.* vii. SARDIS, b. Hard., 1802.
877.* viii. NATHAN, b. Hard., May 31, 1807.

Barnabas Sears was drafted July, 1779, to serve 9 months in Continental Army, under act of June 9, 1779; was in Capt. Powers' Co., age 16; 5 ft. in height; brown complexion.

In his later days he resided in Amherst with his three un-married daughters, and drew a pension.

340.

EDWARD SEARS[5] [*Edw.*[4], *Josiah*[3], *Silas*[2], *Rich.*[1]], b.—— ; m. *Mary* ——, who was adm. to Ch., Halifax, Mass., June 25, 1760. (Edward Sears and Mercy Sears, pub. Yar., June 4, 1764.) Children :

878.* i. HOLMES, b. Hal., July 13, 1757.
879.   ii. MARY, b. Hal., Nov. 8, 1758.
880. iii. LUCINDA, b. Hal., Apr. 26, 1761.
881. iv. MERCY, b. Hal., May 17, 1764.

Edward Sears marched from Halifax to Bristol, on alarm of Dec. 9, 1776, in Lt. Judah Wood's Co., in Lt.-Col. Thos. Lothrop's Regt.; was in camp 11 days; 4 days' service and 80 miles' travel; Sep., 1778, on alarm at Dartmouth and Falmouth, he served 3 days in Lt. Crowell's Co.

344.

JOSIAH SEARS[5] [*Edw.*[4], *Josiah*[3], *Silas*[2], *Rich.*[1]], b. Halifax, Mass., Nov. 17, 1740; m. Plympton, Mass., Feb. 5, 1767, *Lydia Berry.* Child:
882. i. JOSIAH, b. Hal., May 28, 1767.

I give the dates as received from the Town Clerk.
A Lydia Sears m. Plympton, Mar. 15, 1770, Zebulon Robinson; perhaps the above.

346.

Capt. NATHANIEL SEARS[5] [*Sam'l*[4], *Josiah*[3], *Silas*[2], *Rich.*[1]], b. Yarmouth, Mass., Feb. 21, 1731–2; was lost at sea, July 13, 1771; m. Harwich, Nov. 8, 1753, *Phebe Lincoln;* (who m. 2d, Gorham Baker, and had a son Gorham, b. 1781.) Children:
883. i. PHEBE, b. Yar., July 28, 1754; bap. Sep. 18, 1757; m. Yar., Nov. 24, 1774, *Seth Hall,* and rem. to Hawley, Mass.
884. ii. MERCY, b. Yar., May 14, 1756; bap. Sep. 18, 1757; m. Yar., Nov. 7, 1776, *Thomas Blossom.*
885. iii. DESIRE, b. Yar., Aug. 24. 1760; bap. Oct. 19; m. Yar., Dec. 17, 1778, *Joseph Bangs,* he b. July 5, 1757, and rem. to Hawley; children, BANGS: [1.] Phebe, b. Sep. 5, 1779. [2.] Joseph, b. Oct. 10, 1783. [3.] Desire, b. Dec. 9, 1785. [4.] Sarah, b. Jan. 6, 1788. [5.] Polly, b. Feb. 28, 1790. [6.] Jonathan, b. Feb. 9, 1792. [7.] Sabra, b. Feb. 10, 1794. [8.] Olive, b. June 8, 1796. [9.] Washington, b. Oct. 10, 1798. [10.] Freeman S., b. July 11, 1804.
886. iv. REBECCA, b. Yar., Aug. 17, 1762; m. Yar., Mar. 22, 1781, *Heman Gage,* and removed to Hawley.
887.* v. RUFUS, b. Yar., 1770; bap. Mar. 18.
888. vi. JERUSHA, bap. Oct. 13, 1765; m. Yar., Dec. 30, 1787, *Anthony Gage* of Harwich.

He was a ship-master.
Phebe Sears was adm. to 2d Ch., Yar., Aug. 14, 1757, and Nathaniel Sears, "*Jr.*," on Aug. 2, 1767.

355.

DAVID SEARS[5] [*Josiah*[4], *Josiah*[3], *Silas*[2], *Rich.*[1]], b. East-ham, Mass., Apr. 14, 1753; m. there, Jan. 30, 1777, *Martha Cole*. Child:

889. i. DAVID, b. Eastham, Dec. 25, 1777.

David Sears of Eastham was in Capt. Sol. Higgins' Co. from July 13 to Dec. 31, 1775, and enlisted as of Boston, Aug. 16, 1777, for 3 years' service in Col. Jackson's Regt. He perhaps removed to Ashford, Ct., where a David Sears was living in 1840, then aged 87, in receipt of a pension for Revolutionary service.

358.

ZEBEDEE SEARS[5] [*David*[4], *Josiah*[3], *Silas*[2], *Rich.*[1]], b Middleboro, Mass., June 16, 1734; d. Jan. 30, 1775; m. Midd., Mar. 4, 1756, by Peter Oliver, J. P., to *Mary Leonard*, she b. 1737; d. Dec. 5, 1771. Children:

890. i. DANIEL, b. Midd., May 22, 1756.
891. ii. PHEBE, b. Midd., Oct. 7, 1758; m. 1778, *Ezreck Howland*, of Freetown, Mass., (bro. to Judith, who m. Earl Sears;) children, HOWLAND: [1.] John. [2.] Ezreck. [3.] Elkanah. [4.] Polly. [5.] Abigail. [6.] Lucinda.
892.* iii. EARL, b. Midd., Dec. 19, 1761.
893. iv. ELKANAH, b. Midd., Apr. 20, 1764; d. Mar. 18, 1838; he marched to Newport, R. I., in Capt. Abram Washburn's Co., Mar. 10, 1781, 40 miles travel; lived in South Bridgewater, Mass., and was called Captain.
894.* v. LEONARD, b. Midd., Sep. 22, 1771.

Zebedee Sears was a private at Oneida Station, N. Y., Sep. 22, 1758, and in 1775, was in Capt. Sam'l Curtis' Co. in Col. Eben Leonard's Regt.; he enlisted in train June 11, 1775, was in 4th Regt., and had wages allowed him £48 13 7, though not mustered.

One Zebedee Sears from *York*, enlisted June 10, 1775, in Capt. Saml. Laighton's Co., Col. James Scammons' Regt., and deserted July 1.

360.

ABNER SEARS[5] [*David*[4], *Josiah*[3], *Silas*[2], *Rich.*[1]], b. Middleboro, Mass., Feb. 19, 1738–9; m. Bridgewater, Mass.,

July 15, 1764, *Lydia Perkins*, dau. of Sol. Perkins of B.
Children :
895.   i. KEZIA, b. Midd., Apr. 16, 1763.
896. ii. WILLARD, b. Midd., Mar., 30, 1765.
897. iii. LYDIA, b. Midd., Aug. 31, 1766.
898. iv. HOWES, b. Midd., Mar. 26, 1771.
899.   v. ABNER, b. Midd., Oct. 12, 1781.

369.

Capt. PETER SEARS[5] [*Jona.*[4], *Josiah*[3], *Silas*[2], *Rich.*[1]], b.
Halifax, Mass., Nov. 29, 1753; d. 1820, æ. 68 ; m. 1777, *Susanna Coleman*, of Scituate, who d. 1824, æ. 73.   Children :
900.* i. PETER, b. Scit.
901. ii. SARAH, b. Scit.; m. 1811, *Elijah Damon.*
902. iii. MARY, b. Scit. ; m. *Jacob Stockbridge.*
903. iv. LUCY, b. Scit.; m. Dec. 5, 1813, *Abiel Farrar.*
904.   v. DOLLY, b. Scit.; m. *Joseph Stockbridge ;* and 2d,
       Lot Litchfield, of S., he b. June 10, 1781 ; d. s. p.

Peter Sears settled on the John Bryant place, north of
Hoop-pole Hill, Cedar Swamp, Scituate, Mass.

He marched on Lexington alarm, in Capt. Galen Clapp's
Co., and was credited with 24 miles travel, and 5 days' service,
and expense, 9s. 1d. He enlisted at Halifax, Dec. 20, 1775, in
Capt. Nathl. Winslow's Co., in Col. John Thomas' Regt., and
on March 1, 1779, was com. 2d Lieut. in Capt. Noah Nichols'
company of artificers, attached to artillery in the field and later,
captain.

In Gen. Reg. ix, 134, it is erroneously stated that he was
" *son* of *Col. Sears* of Chatham, killed at Culloden," a mythical
personage, and in fact Capt. Peter Sears was not born till 7
years after the battle.

SIXTH GENERATION.

383.

Sergt. JONATHAN SEARS[6] [*Jona.*[5], *Jona.*[4], *Sam'l*[3], *Paul*[2], *Rich.*[1]], b. Harwich, Mass., May 7, 1750; d. Ashfield, Mass., Feb. 18, 1808, æ. 57; m. Yarmouth, Mass., Sep. 23, 1773, *Abigail Hall*, dau. of Joseph and Abigail (Clarke) H., she b. Nov. 2, 1754; d. Nov. 18, 1842; she was adm. to 2d Ch., Yar., June 12, 1774.   Children :

905.   i. BARNABAS CLARK, b. Har., Aug. 3, 1774; bap. E. Yar., Sep. 25; d. Apr. 18, 1799, æ. 25.

906.* ii. JONATHAN, b. Har., Mar. 19, 1777; bap. E. Yar., Apr. 6.

907.* iii. FREEMAN, b. Har., Nov. 28, 1779; bap. E. Yar., Jan. 2, 1780.

908.   iv. HEPSIBAH SWAN, b. Har., Oct. 16, 1783; bap. E. Yar., Nov. 23; m. Rev. *Samuel Parker;* and d. Feb. 13, 1814.

909.* v. AZARELAH, b. Har., July 10, 1789; bap. Oct. 4.

910.   vi. NABBY, b. Har., Jan. 1, 1793; bap. Apr. 21; m. Dr. *Joseph Warren;* and d. Feb. 24, 1881, æ. 88.

911.   vii. CLARINDA, b. Har., July 3, 1795; m. Nov. 24, 1814, Dr. *Atherton Clark*, he b. May 26, 1789; son of Barnabas and Mehitable (Hall) C.; and d. May 3, 1824; (he m. 2d, May 25, 1825, Harriet Smith, dau. of Dr. Enos S.; Dr. Clark's father removed to Westminster, Vt., soon after 1789.   He studied medicine with Dr. Bryant of Cummington, Mass., and practiced several years in Ashfield, then in Cummington.   He removed to Easthampton, Mass., about 1835, and practiced 27 years; d. Guilford, Ct., Sep. 23, 1866); children, CLARK : [1.] Alfred Freeman, b. Jan. 26, 1816; m. Nov. 29, 1838, Harriet Doolittle, she b. Apr. 16, 1817; d. June 6, 1849; and 2d, Mrs.

25

Mary J. Wood, *née* Drake, she b. Aug. 17, 1816 ; d. Mar. 30, 1869 ; he settled on a farm near Princeton, Ill., in 1842, where he d. May 4, 1871 ; had, i. Atherton, b. Sep. 22, 1839. ii. Sarah M., b. Feb. 11, 1841. iii. Clarinda, b. Dec. 31, 1842. iv. Harriet, b. Apr. 30, 1845. v. Alfred P., b. Mar. 18, 1847 ; d. July 22, 1848. vi. Horatio K., b. Jan. 27, 1853. vii. Ellen A., b. Dec. 10, 1855. [2.] Clarinda, b. Dec. 28, 1817 ; d. May 27, 1842. [3.] Atherton, b. Nov. 20, 1819 ; d. Jan. 11, 1841. [4.] William Smith, LL. D., b. July 31, 1826 ; d. 1886 ; m. May 25, 1853, Harriet Richards, dau. of Rev. Wm. R., she b. Lahaina, Maui, Sandwich Islands, Apr. 21, 1829 ; he was a grad. Williston Sem'y, Easthampton, Mass. ; of Amherst Coll., Mass.; of Augusta Univ., Ga. ; and of Gottingen Univ., Germany ; took the degree of Ph. D. ; was Prof. Amherst Coll. several years; Col. 21st Mass. Vol. Inf. in the late war ; Prest. Amherst Agr. Coll., and Prest. Sappero Agri. Coll., which he established in Japan ; resided in Amherst, Mass. ; had, i. Wm. Richards, b. Dec. 2, 1854 ; d. 1855. ii. Emily Williston, b. June 9, 1856 ; m. Feb. 26, 1880, Frank W. Stearns of Boston. iii. Alfred Freeman, b. Aug. 6, 1857 ; d. Aug. 1857. iv. Atherton, b. June 18, 1859 ; grad. Mass. Agri. Coll., address, Grass Valley, Cal. v. Williston, b. Aug. 21, 1860 ; d. young. vi. Fanny, b. Nov. 9, 1863. vii. Mary Richards, b. Mar. 21, 1865. viii. Eliza Smith, b. June 16, 1866. ix. Edith, b. Nov. 20, 1867. x. Hubert Lyman, b. Jan. 9, 1870. xi. Bertha, b. Apr. 14, 1873. Mrs. Clarke resides at Newton, Mass. [5.] Harriet Eliza, b. June 23, 1830 ; a teacher, unm. [6.] Hannah Isabella, b. Nov. 11, 1834 ; m. Oct. 24, 1862, Sidney Ward Leete, he b. Apr. 7, 1833 ; lives in Guilford, Ct. [7.] Sarah Maria, b. Aug. 18, 1836; m. Dec. 9, 1874, Capt. Wm. Byron Churchill, he b. Boston, Aug. 2, 1828 ; d. s. p. Jan. 4, 1883.

912. viii. Priscilla, b. May 16, 1798 ; d. Sep. 7.

Jonathan Sears removed to Ashfield, Mass., and lived on Cape street ; was dism. from Ch., Harwich, Nov. 4, 1800, his wife having been dism. from Ch., Dennis, Nov. 10, 1799.

He served in Capt. Thos. Hamilton's Co., stationed in Barns. county, from July 10, 1775, 6 mos. 7 days ; was Sergt. in Capt. Abijah Bangs' Co.. Col. Dike's Regt., 3 mos. to Dec. 1, 1776 ; marched on alarm at Falmouth, 174 miles travel ; and on alarm at Falmouth and Bedford, in Capt. Benj. Berry's Co., Sep. 7, 1778, marching 112 miles, and doing

7 days' duty. His widow drew a pension in 1840, then aged 85, and living with her son Azarelah.

" In early life he went on whaling voyages, and incidents of hair-breadth escapes are related among his descendants, *e. g.*, that once his boat was thrown so high by a whale that the men in another boat, a mile distant, could see the horizon under it."

In 1785 he was wrecked off Harwich, and barely escaped with his life. From an old and dilapidated paper preserved in the family I copy :

" The Particulars of the HARWICH TRAGEDY.

"Harwich, County of Barnstable, Apr. 8, 1785.

'' On the morning of the Lord's Day last, a most melancholy . . . and Provincetown. The Particulars of this unhappy and sorrowful accident are as follows, viz. :

" A Schooner partly owned and commanded by M^r. Nathan Atwood, sailed from this harbour about six o'clock in the morning, bound to the above Place ; but they had not been on their passage long before a plank started, as is imagined, and she gained water so fast, that before ten o'clock the ill-fated vessel, and unfortunate Schooner sunk down to the bottom headforemost, not leaving the least discovery of even the top of the masts, having on board M^r. NATHAN ATWOOD, and M^{rs}. MARY ATWOOD, his wife, and M^r. HEMAN FINNEY, her brother. A little time before she foundered, M^r. JONATHAN SEARS, and M^r. CYRENIUS FREEMAN, got a raft, which they made of some boards, and started for the shore which was at the distance of some three miles, but M^r. Freeman being very much bruised and chilled, (as these unhappy Persons were on the raft almost nine hours), expired just before he reached the shore, and M^r. Sears was almost expired when he arrived, being scarce able to extricate himself from the surf, which he happily effected by crawling, (though already much bruised and exhausted with the cold), on his hands and knees several rods, the surf breaking over his head several times, before he could get clear of it, after which he was obliged to travel in that wretched manner near a mile before he could discover any building. The first he met with was a barn, that fortunately for him, belonged to a good Samaritan, M^r. SAMUEL HOPKINS of Truro, the owner of which found him in that deplorable state, bruised and exhausted, almost to death, and had he not received immediate relief, which was afforded to him with the utmost humanity, tenderness, and compassion, he must have unavoidably perished in a few hours. M[r]. JOHN CLARKE, got on another raft, but it being very windy, they parted from each other, in a short time after they set out, and M[r]. Sears saw no more of him, but supposed he perished soon after. The wreck was not seen from the shore, as it was very foggy, at the time this sorrowful affair happened, or perhaps some assistance might have been given to the people. One thing we think worthy of remark, and which seems to make this truly Tragical Scene most affecting, is, the almost unparalled conjugal affection showed by M[r]. ATWOOD, one of the unhappy sufferers, to his equally distressed mate, which being so rare an instance of magnanimity, fortitude and a cheerful resignation to the divine will of the ALMIGHTY, that we cannot omit to record it on this Sheet, as we think his conduct an honour to human nature, and ought to be handed down to Posterity, as it will serve to show that there is yet remaining in this Western Hemisphere, some private virtue, founded in a regard to the Fair Sex ; as we find many instances transmitted to us in the History of the Oriental World.

"M[r]. Atwood on perceiving the vessel sinking, jumped on to one of the rafts, that was prepared alongside of her, but on hearing the bitter shrieks and piercing cries of his dear Comfort, the Friend of his bosom, and the other poor drowning souls, which seemed to reach to Heaven, and who were on the verge of eternity, and begging for mercy from GOD, he, like some of the ancient BRAMIST women, when showing their affection for their departing Husbands, heroickly jumped back again into the sinking vessel, chusing rather to perish with her who had been the Partner of his joy, and affliction, than to have the anxiety and horror of mind in beholding so shocking and afflicting a Scene, and not having it in his power to alleviate her distress."

A doleful poem follows, which is not remarkable except for its antiquity, and is addressed especially to the Atwood family. "Sold at the office in Essex Street, near the Liberty Pole, 1785 ; where may be found N[os]. I. II. III. of the 'Bloody Register;' Cash paid for Linen Rags."

386.

JOSEPH SEARS[6] [*Prince[5], Jona.[4], Sam'l[3], Paul[2], Rich.[1]*], b. Harwich, Mass., Apr. 21, 1764; d. Jan. 5, 1846, æ. 82,

gr.-st., W. Br.; m. Har., Jan., 1786, *Kezia Hamblen*, dau. of
Isaac H., she b. Aug. 1, 1764; adm. to Ch., E. Yar., July 25,
1790; d. Dec. 14, 1838, in 75 yr., gr.-st. Children:

913. i. PRINCE, b. Har., Oct. 17, 1787; bap. E. Yar., Aug.
1, 1790 ; d. at sea, Feb. 10, 1810, æ. 23, gr.-st., W. Br.
914. ii. PERSIS, b. Har., Sep. 13, 1789; bap. E. Yar., Aug.
1, 1790 ; m. *David Crowell*, and d. Apr. 5, 1861, æ. 72.
915. iii. OLIVE, b. Har., Dec. 1, 1790; bap. E. Yar., Mar. 6,
1791 ; m. *Zachariah Sears*, No. 810.
916.* iv. NATHAN, b. Har., July 9, 1793.
917. v. BETSY, b. Har., Nov. 26, 1795; bap. Dennis, June
10, 1796; adm. to Ch., Den., May 10, 1818; m. Brewster,
Sep. 27, 1848, *Thacher Clark*, son of Enoch and Lydia
C. of Den., he b. 1787 ; and d. Jan., 1870, æ. 75, gr.-
st., Br.
918.* vi. JOSEPH HAMBLEN, b. Har., Nov. 9, 1801 ; bap. Den.,
Dec. 27, 1801.
919. vii. BENJAMIN, b. Brewster, July 13, 1807 ; was drowned
by the upsetting of a boat, Apr. 15, 1825, æ. 18, gr.-st.,
W. Br.

Jóseph Sears, called "Junior" in church records, lived in
part of Harwich set off in 1803 as Brewster, his house being
in West Brewster.

He served as Selectman 3 years from 1806.

390.

JOSHUA SEARS[6] [*Josh.[5], Josh.[4], Sam'l[3], Paul[2], Rich.[1]*],
b. in Ct., Jan. 8, 1757 ; m. May 18, 1783, *Anna Miles*, she b.
Mar. 8, 1757. Children:

920. i. JOSEPH, b. Mar. 12, 1784; d. Apr. 14, 1843.
921. ii. JOHN, b. Mar. 10, 1786; d. Sep. 30, 1811.
922. iii. BETSY, b. Feb. 22, 1788; m. —— *Hughes;* and d.
Oct. 7, 1864.
923.* iv. ISAAC, b. Dec. 21, 1789.
924. v. ANNA, b. Aug. 31, 1791; d. Apr. 10, 1792.
925. vi. WILLIAM, b. Feb. 11, 1793; lost at sea in 1810.
926. vii. MILES, b. Apr. 12, 1794 ; d. Sep. 7.

Was an Ensign in N. Y. militia.

392.

THATCHER SEARS[6] [*Nath'l[5], Josh.[4], Sam'l[3], Paul[2],*

Rich.[1]], b. Norwalk, Ct., 1752; d. St. John, N. B., July 9, 1819, æ. 67, gr.-st., King St. Cem'y; m. *Rebecca Smith*, dau. of Henry S. of Huntington, Ct., she b. near Brooklyn, N. Y.; d. 1803; and 2d *Abigail Spurr* of Annapolis, Nova Scotia, who d. St. John, Apr., 1761.   Children :

By *Rebecca* :
927.   i. SARAH, b. Norwalk.
928.   ii. MARY, b. Nor.
929.   iii. ANN, b. St. John.
930.   iv. ELIZABETH, b. St. John.
931.   v. REBECCA, b. St. John.
932.   vi. HENRY THATCHER, b. St. John.
933.   vii. GEORGE, b. St. John.
934.   viii. CHARLES, b. St. John.
935.   ix. JAMES, b. St. John; d. there Aug. 3, 1825, æ. 26; was one of the Proprietors of the "New Brunswick Courier."
936·   x. WILLIAM CHARLES, b. St. John.
937.   xi. MARY, b. St. John.
By *Abigail* :
938.   xii. EDWARD, b. St. John, June, 1808; m. *Hannah Hatfield*, who d. s. p.; and 2d, 1874, *Emily Venning*, and lives in St. John.
939.* xiii. ROBERT, b. St. John, June 28, 1810.
940.* xiv. JOHN, b. St. John, 1819.
941.   xv. MARY, b. St. John, 1820; d. 1821.

In early life Mr. Sears was much employed in the Mohawk country, under the patronage of Sir John Johnson, in the purchase of furs.

He was one of the Loyalists of the Revolutionary period, and as such suffered persecution and exile.

He lost heavily in the burning of Norwalk, and his estate there, appraised at £166 13 4 was confiscated by the State, and fell into the hands of the Church family.   (His mother m. 2d, Ebenezer Church of Norwalk.)

He was forced to leave the place, and sought refuge with the British army in New York, removed to St. John, N. B., in 1783, and cut the bush at the foot of King st. for the first settlement of that city, and his daughter Ann, was the first white child born there.

He engaged in business as a furrier and hatter at 397 King street, and his estate there is still in possession of his descendants.

412.

ALDEN SEARS⁶ [*Alden₅ Judah⁴, Sam'l³ Paul², Rich.¹*], b. Dighton, Mass., 1770; d. Bristol, Ont. co., N. Y., Feb. 28, 1829, æ. 59; m. *Thankful Pitts,* who d.; and 2d, *Delancy Vincent,* who d. Aug. 27, 1841. Children:

By *Thankful :*

942.   i. THANKFUL, m. *John Kent* of Bristol, N. Y.; and d. Ohio, about 1877.

943.   ii. NANCY, b. Bristol, Aug. 24, 1804; m. *Cornelius Cline* of Belvidere, N. Y., and d. July 2, 1866; children, CLINE: [1.] George, m. and lives in Belvidere. [2.] Mary, m. D. Homan, and lives in Malta, Ill.

944.   iii. ELIZA, b. Bris., July 10, 1806; m. *B. N. Johnson,* and d. Fayette, Iowa; children, JOHNSON : [1.] Norton B. [2.] William S. [3.] Horace. [4.] David. [5.] Albert. [6.] Betsy. [7.] Nancy. [8.] Anna.

945.*   iv. ALDEN FISHER, b. Bris., Oct. 24, 1807.

946.*   v. AARON V., b. Bris., Mar. 15, 1809.

947.*   vi. LEONARD B., b. Bris., July 10, 1810.

948.*   vii. WASHINGTON Z., b. Bris., Feb. 4, 1812.

949.   viii. HIRAM A., b. Bris., Feb. 4, 1814; d. unm., Aug. 29, 1841.

950.   ix. MARSHALL P., b. Bris., Feb. 5, 1816; m. *Maria Tracy* of Canandaigua, N. Y., and d. s. p. Nov. 12, 1880.

951.   x. ELSIE, b. Bris., Jan. 26, 1818; m. *Frank Griffith* of Garden Prairie, Ill.; rem. to Portland, Oregon, and d. about 1845; children, GRIFFITH : [1.] Henry. [2.] Helen.

952.* xi. HORACE O., b. Bris., Oct. 1, 1819.

Mr. Sears rem. with his parents to Bristol, N. Y., in 1792.

416.

EDWARD SEARS⁶ [*Alden⁵, Judah⁴, Sam'l³, Paul², Rich.¹*], b. Dighton, Mass., Apr. 25, 1778; d. Cincinnati, O., June 10, 1831; m. in Ct., Mar. 19, 1806, *Jemima Root,* she b. Ct., Oct. 17, 1778; d. Aug. 30, 1876. Children:

953.* i. HIRAM, b. N. Y. State, Mar. 18, 1807.

954.* ii. PHILO, b. N. Y. State, Feb. 11, 1809.

955.* iii. IRA, b. N. Y. State, Dec. 29, 1810.

956.* iv. ASAHEL PARKER, b. N. Y. State, June 1, 1816.

957.   v. JULIA ANN, b. Cincinnati, O., Dec. 29, 1819 ; was m. twice, and lives in Walla, Wash'n Ter. ; has a dau., Mrs. M. Hayden, living in Eola, Oregon.

958.* vi. ARTHUR ELLIOTT, b. Cin., June 6, 1823.
959. vii. ANSON, b. Cin., Jan. 18, 1826 ; d. young.

418.

JOHN SEARS[6] [*Alden*[5], *Judah*[4], *Sam'l*[3], *Paul*[2], *Rich.*[1]],
b. Dighton, Mass., June 15, 1783 ; d. Bristol, Ontario county,
N. Y. ; m. *Betsy Low*, she b. 1787; d. Nov. 26, 1815 ; and
2d, Mrs. *Jane (Pendry) Hancock*, she b. 1786; d. Dec. 26,
1829 ; and 3d, *Rhoda Blount*, she b. Oct. 22, 1790.   Children :
By *Betsy :*
960.   i. JOHN ADAMS, b. Bris., Jan. 9, 1809 ; d. Mar. 13, 1813.
961.   ii. RASSELAS L., b. Bris., May 25, 1811 ; d. s. p. May
        11, 1844, æ. 33, in Lima, Ind. ; grad. Union Coll., 1838.;
        Andover Theo. Sem., 1841 ; m. Sep. 11, 1842, *Rebecca
        Walker*, dau. of Eben'r W., of Taunton, Mass., and
        soon after became pastor of the Presb. Church in Lima.
        His memory is still cherished there with devoted affection ;
        in all respects, socially, intellectually and religiously he
        was a superior man.   His widow m. 2d, Rev. O. P. Hoyt
        of Kalamazoo, Mich., Dec. 24, 1855, and has since lived
        in Taunton.
962* iii. JOHN, b. Bris., Apr. 10, 1813.
By *Jane :*
963.* iv. EDWARD H., b. Bris., Dec. 14, 1819.
964.   v. EZEKIEL J., b. Bris., Mar. 14, 1822; d. unm., Nov.
        22, 1844.
965.* vi. DE WITT CLINTON, b. Bris., July 1, 1824.
966. vii. LIZZIE J., b. Bris., Mar. 29, 1827 ; m. July 20, 1853,
        Hon. *C. G. Wicker* of Chicago, Ill.; children, WICKER:
        [1.] Julia Maria, b. July 8, 1854 ; d. Dec. 21, 1856.
        [2.] Sadie Elizabeth, b. July 25, 1856 ; m. May 14, 1879,
        Nathan H. Briggs.   [3.] Isabella Sears, b. Nov. 10, 1857.
        [4.] Frank Geary, b. Oct. 17, 1860 ; d. Dec. 7, 1866.
        [5.] Cora Grace, b. June 23, 1863 ; d. Apr. 7, 1867.
        [6.] Charles Gustavus, b. Sep. 13, 1867.
967. viii. PHEBE, b. Bris., Nov. 30, 1829; d. Mar. 20, 1836.

Mr. Sears was a farmer, and lived on the old homestead in
Bristol, Ontario county, N. Y.

419.

PAUL SEARS[6] [*Nathan*[5], *Judah*[4], *Sam'l*[3], *Paul*[2], *Rich.*[1]],
b. Rochester, Mass., Nov. 11, 1765 ; d. Woodstock, Vt., May

21, 1846; m. Roch., by Rev. Jona. Moore, Feb. 11, 1790, to *Hannah Delano*, dau. of Jabez D. of Roch., who d. Morristown, Vt., July 4, 184–. Children:

968.   i. Eleazar, d. æ. 6 mos.
969.   ii. Betsy, d. Montpelier, Vt., young.
970.   iii. Susan, b. Woodstock, Nov. 22, 1792(?); m. *John Sanderson* of W., and d. ab't 1856; children, Sanderson: [1.] Hannah Delano. [2.] John Sears. [3.] Cynthia Sears; m. Dr. Eben. Deane of Gill, Mass., and lives in Montague, Mass.
971.* iv. Harper D., b. Wood., Jan. 9, 1794.
972.   v. Joseph S., b. Wood., Nov. 2, 1795; d. Morristown, Vt., Apr. 29, 1855; m. *Lurendo Joy* of Cornish, N. H., and had 4 children.
973.   vi. Sarah, b. Wood., Jan. 7, 1799; d. Cedar Rapids, Iowa, June 1876, æ. 77 yrs. 5 mos.; m. Feb., 1822, *Nath'l Seabury* of Stowe, Vt.
974.   vii. Rebecca, b. Montpelier, Sep. 16, 1800; m. 1829, *James G. Barnes* of Ferrisburgh, Vt., who d. Aug. 5, 1881; she lives in Emmett, Calhoun county, Mich.; children, Barnes: [1.] Rich. J., b. June 11, 1830; d. Nov. 1887. [2.] Abner D., b. Nov. 28, 1831; d. Feb. 3, 1855. [3.] Nathan S., b. June 3, 1833; m. Delia Young, and had Fred. and two others. [4.] Martha H., b. May 25, 1835; m. Dec. 24, 1856, John Rees of Battle Creek, Mich., and has Geo. B., who m. Ella E. Pursell, and has Kendall B. [5.] Sarah R., b. Mar. 19, 1841; m. J. W. Fairfax of Chicago, Ill.
975.   viii. Azubah, b. Mont., Aug. 23, 1803; d. unm., Aug., 1869.
976.   ix. Cynthia, b. Mont., Mar. 28, 1805; lives in Woodstock, unm.
977.   x. Stephen D., b. Mont., Jan. 22, 1807; d. unm., Bridgewater, Vt., May 5, 1838, much regretted. He was a doctor, and studied medicine with Dr. Burnell of Woodstock.
978.* xi. Nathan, b. Mont., Jan. 12, 1811.

Paul Sears was a blacksmith by trade. Soon after his marriage he removed to Woodstock, Vt., locating first in the south part of the town, but moved presently to the neighborhood of "the Flats," and set up a blacksmith shop at the foot of the hill where the brook crosses the road, on land purchased of Jesse Williams; he removed to Montpelier in 1800, returning

26

in 1812–13, and remained on his farm till 1827, (1831,) when he sold out and removed to Stowe, Vt., and died there at the house of his son Harper D. Sears.

424.

NATHAN SEARS[6] [*Nathan[5], Judah[4], Sam'l[3], Paul[2], Rich.[1]*], b. Rochester, Mass., Sep. 27, 1785; d. Fairhaven, Mass.; m. Roch., Apr. 7, 1819, by Abram Holmes, J. P., to *Hannah Parker*, dau. of Col. P.,of the Revolutionary Army. Children:

979.   i. THANKFUL, b. Roch., June 12, 1820; m. *Thomas R. Delano* of Fairhaven, and had 10 children.

980.   ii. REBECCA, b. Roch., Feb. 2, 1822; m. *Leander Mayhew* of Westport, and d. leaving a child who resides in New Bedford.

981.   iii. ZALMANNA, b. Roch., Jan. 14, 1823; d. s. p. at sea.

982.   iv. BENJAMIN M., b. Roch., Jan. 15, 1825; m. *Jane Bourne* of Middleboro, Mass., and d. s. p.; the will of Benj. M. Sears of No. Bridgewater, dated Oct. 2, 1848, was allowed May 1, 1849, wife Jane, Exec[x].

983.* v. NATHAN, b. Roch., Oct. 28, 1829.

984.   vi. JOHN P., b. Roch., Dec. 5, 1831; m. *Emma Lawton* of Westport; and 2d, *Lizzie Merrick;* lived in Fairhaven, and had 4 children. He was in Co. A, 18th Mass. Vols., Aug. 7 to Dec. 24, 1862, and was discharged for disability.

426.

LOT SEARS[6] [*David[5], Judah[4], Sam'l[3], Paul[2], Rich.[1]*], b. Rochester, Mass., July 2, 1767; d. N. Y. city, Feb., 1848, æ. 81; m. Oct. 2, 1798, *Lurany Butler*, of N. Y. city. Children:

985.   i. ALICE, b. Newark, N. Y., Dec. 7, 1799; d. Saranac, Mich., Feb. 26, 1873; m. Jan. 1, 1819, *Caleb Woodward*, he b. Dec. 25, 1796; children, WOODWARD: [1.] Allen, b. Dec. 17, 1819; d. Mar. 5, 1884; m. Otsego, Minn., Sep. 17, 1843, Almira R. Lewis, she b. May 27, 1824; d. June 17, 1861; and he m. 2d, Dec. 12, 1866, Eliz'h McCall Cronkite, she b. Nov. 17, 1830; had, i. Caroline Augusta, b. Sep. 9, 1844; m. Sep. 9, 1873, Neal D. Ford. ii. Emily Christiana, b. Mar. 4, 1846; m. Oct. 29, 1866, Asher N.

Williams. iii. Alice Rebecca, b. Nov. 6, 1855; m. May
14, 1874, Thos. Franklin Cronkite. iv. Lucy Lurana, b.
Sep. 20, 1857; m. June 29, 1876, Albro Curtis. v. Frances Anna, b. Nov. 30, 1860; d. June 19, 1861. vi. James
Jesse, b. Nov. 12, 1867. [2.] Albert, b. Apr. 25, 1822;
m. Dec. 31, 1843, Orril Almira Patten, she b. Mar. 7,
1825; and had, i. Adelaide Alzora, b. July 11, 1845; d.
Aug. 9, 1847. ii. Alice Mariah, b. Nov. 3, 1847; m.
July 26, 1862, Augustus Schellworth, he b. Nov. 2, 1837.
iii. Ellen Augusta, b. July 8, 1850; d. Oct. 10. iv. Albert Calvin, b. Nov. 16, 1851; m. Mar. 31, 1878, Martha
Jane Haman. v. Mary Cecilia, b. Feb. 20, 1854; m.
June 29, 1869, Isaac W. Monnett, he b. Oct. 14, 1835;
d. Dec. 23, 1876. vi. Isaac Allen, b. Mar. 6, 1856; d.
Mar. 24. vii. James Alfred, b. July 30, 1857; m. Mar.
10, 1885, Maria Isabel Abel, she b. Mar. 2, 1866.
viii. Wm. Chase, b. Feb. 13, 1862. [3.] Alfred, b. Apr. 25,
1822, *gemini;* d. Aug. 29, 1825. [4.] William, b. Nov.
14, 1824; d. Nov. 5, 1865. [5.] Caroline Augusta, b.
Jan. 28, 1826; d. Jul 22, 1845; m. July 3, 1844, Orlando Bailey, and had yi. Adelaide Augusta, b. July 19,
1845; m. Bridgewater, Mich., Nov. 2, 1861, James Clark
Stiles. [6.] Adelaide A., b. May 6, 1828; d. Feb. 13, 1829.
986.* ii. HENRY, b. New., Feb. 27, 1801.
987. iii. EMANUEL, b. New., Nov. 27, 1802; d. Sep. 16, 1803.
988.* iv. JAMES C., b. New., Feb. 11, 1804.
989. v. PHEBE ANN, b. New., May 8, 1806; m. Aug. 7,
1833, *Harvey Goldsmith*, of Palmyra, N. Y.; children,
GOLDSMITH: [1.] Frances Caroline, b. Dec. 20, 1834; d.
Dec. 22, 1883; m. May 4, 1854, Oscar J. Clark, and had,
i. Oscar, b. Apr. 10. 1855. ii. Ada Josephine, b. Aug.
12, 1857. [2.] James Henry, b. Mar. 19, 1836; m. Nov.
9, 1860, Agnes Jane Hicks, who d. Orland, Ind., May 1,
1865(?); and had, i. Lola Eloise, b. Aug. 9, 1862. ii. Clara
Eloise, b. Dec. 30, 1863. [3.] Edwin, b. Feb. 7, 1838, is
a merchant in Toledo, Ohio; m. Nov. 20, 1866, Emma
Josephine Spaulding, and had i. George, b. Mar. 3, 1868.
ii. Lilian, b. Apr. 16, 1870. [4.] Emma Josephine, b.
June 10, 1843; m. Nov. 15, 1866, G. Brown, an editor
in Angola, Ind., and had, i. Edwin Goldsmith, b. Feb.
27, 1868. ii. Grace Adelaide, b. Oct. 9, 1869. iii. Gertrude May, b. May 13, 1873. [5.] Alice Alzora, b. Sep.
16, 1847; m. Mar. 14, 1867, Frank E. Lovejoy, and has,
i. Lena Goldsmith, b. Oct. 8, 1870.

990.* vi. HIRAM, b. New., June 21, 1808.

991. vii. REBECCA, b. New., Aug. 22, 1810; m. Mar. 2, 1836, *James Dunham,* of Cambridge, N. Y., who d. Aug. 1857, æ. 61; and she m. West Troy, N. Y., Feb. 22, 1863, Laban Wells, who d. 1877; she now lives with her dau. Mrs. Fred. Curtis, Ballston Spa., N. Y.; children, DUNHAM: [1.] Harriet A., m. June 16, 1859, Henry W. Babcock; and 2d, Jan. 8, 1868, Fred. Curtis of Ballston Spa.; she had by 1st husband, i. Lucy J., b. Sep. 9, 1860; m. E. Murray; and by her 2d husband, ii. Hattie; iii. Fred.; iv. Clarence. [2.] James S., b. Jan. 30, 1837; m. Jan. 8, 1868, Nellie M. Brown of Ashtabula, Ohio, and had i. Robert. [3.] Caroline A., b. Apr. 8, 1840; m. June 11, 1859, at West Troy, N. Y., Dr. John F. Miller, he b. Watervliet, N. Y., Aug. 24, 1834; resides No. 15 Lombardy st., Newark, N. J., and had, i. Grace, b. Mar. 22, 1865. ii. Nellie, b. June 2, 1869. iii. Florence, b. Sep. 9, 1874. [4.] Henry Lot, b. July 30, 1844; d. in the army May 6, 1863, æ. 19, of wounds received at Chancellorsville. [5.] Henrietta L., b. July 30, 1844; d. Jan. 7, 1847.

992. viii. ACHSAH, b. New., Oct. 3, 1811; m. *Reuben Griffin,* of N., and d. s. p., 1869.

993. ix. ADELAIDE, d. infancy.

994. x. LUCY L., b. New., Aug. 18, 18—; m. *Julius Phelps,* and d. s. p., Marbletown, N. Y., Aug. 23, 1879.

Lot Sears served in Capt. Stephen Churchill's Co., in Col. Theo. Cotton's Regt., at Newport, R. I., Mar. 9 to Mar. 31, 1781, and was allowed for 60 miles' travel, etc.

He removed to Newark, Wayne county, N. Y.

427.

PRINCE SEARS[6] [*David,[5] Judah[4], Sam'l[3], Paul[2], Rich.[1]*], b. Rochester, Mass., Oct. 25, 1768; d. Taunton, Mass., Oct. 25, 1798, æ. 30; m. Taunton, Apr. 20, 1793, *Sallie Tucker,* dau. of Joseph T. of T.; (who m. 2d, ab't 1800, Solo. Leonard of Raynham, by whom she had, Artemas, Fred. P., Mary, Hannah, Susan and Joséph,) she d. Rayn., Apr. 26, 1833, æ. 58. Children:

995. i. SARAH, b. Taun., 1797; m. Nov. 30, 1815, *Enoch Wilbur* of Rayn.; and d. Nov. 24, 1854, æ. 57; he d. Oct. 14, 1857, æ. 76; children, WILBUR: [1.] Sarah. [2.] Enoch B., m. Clementina E——, who d. Mar., 1852,

æ. 25, at her father's house in Norton; he d. Jan. 10, 1852, æ. 32. [3.] Lloyd, m. Mary ——, who d. Dec. 27, 1862, æ. 36' yrs. 6 mos. 9 days; he d. spring of 1859. [4.] Lydia, m. Daniel Day of Prov., R. I. [5.] Henrietta. [6.] Susan. [7.] Philo, d. Sep. 9, 1874, æ. 42 yrs. 4 mos. 25 days. [8.] Abram G., m. Cynthia ——, who d. Mar. 26, 1862, æ. 23 yrs. 11 mos. 7 days. [9.] Harriet. [10.] Hiram.

996.* ii. PRINCE, b. Taunton, Apr. 23, 1798.

Mr. Sears removed to Taunton in 1793-4.

432.

RICHARD SEARS[6] [*Rich.*[5] *Judah*[4], *Sam'l*[3], *Paul*[2], *Rich.*[1]], b. —— ; m. Middleboro, Mass., Nov. 15, 1857, by Rev. Mr. Putnam, to Mrs. *Rosina Raymond*, she b. Midd.; (m. 2d, Plymouth, Mass., June 15, 1875, Adoniram J. Raymond.) Children:

997. i. LUCY M., b. Midd., Feb. 20, 1860.
998. ii. JAMES F., b. Midd., Nov. 26, 1862; d. Ply., May 2, 1865.
999. iii. HERBERT W., b. Ply., Mar. 14, 1866.

In Middleboro records he is called "son of Richard and Sarah Sears of Hyannis. He would seem rather young to be son of Richard and Sarah (Bumpas) S., and may have been a grand-son. I know of no other Richard and Sarah, so place him here subject to correction.

436.

ROLAND SEARS[6] [*Roland*[5] *Seth*[4], *Sam'l*[3], *Paul*[2], *Rich.*[1]], b. Harwich, Mass., Aug. 23, (12 T. C.) 1750; d. Hawley, Mass., Jan. 18, 1833, æ. 82; m. Yar., Oct. 27, (21 T. C.) 1773, *Thankful Crowell*, dau. of Aaron and Priscilla (Smith) C., she b. Mar. 18, 1748; d. June 12, 1840, æ. 92 (July 23, Hist. Haw.) Children:

1000.* i. ALDEN, b. Har., July 23, 1774; bap. E. Yar., May 7, 1775.
1001.* ii. ALVAN, b. Har., Sep. 26, 1775; bap. E. Yar., Nov. 5.
1002.* iii. ROLAND, b. Har., Apr. 12, 1777; bap. E. Yar., May 18.

1003. iv. MERCY, b. Har., Dec. 19, 1779; bap. E. Yar., Feb. 27, 1780; d. unm.

1004. v. ELIZABETH, b. Har., Dec. 27, 1781; bap. E. Yar., Apr. 7, 1782; m. Nov. 16, 1808, *Joseph Howes*, he b. May 21, 1790; lived in Hawley; children, HOWES: [1.] Roland, b. Nov. 26, 1809. [2.] Joseph, b. Jan. 23, 1811. [3.] Mercy, b. Feb. 18, 1812; m. Aug. 1, 1833, Rev. Anson Dyer; and had, i. Eliz'h, b. July 10, 1834; m. Chester Elmer. ii. Mercy A., d. Oct. 14, 1836. iii. Joseph, b. May 20, 1838. iv. Benj. F., b. May 15, 1841. v. Harriet A., b. June 11, 1843. [4.] Henry, b. Nov. 9, 1813; m. June, 1836, Lucy A. Simons, and lives in Cheshire; had, i. Lucy A., b. May 6, 1838; m. Frank Mason. ii. Lovina, b. Feb. 4, 1840; m. Chas. N. Harlow, and lives in Northampton. iii. Wealthy L., b. Jan. 13, 1842. iv. Augusta M., b. Apr. 21, 1846. v. William H., b. Mar. 14, 1848. vi. Edgar, b. Mar. 8, 1850. vii. Fannie, b. Nov. 13, 1852. viii. Charles, b. Feb. 28, 1854. [5.] Franklin, b. Nov. 28, 1816. [6.] Elizabeth, b. Jan. 16, 1818. [7.] Elijah B., b. June, 1822; m. Mary Jane Simons, and lives in Hawley.

1005.* vi. BENJAMIN, b. Har., Aug. 27, 1783; bap. E. Yar., Oct. 26.

1006. vii. THANKFUL, b. Har., July 31, 1786; bap. E. Yar., Oct. 22, and d. July 28, 1793, æ. 7, gr.-st., W. Br.

1007.* viii. SYLVESTER, b. Har., Feb. 26, 1788; bap. E. Yar., Apr. 27.

Roland Sears and wife were admitted to Church E. Yar., Apr. 30, 1775, and dismissed to Ch. Hawley, Apr. 12, 1795.

He settled soon after 1786, on north line of town, where Lewis W. Temple was living in 1887.

He was in Capt. Benj. Berry's Co., and marched on alarm at Bedford and Falmouth, Sep. 7, 1778, serving 7 days, and traveling 112 miles.

437.

PETER SEARS[6] [*Benj.*[5] *Benj.*[4] *Sam'l*[3] *Paul*[2] *Rich.*[1]], b. South East, N. Y., Dec. 20, 1763; d. Aug. 9, 1822; m. *Susan Webb*. Children:

1008. i. ISAAC, m. *Sophronia Wilkes*.

1009. ii. HENRY, m. *Almira Gardner*.

1010.* iii. CHARLES, b. Litchfield, N. Y., Aug. 4, 1803, (another account says Aug. 20, 1804).

1011.* iv. ALBERT SELIM, b. Richfield, N. Y., Sep. 30, 1810.
1012.   v. SUSAN, m. *Chas. Wells*, and d.
1013.   vi. URSULA, d. unm.
1014. vii. DELLA, d. unm.
1015. viii. CHLOE, b. Rich., Aug. 22, 1802 ; m. June 15,
      1820, *Charles Dudley Clark*, and d. Feb. 19, 1867 ; he
      b. Lebanon, Ct., Sep. 5, 1793, son of Gershom and Lu-
      cretia (Thacher) C.

Peter Sears lived in Litchfield and Richfield, adjoining
towns in N. Y., and is said to have resided for a time in Sardinia, Erie co., N. Y., where he and his wife are buried.
" He was a good man."

438.

HEMAN SEARS⁶ [*Benj.₅ Benj.⁴, Sam'l³, Paul², Rich.¹*],
b. South East, N. Y., Jan. 7, 1767 ; d. Aug. 18, 1817, æ. 50,
gr.-st., Milltown, N. Y., m. *Susie Sears* of So. E.   Child :

1016. i. MARY, b. So. E. ; m. May 12, 1811, Isaac Sears, No.
      772.

Mrs. Sears lived with her daughter, and removed with the
family to Illinois, where their house was destroyed by a
cyclone, and she lost her life.

440.

ISAAC SEARS⁶ [*Benj.₅ Benj.⁴, Sam'l³, Paul², Rich.¹*],
b. South East, N. Y., Mar. 2, 1772 ; d. Brewsters, N. Y.,
Oct. 27, 1839, æ. 67, gr.-st.; m. 1797, *Priscilla Bennett*, who
d. Oct. 18, 1851, æ. 72, gr.-st., Milltown, N. Y.   Children :

1017.   i. HARRIET, b. So. E., Jan. 21, 1800; m. Dr. *Jonah
      Barnum*.
1018.   ii. LYDIA, b. So. E., Jan. 11, 1802 ; m. Dec. 14, 1823,
      Benj. DeForest ; children, DEFOREST : [1.] David L., d.
      Nov., 1888. [2.] Sarah A., m. Jas. L. Crane. [3.] Benj.
      L., m. Jennie Aken.
1019.* iii. BRADLEY, b. So. E., Apr. 23, 1804.
1020.* iv. JOSEPH, b. So. E., April 4, 1806.
1021.   v. AGNES, b. So. E., May 26, 1814 ; m. there Nov. 19,
      1832, *Wm. Northrop*, son of Jas. and Susan N., he b.
      So. E., June 26, 1808; children, NORTHROP : [1.] Wm.
      Asher, b. So. E., 1835.   [2.] Georgianna, b. So. E., May
      22, 1837 ; m. Newark, N. J., 1860, Wm. Baldwin, who

d. 1863 ; and 2d, 1868, Thos. Davis ; has no children.
[3.] Sarah, b. N. Y. city, June 26, 1839 ; m. Oct. 22,
1867, Sam'l D. Davis, and lives in Lakewood, N. J. ;
had, i. Agnes Helen. ii. Archibald Denison. iii. Mary
Elsie. [4.] Theodore F., b. So. E., May 31, 1843 ; m.
1870, Amanda Whitaker, and lives 120 West 131st st.,
N. Y.; had, i. John. ii. William. iii. Georgianna.
[5.] Carrie, b. So. E., Aug. 3, 1841; d. 1854. [6.] Edwin, b. 1845; d. 1846. [7.] Twin, b. 1845; d. 1846.
[8.] Washington Sale, b. So. E., Sep. 20, 1848. [9.] Geo.
Henry, b. So. E., May 16, 1851 ; d. 1860.

1022.   vi. MARY E., b. So. East, May 26, 1814 ; *gemini ;* m.
Oct. 15, 1834, *Thos. Sears Young,* he b. 1813; live in
Lakewood, N. J.; children, YOUNG : [1.] Martha, m.
Wm. Stone of N. Y. city, and had, i. Mary. ii. Helen.
iii. Julia. iv. Alice. [2.] Mary. [3.] Thos. S., m. Caroline E. Swan, dau. of Benj. S., of N. Y. city, and had,
i. May C. ii. Benj. S. [4.] Emma, m. Aug. Talbot of
N. Y. city, and had, i. Ethel. ii. Amy. [5.] Edward,
m. and had, i. Mary ; ii. Jeanette.

441.

SAMUEL SEARS[6] [*Benj.*[5] *Benj.*[4], *Sam'l*[3], *Paul*[2], *Rich.*[1]],
b. South East, N. Y., July 17, 1774; d. Lisbon, Ills., Oct. 10,
1830, æ. 57, gr.-st., Milltown, N. Y.; m. May 20, 1798, *Phebe
Field,* who d. Jan. 3, 1799 ; and 2d, Oct. 2, 1803, *Martha
Bennett,* who d. May 15, 1855.   Children :

By *Phebe :*
1023.   i. PHEBE, b. Dec. 26, 1798 ; d. Apr. 6, 1819, æ. 20,
gr.-st.
By *Martha :*
1024.   ii. SARAH, b. Sep. 10, 1804 ; d.
1025.   iii. STELLA, b. Aug. 21, 1806.
1026.   iv. MARIA, b. June 27, 1808 ; d. Feb. 13, 1870.
1027.   v. CHARITY, b. July 12, 1810.
1028.*   vi. AARON, b. Sep. 18, 1812.
1029.   vii. MELISSA, b. Aug. 1, 1815 ; m. —— *Stone,* and d.
Aug. 25, 1839.
1030.   viii. DELIVERANCE, b. July 19, 1818; d. Sep. 25, 1819,
æ. 1, gr.-st.
1031.   ix. BENJAMIN, b. July 30, 1820 ; d. Sep. 23, 1854.

All the children settled in Illinois.

445.

STEPHEN SEARS⁶ [*Steph.⁵, Benj.⁴, Sam'l³, Paul². Rich.¹*], b. Sharon, Ct., May, 1770; d. Mar. 31, 1812; m. May 7, 1797, *Lois Lovell.* Children:

1032.* i. BENJAMIN, b. Sharon, June 2, 1798.
1033. ii. CHARLES, b. Sharon, Jan. 10, 1800; d. unm., Dec. 7, 1843; was a Deacon.
1034. iii. GEORGE, b. Sharon, Feb. 18, 1802; d. unm., Mar. 4, 1882.
1035. iv. CYNTHIA, b. Sharon, May 8, 1804; d. unm., Dec. 11, 1858.
1036.* v. JOHN, b. Sharon, Feb. 18, 1806.
1037. vi. SEABURY, b. Sharon, July 24, 1809; d. July 4, 1819.
1038.* vii. STEPHEN H., b. Nov. 9, 1811.

447.

Dr. JOHN SEARS⁶ [*Steph.₅ Benj.⁴, Sam'l³, Paul², Rich.¹*], b. Sharon, Ct., about 1784; d. East Bloomfield, N. Y., 1866, æ. 82; m. Dec. 2, 1812, *Almira Gould,* of S., she b. Dec. 15, 1787; d. Jan. 1, 1872; dau. of David and Mary (Brewster) G., and maternally descended from Elder Wm. Brewster, "The Pilgrim." Children:

1039. i. SYBIL B., b. Sharon, Sep. 22, 1813; d. July 15, 1870; m. Oct. 5, 1841, *Henry Haymlin* of E. Bloom-field; children, HAYMLIN: [1.] John S., m. Sep. 13, 1855, Elizabeth Holcomb. [2.] Agnes D., m. Sep. 11, 1872, Chas. E. Steele. [3.] Frank D., m. Sep. 25, 1872, Elizh. Puriquet; and 3 others.
1040. ii. MARY, b. Sharon, Apr. 9, 1815; d. June 12, 1840.
1041.* iii. SIMEON B., b. Sharon, Sep. 6, 1816.
1042.* iv. JOHN, b. Sharon, May 20, 1818.
1043.* v. VINCENT G., b. Sharon, Aug. 24, 1823.
1044. vi. ALBERT R., b. Sharon, Aug. 17, 1826; d. Aug. 1, 1847.
1045. vii. SARAH A., b. Sharon, June 6, 1828; m. Dr. *David Atwater* of Springfield, Mass.
1046. viii. FRANCES, b. Sharon, Nov. 6, 1830; d. Oct. 7, 1854.

Dr. John Sears practiced in Sharon for 40 years, then re-moved to East Bloomfield, where he resided until his death.

27·

451.

IRA SEARS[6] [*Enoch*[5], *Benj.*[4], *Sam'l*[3], *Paul*[2], *Rich.*[1]], b. Dutchess county, N. Y., Mar. 7, 1774; d. Bennington, Vt., Nov. 9, 1818, æ. 44; m. there, 1794, *Sally Cushman*, 3d child of Chas. C., she b. there May 7, 1775; d. Albion, N. Y., Apr. 26, 1858, in 83 yr.; (having m. 2d, Ezekiel Noble, and 3d, Capt. John Mason of Castleton, Vt.;) she was a lineal descendant in the 7th gen. from Elder Robert C., "The Pilgrim," (Chas.[6], Chas.[5], John[4], Eleazar[3], Thos.[2], Robt.[1])   Children:

1047.   i. IRA, b. Dorset, Vt., Aug. 5, 1795; was a soldier in War of 1812, sickened and died on his way home, at St. Albans, Vt., Apr. 24, 1814.

1048.   ii. PAMELIA, b. Dor., Apr. 5, 1797; m. Castleton, Vt., Feb., 1824, *Asa Stark Jones*, from Hadley, Mass., (a gr.-son of Capt. Stark, who was cousin to Gen. S., of Rev'y War;) he b. Pawlet, Vt., 1798; d. Albion, N. Y., Jan. 29, 1873, æ. 77; she d. there Mar. 3, 1882; children, JONES; all b. Pawlet: [1.] Jane Maria, b. Dec. 3, 1824; m. July 10, 1848, Rev. Elijah H. Bonney, then preaching in Paw., rem. to Vernon Castle, N. Y.; Lenox, N. Y.; Somerset, N. Y., and Clarkson, N. Y., where he d. June 26, 1882; she d. Potsdam, N. Y., July 5, 1885; leaving a dau. Emma Jane, b. July 7, 1849.   [2.] Julia L., b. June 2, 1835; m. Albion, N. Y., May, 1866, Richard H. Downing of Red Wing, Minn., and d. there Oct. 18, 1874; had, i. Jennie, b. June 16, 1867; lives La Delle, Dak. ii. Harry, b. Aug. 8, 1869; d. La Delle, Oct. 30, 1884.   [3.] Anna E. Sears, b. Jan. 10, 1840; lives Albion, N. Y.

1049.   iii. CHARLES CUSHMAN, b. Dor., Feb. 16, 1799; m. Hinsdale, Mass., Sep. 3, 1833, *Ann Emmons*, she b. there Jan. 9, 1814; and d. s. p., Princeton, N. J., Nov. 24, 1838; (she m. 2d, T. B. Bigelow, and d. s. p., Oakland, Cal., July, 1876.)   Mr. Sears read law in Adams, Jefferson county, N. Y., together with Rev. C. G. Finney, and both were converted to Christianity; he discontinued the study of law, grad. Ham. Coll. 1826, and prepared for the ministry.   The last year of his life was spent at Princeton, where he was proprietor of a school for boys, preparing them for college.

1050.   iv. DESIAH, b. Dor., Apr. 28, 1801; m. Rutland, Vt., 1820, *Whitman Haskins*, and d. there July 21, 1821.

1051.* v. Isaac Underhill, b. Bennington, Vt., Sep. 19, 1803.
1052. vi. Joshua Atkins, b. Benn., July 5, 1806; d. Castleton, Vt., Jan. 1, 1835.
1053. vii. Alpheus, b. Benn., Aug. 21, 1808; d. Pawlet, Vt., Sep. 8, 1830.
1054.*viii. Henry, b. Benn., Nov. 8, 1810.
1055. ix. Sarah Ann, b. Benn., July 19, 1813; m. Paw., May 11, 1853, *Thos. J. Swallow*, he b. Weston, Vt., May, 1806; d. Albion, N. Y., Aug. 28, 1870, where his widow still lives.
1056. x. Ira Cushman, b. Benn., Jan. 9, 1815; m. Broadalbin, N. Y., Aug. 13, 1838, *Phebe Hunt*, she b. Mayfield, N. Y.; and d. B., June 5, 1860; (she m. 2d, Edmund Berry, and lives in B.)

453.

Dr. ISAAC SEARS[6] [*Sunderland[5], Benj.[4], Sam'l[3], Paul[2], Rich.[1]*], b. Nov. 22, 1778; d. Stillwater, N. Y., Feb. 8, 1824, æ. 45; m. Nov. 10, 1803, *Fanny Thompson*. Children:
1057.* i. Robert.
1058. ii. Isaac, lived in Mechanicsville, near Waterford, Sar. co., N. Y.
1059. iii. Ellen, lives with a niece near Mechanicsville. —— and 6 daus.

Isaac Sears was a physician, and at the organization of the Herkimer Co. Med. Soc., was chosen one of the Censors. In 1807 he was a Mem. of the State Med. Soc., and in 1812 Trustee of Fairfield Med. Coll., under charter of that date.

454.

Rev. REUBEN SEARS[6] [*Sunderland[5], Benj.[4], Sam'l[3], Paul[2], Rich.[1]*], b. Nov. 22, 1778; d. Prophetsville, Ill., Aug. 5, 1846; m. Nov. 10, 1803, *Sally Fitch*, dau. of Capt. Eliphalet F. of Canaan, Ct., who d. Sep. 5, 1846. Children:
1060. i. Charlotte, m. Hon. *Vernon Tichenor*, an att'y of Waukesha, Wis.; children, Tichenor: [1.] Willis V., lives in Mason City, Iowa; m. Helen A. Howard, and had, i. Vernon Howard. ii. Charlotte Sears. iii. Mary.
1061. ii. Mary, m. *Samuel F. Pruyn* of Burkett's Bridge, N. Y.; children, Pruyn: [1.] Mary, m. Warren F. Caulkins, Anita, Iowa. [2.] Sarah. [3.] Marion V. S., m.

—— James of Ireland, Neb. ⌊4.] Anna is a teacher, in Yakima City, Wash. Ter., unm. [5.] Edward, an att'y in
Yakima City. [6.] Emma D., m. Geo. Schmitz, a merchant in Davenport, Iowa. [7.] Fred. S., a printer in
Clark, Dak.

1062. iii. CATHERINE, m. *Hubbard S. Cabot* of Prophetstown,
Ill.; children, CABOT: [1.] Sarah. [2.] Mary. [3.] Norman, d. [4.] William.

1063.* iv. REUBEN E., b. July 31, 1824.

1064.   v. SARAH F., unm., lives with her sister Catherine.

Reuben Sears grad. Union Coll., and was settled over a
church in Hudson for several years, but his health failing, he
removed to Ballston Spa, where he wrote a poem, extolling
the virtues of the mineral waters, which was pub. in pamphlet
form in 1819.

He was afterward settled in Dracut, Mass., and in New
Scotland, Albany co., N. Y. and died in Prophetsville, Ill., 1846.

He was a Presbyterian clergyman, and one of the most conscientious and devoted persons in existence.

His whole life was made up of untiring effort for the good
of men.

He was one of the first to advocate total abstinence.

In one of his early sermons on the evils of intemperance, he
depicts the sad condition from this cause existing among the
clergy and elders, also the members of the church, and tells
them of the ruin and disgrace they are bringing upon themselves and the church : — and here the very first idea of the
possibility of total abstinence seems to have entered his mind,
as he exclaims: " Brethren, these things ought not to be; far
better than such a state of things should exist, would it be for
all to even totally abstain from the use of all intoxicating bev-
erages."

As an anti-slavery man he was " a thorn in the flesh " of the
Presbytery and Synod to which he belonged, by his persistent
introduction of resolutions denouncing the institution of slavery as " wrong in principle and opposed to true godliness."

He died in the firm conviction that God would order it
otherwise in His own good time.

455.

Dr. WILLIAM SEARS[6] [*Sunderland*[5], *Benj.*[4], *Sam'l*[3],
Paul[2], *Rich.*[1]], b. June 10, 1781; d. St. Louis, Mo., May 12,
1846, æ. 65; m. Nov. 12, 1812, *Hannah Gregory*, dau. of Col.

Uriah and Tamar (Rowland) G., of Ballston Centre, N. Y., she b. June 6, 1781 ; d. St. Louis, Mo., June 28, 1847, æ. 66. Children :

1065. i. ELIZABETH, b. Feb. 20, 1815 ; d. Aug. 3, 1822.
1066.* ii. SUNDERLAND GREGORY, b. Saratoga, N. Y., Sep. 27, 1817.
1067. iii. HENRY W., b. St. Louis, Mo., Mar. 21, 1822 ; m. and d., leaving 2 sons.

Wm. Sears was a physician, and practised in St. Louis, Mo.

456.

ABRAM SEARS[6] [*Sunderland*[5], *Benj.*[4], *Sam'l*[3], *Paul*[2], *Rich.*[1]], b. Oct. 27, 1783 ; d. Cortland, N. Y., June 12, 1863 ; m. Oct. 25, 1802, *Anne Barnum*, (3d cousin to P. T. B.,) who d. Sep. 20, 1812.   Children :

1068. i. WILLIAM, styled " Captain," has been Mayor of Dunlap City, Iowa.
1069. ii. EGBERT, lived in Groton, Tompkins county, N. Y.
1070. iii. ELI, lived in Groton, Tompkins county, N. Y.
1071. iv. ALBERT, lived in Cortlandville, N. Y.
1072. v. HIRAM.
—— and two daus.

459.

LEVI SEARS[6] [*Sunderland*[5], *Benj.*[4], *Sam'l*[3], *Paul*[2], *Rich.*[1]], b. Nov. 1, 1790 ; d. June 13, 1833, æ. 43 ; m. ——.   Children :
1073. i. MARCUS.
1074. ii. FRANK, lived in Groton, Tompkins county, N. Y.

464.

WILLIAM SEARS[6] [*Seth*[5] *Benj.*[4], *Sam'l*[3], *Paul*[2], *Rich.*[1]], b. South East, N. Y., Oct. 19, 1775 ; d. Neversink, N. Y., May 24, 1864 ; m. Ridgefield, Ct., Oct. 24, 1796, *Thirza Sears*, No. 782, dau. of Comfort and Eunice (Crane) S., she b. Mar. 22, 1779 ; d. Jan. 3, 1861.   Children :
1075.* i. MILES, b. Dec. 1, 1798.
1076. ii. CLARISSA, b. Oct. 18, 1801 ; m. *S. M. Hoyt ;* rem. to Bridgeville, N. Y., and d. Thompson, Apr. 5, 1824 ; had 1 son.

1077.   iii. EUNICE, b. Jul 9, 1803; m. *Sturges Andrus* of Mountaindale, N. Y. and had Frank, a clergyman.

1078.   iv. POLLY MATILDA, b. Apr. 6, 1805; m. *E. T. Partridge*, and rem. to Jamestown, N. Y., and d. Nov. 3, 1853; had 4 sons and 2 daus.

1079.   v. CAMILLA, b. Apr. 13, 1807; m. *Alson Lord* of Bridgeville, N. Y., and d. Apr. 1, 1827.

1080.   vi. JAMES WILLIAM, b. Mar. 12, 1809; m. *Jennet Bowers*, and had several children.

1081.   vii. HIRAM, b. Mar. 9, 1811; m. *Laurilla Shepardson;* and 2d, *Lucretia Brush;* and 3d, *Mary A. Gates;* he rem. to Gerry, N. Y., and had 2 sons, and a dau. who m. and lives on farm near her father, and has 4 daus.

1082.   viii. ESTHER, b. Mar. 9, 1813; m. *Wm. Bowers* of Bridgeville, N. Y., and had a large family.

1083.   ix. GEORGE E., b. Mar. 3, 1815; m. twice; and d. s. p., 1884.

1084.   x. PATTY MARIA, b. Mar. 19, 1817; m. *Henry Race;* had several children; and m. 2d, *Walter Hoyt*.

1085.   xi. MARY ANN, b. Apr. 18, 1819; m. *Robert Knapp*, and d. s. p.

1086.   xii. CAROLINE OPHELIA, b. May 18, 1824; m. *James O. Neil*, lived in Thompsonville, N. Y., and had a large family.

471.

Lt. DAVID SEARS[6] [*Eben'r*[5], *Eben'r*[4], *Paul*[3], *Paul*[2], *Rich.*[1]], b. Chatham, Ct., Nov. 27, 1757; d. Apr. 29, 1842; m. *Lucy Hall* of C. Children:

1087. i. CHARLES, b. Chat., 1792; bap. Oct. 18, 1795; d. Cuba, Apr. 26, 1819.

1088. ii. LUCY, b. Chat., 1794; bap. Oct. 18, 1795; d. Apr. 17, 1862, æ. 69; m. Apr. 18, 1826, *Patrick Derby, Jr.*, of Middletown, Ct., who d. Hampton, Ct., at a very advanced age; children, DERBY: [1.] Sarah. [2.] Harriet. [3.] Mary. [4.] Albert, lives in E. Hamp. [5.] Charles, lives in E. Hamp.

July 23, 1776, David Sears was app. Lt. 2d Reg. Ct. Mil., and his name appears as a pensioner in census of 1840, then æ. 85(?).

484.

JOHN SEARS[6] [*Paul*[5] *Eben'r*[4], *Paul*[3] *Paul*[2], *Rich.*[1]], b. Winthrop, Me., Sep. 3, 1778; d. Knox, Me., Mar. 4, 1853;

m. in Knox or Thorndike, Me., Apr. 28, 1805, *Achsah Whit-comb*, she b. Thorn., Oct. 11, 1784 ; d. June 29, 1828, æ. 44 ; and 2d, Jan., 1830, Mrs. *Maria Walker*, dau. of Wm. Stover, and widow of Joshua W., of Albion, Me., she b. Penobscot, Me., Nov. 17, 1793 ; d. Jan. 30, 1853 ; (by her 1st marriage she had a dau., Sarah Milby W., who m. David Sears, No. 1093.) Children :

By *Achsah* :

1089. i. SAMUEL, b. Knox, Me., Jan. 10, 1806; m. Nov. 6, 1833, *Orpah Dorman*, of Cherryfield, Me., she b. Jan. 11, 1810 ; d. Oct. 30, 1871 ; and he m. 2d, Dec. 14, 1872, Mrs. *Elizabeth Ward*, she b. Aug. 13, 1807 ; he was educated in public schools and China and Bluehill Acad.; was a teacher, farmer, millwright and J. P., settled in Lagrange, rem. to Machias, and now lives in Augusta, Me.

1090. ii. MARY ELIZA, b. Knox, May 20, 1807; d. Dec. 10, 1815-16.

1091. iii. LYDIA, b. Knox, Feb. 6, 1809 ; m. *Jesse Clark*, and had 3 children ; lived in Unity, Me., and Lowell, Mass., and just before the war, rem. to Balt., Md., married a Kentuckian, and settled near Salt Lake.

1092. iv. MERCY, b. Knox, Jan. 28, 1811 ; d. Dec. 20, 1811 or 1820.

1093.* v. DAVID, b. Knox, Aug. 19, 1813.

1094.* vi. JOHN, b. Knox, Aug. 22, 1815.

1095.* vii. THOMAS, b. Knox, Oct. 18, 1819.

John Sears was a joiner, farmer, merchant and mill-owner.

He came to Knox from Winthrop and Sebago, moving into a new country, with but a few scattering neighbors.

They had no roads but a track or spotted line through the woods, and kept up a little winter communication with Winthrop.

486.

PAUL STICKNEY SEARS[6] [*Paul*[5] *Eben'r*[4], *Paul*[3], *Paul*[2], *Rich.*[1]], b. Winthrop, Me., July 4, 1781 ; d. there, Mar. 22, 1833, æ. 52 ; m. 1805, *Susan Billington*, she b. Wayne, Me.; d. Winth., æ. 84. Children :

1096.* i. MOSES B., b. Winth., Dec. 2, 1806.

1097. ii. LOUIZA, b. Winth.; d. there.

1098.   iii. OLIVE E., b. Winth.; d. Oxford, Me.
1099.   iv. SUSAN E., b. Winth.
1100.   v. ELEANOR W., b. Winth.; d. Mar. 28, 1842.
1101.* vi. FRANCIS B., b. Winth., Dec. 2, 1822.
1102.   vii. WILLIAM HENRY, b. Winth.; lives Livermore, Me.
1103.   viii. NATHANIEL, b. Winth.; d. æ. 4.
1104.   ix. SAMUEL J., b. Winth.; d. Apr. 8, 1840, æ. 22.

Mr. Sears was a farmer; lived and died on the old homestead in Winthrop.

488.

SILAS SEARS[6] [*Paul5 Eben'r4, Paul3, Paul2, Rich.1*], b.
Winthrop, Me., Mar. 17, 1783; d. North Adams, Mich., 1867–
69; m. *Abigail Burgess.* Children: 1110. EMELINE NEWCOMB m. Don C. Hampton more
1105. i. FRANKLIN, d. 1849 N. Adams
1106. ii. IRENE, m. Addison La Core, and lives near Hillsdale,
Mich.
1107. iii. CAROLINE, is a widow with 2 children, and lives on
the homestead. Wisconsin   m. Henry Lewis
1108. iv. SILAS, m., and lived in Winslow, Ill., for some years,
then removed to Marshalltown, Iowa.
1109. v. DAVID, m., and in 1866, had 8 children; he carried
on the farm. Eliza Sears Corbett N. Adams Mich. Mary & Frank Silas
Silas Sears was settled at Glenburn, Me., for some 25 years,
then removed to North Adams, 6 miles from Hillsdale, Mich.,
where he had a farm.

493.

EBENEZER SEARS[6] [*Wm.5, Paul4, Paul3, Paul2,
Rich.1*], b. Rochester, Mass., Dec. 15, 1754; d. Dover, Vt.,
Jan. 24, 1849, æ. 94; m. Oct. 21, 1779, (1777, T. C.,) *Jane
White,* dau. of Justin and Jane W. of Roch., she b. Oct. 17,
1758; d. Dover, Nov. 14, 1833.   Children:
1110.   i. CHARITY, b. Dover, May 28, 1781; m. *Horatio G.
Sadler,* and d. 184–.
1111.   ii. RESOLVED, b. D., Nov. 3, 1783; d. Dec. 16, 1795.
1112.   iii. JANE, b. D., Dec. 20, 1785; m. Feb. 10, 1808,
Aholiab Gould, he b. Oct. 10, 1777; d. Aug. 2, 1840;
she d. Jan. 12, 1864, Carroll, N. Y., had 1 son and 5
daus.

1113.* iv. WILLIAM, b. D., Feb. 29, 1788.
1114.   v. LUCINDA, b. D., July 27, 1790 ; m. *Elijah Braley*,
      and d. Carroll, N. Y., Jan. 10, 1817.
1115. vi. SUSANNA, b. D., Jan. 25, 1792 ; m. Jan. 28, 1813,
      Obida Dean, he b. Feb. 12, 1789 ; she d. Carroll, N. Y.,
      Jan. 9, 1835 ; had 2 sons and 7 daus.
1116. vii. PHILENA, b. D., Feb. 23, 1794 ; d. Sep. 16, 1795.
1117.*viii. EBENEZER, b. D., Aug. 11, 1796.
1118. ix. ELECTA, b. D., June 18, 1799 ; m. *Ira Blashfield*,
      and d. Marlboro, Vt., May 15, 1876 ; he was killed at
      Williamsville, Vt., Mar., 1856.

Mr. Sears removed with his parents to Douglass, Mass., and
thence to Dover, Vt., where he lived until his death.

His name appears in the list of Revolutionary pensioners in
1840, then aged 85.

496.

WILLIAM SEARS[6] [*Wm.*[5], *Paul*[4], *Paul*₃ *Paul*[2], *Rich.*[1]],
b. Rochester, Mass., May 9, 1762 ; d. Dover, Vt., Jan. 1, 1813 ;
m. Jan. 6, 1788, *Hannah Stearns* of Douglass, Mass., she b.
Rehoboth, Mass., July 16, 1769 ; and 2d, Mrs. *Urania Hol-
brook*, dau. of Lt. Sam'l Freeman, and widow of Elijah H.,
(by her 1st marriage she had, Rachel and Urania, *gemini*, Sanford, Laura, and Julia.)   Children :
By *Hannah :*
1119.   i. DRUSILLA, b. Dover, late in 1788 ; m. *George Ben-
      nett*, and d. ab't 1860.
1120.* ii. OTIS, b. D., ab't 1789.
1121.* iii. CLARK, b. D., ab't 1794.
1122. iv. POLLY, b. D., ab't 1796 ; m. *Jacob Perkins*, and d.
      ab't 1850.
1123.   v. BETSY, b. D., ab't 1798 ; m. *David Dillingham*,
      and d. ab't 1850.
1124. vi. HANNAH, b. D., ab't 1800 ; m. *John Tubbs*, and
      rem. to Galway, N. Y.
1125. vii. SALLY, b. D., ab't 1802 ; m. *Wm. Sherman*, and d.
      early in 1875.
1126. viii. RESOLVED, b. D., Apr. 6, 1804 ; m. Randolph, N.
      Y., 1836, *Eliza Semple*, and lives in R. ; had 2 sons.
1127. ix. ALVIN, b. D., 1806 ; m. and d. ab't 1840.
1128.   x. ELIZA, b. D., Oct., 1808 ; d. unm., 1865.
28

501.

SILAS SEARS[6] [*Nath'l*[5], *Paul*[4], *Paul*[3], *Paul*[2], *Rich.*[1]],
b. Rochester, Mass., Nov. 26, 1762; (another account says Oct.
10,) d. Jan. 23, 1838, æ. 76; m. Dartmouth, Mass., July 11,
1782, by Rev. Sam'l West, to *Elizabeth West* of Roch., she b.
May 24, 1762; d. Weathersfield, Vt., Nov. 22, 1813, æ. 51;
and he m. 2d, —— ——.   Children:

By *Elizabeth* :
1129.*   i. JOSEPH, b. Weathersfield, Apr. 11, 1783.
1130.   ii. SALLY, b. W., Mar. 3, 1785; d. Jan. 24, 1794.
1131.* iii. SILAS, b. W., Mar. 30, 1788.
1132.* iv. NATHANIEL, b. W., Sep. 15, 1790.
1133.   v. JESSE, b. W., July 26, 1793.
1134.   vi. SALLY, b. W., July 10, 1795; d. of spotted fever,
        Nov. 23, 1813.
1135.* vii. ALDEN, b. W., Aug. 6, 1797.
1136. viii. BETSY, b. W., Oct. 24, 1799; d. of spotted fever,
        Nov. 17, 1813.
1137.* ix. LEONARD, b. W., May 12, 1802.
By *2d wife* :
1138.   x. ELIZABETH, b. W., Sep. 22, 1822.

Family tradition says Silas Sears served during the whole of
the Revolutionary war, and that he was one of the first chosen
by Lafayette to go into his corps.

Silas Sears, called " of Scituate," was in Capt. Nath'l Winslow's Co., in Col. Whitney's Regt., from June to Nov., 1776,
and was allowed for 77 miles' travel ; — he, then of Rochester;
was in Capt. Edw'd Hammond's Co., in Col. Sam'l Fisher's
Regt., Aug. 15, to Sep. 13, 1779, 80 miles' travel, wages and
subsistence, £2.12 0; served in Continental service with six-
months' men, from July 6 to Dec. 8, 1780; arriving in Springfield for service in Northern army, July 8, 1780; was allowed
for 5 mos., 14 days' service and 240 miles' travel, £12 2 10; description : Silas Sears from Rochester, aged 17, 5 ft. 10 inches
height, dark complexion.

He afterward removed to Vermont, and settled on a farm
near River Lamoille.

He is said to have married against his father's wishes, which
occasioned a breach in the family relations.

In 1813 he started for Boston on horseback, but was over-
taken by a messenger on the third day from home, and informed of the sudden and severe sickness of his family.

He at once retraced his steps, but when he reached home his wife and daughter Betsy were dead and Sally dying of spotted fever.

503.

NATHANIEL SEARS⁶ [*Nath'l⁵, Paul⁴, Paul³, Paul², Rich.¹*], b. Rochester, Mass., 1766 ; d. Mar. 30, 1816, æ. 51 ; m. New Bedford, Mass., 1786, (pub. Roch., Apr. 19, 1785,) *Hannah Keene* of Freetown, Mass., she b. Feb. 18, 1768 ; d. Roch., Sep. 25, 1846, æ. 78 ; (she was sister to Jesse K.) Children :

1139.   i. STEPHEN, b. Roch., Aug. 5, 1787 ; d. Charleston, S. C., Nov. 2, 1809 ; (Nov. 20, T. Rec.) m. Nov. 20, 1807, by Abram Holmes, J. P., to *Lucy Bennett*, and had 2 daus. mentioned in his father's will in 1811.

1140.* ii. WILLIAM, b. Roch., Aug. 31, 1789.

1141.   iii. HANNAH, b. Roch., Jan. 23, 1792 ; m. *Jona. Tobey*, of New Bedford, and d. 1879, leaving a large family.

1142.   iv. BETSY, b. Roch., May 20, 1794 ; d. Apr. 9, 1795.

1143.* v. JESSE, b. Roch., Apr. 3, 1796.

1144.   vi. BETSY, b. Roch., July 7, 1798 ; d. July 13.

1145.* vii. NATHANIEL, b. Roch., Aug. 15, 1799.

1146. viii. LUCY, b. Roch., Feb. 15, 1802 ; m. Roch., Mar. 31, 1822, by Rev. Oliver Cobb, to *John Snow* of Fairhaven, and had 5 children.

1147.* ix. JOSEPH, b. Roch., Mar. 15, 1804.

1148.   x. CLARISSA ROGERS, b. Roch., Dec. 15, 1806 ; m. there, Mar. 9, 1830, *Calvin Staples*, of New Bedford ; he b. Taunton, Mar. 29, 1806 ; d. June 27, 1860 ; children, STAPLES : [1.] Clarissa Sears, b. Dec. 16, 1830 ; lives in N. B., unm. [2.] Hannah James, b. Sep. 19, 1832 ; d. Dec. 28, 1838. [3.] Almira Maltby, b. Nov. 16, 1834 ; d. Dec. 28, 1838. [4.] Calvin Sylvester, b. Oct. 17, 1836 ; d. Aug. 6, 1837. [5.] Isabella Graham, b. Dec. 12, 1837; m. Sep. 21, 1858, Rev. Jas. Russell Bourne of N. Bed., he b. there, June 25, 1833, lives in Sharon, Ct., and had, i. Edward Gaylord, b. June 24, 1860 ; grad. Yale, 1883, took Cobden Medal, Foote scholarship and Berkeley scholarship. ii. Henry Eldredge, b. Apr. 13, 1862 ; grad. Yale, 1883 ; during Senior year stood 3d in class of 149, and 2d on examina-

tion ; Principal of High School, Thomaston, Me.; ent.
Yale Theo. Sem. 1884. iii. Richard Sears, b. Nov. 5,
1864 ; d. June 6, 1865. [6.] Samuel Maltby, b. Feb. 17,
1840 ; d. at sea, Mar. 26, 1864. [7.] John Calvin, b.
Jan. 31, 1842 ; is a Cong. Min., Deerfield, Mass.; m.
Marietta, O., Jan. 7, 1868, Helen Maria Eels, and had,
i. Kate Tileston. ii. Samuel Meade. ⌐8.] Lucy J., b.
Jan. 24, 1844; m. July 8, 1867, Edw. H. Rice of Winchester, Mass., and d. June 28, 1878 ; had, i. Calvin
Winsor, b. Nov. 4, 1868. [9.] James Sylvester, b. Mar.
29, 1846; m. June 24, 1869, Emma G. Tripp, and lives
N. Bed.; had, i. Walter Clifton, b. Oct. 3, 1872.
[10.] Abby Kingsbury, b. Jan. 22, 1848; d. Aug. 13,
1851.

1149.   xi. SUSANNA, b. Roch., Feb. 21, 1809; (Feb. 25, T. C.)
m. *Dan'l Knowles*, who d.; she lives in Prov., R. I.

1150.* xii. STEPHEN, b. Roch., Sep. 18, 1813.

Nathaniel Sears did duty for a short time in Rhode Island
during the Revolutionary war; he was then very young.

He engaged largely in building, farming, etc., and by his industry accumulated during his short life quite a large estate
for those days.

He lived opposite his parents, and his house was a regular
stopping place for the ministers who traveled from place to
place preaching, and many a time was crowded by those who
came to meeting.

His will, dated Nov. 27, 1811, was proved Apr. 10, 1816,
and mentions wife Hannah ; sons William, Jesse, Nathaniel
and Joseph; daus. Hannah, wife of Jona. Tobey; Lucy,
Clarissa and Susanna ; and grand-daus., children of deceased
son Stephen. Wm. Sears was app. Execr.

504.

PRINCE SEARS[6] [*Nath'l[5], Paul[4], Paul[3], Paul[2], Rich.[1]*],
b. Rochester, Mass. ; m. June, 1794, Mrs. *Rebecca Fuller* of
Portsmouth, R. I.

1151. i. PAUL D., lived in Ludlow, Vt., married twice, but
having no children, adopted Paul, son of his bro. Leonard ; d. ab't 1878, leaving a widow. *d. '84*

1152.* ii. LEONARD W. *b. Apr. , 1792 d. '84*

1153. iii. CALVIN R., d. unm., æ. ab't 20.

1154. iv. SOPHIA, m. —— *Bettis*, a Canadian, and had issue, of whom, the eldest, La Fayette B., lives some 30 miles west of Ludlow, "over the mountains."

Prince Sears removed from Rochester to Calais, Vt., about 1800, and thence about 1836, to Ludlow, Vt.

His farm in Calais adjoined that of Ezekiel D. Nye's father, which was in North Montpelier, and to Mr. Nye I am indebted for most of the data concerning this family.

510.

JOHN SEARS[6] [*Nath'l*[5], *Paul*[4], *Paul*[3], *Paul*[2], *Rich.*[1]], b. Rochester, Mass., about 1786; d. Feb. 7, 1827; m. Roch., Sep., 1806, *Nancy Gifford*, she b. Fairhaven, Mass., Oct. 25, 1786; d. New Bedford, Mass., 1864, æ. 76.   Children:

1155.* i. MARSHALL GIFFORD, b. Roch., Feb. 15, 1807.
1156. ii. SOPHRONIA, b. Roch., Feb. 25, 1808; m. Jan. 14, 1829, *Jona. Cowing;* d.
1157. iii. CHARITY, b. Roch., Nov. 28, 1809; d.
1158. iv. THOMAS GIFFORD, b. Roch., Feb. 12, 1812; d. Middleboro, Nov. 17, 1870, æ. 59.
1159. v. ALMODA, b. Roch., Apr. 18, 1814; d. Mar. 7, 1816.
1160. vi. MARY ANN, b. Roch., Sep. 25, 1816.
1161. vii. BETSY, b. Roch., Dec. 19, 1818; d.
1162. viii. LUCY AUGUSTA, b. Roch., June 25 (18 T. C.), 1821; d.
1163. NATHAN PIERCE, b. Roch., Nov. 1, 1823; d.

John Sears lived on the old homestead farm in Rochester.

511.

THOMAS SEARS[6] [*Thos.*[5], *Thos.*[4], *Paul*[3], *Paul*[2], *Rich.*[1]], b. Plymouth, Mass., 1771; d. there, Sep. 28, 1845, æ. 74; m. Nov. 7, 1797, *Susanna Morton* of Ply., who d. there, Mar. 29, 1841.   Children:

1164.* i. THOMAS BARTLETT, b. Ply., July 19, 1808.
1165. ii. FANNY, m. —— *Rowell* of Oregon.
1166. iii. SUSAN, d. Ply., June 26, 1841.
1167. iv. BATHSHEBA DREW, m. *Francis Thompson.*

516.

ELEAZAR SEARS[6] [*Will'd*[5], *Thos.*[4], *Paul*[3], *Paul*[2], *Rich.*[1]], b. Plymouth, Mass., May, 1778; d. there, Mar. 24,

1855, æ. 76 yrs. 10 mos. ; m. Ply., Aug. 22, 1805, *Polly Morton* of Ply., who d. Aug. 2, 1867, æ. 81.   Children :

1168.   i. MARY ANN, b. Ply., 1806. ·
1169.* ii. WILLIAM, b. Ply., Jan. 5, 1808.
1170.   iii. HIRAM, b. Ply. ; d. æ. 2½ yrs.
1171.* iv. DANIEL H., b. Ply., Mar. 20, 1811.
1172.*   v. HIRAM B., b. Ply., May 19, 1816.
1173.   vi. LUCY H., b. Ply., 1819 ; d. Apr. 30, 1856, æ. 37.
1174. vii. HARRIET NEWELL, b. Ply., 1822 ; d. Dec. 31, 1840,
        æ. 18.
1175.*viii. WINSLOW.
1176.   ix. EUNICE B.

Eleazar Sears was a chairmaker, and prior to 1814 bought land at " Hob's Hole " or Wellingsley, in Plymouth, which he subsequently sold to Thaddeus Churchill.

517.

DAVID SEARS[6] [*Will'd*[5], *Thos.*[4], *Paul*[3], *Paul*[2], *Rich.*[1]], b. Plymouth, Mass., Aug. 1, 1786 ; d. there, Mar. 23, 1865 ; m. Dec., 1819, (pub. 5,) *Nancy Manter*, dau. of Belcher and Sarah (Wright) M.; and 2d, Jan. 4, 1830, Mrs. *Jane Doten*, dau. of Benj. Warren of Ply., who d. Oct. 25, 1866, æ. 70 yrs. 3 mos.   Children:

By *Nancy:*
1177.   i. SARAH P., b. Ply., Nov. 28, 1820.
1178.   ii. NANCY, b. Ply., Nov. 23, 1822 ; m. *Lemuel Doty ;*
        children, DOTY :   [1.] Lemuel W. [2.] Charles H., 1844.
1179.   iii. DAVID, b. Ply., Dec. 6, 1824 ; d. at sea, Jan., 1838.
1180.   iv. STEPHEN, b. Ply., Feb. 26, 1827 ; lost at sea ; unm.
1181.   v. ALBERT M., b. Ply., Mar. 15, 1829 ; m. *Mary Ann
        Mead ;* was mate of a vessel, and drowned at sea, being
        knocked over by the boom ; his will, dated Dec. 10, 1853,
        was allowed Jan. 16, 1854 ; wife Mary A., Exec[x], had
        the house and lot, (she m. 2d, June 20, 1854, Patrick
        Kirwin.)
By *Jane :*
1182.   vi. ANGELINE WARREN, b. Ply., 1830.
1183.* vii. BENJAMIN WARREN, b. Ply., Oct. 4, 1831.
1184. viii. MERCY ANN, b. Ply., Oct. 3, 1832 ; m. Ply., July
        4, 1861, *Charles Whitten, Jr.*, of Ply.
1185.   ix. RUFUS WARREN, b. Ply., Oct. 2, 1834 ; d. Oct. 5,
        1837.

1186.* x. JOSEPH HENRY, b. Ply., Oct. 1, 1836.
1187. xi. RUTH WARREN, b. Ply., Apr. 17, 1838; m. there, Dec. 23, 1857, *Abram Whitten* of Ply.

518.

EDMUND SEARS[6] [*Will' d*[5], *Thos.*[4], *Paul*[3], *Paul*[2], *Rich.*[1]], b. Plymouth, Mass.; d. 1868; pub. Ply., Aug. 31, 1805, to *Lucy Holmes* of Ply., who d.; and he m. 1st, *Elizabeth Bartlett;* and 2d, 1807, *Rebecca Lucas*, dau. of Abijah and Mary (Robbins) L. of Plympton, she b. 1782; and 3d, widow *Ruby Maxima,* dau. of Wm. and Temperance Hall. Children:

1188.* i. EDMUND L., b. Carver, Mass.
1189. ii. THOMAS LEWIS, b. Car., lives in Somerset, Mass.
1190. iii. REBECCA, b. Car.
1191.* iv. IVORY H., b. Car., Mar. 5, 1810.
1192. v. ELIZABETH, m. *Lyman Sayles*, and had a dau., Ella, m. Eugene Jllson, and lives Milton, Mass.
1193. vi. SOLOMON, d. Providence, R. I.
1194. vii. ROBERT B., went west; a dau. m. George Cole.

520.

JOSEPH SEARS[6] [*Will' d*[5], *Thos.*[4], *Paul*[3], *Paul*[2], *Rich.*[1]], b. Plymouth, Mass.; d. Carver, Mass., æ. 85; m. (pub. Ply., June 19, 1808,) *Hannah Robbins,* of C., who d. there. Children:

1195. i. WILLARD, b. Car., Nov. 5, 1810; unm.
1196.* ii. ALLEN, b. Car., Jan. 9, 1812.
1197. iii. ELMIRA, b. Car., 1816; m. *George Cummings* of Lakeville.
1198.* iv. LEANDER, b. Car., Mar. 20, 1820.

521.

THOMAS SEARS[6] [*Will' d*[5], *Thos.*[4], *Paul,*[3] *Paul*[2], *Rich.*[1]], b. Plymouth, Mass., 1799; d. June 6, 1863, æ. 74; m. 1815, *Rebecca Collins* of Ply., dau. of John C., she d. Ply., Aug. 22, 1872, æ. 74 yrs. 1 mo. 28 d. Children:

1199.* i. JAMES T.
1200.* ii. HORATIO.
1201.* iii. ELBRIDGE G.

1202.* iv. OTIS.
1203.   v. AUGUSTUS, b. 1831; enlisted in Seventh Mass. Vols.
        Jan. 31, 1862, and was discharged Apr. 11, 1862.
1204. vi. REBECCA, m. *Benj. Suter.*
1205. vii. CAROLINE, d. æ. 18.

525.

ISAAC SEARS[6] [*Elkanah*[5], *Josh.*[4], *Paul*[3], *Paul*[2], *Rich.*[1]],
b. Chatham, Ct., Nov. 3, 1757; d. New Durham, N. Y., 1842,
æ. 85; m. *Grace* ——.   Children:
1206.   i. ISAAC, bap. Chat., Sep. 24, 1786; rem. to Huron,
        Wayne co., N. Y., and d. leaving issue.
1207. ii. ANNA, bap. Chat., Sep. 24, 1786.
1208. iii. LUCY, bap. Chat., Sep. 24, 1786.
1209. iv. POLLY, bap. Chat., Feb. 3, 1788.
1210.   v. SALLY, bap. Chat., June 6, 1790.
1211.* vii. CHAUNCEY, b. 1787.
1212. viii. SELDEN.
1213. ix. *Daughter.*

Isaac Sears served in the Revolutionary Army.
In 1780, he was appointed on Com. at Chatham to provide
for the wants of the Continental Army.
He removed to New Durham, Greene co., N. Y., being dism.
from the Ch., East Hampton, in 1798.
May 9, 1778, he deeded to Isaac Sears 6 acres of land in E.
Hamp.; 1796, he signed deed to Willard Sears; 1821, Isaac
Sears of New Durham, and Benjamin Sears signed deed to
Willard Sears.

526.

WILLARD SEARS[6] [*Elkanah*[5], *Josh.*[4], *Paul*[3], *Paul*[2],
Rich.[1]], b. Chatham, Ct., Sep. 8, 1760; d. East Hampton, Ct.,
Aug. 23, 1838, æ. 78; m. Nov. 23, 1785, *Rhoda Bailey*, she
b. Mar., 1766; d. Feb. 17, 1794; and 2d, May 22, 1796, Mrs.
Betsy (Clark) Stevens, who d. Jan. 9, 1831, æ. 58.   Children:
By *Rhoda:*
1214.   i. *Child*, b. and d. E. Hamp., Apr. 2, 1787.
1215. ii. RHODA, b. E. Hamp., Mar. 29, 1789; m. May 3,
        1820, *Ezra Ayres* of Greenwich, Mass.; children,
        AYRES: [1.] Adeline Elizabeth, b. Oct. 12, 1822.

[2.] Augustus Willard, b. Apr. 16, 1827. [3.] Ezra
Smith, b. Feb. 18, 1831.

·1216.   iii. RACHEL, b. E. Hamp., Feb. 11, 1794; m. Mar. 7,
1813, *Erastus Sheldon* of New Marlboro, Mass., and d.
Jan. 22, 1834, æ. 40; he d. Apr., 1860, æ. 80; children,
SHELDON: [1.] Elizabeth, b. Jan. 20, 1817. [2.] Oliver, b. Sep. 18, 1819. [3.] Erastus Martyn, b. Apr.
10, 1821. [4.] Eunice M., b. Dec. 28, 1823. [5.] Edmund Sears, b. July 25, 1829.

By *Betsy:*
1217.   iv. BETSY, b. E. Hamp., Mar. 23, 1797; m. Sep. 6,
1821, *Harvey Arnold* of E. Hamp., who d. Feb. 18, 1847;
she d. Jan. 16, 1850; children, ARNOLD: [1.] Joshua
M., b. Sep. 11, 1832; d. Feb. 25, 1888. [2.] James
Prescott, b. Jan. 10, 1826. [3.] Lavinia B., b. Mar. 4,
1828. [4.] Edwin H., b. Nov. 27, 1830.
1218.*   v. OGDEN, b. E. Hamp., Aug. 19, 1798.
1219.*   vi. WILLARD, b. E. Hamp., Oct. 19, 1799.
1220.   vii. EUNICE, b. E. Hamp., May 11, 1801; m. Sep. 21,
1834, *Henry Snow, Jr.*, of E. Haddam, Ct., and d. June
10, 1875, æ. 74; children, SNOW: [1.] Henry, b. July
31, 1839; lives E. Hamp. [2.] Lavinia, b. Nov. 3, 1840.
1221.* viii. STEPHEN GRIFFITH, b. E. Hamp., Sep. 27, 1803.
1222.*   ix. ELIJAH CLARK, b. E. Hamp., June 23, 1805.
1223.*   x. SELDEN PHILO, b. E. Hamp., July 21, 1813.

Willard Sears was a reliable, Christian man, and unusually
conscientious.

It is related of him that on one occasion having found a
pocket-book with money in it, and no owner appearing, he
mounted his horse and rode continuously for three days, until
he placed it in the hands of its owner.

530.

Rev. BENJAMIN SEARS[6] [*Elkanah*[5], *Josh.*[4], *Paul*[3],
Paul[2], *Rich.*[1]], b. Chatham, Ct., Feb. 21, 1771 (?1773); d.
Delaware, Ohio, Oct. 11, 1822; m. Feb. 2, 1794, *Ann Bige-
low*, dau. of David and Patience (Foster) B., she b. Marlboro,
Ct., Jan. 15, 1773; d. Mecklenburg, N. Y., May 14, 1842.
Children:

1224.* i. ELKANAH, b. New Durham, N. Y., June 22, 1795.
1225.* ii. JOHN, b. New Dur., Apr. 20, 1797.
29

1226. iii. BENJAMIN, b. New Dur., June 16, 1800; bap. 1815; d. Fort Wayne, Ind., Nov. 24,(?) 1822, of typhus fever. "Although he made no pretensions to the ministry, he was much drawn toward the Indian Mission, and proposed to consecrate his life to such useful Christian labors among the natives as he could perform. Having ordered his clothing and effects to be applied to the use of the mission, he departed this life, Nov. 3, 1822, in full assurance of a blissful immortality."

1227.* iv. DAVID, b. Meredith, N. Y., July 17, 1803.

1228.* v. ORIN, b. Mere., Dec. 12, 1805.

1229. vi. LUCRETIA, b. Mere., 1808, m. *Harvey Munson*, and after his death removed to New Haven, Ct., where she and her daus. reside; children, MUNSON: [1.] Elizabeth, m. Charles Peek, and had, i. Emily. ii. Robert. [2.] Martha, m. Alex'r H. Bush, and had, i. Alfred H. ii. Julia E. iii. Mary E. iv. Albert. v. Martha.

1230.* vii. HIRAM, b. Mere., May 25, 1811.

1231. viii. RUFUS, b. Mere., 1817; prepared for the office of a Baptist clergyman, and d. Bath, N. Y., Apr. 7, 1842.

" In early life Mr. Sears followed farming and coopering, with his father ; rem. from Chatham, Ct., to New Durham, Greene co., N. Y., and thence, after two years, he penetrated the forest still further, to Delaware, Ohio, where he resided till his death.

" He filled with honor and esteem various military offices.

" Changing his views of the Christian religion, he joined the Baptist Church, devoted himself to the ministry, received ordination, and after serving his church for some years, to its great increase, took his leave for a more extended field.

" He received his appointment as missionary, and traveling with his two sons, John and Benjamin, and John's wife, he went to Fort Wayne, Ind., his sons having received appointments to labor as missionaries among the Indians.

" He aided them in the constitution of a church at Fort Wayne, the first one established in Indiana.

" He returned from the mission to Delaware, and died soon afterward, much lamented as a man of energy and piety."

532.

DAVID SEARS[6] [*Josh.[5], Josh.[4], Paul[3], Paul[2], Rich.[1]*], b. Sandisfield, Mass., Oct. 2, 1762; m. —— ——. Children:

1232. i. SARAH, b. Sand., m. —— *Wheeler*, and rem. to N. Y. State.

1233. ii. MARY, b. Sand.; m. *Isaac Gamble;* children, GAM-
    BLE: [1.] Emily. [2.] Mary. She m. 2d, *Immar
    Hubbard* of Sand., and had issue.

"David Sears of Sandisfield, laborer, age 18, 5 ft. 9 in. height,
light complexion, brown hair," enlisted in Capt. Robins' Co.,
in Col. Ashley's Regt., July 2, 1780, and was discharged Jan.
5, 1781, having served 6 mos. 7 days, travel 75 miles from
home, wages £12 9 4; he was in Capt. John Barrows' Co.
Col. Caleb Hyde's Regt., and served at Stillwater, N. Y., Oct.
20 to Oct. 28, 17—; 9 days, 60 miles' travel.

Rev. E. H. Sears says: " He enlisted in the war of the
Revolution, was in Washington's Army, and passed though the
trying scenes of the New Jersey Campaign."

534.

JOSHUA SEARS[6] [*Josh.[5], Josh.[4], Paul[3], Paul[2], Rich.[1]*],
b. Sandisfield, Mass., Nov. 7, 1766; m. —— ——. Children:
1234   i. FREDERIC.
1235. ii. HARVEY.

Joshua Sears served in Capt. Jere. Hickok's Co., Lt.-Col.
Sears' Regt., Aug. 6 to Nov. 8, 1781, 3 mos. 7 days.

He removed to New York State.

535.

Capt. DANIEL SEARS[6] [*Josh.[5], Josh.[4], Paul[3], Paul[2],
Rich.[1]*], b. Sandisfield, Mass., Feb. 2, 1769; d. May 30, 1853,
æ. 84; m. *Edy Bosworth,* who d. Aug. 18, 1851, æ. 83, of
lung fever. Children:
1236. i. ALBERT, b. Sand., Apr. 10, 1792; rem. to Georgia;
    was a speculator, and acquired a large property, but lost
    considerable of it during the late war; he died unm.,
    leaving some $50,000 to be divided among his relatives.
1237. ii. SARAH, b. Sand., Jan. 12, 1794; m. —— *Baldwin*
    of Goshen, Ct.; children, BALDWIN: [1.] Son, murdered
    by Indians in California. [2.] Son, went South, and en-
    tered into partnership with Jason Sears; was a soldier in
    the Confederate army, where he lost his health, and died
    of consumption. [3.] Laura, m. James Shepard of Sand.,
    (bro. to Geo. A. Shepard, Town Clerk,) rem. to Ohio,
    where both died; had five children, one of whom is a
    practicing physician in Westfield, Mass. Mrs. Baldwin

lives in Gates Mills, Cuyahoga co., Ohio, with her gr.-children; address, care Albert Shepard.

1238. iii. MARCUS AURELIUS, b. Sand., July 11, 1796; was a teacher, and d.

1239.* iv. JASON, b. Sand., Feb. 29, 1803.

1240. v. MARY, b. Sand., Mar. 29, 1806; m. —— *Baldwin*, of Colebrook, Ct., and lives there a widow; address, care Dan'l Baldwin.

1241.* vi. HENRY MORRIS, b. Sand., Mar. 10, 1808.

Daniel Sears is styled "Captain" in town records. He lived to a great age, held many offices of trust, and died venerable for character and years.

539.

JOSEPH SEARS[6] [*Josh.[5], Josh.[4], Paul[3] Paul[2], Rich.[1]*], b. Sandisfield, Mass., 1778; d. Sep. 8, 1851, æ. 73, in a fit; m. *Lucy Smith*, dau. of Silas S., who d. Oct. 4, 1855. Children:

1242.* i. DANIEL, b. Sand., Apr. 13, 1801.

1243. ii. EDY, b. Sand., May 11, 1804; d. May 1, 1805.

1244.* iii. JOSHUA MILTON, b. Sand., Sep. 19, 1808.

1245.* iv. EDMUND HAMILTON, b. Sand., 1810.

Mr. Sears was a prominent man, and held various offices, Rep. to State Leg., 1819, 1820, 1822.

542.

PAUL SEARS[6] [*Paul[5] Josh.[4], Paul[3], Paul[2], Rich.[1]*], b. Sandisfield, Mass., Feb. 2, 1769; d. Sep. 25, 1851, æ. 83, of consumption; m. *Rachel Granger* of S.; she b. Aug. 4, 1771; d. Aug. 23, 1846. Children:

1246. i. MARY, b. Sand., July 2, 1788; m. *James Burt*, for many years of firm Burt, Sears & Co., Hartford, Ct., and d. Orange, N. J.; children, BURT: [1.] Edwin C., manuf. of "Burt's shoes;" d. [2.] Adelia, m. Horatio Day of Hartford. [3.] James, manuf. of "Burt's boots." [4.] Mary Jane, m. —— Price. [5.] John, manuf. " Burt's cable wire boots." [6.] Anna, m. —— Gallatin, wholesale druggist, N. Y.

1247.* ii. ALFRED, b. Sand., Sep. 27, 1795.

1248. iii. BELINDA, b. Sand., Aug. 23, 1798; m. *Luman Davis*, who d.; and 2d, *Anson Avery;* and 3d, —— *Truesdale* of Youngstown, Ohio; she d. Nov. 30, 1868;

children, DAVIS: [1.] Mary, m. —— McKee of Y., where she lives.

1249. iv. SALLY, b. Sand., July 1, 1801; m. *Wm. Bolles*, and rem. to Central New York, where he engaged in manufacturing scythes; was foreman of E. Remington & Son's works for many years, now lives in Fountain, So. Minn.; children, BOLLES: [1.] Jason. [2.] Clarinda. [3.] Jane. [4.] Sarah. [5.] William.

1250.* v. BARNAS, b. Sand., Nov. 17, 1802.
1251.* vi. LYMAN, b. Sand., Sep. 19, 1804.
1252.* vii. DAVID G., b. Sand., June 29, 1806.
1253.* viii. JOHN R., b. Sand., Jan. 11, 1809.
1254.* ix. HIRAM, b. Sand., July 8, 1811.
1255.* x. HENRY, b. Sand., Aug. 3, 1815.

544.

Dea. SIMEON SEARS[6] [*Paul*₅ *Josh.*⁴, *Paul*³, *Paul*², *Rich.*¹], b. Sandisfield, Mass., 1776; d. Penn., 1864, æ. 88; m. 1795, *Tryphena Hurlburt*, she b. 1777; d. ; 2d, E. Hartford, 1801, *Lovisa Spencer*, who d. Sand., 1844, æ. 67. Children:

By *Tryphena:*

1256. i. POLLY HURLBURT, b. Sand., Nov. 23, 1800; d. Va., Dec. 22, 1861, æ. 60; m. 1822, *Benj. Heath.*

By *Lovisa:*

1257. ii. ARTEMESIA, b. Sand., Dec. 8, 1802; d. 1848, æ. 45; m. 1825, *Calvin Chapin;* previous to her marriage she taught school several terms; children, CHAPIN: [1.] Clarissa, d. New Milford, Ct., 1854; was a school teacher and much beloved by all who knew her. [2.] Newton, a fine scholar and teacher, lives in Illinois. [3.] Samuel, a carpenter and cabinet-maker, m. and had, i. Jenny, b. Mar. 14, 1868; grad. High School, New Britain, Ct., 1886, with highest honors in her class, and is now a teacher in State Normal School in that place. ii. Wilfred, b. 1872. iii. Gertrude, b. Nov. 16, 1874. The Chapins are all Baptists.

1258.* iii. NORMAN SPENCER, b. Sand., Jan. 7, 1805.
1259.* iv. JULIUS, b. Sand., Apr. 3, 1807.
1260. v. EMILY, b. Sand., Apr. 17, 1809; d. Stockbridge, Mass., Nov. 27, 1886, æ. 77; m. Sep. 21, 1832, *Sam'l Thompson* of So. Tyringham, (now Monterey) he b.

Aug. 23, 1805; d. Athens, Pa., Jan. 29, 1886; removed in 1866 to Hammonton, N. J., and in 1886 to Athens, Pa.; children, THOMPSON: [1.] Merrick Samuel, b. Sep. 15, 1833; is a cabinet-maker in Nashua, N. H.; m. June 7, 1853, Clarinda M. Walker, and had, i. Arthur Samuel, b. Nov. 11, 1854; grad. High Sch., Nashua, at 15, Dart. Coll. at 20; was licensed to preach by Methodists; taught High Sch., Nashua; joined Congregationalists, and entered Divinity Sch., Yale Coll., Sep., 1877; was accidentally shot on the Sound, Dec. 1, 1877. ii. Ina Viola, b. Sep. 8, 1857; was highly educated and taught in High Sch., Nashua, several years; m. Sep., 1882, Edw'd Booth of Burlington, Vt. iii. Ida Clarinda, b. Jan. 24, 1864; is teacher in a graded school in Nashua. iv. Josiah Graves, b. Feb. 26, 1868; grad. Dart. Coll., 1889. [2.] George Edward, b. Mar. 3, 1835; is a cabinet-maker and machinist in Lynn, Mass.; m. Nov. 4, 1854, Eliza W. Blanding; and 2d, Ithaca, N. Y., —— ——; he served in army as fifer 9 mos., and had, i. Ellen Josephine, b. Franconia, N. H., Nov. 29, 1855; d. May 21, 1869. ii. Nellie Bertha, b. Monterey, Mass., Oct. 6, 1859; m. Nov. 26, 1881, Bradbury H. Huff, and lives in Annisquam, Mass. iii. Carrie Agnes, b. Otis, Mass., Dec. 25, 1861; m. Dec. 25, 1878, Gus. J. Lull, who d. soon. [3.] Frances Emeline, b. Dec. 22, 1836; educ. at Sem'y New Milford, Ct., and taught school $3\frac{1}{2}$ years; m. Dec. 5, 1855, W. H. Cheney, and 2d, July 23, 1868, Isaiah Potter, and lives in Athens, Pa.; had by 1st marriage, i. Chas. Henry, b. Nov. 12, 1859; d. Sep. 7, 1863. ii. Bertha Delphine, b. May 26, 1862. iii. Francis Judson, b. Mar. 11, 1865. [4.] James Emerson, b. May 13, 1839; enlisted Sep., 1861, in 27th Regt. Mass. Vols.; was in more than 20 battles, and was promoted Sergt. for bravery, and killed Cold Harbor, June 3, 1864. [5.] Julia Ann, b. Sep. 7, 1841; educ. New Marlboro and Westfield, Mass., and taught school 4 years; m. Jan. 18, 1866, John S. Sears, No. 2516 a, vi, of Monterey, and removed to Stockbridge, 1872. [5.] Rosina Amelia, b. July 21, 1844; taught school several years; m. Dec. 25, 1865, Judson A. Potter, and lives in Willington, Ct.; had, i. Estelle E., b. Apr. 9, 1868. ii. Clarence Thompson, b. Apr. 10, 1870; lives in Wash. Ter. iii. Arthur Judson, b. Feb. 5, 1872. iv. Geo. Boardman, b. Feb. 27, 1874. v. Orrilla Adel, b. Sep. 27, 1876. vi. Bessie, b. Oct. 11, 1882. (19, 1883.)

[6.] Millicent Jemima, b. July 29, 1848; finished her education at a select school in Hammonton, N. J., and taught school several years; m. July 17, 1870, Geo. H. Perkins of H.; lived in Kansas 3 years, and died of consumption at Atlantic City, N. J., Aug. 6, 1877; had no children. He m. 2d, Bertha D. Thompson.

1261.* vi. SIMEON, b. Sand., July 13, 1811.
1262. vii. EDWARD, b. Sand., Dec. 9, 1813.
1263. viii. SARAH LOVISA, b. Sand., 1822; m. 1847, Rev. *Henry Barlow*, who d. 1853, leaving 2 daus. m., and live with their mother in Dundee, Ill.

Mr. Sears was a farmer in Sandisfield, Mass., a deacon of the Baptist Ch., and a very exemplary Christian man.

547.

SIMEON SEARS[6] [*Sim.*[5], *Josh.*[4], *Paul*[3] *Paul*[2], *Rich.*[1]], b. ——; m. —— ——. Children :
1264.* i. JAMES, b. N. Y. State, Nov. 6, 1790.
1265. ii. ISAAC.
1266. iii. ABRAHAM.
1267. iv. HENRY.
1268. v. MELINDA.
1269. vi. CHARLOTTE.
1270. vii. SMITH.

550.

JOSEPH SEARS[6] [*Sim.*[5], *Josh.*[4], *Paul*[3], *Paul*[2], *Rich.*[1]], b. ——; m. 1800, *Sarah Pitts*. Children :
1271.* i. DAVID BENTON, b. Lima, N. Y., Apr. 28, 1804.
1272. ii. CHAUNCY,   ⎫
1273. iii. *Dau.*,   ⎬ drowned in Sciota river, 1812.
1274. iv. *Dau.*,   ⎭
1275. v. POLLY, m. —— *Jackson ;* 2d, *Donohue Williams.*
1276. vi. REBECCA, m. *Tim. Wood,* and lives in Creston, Iowa.
1277. vii. DEBORAH, m. *Wm. L. Lee,* Rock Island, Ill., and lives in Eureka Sp'gs, Ark.

Mr. Sears removed to Lima, N. Y., in 1796, and thence in the fall of 1811, to Huron co., Ohio, and in 1814, to Switzerland co., Ind., and finally to Wabash Valley, Ill., in 1818.

His family suffered great hardships while residing in the Sciota Valley during the war of 1812, and were frequently imperiled by the attack of marauding Indians.

They were finally obliged to flee to Fort Erie for safety, but in crossing the Sciota river their boat was upset, and three of the children were drowned.

560.

HENRY SEARS[6] [*Micajah[5], Dan'l[4], Paul[3], Paul[2], Rich.[1]*], b. Yarmouth, Mass., Aug. 8, 1775; d. East Dennis, Feb. 22, 1839, æ. 63, gr.-st., Br.; m. Harwich, Apr. 1, 1802, *Elizabeth Snow*, dau. of Thomas S. of Har., who d. Aug. 24, 1829, æ. 47, gr.-st.; 2d, (pub. Den., Feb. 2, 1831,) *Ruth Turner* of Yar. Children:

By *Elizabeth* :
1278. i. NABBY S., b. Den., Jan. 25, 1803; m. —— *Jacobs;* 2d, Brewster, July 28, 1861, *Thomas Sears*, No. 663.
1279. ii. HENRY, b. Den., July 21, 1806; drowned by upsetting of a boat, Apr. 15, 1825, æ. 18, gr.-st.
1280. iii. ELIZABETH A., b. Den., Aug. 15, 1810.
1281. iv. MICAJAH, b. Den., Dec. 10, 1813.
1282. v. POLLY S., b. Den., Oct. 8, 1820.
1283. vi. CLARISSA, b. Den., Mar. 26, 1823.
By *Ruth:*
1284. vii. LAVINIA H., b. Den., Feb. 27, 1832.
1285. viii. RUTH ANN, b. Den., Mar. 1, 1835; d. Nov. 19, 1836, gr.-st.

568.

LEMUEL SEARS[6] [*Paul[5] Dan'l[4], Paul[3], Paul[2], Rich.[1]*], b. Dec. 30, 1785; d. May 28, 1829, having long been an invalid; m. ——. Child:
1286. i. LEMUEL.

571.

Dr. NATHAN SEARS[6] [*Paul[5] Dan'l[4], Paul[3], Paul[2], Rich.[1]*], b. Ashfield, Mass., Feb. 14, 1791; d. Feb. 1, 1848; m. Mrs. *Grace Newkirk, née* Loper, of New Jersey, who d. Mt. Carmel, Ill., Nov. 24, 1863. Children:
1287.* i. PAUL, b. near Zanesville, Ohio, June 5, 1820.
1288. ii. CLARISSA, m. *E. B. Bishop*, and lives 300 18th st., San Francisco.
1289. iii. NATHAN HENRY, d. Nov. 20, 1862.

Dr. Sears studied medicine in the office of Dr. Bryant, father of Wm. Cullen B., the poet, who was then studying law.

After his graduation he removed to Zanesville, Ohio, where he practiced until 1834, when he removed to Wayne co., Mich., and in 1839, to Mt. Carmel, Wabash co., Ill., where he died.

When young he made a six months' cruise in one of his father's whaling vessels.

578.

DANIEL SEARS[6] [*Enos*[5] *Dan'l*[4], *Paul*[3], *Paul*[2], *Rich.*[1]], b. Ashfield, Mass., Oct. 6, 1779; d. there, July 31, 1858, æ. 78; m. Buckland, Mass., May 14, 1804, *Electa Rawson;* she b. Conway, Mass., Mar. 17, 1788; d. Ash., Apr. 14, 1861, æ. 73. Children:

1290.   i. REBECCA, b. Ash., Apr. 7, 1805; m. Dec. 2, 1823, *Milton Bussey;* rem. to Caledonia, Wis., and Lake City, Minn.; children, BUSSEY: [1.] Harriet J. [2.] Mary Ellen. [3.] Sarah A.
1291.* ii. LEWIS, b. Ash., Dec. 24, 1806.
1292.* iii. WILLIAM, b. Ash., Dec. 17, 1808.
1293.* iv. LUTHER RAWSON, b. Ash., Dec. 9, 1810.
1294.   v. ESEK BUSSEY, b. Ash., Jan. 11, 1815; m. Mar. 31, 18–4, *Esther F. Olin;* rem. to Caledonia, Wis., in 1837; has no children.
1295.   vi. SARAH ANN, b. Ash., Dec. 23, 1819; d. Apr. 25, 1837.
1296.* vii. DANIEL, b. Ash., Mar. 28, 1824.

The five eldest children removed to the vicinity of Racine, Wis., about 1830, when the country was yet a wilderness.

Their efforts were met with success, both in regard to farming, and the rise in value of land.

Daniel Sears did not become interested in the subject of religion until he had quite a family, after which he was prompt in his attendance on divine worship, and was called very liberal to benevolent objects.

579.

WILLIAM SEARS[6] [*Enos*[5], *Dan'l*[4], *Paul*[3] *Paul*[2], *Rich.*[1]], b. Ashfield, Mass., ab't 1785; d. there Aug., 1829, æ. ab't 44;
30

m. Ash., *Tamsen Eldridge;* she b. there, 1786 ; d. 1880, æ.
94. Children :

1297.   i. LAVINIA, b. Ash., ab't 1810 ; m. ab't 1830, *Ephraim
   Williams* of Ash.
1298.* ii. NATHAN, b. Ash., ab't 1813.
1299.* iii. WILLIAM, b. Ash., June 20, 1818.
1300.* iv. SAMUEL, b. Ash., July 28, 1820.
1301.* v. STEPHEN, b. Ash., Sep. 11, 1822.

584.

JACOB SEARS[6] [*Edm'd[5], Edm'd[4], Paul[3], Paul[2], Rich.[1]*],
b. East Yarmouth, Mass., Oct. 9, 1771 ; d. Dennis, Dec. 27,
1846, æ. 75; m. Harwich, Jan. 7, 1797, *Elizabeth Foster,* she
b. Har., Nov. 4, 1772; d. Feb. 21, 1844.   Children :

1302.* i. DANIEL, b. Den., Oct. 20, 1797.
1303.* ii. NATHAN FOSTER, b. Den., Sep. 26, 1800.
1304. iii. JACOB, b. Den., July 26, 1802 ; bap. Sep. 19; d.
   Apr. 23, 1803, gr.-st., W. Br.
1305. iv. ELIZABETH, b. Den., July 9, 1804 ; bap. Mar. 3,
   1805 ; d. July 5, gr.-st., No. Den.
1306. v. ELIZABETH F., b. Den., Nov. 25, 1806 ; bap. Dec.
   28; m. Oct. 5, 1826, *Thomas Sears,* No. 663.
1307. vi. POLINA, b. Den., Nov. 5, 1808; d. Oct. 14, 1864.

Jacob Sears and wife were adm. to Ch., Dennis, Mar. 28,
1802.   He was chosen Town Collector, Mar. 5, 1799.

585.

JUDAH SEARS[6] [*Edm'd[5], Edm'd[4], Paul[3], Paul[2], Rich.[1]*],
b. East Yarmouth, Mass., Oct. 6, 1773 ; adm. to Ch., Dennis,
Apr. 8, 1802 ; d. there, Jan. 18, 1850, æ. 76; m. Den., Jan.
18, 1798, *Sarah Hale,* she b. Sandwich, Mass., Oct. 13, 1778 ;
adm. to Ch., Den., Oct. 25, 1801 ; d. Hyannis, Oct. 31, 1855,
æ. 77.   Children :

1308.   i. BETHANY, b. Den., Sep. 29, 1799 ; m. Oct. 27,
   1818, *Eli Howes,* and d. Oct. 22, 1824.
1309.* ii. EBENEZER, b. Den., July 3, 1802 ; bap. July 18.
1310.* iii. JUDAH, b. Den., Nov. 17, 1804 ; bap. Jan. 2, 1805.
1311. iv. ZENAS, b. Den., Nov. 17, 1806, bap. Dec. 21; d.
   Mar. 15, 1808.
1312. v. SALLY, b. Den., Jan. 12, 1809 ; m. May 9, 1836,
   Ralph Dwight, he b. Thompson, Ct., July 30, 1809 ;

rem. to Dudley, Mass.; children, DWIGHT: [1.] Sarah,
b. Sep. 12, 1837; m. Apr. 27, 1873, Zephaniah Baker of
Dudley. [2.] Caroline, b. June 12, 1839; d. May 4,
1869. [3.] Martha, b. Mar. 4, 1843; m. Dec. 3, 1863,
Franklin Jacobs of Southbridge, Mass. [4.] Susan, b.
Dec. 7, 1846; d. Aug. 17, 1849.

1313.　vi. LYDIA, b. Den., Dec. 14, 1812; d. W. Br., Feb. 16,
1888; m. July 4, 1833, *Nathan Foster*, he b. W. Br.,
Mar. 6, 1807; children, FOSTER: [1.] Polly D., b. July
15, 1835; d. Mar. 6, 1836. [2.] Lydia S., b. Sep. 27, 1837;
m. Nov. 14, 1858, Stephen Burgess of Harwichport.
[3.] Martha S., b. Nov. 16, 1840; m. Nov. 17, 1858, Ambrose N. Doane of Har. [4.] Dau. b. and d., Sep. 8,
1842. [5.] Polly D., b. Sep. 17, 1843; m. Dec. 6, 1867,
Chris. C. Crowell of E. Den., and rem. to Blair, Neb.
[6.] Nathan, b. Sep. 19, 1846; m. Oct. 15, 1874, Carrie
Moody of Har.; and is a lumber and grain dealer in
Herman, Neb. [7.] Laura A., b. Apr. 12, 1849; d. July 2,
1853. [8.] Dau., b. Jan. 25, 1851; d. Jan. 26. [9.] Judah
E., b. Oct. 30, 1852; m. Sep. 17, 1878, Sarah P. Weekes
of Har.; is a clothing dealer in Newport, Vt. [10.] Persis S., b. Aug. 28, 1855.

1314.　vii. BETSY PAINE, b. Den., Apr. 14, 1816; m. Oct. 5,
1837, *Prince Crowell* of Sandwich, who was lost at sea,
Mar. 21, 1840, æ. 28; 2d, Jan. 10, 1841, *Ellis M.
Swift* of Bourne, Mass., who d. Oct. 7, 1876, æ. 78; children, SWIFT: [1.] Ordello R., b. Aug. 7, 1847. [2.] Lucy
G., b. Oct., 1853; m. Oct. 2, 1873, —— Eldridge.
[3.] Deborah H., b. July 24, 1854; d. May 31, 1875.

1315.　viii. PERSIS, b. Den., Sep. 17, 1818; m. Oct. 8, 1839,
Edwin Baker of Hyannis, and d. Mar. 31, 1850.

1316.　ix. MARTHA, b. Den., Sep. 7, 1822; m. Boston, Mar.
1, 1852, *Edwin Baker* of Hyannis, his 2d wife, and d.
there, Jan. 30, 1856.

587.

PAUL SEARS[6] [*Edm'd[5], Edm'd[4], Paul[3], Paul[2], Rich.[1]*], b.
East Yarmouth, Mass., Nov. 22, 1777; d. East Dennis, Nov.
23, 1854, æ. 77; m. Den., Jan. 1, 1801, *Ruth Howes*, dau. of
Barnabas H., she. b. E. Yar., Sep. 9, 1781; d. Jan. 5, 1865,
æ. 83. Children:

1317.* i. DEAN, b. Den., Feb. 22, 1802; bap. Aug. 2, 1807.

1318. ii. BETSY, b. Den., June 4, 1806; m. Dec. 8, 1825, *Joseph Knowles Mayo*, of So. Orleans, Mass.
1319. iii. RUTH, b. Den., Sep. 15, 1808; m. Nov. 27, 1828, *Daniel Crowell*, and d. Sep. 29, 1838, æ. 30, gr.-st., Br.; he d.
1320.*iv. PAUL, b. Den., Dec. 3, 1812.
1321.* v. BARNABAS H., b. Den., June 27, 1815.

Paul Sears and wife were adm. to Ch., Dennis, June 21, 1807.

593.

EDMUND SEARS[6] [*Edm'd[5], Edm'd[4], Paul[3] Paul[2], Rich.[1]*], b. East Yarmouth, Mass., Apr. 8, 1792; d. East Dennis, Jan. 17, 1867, æ. 75; m. Den., Nov. 28, 1815, *Elizabeth Crowell*, dau. of Nath'l C. of Den., she b. Jan. 22, 1797; d. Jan. 22, 1865.   Children :
1322.   i. MARY, b. Den., Nov. 17, 1817; m. Dec. 6, 1838, *Asa Shiverick*, he b. E. Den., Jan. 14, 1816; and d. July 21, 1847.
1323.   ii. BETSY CROWELL, b. Den., Oct. 4, 1819; m. Jan. 25, 1838, *Jotham Howes*, he b. Feb. 5, 1813; d. at sea, Oct. 4, 1841; 2d, July 16, 1848, *Asa Shiverick*, his 2d wife, and d. Nov. 13, 1855.
1324.*iii. NATHAN, b. Den., Aug. 30, 1821.
1325. iv. CHLOE C., b. Den., Oct. 4, 1826; m. Nov. 19, 1846, *Ezra Sears*, No. 1330.
1326.* v. SETH, b. Den., Sep. 15, 1829.
1327. vi. HANNAH CROWELL, b. Den., June 12, 1833; m. May 16, 1854, *Joshua G. Sears*, No. 1738.

Edmund Sears was Selectman 5 years from 1839.

599.

EZRA SEARS[6] [*Josh.[5], Edm'd[4], Paul[3], Paul[2], Rich.[1]*], b. East Yarmouth, Mass., Mar. 31, 1789; d. East Dennis, Nov. 24, 1830, æ. 41; m. Den., Dec. 26, 1815, Mary Seabury, dau. of David S. of Den., who was living 1884, æ. 91.   Children :
1328.* i. JOSHUA, b. Den., June 10, 1817.
1329. ii. LOT, b. Den., July 25, 1819; was a farmer, and drowned June 24, 1840.
1330. iii. EZRA, b. Den., June 11, 1821; m. Nov. 19, 1846, *Chloe Sears*, No. 1325, she b. Oct. 4, 1826; d. Jan. 30,

1852; he was a seaman, and d. Baltimore, Md., Dec. 3, 1846.

1331.* iv. DAVID S., b. Den., Jan. 16, 1823.

1332. v. WARREN, b. Den., July 13, 1825; d. July 5, 1845, on board ship in Boston Bay.

1333.* vi. HEMAN G., b. Den., Sep. 1, 1829.

Ezra Sears was a cabinet-maker, and lived in East Dennis.

June 14, 1831, Prob. Court made an allowance to his widow Polly.

602.

Capt. GEORGE SEARS[6] [*Josh.*[5], *Edm'd*[4], *Paul₃ Paul²*, *Rich.*[1]], b. East Dennis, Mass., Sep. 8, 1795 , d. Boston, Oct. 12, 1845; m. Aug. 24, 1820, *Susan Gray*, dau. of John G. of Barnstable; she b. there, Jan. 3, 1798; d. Aug. 7, 1860. Children:

1334. i. OLIVE, b. June 9, 1822; d. Apr. 28, 1832.

1335. ii. SUSAN GRAY, b. June 12, 1825; d. Apr. 26, 1832.

1336. iii. OLIVER GRAY, b. Mar. 7, 1828; d. May 10, 1832.

1337. iv. GEORGE, b. May 2, 1830; d. Sep. 15, (14 T. Rec.) 1830.

1338.* v. GEORGE OLIVER, b. Boston, Jan. 31, 1835.

1339. vi. ELLEN VICTORIA, b. Boston, Dec. 7, 1837; lives with her bro. in Boston; unm.

George Sears was a shipmaster, removed to Boston, resided and died in Rowe place.

611.

WILLIAM SEARS[6] [*Chris.*[5], *Edm'd*[4], *Paul³*, *Paul²*, *Rich.*[1]], b. East Yarmouth, Mass., July 9, 1791 ; d. Dorchester, Mass., Jan. 5, 1830; m. (pub. Dennis, Apr. 13, 1822,) *Mary Hallet*, dau. of James H. of Yar. Children:

1340. i. LUCY HALLET, b. Den., Apr. 20, 1823.

1341. ii. WILLIAM, b. Yar., Dec. 19, 1826; d. Jan. 25, 1828.

1342. iii. HARRIET, b. Boston, Mar. 23, 1825.

621.

ELKANAH SEARS[6] [*Elk.*[5], *Edm'd*[4], *Paul³*, *Paul²*, *Rich.*[1]], b. East Dennis, Mass., Feb. 16, 1800 ; adm. to Ch., Den., Oct.

24, 1818; d. Jan. 20, 1876, æ. 75, gr.-st., W. Br.; m. Feb., 1827, *Clarissa Hall* of Den., who d. Nov. 14, 1835, æ. 32, gr.-st.; and 2d, Yar., Dec. 8, 1836, *Sarah Berry*, she b. Yar., 1802; d. Mar. 18, 1889, æ. 87. Children:

By *Clarissa* :
1343.   i. Lucy T., b. Den., Aug. 12, 1828; m. 1860, *Shubael Howes* of Den.
1344. ii. Emeline, b. Den., Sep. 15, 1830; m. 1872, *Wm. Howland* of New Bedford, who d. 1880.

By *Sarah* :
1345. iii. Sarah H., b. Den., Nov. 30, 1838; m. 1871, *Wm. C. Downes* of Vineyard Haven, and had 2 children.

622.

THOMAS SEARS[6] [*Elkanah*,[5] *Edm'd*,[4] *Paul*,[3] *Paul*,[2] *Rich.*[1]], b. East Dennis, Mass., Feb. 16, 1800; m. West Yarmouth, Mass., Dec. 28, 1825, *Azubah Crowell*, dau. of Abner C., she b. Yar., June, 1800; d. E. Den., Jan. 4, 1867, æ. 66, gr.-st., W. Br.; and 2d, Nov. 1, 1867, *Louiza G. Ainsworth* of Yar. Children:

By *Azubah* :
1346.   i. *Child*, b. Den., Dec. 21, 1826; d. Dec. 28.
1347. ii. Mercy, b. Den., 1827.
1348. iii. George, b. Den., Oct. 20, 1829; d. Nov., 1853; was owner and master of brig "Sophia," which sailed from San Francisco for Brigham City, Oregon, and was never heard from after.
1349. iv. Olive B., b. Den., June 15, 1832; m. (pub. Yar., Apr. 17, 1854,) *Rufus White* of So. Yar., and had [1.] Rufus Winfield.
1350.* v. Isaiah C., b. Den., Dec. 9, 1833.
1351. vi. *Child*, b. Den., 1843; d. inf.

Mr. Sears has always taken much interest in the family history, and possessing a retentive memory, has a great fund of anecdote to relate.

He resides in East Dennis, was in good health at last accounts (1888), though feeling some of the infirmities of age.

623.

Capt. WILLIAM SEARS[6] [*Elkanah*[5], *Edm'd*[4], *Paul*[3], *Paul*[2], *Rich.*[1]], b. East Dennis, Mass., Apr. 4, 1808; m. South Yar-

mouth, Mass., Jan. 21, 1836, *Ruth Berry*, she b. Yar., Dec. 15, 1807; d. Feb. 27, 1876; and 2d, Den., Mar. 7, 1886, *Laura A. Smalley*, dau. of James A. S. Children:
By *Ruth:*
1352.* i. WILLIAM G., b. Den., Oct. 4, 1838.
1353.* ii. ISAAC B., b. Den., Mar. 25, 1841.
1354.* iii. ELKANAH H., b. Den., Apr. 25, 1849.

624.

ELISHA SEARS[6] [*Elisha*,[5] *Elisha*,[4] *John*,[3] *Paul*,[2] *Rich.*[1]], b. East Dennis, Mass., Aug. 25, 1795; d. there, Dec. 14, 1838, æ. 42; gr.-st., W. Br.; m. (pub. Den., Mar. 27, 1824,) *Hitty Wing*, dau. of Lemuel W. of Sandwich, Mass., who d. about 1856. Children:
1355.* i. FRANKLIN, b. Den., Sep. 4, 1826.
1356.* ii. ELISHA HARVEY, b. Den., Jan. 17, 1829.
1357. iii. *Dau.*, d. May 12, 1830.
1358. iv. KEZIA, b. Den., Aug. 17, 1833; d. Mar. 17, 1834.
1359. v. MERCY WING, b. Den., Dec. 15, 1835; m. *John Poe*, a relative of the Indian Fighter of historic fame, who d. in Salisbury prison pens, during the Rebellion; and 2d, Bowling Green, Ohio, 1866, Rev. *John Poucher* of the M. E. Ch., and lives in Elmore, Ohio; children, POE: [1.] Theodocia, d. 1884, æ. 20. POUCHER: [2.] Frank. [3.] Naomi. [4.] Edward. [5.] George. [6.] Robert.

627.

Capt. CONSTANT SEARS[6] [*Elisha*[5], *Elisha*[4], *John*[3], *Paul*[2], *Rich.*[1]], b. East Dennis, Mass., July 26, 1802; d. Brewster, Mass., July 13, 1887; m. Br., Apr. 8, 1824, *Deborah Hopkins*, dau. of John and Nabby H., she b. there, Apr. 19, 1801; d. May 2, 1861, æ. 60; and 2d, *Dorothy Eldridge*, dau. of Samuel E., who d. Sep. 21, 1877, æ. 67 yrs. 5 mos.; and 3d, Dennis, Mar. 28, 1879, Mrs. *Dinah H. Thacher*, dau. of Richard and Olive Nickerson, she b. 1823, (her son by 1st marriage, Capt. Geo. Thacher, m. a dau. of Capt. Jepthah B. Sears.) Children:
By *Deborah:*
1360. i. THANKFUL, b. Den., Mar. 1, 1826; m. Dec. 17, 1848, *Sam'l S. Hall*, son of Edm'd H. of Den., he b.

Aug. 21, 1824; d. Apr. 3, 1878; was a shoemaker and salt manufacturer; children, HALL: [1.] Helen A., b. Jan. 3, 1850. [2.] Thomas S., b. Jan. 27, 1852. [3.] Samuel C., b. Jan. 18, 1854. [4.] Charles E., b. Sep. 23, 1855. [5.] Frederic, b. June 14, 1858. [6.] Susie D., b. Nov. 5, 1860. [7.] Elisha S., b. Nov. 6, 1861. [8.] James C., b. Aug. 5, 1867.

1361.   ii. EMILY, b. Den., Aug. 23, 1828; m. Brewster, Aug. 11, 1858, by Rev. S. P. Snow, to *Lathrop Baker*, son of Braddock B. of Yar., he b. 1829.

1362.   iii. MARY ANN, b. Den., Apr. 22, 1831; d. Nov. 10, 1832.

1363.   iv. SARAH R., b. Den., Dec. 18, 1833; m. Brewster, June 29, 1857, by Rev. Enoch Pratt to *Milton B. Crowell*, son of Zenas and Jerusha C. of Yar., he b. 1828; lives in Brockton, Mass.

1364.   v. BETSY T., b. Den., Nov. 27, 1836; m. Brewster, Nov. 26, 1868, by Rev. A. Parke Burgess, to *Rufus Smith*, son of Stephen and Clarissa S. of Chathamport, he b. 1827.

1365.   vi. JULIA ANN, b. Den., Mar. 19, 1839; is a teacher in Normal School, Nashville, Tenn.

1366.   vii. AMANDA F., b. Den., Dec. 10, 1841; is a teacher.

Capt. Constant Sears was born, and long resided in the ancient house built by his great-gr.-father, Capt. John Sears, in East Dennis, but after the death of his first wife removed to the house which he built in West Brewster, on the site of the old Capt. Samuel Sears' house.

In early life he followed the sea, and became a shipmaster; after retiring he was a farmer and salt manufacturer.

He held many places of trust and honor, and at times taught school.

He was esteemed by all who knew him as a kind and upright citizen.

632.

SAMUEL RIPLEY SEARS[6] [*Noah[5], Elisha[4], John[3], Paul[2], Rich.[1]*], b. Brewster, Mass., Nov. 3, 1810; d. Nov. 28, 1881; m. Dennis, Dec. 4, 1834, *Susannah Hall*, dau. of Edm'd and Thankful H. of Den., she b. July 24, 1810; d. July 7, 1874.   Child:

1367.   i. SARAH H., b. Brew., July 23, 1848; m. there, Feb.

20, 1873, by Rev. Earnest H. Leesman, to Capt. *John
W. Robbins*, son of John and Duty R. of Harwich, he
b. 1849.

636.

HEMAN SEARS⁶ [*John⁵, John⁴, John³, Paul², Rich.¹*], b.
Yarmouth, Apr. 10, 1780; d. Feb. 27, 1836; m. Dennis, Oct.
2, 1800, *Olive Howes*, dau. of Joseph H., she b. Mar., 1775;
adm. Ch., Den., Sep. 24, 1803; d. Feb. 15, 1804, æ. 26, gr.-st.,
No. Den.; and 2d, (pub. Den., Mar. 2, 1818,) *Abigail Sears*,
No. 661, dau. of Reuben S., she b. Aug. 9, 1773; d. Nov.
18, 1880. Children:

By *Olive :*
1368.   i. HANNAH, b. Den., July 12, 1801; bap. Sep. 24,
        1803; d. Aug. 11, 1818.
1369.   ii. HULDAH, b. Den., Oct., 1802; bap. Sep. 24, 1803;
        d. Nov. 12, 1803.
By *Abigail :*
1370.   iii. OLIVE HOWES, b. Den., Dec. 29, 1818; m. 1836,
        Stillman Kelly, and d. Feb. 1, 1879; she compiled and
        published a Genealogical Tree of the Sears family;
        children, KELLY: [1.] Heman S., b. Oct. 25, 1837.
        [2.] Olive F., b. July 18, 1840; m. Apr. 29, 1860,
        Jacob Sears, No. 2581. [3.] Abbie S., b. Sep. 18, 1842.
        [4.] Hannah S., b. Feb. 13, 1844. [5.] Ellen M., b. Jan.
        27, 1846. [6.] Fannie L., b. Apr. 19, 1848. [7.] Still-
        man F., b. Feb. 28, 1851; m. Chloe C. Sears, No. 2619.
        [8.] Zebina D., b. Nov. 17, 1852; m. Hannah C. Sears,
        No. 2624. [9.] Elsie M., b. Mar. 17, 1857. [10.] Car-
        rie W., b. Apr. 29, 1860.
1371.   iv. HANNAH, b. Den., Feb. 11, 1821; m. Boston,
        May 1, 1840, by Rev. Jas. Mudge, Jr., to *Jotham Salis-
        bury* of Weymouth, Mass., and d. Jan. 26, 1844.
1372.   v. ABBIE, b. Den., Apr. 6, 1823; m. Dec. 30, 1852,
        Martin D. Dunbar, and lives in Hingham, Mass.
1373.* vi. ELIJAH BAILEY, b. Den., June 7, 1826.
1374.* vii. ORIN, b. Den., Aug. 7, 1828.
1375.   viii. HULDAH H., b. Den., Jan. 6, 1831; d. Jan. 3,
        1839, gr.-st., Br.
1376.   ix. FANNIE ANN, b. Den., June 25, 1833; d. July 2,
        1833, gr.-st., Br.

31

1377.   x. HEMAN, b. Den., Oct. 23, 1835; d. Sep. 8, 1836,
    gr.-st., Br.

638.

ENOS SEARS[6] [*John5 John4, John3, Paul2, Rich.1*], b.
Yarmouth, Mass., Oct. 10, 1873; m. —— ——.   Children :

1378.   i. JOSHUA, b. Den., Oct. 19, 1807.
1379.* ii. BARZILLAI, b. Den., Oct. 21, 1809.
1380. iii. SALLY, b. Den., Jan. 19, 1813.
1381.* iv. LYMAN.
1382.* v. ENOS.

Enos Sears is said to have removed to Colerain, Mass.

640.

MOODY SEARS[6] [*John5, John4, John3, Paul2, Rich.1*], b.
Yarmouth, Mass., Nov. 19, 1788; d. May 28, 1865; m. (pub.
Dennis, Jan. 13, 1810,) *Betsy Crowell* of Den.; 2d, Harwich, Nov. 9, 1812, *Jane Davis* of Har., who d. Oct. 24,
1849; 3d, Har., Dec. 22, 1850, *Susan* (*Bassett*) *Cahoon*,
dau. of Michael Bassett, she b. 1803; kept the "Sears House"
at Brewster at a very advanced age.   Children :
By *Jane :*
1383.*   i. GILBERT, b. Oct. 13, 1813.
1384.* ii. ENOS, b. Nov. 5, 1816.
1385.* iii. JOHN, b. Sep. 19, 1818.
1386.   iv. ASA W., b. June 29, 1820; drowned July 10, 1834,
    gr.-st., Br.
1387.   v. LARNED, b. Sep. 20, 1823; lost in sch. "Bride,"
    near Race Point, Oct. 3, 1841, gr.-st., Br.
1388.   vi. BETSY JANE, b. Apr. 30, 1826; d. Feb. 4, 1876.
1389. vii. NANCY C., b. June 5, 1828; d. June 11, 1829.
1390. viii. *Child*, b. and d. Nov. 29, 1829.

653.

JOHN SEARS[6] [*Edw'd5, Will'd4, John3, Paul2, Rich.1*],
b. Harwich, Mass., Dec. 31, 1794; m. Dennis, Dec. 25, 1817,
Mercy Howes, dau. of Abijah and Lydia (Bassett) H., who d.
1822; 2d, *Hannah Snow*, who was dism. from Ch., Br., to Ch.,
Den., June, 1825.   Children:
1391.* i. PHILIP HOWES.

1392. ii. MERCY, m. *Eben'r Howes*, and rem. to Malden, Mass.
1393. iii. TAMSEN, b. Den., Sep., 1827 ; bap. May 25, 1828 ; d. Aug. 30, 1828, gr.-st., W. Br.
1394. iv. *Child*, d. Mar. 1, 1828, gr.-st., W. Br.
1395. v. BETHIA, b. Den., Apr., 1830 ; d. Aug. 15, 1830, gr.-st., W. Br.

660.

REUBEN SEARS[6] [*Reuben*[5], *Will'd*[4], *John*[3], *Paul*[2], *Rich.*[1]], b. Harwich, Mass., July 29, 1791 ; d. Brewster, Feb. 21, 1845, gr.-st., Br.; m. Har., Nov. 6, 1814, *Nancy Sears*, No. 612, dau. of Christopher and Mary (Snow) S., she b. Nov. 9, 1794 ; d. May 2, 1872, gr.-st. Children :
1396. i. NANCY, b. Br., Aug. 12, 1815.
1397.* ii. ELIJAH BAILEY, b. Br., Nov. 9, 1817.
1398. iii. CHRISTOPHER, b. Br., Jan. 1, 1820 ; d. Aug., 1885.
1399.* iv. REUBEN, b. Br., Aug. 8, 1822.
1400. v. WILLARD, b. Br., Nov. 2, 1827 ; d. July 11, 1838.
1401. vi. MARY, b. Br., June 14, 1831 ; m. there, Mar. 22, 1854, by Rev. W. R. Tisdale, to *Thos. Whitcomb*, son of Thos. and Louisa W. of Cohasset, Mass. ; he b. 1827.
1402. vii. OLIVE H., b. Br., Mar. 21, 1834 ; m. Dec. 2, 1852, by Rev. W. R. Tisdale to *Eliot Wefer* of Cohasset. Lives in E. Dennis.
1403.* viii. HEMAN, b. Br., Feb. 25, 1836.
1404. ix. WILLARD, b. Br., Mar. 26, 1840. Is a builder in Malden, Mass.
1405. x. (?) PAMELIA.

662.

PHILANDER SEARS[6] [*Reuben*[5], *Will'd*[4], *John*[3], *Paul*[2], *Rich.*[1]], b. Harwich, Mass., Dec. 29, 1795 ; m. (pub. Dennis, Oct. 27, 1821,) *Bethia Sears*, No. 626, dau. of Elisha S., she b. Nov. 27, 1799. Children :
1406.* i. ALDEN.
1407.* ii. SYLVANUS.
1408. iii. PHILANDER F., b. 1838 ; served in Co. B, 4th Mass. Heavy Art'y, Aug. 24, 1864, to June 17, 1865.
1409. iv. CHARLES, m.
1410. v. RHODA A., b. Feb. 27, 1827 ; m. Nov. 27, 1849, *Justin Forbush* of Grafton, Mass., he b. Jan. 24, 1820 ;

was killed by the cars at Dundee, Ill., Nov. 4, 1859; children, FORBUSH: [1.] Emma J., b. Dec. 28, 1854; grad. State Normal School, Framingham, Mass. [2.] Susie C., grad. Nor. School, Framingham.

1411. vi. LOUISA, m. —— *Bellows.*
1412. vii. LAURA, b. Worcester, Jan. 27, 1839.

Removed to Worcester, Mass.

663.

THOMAS SEARS[6] [*Reuben[5], Will'd[4], John[3], Paul[2], Rich.[1]*], b. Harwich, Mass., Dec. 11, 1797; d. Brewster, Apr. 23, 1873; m. E. Dennis, Oct. 5, 1826, *Elizabeth F. Sears,* No. 1306, dau. of Jacob and Elizabeth (Foster) S., she b. Nov. 25, 1806; d. Feb. 15, 1860; 2d, Brewster, July 28, 1861, *Nabby (Sears) Jacobs,* No. 1278, dau. of Henry and Elizabeth Sears, she b. Br., Jan. 25, 1803; d. Pembroke, Mass., Jan. 10, 1889, æ. 86. Children:

By *Elizabeth :*
1413.   i. ELIZABETH F., b. Br., Mar. 17, 1828; m. Nov. 1, 1849, *James A. Smalley,* son of Anthony and Laura A. S. of Br.; lives in E. Dennis.
1414.   ii. THOMAS, b. Br., Mar. 12, 1830; drowned July 11, 1838, gr.-st., Br.
1415.* iii. CHARLES, b. Br., Oct. 16, 1832.
1416.* iv. DAVID H., b. Br., Mar. 16, 1836.
1417.   v. THOMAS D., b. Br., Feb. 22, 1845; m. there, Dec. 25, 1869, *Asenath Paine,* dau. of Augustus and Relief P. of Br., she b. 1850.

Mr. Sears was well known, and loved by all.
His death was, as his life, calm and peaceful, with a full assurance that he was ready.

665.

ORIN SEARS[6] [*Reuben[5], Will'd[4], John[3], Paul[2], Rich.[1]*], b. Harwich, Mass., Sep. 9, 1802; m. Brewster, Dec. 10, 1829, *Hannah M. Hopkins,* she b. Provincetown, Mass., Sep. 18, 1808. Children:

1418.* i. NATHAN HENRY, b. Br., Nov. 28, 1830.
1419.* ii. LORENZO JOHNSON, b. Br., Feb. 27, 1832.

1420. iii. HANNAH MARIA, b. Br., Mar. 29, 1836; m. Hingham, Nov. 22, 1866, *John Lincoln, Jr.*, he b. there; lives at Northbridge Centre, Mass.

1421. iv. LORENZA DUNHAM, b. Br., May 7, 1839; d. Nov. 26, 1867.

1422.* v. ORRIN BREWSTER, b. Br., Mar. 8, 1845.

Mr. Sears removed to Hingham, Mass., where he carried on salt works, and a farm.

He was for many years a local preacher, class leader and steward in the Methodist Episcopal Church, and has served the town as Selectman and Clerk.

668.

CHARLES SEARS[6] [*Eben'r*[5], *Will'd*[4], *John*[3], *Paul*[2], *Rich.*[1]], b. Yarmouth, Mass., July 31, 1789; d. Yarmouthport, Mar. 4, 1865; m. Yar., 1814, *Elizabeth Hallet*, dau of Eben'r H. of Yar.; she b. Feb. 4, 1790; d. Aug. 10, 1866.   Children:

1423.   i. JOSHUA, b. Yar., Apr. 2, 1815; d. Burlington, Wis., Oct. 8, 1837.

1424.   ii. EBENEZER, b. Yar., Aug. 11, 1817; d. Boston, May 29, 1845.

1425.* iii. CHARLES, b. Yar., Mar. 21, 1819.

1426.   iv. ELIZABETH H., b. Yar., Feb. 7, 1821; m. Yar., Feb. 18, 1847, *Lot Hallet;* he b. Yar., June, 1815; lives in Hyannis, Mass.

1427.   v. LUCY ANN, b. Yar., May 15, 1823; m. Yar., June 8, 1847, Capt. *Winthrop Sears*, No. 1568, his 2d wife.

1428.   vi. HANNAH, b. Yar., Feb. 14, 1827; d. unm., Boston, Apr. 9, 1868.

1429.   vii. THOMAS, b. Yar., July 13, 1828; d. July 15.

1430.   viii. MARY, b. Yar., July 13, 1828, *gemini;* d. July 15.

1431.   ix. MARY, b. Yar., July 21, 1832; m. Yar., July 6, 1853, *Orel Towle*, a fur dealer in Boston; he b. Exeter, Me., Mar. 1, 1812; lives in Somerville, Mass.; children, TOWLE: [1.] Minnie, b. Mar. 31, 1855. [2.] Harvey Parker, b. Mar. 15, 1867; student Har. Coll., 1886. [3.] Elizabeth Sears, b. Sep. 21, 1869. [4.] Orel, b. July 1, 1873.

1432.   x. CATHARINE AMY, b. Yar., Jan. 29, 1837; d. Oct. 6, 1863; m. Nov. 25, 1858, *John Preston* of Dorchester, Mass.

Charles Sears was a very genial and pleasant man, and although deputy sheriff of the county, never made an enemy.

His method when he had an unpleasant duty to perform was to do it in a friendly way, often himself giving bonds for an unfortunate debtor, and encouraging and assisting him to discharge his obligations.

He kept the "Sears Hotel" at Yarmouthport many years; was mail contractor, stage proprietor, etc.

He was a large, portly man, of fine appearance, and courteous in manner to all.

669.

JOSHUA SEARS[6] [*Eben'r*[5], *Will'd*[4], *John*[3], *Paul*[2], *Rich.*[1]], b. Yarmouth, Mass., Aug. 20, 1791; d. Feb. 7, 1857; m. Boston, Feb., 1854, *Phebe C. Snow*, dau. of Dea. Robert S. of Brewster, who d. Jan. 1, 1855. Child:

1433.* i. JOSHUA MONTGOMERY, b. Dec. 25, 1854.

Mr. Sears was long known as an industrious and successful merchant, capitalist and ship-owner.

He removed from Yarmouth to Boston in 1808, and soon engaged in business on Long Wharf, continuing in the same store till the close of his life, and accumulated a large property.

He was just in his dealings, painstaking, frugal, temperate, assiduous and far-seeing.

He was an original thinker, a great reader, with a tenacious memory, enabling him to repeat much that he had read, even whole pages of the Iliad, (Pope's translation).

Articles of noticeable ability were often written by him for the papers, and he would doubtless have stood high in any profession he might have chosen.

His married life was brief, but happy.

"Man proposes but God disposes," was the exclamation with which he bowed to the severity of bereavement.

Carrying his infant in his arms to the baptismal font, he seemed ever after especially solicitous that the education of the child should be religious, and when himself about to depart, his interest in this was deeply marked in the charge to his son's guardians.

Mr. Sears left legacies to numerous relatives, to the Seaman's Friend Society, and for a nautical school at Yarmouth.

The balance of his large property was left in trust for his son, Joshua M. Sears.

670.

WILLARD SEARS[6] [*Eben'r*[5], *Will'd*[4], *John*[3], *Paul*[2],

Rich.[1]], b. Yarmouth, Mass., Apr. 2, 1794; d. New Bedford, June 1, 1878, æ. 84; m. *Ruth Cushman,* she b. July 25, 1799; d. Jan 22, 1885. Children:

1434.   i. HANNAH GRAY, b. New Bed., Oct. 24, 1824; d. Apr. 9, 1826.

1435.   ii. HANNAH GRAY, b. New Bed., Jan. 3, 1827.

1436.   iii. RUTH BARKER, b. New Bed., Nov. 23, 1829; d. Sep. 17, 1830.

1437.   iv. RUTH BARKER, b. New Bed., Dec. 2, 1831; m. *John Simpkins, Jr.,* a wealthy stock broker of New York, and died suddenly at Newport, R. I., June 11, 1882; children, SIMPKINS: [1.] Willard Sears, who was thrown from his horse in Central Park, N. Y., Oct. 9, 1886, and killed, æ. 21; was student in Columbia Coll.

1438.   v. MARY CROCKER, b. New Bed., June 29, 1833; m. —— *Sisson ;* and 2d, Dr. *John Millard* of Paris, France.

1439.   vi. ELIZABETH WILLARD, b. New Bed., Jan. 7, 1835; m. *Charles W. Seabury* of Boston.

1440.* vii. WILLARD THOMAS, b. New Bed., Nov. 5, 1837.

Mr. Sears removed to New Bedford, Mass., about 1818, established himself in the tannery business and was for many years actively identified with the progress of that city.

667.

THOMAS WARREN SEARS[6] [*Eben'r*[5], *Will'd*[4], *John*[3], *Paul*[2], *Rich.*[1]], b. Yarmouth, Mass., May 10, 1812; d. Boston, Aug. 1, 1843, æ. 31; m. Boston, July 14, 1835, *Eliza Alger,* dau. of Cyrus A. of So. Boston (who. m. 2d, Holmes Hinckley.) Children:

1441.*   i. ALEXANDER POMROY, b. Boston, Feb. 12, 1836.

1442.   ii. OLIVIA RICHARDSON, b. Boston, July 21, 1838; m. there, Oct. 25, 1866, *Preston Carpenter Firth West;* children, WEST: [1.] Elise Alger, b. Boston, July 22, 1867. [2.] Montgomery Sears, b. Boston, May 14, 1869.

1443.* iii. CYRUS ALGER, b. Boston, June 20, 1841.

Mr. Sears removed to Boston, and engaged in business as a merchandise broker and auctioneer, making a specialty of groceries and fruit, selling from the wharf and vessel.

He was one of the prominent citizens of South Boston, (at that time a beautiful and favorite portion of the city,) but died in the prime of manhood.

For years he had been marked with the seal of consumption, and no one knew it better than he, but he fought it, inch by inch, to the very last.

His last sale was in 1843, when the old brig " Pleiades," belonging to the Peabodys, just returned from a pepper voyage, was advertised by T. W. Sears & Co., at the head of India wharf.

The friends of Sears endeavored to persuade him not to attempt the sale in person, but he did, and his voice could hardly be heard as he leaned against the bulwarks, and told off the bids.

Though dying at the age of thirty-one, Mr. Sears had established the reputation of possessing abilities of the highest order in his profession, and gave promise of a very brilliant future.

Many are the stories that are told of his sense of humor, and his quick repartee, but he had finer traits of character, which formed a strong background and support to his external accomplishments.

At heart he was deeply religious and devotional, as may be seen in several prayers which he wrote, and which were printed in the " Christian World."

But the quality that most endeared him to his friends was his sensitive sympathy for others.

Generous from his sense of human brotherhood, he was also just from a sense of duty, and in winning men's love, he failed not to win their respect.

681.

EBEN SEARS[6] [*Will'd[5]*, *Will'd[4]*, *John[3]*, *Paul[2]*, *Rich.[1]*], b. Brewster, Mass., Jan. 17, 1795 ; d. Boston, Sep. 17, 1849, æ. 54 ; m. there, Apr. 28, 1822, by Rev. Sereno E. Dwight, to *Eliza Fair Crease*, dau. of Samuel and Elizabeth (Warden) C., of Boston ; she b. there, June 6, 1799 ; d. there, Apr. 22, 1846. Children :

1444.   i. ELIZA CREASE, b. Boston, Apr. 9, 1823 ; d. Nov. 23, 1831 ; a remarkably beautiful and interesting child, still remembered and spoken of with admiration and affection, after a lapse of more than fifty years.

1445. ii. CAROLINE, b. Boston, Dec. 23, 1824; d. Sep. 23, 1825.

1446. iii. MARY JANE, b. Boston, Apr. 29, 1828 ; d. Somerville, Mass., of pneumonia, Apr. 5, 1860 ; m. Boston, Nov. 29, 1852, by Rev. Nehemiah Adams, to *Samuel Pearce*

May, son of Jean and Marianne (Bichard) Mahy, of the Island of Guernsey, Eng.; he b. Boston, May 14, 1828. (The family name was changed to May by act of Mass. Leg., Apr., 1833;) he m. 2d, her sister Emma Elizabeth; children, MAY: [1.] Richard Crease, b. Brooklyn, N. Y., Nov. 20, 1853; d. Somerville, Mass., Jan. 31, 1858. [2.] Lucy Rogers, b. East Braintree, Mass., Feb. 17, 1856; d. Somerville, Feb. 14, 1858. [3.] Adelaide Sears, b. Somerville, June 26, 1858; d. Newton, Mass., Feb. 14, 1869. [4.] Emma Sears, b. Somerville, Mar. 20, 1860; d. Newton, Feb. 28, 1869.

1447.* iv. EBEN, b. Boston, July 15, 1829.

1448. v. WILLIAM CREASE, b. Boston, Nov. 15, 1831; d. May 6, 1837.

1449. vi. RICHARD WILLARD, b. Boston, Nov. 22, 1835; d. Boston, Sep. 15, 1880. He was educated at Phillips Acad., Exeter, N. H., and at Wilbraham, Mass., received a business education in the counting-rooms of Wm. Tucker, Boston, and Coolbaugh & Brooks, Bankers, Burlington, Iowa; entering business with his brother, under the firm of E. & R. W. Sears, shipping and commission merchants, Boston. The business being broken up by the war, they engaged in real estate and mining enterprises. Of an eminently social nature, he made friends of all he met, was extremely fond of children, and had a peculiar faculty for entertaining them, liberal with his friends, and generous to a fault, his purse was ever open. He was a member of the Cadets, N. E. Hist. Gen. So., Art Club, Apollo Club, etc., Revere Lodge, St. Andrew's R. A. Chapter, St. Bernard Encampment, and Sov. Consistory of Boston.

1450. vii. EMMA ELIZABETH, b. Boston, May 10, 1838; m. there, June 15, 1864, by Rev. A. L. Stone, to *Samuel Pearcé May*, his 2d wife, lived for three years at Jamaica Plains, Mass., removing thence in the spring of 1867 to their present residence in Newton, Mass. He has spent several years in compiling this book; children, MAY: [1.] Jeannie Sears, b. Jamaica Plains, Mar. 27, 1865. [2.] Stella, b. Newton, July 25, 1867; grad. N. H. S., 1886. [3.] William Rogers, b. Newton, May 13, 1869; grad. Bigelow School and entered at High School, but left to accept a clerkship in Boston. [4.] Florence, b. Newton, Apr. 28, 1871. [5.] John Bichard, b. Newton, Aug. 8, 1876.

32

1451. viii. ADELAIDE LOUISA, b. Boston, Feb. 12, 1840 ; m.
Newton, May 6, 1874, by Rev. F. B. Perkins to *Gorham
Dummer Gilman* of Newton, son. of Sam'l and Lucy
Gorham (Dummer) G. of Hallowell, Me., his 2d wife,
he b. May 29, 1822 ; is of firm Gilman Bros., wholesale
druggists, Boston ; he lived many years in Sandwich
Islands, and in 1887, received the order of Kapiolani
from King Kalakaua, in recognition of services to the
Queen, and was the next year advanced a grade ; has
served several terms in Common Council and as Alderman in Newton, and Rep. to Leg., 1889 and 1890 ; child,
GILMAN : [1.] Ethel Sears, b. Feb. 3, 1878.
1452.   ix. WILLIAM ALBERT, b. Boston, Feb. 10, 1845;
drowned Worcester, Mass., Aug. 25, 1847.

Mr. Sears served in the militia at Yarmouth, during the war
of 1812, acting as drill-master.

At the close of the war he removed to Boston, and learned
the trade of carpenter under an Englishman named Hill, working for him three years upon the elegant mansion corner of
Somerset and Beacon streets, built by David Hinckley, afterward occupied by the Somerset Club, and later by the Congregational House, and became an unusually careful and thorough
workman.

He afterward worked at organ building, and assisted in putting up the organs in the old South Church, Boston, and
Trinity Church, New York.

In 1822 he married Eliza F. Crease, whose father, a furrier,
owned and lived on the estate cor. Washington street and
Norfolk place, where R. H. White & Co.'s store now stands.

For several years he was associated in business with his bro.
Willard as builders and contractors, during which time they
laid out and fenced Mt. Auburn Cemetery, and erected the
original buildings and gateways connected with it.

He was dignified and commanding in appearance, hasty in
temper naturally, he kept it entirely under control, but was
quick to resent an indignity.

Thoroughly conservative, he did not agree with his brother
in many of his radical theories, but was through life a temperate man.

684.

WILLARD SEARS[6] [*Will'd[5], Will'd[4], John[3], Paul[2],
Rich.[1]*], b. Brewster, Mass., Nov. 29, 1803; m. Boston, Jan.

24, 1833, by Rev. Wm. Jenks, to *Mary Easterbrooks Crease*, dau. of Sam'l and Eliz'h (Warden) C. of B., (sister to his bro. Eben's wife,) she b. Apr. 13, 1801 ; d. Sep. 13, 1835 ; and 2d, N. Y. city, Apr. 18, 1837, *Susan Hatch*, dau. of David and Olive (Wright) H. of Chelsea, Vt., she b. Nov. 30, 1813. Children :

By *Mary* :

1453. i. WILLARD, b. and d. Boston, Nov. 23, 1833.
1454. ii. SAMUEL GREENE, b. and d. Boston, Sep. 13, 1835.

Willard Sears received an ordinary " district school " education in his native town of Brewster, and grew up pretty much like other Cape Cod boys, working on the farm, helping at the salt-works, and at his father's trade of carpenter, and early learning the lesson of self-reliance. At the age of 9, wishing to visit his brother who was learning a trade in Boston, he embarked on board the packet, and worked his passage by cooking for the crew, viz., captain and mate.

Mar. 26, 1822, he left the old homestead, and became an apprentice with Mr. Wm. Goodrich, an organ-builder on Harlem place, Boston, next the " Lion Theatre," who failed in the course of a year. Young Sears then worked for a few months on looking-glass frames, and later on gas-meters in the shop corner of Washington and Bromfield streets ; there was on the premises a steam-engine, the first in Boston, which blew up one fine day, and scared the neighbors out of their wits, and in consequence the owner was forbidden to use it again.

This failed the man, a good Baptist, and the first Christian whose acquaintance Mr. Sears made in Boston ; however, he recovered, and went on with his business. Mr. S. then left, and went to work for his brother in putting up the organ in the Old South Church ; it was made in London, and as the builders in this country were opposed to its importation, they refused to put it up. A Mr. Cory was, therefore, engaged to come over and erect it, and keep it in tune for a year ; he remained and went into business here.

During the winter of 1824, Mr. C. and Eben Sears went to New York to set up the Trinity Church organ. Christmas eve the boss invited all hands to his house to celebrate ; they drank and sung until pretty drunk, and at 10 P. M. the brothers Sears went home, leaving the rest to make a night of it.

Upon his departure for New York, his employer left with Willard checks to make weekly payments to the men, and with which to buy stock. The rest of the men were foreigners, and kept up their carouse for three weeks until delirium tremens set in. Their poor wives came to Mr. Sears for money with which to buy food, which he gave them, without authority, and was much perplexed what to do. He then made a vow that he would never take alcoholic drinks, and this resolution he has adhered to, except in two instances; first, when urged by his pastor in Brewster while calling on him; and second, when about to join Essex St. Ch., Boston, he called upon the Deacon, an Englishman by birth, who would take no refusal.

In 1826, while building a block of brick houses on Haymarket place, he wished to break up the custom of furnishing grog to the men at 11 and 4 each day. About July 3 the ridgepole was to be raised, and the usage then was that the men were at liberty to drink as often and as much as they pleased. The day was hot, and the men drank all the more; the staging was insecurely built and broke down, and some of the men had broken bones as well as bruises. Mr. Sears' brother had his collar-bone broken, and received other injuries which confined him to the house several weeks.

During his illness Willard offered the men ten cents more per day to give up their rations, and about one-half agreed to do so. In three days he had a full gang of young, smart and good men at work, and the next month's pay, for an equal amount of work, was one-third less than in grog-days. Seeing this result, the brothers never after furnished any liquor or drank any themselves.

The same year that the municipal government was established, Mr. Sears came to Boston, and soon became prominent in a series of events which resulted in a complete revolutionizing of the city fire department. He was at that time a member of the "Young Men's Moral Association," devoted to exposing and breaking up gambling, dance-houses, etc. As a Mayor's detective, young Sears discovered the weakness of the department, and its remarkable strength also.

There was a body of 1,500 young, smart, athletic men, organized in such a way as to be scarcely at all under the control of the city government. The city furnished the engines, and kept them in repair, and then the companies did about as they pleased, except when at fires, they were nominally under the control of the fire wardens, and even this was more by sufferance than discipline.

The volunteers worked well at a fire, and were prompt in getting there. Cash presents, gifts of liquors and eatables, were freely donated to the firemen by grateful persons whose property had been in danger ; then followed the inevitable carousal, which did not cease so long as the materials lasted. The firemen represented every social degree, each having its own company, and none had more elegant, luxurious and prolonged carousals than the swell company of Beacon Hill.

Needless to say, fires were frequent.

One Sunday morning in 1828, Mr. Sears entered an engine-house. The members of that company were not graded low in the social scale, but were all the sons of reputable parents.

It was the morning after a fire, and sitting round, in a dazed condition, were half a dozen members, just recovering from their debauch, while more than 20 young men lay helplessly drunk on the floor, and among them several women, also stupefied. Such was the condition of things when Mr. Sears joined the Boston fire department.

His principles having become known, he was refused admission to the existing organizations, but procured leave to form a company, and became the Captain of it. No. 8, as it was called, was the entering wedge that finally split, and broke up the existing system.

Mr. Sears organized with young men pledged to reform.

On the wall of the engine-house hung the roll of membership, at the top of which were these words: "*No drinking of liquor*," "*No using of tobacco*," "*No profanity while on duty*." Each pledge had its vertical column, and list of members underneath. Every name *must* be in the first column, and most of them were in all.

In consequence of this innovation all the old companies were down on No. 8, and it was annoyed in all possible ways, and systematically obstructed whenever it started for a fire, and the bitterness was not softened by the fact that No. 8 was the most efficient company in Boston.

Capt. Sears resolved to bring things to a head, and on the next alarm of fire, No. 12 purposely obstructing his path, he gave his men orders to pass them at all hazards,— and as the result, No. 12 was a wreck. He was arraigned before the Mayor, who was very wroth, and threatened to disband the company. In reply, Mr. S. referred to the ordinance: "You will proceed at once to the fire, and break down all obstructions."

"There, Mr. Mayor, is the law, and we only obeyed it, and now I will resign ; I have had trouble and annoyance enough, and will have nothing more to do with it."

At the Mayor's request he finally consented to continue in the department, but the annoyances did not cease, the city government would not repair the engine, and the work was done at his own expense. He finally disbanded the company.

For a few years thereafter the fire department went from bad to worse, until it came to a crisis brought on by the efforts of the municipal government to bring about a reform, and all the companies disbanded, leaving the city without a single company to protect property in case of fire.

At this juncture Mr. Sears was called upon by the presidents of the insurance companies, and requested to take charge of a company they had organized, composed of leading men of Boston, such as Capt. Williams, Dr. Hayward, Hon. Mr. Wheeler, Dea. Charles Scudder, and other gentlemen from Beacon street and Colonnade Row.

After some demur he finally consented, but at the first trial satisfactorily convinced them that they were not the right material for such dirty and laborious work, and that the only true, and the cheapest system for the insurance companies and property holders was a paid fire department, and this, too, out of regard for the morals of the youth of the city.

A committee was thereupon raised to wait upon the Mayor and Aldermen, and state their views upon the subject, and as a result the city established the paid fireman's system in 1838, the first in the United States.

About the year 1837, Rev. Sylvester Graham lectured in Boston, on Temperance, Physiology and Hygiene, advocating a vegetable diet, and the use of unbolted flour, now so popular under the name of " Graham flour."

The bakers and rummies became much incensed, mobbed him, and drove the ladies, to whom he was lecturing, into the street.

The ladies then applied to Mr. Sears for the use of the hall attached to the Marlboro Hotel, owned by him, and a day being set for the lecture, notice was printed in three papers that Graham would be mobbed.

The Mayor sent the City Marshal to Mr. Sears, ordering him forthwith to appear at the City Hall. Mr. S. was at the time employed with his men in pulling down some old plastering in the hotel, and was covered with mortar and dirt. He told the Marshal he was busy, had violated no law, and would not go. The Marshal then left, but shortly returned with a carriage, and the Mayor's compliments, requesting the favor of an interview, to which Mr. S. then consented.

An account of the interview may be found in the "Liberator" of March 24, 1837, under the head of "Mob Law."

The result was that the Mayor told him the building would be mobbed, and he could not protect him with the force at his disposal, and if he persisted in letting it be used by Graham he must take the consequences. Mr. S., seeing that little was to be expected from the city officials, decided to protect his property himself at all hazards.

He directed his workmen to place the old plaster in heaps by the windows, together with a quantity of lime, and await orders which he would transmit through his clerk. After parleying some time with the mob which assembled outside the barricade that had been erected to protect passers-by during the alterations, and finding they were bent on mischief and could no longer be delayed, he retired through a small door and gave a preconcerted signal. At once the workmen commenced shoveling out the lime and mortar from the upper windows. The mob, looking up to see what was to pay, in a moment had their eyes and mouths filled with the pungent dust, there was a strong wind blowing, and the street was presently filled with a cloud of lime. Flesh and blood could not stand this; the mob broke and retired, and Mr. Sears had won a bloodless victory.

The papers discussed the matter thoroughly, and the public finally decided for the right of free speech.

In a few weeks the Mayor called upon Mr. Sears and said: "If you will stop Garrison from writing any more about me, when you dedicate your chapel, I will protect you and your property, if I have to call in the State and navy soldiers, with all the police.— Sir, I was wrong, but do stop Garrison ; he is ruining my character, and bringing me to disgrace."

At the dedication of Marlboro Chapel, he, without solicitation, put 30 police inside, 40 outside, and held the military in reserve.

Of course, Mr. Sears was one of the earliest abolitionists and free-soilers.

In 1834, Geo. Thompson, an English emancipationist, on his return from the W. I., came to Boston to deliver a lecture.

The use of "Faneuil Hall" was granted, but permission revoked by the city authorities. Mr. Sears and Amasa Walker then hired "Julien Hall" for the purpose, giving their bond for $17,000 to pay any damage that might be done by a mob. This also was revoked, and the only place that could be procured was "Ritchie Hall," over Dea. Gulliver's carpet store, corner of Temple place. The entrance was soon surrounded by an armed mob of Southerners and their sympathizers, and Thompson was finally taken out through a hoisting scuttle in the rear, placed in a carriage with J. S. Withington, and driven to the house of J. G. Whittier in Amesbury. He did not dare to return, but embarked shortly for England. During the disturbance Mr. Sears was on guard at the door; was struck several times, but not materially injured, and held the fort until Thompson had retired.

In 1836 Mr. Sears and Dea. Charles Scudder fitted out the first missionary to Jamaica (an Oberlin student), and established the first station there.

He was the first to take a colored apprentice, later procuring for him a commission as Justice of the Peace, guaranteeing his good conduct.

He was intimately connected with the " Underground Railway," and aided many fugitives on their way to Canada and freedom.

The " Marlboro Hotel " was opened by him as a temperance house, the first in this country. No liquor was to be sold in it, and at first no smoking was allowed, but this latter was conceded later.

The ladies and gentlemen's parlors were thrown open morning and evening for religious services. Grace was said before every meal, and for twenty-six years the observance of the services was continuous and uninterrupted. The chapel in the rear was a free hall for lectures and discussions on all moral and social questions. It was opened in May, 1838, and was run as a free hall and chapel for fourteen years. It was afterward let for the " Lowell Institute " Lectures. The house was patronized by a class of quiet, religious people who wanted such a stopping-place when they came to the city. John G. Whittier, Mr. Longfellow and Henry Wilson were frequent guests.

During a long life, Mr. Sears has contracted for and built innumerable edifices, both public and private, among them the Fitchburg Depot, Boston, and all stations and freight-houses to Fitchburg; eastern railway stations and old ferry-houses; Boston & Worcester Depot in Boston, and stations and freight-houses to Worcester; Old Colony Depot and stations to Sandwich; and much other railroad work in the east and west; some thirty churches, among them, the Swedenborgian, Dr. Kirk's, and Essex St., Boston; Catholic Ch., So. Boston; Cong. Ch., Bunker's Hill, Charlestown; Dr. Thompson's, Roxbury; Dr. Langworthy's, Chelsea; West Newton and Brookline churches, etc.; built and owned Marlboro Hotel and Chapel, and reconstructed the State's Prison at Charlestown.

He was one of the petitioners and obtained the charter for the Female Medical College, Boston, and a Trustee; put up the first sixty buildings in San Francisco, but lost by fire and shipwreck $250,000, being uninsured. He owned the ship "Roland" and cargo, and the cargo in bark "Henry Ware," both of which were lost upon the voyage.

Mr. S. obtained the charter, and called the first meeting to organize the Northern Pacific R. R., and was in the board of direction for five years.

For some years he has done little business beyond supervising the Alburgh Springs Hotel, Vermont, and the Mineral Springs connected therewith, which he purchased after having himself experienced their marvelous curative powers.

Mr. Sears is as we have seen by nature a radical reformer, a teetotaller, and anti-tobacconist, abolitionist and free-soiler; for a time a vegetarian, but this did not hold; he early took the anti-mason infection, and has never got over it.

He is a strict Sabbatarian, and a perfect type of the old Puritan; of downright and combative disposition, had he lived in Cromwell's time, he would doubtless have fought at his side.

Charitable by nature, his benefactions have been large and constant. Oberlin College long found in him a liberal patron, and it is estimated he gave in all $100,000 to that institution; as a trustee, he took the place of Ossawattomie Brown, and served many years. Many other religious, educational and charitable institutions have partaken of his bounty.

The poor and oppressed have ever found his heart and purse open, and many a fugitive from oppression has had cause to bless him.

Of a large and muscular mould, Mr. Sears has possessed great strength and endurance; dark in complexion, his jet black hair has only lately become an iron-gray; quick spoken, and decided in manner, he has had great success in managiug large gangs of men.

Soon after his marriage he went to reside in Brookline, removing thence to West Newton, and later to the banks of the winding Charles at Watertown.

His pleasant estate there being absorbed by the government as a portion of the arsenal grounds, he removed to Newtonville, and now, (1887,) in his old age, resides in Newton with his wife and his only surviving sister, a wonderfully smart and active maiden lady of 88.

686.

ARNOLD SEARS[6] [*Nath'l*[5], *Nath'l*[4], *John*[3], *Paul*[2], *Rich.*[1]], b. Yarmouth, Mass., Dec. 25, 1781 ; d. Pawtucket, R. I.; m. (pub. Dennis, Oct. 3, 1807,) *Thankful Marchant* of Yar. Children :

1455.*   i.   OBED, b. Yar., Jan. 16, 1808.
1456.   ii.   ABRAHAM, b. Yar., Sep. 6, 1809.
1457.   iii.   CAROLINE, b. Yar., July 12, 1811.
1458.*   iv.   ARNOLD HOWES, b. Yar., Sep. 1, 1815.
1459.   v.   LAURA ANN, b. Yar., Jan. 16, 1817.
1460.   vi.   ORLANDO, b. Yar., Jan. 24, 1820.
1461.   vii.   SUSAN, b. Yar., Oct. 16, 1824; pub. Yar., Oct. 1, 1856, to *Wm. Crowell* of Yar.

"Arnold Sears' child d. July 1, 1822." (T. Rec.) He removed to Providence, R. I.

689.

NATHANIEL SEARS[6] [*Nath'l*[5], *Nath'l*[4], *John*[3], *Paul*[2], *Rich.*[1]], b. Yarmouth, Mass., Aug. 12, 1785 ; m. Harwich, Apr. 2, 1806, *Thankful Chase ;* 2d, (pub. Dennis, Aug. 5, 1813,) *Hitty Ellis* of Den.; 3d, Brewster, Apr. 9, 1830, *Thankful Walker*, dau. of Benj. W.   Children :

By *Hitty :*
1462.   i.   THANKFUL, b. Den., Jan. 24, 1814; m. Dec. 17, 1835, *Abiel Ellis* of Har.
1463.   ii.   POLLY, b. Den., Oct., 1815 ; d. inf.
1464.   iii.   MARY ANN, b. Den., Aug. 1, 1817; m. Feb. 9, 1837, *Carmi Hall* of Har.; 2d, Feb. 22, 1841, Isaac Smith of Har.
1465.   iv.   ACHSAH, b. Den., Sep. 2, 1819 ; m. May 8, 1842, *Benj. Baker* of Har., and d. Apr. 11, 1883, æ. 63 yrs. 7 mos. 9 days.
1466.*   v.   ALVIN, b. Den., Jan. 10, 1822.
By *Thankful :*
1467.   vi.   MEHITABLE, b. Den., July 20, 1833; m. Br., June 14, 1868, *John H. Crowell*, son of John and Phebe C. of Den.; he b. 1833.
1468.*   vii.   NATHANIEL, b. Br., May 1, 1836.
1469.*   viii.   HENRY CLARK, b. Br., Mar. 16, 1845.
1470.   ix.   JEDIDAH, b. Br., Jan. 10, 1847; m. there, Nov. 23,

1865, *Washington A. Eldredge* of Chatham, son of Washington and Elizabeth E. of Br.; he b. 1843.

1471.   x. (?) Greene, b. Br.

Was a fisherman, and lived in Dennis and Brewster.

691.

LOT SEARS[6] [*Nath'l[5], Nath'l[4], John[3], Paul[2], Rich.[1]*], b. Yarmouth, Mass., Apr. 11, 1791; d. May 25, 1860; m. Nov. 11, 1821, *Jemima Marchant* of Yar., who d. Jan. 26, 1852. Children :

1472.   i. Barnabas, b. Den.
1473.   ii. Bethia, b. Den., Aug. 24, 1824; m. 1848, *Baxter Studley*, and lives in Rhode Island.
1474.   iii. Lot Hallet, b. Den., July 31, 1826; m. Mrs. *Charity* ——, and lives in So. Yar.; has no children.
1475.* iv. Benjamin, b. Den., Nov. 20, 1828.
1476.   v. Asa, b. Den., Sep. 13, 1831.
1477.   vi. Emeline, b. Den., May 23, 1834; m. Har., Jan. 29, 1855, *David H. Snow* of Har., and lives Pawtucket, R. I.

694.

FREEMAN SEARS[6] [*Nath'l[5], Nath'l[4], John[3], Paul[2], Rich.[1]*], b. Dennis, Mass., Jan. 24, 1799; d. East Den., Apr. 19, 1879, æ. 80 yrs. 2 mos. 16 days, gr.-st., Br.; m. Den., Dec. 20, 1821, *Hitty Crosby* of Den., she b. Aug. 2, 1796; d. July 22, 1848, æ. 52, gr.-st., Br. ; 2d, Brewster, Feb. 20, 1849, *Mary Davis*, dau. Rev. Joshua and Esther D. of Br., who d. Apr. 19, 1855, æ. 40, gr.-st.; 3d, Den., May 25, 1856, *Patty Baker* of Den., who d. Sep. 20, 1859, æ. 72, gr.-st. ; 4th, Den., Sep. 27, 1860, *Sally J. Crosby*, who d. Oct. 17, 1875, æ. 58, gr.-st.; 5th, Den., May 2, 1876, *Mary Mayo*, who d. Oct. 18, 1876, æ. 58, gr.-st; 6th, Den., Feb. 15, 1877, *Temperance D. Tobey*, who survived him.   Children :

By *Hitty* :

1478.   i. Deborah, b. Den., Oct. 26, 1822 ; m. *Ahira Clark*.
1479.   ii. Barnabas, b. Den., Jan. 9, 1826; d. Mar. 11, 1826.
1480.* iii. Freeman F., b. Den., June 9, 1828.
1481.   iv. Mary A., b. Den., Nov. 8, 1831; m. Br., Feb. 9, 1859, *Nath'l Porter Keene* of No. Weymouth, Mass., son of Nath'l and Margery K. of Pembroke ; he b. 1833.

1482.   v. CALVIN, b. Den., Mar. 14, 1834; d. Feb. 12, 1839.
1483.   vi. BARNABAS, b. Den., Mar. 30, 1837; m. Har., Jan. 19, 1860, *Susan S. Rogers*, and lives No. Harwich.
1484.   vii. RACHEL, b. Den., Jan. 14, 1840; m. *Pembroke Mayo*, and d. Mar. 10, 1860.
By *Mary :*
1485.   viii. JOSHUA D., b. Den., Jan. 8, 1850; m. Jan. 11, 1872, *Elenor B. Studley* of Har.
1486.   ix. ESTHER J., b. Den., Nov. 5, 1851.
1487.   x. BENJAMIN, b. Den., Aug. 29, 1854; d. Oct. 1, 1855.

701.

Hon. DAVID SEARS[6] [*David[5], Dan'l[4], Dan'l[3], Paul[2], Rich.[1]*], b. Boston, Mass., Oct. 8, 1787; d. Jan. 14, 1871, æ. 83; m. Boston, June 13, 1809, by Rev. John S. J. Gardiner to *Miriam Clarke Mason*, dau. of Hon. Jona. M. of B. Children :

1488.   i. DAVID MASON, d. young in Falmouth, Eng.
1489.   ii. ANNA POWELL GRANT, b. 1813; m. Boston, Jan. 17, 1833, *Wm. Amory;* children, AMORY : [1.] William, m. Ellen Brewer, dau. of Gardner B. of B. [2.] Harriet, m. Joseph Peabody Gardner of B. [3.] Ellen, m. John F. Anderson of B. [4.] Charles Walter, m. Eliz'h Gardner of B. [5.] Francis Inman, m. Grace Minot of B.
1490.   iii. HARRIET E. DICKASON, b. 1814; m. *Geo. Caspar Crowninshield;* children, CROWNINSHIELD : [1.] Caspar (Gen.); m. Eliz'h Copley Greene of B. [2.] Fanny, m. John Quincy Adams of Quincy. [3.] Cora, m. Chas. Boyden of B.
1491.   iv. CORDELIA MASON, b. 1816; d. unm.
1492.   v. ELLEN, b. 1819; m. Canton de Vaud, Switzerland, Aug. 22, 1837, *Paul Daniel Gonsalve Grand d'Hauteville*, who d. recently; child, GRAND d'HAUTEVILLE : [1.] Frederic Sears, b. Sep. 27, 1838; m. Eliz'h Fish, dau. of Hon. Hamilton F. ; 2d, Susan Macomb, dau. of Maj. Alex. M. of New York. He was capt. on staff Civil war.
1493.* vi. DAVID, b. 1822.
1494.* vii. FREDERIC RICHARD, b. 1824.
1495.   viii. WINTHROP, d. young.
1496.   ix. GRACE WINTHROP, b. 1828; m. Boston, May 15, 1849, *Wm. Cabel Rives, Jr.*, of Virginia, who d. Apr.,

1889, in Washington, D. C.; children, RIVES : [1.] Wm. Cabel, M. D., m. Ethel Rhinelander of N. Y. [2.] Alice, d. Denver, Col., Mar. 29, 1887. [3.] Arthur Landon.

1497.* x. WINTHROP, b. 1832; name changed by act of Mass. Leg., Mar. 24, 1849, to Knyvet Winthrop.

" Mr. Sears was educated in the best schools that Boston at that time afforded, and after a preparatory course of study in the Latin School, entered Harvard College in 1803, at the age of 16, taking his Bachelor's degree in 1807.

" He read law for a time, and soon after his marriage in 1809, sailed for Europe with his wife, and passed several years in foreign travel, at a most interesting period in Continental history.

" The sudden death of his father devolved on him the care of a large estate, and before he was thirty years of age he was called to assume that responsible position among the very richest men of Boston, which he continued to hold during half a century.

" Building for himself a costly and elegant mansion fit for the generous hospitalities which belong to wealth, he began early to make plans for doing his share in acts of public and private beneficence.

" In 1820 he was actively associated with the erection of St. Paul's Church, on Tremont street, and he subsequently gave that parish a fund which now exceeds forty thousand dollars in value; this was followed in succeeding years by various provisions for other religions, literary and charitable objects, which, while accomplishing valuable purposes at once, may not exhibit their full fruit for a long time to come.

" The 'Sears Tower' of the Observatory at Cambridge, built at his cost, gave the first encouragement to an establishment which has been munificently endowed by others, and to whose permanent fund he was also a handsome contributor.

"About 1820 Mr. Sears purchased some 200 acres of land in the suburbs of Boston, which has since become the beauti- ful village of Longwood, which he proceeded to lay out and beautify at great expense, giving to many of the streets and squares names which he believed to be identified with the family in this country and England.

"A capacious stone chapel, built after the design of St. Peter's Church in Colchester, Eng., and to which he gave the name of ' Christ's Church in Longwood,' contains, in its basement, vaults constructed as a last resting-place for himself and those most dear to him.

" For this church he prepared a form of service in accordance with his peculiar views, and which has been described as 'the Book of Common Prayer, with any thing of the nature of Calvinism carefully weeded out, mildly tinctured with the writings of Channing, but more strongly flavored with Romanism,' and stated service was maintained during the last eight years of his life.

"A block of houses near by, destined ultimately for the dwellings of such as had seen better days, and to be known as 'The Scearstan Charter House,' and an accumulating fund under the control of the Overseers of the Poor, Boston, which has added not a little, year by year, to the comfort and support of a large number of poor women, will bear testimony to his thoughtful and well-considered benevolence."

After the death of Mr. Sears, by an arrangement between his heirs and the city of Boston, his various endowments for the poor of his native place were amalgamated under the comprehensive title of " The David Sears Charity."

In 1886 this fund amounted to near $280,000, and will be much further increased by the rise in real estate.

" Mr. Sears often enjoyed such public honors as he would accept, and served as a Representative to the Mass. Leg. in 1816–18, 1824–25 and 1828, and as a Senator in 1826 and 1851.

" He was a Presidential Elector in 1868, and invited his colleagues of the State Electoral College to meet the President elect, General Grant, at his house in Boston.

" In early life he was a member of the Independent Corps of Cadets and Com'd Ensign. In 1818 he presented the company with a new standard, and provided for them an elegant entertainment.

" He occasionally mingled in the public discussions of the day, and an elaborate letter which he addressed to John Quincy Adams on the best method of abolishing slavery, while that was still a living question, will be particularly remembered among his contributions to the press."

In middle life Mr. Sears became interested in the subject of family history and genealogy, and employed the late Mr. H. G. Somerby to make searches in England to trace his ancestry, and expended a large sum in these researches. His kinsman, Rev. Edmund H. Sears, undertook to edit the material collected, but he had no practical acquaintance with genealogy, and allowed himself to become responsible for a series of romantic legends under the title of " Pictures of the Olden Time," to which was added, in a private edition for the family, a genealogical account of the English and American branches.

About the year 1848 Mr. Sears erected monuments and mural tablets to various members of the family in Yarmouth and Chatham, Mass., Newport, R. I., and in St. Peter's Church, Colchester, Eng., to which church he presented in 1852 a flagon and paten of elegant design and elaborate workmanship inclosed in a handsome wainscot box.

In 1855 he endowed the church with £100, in trust, for charitable purposes, to which he added, in 1858, a further sum, now known as " The Sears Dole."

Mr. Sears deposited with the N. E. Hist. Gen. Society, medals to be given those of the name of Sears proving their descent from Richard and Dorothy Sares, a description of which may be found in Gen. Reg., vol. 26, p. 182.

Subsequent investigation has developed that Mr. Sears was grossly deceived in regard to many particulars of the pedigree and early history of his family, so that the monuments erected by him, and the genealogies he printed, now for the most part only serve to perpetuate unfortunate delusions.

" Mr. Sears was one of the first to own and occupy a summer residence at Nahant, but finding it too bleak for his own taste, and tempted by the softer atmosphere of the Gulf Stream, he built, in 1845, a marine villa at Newport, to which he gave the name of 'Red Cross.'

" Its extensive grounds are built over, but the immediate neighborhood is still pleasantly associated in many minds with the remembrance of his refined, graceful and unostentatious hospitality.

" With his characteristic generosity, he conveyed to the municipality a fund of five thousand dollars, the income to be applied to benevolent objects.

" The summer of 1869 was his last at Newport; the next year his health became seriously impaired, and he died in Boston, Jan. 14, 1871, at the advanced age of eighty-three, his wife, with whom he had lived near sixty-three years, having preceded him by a few months.

" He will be long remembered by all who have known him as one of the courteous and dignified gentlemen of the old school, of whom so few are now left to remind us of the manners and bearing of other days."

706.

EDWARD SEARS[6] [*Edw'd*[5], *Silas*[4], *Silas*[3], *Silas*[2], *Rich.*[1]], b. Yarmouth, Mass., Apr. 9, 1779; d. So. Dennis, Oct. 10,

1858; m. Harwich, Apr. 20, 1807, by Rev. Abner Lewis, to *Abigail Baker*, dau. of Shubael and Rebecca (Chase) B., she b. Har., Nov. 22, 1783'; d. So. Den., Sep. 18, 1853. Children:

1498.* i. GRAFTON, b. Den., Feb. 9, 1805.(?)
1499.* ii. EDWARD, b. Den., July 4, 1808.
1500.* iii. SHUBAEL B., b. Den., July 27, 1810.
1501.* iv. MICHAEL, b. Den., Aug. 30, 1812.
1502.* v. SYLVANUS, b. Den., Sep. 4, 1815.
1503.* vi. JEPTHAH B., b. Den., June 8, 1817.
1504. vii. HENRY B., b. Den., Oct. 12, 1819 ; drowned Feb. 5, 1833.
1505. viii. ABIGAIL, b. Den., Dec. 12, 1821 ; m. *Abiathar Doane*, and d. July 20, 1855.
1506.* ix. BENJAMIN, b. Den., Sep. 27, 1826.

709.

JAMES SEARS[6] [*Moody[5], Silas[4], Silas[3], Silas[2], Rich.[1]*], b. Yarmouth, Mass., Apr. 12, 1766; d. Yar., Oct. 8, 1830; m. Dec. 10, 1789, *Thankful Hallet*, dau. of Jere. and Hannah (Griffith) H., she b. Oct. 6, 1764 ; d. May 13, 1791; 2d, (pub. Har., Dec. 15, 1792, to *Mary* Sears, and again Apr. 12, 1793, to *Betsy* Sears of Dennis) ; m. Apr. 14, 1793, *Elizabeth Sears*, who d. July 2, 1827; 3d, Yar., Nov., 1827, *Rebecca Crowell*. Children:

By *Thankful :*
1507. i. THANKFUL, b. Yar., May 13, 1791; d. May 14.
1508. ii. JERUSHA, b. Yar., May 13, 1791 ; d. May 14, *gemini;* they were buried in the same coffin with their mother.

By *Elizabeth :*
1509. iii. *Child*, d. July, 1795.
1510. iv. THANKFUL, b. Yar., Jan. 8, 1798; m. Yar., 1817, *Edw'd Crowell*, 3d, of Den.
1511.* v. JAMES, b. Yar., Sep. 28, 1799.
1512. vi. FREEMAN, b. Yar., Sep. 9, 1802; pub. Yar., Oct. 29, 1824, to *Patience Eldridge.*
1513. vii. LAVINIA, b. Yar., July 3, 1804; pub. Yar., Aug. 25, 1825, to *Gorham Baker.*
1514. viii. OTIS, b. Yar., Jan. 20, 1806 ; d. July 31, 1827.
1515. ix. BETSY, b. Yar., Jan. 13, 1808; m. July, 1827, *Reuben Worth* of Nantucket.
1516. x. FESSENDEN, b. Yar., Apr. 1, 1818.

711.

PRINCE SEARS[6] [*Moody*[5], *Silas*[4], *Silas*[3], *Silas*[2], *Rich.*[1]], b. Yarmouth, Mass., Dec. 20, 1769; d. South Dartmouth, Mass., Aug. 13, 1808, æ. 38; m. (pub. Dennis, Mar. 4, 1794,) *Achsah Collins* of Den., dau. of David C. of Chatham; she b. July 28, 1776; d. Monument, Mass., Feb. 16, 1858, æ. 81; (was sister of Anna Collins, who m. Isaiah Sears, No. 714.) Children:

1517.   i. COLLINS, b. Den., Apr. 27, 1795; d. May 14.
1518.* ii. PRINCE, b. Den., Aug. 15, 1797.
1519. iii. EZRA, b. Den., Aug. 20, 1799; d. Sep. 8.
1520. iv. DAVID, b. Den., Aug. 6, 1800; d. Aug. 19.
1521.   v. EUNICE, b. Den., July 7, 1801; m. So. Dartmouth, *Gorham Thacher*, a ship carpenter, his 2d wife, and d. Oct. 21, 1878; children, THACHER: [1.] Prince S. [2.] Preserved D. [3.] Phebe, m. Alfred Washburn. [4.] Eunice, m. Edw'd Curtis. [5.] George L.
1522. vi. CLARISSA, b. Den., June 2, 1803; d. Oct. 24, 1823, æ. 20.
1523. vii. SALLY HOWES, b. Den., Aug. 13, 1805; m. *Lurin Bourne*, and d. Newport, R. I., Mar. 30, 1879, æ. 73.
1524. viii. *Son*, b. and d. Den., July, 1806.
1525. ix. ACHSAH COLLINS, b. So. Dartmouth, Mar. 9, 1808; m. Jan. 26, 1830, Capt. *Ezekiel Harding*, who d. Oct. 18, 1850; she lives in Middleboro, Mass.; children, HARDING: [1.] Andrew Sears, d. May, 1867, æ. 17. [2.] Watie Anna. [3.] Achsah Sears, m. Fred. Wood. [4.] George Gideon. [5.] Andrew Alvin.

714.

ISAIAH SEARS[6] [*Moody*[5], *Silas*[4], *Silas*[3], *Silas*[2], *Rich.*[1]], b. Yarmouth, Mass., Mar. 18, 1777; d. Dartmouth, Mass., Feb. 14, 1864, æ. 87; m. Chatham, Feb. 25, 1797, *Sarah Ann Collins*, dau. of David C., she b. May, 1778; d. So. Dartmouth, Aug. 13, 1845, æ. 67. Children:

1526.   i. MEHITABLE, b. Yar., Apr. 9, 1798; m. *Gideon Berry*, his 2d wife, and d. Aug., 1820.
1527.* ii. MOODY, b. Yar., Dec. 13, 1799.
     34

1528.   iii. ELIZABETH, b. Yar., Sep. 1, 1801; m. Feb. 15, 1821, *Freeman Crowell, Jr.*, of West Den., and d. Dec., 1851.

1529.   iv. ROSANNA, b. Yar., July 25, 1803; d. unm., New Bedford, Aug. 22, 1879.

1530.   v. DEBORAH, b. Yar., June 26, 1806; m. *Josephus Ellis* of Sandwich, and d. New Bed., Apr., 1852.

1531.   vi. SUSAN C., b. Yar., Oct. 25, 1808; d. So. Dart., Oct. 6, 1859.

1532.   vii. CHARLOTTE, b. Yar., Oct. 25, 1808, *gemini;* d. Nov., 1808.

1533.* viii. ISAIAH, b. Yar., Oct. 11, 1810.

1534.   ix. PETER C., b. Yar., Oct. 6, 1812; (Sep. 29, T. C.;) d. unm., Nov. 13, 1832, Sandwich.

1535.   x. EUNICE, b. Yar., Nov. 13, 1814; m. So. Dart., Dec. 14, 1834, *Eben R. Smith;* he b. Chatham, Aug. 28, 1811; d. New Bed., Aug., 1871; she lives in New Bed.; children, SMITH: [1.] Marynette C., b. 1837; d. [2.] Arabella J., b. 1839; d. [3.] Theophilus, b. Oct. 7, 1841; m. Sep. 6, 1861, Mary W. Allen; she b. So. Westport, Mass., May 21, 1842; had, i. Eben R. ii. Marynette. iii. Almira. [4.] Susan C., b. Feb., 1843; m. —— Ricketson, and lives New Bed.

1536.   xi. MARY ANN, b. Yar., Dec. 6, 1816; (1817, T. C.) m. *Hiram Norton* of Edgartown, and d. New Bed., June, 1853.

1537.   xii. SARAH HOWES, b. Yar., May 7, 1822; m. *Joseph Howland* and lives in New Bed.

Isaiah Sears was a fisherman, and taught school during the winters in Yarmouth and Dennis.

715.

ENOCH SEARS[6] [*Moody*[5], *Silas*[4], *Silas*[3], *Silas*[2], *Rich.*[1]], b. Yarmouth, Mass., June 28, 1779; d. at sea, June, 1839; m. Harwich, Dec. 5, 1799, *Bethia Kelly* of Har.   Child:

1538.   1. MERCY, b. 1801; m. Har., Oct. 14, 1824, *Freeman Ryder* of Har., he b. 1800, son of Paul and Hannah R.; children, RYDER: [1.] Bethia, b. 1825. [2.] Freeman, b. 1829. [3.] Rosalinda, b. 1833; d. 1839. [4.] David, b. 1836; d. 1839. [5.] John, b. 1840.

720.

Capt. LEWIS SEARS[6] [*Eleazar*[5], *Silas*[4], *Silas*[3], *Silas*[2], *Rich.*[1]], b. Yarmouth, Mass., Oct. 26, 1768; (1767, T. C.) d.

So. Yar., Sep. 20, 1848, æ. 80, gr.-st., S. Yar.; m. Yar., Apr. 9, 1792, (Apr. 18, T. C.) *Ruth Baker*, dau. of Sylvanus and Jane B., she b. Yar., Aug 29, 1772 ; d. Brewster, Oct. 26, 1856, æ. 84, gr.-st. Children :

1539.* i. JONATHAN, b. Yar., Dec. 12, 1792.
1540.* ii. LEWIS, b. Yar., Sep. 14, 1795.
1541. iii. RUTH, b. Yar., Nov. 4, 1797; d. Mar. 31, 1801.
1542. iv. ELEAZAR, b. Yar., Oct. 16, 1800 ; d. Aug. 31, 1823, gr.-st.
1543.* v. HIRAM, b. Yar., Oct. 10, 1803.
1544. vi. RUTH, b. Yar., Feb. 10, 1806 ; m. Aug. 7, 1825, Capt. *John Freeman* of Br., he b. Mar. 25, 1800 ; d. July 2, 1864 ; she d. Oct. 4, 1875 ; children, FREEMAN : [1.] John, b. Aug. 24, 1835; m. Jane S. Nickerson of Den. [2.] Benjamin, b. Sep. 8, 1843 ; m. Sarah F. Freeman of Sandwich.
1545. vii. ALFRED, b. Yar., Sep. 10, 1809 ; d. Dec. 17, 1820, gr.-st.
1546. viii. *Child*, b. Yar.; d. 1813, æ. 4 yrs.
1547. ix. JANE, b. Yar., July 31, 1811; m. (pub. Yar., Jan. 21, 1832,) *Israel Nickerson* of Den., and d. Jan. 25, 1838.
1548. x. BENJAMIN, b. Yar., Apr. 1, 1814; lives in Burgettville, Shasta co., Cal., unm.
1549. xi. HARRIET, b. Yar., Apr. 26, 1817; m. Nov. 21, 1847, *Nelson White* of Yar., and d. Oct. 16, 1873, gr.-st.

He was a master mariner.

723.

EDWARD SEARS[6] [*Eleazar*[5], *Silas*[4], *Silas*[3], *Silas*[2], *Rich.*[1]], b. Yarmouth, Mass., July 11, 1777 ; d. Apr. 29, 1859, gr.-st., So. Yar.; m. Yar., Mar. 7, 1797, *Susan Crowell* of Dennis, who d. Aug. 15, 1820 ; 2d, Yar., Apr. 9, 1821, *Ruth Taylor*, who d. June 23, 1864, æ. 72, gr.-st. Children :
By *Susan :*
1550. i. JOHN, b. Yar., Jan. 3, 1798 ; d. Oct., 1799.
1551.* ii. EDWARD, b. Yar., May 12, 1800.
1552.* iii. SAMUEL, b. Yar., Jan. 22, 1803.
1553.* iv. EMERY, b. Yar., Aug. 25, 1806.
1554. v. PAULINA, b. Yar., Apr. 12, 1809 ; d. inf.
1555. vi. SUSAN, b. Yar., Nov. 24, 1812; m. Yar., Feb., 1834, *Peregrine White*.

1556. vii. Lois, b. Yar., Sep. 21, 1814; m. (pub. Yar., Dec. 24, 1836,) *Joshua Baker*.

1557. viii. PAULINE, b. Yar., June 23, 1820; m. Yar., Dec. 30, 1841, *Francis Kelly*.

By *Ruth* :

1558. ix. NATHAN, b. Yar., Jan. 19, 1822.

1559. x. REBECCA, b. Yar., Aug. 4, 1824; m. (pub. Yar., Apr. 1, 1848,) *Abraham Berry ;* 2d, —— ——.

1560. xi. ABBY T., b. Yar., Apr. 14, 1827 ; m. Yar., Oct. 29, 1846, *Winthrop Crowell*.

1561. xii. CORNELIA, b. Yar., Apr. 4, 1830; d. Oct. 15, 1860, gr.-st.

727.

ALLEN SEARS[6] [*Thos.*[5], *Thos.*[4], *Silas*[3], *Silas*[2], *Rich.*[1]], b. Yarmouth, Mass., Aug. 5, 1760 ; m. Yar., Aug. 4, 1789, *Sarah Howes*, dau. of Isaac and Temperance (Crowell) H., she b. Mar. 21, 1761. Children :

1562. i. ALLEN, b. N. Y. State, 1806; d. s. p., Spencer, Owen co., Ind., Dec. 4, 1846 ; m. Vigo co., Ind., 1846, *Sarah A.* ——, she b. Licking co., Ohio, Jan. 5, 1827; lives in Sullivan, Ind., having m. 2d, —— Julian. He rem. when a young man to Western Penn., thence to Cincinnati, Ohio, where he remained but a short time, and thence to Kentucky. He joined the Meth. Epis. Ch. previous to 1838, and was licensed to preach in that year, and appointed to the Taylorsville Circuit as junior preacher ; was transferred to Ind. Conference in 1845, and appointed to Vincennes Station, and in 1846 to Spencer Circuit. " Bro. Sears was a man of very strong faith, deep piety, a truly evangelical preacher, and a good pastor."

1563. ii. *Dau.*, m. —— *Annis*, and lived near Battlecreek, Mich.

1564. iii. *Son*, left a widow at Battlecreek, Mich.

Allen Sears was in Capt. Abial Pierce's Co., in Col. Dike's Regt., Aug. 20, 1776, 120 miles' travel ; in Capt. Sam'l Briggs' Co., Col. Thomas Collins' Regt., Sep. 29, 1777, at Tiverton, R. I., 32 days' service, £1 1 4 ; in Capt. John Barrows' Co., Col. Abijah Sterne's Regt., Apr. 4 to July 2, 1778, 2 mos. 21 days, £5 8 0. Service at or near Boston, 2 days allowed to travel home; in Lt. John Doty's Co., Col. Eben. Sproul's Regt., alarm at Dartmouth, Sep. 5 to Sep. 11, 1778; also May 1 and 7, 1776, 6 days, £1 12 0; was in Capt. Wm. Tupper's Co., Col. Titcomb's Regt., expedition to R. I., 65 days under Maj.-Gen. Spencer, £4 6 8. "Allen Sears of Rochester, age 19, 5 ft. 6 inches height, light complexion," arrived at Springfield, July 8, 1780; then went to reinforce Northern Army, near Lake George; served July 6 to Dec. 18, 1780, 5 mos. 14 days, and 240 miles' travel, £12 2 10.

After the war he removed to Portage, Allegany co., N. Y. (now Livingston co.), and in the census of 1840 is set down as a Revolutionary pensioner, and living with Nath'l Rathbun.

731.

WINTHROP SEARS[6] [*Eleazar*[5], *Thos.*[4], *Silas*[3], *Silas*[2], *Rich.*[1]], b. Yarmouth, Mass., May 1, 1772; d. Nov. 17, 1838; m. Yar., Dec. 11, 1794, *Betsy Crowell*, who d. July 30, 1809, in 36 yr.; 2d, Yar., 1809, Mrs. *Susannah Crowell*, who d. May 5, 1853. Children:

By *Susannah:*

1565.* i. ODLIN PAGE, b. Yar., Dec. 25, 1810.
1566. ii. SUSAN, b. Yar., Dec. 26, 1811; m. Yar., Jan., 1832, *Christopher Lewis.*
1567. iii. NABBY, b. Yar., Mar. 10, 1815; m. Yar., Nov., 1835, *Higgins Crowell.*
1568.* iv. WINTHROP, b. Yar., Jan. 2, 1818.
1569. v. MARY, b. Yar., June 1, 1821.

726.

THOMAS SEARS[6] [*Eleazar*[5], *Thos.*[4], *Silas*[3], *Silas*[2], *Rich.*[1]], b. Yarmouth, Mass., Mar. 16, 1781; m. Yar., July 16, 1805, *Lydia Atwood Gray.* Children:

1570. i. SHERBURNE, b. Yar., Mar. 12, 1806.
1571. ii. THOMAS, b. Yar., Apr. 30, 1807.
1572. iii. LYDIA A., b. Yar., Apr. 17, 1809.
1573. iv. ALMIRA, b. Barnstable, July 31, 1811; m. Yar., 1832, *Henry Cotton* of Nantucket.
1574. v. SABRA, b. Barns., May 10, 1813; m. (pub. Den., Nov. 20, 1847,) *John Sears, Jr.*, of Den., No. 1385(?).

735.

Capt. RICHARD SEARS[6] [*Eleazar*[5], *Thos.*[4], *Silas*[3], *Silas*[2], *Rich.*[1]], b. Yarmouth, Mass., July 22, 1783; d. Goshen, N. Y.,

July 18, 1851, æ. 67 ; m. Yarmouth, Mass., Aug. 16, 1810, *Ruth Hedge*, she b. Apr. 21, 1789 ; d. Goshen, Jan. 5, 1871, æ. 81.   Children :

1575.   i. EDWIN, b. Oct. 30, 1812 ; d. Goshen, Sep. 20, 1853.
1576.   ii. EDMUND HALL, b. Dec. 29, 1814 ; d. at sea, Aug. 14, 1837.
1577.   . RUTH HEDGE, b. June 16, 1819 ; d. Goshen, Dec. 31ḷịi1836.
1578.   iv. JANE, b. May 24, 1821, at 147 Grand st., N. Y. ; m. Goshen, N. Y., Feb. 6, 1844, *Wm. Murray Sayer*, he b. Minisink, N. Y., Mar. 14, 1820 ; children, SAYER : [1.] Edmund Sears, b. Nov. 28, 1844 ; m. Meadsville, Pa., Oct. 12, 1869, Mary Elizabeth Dick. [2.] William, b. Sep. 14, 1846 ; d. May 18, 1849. [3.] Ruth Sears, b. July 5, 1848 ; m. Oct. 9, 1873, Frank A. Merriam, and lives Kansas City, Mo. [4.] Richard Sears, b. Nov. 9, 1850 ; m. Middletown, N. Y., June 16, 1881, Frank(?) Willard Low, and lives Brooklyn, N.Y. [5.] William Murray, b. Dec. 20, 1852 ; m. Jan. 11, 1883, Clara Halstead, and lives Brooklyn, N. Y. [6.] Alice Emma, b. Mar. 9, 1855. [7.] Jane, b. Sep. 19, 1857; m. Oct. 23, 1879, Joseph Wadsworth Gott. [8.] Antoinette, b. Jan. 22, 1860. [9.] Sally Lavinia, b. May 31, 1863.
1579.   v. LAVINIA, b. Feb. 3, 1824 ; d. New York, Oct. 7.
1580.   vi. JULIA, b. Mar. 20, 1827 ; d. Goshen, June 27, 1832.
1581.   vii. SARAH LAVINIA, b. June 30, 1829 ; m. Goshen, June 13, 1850, *James W. Oliver*, and died there, Nov. 2, 1861.
1582. viii. RICHARD, b. Dec. 23, 1833 ; m. Goshen, Oct. 10, 1860, *Jane Augusta Smith*, and died Feb. 1, 1865.

Was a sea captain.

736.

Corp. PHILIP SEARS[6] [*David*[5], *Jas.*[4], *Silas*[3], *Silas*[2] *Rich.*[1]], b. North East, N. Y., 1759; d. Lenox, Mass., July 17, 1831, æ. 72 ; m. Pittsfield, Mass., (pub. Lenox, Nov. 25, 1798,) *Lavinia Gunn*, she b. Pitts., 1771 ; d. Lenox, Mar. 16, 1847, æ. 76.   Children :

1583.*   i. CHAUNCY, b. Len., June 30, 1799.

1584. ii. LAURA D., b. Len., June 11, 1801 ; m. (pub. Lenox, Sep. 14, 1822,) *Chauncy Brooks*, and lives Sugar Grove, Ill.

Philip Sears served in Capt. Ezra Whittlesey's Co., Sep. 7 to Sep. 30, 1777 ; in Capt. Chas. Dibbet's Co. on alarm of Oct. 18, 1780, four days' service; and was Corporal in Capt. Wm. Wells' Co., alarm at Saratoga, Oct. 30 to Nov. 7, 1781.

Dec. 3, 1777. "Voted, John Whitlock, Ephraim Smith, David Sears, Philip Sears and Edward Martingale are dangerous to the United States of America," etc. (Town Rec.)

He was a farmer.

737.

DAVID SEARS[6] [*David*5 *Jas.*4, *Silas*3, *Silas*2, *Rich.*1], m. Lenox, Mass., *Huldah Carr;* and 2d, Milton, Sar. co., N. Y., *Jennie Cole*, she b. Scotland. Children:

By *Huldah:*

1585.* i. DAVID, b. Lenox, June 13, 1785.

1586. ii. LOVILLY, b. Milton, N. Y., Oct. 25, 1786; m. Auburn, N. Y., *Wm. Hoffman*, and d. Nunda, Ill.

1587. iii. ABIGAIL, b. Milton ; m. *Hezekiah Hoyt*, and d. Mar. 16, 1859.

1588. iv. HULDAH, b. Milton, Jan. 28, 1798; m. there, Apr. 26, 1815, *Alex'r Shearer*, he b. there, June 9, 1786 ; settled in Camillus, N. Y., when it was a wilderness ; he was a farmer and Deacon of Presb. Ch.; d. Sep. 29, 1845 ; his widow lives on the old homestead in Cam.; children, SHEARER : [1.] Abigail, b. May 27, 1816 ; m. Jan. 29, 1834, Jas. Van Alstine. [2.] Harriet, b. June 28, 1818. [3.] David, b. Mar. 1, 1821; m. Jan. 10, 1844, Almira Van Alstine, and d. June 12, 1883. [4.] Huldah, b. Sep. 8, 1822 ; m. May 13, 1847, Albert G. Townsend, he b. Pompey, N. Y., Apr. 29, 1823 ; d. Feb. 8, 1875. [5.] Alexander, b. July 28, 1825 ; m. Jan. 2, 1856, Margaret Hopkins, she b. Amboy, N. Y., Oct. 24, 1831. [6.] Lovilly, b. Mar. 3, 1828; m. May 1, 1845, Wm. B. Preslow, he b. England ; Jan. 11, 1881, was a miller, and after a red-potter. [7.] Mary Jane, b. Apr. 5, 1833.

1589.* v. ELEAZAR, b. Milton, July 31, 1801.

1590. vi. ISAAC, b. Milton ; d. Ballston Spa, N. Y., Dec. 17, 1834 ; m. *Visonia Jones*, (who m. 2d, —— St. John, and lives in Wolcott, N. Y.)

1591. vii. EDWARD, b. Milton; d. Kalamazoo, Mich.; m. Camillus, N. Y., Rebecca Hand, (another account says, Martha Lamb,) who d. Kal.
1592. viii. JOHN, b. Milton; died Kalamazoo, Mich.
1593. ix. MAJOR, b. Milton; d. Saratoga, N. Y., æ. 19.

David Sears was in Capt. Wm. Ford's Co., Col. John Brown's Regt., at Stone Arabia, N. Y., July 21 to Oct. 27, 1780, and marched to Stillwater in Capt. Josiah Yale's Co., Oct. 12, 1781, doing 12 days' service.

738.

ISAAC SEARS[6] [*David*[5], *Jas.*[4], *Silas*[3], *Silas*[2], *Rich.*[1]], m. *Priscilla Stearns*, dau. of Oliver S. of Mansfield, Ct., she b. about 1768; d. Lenox, Mass., May 1, 1799. Children:
1594. i. ELIJAH, b. Lenox, May 11, 1794.
1595. ii. POLLY, b. Lenox, July 12, 1796.
1596. iii. MELISSA.

739.

LUTHER SEARS[6] [*David*[5], *Jas.*[4], *Silas*[3], *Silas*[2], *Rich.*[1]], b. Lenox, Mass., 1772; d. Volney, N. Y., July, 1857, æ. 85; m. Lenox, Feb. 5, 1798, by Eldad Lewis, J. P., to *Anna Foster*. Children:
1597.* i. NELSON, b. Lenox, Aug. 12, 1798.
1598. ii. NANCY, b. Lenox, 1800; m. there, Nov. 1, 1821, *Levi Butler*, lived in L., and d. 1883, æ. 83; children, BUTLER: [1.] Luther. [2.] A. C. [3.] John. [4.] Marshall, of Richmond, Mass. [5.] Maria, m. —— Howland of Lenox.
1599.* iii. MARSHALL, b. Lenox, 1802.
1600.* iv. ZACHARIAH P., b. Lenox, 1804.
1601.* v. LUTHER, b. Lenox, 1806.
1602. vi. MARIETTA, b. Lenox, 1809; m. May 14, 1829, *Ira Carrier*, and rem. to Fulton, N. Y.; child, CARRIER: [1.] Ira, lives in F.
1603. vii. ANN MARIA, b. Lenox; m. *Lyman Judd*, and d. Volney, N. Y.; children, JUDD: [1.] Alphonse, lives in F. [2.] Sarah.
1604. viii. HARRIET, b. Lenox, 1819; m. *Fred. Washburn* of L.; child, WASHBURN: [1.] George, lives in L.

740.

JAMES SEARS[6] [*David[5], Jas.[4], Silas[3], Silas[2], Rich.[1]*],
b. Lenox, Mass., May 15, 1776; d. Richford, N. Y., Feb. 22,
1847; m. Lenox, Dec. 23, 1798, by Rev. Sam'l Shepard, to
Lucy Judd, she b. Pittsfield, Mass., Nov. 28, 1776; d. Richford. Children:

1605.   i. LUCY, b. Lenox, Nov. 18, 1802; m. there, Sep. 11,
1828, *Geo. Cargill,* he b. Goshen, Mass., Jan. 31, 1802,
son of John and Mary (Crow) C., d. Newark Valley, N.
Y., Sep. 22, 1872; she d. June, 1872.

1606.   ii. PATTY, b. Lenox, May 18, 1806; m. *James Bristol*
and rem. to Castle Creek, Broome co., N. Y.

1607.* iii. DIOCLESIAN, b. Lenox, Nov. 15, 1808.

1608.   iv. SALLY, b. Lenox, Apr. 9, 1810; m. (pub. Len., Dec.
25, 1831,) *Lucius D. Rogers* of L.; removed to Richford,
N. Y., where he d.; child, ROGERS: [1.] Sarah, m.
Horatio Sykes, and lived in Berkshire, N. Y., she m. 2d,
—— Cross, an old man of B.; had several children.

1609.* v. PHILIP, b. Lenox, May 21, 1812.

741.

ZACHARIAH SEARS[6] [*David[5], Jas.[4], Silas[3], Silas[2],
Rich.[1]*], b. Lenox, Mass., Apr., 1778; d. there, Nov. 17, 1865,
æ. 87, of old age; m. (pub. Lenox, July 29, 1805,) *Sally Hall*
of Ashfield; 2d, *Almira Butler,* who d. Len., Mar. 13, 1857,
æ. 71, of consumption. Children:

By *Sarah :*

1610.   i. ZACHARIAH PADDOCK, b. Lenox; m. *Mary Ann
Millard,* and d.

1611.   ii. DAVID, b. Lenox; m. a Virginia lady, and d.

1612.* iii. SAMUEL H., b. Lenox, 1808.

By *Almira :*

1613.* iv. JOHN, b. Lenox, Dec. 3, 1812.

1614.* v. ELIJAH, b. Lenox.

1615.   vi. SARAH, b. Lenox; m. *John Parker,* and d.

1616.* vii. JAMES, b. Lenox.

1617.* viii. LEVI L., b. Lenox, Apr. 8, 1825.

1618.   ix. POLLY, b. Lenox; m. —— *Whitaker* of Pittsfield.

1619.   x. MARIA, b. Lenox.

35

742.

CALVIN SEARS[6] [*David[5], Jas.[4], Silas[3], Silas[2], Rich.[1]*], b. Lenox, Mass., about 1769 ; d. there, Mar. 6, 1859, æ. 90, of old age; m. (pub. Lenox, Dec. 25, 1792,) *Mary Hubby* of Pittsfield, Mass. Children:

1620.   i. MARY MARIA, b. Lenox, May 14, 1800.
1621.   ii. FANNIE, b. Lenox, Mar. 30, 1802; m. there, July 15, 1823, *John A. Phelps* of Len.

Mr. Sears kept tavern in Worthington, Mass.

747.

ENOCH HAMLIN SEARS[6] [*Seth[5], Jas.[4], Silas[3], Silas[2], Rich.[1]*], b. —— ; m. —— *Smith*, dau. of Jeremiah S. of Charlton, N. Y. Children:

1622.*   i. ALEXANDER, b. Aug. 9, 1782.
1623.   ii. BETSY, m. *Jonathan Hedges;* children, HEDGES: [1.] Elias, d. [2.] William, d. [3.] Henry, d.
1624.   iii. RUTH, m. *Jona. Curtis;* children, CURTIS: [1.] Thomas. [2.] Caroline.
1625.   iv. SALLY, m. —— *Pierson;* and d. six weeks later, of consumption.
1626.   v. LEWIS, d. of consumption.
1627.   vi. SMITH; was taken West by relatives, and not heard from since.

748.

SETH SEARS[6] [*Seth[5], Jas.[4], Silas[3], Silas[2], Rich.[1]*], b. ab't 1771; d. Milltown, N. Y., May 1, 1819, æ. 48, gr.-st.; m. *Ruhamah Andrews*, who d. Dec. 9, 1813, æ. 31; 2d, Mrs. *Eunice (Paddock) Crosby*, (a cousin of Joseph Crane Sears, through his mother; she had two daus. by her 1st husband, viz.: "Blind Fanny J. Crosby," the hymn writer, and Mrs. Morris, who was living in Bridgeport, Ct., in 1885, æ. 86, to whom I am indebted for data relative to this and connected families.) Children :

1628.   i. EBENEZER, m. and had a dau.
1629.   ii. PETER, d. unm.
1630.   iii. NAOMI.

1631. iv. ROXANNA.
1632. v. SETH, m. *Polly* ——, and d. s. p., Norwalk, Ct.
1633. vi. LEWIS, m. and went West.
1634. vii. RUHAMAH.

749.

ELEAZAR H. SEARS[6] [*Seth*[5], *Jas.*[4], *Silas*[3], *Silas*[2], *Rich.*[1]],
b. South East, N. Y., or Danbury, Ct., 1771; d. De Ruyter,
N. Y., 1855, æ. 84; m. So. East, *Betsy Marvin*, who d. De R.,
1854, æ. 76. Children :
1635. i. STEPHEN GREGORY, b. So. E., 1798; d. De R., 1868.
1636. ii. ANN M., b. So. E., 1800; d. Cazenovia, N. Y., 1874.
1637. iii. GEORGE, b. So. E., 1804; d. De R., 1858.
1638. iv. FRANCIS, b. So. E., 1808; d. Homer, N. Y., 1870;
(either he or a son Francis m. a sister of Gov. Nye of
Colorado, and had a dau. Mary, who lived in Clinton,
Iowa.)
1639.* v. ODELL M., b. De R., 1815.

752.

DANIEL SEARS[6] [*Knowles*[5], *Jas.*[4], *Silas*[3], *Silas*[2], *Rich.*[1]],
b. Ridgefield, Ct., May 14, 1762; d. Van Buren, N. Y., Feb.
18, 1840; m. Mar. 30, 1787, *Catharine Warin*, she b. Oct.
10, 1767; d. Apr. 3, 1860. Children :
1640. i. ALFRED, b. Jan. 14, 1789; d. unm., July 28, 1856.
1641.* ii. ARZA, b. Rensselaerville, N. Y., Oct. 17, 1790.
1642. iii. AMBROSE, b. Aug. 17, 1793; m. *Ruth* ——, and d.
Ellington, N. Y., Aug. 9, 1843.
1643.* iv. AHIRAM, b. Apr. 5, 1795.
1644. v. RUHAMAH, b. Dec. 22, 1796; m. *Sam. Barager;*
he b. 1794; d. 1871; rem. to Candor, N. Y., and d. Apr.
4, 1878; children, BARAGER: [1.] Mahala Ann, m. June
15, 1841, Thos. Marshall; she was a school teacher.
[2.] Emeline, m. —— Smith. [3.] Samantha, d. unm.
[4.] Herbert A., b. 1830; m. Hattie Currie of Hudson.
[5.] George T., b. 1832; m. Nettie Coburn of Mead-
ville, Pa. [6.] Charles F., member N. Y. Assembly,
1884; m. Mary Markell, lives Candor, N. Y. [7.] James,
d. young. [8.] William, d. young.
1645. vi. ABIJAH, b. Nov. 25, 1798; d. unm., June 26, 1837.
1646. vii. RUFUS, b. Sep. 2, 1802; d. Nov. 26, 1866; m.
Amanda Townsend (sister of Benajah T.); rem. to Scho-

harie, N. Y., thence to Susquehanna, Pa., and in 1854, to Crown Point, Lake co., Ind.

1647. viii. MARIA, b. Mar. 1, 1805; m. *Asa West Bushnell*, a Presb. Min'r, and rem. to Le Roy, Calhoun co., Mich., in 1840, where she d. Oct. 19, 1841; children, BUSHNELL: [1.] Asa. [2.] John.

Daniel Sears removed about 1793 to Rensselaerville, N. Y., and in 1835 to Van Buren, where he dwelt with his son Arza until his death in 1840.

757.

JOHN SEARS[6] [*Knowles[5], Jas.[4], Silas[3], Silas[2], Rich.[1]*], b. Oct. 15, 1772; d. Sep. 1, 1839; m. *Mary Townsend*, dau. of Uriah and Hannah T., she b. July 25, 1772; d. Aug. 6, 1819; 2d, Apr. 20, 1820, *Phebe Lusk*, she b. Aug. 27, 1784; d. Apr. 28, 1855. Children:

By *Mary:*

1648.   i. SUSANNA, b. Camillus, N. Y., Nov. 30, 1793; d. Aug. 22, 1808.

1649.   ii. TAMMA, b. Cam., Oct. 26, 1795; m. *John H. Lamerson*, he b. Nov. 16, 1785; d. July 24, 1863; she d. Sep. 24, 1864; children, LAMERSON: [1.] Susan, b. Dec. 18, 1814; m. Oct. 17, 1833, Brinkerhoff La Duc, who d. Van Buren, N. Y., in fall of 1883. [2.] Jacob, b. July 17, 1817; m. Caroline Waterman, and d. June 6, 1860. [3.] Betsy, b. June 7, 1819. [4.] Tamma, b. July 12, 1821; m. Isaac Peck. [5.] John Sears, b. Nov. 14, 1823; m. Catherine Stevens, and d. Feb. 8, 1862. [6.] Mary, b. Apr. 3, 1826; m. Zora Hayden. [7.] Sears, b. July 29, 1828; m. Sarah Allen, and d. Apr. 28, 1866. [8.] Matilda, b. May 17, 1831; m. William Peck. [9.] George, b. Sep. 7, 1833; d. May 13, 1849. [10.] Wayne, b. Jan. 17, 1836; m. Henrietta Williams.

1650.   iii. HANNAH, b. Cam., Dec. 12, 1797; m. there, Nov. 6, 1815, *Cyrus H. Kingsley*, he b. Lebanon, Ct., Aug. 21, 1789; d. Dec. 16, 1878; children, KINGSLEY: [1.] Oliver, b. Aug. 16, 1816. [2.] Polly, b. Jan. 1, 1819. [3.] Emily, b. Mar. 17, 1823. [4.] Knowles, b. Oct. 18, 1825; d. Feb. 15, 1827. [5.] Edward, b. Apr. 25, 1828; d. Oct. 14, 1858. [6.] Cyrus, b. July 29, 1830. [7.] Ulysses, b. Jan. 23, 1834; d. Sep. 11, 1836. [8.] Algernon, b. Jan. 2, 1839.

1651. iv. Knowles, b. Cam., May 18, 1800 ; d. Aug. 18, 1820.
1652. v. Betsy, b. Cam., Nov. 13, 1802 ; d. Aug. 7, 1819.
1653. vi. Adeline, b. Cam., Apr. 14, 1805 ; d. Aug. 31, 1876.
By *Phebe :*
1654. vii. John, b. Cam., Jan. 15, 1821 ; d. Jan. 29, 1857.
1655. viii. Phebe, b. Cam., Aug. 12, 1823.

Mr. Sears removed to Camillus, N. Y., and after the death of his first wife, to Red Creek, Wolcott co., N. Y.

758.

ABIJAH SEARS[6] [*Knowles*5 *Jas.*[4], *Silas*[3], *Silas*[2], *Rich.*[1]], b. Danbury, Ct., Aug. 8, 1774 ; d. near head of Seneca lake, N. Y. (perhaps at Hector); m. Dan., Jan. 8, 1797, *Catharine Boughton*, dau. of Matthew B., who d. May, 1816 ; 2d, *Sally (Hendricks) Catlin*, widow of Sam'l C., who d. Mar., 1883 ; 3d, *Anna Browne*, whose first husband was named Hooker, who d. Newark Valley, N. Y., about 1856. Children :

By *Catharine :*
1656.* i. James, b. Eaton, N. Y., May 12, 1797.
1657.* ii. Charles, b. Eaton, ab't 1800.
1658. iii. Mary Ann, b. Eaton, Apr. 16, 1805 ; m. Newark Valley, Jan. 1, 1826, *Oliver Rewey*, a blacksmith, he b. Stockbridge, Mass., July 16, 1804, son of John and Lucy (Taylor) R., lived in New. Val., and d. Mar. 18, 1839 ; (he m. 2d, Emeline Allen, and d. Jan. 19, 1883;) children, Rewey : [1.] Martha Ann, b. Dec. 12, 1826 ; m. Oct. 3, 1847, Daniel Birchard Allen. [2.] Angeline, b. Jan. 14, 1829 ; m. Apr. 15, 1855, Robert Franklin Clark. [3.] Mary Augusta, b. Apr. 21, 1836 ; m. Dr. Roberts.
1659.* iv. Hart Boughton, b. Eaton, Aug. 15, 1807.
1660. v. Erastus, b. Eaton, d. æ. ab't 18 mos.
By *Sally :*
1661. vi. Lucy, b. Danby, N. Y., kept a millinery store in Elmira, N. Y.
1662. vii. Isaac.

Mr. Sears removed to Eaton, Mad. co., N. Y., and later to the head of Seneca lake, perhaps to Hector, where he died a few years after.

759.

ISAAC SEARS[6] [*Knowles*[5], *Jas.*[4], *Silas*[3], *Silas*[2], *Rich.*[1]],
b. Danbury, Ct., Aug. 7, 1776 ; d. Sep. 20, 1848 ; m. ——
——, who d.; 2d, *Polly Woods*, who d. s. p., June 27, 1858.
Children :

By 1*st wife :*
1663.   i. KATE, m. *Noah Sherwood ;* child, SHERWOOD :
        [1.] John, who lives West Somerset, Niag. co., N. Y.
1664.   ii. ANGELINE, m. —— *Jones.*
1665. iii. SOPHY, was adopted by Elijah Benedict, and d. unm.,
        Aug. 17, 1826, æ. 22, gr.-st., " Bogg's District," Dan-
        bury, Ct.
1666.* iv. HEMAN, b. May 23, 1807.
1667.* v. HAMAN, b. May 23, 1807, *gemini.*

He was a farmer, and settled in Newfane, Niagara co., N. Y.

761.

CHARLES SEARS[6] [*Knowles*[5], *Jas.*[4], *Silas*[3], *Silas*[2], *Rich.*[1]],
b. Danbury, Ct., Aug. 3, 1780; d. Ridgefield, Ct., Apr. 22,
1836 ; m. there, Mar. 17, 1804, *Betsy Smith*, dau. of Job and
Esther (Benedict) S. of R., she b. there, Oct. 26, 1784 ; d.
Aug. 15, 1869, æ. 85, (see Whitney Gen., No. 710.) Children :
1668.   i. CLARA M., b. Ridge., Nov. 18, 1804 ; d. Sep. 7,
        1821.
1669.* ii. EDWIN COLLINS, b. Ridge., Jan. 17, 1808.
1670.* iii. GEORGE, b. Camillus, N. Y., Mar. 12, 1823.

Mr. Sears removed to Camillus, Onon. co., N. Y., but returned,
and died in Ridgefield ; he was a farmer, and was found dead
in a field.   He and his wife were buried in Titicus Cemetery.

766.

ELI SEARS[6] [*Thos.*[5], *Jas.*[4], *Silas*[3], *Silas*[2], *Rich.*[1]], b. Oct.
16, 1768 ; d. Carmel, N. Y., Mar. 16, 1800 ; m. there, Feb. 24,
1788, *Hanna Bull*, she b. Mar. 17, 1769 ; d. Searsburg, N. Y.,
Feb. 4, 1850.   Children :
1671.* i. THOMAS BALDWIN, b. Mar. 2, 1789.
1672.* ii. DAVID F., b. Apr. 17, 1791.

769.

JAMES SEARS[6] [*Thos.*[5], *Jas.*[4], *Silas*[3], *Silas*[2], *Rich.*[1]], b. 1778 (?); d. Mar., 1857; m. Nov. 19, 1797, —— ——. Children :

1673. i. ARCHIBALD.
1674. ii. JAMES.

770.

ARCHIBALD SEARS[6] [*Thos.*[5] *Jas.*[4], *Silas*[3], *Silas*[2], *Rich.*[1]], b. Carmel, N. Y., Aug. 8, 1780 ; d. So. East, N. Y., Oct. 27, 1864, æ. 84 yrs. 2 mos. 19 days, gr.-st. ; m. there, Jan. 25, 1829, *Polly Sellick,* dau. of Jesse S., she b. there, July 11, 1798 ; d. May 26, 1868, æ. 69 yrs. 10 mos. 24 days, gr.-st. Children :

1675. i. MARY E., b. So. East, May 30, 1830; m. *Rich. T. Haviland* of Patterson, N. Y. ; he b. there, Feb. 23, 1829; children, HAVILAND: [1.] Fred. Sears, b. Jan., 1854; d. Mar. 13, 1856. [2.] Gertrude Algetta, b. Oct. 9, 1858. [3.] Edward Sears, b. June 2, 1864.
1676. ii. FANNIE, b. So. East, May 26, 1832 ; lives with sister Kate, unm.
1677. iii. KATE, b. So. East, Sep. 27, 1834; m. Oct., 1866, Rev. *Roswell Smith,* and lives in New York city.
1678. iv. THOMAS, b. So. East, Apr. 16, 1836 ; m. Nov., 1878, —— ——. He was Capt. 4th Heavy Arty., N. Y., during the Civil war, and promoted Major, now lives in Denver, Col.

Archibald Sears lived on part of the old homestead in South East, Putnam co., N. Y., and joined the church there at the age of 80.

772.

ISAAC SEARS[6] [*Thos.*[5], *Jas.*[4], *Silas*[3], *Silas*[2], *Rich.*[1]], b. July 23, 1786 ; m. May 12, 1811, *Mary Sears,* No. 1016, dau. of Heman and Susie S., she b. 1791 ; d. Apr. 11, 1821, æ. 30, gr.-st. Children :

1679. i. GEORGE, b. So. East, N. Y.
1680. ii. HEMAN, b. So. East.
1681. iii. SUSIE, b. So. East.
1682. iv. ISAAC, b. So. East, 1821 ; d. Jan. 21, 1823.

Mr. Sears, called *" Tanner Ike,"* to distinguish him from *" Tailor Ike,"* No. 440, removed from South East, N. Y., to Illinois, about 1833, with his family, where his house was destroyed by a cyclone, and his mother-in-law killed.

778.

JARED SEARS[6] [*Jas.*[5], *Jas.*[4], *Silas*[3], *Silas*[2], *Rich.*[1]], b. Lenox, Mass., Aug. 12, 1779 ; d. Knowlesville, N. Y., Feb. 6, 1828; m. Bennington, Vt., Feb. 11, 1802, *Betsy Robinson*, dau. of Col. Samuel and Esther (Safford) R., she b. Benn., Apr. 18, 1780 ; d. there in 1843. (Her father was a Capt. at the battle of Bennington; was one of the first settlers there, and for many years the most prominent man in the township.) Children :

1683.   i. MARY ANN, b. Swanton, Vt., Apr. 5, 1804 ; m. Benn., May 10, 1830, *Martin S. Norton*, he b. there, Nov. 21, 1788 ; d. Grass Valley, Cal., where his widow resides.
1684.   ii. EMILY HYDE, b. Swan., Sep. 20, 1805 ; m. Benn., *Henry Robinson*, he b. there, Feb. 5, 1809; lives Charlotte, Mich.
1685.* iii. BENJAMIN ROBINSON, b. Benn., Dec. 21, 1807.
1686.   iv. LUCY ROBINSON, b. St. Albans, Vt., Feb. 13, 1810 ; m. there, Nov. 20, 1831, *Zebina E. Fobes*, he b. Middleboro, Mass., Nov. 19, 1804 ; lives in Benn. Centre, Vt.
1687.   v. CHARLES FOLLETT, b. Benn., Aug. 26, 1817 ; d. New Orleans, La., in 1841, of yellow fever.
1688.   vi. DELIA MARIA, b. Benn., Aug. 25, 1821 ; m. there, Mar. 19, 1846, *Zimri Haswell*, he b. Shoreham, Vt., Sep. 1, 1817; d. San Francisco, Cal. ; she d. Aug. 1, 1853.

781.

JAMES SEARS[6] [*Jas.*[5], *Jas.*[4], *Silas*[3], *Silas*[2], *Rich.*[1]], d. Knightstown, Henry co., Ind., 1847; m. *Elinor Wilson*, she b. 1793, of Scotch-Irish parentage ; d. at the residence of Washington Sears, near Fishersburgh, Mad. co., Ind., June 14, 1869, æ. 76.   Children :

1689.* i. JOHN, b. ab't 1810.
1690.   ii. ANNA, b. N. Y. State ; m. Brown co., Ohio, *John Steel*, and d. 1877 ; children, STEEL : [1.] James, lives in Knightstown, Ind., and others.

1691.* iii. DAVID, b. N. Y. State.
1692.* iv. JAMES, b. Canada, Oct. 20, 1812.
1693. v. *Son*, d. inf.
1694. vi. ALEXANDER, b. Ohio; d. 1860; m. Hancock co., Ind., Mary Ann Gobal, who lives in Nebraska, had several children, who m. and lived in Iowa and Ind.
1695.* vii. WILSON, b. Ohio, Oct. 6, 1815.
1696.* viii. GEORGE WASHINGTON, b. Ohio or Ind.
1697. ix. HARRISON, b. Henry co., Ind.; m. there, *Sarah Burkett*, and both d. near Mattoon, Ill.
1698. x. WILLIAM, b. Henry Co., Ind.; m. Hancock co., Ind., *Charity McClelland*, who d.; he owns a large farm in Greenfield, Ind.
1699. xi. MARY JANE, b. Henry co., Ind.; m. there, Henry Graham, who d.; she lives in Lapel, Ind.
1700. xii. SARAH ELLEN, b. Ohio(?), 1835; m. Rush co., Ind., *Samuel S. Allen*, and lives Dayton, Ohio; children, ALLEN: [1.] Alonzo W., m. Mary Davis. [2.] Alice R., m. James Dobbin. [3.] Edgar H., b. 1856. [4.] Helen M., b. 1857; m. Wm. Davis. [5.] Anna A., b. 1861. [6.] Ulysses Grant, b. 1864; m. Anna Hoffman. [7.] Minna M., b. 1867.
1701. xiii. ALMIRA, b. Rainsville, Ind.; m. *John Griffin*, who d.; 2d, *Joseph Forbes*, who d.; she lives in Greenfield, Ind., with her children.

James Sears removed to Canada with his father, and was pressed into the British service in the war of 1812.

He was with his command, within hearing of the guns at Perry's fight on Lake Erie, and heard a British officer remark: " This seals our salvation or our damnation."

" Yankee Sears " always declared that he never fired a gun at his countrymen, but took care to aim over their heads.

After his discharge from the service, he got over into New York State as soon as possible, his departure being hastened by turbulent Indians, who rifled his cabin, and drove him with his family into the woods.

From thence he removed to Ohio, and in 1819 to Indiana, where he settled at Knightstown, in Henry co., and where he died.

He is buried with his wife in the Quaker Cemetery in Roysville.

36

787.

Dea. JAMES SEARS[6] [*Comfort*[5], *Jas.*[4], *Silas*[3], *Silas*[2], *Rich.*[1]], b. Ridgefield, Ct., Nov. 10, 1788; d. Seneca Castle, N. Y., Jan. 19, 1878, æ. 89 ; m. South East, N. Y., Oct. 11, 1808, *Deborah Crosby*, dau. of Enoch C., she b. there, Oct. 11, 1790; d. Phelps, N. Y., Feb. 3, 1849 ; 2d, Mrs. *Charity (White) Hopkins*, who d. Apr. 11, 1883, (having been thrice married.)   Children :

By *Deborah :*

1702.* i. GEORGE BELDEN, b. Millplain, Ct., June 25, 1809.

1703.* ii. GOULD BOUGHTON, b. Millplain, Apr. 18, 1811.

1704. iii. CAMILLA MARIA, b. Millplain, Aug. 9, 1816 ; m. Ridgefield, Ct., Dec. 25, 1833, *Francis B. Northrop*, son of Jas. N., he b. North Salem, N. Y., May 1, 1809 ; lives in Millburn, N. J.; children, NORTHROP :   [1.] Marietta, b. Oct. 1, 1834 ; m. Bethel, Me., Sep. 30, 1867, Adelbert B. Twitchell ; lives Newark, N. Y., and had, i. Richard Sears, b. Aug. 22, 1868.   ii. Adelbert B., b. Dec. 28, 1869.   iii. Harry Francis, b. Jan. 16, 1871. iv. Samuel Alphin, b. June 3, 1874 ; d. Mar. 18, 1876. [2.] James Francis, b. Feb. 15, 1840 ; m. Feb. 15, 1864, Annie D. Tucker, who d. s. p., Aug. 20, 1882. [3.] Henry Daw, b. Nov. 24, 1843 ; m. June 20, 1866, Sarah A. Weeks, who d. Aug. 4, 1867 ; and 2d, Oct., 1870, Annie E. Douglass ; had, i. Harry A., b. Apr. 19, 1867; d. Aug. 4.   ii. Fred. D., b. Nov., 1871 ; d. Nov., 1875. iii. Grace, b. Sep. 8, 1874. iv. Sarah, b. Jan. 1, ——. v. Harry D., b. Dec. 1, 1880.   [4.] George B. Sears, b. Apr. 18, 1850 ; m. Apr. 18, 1875, Sarah G. Berdan née Crosby, and had, i. Sadie Camilla, b. Apr., 1876, d. June.

1705. iv. ELIZA ANN, b. Millplain, May 13, 1823 ; m. Mar., 1840, *John Wright*, and d. Aug., 1879 ; children, WRIGHT: [1.] W. H.; lives Clifton Springs, N. Y. [2.] Dau., m. Charles Ellsworth, and lives Bay City, Mich.

1706.* v. CLARKE CROSBY, b. Millplain, Oct. 23, 1827.

James Sears removed from Millplain, Ct., to Seneca Castle, N. Y., in 1836, having sold his farm (which adjoined his bro. Lewis', and was 2 miles from the old homestead,) to his bro. Joseph C.

" He was a well-to-do farmer, of excellent literary taste, and of much spiritual culture.

" His idea of honesty was, 'good measure, pressed down and running over,' and every thing was done heartily, and as unto the Lord, who seemed ever present with him.

" He was single-hearted, pure-minded beyond most Christians, and had great humility.

"All his children were taught by example as well as precept.

" He was a Deacon for 30 years, and was blessed with two most excellent wives."

789.

JOSEPH CRANE SEARS[6] [*Comfort*[5], *Jas.*[4], *Silas*[3], *Silas*[2], *Rich.*[1]], b. Ridgefield, Ct., Dec. 18, 1792; d. Millplain, Ct., May 29, 1857, æ. 64; m. Oct. 26, 1814, *Patty M. Barnum*, she b. South East, N. Y., Dec. 9, 1793; d. there, Nov. 14, 1815, æ. 22, gr.-st., Old Cem., Milltown, N. Y.; 2d, Feb. 22, 1818, *Mary A. Brush*, she b. Jan. 3, 1796; d. Dec. 13, 1872, æ. 76, at the house of her dau. Camilla in Camden, N. J. Children:

By *Patty:*

1707.* i. HERMAN BARNUM, b. So. East, Nov. 11, 1815.

By *Mary:*

1708. ii. MARTHA MATILDA, b. So. E., Mar. 5, 1821; m. Aug. 7, 1853, *Lyman Platt* of Danbury, Ct., he b. Jan. 1, 1819, and d. July 23, 1866; children, PLATT: [1.] Anne S., d. inf. [2.] Joseph Elmore, b. July 29, 1862; lives in Dan.

1709.* iii. JACOB BRUSH, b. So. E., Apr. 9, 1823.

1710.* iv. ALONZO ELMORE, b. So. E., Oct. 3, 1825.

1711. v. ESTHER CAMILLA, b. Ridge., Aug. 21, 1829; m. Dan., June 28, 1854, *James A. Perry*, he b. Patterson, N. Y., Mar. 15, 1821; was a lumber merchant in Buffalo, N. Y., and rem. to 2642 Brown st., Phila., Penn.; children, PERRY: [1.] Norman Albert, b. June 3, 1855. [2.] Emma Camilla, b. Jan. 17, 1857; m. Albert G. Smith, he b. Ridgeley, Md., 1848, and had, i. Gertrude, b. July 25, 1879(?). ii. Norman, b. Nov. 21, 1878(?). [3.] Anna Sears, b. Nov. 3, 1863. [4.] Mary Eliza, b. 1867; d. inf.

1712. vi. MARGARET ELIZA, b. Ridge., Aug. 27, 1831; is Prop'r Tallman Sem'y, Paterson, N. J.; she has rendered much assistance in collecting data relative to the Ridgefield and other connected Sears families.

1713. vii. HENRIETTA LOUISA, b. Ridge., Mar. 31, 1835; m.
      Dan., Mar. 22, 1835, *Charles H. Crosby*, he b. Cold
      Spring, N. Y., May 25, 1831; lives in Bridgeport, Ct.;
      children, CROSBY: [1.] Charles Edward, b. Dec. 4, 1861;
      d. Oct. 19, 1865. [2.] *Adopted*, Mar. 17, 1874, Fannie
      L. Hoyt, she b. Nov. 26, 1873.

Mr. Sears lived in South East, N. Y., till 1827–8, when he
removed to his father's place, remaining there till 1836, when
he purchased the farm of his brother James in Millplain, Ct.

The house that Herman B. Sears was born in, was also the
birthplace of George Belden Sears.

The old boundary line between Connecticut and New York
passed through the house, and the room they were born in was
on the New York side.

By a later survey the whole house is in Connecticut.

Mr. Sears was a public-spirited man, and interested in all
improvements.

He was Rep. to State Leg. in 1835–6, and 1842.

He was greatly beloved by all his neighbors, especially the
young, was an active church member, often on committees, and
in 1829 sent to the Presbytery.

790.

Dea. LEWIS SEARS⁶ [*Comfort⁵, Jas.⁴, Silas³, Silas²,
Rich.¹*], b. Ridgefield, Ct., June 26, 1795; d. Danbury, Ct.,
Nov. 10, 1868, æ. 73; m. Phelps, N. Y., Sep. 30, 1824, *Sarah
Crosby*, she b. South East, N. Y., June 27, 1800; d. Buffalo,
N. Y., May 31, 1869; (her sister Deborah m. James Sears,
No. 787.)   Children:

1714.* i. THEODORE CROSBY, b. Dan., Aug. 4, 1828.
1715.   ii. WILLIAM HENRY, b. Dan., Dec. 23, 1830; m. *Rose
        Richmond;* lives in Kansas or Colorado, and has several
        children.
1716.* iii. FRANCIS AUGUSTUS, b. Dan., Sep. 18, 1833.
1717. iv. MARY ELIZA, b. Dan., Oct. 15, 1836; lives in Buf-
        falo with brother Francis.

Mr. Sears was a Deacon in Cong. Ch., Danbury.

792.

GEORGE SEARS⁶ [*Geo.⁵, Seth⁴, Rich.³, Silas², Rich.¹*], b.
Newport, R. I., 1765; d. Christiania, Del., Sep. 17, 1800,

æ. 35 ; m. *Lucretia Fry*, dau. of —— and Mary (Greene) F. Children :

1718.   i. GEORGE, d. young, unm.
1719. ii. RICHARD, d. young, unm.
1720. iii. ABIGAIL, m. *James Wm. McCulloh*, who was a shipping agent at Balt., and later a commercial lawyer. Was app. 1st Comptroller U. S. Treasury, 1842–49. He was a son of Maj. John McC., who emigrated to this country before the war, and with Col. Porter, commanded the art'y of the Pa. line in Washington's army. Col. P. and Maj. McC. married sisters. (Col. P. was father of Geo. P., Territorial Gov. of Mich., of David P., Gov. of Pa., and James Madison P., Sec. of War ;) their wives were Todds, relatives of Mrs. Abraham Lincoln, and the Todds of Ky. Mr. McC. was wounded in the war of 1812, and went on crutches for seven years ; children, McCULLOH : [1.] John Sears, lives Glencoe, Balt. co., Md. [2.] Richard S., lives in Glencoe, and writes his name McCulloch. [3.] Mary L., m. Henry Upham, and lives in Longwood, Mass. [4.] Isabella W., m. Copley Greene of Boston, Mass. [5.] James W., of Englewood, N. J. ; a son, Walter, lives at Brewsters, N. Y. [6.] Annie L., m. Wm. I. Brown. [7.] Adelaide, m. John P. Hubbard, and lives in Phila., Pa. [8.] Margaret C., m. Russell Sturgis, Jr., of Boston.

Mr. Sears was a clerk in the store of George Gibbs, a merchant of Newport, R. I., (father of Mrs. Channing,) went to Baltimore, to take charge of a branch there, became a general shipping merchant, and was prosperous and highly respected.

He was Secretary of the " Republican Society," in Aug., 1795.

He died suddenly of yellow fever, Sep. 17, 1800, at Christiania, Del., whither he had fled with his family to escape the pestilence, then epidemic in Baltimore.

His wife's mother, Mary (Greene) Fry, was sister of Nath'l Greene's father, and first cousin to Gen. Nath'l G., of the Revolutionary army.

The Greenes and Frys were Quakers, and had intermarried for several generations in Rhode Island.

Amy F., sister of Lucretia, m. —— Bailey of Tiverton, R. I., and her sister, Mary, m. —— Ganot, an officer of Rochambeau's staff, who disappeared mysteriously, and was never heard of again.

Christopher F., a brother, lived in Norfolk, Va., and d. New-port, æ. 94.

Gen. George Sears Greene, civil eng. of the Aqueduct Com., N. Y., was named for George Sears, Senior, out of intimate family friendship.

796.

JOHN T. SEARS[6] [*Geo.[5], Seth[4], Rich.[3], Silas[2], Rich.[1]*], d. in the West Indies, 1819–20 ; m. Danvers, Mass., 1813, *Betsy Wilkins*, who died there, June 14, 1870.　Children :

1721.* i. John Augustus, b. Danvers.
1722. ii. Mary Ann, b. Dan.; d. s. p., 1850.

According to family tradition, John T. Sears was brought to Marblehead, Mass., when a small boy, by Capt. John Chandler of that place.

It is said that his family lived in the *interior*, and that he was at school in a *seaport* town, with his *brother George* and *sister Mary*, when Capt. Chandler enticed him on board his vessel, and brought him away.

In 1812 he commanded the privateer "Lyon," and after the war, opened a ship-chandlery in Marblehead, and started and worked the anchor foundry at Danversport; he refitted and sailed the Herm. brig "Hannibal," in which he went as super-cargo with Capt. Williams of Salem, and died of yellow fever while on the voyage.

In tracing the parentage of Mr. Sears, I find but one family in which the name of *George* occurs prior to 1800, viz., that of George Sears of Newport, R. I.

Unfortunately the family records are very imperfect, and town and church records afford few data of the family, and nothing is to be learned from those of the Probate Court.

Possibly the records of the Quaker Church may throw some light on the family genealogy.

The romantic story of John T. Sears is unknown to the de-scendants of George Sears, Jr., but I place him here for the benefit of future investigators, and give his story as it was told to me.

798.

Col. JASPER PECK SEARS[6] [*John[5], John[4], Rich.[3], Silas[2], Rich.[1]*], b. Lyme, Ct., July 7, 1763 ; bap. Aug. 4, 1771 ; d. West Bloomfield, N. Y., May 17, 1811, æ. 48, gr.-st. ; m. West

Springfield, Mass., Jan. 29, 1793, *Martha Parsons*, (who m. 2d, —— *Dobbins ;*) she d. Nov. 20, 1828, æ. 64. Children :

1723. i. Mary Parsons, b. W. Bloom., May 9, 1794 ; m. Oct. 24, 1809, *Erastus Hunt* of W. Bloom., who d. 1822; 2d, *Josiah Taft* of W. Bloom., she d. Hamburg, N. Y., Jan. 19, 1878. E. A. Hunt, a grand-son, lives in Hamburg.

1724. ii. John, b. W. Bloom., Aug. 28, 1796 ; d. unm., Lancaster, N. Y., Apr. 24, 1837.

1725. iii. Orra Sophronia, b. W. Bloom., July 12, 1798 ; m. Buffalo, N. Y., Apr. 27, 1841, Dr. *Edwin Cook*, and d. Tonawanda, N. Y., Apr. 24, 1872.

1726.* iv. Richard, b. W. Bloom., Apr. 24, 1800.

1727.* v. Jasper Peck, b. W. Bloom., May 17, 1807.

1728.* vi. Israel Parsons, b. W. Bloom., Aug. 6, 1810.

Mr. Sears emigrated to West Bloomfield, Ont. co., N. Y., then called the "Geneseo settlement," in 1790, in company with Mr. Clark Peck and a Mr. Marvin.

They bought farms together, their purchase being a mile square.

Col. Sears, as he was styled, kept the pioneer tavern, and his farm is now occupied by Henry O. Brown, son-in-law of Simeon Sears, No. 1041.

803.

ZACHARIAH SEARS⁶ [*Roland*₅ *Zach.*⁴, *Jos.*³, *Silas*², *Rich.*¹], b. Ashfield, Mass., Mar. 19, 1782 ; (Mar. 11, another account;) d. June 3, 1842; m. Jan. 15, 1806, *Delight Coolidge*, she b. Jan. 8, 1783 ; d. 1850. Children :

1729.* i. Lorenzo, b. Fabius, N. Y., Dec. 23, 1806.

1730.* ii. Orange S., b. Fabius, Feb. 3, 1811.

1731.* iii. Warren C., b. Fabius, Dec. 20, 1812.

1732. iv. Ahira, b. Fabius, Feb. 4, 1817 ; d. unm., Aug. 29, 1886, Jackson, Mich.

1733. v. Louisa, b. Fabius, July 7, 1819 ; m. Ann Arbor, Mich., Mar. 23, 1837, *Dennis F. Boyden*, he b. Sep. 18, 1800 ; d. July 3, 1844 ; 2d, Jackson, Mich., *Charles French*, and lives in Rives, Mich. ; children, Boyden : [1.] Julia E., b. July 3, 1838 ; d. June, 30, 1872. [2.] Ellen Delight, b. Aug. 30, 1840 ; m. Ann Arbor, Mich., May 30, 1865, Henry Walter Nichols, he b. there, Jan. 2, 1838 ; they *adopted* Julius S. Kimberly, b. Apr. 22, 1872.

1734.* vi. LYSANDER, b. Fabius, July 21, 1822.

Mr. Sears was a farmer, lived' in Fabius, Onondaga co., N. Y., where all his children were born, and removed in 1829 to Ann Arbor, Mich.

804.

AHIRA SEARS[6] [*Roland*₅ *Zach.*[4], *Jos.*[3], *Silas*[2], *Rich.*[1]], b. Ashfield, Mass., Dec. 12, 1783; d. there, Jan. 13, 1870, æ. 86; m. Ash., Apr. 4, 1815, *Aurora Griffith*, she b. Haddam, Ct., Nov., 1791; d. Shelburne Falls, Mass., Mar. 17, 1881, æ. 89. Children:

1735.   i. THOMAS CONANT, b. Ash., Nov. 22, 1815; d. unm., Sep. 26, 1883.
1736.   ii. DARWIN DWIGHT, b. Ash., Aug. 11, 1818; m. July 16, 1845, *Huldah J. Thomas.*
1737. iii. SALLY, b. Ash., Aug. 11, 1820; m. June 8, 1854, *Enos Hall*, son of Joseph H., lived in Ash.; child, HALL: [1.] Ellen T.
1738.   iv. JOSHUA GRIFFITH, b. Ash., Sep. 5, 1822; m. East Dennis, Mass., May 16, 1854, *Hannah C. Sears*, No. 1327, and lives in Shelburne Falls, Mass.
1739.   v. BETSY JANE, b. Ash., Nov. 15, 1824.
1740.   vi. HARRIET BENNETT, b. Ash., Aug. 13, 1827; m. Nov. 29, 1849, *Onslow G. Spellman*, and lives in Williamsburg, Mass.

Mr. Sears was a farmer, lived and died on the old homestead, Cape street, Ashfield.

805.

Lt. PETER SEARS[6] [*Roland*₅ *Zach.*[4], *Jos.*[3], *Silas*[2], *Rich.*[1]], b. Ashfield, Mass., Aug. 23, 1787; d. Northfield, Mich., Jan. 18, 1867, æ. 80; m. Ash., Mar. 15, 1808, *Lucy Fuller*, she b. there, Feb. 22, 1789; d. North., Jan. 23, 1875, æ. 86. Children:

1741.   i. THANKFUL, b. Ash., Feb. 3, 1809; m. *Orville Barnes*, and lives in Ann Arbor, Mich.; children, BARNES: [1.] Lucy Ann, m. —— Tubbs. [2.] Emily, m. —— Moore. [3.] Elizabeth, m. —— Alvord. [4.] Albert.
1742.* ii. PETER, b. Ash., June 3, 1811.

1743. iii. MARY ANN, b. Ash., Sep. 1, 1813; m. there, *Abram Moe*, and d. Adrian, Mich., Aug. 15, 1877; children, MOE: [1.] Orville. [2.] Martha, m. —— Sperry. [3.] George. [4.] Thomas. [5.] Alice. [6.] Ida.

1744.* iv. SOLOMON F., b. Ash., June 22, 1816.

1745.* v. SAMUEL D., b. Ash., Oct. 9, 1818.

1746. vi. RUSSELL, b. Ash., Apr. 5, 1821; served 6 mos. in 26th Regt. Mich. Vols., and d. of small-pox in Louisville, Ky., Feb. 18, 1864.

1747.* vii. GEORGE, b. Charlemont, Mass., Mar. 13, 1824.

1748. viii. LEWIS C., b. Charl., Nov. 13, 1826; d. Chelsea, Mich., Oct. 1, 1870.

1749. ix. WILLIAM FRANKLIN, b. Webster, Mich., Sep. 22, 1829; d. Boulder, Col., Oct. 19, 1875.

1750. x. JOHN, b. Webster, Oct. 31, 1832; lives in Leadville, Col.

Peter Sears was a farmer, lived for a time in Charlemont, Mass., and removed to Ann Arbor, Mich., in 1826, where he died in 1867, on the farm which he purchased of the government, (and now in Northfield.)

His commission as Lieut., 5th Regt., dated Apr. 10, 1818, and signed by Gov. John Brooks of Mass., is in possession of his son Solomon F., who has preserved many ancient family letters and papers.

806.

ROLAND SEARS[6] [*Roland[5], Zach.[4], Joseph[3], Silas[2], Rich.[1]*], b. Ashfield, Mass., Feb. 3, 1789; d. Clay, N. Y., Apr. 16, 1872; m. Feb. 10, 1815, *Experience Clarke*, she b. Jan. 7, 1791; d. Clay, May 23, 1833; 2d, Dec. 18, 1833, *Hepsibah Hill.* Children:

By *Experience:*

1751.* i. SILAS C., b. Dec. 20, 1815.

1752. ii. EMILY, b. Oct. 14, 1819; m. Apr., 1835, *Stephen Hinckley*, and lives in Pennelsville, N. Y.

1753. iii. BETSY, b. Aug. 14, 1826; m. Jan. 1, 1845, *George Hills*, and d. Aug. 1, 1864.

1754. iv. MARIA, b. Jan. 14, 1831; m. Apr. 12, 1854, *James Osborne*, and d. Pennelsville, N. Y., Sep. 14, 1854.

By *Hepsibah:*

1755.* v. WARREN J., b. Clay, Jan. 14, 1836.

Mr. Sears served during the war of 1812, and subsequently removed to Clay, Onon. co., N. Y., where his widow was living, with her son Warren J., in 1884, æ. 80, in receipt of a pension from the U. S.

807.

Dr. THOMAS SEARS[6] [*Roland₅ Zach.*[4], *Joseph*[3], *Silas*[2], *Rich.*[1]], b. Ashfield, Mass., Jan. 29, 1791; d. Chelsea, Mich., Aug. 25, 1839, æ. 48; m. Goshen, Mass., May 11, 1815, *Sophia James*, dau. of Capt. Malachi J., she b. there Nov. 18, 1791; d. Chelsea, Jan. 16, 1879, æ. 87.   Children:

1756.   i. Darwin Rush, b. Peru, Mass., Jan. 30, 1816; d. there, Apr. 5, 1817.
1757.* ii. Claudius Wistar, b. Peru, Nov. 8, 1817.
1758.   iii. Frances Maria, b. Peru, June 1, 1819; m. *Wm. S. Martin*, who d.; she lives in Reading, Mich.; child, Martin : [1.] Dau., m. Frank Perry, and lives Jefferson, Texas.
1759.   iv. Sophia Antoinette, b. Peru, Feb. 13, 1821; m. Dr. *Alex'r Ewing*, who d.; she lives Chelsea, Mich.
1760.   v. Thomas Spencer, b. Peru, Mar. 9, 1823; d. there, Sep. 15.
1761.   vi. Clarissa Cecilia, b. Canaan Four Corners, N. Y., July 28, 1824; m. *Henry H. Noble*, and d. Elk Rapids, Mich., Feb. 4, 1868.
1762.   vii. Thomas Spencer, b. Can. Four Cor., Oct. 14, 1826; m. Chelsea, Mich., Dec. 23, 1858, *Anna E. Congdon;* is a farmer and banker in Chelsea, Mich.; no children.
1763.   viii. Elizabeth Lyman, b. Can. Four Cor., Sep. 18, 1828; m. *Freeman M. Rowley*, Beloit, Iowa.
1764.   ix. Sarah James, b. Can. Four Cor., Apr. 8, 1831; m. *Edwin A. Rowley*, who d.; she lives in Beloit, Ia.
1765.   x. Mary Robinson, b. Can. Four Cor., Apr. 22, 1835; d. there, Jan. 24, 1837.

Dr. Sears was educated in Ashfield Academy, and studied medicine with Dr. Peter Bryant of Cummington, Mass., grad. Mass. Gen. Hospital, Boston, and practiced in Peru, Mass., at Canaan Four Corners, N. Y., and in Chelsea, Washtenaw co., Mich., where he died in 1839.

810.

ZACHARIAH SEARS[6] [*Jos.*[5], *Zach.*[4], *Jos.*[3], *Silas*[2], *Rich.*[1]], b. Yarmouth, Mass., Dec. 29, 1783; d. Dennis, Aug. 25, 1845;

m. there, Dec. 2, 1813, *Olive Sears*, No. 915, dau. of Joseph
S. of Brewster, she b. Dec. 1, 1790; d. July 3, 1872. Children :

1766.   i. JOSEPH BAINBRIDGE, b. Den., Oct. 25, 1814; d. at
        sea, Oct. 9, 1836.
1767.   ii. ISAAC H., b. Den., Oct. 7, 1816 ; d. Apr. 27, 1838.
1768.* iii. BARZILLIA, b. Den., Nov. 22, 1822.
1769.* iv. BENJAMIN, b. Den., Oct. 27, 1826.
1770.   v. ELIZABETH LOWE, b. Den., Nov. 9, 1828; m. Aug.
        15, 1848, Capt. *Milton P. Hedge*, son of John and
        Nabby (Sears) H., he b. Aug. 15, 1825, lives in East
        Den.; children, HEDGE: [1.] Milton Lee, b. Mar. 6,
        1855 ; d. young. [2.] John M., b. Aug. 3, 1857; m.
        Dec. 6, 1879, Hattie Phelps, she b. Dec. 6, 1861 ; is a
        lumber dealer at Clear Creek, Neb. [3.] Joseph, b.
        Jan. 27, 1860; m. Aug. 22, 1882, Julia Smalley, she b.
        Sep., 1861 ; runs a sheep ranch in Cambridge, Kan.
        [4.] George Sears, b. July 4, 1865.

Was a mariner, and lived in East Dennis; was insane many
years previous to his death.

811.

Dea. HENRY SEARS[6] [*Jos.*[5], *Zach.*[4], *Jos.*[3], *Silas*[2], *Rich.*[1]],
b. Yarmouth, Mass., May 5, 1785; d. East Dennis, May 28,
1823, æ. 38, gr.-st., Br. ; m. (pub. Den., Apr. 6, 1807,) *Rhoda
Howes*, dau. of Joseph H., she b. Den., Apr. 2, 1787; d. June
14, 1846. Children :

1771. i. CALVIN, b. Den., Jan. 11, 1808; m. Brewster, June
      23, 1851, *Phebe Cole*, dau. of Elkanah C. of Eastham,
      and d. s. p., Dec. 11, 1881.
1772. ii. CHARLES, b. Den , Oct. 26, 1809; d. Rondout, N.
      J., Sep. 15, 1832, æ. 23, gr.-st., Br.
1773. iii. HITTY, b. Den., Mar. 20, 1813; d. Jan. 18, 1842,
      æ. 28, gr.-st.
1774. iv. LYDIA H., b. Den., Nov. 28, 1815 ; d. Feb. 27, 1839,
      æ. 23, gr.-st.
1775. v. ZEBINA, b. Den., Dec. 9, 1818; d. Dec. 16, 1867.
1776. vi. REBECCA, b. Den., Apr. 11, 1822; m. Dec. 1, 1846,
      Rev. *Chas. Hammond*, he b. Petersham, Mass., Feb. 26,
      1819 ; is of Conf. M. E. Ch., and lives West Thompson,
      Ct.; children, HAMMOND : [1.] Sabrina D., b. Oct. 15,
      1847. [2.] Charles Henry, b. Jan. 11, 1851; m. Mar. 9,

1875, Cynthia B. Smalley of So. Harwich; is a book-keeper for Washburn & Moen, Worcester, Mass. [3.] Lizzie J., b. May 23, 1857; m. July 19, 1881, W. A. Dickenson of Springfield, Mass., and had, i. Daisy Maude, b. Apr. 13, 1882.

Mr. Sears lived in East Dennis; was a sea captain and a Deacon.

813.

Capt. ZEBINA SEARS⁶ [*Jos.⁵, Zach.⁴, Jos.³, Silas², Rich.¹*], b. Yarmouth, Mass., Mar. 11, 1790; d. East Dennis, Aug. 27, 1835, æ. 45, gr.-st., Br. ; m. Aug. 9, 1812, by Rev. Thos. Baldwin, to *Elizabeth Lloyd Dexter* of Boston, she b. May 6, 1796; d. there, Apr. 28, 1880.   Children :

1777.* i. CHARLES ZEBINA HARRIS, b. Boston, May 11, 1813.
1778. ii. HANNAH ELIZABETH, b. Boston, Apr. 20, 1817 ; d. unm., Harrisburg, Pa., June 6, 1882.
1779.* iii. JOSEPH HENRY, b. Boston, Mar. 13, 1821.
1780.* iv. ALFRED FRANCIS, b. Boston, Nov. 10, 1826.
1781. v. EDWIN DEXTER, b. Boston, Sep. 23, 1828 ; d. Pensacola, Fla., Mar., 1860.
1782. vi. FRANKLIN A., b. Boston, Oct. 18, 1830 ; d. there, Mar. 30, 1868.
1783. vii. AUGUSTUS M., b. Boston, May 30, 1833 ; d. there, July 27, 1835.

Mr. Sears was a sea captain, and resided on Washington place, Fort Hill, Boston, but died in East Dennis, in the same house in which he was born.

His children have a tradition that they descend from Col. Isaac Sears of New York ; —— the Lloyds of Boston were connections of Paschal N. Smith, who married Hester Sears, dau. of Col. Isaac S., and their mother was perhaps of that family.

814.

JOSEPH SEARS⁶ [*Jos.⁵, Zach.⁴, Jos.³, Silas², Rich.¹*], b. Yarmouth, Mass., June 24, 1792 ; (June 23, 1793, Fam. Bible,) d. Fayette, Mo., Feb. 10, 1852; m. Oct. 23, 1817, *Elizabeth Loe*, dau. of Thomas and Fanny L., she b. Dec. 27, 1800; d.

Sep. 27, 1841; 2d, Nov. 10, 1842, *Ann Maria Turner*, who d. Fayette, Nov. 10, 1860. Children :

By *Elizabeth:*

1784. i. CLARISSA, b. Oct. 16, 1819 ; m. May 31, 1838, *Robt. H. Jordan ;* children, JORDAN : [1.] William H., a minister in Carrollton, Mo.

1785. ii. THANKFUL A., b. Oct. 17, 1821 ; m. May 31, 1838, *Edw'd Currell.*

1786. iii. FANNY, b. Jan. 18, 1824 ; m. Oct. 22, 1843, *Chas. Wesley Baker*, and d. Oct. 6, 1844.

1787.* iv. HENRY, b. Nov. 4, 1825.

1788. v. ELIZABETH, b. Jan. 14, 1828 ; m. *John G. Treadway*, and d. Kansas City, Mo.

1789. vi. MARY, b. Apr. 27, 1830; d. unm.

1790. vii. AUGUSTUS, b. May 11, 1832; d. unm., Fayette, Mo., Feb. 18, 1884.

1791. viii. THOMAS, b. May 22, 1834; d. about 1840.

1792. ix. MIRANDA, b. June 5, 1836 ; m.

1793. x. JOSEPH G., b. July 26, 1838; d. unm., Excelsior Springs, Mo., 1884.

1794.* xi. PETER R., b. Jan. 2, 1841.

By *Ann :*

1795.* xii. JOHN T., b. Sep. 18, 1843.

1796. xiii. EDWARD J., b. Sep. 13, 1845 ; d. Aug. 17, 1846.

1797. xiv. KATE, b. Aug. 31, 1847 ; m. Cyrus Fox, and lives in Richmond, Ky.

1798.* xv. ROBERT C., b. Apr. 27, 1849.

1799. xvi. SQUIRE A., b. May 30, 1852 ; lives in Kansas City, Mo., unm.

Mr. Sears removed to Missouri, and settled on a farm in Fayette, Howard co.; was a member of Meth. Ch.

816.

PETER SEARS[6] [*Jos.[5], Zach.[4], Jos.[3], Silas[2], Rich.[1]*], b. East Dennis, Mass., May 9, 1796; d. Geneva, Ill., ab't 1859 ; m. July 24, 1824, *Sarah Griffith Clark*, she b. Westminster, Vt., Feb. 11, 1801; d. 1837; dau. of Abraham and Temperance (Hallet) C. Child :

1800. i. FRANKLIN, d. inf.

Mr. Sears was for many years a partner with Scotto Clark in the wholesale and retail hardware business on Kilby st., Bos-

ton, and removed with him to Geneva, Ill., where he died
about 1859.

817.

ROLAND SEARS[6] [*Jos.*[5], *Zach.*[4], *Jos.*[3], *Silas*[2], *Rich.*[1]], b.
East Dennis, Mass., Nov. 23, 1798; d. there, May 24, 1857;
m. July 5, 1838, *Mehitable Sears Berry*, dau. of Watson B. of
Belfast, Me., she b. Brewster, Mass., July 10, 1808, (was for
10 years from 1828 in the family of Richard Sears of Chatham, as companion to Madame S., and now lives 29 Quincy st.,
East Somerville, Mass.)   Children :

1801.   i. SARAH FRANCIS, b. Dennis, Apr. 2, 1839 ; m. May
          8, 1861, *Wm. Henry Souther*, he b. Aug. 24, 1836 ; is
          in gas-fixture business, Brooklyn, N. Y.; children,
          SOUTHER: [1.] Henry, b. Jan., 1863. [2.] Maria Louisa,
          b. Jan. 2, 1868.
1802.   ii. LYDIA ALICE, b. Den., July 7, 1840 ; m. *Chas. H.
          Nason*, a tailor of Boston ; no children.
1803.* iii. JOSEPH BAINBRIDGE, b. Den., Apr. 18, 1842.
1804.   iv. RICHARD FRANKLIN, b. Den., Dec. 22, 1843 ; m.
          Emma Bort ; is of firm of Sears & Co., lumber and rub-
          ber dealers, Para, Brazil.
1805.* v. GEORGE FULTON, b. Den., Feb. 20, 1847.
1806.   vi. ELIZABETH WATSON, b. Den., Jan. 3, 1849 ; m.
          1875, *Jas. Carter Huston*, clerk in custom-house, Boston ;
          children, HUSTON: [1.] George Arthur, b. Feb. 20, 1876.
          [2.] Clarence Eugene, b. Dec. 10, 1878.
1807.   vii. WILLIAM HAYMAN, b. Den., Aug. 12, 1850 ; d.
          July 24, 1851.
1808. viii. MARY HARRIET, b. Den., Sep. 10, 1852 ; m. George
          Arthur Fullerton.

Mr. Sears lived in the old homestead in Dennis, which had
been occupied in turn by his great-gr.-father, gr.-father and
father.

820.

ISAAC SEARS[6] [*Steph.*[5], *Jos.*[4], *Jos.*[3], *Silas*[2], *Rich.*[1]], bap.
Harwich, Mass., Oct. 19, 1766; was found dead in the road,
Mar., 1816 ; m. Chatham, Nov. 3, 1784, *Sarah Eldridge* of C.,
she bap. and adm. to Ch., Den., July 10, 1796.   Children :

1809.* i. MULFORD, b. Den., Nov. 1, 1785,
1810.   ii. PATTY, b. Den., Nov. 1, 1785, *gemini*,   } bap. July
1811.* iii. ELDRIDGE, b. Den., Sep. 25, 1790,   } 10, 1796.

822.

LARNED SEARS[6] [*Steph.*[5], *Jos.*[4], *Jos.*[3], *Silas*[2], *Rich.*[1]], b. East Yarmouth, Mass., Feb., 1766; bap. Har., Oct. 19; d. Oct. 28, 1822; m. Yar., Jan. 24, 1788, *Kezia Baker*, dau. of Eldridge B. of Yar., who was adm. to Ch., Den., Aug. 21, 1806, and d. June 3, 1857. Children:

1812.* i. DAVID, b. Yar., Dec. 7, 1789.
1813. ii. URIAH, b. Yar., Feb. 8, 1791; m. Oxford, Mass., *Chloe Rawson*, and d. Sep. 22, 1877. He was for many years a sea captain. On a return voyage in 1812, he was captured by a British cruiser, taken to Gravesend, Eng., and imprisoned a year.
1814. iii. LAVINIA, b. Yar., Mar. 25, 1793; (another account says, Apr. 25, 1794;) m. Yar., *Josiah Baker*, and d. Sep. 22, 1867.
1815.* iv. LARNED B., b. Den., Apr. 29, 1795; (1796, another account.)
1816. v. MERCY, b. Den., Oct. 8, 1797 or 98; d. unm., Feb. 15, 1826.
1817. vi. SERVILLA, b. Den., Apr. 18, 1801; d. unm., Apr. 15, 1835.
1818. vii. ROZILLA, b. Den., Sep. 9, 1803; m. *John B. Darling* of Killingly, Ct.; was a milliner, and d. Sep. 8, 1875.
1819. viii. ELIZA, b. Den., July 9, 1805; m. *George Geer* of Griswold, Ct., and d. Feb. 17, 1822.
1820. ix. KEZIA, b. Den., Jan. 14, 1808; m. *John Bartlett* of Killingly, Ct., and d. Mar. 15, 1875.
1821. x. OLIVE, b. Den., Apr. 23, 1810; d. unm., Mar. 23, 1879.
1822. xi. SUSAN, b. Den., Apr. 18, 1814; was a milliner with her sister, Rozilla, 30 years, and now lives unm. in Putnam, Ct.
1823. xii. DUTEE, b. Oxford, May 31, 1817; bap. Den., Aug., 1824; m. *Hannah P. Chase*, Southbridge, Mass., and d. Dec. 21, 1879; was a jeweler in Killingly, Ct.

Larned Sears followed the sea, was resident of Harwich when married, was chosen Collector of Dennis, Mar. 3, 1795, removed to Oxford, Mass., between 1814 and 1817, and died there. After his death his widow returned to Dennis.

823.

LEVI SEARS[6] [*Steph.[5], Jos.[4], Jos.[3], Silas[2], Rich.[1]*], b. Harwich, Mass., Dec. 13, 1770; d. Dennis, Dec. 5, 1827, gr.-st.,
W. Br.; m. Har., Dec., 1796, *Jerusha Foster*, dau. of John F.
of Har., she b. 1774; d. 1858.   Children :

1824.   i. JONATHAN, b. Har., May 30, 1798; bap. Aug. 19;
m. Nov. 10, 1864, *Sarah Hallet* of Yar., dau. of Aaron
and Phebe (Sears) Crowell, and widow of Barnabas Hallet, she b. Mar. 4, 1800; d. July 10, 1871, æ. 71; he d.
July 18, 1871, æ. 73, gr.-st., W. Br.
1825.   ii. ALMIRA, b. Har., Apr. 27, 1801; bap. June; d.
Aug. 20, 1863, gr.-st.
1826.   iii. LABAN, b. Brewster, Oct. 5, 1805; bap. Nov. 17;
d. Aug. 10, 1819, gr.-st.
1827.   iv. LEVI, b. Br., Aug. 23, 1812; m. Feb. 10, 1850,
Lucy H. Homer of Den., she b. Apr. 7, 1822.
1828.*   v. LUTHER, b. Br., 1815.
1829.   vi. *Dau.*, b. Br.
1830.* vii. JOSIAH F., b. Den., Dec. 12, 1818.

825.

STEPHEN SEARS[6] [*Steph.[5], Jos.[4], Jos.[3], Silas[2], Rich.[1]*],
m. Yarmouth, Mass., Apr. 3, 1791, *Lydia Sears*, No. 861,
dau. of Stephen S. of Yar., she b. July 24, 1771; was received in full com'n, Har., July 14, 1793.   Children :

1831.   i. BARZILLAI, d. May 19, 1793, gr.-st., W. Br.
1832.   ii. WARREN, bap. Har., 1795 ; not ment'd in father's
will, 1819.
1833.* iii. BARZILLAI, bap. Har., Oct. 19, 1805.
1834.* iv. STEPHEN.
1835.   v. CLARISSA, m. —— *Miller*.
1836.   vi. LYDIA, (perh. m. *Rufus Ellis*, he. b. 1803.)
1837. vii. ELIZA.

Stephen Sears removed to Sandwich, Mass.
His will, dated Apr. 17, 1819, was presented for probate,
Nov. 14, 1826, by his widow Lydia Sears, and Benj. Burgess.

827.

Capt. JOSEPH SEARS[6] [*Steph.[5], Jos.[4], Jos.[3], Silas[2],
Rich.[1]*], b. Aug. 26, 1776; d. Brewster, Feb. 22, 1843, æ. 66,

gr.-st., Br.; m. Dennis, Dec. 19, 1799, *Marabah Howes*, dau. of Elkanah H., she b. there, Dec. 14, 1779 ; d. Br., Apr. 27, 1857, æ. 77 yrs. 4 mos. 13 days, gr.-st., Br.   Children :

1838. i. CAROLINE, b. Har., May 24, 1801 ; m. —— *Slocum*.
1839. ii. DESIRE, b. Har., Sep. 9, 1802 ; m. *Isaiah Parlow*, and d. Mar. 15, 1877.
1840. iii. JOANNA, b. Br., June 18, 1804 ; m. *Charles Briggs*, and d. Nov. 20, 1840.
1841. iv. LORING, b. Br., Nov. 29, 1805 ; d. unm., Aug. 20, 1826.
1842.* v. FRANKLIN, b. Br., Aug. 8, 1808.
1843. vi. BELINDA, b. Br., June 23, 1810 ; m. (pub. Yar., Apr. 30, 1831,) *Wm. Homer* of Dennisport.
1844.* vii. FREDERIC, b. Br., June 30, 1812.
1845.* viii. JOSEPH ELLERY, b. Br., Sep. 4, 1814.
1846. ix. HARRIET NEWELL, b. Br., Mar. 16, 1818 ; m. *Thos. Snow Crosby* of Worcester, Mass.
1847. x. EDWIN, b. Br., Jan. 12, 1820 ; d. Sep. 21, 1822.

Was a sea captain.

829.

WASHINGTON SEARS[6] [*Steph.*[5], *Jos.*[4], *Jos.*[3], *Silas*[2], *Rich.*[1]], b. Harwich, Mass., Oct. 26, 1781 ; m. Brewster, Mar. 24, 1805, *Betsy Mack* of Br.   Children :

1848. i. LYMAN, b. Br., Oct. 18, 1806 ; m. *Hannah* ——, and had Elizabeth V., who m. Plymouth, Apr. 30, 1856, Stephen H. Jackson of Duxbury.
1849.* ii. GEORGE, b. Br., Oct. 2, 1808.
1850.* iii. WILLIAM, b. Br., Sep. 6, 1810.
1851. iv. SUKEY, b. Br., Dec. 19, 1812.
1852. v. FRANCIS, b. Br., June 4, 1815.
1853. vi. WASHINGTON, b. Br., Dec. 12, 1820.
1854. vii. CHARLES, b. Br., June 9, 1823.

Mr. Sears removed to Plymouth, Mass.

831.

Dea. ROLAND SEARS[6] [*Freeman*[5], *Roland*[4], *Jos.*[3], *Silas*[2], *Rich.*[1]], b. Hardwick, Mass., Dec. 24, 1762 ; d. Greenwich, Mass., Mar. 22, 1851, æ. 89 ; m. Barre, Mass., Nov. 29,

38

1785, *Mary Fletcher*, she b. there, July 1, 1767; d. Greenwich, Feb. 1, 1849, æ. 82. Children : .

1855.   i. Freeman, b. Green., Sep. 15, 1786 ; d. Aug. 24,
          1803.
1856.   ii. Polly, b. Green., June 2, 1789; m. there, Oct. 12,
          1809, *Levi Mellen*, he b. there, Dec. 2, 1777. She was a
          favorite child, and partook largely of her father's char-
          acteristics ; conscientious in the highest degree, loyal
          and loving to friends, and to truth and religion. A friend
          said of her, " she was like a tower set upon a hill, whose
          light reflected far below the horizon of most people's ex-
          istence ; " children, Mellen : [1.] Mary A., b. Aug. 1,
          1811 ; m. Oct. 29, 1838, Alfred Bond, he b. Wilbraham,
          Mass., Dec. 31, 1811, lived in Detroit, Mich. [2.] So-
          phronia R., b. May 28, 1813 ; m. Barre, Mass., Sep. 15,
          1841, Wm. R. Haskell, he b. New Salem, Mass., Nov.
          18, 1813. [3.] Amy A., b. July 25, 1816; m. Green-
          wich, Sep. 30, 1834, Gregory Ellis, he b. New Salem,
          Dec. 22, 1809 ; rem. to Warren, Mass., and Hartford, Ct.,
          had, i. Augustine L., b. July 15, 1835 ; m. Hartford,
          Oct. 13, 1859, Abigail Daniels of H. ii. Julia A., b.
          Jan. 29, 1838 ; m. Har., T. Jefferson Boardman of
          Weathersfield, Ct., and d. 1858. iii. Mary Charlena, b.
          Sep. 11, 1843 ; m. Hart., Oct. 25, 1861, T. Jefferson
          Boardman, her brother-in-law, and lives in H. iv. Hat-
          tie Mellen, b. June 25, 1848 ; m. Hart., Nov. 16, 1869,
          F. Crayton Sturtevant, he b. Hartland, Vt., Dec. 13,
          1838, lives in Hartford, Ct. v. Kate Florence, b. July
          1, 1851, lives in Boston. [4.] Charles W., b. June 29,
          1818 ; m. Fitzwilliam, N. H., Apr. 21, 1840, Mary B.
          Blood, she b. Sterling, Mass., May 13, 1814 ; was a min-
          ister, and d. Taunton, Mass., Oct. 22, 1866. [5.] Wil-
          liam Roland, b. June 29, 1822 ; m. Milford, Mass., Dec.
          9, 1844, Diana Nelson, she b. there. [6.] Harriet A., b.
          Mar. 20, 1828 ; m. Warren, Mass., Nov. 26, 1846, James
          M. Ward, he b. Bradford, N. H.; and d. June 7, 1848.
1857. iii. Jonathan Fletcher, b. Green., May 6, 1791; m.
          Sally Towne, and d. July 8, 1849 ; Rep. to Leg., 1835–
          36 ; a dau. m. Dr. Vining, and had issue.
1858. iv. Anna Fletcher, b. Green., May 16, 1795; m. Nov.
          23, 1820, *Smith Robinson*, he b. Mar. 31, 1795 ; d. Nov.
          7, 1871, æ. 76; she d. Jan. 17, 1828, æ. 33; children,
          Robinson : [1.] Franklin Smith, b. Feb. 20, 1822 ; d.

Aug. 3, 1826. [2.] Harriet Emilia, b. Nov. 26, 1823; m. Enfield, Mass., May 23, 1844, Benj. F. Kendrick, and lives in Amherst, Mass. [3.] Mary Relief, b. May 26, 1825; m. Enfield, May 23, 1844, Horace Ward, he b. Belchertown, Mass., Sep. 3, 1839; lived in Amherst, and had, i. Anna Howard, b. May 6, 1845. ii. Mary Sears, b. June 5, 1846; m. Frank Coburn of Lowell. iii. Harriet Frances, b. Apr. 5, 1848; m. Chas. Harrington of Worcester. iv. Kate, b. May 26, 1849; m. Whitfield Drake of Knoxville, Tenn. v. Fannie Louise, b. June 13, 1852; d. Aug., 1853. vi. Alice, b. Apr. 30, 1857; m. Alfred Bailey of Utica, N. Y. vii. Josephine, b. Oct. 20, 1860. [4.] Anna Amanda, b. Dec. 11, 1827; m. 1852, Horace Taylor of Granby, Mass., and lives in Rockford, Ill.

1859. v. RELIEF, b. Green., Mar. 2, 1798; m. *Calvin Sears*, No. 1865.

1860. vi. EMILIA, b. Green., May 1, 1800; d. Mar. 21, 1814.

1861. vii. ALPHEUS, b. Green., Oct. 24, 1802; d. Aug. 26, 1803.

1862.*viii. ALPHEUS FREEMAN, b. Green., May 7, 1808.

1863. ix. EMILIA, b. Green., Aug. 5, 1814.

" A tall, erect figure, very kindly and benevolent to the poor, industrious, and with large executive ability, claiming that six hours' sleep was enough for any man.

" He had a sterling sense of honesty, and fair dealing.

" He was a patriot, and loved his country, enlisting in its service when but a mere lad of sixteen, and he often astonished his grand-children and friends with recitals of their privations and sufferings during the war.

Roland Sears of Greenwich, Hamp. co., Mass., 17 years, 5 feet, 8 inches in height, dark complexion, arrived Springfield, July 18, 1780, for service in northern army; he had previously served, Aug. 17 to Aug. 21, 1777, in Capt. Ephraim Jennings' Co., Col. David Field's Regt. at Bennington, 30 miles; Sept. 12, 1777, to Jan. 4, 1778, in Capt. Eben. Newell's Co., Col. Key's Regt.; and July 21 to Aug. 25, 1779, at New London, Ct., in Capt. Elisha Dwight's Co., Col. Elisha Porter's Regt., 85 miles from home. In 1787 he took the oath of allegiance, having been concerned in Shay's rebellion. His name appears in census of 1840, as a Revolutionary pensioner, then aged 77.

" Dea. Roland," as he was called, to distinguish him from his brothers, " Dea. Andrew " and " Dea. John," who lived near by, was a very conscientious, religious man, quite after the Pilgrim type.

"He offered grace at every meal.

"With the greatest reverence I recall my grand-father on his knees in the family prayers, in his earnest and devout expressions of gratitude and thankfulness; and his confessions of shortcomings. And the closing words of the prayer have never left my childish memory, and I often find myself closing the petition with them: 'And now Lord, what wait we for? Our wants and complaints are spread before Thee, and Thou knowest what we need, better than we can think, or even ask.'

"Many years ago, in a great movement in the Congregational Church, Dea. Sears avowed himself a believer in one God, a Unitarian; quite a grief to his wife, a sweet Christian lady.

"Later on, they both accepted the faith, that evil can never perpetuate itself, in the other life, and as the result every soul shall confess, and glorify God forever."

832.

Dea. ANDREW HASKELL SEARS[6] [*Freeman*[5], *Roland*[4], *Jos.*[3], *Silas*[2], *Rich.*[1]], b. Hardwick, Mass., Mar. 29, 1765; d. Apr. 14, 1846, æ. 81; m. Greenwich, Mass., Mar. 14, 1787, *Rachel Stetson*, who d. there, Aug. 2, 1835, æ. 67; 2d, *Rachel Leonard* of Oakham, Mass., who d. Oct. 14, 1864, æ. 84. Children:

By *Rachel S.:*

1864.	i. HETTY, b. Green., Feb. 13, 1788; m. July 6, 1808, *Daniel Mills* of G., and d. May, 1857.

1865.* ii. CALVIN, b. Green., Oct. 30, 1790.

1866.	iii. CYNTHIA, b. Green., Apr. 13, 1792; m., and d. in Ohio.

1867.	iv. MERCY, b. Green., Oct. 13, 1795; m. *Artemas Loring* of Petersham, Mass., a farmer, and d. there.

1868.* v. TURNER, b. Green., Apr. 4, 1798.

1869.	vi. CLARK, b. Green., Apr. 7, 1800; m. —— —— of Petersham, and d. Charlestown, Mass., Aug., 1863.

1870.	vii. LYDIA, b. Green., Apr. 17, 1802; m. Oct., 1823, Capt. *Norman Pease* of Hartford, Ct., and d. Oct. 4, 1833.

1871.	viii. MARY FLETCHER, b. Green., Aug. 16, 1804; m. *Hiram Bundy* of Woodstock, Ct., and d. DeKalb, Ill., Oct., 1870.

1872.* ix. ANDREW HASKELL, b. Green., Oct. 10, 1806.
1873. x. PHEBE POWERS, b. Green., Apr. 17, 1809; m. *Sam'l Holt*, a portrait painter of Hartford, Ct., and d. Feb. 14, 1831.

Mr. Sears was a Deacon in the Church for many years, and led the choir 40 years.

He was a farmer and cooper, and a very exemplary man.

841.

JOSEPH SEARS[6] [*Barnabas[5], Roland[4], Jos.[3], Silas[2], Rich.[1]*], b. Apr. 12, 1769; d. Pelham, Mass., May 14, 1801, æ. 33; m. —— ——. Child:

1874. i. JAMES S., b. Pelham; d. s. p.

Roland Sears administered upon the estate of Joseph Sears of Pelham, and Moses Sears was appointed guardian of James S. Sears, minor son of Joseph S.

842.

MOSES SEARS[6] [*Barnabas[5], Roland[4], Jos.[3], Silas[2], Rich.[1]*], b. Hardwick, Mass., Apr. 22, 1771; d. Otisco, Onon. co., N. Y., Sep. 11, 1805, æ. 35; m. —— *Clark*, (who m. 2d, —— *Taylor*, and removed to Franklin, Pa., and had son, Judge Charles T.) Children:

1875. i. *Son.*
1876. ii. *Dau.;* lives in Cleveland, Ohio.
1877. iii. *Dau.*

847.

BARNABAS SEARS[6] [*Barnabas[5], Roland[4], Jos.[3], Silas[2], Rich.[1]*], b. Greenwich, Mass., May 1, 1782; d. Lockport, N. Y., Oct. 29, 1856, æ. 74; m. Bennington, Vt., Sep. 3, 1810, *Lucy E. Stone*, dau. of Archibald and Rhoda (Dewey) S., she b. there, Dec. 25, 1782; d. Lockport, Feb. 18, 1874, æ. 92. Children:

1878. i. ANNIS, b. June 18, 1811; d. unm., June 5, 1833.
1879.* ii. ROWLAND, b. Scipio, N. Y., Mar. 24, 1816.

Mr. Sears, when a young man, was employed in the U. S. Arsenal in Springfield, Mass.

In 1811 he removed to Scipio, N. Y., and in 1827 to the "Holland Purchase," buying a large tract of land near Lockport, N. Y., and after 1829 resided permanently in the village until his death.

850.

BARNABAS SEARS[6] [*Elisha*[5], *Roland*[4], *Jos.*[3], *Silas*[2], *Rich.*[1]], b. Barre, Mass., June 11, 1777; d. Hardwick, Mass., Oct. 3, 1838, æ. 61; m. Barre, Oct. 21, 1800, *Abigail Witherell*, who d. Dec. 4, 1860, æ. 80. Children:

1880.   i. ASHBEL, b. Barre, June 28, 1801.
1881.* ii. SUMNER, b. Barre, Feb. 9, 1804.
1882. iii. ENOS, b. Barre, June 24, 1806.
1883. iv. ALONZO, b. Barre, Jan. 28, 1808.
1884.   v. MERCY, b. Barre, May 1, 1810; d. Apr. 19, 1825.
1885. vi. ARETHUSA, b. Barre, Dec. 13, 1816.
1886.* vii. BARNABAS, b. Barre, Aug. 12, 1819.
1887. viii. CAROLINE H., b. Barre, Apr. 15, 1831. (?1821.)

"Abigail Sears m. Chas. S. Smith of Barre, Sep. 21, 1841." (T. Rec.)

A grand-daughter of Barnabas Sears married Bishop James T. Peck of Meth. Epis. Ch.

855.

FRANKLIN SEARS[6] [*Elisha*[5], *Roland*[4], *Jos.*[3], *Silas*[2], *Rich.*[1]], b. Barre, Mass., Oct. 3, 1785; d. Livingston co., N. Y., Jan. 4, 1869, æ. 83; m. Groveland, N. Y., Dec. 9, 1819, *Elizabeth Shadders*, she b. Hagerstown, Md., Jan. 22, 1801; d. Moscow, N. Y., Feb. 9, 1872, æ. 71. Children:

1888.   i. *Dau.*, d. æ. 3 mos.
1889.* ii. EDMUND WINSLOW, b. Groveland, N.Y., Oct. 9, 1821.
1890. iii. ELIZABETH, b. Grove., m. *Harry Ewart*, and lives G.; no children.
1891. iv. WILLIAM WALLACE, b. Grove., Apr. 21, 1828; m. *Margaret Poorman*, had 2 sons and 3 daus., and lives Chatsworth, N. Y.
1892.   v. JANE MARIA, b. July 21, 1830; m. *D. T. Barnum*, and lives in Moscow, N. Y.; children, BARNUM: [1.] Daniel P., lives in Sparta, Ill. [2.] Benjamin, is a clerk in Barnum's Iron Works, Detroit, Mich. [3.] Dau., m. Rev. F. Gutelius, a Presb. Min. in Moscow.

1893. vi. JULIA A., b. Apr. 29, 1833; m. *Wm. Crawford*, who d.; she lives in Cuylerville, N. Y.
1894. vii. ELLEN, b. Oct. 26, 1835; d. Mar. 2, 1843.
1895. viii. MARY, b. Oct. 26, 1837; m. *Edward O. Bickford,* and d. 1861; had a dau. (he m. again).
1896. ix. MATILDA, d. inf.

Mr. Sears was a shoemaker; removed to Livingston co., N. Y., where all his children were born.
His wife and all her daughters were Presbyterians.

859.

STEPHEN SEARS[6] [*Steph.*[5], *Barnabas*[4], *Jos.*[3], *Silas*[2], *Rich.*[1]], b. Yarmouth, Mass., Oct. 2, 1765; d. East Dennis, Mass., May 24, 1851, æ. 85; m. Yar., Nov. 10, 1785, *Sarah Gorham*, dau. of David G., who d. Apr., 1811; was adm. Ch., E. Yar., Jan. 28, 1787; he m. 2d, —— ——, who d. Jan., 1825. Children:

By *Sarah :*
1897.   i. ELIZABETH, b. Yar., Aug. 20, 1786; bap. Jan. 28, 1787.
1898. ii. PRISCILLA, b. Yar., June 25, 1788; bap. Aug. 3, 1788; "gone to Meth.," June 22, 1817.
1899.* iii. BARNABAS, b. Yar., July 30, 1790; bap. Aug. 15.
1900. iv. LYDIA, b. Yar., Sep. 3, 1792; bap. Nov. 4; d. Oct. 1, 1826.
1901.   v. DAVID GORHAM, b. Den., Nov. 16, 1794; m. Yar., Nov. 30, 1822, *Nabby Miller.*
1902.* vi. ALMOND, (*Alfred*, Ch. Rec.) b. Den., May 1, 1798; bap. July 1, 1798.
1903. vii. STEPHEN, b. Den., Mar. 16, 1800; bap. May 18, and d. Dec. 8.
1904.* viii. STEPHEN, b. Den., July 5, 1804; bap. Dec. 2.

863.

JOHN SEARS[6] [*Rich.*[5], *Silas*[4], *Jos.*[3], *Silas*[2], *Rich.*[1]], b. (prob. in Mass.), Feb. 22, 1773; d. Monkton, Vt., Dec. 1, 1852, in 80th year; m. *Betsy Chapman*, she b. 1778; d. Monk., Oct. 28, 1842, in 65th year. Children:
1905.   i. EDMUND, b. Hinesburg, Vt., was drowned in Lewis' creek near Charlotte, Vt., æ. ab't 9 yrs.

1906.   ii. BETSY, b. Hines., d. æ. 3 mos.
1907.   iii. HARRIET, b. Hines., Apr. 7, 1798; m. there, Jan.
1, 1815, *Harvey Vidito,* he b. Cambridge, N. Y., July
16, 1796; was a carpenter, and d. Starksboro, Vt., Nov.
25, 1880, æ. 84; she d. Hines., Nov. 22, 1847, æ. 49;
" both good Methodists;" children, VIDITO: [1.] Cornelia, b. Oct. 1, 1816; m. Nov. 8, 1839, Prentiss Waldo,
he b. Moriah, N. Y., was a blacksmith and farmer, and a
prominent man in Meth. Ch.; had, i. Lucius, b. Mar.,
1841; d. inf. [2.] Melinda, b. Mar. 8, 1818; d. July
17, 1820. [3.] Clarinda, b. Jan. 22, 1821; m. Williston,
Vt., Feb. 18, 1841, Chester Wells, he b. there, a farmer;
she d. Columbus, Ohio, Aug. 7, 1842, æ. 21; had, i.
Harriet, b. July, 1842. [4.] Jane, b. Mar. 14, 1823;
d. unm., Williston, Vt., May 18, 1844. [5.] Harvey, b.
Apr. 14, 1825; d. San Francisco, Cal., Oct. 17, 1857.
[6.] Laura, b. Feb. 1, 1827; d. Williston, May 22, 1845;
[7.] Lucius, b. Feb. 1, 1827, *gemini;* d. Sep. 27, 1828.
[8.] Huldah, b. Dec. 28, 1828; d. Mar. 18, 1832. [9.]
Byron, b. Mar. 19, 1831; d. Mar. 19, 1832. [10.] Wel-
come, b. Sep. 12, 1833; d. July 4, 1849. [11.] Phila, b.
Apr. 18, 1836; m. Nov. 13, 1862, Alfred W. Bostwick of
Hines., he b. Aug. 15, 1815; d. s. p., Starksboro, Vt.,
Mar. 11, 1883. [12.] Elida, b. Mar. 2, 1838; d. Aug.
5, 1853.
1908.   iv. AURELIA, b. Hines., m. *Joseph Browne,* he b. Canada; lived in Charlotte, Vt.; she d. Dickinson, N. Y.;
children, BROWNE: [1.] Minerva, b. July 27, 1823; m.
Williston, Jan. 15, 1848, Thos. Bell, he b. Ottawa, Can.,
1820; lives in Sparta, Wis.; had, i. Thomas, b. Apr. 11,
1849; a book-keeper; m. Grand Rapids, Wis., 1878,
Julia Trace, she b. Wansum, Wis., 1845; d. 1885.
ii. Joseph, b. July 18, 1850; m. 1883, Stella Beach; is
a R. R. bridge builder.   iii. Benjamin, b. 1851; a surveyor.   iv. Nellie, b. 1854; a teacher.   v. John S., b.
1861; a teacher.   vi. Aurelia, b. 1866; a teacher. [2.] Simeon, b. 1825; lives Sparta, Wis. [3.] Aurelia, b. 1827;
d. [4.] Joseph, b. 1831; lives in Minneapolis, Minn.
[5.] Hubert, b. 1833. [6.] Child.
1909.*   v. HIRAM, b. Hines.
1910.   vi. CAROLINE, b. Charlotte, Vt., Oct. 21, 1806; m.
Hines., July 15, 1830, *Byron Sutton,* he b. Shelburne,
Vt., May 6, 1800; d. Feb. 9, 1858; she d. Charlotte,
Jan. 13, 1872, æ. 65; children, SUTTON: [1.] Lucretia,

b. May 17, 1831; m. May 27, 1852, Nath'l G. Norton, he b. Hines., Feb. 3, 1831; lives Vergennes, Vt.; is proprietor "Island Mills"; she d. Oct. 5, 1876; (and he m. 2d, 1878, Sarah A. Sutton, her sister;) had, i. Emma Amanda, b. Nov. 29, 1852; d. May 28, 1856. ii. Ella Caroline, b. Dec. 19, 1854; d. Dec. 9, 1864. iii. John Nathaniel, b. Oct. 9, 1856; m. Aug. 29, 1884, Lizzie E. Horton. iv. Eugene Galen, b. May 1, 1859; m. June 19, 1883, Carrie F. Foster. v. Lilla Imogene, b. June 7, 1861; d. July 28, 1863. vi. Imogene Lucretia, b. July 8, 1865; d. Dec. 26. vii. Arthur William, b. May 8, 1867. viii. Son, b. Aug. 5, 1869; d. Aug. 26. ix. May Cornelia, b. Feb. 20, 1871. [2.] James B., b. Sep. 10, 1832; m. June 16, 1858, Abbie M. Slocumb, and had, i. George S., b. May 19, 1859. ii. Emma M., b. Sep. 28, 1862. iii. Walter E., b. Aug. 24, 1864. iv. Benj. F., b. May 9, 1868. v. Fannie M., b. June 19, 1874. [3.] John M., b. Dec. 22, 1833; d. Apr. 25, 1863, in Union Army. [4.] Benjamin F., b. Aug. 10, 1835; grad. Med. Univ., Vt., 1860; m. Nov. 19, 1860, Fannie E. Smith, dau. Luman B. S. of Monkton; lives Middlebury, Vt., and had, i. Lucia Caroline, b. Jan. 8, 1862; m. July 15, 1885, John H. Stewart of Midd. [5.] Sarah A., b. Nov. 8, 1836; m. 1878, Nath'l G. Norton, her brother-in-law; no issue. [6.] George T., b. Nov. 25, 1837; grad. Univ., Vt., 1861; m. Feb. 24, 1863, Julia Hubbard, she b. Greenwich, N. Y., Apr. 20, 1838; he is a minister M. E. Ch., Starksboro, Vt., had, i. James Brainard, b. Nov. 4, 1864. ii. Caroline Miller, b. Dec. 13, 1865. iii. Mary Frances, b. Feb. 11, 1867; m. Luther D. Knox. iv. Cornelia Jemima, b. Jan. 17, 1871; d. Sep. 2. v. Cornelia Jemima, b. June 4, 1872. vi. George Byron, b. Mar. 13, 1879. vii. Jessie May, b. Mar. 9, 1881. [7.] Caroline M., b. Oct. 18, 1840; m. July 2, 1861, Abel Warren Jennison, he b. St. Lawrence co., N. Y., Feb. 22, 1839; lives Janesville, Minn., and had, i. Alice Caroline, b. Sep. 13, 1862. ii. John Wesley, b. Feb. 24, 1865. iii. Jessie Mabel, b. Sep. 30, 1869; d. July 10, 1870. iv. Sarah Sutton, b. Dec. 25, 1876; d. May 20, 1877. [8.] Frederic M., b. Feb. 28, 1844; d. Mar. 24, 1845. [9.] Cornelia J., b. Mar. 29, 1846; d. Dec. 28, 1870.

1911. vii. CASSIUS, b. Charlotte; m. N. Y. city, *Adeline Gruna;* had a son, and were all lost at sea; was a machinist.

39

1912. viii. John, b. Char., was a saddler, and d. unm., Monkton, Feb. 27, 1834.

1913. ix. Emeline, b. Hines.; m. 1837, *John Thomas Moore* of Middlebury, Vt., he b. Ireland; she d. Monkton, Mar. 9, 1842; children, Moore: [1.] John T., b. 1837; a Meth. preacher; d. unm., Mar. 4, 1861.

1914. x. Mary Elizabeth, b. Hines., 1816; a teacher; d. unm., Monkton, Oct. 17, 1841.

1915. xi. Anna B., b. Hines., Feb. 17, 1817; m. Aug. 8, 1838, *David L. Fisk* of Dickinson, Vt., and d. Columbus, Ohio, Sep. 11, 1881; she was a teacher, and a devoted member of Meth. Epis. Ch.; children, Fisk: [1.] George William, b. June 13, 1839. [2.] Wallace Wilbur, b. Jan. 20, 1841; m. Mrs. Melissa D. Mason, and had, i. Desdemona Grace, b. Feb. 1, 1874. ii. Jessie Hoyt, b. Apr. 4, 1875; d. Sep. 19, 1877. iii. Pearly May, b. Mar. 27, 1877. [3.] Ella Maria, b. Aug. 15, 1843; m. Oct. 22, 1870, Jerome Jefferson Jones; 2d, Apr. 1, 1880, James H. Slawson; had by 1st marriage, i. Julia Margaret, b. Feb. 21, 1874; d. Apr. 14, 1875. ii. Julietta; and by 2d mar., iii. Charles Meek, b. Mar. 2, 1881; d. July 19. iv. Dottie May, b. June 7, 1882. v. Lewis Gwinn, b. June 22, 1884. [4.] Emma Frances, b. Apr. 4, 1847; m. Dec. 25, 1869, Peter Pfeiffer, and had, i. George W., b. Sep. 30, 1870. ii. Charles A., b. Apr. 18, 1872. iii. Rosabel, b. Dec. 14, 1873. iv. Francis Sessions, b. Nov. 1, 1875. v. Jennie, b. Mar. 27, 1878; d. Jan. 10, 1885. vi. Clara Pearl, b. Oct. 2, 1881. vii. Son. [5.] Sarah Ann, b. Feb. 1, 1851.

1916. xii. Rufus Chapman, b. Hines., Dec. 15, 1818; d. Monkton, Aug. 29, 1838.

1917.*xiii. Henry Lee, b. Hines., Mar. 24, 1820.

John Sears was apprenticed to Godfrey Stocks, a cordwainer of Schoharie, N. Y., and after learning his trade returned to Vermont, and died in Monkton.

He was a man of considerable ability, and a great reader.

864.

RICHARD SEARS[6] [*Rich[5].*, *Silas[4]*, *Jos.[3]*, *Silas[2]*, *Rich.[1]*], b. (prob. in Mass.), Oct. 9, 1775; d. Rome, N. Y., May 2, 1830, and bur. Old City Cem.; m. Feb., 1798, *Mary Ash* of

Ct., she b. Oct. 14, 1782; d. Camden, N. Y., June 8, 1845, and bur. Westmoreland. Children:

1918.   i. MARY, b. Rome, Dec. 25, 1798; m. there, Nov. 10, 1825, *Alfred Estey*, a Scotchman, and d. Albany, July 27, 1832; child, ESTEY: [1.] Harriet, d. s. p., Camden, N. Y.

1919.* ii. RICHARD, b. Rome, Aug. 21, 1801.

1920. iii. JONAS, b. Rome, Feb. 24, 1804; d. unm., Mar. 20, 1833.

1921. iv. SILAS, b. Rome, Aug. 8, 1806.

1922.   v. PRISCILLA, b. Rome, Jan. 28, 1810; m. there, Jan. 1, 1832, *Orin Hungerford* of Henderson, N. Y., and d. there, Jan. 7, 1837; child, HUNGERFORD: [1.] Orin, who rem. to Texas.

1923.   vi. SABRINA, b. Rome, July 8, 1812; m. Westmoreland, N. Y., Sep. 26, 1831, *Reuben Seelye*, son of Daniel and Betsy (Doolittle) S., he b. Jan. 19, 1811; and d. there, Mar. 30, 1851; (he m. 2d, Aug. 12, 1851, Abby D. Dunham, by whom he had, Nathan L., b. Nov. 8, 1852; m. Ida Fluker. Norman Lee. Eva B., b. Feb. 4, 1855; m. G. E. Cheney, and Rose M., b. Apr. 18, 1857;) children, SEELYE: all b. Westmoreland, [1.] Henry, b. Oct. 2, 1832; d. Nov. 24, 1853. [2.] Mary E., b. May 1, 1834; d. Mar. 15, 1847. [3.] Nancy M., b. Nov. 4, 1836; d. Feb. 4, 1853. [4.] Martha M., b. Feb. 6, 1839; d. Sep. 16, 1839. [5.] Norman, b. Sep. 24, 1840; m. Clinton, Mar. 24, 1869, Martha Egan, and had, i. Edith Mabel, b. Aug. 21, 1870; he served in 2d N. Y. Heavy Art'y during the war. [6.] Duane, b. Oct. 20, 1842; d. in army, Fredericksburg, Va., Dec. 15, 1862. [7.] Rispah O., b. Apr. 7, 1845; m. Nov. 18, 1869, Alpha P. Powers of Adrian, Mich., he b. Cleveland, O., June 14, 1847; d. Adrian, Apr. 11, 1872; she m. 2d, Aug. 16, 1882, Chas. F. Crozier, he b. Piqua, O., Jan. 13, 1854; d. s. p., Jan. 4, 1886; she lives near Aberdeen, Dakota, had by 1st husband, i. Eddie A., b. June 18, 1871.

1924.   vii. JOHN ASH, b. Rome, Aug. 26, 1820; d. unm., Aug. 20, 1845.

1925.* viii. WALTER S., b. Rome, Oct. 19, 1823.

Richard Sears removed with his father to the vicinity of Hoosick, Rens. co., N. Y., and later to Rome, Oneida co., N. Y., then known as Fort Stanwix, there being at that time but one house outside of the Fort ; was a farmer, and a Methodist.

His wife was blind for many years previous to her death.

865.

ORANGE SEARS[6] [*Rich.[5], Silas[4], Jos.[3], Silas[2], Rich.[1]*], b. Amherst, Mass., Dec. 4, 1776; d. Lyons, N. Y., 1854; m. Valley Falls, N. Y., 1809, Mrs. *Annis (Bissell) Silliman*, widow of Robert S., she b. Litchfield, Ct., July 29, 1782 ; d. West Butler, N. Y., Sep. 17, 1841; (by her 1st husband she had, Daniel D., b. 1804, lives No. Wolcott, N. Y., and Rhoda, m. Adolphus Grant, had a numerous family and d. ab't 1879, Newark, N. Y.)   Children :

1926.   i. ORIN, b. Valley Falls, N. Y., Nov. 27, 1810 ; d. unm., Aug., 1839.

1927.*   ii. OSCAR, b. Arlington, Vt., June 23, 1812.

1928.   iii. AMANDA, b. Val. F., Mar. 1, 1815 ; m. Dec. 25, 1836, *Merritt Purdy* of Pittstown, N. Y., settled in West Butler, N. Y., and d. Oct. 12, 1869 ; he d. 1873, an honored citizen and J. P. ; children, PURDY : [1.] Charles E., b. Dec. 31, 1837; m. Feb. 24, 1863, Mary Chatfield, no chil. [2.] Maria B., b. Nov. 16, 1840 ; m. Sep. 8, 1865, Dr. Washington F. Peck, he b. Galen, N. Y., Jan. 22, 1841, lives in Davenport, Iowa, and had, i. Jessie Allen, b. Oct. 11, 1866. ii. Mary Alida, b. Dec. 25, 1869. iii. Robertson Irish, b. July 6, 1871. [3.] Caroline, b. Apr. 17, 1842; d. May 18, 1845. [4.] Hiram J., b. Jan. 18, 1847; m. Dec. 19, 1867, Emma R. Roberts; lived Seneca Falls, N. Y., had, i. Alice Amanda, b. July 11, 1872.

1929.*   iv. HIRAM, b. Val. F., July 17, 1818.

Was a wagon builder.

869.

ABNER SEARS[6] [*Rich.[5], Silas[4], Jos.[3], Silas[2], Rich.[1]*], b. (prob. in Mass.), June 15, 1787 ; d. near Naples, Ill., Aug. 22, 1842, in 56 year ; m. near Troy, N. Y., Dec. 30, 1807, *Mary Van Pelt*, dau. of Alexander and Hannah Van P., she b. Essex co., N. J., Mar. 6, 1789 ; d. Aug. 3, 1865, in 77 year ; (her father was a thriving blacksmith, and an honored local preacher in the Meth. Ch., in and about the city of Troy during many years.) Children:

1930. i. CHARLOTTE, b. Rens. co., N. Y., July 9, 1809; rem. with her parents to Yankeetown, Ohio, in fall of 1818, and m. there, Apr. 24, 1825, *John Davis*, he b. Pickaway co., Ohio, Jan. 24, 1800; d. near Mt. Pleasant, Ill., Feb. 21, 1886, in 87 yr.; a farmer and Methodist; she d. there, Apr. 16, 1873; was a member of Meth. Ch. there; children, DAVIS: [1.] Diantha, b. July 22, 1826; m. Abram H. Scholl, and d. s. p., Oct. 23, 1853; he d. Oct. 28, 1855. [2.] Rachel, b. Nov. 28, 1827; m. Simon Peter Beckmann, who d. Apr. 10, 1873; she lives Main Prairie, Minn., had, i. Diantha, d. inf. ii. John, d. inf. iii. Mary, d. inf. iv. Levi, d. inf. v. Washington, m. Nellie Greeley, Main Prairie, Minn. vi. Addison, d. inf. vii. Addie, m. Aug. 15, 1879, George R. Whiteside. viii. Mary Frances. [3.] James, b. Sep. 2, 1829; lives Ketchum, Idaho. [4.] Alexander, b. Nov. 20, 1831; d. Aug. 20, 1832. [5.] Mary Jane, b. Sep. 8, 1833; m. Jan. 4, 1855, Wm. N. Mumford, he b. Newport, Nova Scotia, Jan. 26, 1824; was Capt. Co. E, 119th Regt., Ill. Vols., during the war; she d. June 16, 1868; (he m. 2d, Apr. 4, 1869, Mrs. Rebecca Poe, dau. Rev. Granville Bond;) had, i. Augustus, b. Oct. 23, 1855; m. Nov. 1, 1883, Arminta Petty. ii. William, b. Oct. 25, 1858; m. Sep. 4, 1883, Kate Barry. iii. Mary Estelle, b. Jan. 14, 1861; d. June 11, 1862. iv. Lorena Belle, b. Dec. 1, 1862; d. Oct. 13, 1864. v. Charlotte, b. Dec. 31, 1865; m. Oct. 1, 1884, Arthur K. Thompson. [6.] William H., b. Dec. 9, 1836; m. Mar. 10, 1864, Cordelia M. Lee, she b. June 26, 1842; he was in Co. E, 119th Ill. Vols., during the war, had, i. Lee, b. Dec. 30, 1864; d. Sep. 12, 1865. ii. Albertie, b. Oct. 15, 1866; d. Sep. 10, 1868. iii. Homer, b. Feb. 3, 1869; d. Mar. 21. iv. William, b. June 16, 1870. v. George C., b. Jan. 10, 1876. [7.] Abner, b. Jan. 15, 1839; d. Jan. 28. [8.] Milton, b. Oct. 13, 1841; d. unm., Aug. 17, 1863; Corp., Co. G, 3d Regt., Ill. Vols. [9.] Hiram, b. Mar. 22, 1844; m. Mar. 27, 1876, Nancy Ellen Hahn, she b. June 8, 1852; he was in Co. E, 119th Regt. Ill. Vols.; wounded at Fort Blakesley, Ala., Apr. 9, 1865, and discharged, Greenville Hospital, La., June 18, 1865; had, i. Lottie, b. June 16, 1877. ii. Lena, b. Nov. 29, 1878. iii. Hiram Frederic, b. Aug. 1, 1880. iv. Lulu, b. Dec.

31, 1882. v. Wm. Arthur, b. Dec. 27, 1884. [10.] Sam uel, b. Jan. 28, 1847; d. Jan. 20, 1852. [11.] Jerome, b. Feb. 26, 1849; d. Mar. 11, 1859. [12.] John H., b. Mar. 23, 1850.

1931.   ii. ANGELINE, b. Duanesburg, N. Y., Nov. 26, 1810; d. Aug. 4, 1813, near Cherry Valley, N.Y., from accident.

1932.   iii. DIANTHA, b. Duanes., Mar. 30, 1812; rem. with her parents to Madison, Ohio, in 1818; m. Yankeetown, O., Oct. 14, 1830, *Henry L. Farmer*, he b. near Chillicothe, O., July 19, 1809; rem. to Warsaw, Ind., 1837; to Montezuma, Iowa, in 1856; he was a farmer, and an honored member and officer of the United Brethren Church; d. near Ewart, Iowa, July 25, 1883; she lives near Montezuma, and is a faithful member of U. B. Ch.; children, FARMER: [1.] Joseph, b. Oct. 4, 1831; m. Sep. 22, 1850, Jemima E. Linn, had no children, but adopted Anna Laura ——; he became a popular and useful minister in the U. B., and d. Feb. 15, 1861; his wid. m. 2d, Martin Tridell. [2.] John Wesley, b. Dec. 22, 1833; m. Aug. 12, 1855, Sarah G. Arnold, she b. Aug. 8, 1836; d. Oct. 14, 1880; he m. 2d, Nov. 20, 1884, Alice Virginia Hunnicutt, she b. Apr. 4, 1850; he entered the Union army as a private in 1862, and was promoted to 1st Lt.; has been twice Sheriff of the co.; had, i. Andrew M., b. Apr. 23, 1856; m. Ella M. Holcomb, in 1877. ii. Joel T., b. Oct. 5, 1860; d. Dec. 14, 1862. iii. Madge B., b. Jan. 13, 1868. iv. Alfred T., b. June 27, 1880; d. Dec. 18. [3.] Lewis W., b. Jan. 30, 1836; m. Jan. 23, 1859, Mary Louiza Farmer; he was in Co. B, 40th Regt. Iowa Vols.; had, i. Elmira C., b. Nov. 13, 1859; m. Mar. 3, 1878, John H. Palmer. ii. Ida, b. May 29, 1861; m. Mar. 2, 1882, Archibald J. Finch. iii. James J., b. July 26, 1863. iv. Clara A., b. Sep. 3, 1866. v. Charles E., b. Apr. 5, 1870. vi. Nellie J., b. June 23, 1872. [4.] Mary Catherine, b. July 25, 1838; m. Apr. 11, 1858, Joseph H. Gwinn, a J. P., and Not. Pub.; had, i. Henry T., b. Dec. 28, 1858. ii. Diantha M., b. Aug. 6, 1860; m. June 13, 1884, Wm. T. Collins. iii. Jemima R., b. Sep. 18, 1861; m. Sep. 20, 1885, Seneca S. Maple. iv. Effa A., b. Sep. 3, 1862. v. Ida M., b. Sep. 19, 1864. vi. William G., b. May 23, 1868. vii. Leovell A., b. Feb. 22, 1870; d. Feb. 14, 1871. viii. Dau., b. July 25, 1873; d. Aug. 17. ix. Grace D., b. Mar. 16, 1878. [5.] Julia Elizabeth, b. June 22, 1841; m. Apr. 29, 1860, John

Butts, and had, i. Diantha J., b. Mar. 6, 1861; d. Jan.
9, 1871. ii. William H., b. July 29, 1863. iii. Anthony
M., b. July 26, 1866. iv. Homer E., b. Jan. 31, 1873.
[6.] Susan, b. Mar. 23, 1843; d. Nov. 22. [7.] Charlotte M., b. May 27, 1846; m. May 9, 1869, George M.
Stevens, and had, i. Oscar O., b. Nov. 4, 1870. ii. Howard W., b. Jan. 9, 1872. iii. John L., b. Mar. 7, 1873;
d. Oct. 9. iv. Ida F., b. Dec. 31, 1874. v. Miles M.,
b. May 27, 1876. vi. Edgar E., b. Aug. 30, 1877.
vii. Otho R., b. Apr. 23, 1879. viii. Ida F., b. Mar.
10, 1881. ix. Thaddeus Stevens, b. Feb. 20, 1883.
[8.] Abner Sears, b. Aug. 30, 1848; m. Mar. 7,
1872, Harriet M. Bryan, and d. Apr. 7, 1886; had,
i. Martha E., b. Dec. 29, 1872. ii. Charles M., b. Dec.
2, 1874. iii. Edith M., b. Jan. 31, 1878. iv. Joseph R.,
b. Feb. 27, 1883.

1933.* iv. ALEXANDER, b. near Cherry Valley, N. Y., Mar.
16, 1814.

1934.* v. WASHINGTON, b. near Cherry Valley, N. Y., June
3, 1816.

1935. vi. HANNAH JANE, b. near Cherry Valley, N. Y., Mar.
1, 1818; removed with her parents to Yankeetown, Ohio,
in fall of 1818, and to near Naples, Ill., in fall of 1836;
m. there, Aug. 8, 1844, *James G. Killpatrick* of Winchester, Ill., he b. Franklin co., Ohio, Sep. 2, 1820; was
a red-potter by trade; removed to vicinity of Maroa,
Ill., and became a farmer. He was bro. to Lt.-Col.
Thos. M. Killpatrick of Ill., and a relative of Gen. K.,
U. S. Army; was a devoted member of Meth. Ch., and
d. Mar. 8, 1863; his wife, a noble Christian woman, d.
Nov. 30, 1879, and was buried with her husband in Winchester; children, KILLPATRICK: [1.] Mary Malvina, b.
July 12, 1845; d. Sep. 2, 1852. [2.] Thomas William,
b. Oct. 18, 1847; d. Sep. 8, 1852. [3.] James Addison,
b. Dec. 26, 1849; m. Feb. 5, 1879, Mary Elizabeth Green,
she b. Feb. 5, 1855, dau. Thos. and Mary G.; no children.
[4.] Matilda Jane, b. Feb. 19, 1851; d. Apr. 3, 1852.
[5.] Vesta Angeline, b. Apr. 18, 1853. [6.] Eliza Caroline, b. Jan. 16, 1855; d. Apr. 15, 1882, unm. [7.] Frank
Ely, b. Mar. 12, 1857; d. July 30, 1883. [8.] Hiram
David, b. Aug. 27, 1859; m. Feb. 2, 1882, Julia Etta
Burrus, and had 2 children, d. inf.

1936.* vii. RICHARD RENSELLAER, b. Yankeetown, Ohio, Nov.
5, 1819.

1937. viii. ANGELINE, b. Yank., Sep. 10, 1822 ; removed with her parents to vicinity of Naples, Ill., in fall of 1836; was educated at Meth. Female Coll., Jacksonville, Ill., and d. near Naples, Aug. 20, 1852, unm. ; was a teacher, and a devoted member of the Meth. Ch.

1938.* ix. HIRAM, b. Yankeetown, O., Apr. 10, 1825.

1939.   x. CAROLINE, b. Yankeetown, O., Apr. 30, 1827; removed to near Naples, Ill., with her parents in fall of 1836, and m. there, Aug. 10, 1843, *Henry B. Morrison*, a farmer; both are devoted members of Meth. Ch., and live in Monticello, Ill. ; children, MORRISON : [1.] Alexander Franklin, b. Dec. 24, 1844; was in Union Army ; m. Oct. 2, 1865, Maggie Shurtleff of Clinton, Ill., and is book-keeper in Bank Monticello ; had, i. Lillian, b. Oct. 2, 1866 ; d. inf. ii. Henry Baker, d. inf. iii. Emily Estelle, b. Aug. 27, 1869. iv. Blanche, b. Jan. 9, 1871. v. Sylvanus Shurtleff, b. Jan. 22, 1874. vi. Mabel Frances, b. Feb. 1, 1880. [2.] John Washington, b. Nov. 16, 1846 ; d. Oct. 17, 1848. [3.] Mary Angeline, b. Feb. 26, 1849 ; m. Nov. 23, 1875, Rev. Thos. J. Coultas of the Ill. Conf. M. E. Ch., and had, i. Aldo Bliss, b. Mar. 10, 1877. ii. Edna Berenice, b. Mar. 16, 1879. iii. Lotas Bertena, b. Dec. 8, 1883. [4.] James Addison, b. Apr. 3, 1852 ; d. July 4, 1854. [5.] Matilda Jane, b. Apr. 3, 1852, *gemini;* d. Oct. 1, 1855. [6.] Louisa Adelaide, b. Jan. 16, 1854 ; d. Feb. 20, 1855. [7.] Edna Alethea, b. Aug. 3, 1857; m. Nov. 12, 1879, Rev. Joseph W. Cornish of Minn. Conf. M. E. Ch., and had, i. Edna Belle, b. Feb. 13, 1881. ii. Carrie Josephine, b. Jan. 9, 1883. iii. Thomas Kynett, b. Mar. 14, 1884. [8.] Julia Elizabeth, b. Oct. 21, 1858 ; m. Sep. 7, 1880, Prof. Franklin F. Roose of Lincoln, Nebraska, and had a child, d. inf. [9.] Ida Caroline, b. Sep. 18, 1860 ; m. June 14, 1882, S. W. Battelle of Quincy, Ill., and had, i. William Morrison, b. Nov. 17, 1883. ii. Joseph Ernest, b. Sep. 4, 1886.

1940.* xi. ADDISON, b. Yankeetown, Ohio, Jan. 1, 1830.

Abner Sears lived for a time in Rensselaer, Schenectady and Otsego counties, New York, working at his trade of wagon-builder.

In the fall of 1818, he emigrated to Ohio, and settled in Yankeetown, Madison township, Fayette co., and became a thrifty farmer, removing in the fall of 1836 to the vicinity of Naples, Morgan (now Scott) co., Illinois.

He was an honored member and exhorter in the Methodist church.

His wife was a woman of remarkable ability for planning wisely in the industrious and religious cultivation of the family.

She is said to have been a second cousin to the late Maj. Anderson, the hero of Fort Sumter, and connected on her mother's side with the family of Richard Stockton, signer of the Declaration of Independence.

870.

BARNABAS SEARS⁶ [*Barnabas⁵, Silas⁴, Jos.³, Silas², Rich.¹*], b. Hardwick, Mass., 1787; d. Savannah, Ga., Sep. 20, 1820, of yellow fever; m. Pelham, Mass., May 21, 1818, *Mary Gray*. Child:

1941.* i. CHARLES OLIVER, b. Hadley, Mass., Jan. 29, 1819.

Polly Sears was appointed administratrix of Barnabas Sears, Jr., of Pelham, Mar. 6, 1821; Barnabas Sears and Wm. M. Gray, sureties.

876.

SARDIS SEARS⁶ [*Barnabas⁵, Silas⁴, Jos.³, Silas², Rich.¹*], b. Hardwick, Mass., 1802; d. Mar. 18, 1861, æ. 59; m. ——— ———. Children:

1942. i. ROSANNA, m. *Hubbard Lawrence* of Hadley, Mass., and d.
1943. ii. IDELLA, m. *Charles Snow* of Ware, Mass., and d.
1944. iii. HENRY, lives in Shutesbury, Mass.
1945. iv. FRANK, removed to New Hampshire.
1946. v. ARTHUR, b. 1846; enlisted in Co. D, 27th Mass. Vols., Aug. 15, 1862, and d. Amherst, Mass., June 22, 1864.
1947. vi. CLARENCE, d.

877.

NATHAN SEARS⁶ [*Barnabas⁵, Silas⁴, Jos.³, Silas², Rich.¹*], b. Hardwick, Mass., May 31, 1807; d. Amherst, Mass., Jan. 20, 1878, æ. 71; m. Leverett, Mass., Feb. 2, 1842, *Julia A. Field*, she b. there, Sep. 29, 1811. Children:

1948. i. ELIZABETH E., b. Feb. 15, 1843; m. Brattleboro, Vt., Feb. 21, 1860, *John E. Guestin* of Amherst, he b.

40

Canada, Dec. 25, 1832; children, Guestin: [1.] Edward
A., b. Sep. 6, 1862; d. July 27, 1864. [2.] Cora L., b.
Sep. 23, 1866; m. Keene, N. H., May 8, 1883, Frank J.
Ingram, he b. Amherst, May 6, 1861. [3.] Lena M.,
b. Mar. 28, 1870.

1949. ii. ERASTUS F., b. May 18, 1845.

878.

HOLMES SEARS[6] [*Edw'd[5], Edw'd[4], Josiah[3], Silas[2],
Rich.[1]*], b. Halifax, Mass., July 13, 1757; d. there, Nov. 5,
1836; m. Mar. 18, 1781, *Mercy Cushing* of Hal., and 2d,
Plymouth, Mass., Nov. 25, 1790, *Mercy Bradford*, dau. of
John and Eliz'h (Holmes) B., she b. 1761; d. Mar. 4, 1847.
Children:

1950. i. MERCY C., b. Hal., Sep. 29, 1793; d. before 1834.
1951.* ii. WILLIAM, b. Hal., Sep. 4, 1796.
1952. iii. JOSIAH, b. Hal., Oct. 20, 1797; m. there, 1817,
   Polly Porter of Bridgewater, Mass., and d. before 1834.
1953. iv. WARD, b. Hal., Mar. 17, 1798; m. *Hannah Larra-
   bee*, and d. Sep. 20, 1838.
1954. v. LUCINDA, b. Hal., Sep. 10, 1801; m. *Ebenezer
   Johnson*, and d. Feb. 26, 1840; he d. Dec. 5, 1838.

November, 1776, Holmes Sears was allowed for rations
£5 10, and for travel £2 4; he was in Lt. Judah Woods' Co.
in Lt.-Col. Thos. Lothrop's Regt., and marched from Halifax
to Bristol on alarm of December 9, 1776; was 11 days in
camp, and allowed for 80 miles and 4 days' travel. He probably served in regular army also, as his widow drew a pension
in 1840; she was then aged 77, and living with her son
William.

His will, dated Sep. 2, 1834, was allowed Jan. 16, 1837, and
mentions wife Mercy, sons Ward and William, dau. Lucinda
Johnson, and grand-sons, William Holmes Sears and Henry
Ward Sears. William Sears, Exec'r.

887.

Dea. RUFUS SEARS[6] [*Nath'l[5], Sam'l[4], Josiah[3], Silas[2],
Rich.[1]*], b. Yarmouth, Mass., Jan. 9, 1770; d. Hawley, Mass.,
Nov. 16, 1856, æ. 87; m. Ashfield, Mass., ab't 1793, *Priscilla
Sears*, No. 564, dau. of Daniel and Priscilla (Sears) S., she b.
Yar., Feb. 27, 1775; d. Hawley, Nov., 1802, æ. 28; he m.

2d, Mar., 1803, *Maria Howes*, she b. Yar., July 6, 1775 ; d. May 25, 1864.   Children :

By *Priscilla :*

1955.   i. VIENNA, b. Haw., Jan. 23, 1795 ; m. ab't 1812, and
         d. 1835.
1956.* ii. NATHANIEL, b. Haw., Aug. 3, 1796.
1957.   iii. PRISCILLA, b. Haw., Mar. 25, 1798 ; d. Nov., 1802.
1958.   iv. DANIEL, b. Haw., Jan. 31, 1800; d. Nov., 1802.
1959.   v. RUFUS, b. Haw., d. Nov., 1802.

By *Maria :*

1960.* vi. RUFUS, b. Haw., Dec. 23, 1803.
1961.* vii. ANTHONY, b. Haw., Aug. 18, 1805.
1962.   viii. MARIA, b. Haw., Apr. 10, 1806 ; m. there, Aug.
         10, 1830, *Timo. Baker*, son of Rufus and Olive (Hall)
         B., he b. Oct., 1807 ; lives in Adams, Mass.
1963.   ix. PRISCILLA, b. Haw., Mar. 3, 1807.
1964.*   x. FREDERIC H., b. Haw., June 25, 1811.
1965.* xi. BENJAMIN FRANKLIN, b. Haw., Mar. 15, 1813.

Rufus Sears was born in the east precinct of Yarmouth, now Dennis, Mass., in 1770, and was but a few weeks old when his father died.

He lived with his mother until eleven years old, (who meanwhile had married Gorham Baker,) and then removed with his sister, Desire, wife of Dea. Joseph Bangs, to Hawley, then an almost unbroken wilderness, with a few scattering log-houses, and lived with her until 21.

He then made a visit to his mother on Cape Cod, carrying his clothes and provisions in a pack, and traveling all the distance on foot ; spent the winter with her, and in March, not wishing to go to sea, as the other young men were then doing, he shouldered his pack and trudged back to Hawley again.

When he left the Cape the farmers were planting ; arriving at Hawley, he found the land still covered with the last winter's snow.

He then purchased and cleared a tract of land, put up a small house, and about 1793 married Priscilla Sears.

He professed to be a follower of the meek and lowly Jesus before he was 21, endeavored to train up his children in the right way, and was a Deacon in the Congregational Church for many years.

892.

EARL SEARS[6] [*Zebedee[5], David[4], Josiah[3], Silas[2], Rich.[1]*], b. Middleboro, Mass., Dec. 19, 1761 ; d. there, Jan. 10, 1842 ;

m. Midd., Apr. 27, 1793, by Rev. Eben'r Hinds, to *Judith Howland*, dau. of John and Abigail H. of Freetown, Mass., she b. Feb. 25, 1755; d. Midd., July 20, 1846. Children:

1966. i. MARY, b. Midd., Aug. 3, 1794; d. Feb. 29, 1796.
1967.* ii. EARL, b. Midd., Dec. 2, 1796.

Earl Sears marched to R. I., on alarm of July 29, in Capt. Henry Pierce's Co., Lt.-Col. White's Regt., did 9 days' service, and traveled 40 miles.

894.

LEONARD SEARS[6] [*Zebedee[5], David[4], Josiah[3], Silas[2], Rich.[1]*], b. Middleboro, Mass., Sep. 22, 1771; m. there, Mar. 22, 1795, by Rev. Caleb Turner, to *Remember Leonard* of M., who d. there, Feb. 26, 1803; 2d, by Willis Wood, J. P., June 3, 1804, to *Abiah L. Simmons*, dau. of Joseph Leonard, and widow of Sebra Simmons, who d. 1828, æ. ab't 55. Children:
By *Remember:*

1968.* i. OLIVER LEONARD, b. Midd., Mar. 1, 1795.
1969. ii. DANIEL, b. Midd., Aug. 16, 1797; settled in Troy, N. Y., when a young man, m. and had 3 children.
1970. iii. ZEBEDEE, b. Midd., July 6, 1799.
1971. iv. MARY, b. Midd., Sep., 1802.

900.

PETER SEARS[6] [*Peter[5], Jona.[4], Josiah[3], Silas[2], Rich.[1]*], b. Scituate, Mass., m. (pub. Boston, Jan. 15, 1806,) *Delight Beals*. Children:

1972.* i. ISAAC, b. Boston, Aug. 9, 1806.
1973. ii. CHARLES, d. Boston, Oct., 1834, æ. 29.
1974. iii. NANCY D.
1975. iv. MARY D., m. Boston, Nov. 4, 1838, *Warren Gill*.
1976. v. CATHARINE C., m. Boston, Aug. 17, 1848, *Edward Ricker*.

906.

JONATHAN SEARS[7] [*Jona.*[6], *Jona.*[5], *Jona.*[4], *Sam'l*[3], *Paul*[2], *Rich.*[1]], b. Harwich, Mass., Mar. 19, 1777; d. Ashfield, Mass., Aug. 2, 1859; m. Feb. 3, 1803, *Hannah Foster*, she b. Tisbury, Mass., Aug. 9, 1782; d. July 30, 1855. Children:

1977.*   i. CLARK, b. Ash., Jan. 31, 1804.
1978.   ii. OLIVE, b. Ash., May 27, 1806; m. *Heman Cargill*, (who married again but had no issue;) children, CARGILL: [1.] Julius, b. May, 1846; lives in Newark Valley, N. Y. [2.] Son, lives New. Vall.
1979.* iii. WILLIAM, b. Ash., Mar. 28, 1808.
1980.* iv. FREEMAN, b. Ash., Aug. 30, 1810.
1981.   v. PHILENA, b. Ash., Sep. 3, 1812; m. *Charles Cargill*, and d. s. p., Tyringham, Mass., July 23, 1836.
1982.* vi. STILLMAN, b. Ash., Sep. 23, 1815.
1983.* vii. JONATHAN, b. Ash., Oct. 27, 1818.
1984. viii. MILTON FOSTER, b. Ash., Feb. 9, 1821; d. 1853; m. *Mercy D. Williams*, she b. there, Nov. 28, 1824, dau. of Apollos and Annis (Smith) W., had, [1.] Son, b. Jan. 7, 1851; d. Jan. 11, 1851. [2.] Dau., b. and d. Oct. 26, 1852; —— she lives in Kidder, Mo.
1985.   ix. HANNAH, b. Ash., Nov. 8, 1823; m. Feb. 10, 1846, *Henry Eldridge* of Ash., and d. Shelburne, Mass., June 1856, leaving a dau.; he lives in Dwight, Ill.

Mr. Sears removed to Ashfield, with his parents, lived and died on Cape street.

He was Selectman in 1820–22, 1824–26, 1829–31, and Rep. to State Legislature in 1833 and 1836.

In early life he went on fishing voyages with his brother, Barnabas C., to the banks of New Foundland and the Magdalen Islands.

907.

Rev. FREEMAN SEARS[7] [*Jona.*[6], *Jona.*[5], *Jona.*[4], *Sam'l*[3], *Paul*[2], *Rich.*[1]], b. Harwich, Mass., Nov. 28, 1779; d. 1811; m. July 7, 1808, by Rev. Joshua Bates to Lydia Badlam of Dedham, Mass., she b. Oct. 30, 1780, dau. of Lemuel and Lydia (Gibbens) B., (who m. 2d, Boston, Jan. 18, 1818, David Colburn of Dedham.) Child:

1986. i. LYDIA GIBBENS, d. ab't 1857; m. Boston, May 10, 1830, *S. F. Haven,* he b. Dedham, May 28, 1806; d. Sep. 5, 1881; (m. 2d, Dec. 3, 1872, *Frances W. Allen;*) was for many years Librarian of Am'n Antiq. So., Worcester, Mass.; children, HAVEN: [1.] Samuel Foster, b. Dedham, May 20, 1831; was Asst. Sur. 15th Mass. Vol. Inf., Aug. 5, 1861; Surgeon, July 21, 1862, and killed Fredericksburg, Va., Dec. 13, 1862.

Mr. Sears graduated at Williams College, settled as a clergyman in Natick, Mass., and was the first minister of the Central Church in that town, in 1802.

His will was proved in 1811.   Inventory, $3,000.

His daughter, Lydia, was named in her great-grand-mother's will, Jan. 7, 1815.   See *ante.*

909.

AZARELAH SEARS[7] [*Jona.*[6], *Jona.*[5], *Jona.*[4], *Sam'l*[3], *Paul*[2], *Rich.*[1]], b. Ashfield, Mass., July 10, 1789; d. there, Feb. 17, 1875; m. *Hannah Maynard* of Conway, Mass. Children :

1987.* i. OLIVER M., b. Ash., Nov. 21, 1817.
1988.   ii. HEPSIBAH, b. Ash., Mar. 10, 1819; m. *William Thayer.*
1989.* iii. JOSEPH, b. Ash., June 4, 1820.
1990.   iv. HARRIET, b. Ash., Apr. 4, 1822; m. Jan. 20, 1847, *Isaac Jones.*
1991.   v. LUCY ANN, b. Ash., May 25, 1824; d. Feb. 27, 1852.
1992.* vi. WILLIAM HALE, b. Ash., Aug. 8, 1826.
1993. vii. SAMUEL, b. Ash., Sep. 15, 1829; d. July 20, 1852.
1994.* viii. EDWIN, b. Ash., Apr. 17, 1832.
1995.   ix. HENRY LYMAN, b. Ash., Aug. 20, 1836; d. 1861.

916.

NATHAN SEARS[7] [*Jos.*[6], *Prince*[5], *Jona.*[4], *Sam'l*[3], *Paul*[2], *Rich.*[1]], b. July 9, 1793; d. Brewster, Mass., Apr. 27, 1841, æ. 47; m. July 9, 1818, *Sarah Winslow*, dau. of Abraham W., she b. Jan. 20, 1795; d. Camden, N. J., Mar. 26, 1875. Children:

1996. i. SUSAN, b. Br., July 4, 1820; d. Feb. 20, 1821.
1997. ii. SUSAN, b. Br., Nov. 23, 1822; m. there, June 9, 1847, *Anthony Howes*, son of Wm. and Lydia H. of Dennis, he b. 1821; she d. Apr. 6, 1851, æ. 28.
1998. iii. SALLY WINSLOW, b. Br., May 12, 1824; m. there, Dec. 25, 1845, Capt. *Asa H. Howes* of Den., son of Christopher and Susan H., he b. 1820; 2d, Jan. 8, 1854, —— ——; she d. Shreveport, La., Apr. 10, 1876.
1999. iv. EMELINE, b. Br., Aug. 20, 1827; d. Sep. 24, 1831.
2000. v. NATHAN FREDERIC, b. Br., May 12, 1832; m. Jamaica Plain, Mass., Apr. 28, 1858, —— ——, and d. Boston, May 11, 1869, æ. 37.
2001.* vi. ABRAHAM WINSLOW, b. Br., Feb. 14, 1835.

Mr. Sears was chosen Selectman of Brewster, 1835-39.

918.

Capt. JOSEPH HAMBLEN SEARS[7] [*Jos.*[6], *Prince*[5], *Jona.*[4], *Sam'l*[3], *Paul*[2], *Rich.*[1]], b. Harwich, Mass., Nov. 9, 1801; d. Brewster, Mass., Feb. 3, 1885, æ. 83; m. there, Dec. 2, 1824, *Olive Bangs*, dau. of Elkanah B., she b. Har., Sep. 10, 1802; was adm. to Ch., Br., July 2, 1848; d. 1889. Children:

2002. i. KEZIA H., b. Br., Oct. 17, 1827; d. Sep. 28, 1828.
2003.* ii. JOSEPH HENRY, b. Br., June 8, 1829.
2004.* iii. ELISHA FREEMAN, b. Br., Mar. 28, 1831.
2005. iv. ELLEN, b. Br., Oct. 10, 1834; m. there, Apr. 9, 1854, *Josiah M. Knowles*, son of Winslow and Sarah K. of Br., he b. 1831.
2006. v. BENJAMIN B., b. Br., Sep. 5, 1836; d. Sep. 15, 1837.
2007. vi. SUSAN OLIVIA, b. Br., Oct. 29, 1839; m. there, Oct. 16, 1862, *Andrew Nickerson* of Boston, son of David and Emily N., he b. 1832.

2008. vii. Sarah Louise, b. Br., Feb. 26, 1845 ; m. Nov. 15, 1871, *Walter T. Winslow*, son of Elisha D. and Nancy (Healey) W. of Br., he b. Feb. 13, 1843 ; is an architect in Boston.

Was a sea captain.

923.

ISAAC SEARS[7] [*Josh.*[6], *Josh.*[5], *Josh.*[4], *Sam'l*[3], *Paul*[2], *Rich.*[1]], b. (perh. in New Haven, Ct.,) Dec. 21, 1789 ; was lost at sea, May, 1836 ; m. Boston, Mass., Mar. 1, 1827, by Rev. James D. Knowles, to *Sarah M. (Jenks) Edgar*, she b. there, Mar. 4, 1796 ; d. Chelsea, Mass., July 28, 1884. Children :

2009.   i. Eliza Fenno, b. Boston ; d. Aug., 1828, æ. 3 mos.
2010.* ii. Isaac Henry, b. Boston, Sep. 17, 1833.
2011. iii. William J., b. Boston ; d. Oct., 1834, æ. 2 yrs. 6 mos.

Isaac Sears and Mary Johnson were published Boston, Jan. 3, 1826, but not married.

939.

ROBERT SEARS[7] [*Thatcher*[6], *Nath'l*[5], *Josh.*[4], *Sam'l*[3], *Paul*[2], *Rich.*[1]], b. St. John, N. B., June 28, 1810 ; m. N. Y. city, Jan. 12, 1832, *Harriet Howard Martin*, eldest dau. of Dr. Nath'l Martin of New Jersey, she b. Feb. 12, 1809 ; d. Toronto, Canada, June 4, 1881, æ. 73. Children :

2012.   i. Henry Thatcher, b. N. Y., Oct. 17, 1832 ; d. Jan. 17, 1834.
2013.   ii. Mary Elizabeth, b. N. Y., Dec. 14, 1834 ; d. Mar., 1835.
2014. iii. Harriet Howard, b. N. Y., Apr. 19, 1836 ; m. Dec. 11, 1861, Dr. *Wm. F. Humphrey* of St. John, N. B., a graduate of Yale Coll., who d. Valetta, Malta, in 1865 ; she lives in Toronto, Can. ; has no children.
2015.   iv. George Edward, b. N. Y., Sep. 13, 1838 ; lives in N. Y. city.
2016.* v. Robert, b. N. Y., Dec. 7, 1841.
2017.   vi. John Carle, b. N. Y., July 1, 1844 ; d. Apr. 25, 1846.
2018. vii. David, b. N. Y., Jan. 3, 1847 ; d. same year.
2019. viii. Frederic, b. N. Y., July 28, 1848 ; d. Rio Janeiro, Mar. 16, 1873, of yellow fever.

Mr. Sears removed from St. John to New York city, and engaged in the publication of popular works, biblical, historical, travels, etc.

He retired from business many years since, and resides in Toronto, Can., with his dau., Mrs. Humphrey.

940.

JOHN SEARS[7] [*Thatcher*[6], *Nath'l*[5], *Josh.*[4], *Sam'l*[3], *Paul*[2], *Rich.*[1]], b. St. John, N. B., 1819 ; m. *Ann Blackwood*, dau. of Rev. Robert B., and grand-dau. of Rev. John Macara of Edinburgh, Scotland, she b. Tatamagouche, N. S. Children :

2020.   i. HENRY THATCHER, b. St. John, June 22, 1840 ; is an M. D., and lives 257 W. 52d st., N. Y.
2021.   ii. ROBERT BLACKWOOD, b. St. John ; address, 1 William st., N. Y.
2022.* iii. GEORGE, b. St. John, Jan. 11, 1844.
2023.   iv. EDWARD, b. St. John, and lives there.
2024.   v. JOHN BOURCHIER, b. and d., St. John.
2025.   vi. WILLIAM MACARA, b. St. John, June 21, 1850 ; d.
2026. vii. DAVID, b. St. John, and lives there.
2027. viii. ANNIE, b. St. John.
2028.   ix. JAMES WALTER, b. St. John. Lieut. Sears was gazetted to H. M. 38th Regt. Foot, 25th June, 1881, served through the Egyptian campaign of 1882, received the Egyptian War Medal, and Khedive's Star. Now serving in Canada, having an appointment in one of the Military Schools lately established by the Canadian government.
2029.   x. THATCHER, b. St. John.

Mr. Sears resides 71 St. James st., St. John, N. B.

945.

ALDEN FISHER SEARS[7] [*Alden*[6], *Alden*[5], *Judah*[4], *Sam'l*[3], *Paul*[2], *Rich.*[1]], b. Bristol, N. Y., Oct. 24, 1807 ; d. Garden Prairie, Ill., Dec. 7, 1868 ; m. *Harriet Warner*. Children :

2030. i. MARY A., b. Gar. Pr., Dec. 20, 1845 ; m. *Alex'r McGlashan;* children, McGLASHAN : [1.] Maud, b. Nov. 4, 1871 ; d. Jan. 31, 1882. [2.] Jessie, b. Aug. 24, 1875 ; d. Jan. 29, 1882. [3.] ALDEN A., b. Feb. 24, 1883.

41

2031. ii. HARRIET EMILY, b. Gar. Pr., Mar. 20, 1848; m. *Thomas Munn*, and lives in Sumner co., Kan.; child, MUNN: [1.] Alden T., b. Oct., 1878; d. May, 1879.

Mr. Sears removed in 1838, to Garden Prairie, Ill., and settled on a farm.

946.

AARON V. SEARS[7] [*Alden*[6], *Alden*[5], *Judah*[4], *Sam'l*[3], *Paul*[2], *Rich*.[1]], b. Bristol, N. Y., Mar. 15, 1809; d. Riley, Ill., May 21, 1882; m. *Sarah Harris*. Children:

2032. i. PERSIS, b. Riley, Aug. 8, 1846; m. *Dwight Babcock*, and lives in Boone co., Iowa.
2033. ii. EMILY, b. Riley, Nov. 14, 1848, and lives there.
2034.* iii. ADELBERT H., b. Riley, May 25, 1851.
2035. iv. SUSIE M., b. Riley, June 6, 1853; m. *Rozell Curtis*, and lives in Dakota.
2036. v. CORA H., b. Riley, May 15, 1855; lives there.
2037. vi. FREDERIC, b. Riley, May 3, 1863; lives on the homestead in R.

Was a farmer.

947.

LEONARD BROWNELL SEARS[7] [*Alden*[6], *Alden*[5], *Judah*[4], *Sam'l*[3], *Paul*[2], *Rich*.[1]], b. Bristol, N. Y., July 10, 1810; d. Belvidere, Ill., June 3, 1864; m. May 16, 1839, *Maria H. Burghardt* of Allen's Hill, Ont. co., N. Y., she b. Nov. 25, 1818. Children:

2038. i. HORACE B., b. Belv., Sep. 27, 1841; d. Apr. 9, 1862, from exposure on battle-field of Fort Donaldson; was in Co. F, 45th Regt., Ill. Vols.
2039.* ii. IRVING COE, b. Belv., Aug. 2, 1843.
2040. iii. MARIA LOUISE, b. Belv., Sep. 16, 1846; m. May 15, 1879, *J. D. Lowe*, and lives in Vinton, Iowa; child, LOWE: [1.] Addie G., b. Oct. 16, 1880.
2041. iv. ADDIE CYNTHIA, b. Belv., May 11, 1848; m. there, Dec. 23, 1886, *Harvey A. Gould*, and lives there; child, GOULD: [1.] Jennie Louise, b. 1888.

Removed to Belvidere, Ill., and settled on a farm.

948.

WASHINGTON ZEPHANIAH SEARS[7] [*Alden*[6], *Alden* , *Judah*[4], *Sam'l*[3], *Paul*[2], *Rich*.[1]], b. Bristol, N. Y., Feb. 4, 1812;

d. Garden Prairie, Ill., Mar. 11, 1885, æ. 73 ; m. *Louisa Harris.*
Children :

2042.   i. FRANCES V., b. Gar. Pr.. Aug. 22, 1847; unm.
2043.   ii. LAURA E., b. Gar. Pr., Feb. 26, 1849 ; unm.
2044.* iii. HIRAM A., b. Gar. Pr., Apr. 19, 1851.
2045.* iv. HENRY W., b. Gar. Pr., Sep. 3, 1858.

" Mr. Sears was one of the pioneers of northern Illinois, having removed from Bristol, N. Y., in 1838, with his widowed mother, six brothers, and three sisters.

" All of the family settled on farms within six miles of each other.

" Two of the sisters eventually went West and died, one in Oregon, and one in Iowa ; and all have now passed away except the youngest, Mr. H. O. Sears of Garden Prairie.

" Mr. Sears was a sincere Christian, a member of the Congregational Church, and was dearly loved by all of us who were his kindred, and highly respected by every one who knew him."

952.

HORACE O. SEARS[7] [*Alden[6], Alden[5], Judah[4], Sam'l[3], Paul[2], Rich.[1]*], b. Bristol, N. Y., Oct. 1, 1819 ; m. May 12, 1842, *Harriet Ames.* Children :

2046.   i. HENRY O., b. Gar. Pr., May 22, 1843; d. Dec. 6, 1857.
2047.* ii. EDWARD C., b. Gar. Pr., Mar. 27, 1845.
2048. iii. CHARLES A., b. Gar. Pr., Nov. 29, 1846 ; m. ——
——, and had a dau. b. 1887; he lives on the farm.
2049.* iv. THERON M., b. Gar. Pr., Apr. 7, 1849.

Mr. Sears is a farmer at Garden Prairie, McHenry co., Ill.

953.

HIRAM SEARS[7] [*Edw'd[6], Alden[5], Judah[4], Sam'l[3], Paul[2], Rich.[1]*], b. Oswego co., N. Y., Mar. 18, 1807; d. Ohio, 1834-5; m. *Sarah Lemon.* Children :

2050.   i. CHRISTOPHER, lives in Wisconsin.
2051.   ii. MARY JANE. (A Mary Jane Sears, b. Butler, Wayne co., N. Y., Mar. 15, 1829; m. Oct. 16, 1851, at Rush, Monroe co., N. Y., Warren Sumner Keyes, a farmer; he b. May 10, 1829, son of Sol. and Esther K., and settled at Henrietta, N. Y.; had Mary Adelaide, b. May 30, 1856.)

954.

PHILO SEARS[7] [*Edw'd[6], Alden[5], Judah[4], Sam'l[3], Paul[2], Rich.[1]*], b. Oswego co., N. Y., Feb. 11, 1809 ; d. Cincinnati, Ohio, 1850 ; m. there, 1835, Mrs. *Julia A. Cline,* who d. Feb., 1885. Children:

2052.   i. IRA P., b. 1836; m. and has 5 children ; lives in Mt. Summit, Benton co., Oregon.
2053.   ii. CHARLES ELLIOTT, b. Oct., 1839 ; d. Aug., 1840.
2054.   iii. SUSAN E., b. July 13, 1843; m. 1862, *John W. Sorrell;* children, SORRELL : [1.] Clyde P., b. Apr. 22, 1863. [2.] Otho, b. Aug. 8, 1866. [3.] John A., b. Feb. 27, 1869; d. 1873. [4.] BESSIE F., b. Oct. 20, 1871; d. Sep., 1872. He d. July, 1873, and she m. 1878, *Decatur Pitman* of Milan, Mo.; child, PITMAN: [5.] Mary, b. Jan., 1879.
2055.   iv. JAMES E., b. May, 1845 ; d. July, 1849.
2056.   v. JEMIMA, b. Jan., 1848; d. Apr., 1853.

955.

IRA SEARS[7] [*Edw'd[6], Alden[5], Judah[4], Sam'l[3], Paul[2], Rich.[1]*], b. Oswego co., N. Y., Dec. 29, 1810; d. Mar. 2, 1884 ; m. Nov. 27, 1836, *Amanda M. Stockton* of Clermont co., Ohio, who d. Feb. 9, 1883. Children :

2057.   i. ALMIRA, b. May 25, 1838 ; d. Aug. 2.
2058.   ii. ALONZO P., b. Dec. 6, 1840 ; m. Apr. 19, 1866, ——— ———.
2059.   iii. JULIA A., b. Dec. 6, 1842 ; m. Oct. 31, 1860, ——— ———.
2060.   iv. WILLIAM W., b. Dec. 3, 1844; m. Mar. 3, 1872, ——— ———.
2061.   v. LAURA Y., b. May 8, 1846 ; m. Sep. 10, 1868, ——— ———.
2062.   vi. ARTHUR E., b. Feb. 20, 1848 ; m. Apr. 2, 1871, ——— ———.
2063.   vii. OSCAR P., b. Feb. 12, 1850 ; m. Mar. 9, 1876, ——— ———, lives Milan, Mo.
2064.   viii. MARY M., b. June 14, 1852 ; m. Apr. 3, 1871, ——— ———.
2065.   ix. IRA L., b. May 10, 1857 ; m. May 13, 1886, ———

2066. x. AMANDA M., b. Oct. 31, 1859; m. Mar. 30, 1878,
—— ——, who d. 1879; she m. 2d, June 12, 1880,
—— ——.

956.

Rev. ASAHEL PARKER SEARS[7] [*Edw'd*[6], *Alden*[5],
Judah[4], *Sam'l*[3], *Paul*[2], *Rich.*[1]], b. Ontario co., N. Y., June 1,
1816; d. Auburn, Ill., Dec. 17, 1874; m. Apr. 7, 1839,
Eleanor Hall of Williamsburg, Ohio, who was living in '87.
Children:
2067.   i. LAURA, b. Feb. 17, 1840; m. Blanchard, O., July
    13, 1856, *Jacob Neigh;* no children.
2068.   ii. MARY J., b. July 18, 1842; d. Sep., 1845.
2069. iii. ALMIRA, b. Nov. 27, 1844; d. Dec. 25, 1863.
2070.   iv. LEONIDAS HAMLIN, b. Apr. 30, 1847; d. Nov. 1,
    1864.
2071.* v. THOMAS MILLVILLE, b. Sep. 7, 1849.
2072.* vi. OLIVER TRIMBLE, b. June 25, 1852.
2073. vii. CLARA VICTORIA, b. Oct. 28, 1857; m. Monterey,
    Ill., Aug. 18, 1875, *George W. Howe;* children, HOWE:
    [1.] Walter Parker. [2.] Harry Fremont. [3.] Laura.
    [4.] Jessie. [5.] Child.
2074.* viii. WILLIE LINCOLN, b. June 25, 1860.

At the age of 25 Mr. Sears commenced preaching, and continued laboring with the "Christian Church," until a short
time before his death.

958.

Rev. ARTHUR ELLIOTT SEARS[7] [*Edw'd*[6], *Alden*[5],
Judah[4], *Sam'l*[3], *Paul*[2], *Rich.*[1]], b. Cincinnati, Ohio, June
6, 1823; m. Shelbyville, Mo., Apr. 17, 1848, *Julia A. Hawkins,* she b. there, Feb. 10, 1831; d. Carroll co., Mo., May 10,
1859; 2d, Milan, Mo., Jan. 10, 1860, *Eliza E. DeFrance,*
she b. Pa., Feb. 16, 1830. Children:
By *Julia:*
2075.   i. MARY C., b. Boone co., Mo., June 27, 1849; m.
    —— *Holden,* and lives in Wardner, Idaho.
2076.   ii. ALVA L., b. Monroe co., Mo., July 31, 1850.
2077. iii. CLARA L., b. Randolph co., Mo., Jan. 14, 1853.

2078. iv. LAURA ROSS, b. Lincoln co., Mo., Apr. 23, 1855 ; m. Independence, Oregon, May 9, 1875, *William H. Osborn,* he b. Mill Rock, Iowa, Mar. 5, 1851 ; are both members of 1st Ch., Salem, Oregon ; children, OSBORN : [1.] Guy Ray, b. Apr. 7, 1879. [2.] Della Ouda, b. Sep. 3, 1880.

2079. v. ARTHUR L., b. Lincoln co., Mo., Mar. 31, 1857.

By *Eliza :*

2080. vi. WILLIAM A., b. Milan, Mo., Dec. 14, 1860.

Mr. Sears was a traveling preacher of the Meth. Epis. Church for over 30 years, and is now a local at Wright's, Santa Clara co., Cal.

962.

JOHN SEARS[7] [*John[6], Alden[5], Judah[4], Sam'l[3], Paul[2], Rich.[1]*], b. Bristol, N. Y., Apr. 10, 1813; d. near Lockport, Ill., Jan. 25, 1867; m. *Moranda Blount,* who d. 1847; 2d, 1849, *Mary Jane Curtis,* who d. Nov., 1858; 3d, 1860, *Lucy Evans Hosmer.* Children :

By *Moranda :*

2081.   i. RASSELAS LOW, b. Des Plaines, Ill., Apr. 10, 1838 ; d. San Antonio, Texas, Mar. 27, 1859.

2082.   ii. JOHN, b. Des Pl., Jan. 22, 1841 ; d. Colorado, Apr. 1, 1863.

2083.* iii. JOSEPH, b. Des. Pl., Jan. 22, 1841, *gemini.*

2084.   iv. MORANDA, b. Chicago, Ill., Aug. 14, 1846; d. Aug. 27.

2085.   v. EDWARD, b. Chicago, July 26, 1847; d. Aug. 6.

By *Mary Jane :*

2086.   vi. MYRA LOUISA, b. Chicago, July 6, 1850 ; m. Feb. 10, 1870, *Wm. H. Burnet,* and lives 2342 Indiana ave., Chicago ; children, BURNET : [1.] Anna Louisa, b. Jan. 4, 1871. [2.] John Sidney, b. Sep. 15, 1874. [3.] Bessie Curtis, b. Nov. 6, 1877.

2087.* vii. WILLIAM HENRY HOSMER, b. Chicago, Jan. 17, 1853.

2088. viii. HIRAM LOW, b. Chicago, June 17, 1855 ; d. Aug. 17.

By *Lucy :*

2089.   ix. GEORGE HOSMER, b. Chicago, Aug. 13, 1861; lives there.

2090.   x. KATHERINE ELIZABETH, b. Chicago, Aug. 8, 1863.

2091.   xi. LUCY TALCOTT, b. Chicago, July 21, 1865 ; d. Delaware, Ill., Mar. 4, 1882.

Mr. Sears removed from Bristol, N. Y., to Des Plaines, Cook co., Illinois; thence to Chicago, and later to Delaware, near Lockport, Will co., Ill.

963.

EDWARD H. SEARS[7] [*John*[6], *Alden*[5], *Judah*[4], *Sam'l*[3], *Paul*[2], *Rich.*[1]], b. Dec. 14, 1819; m. June 13, 1850, *Julia M. Jones* of Chicago, Ill. Children:

2092.   i. CAROLINE MATILDA, b. Feb. 1, 1854; d. Oct. 11.
2093.   ii. EDWARD JONES, b. Chicago, June 19, 1858; d. May, 1883; was educated in Todd's Sem'y, Woodstock, Wis., and in Wesleyan Acad., Wilbraham, Mass., and grad. with high honors. He engaged for a time in sheep raising, and later was of firm Keefer, Sears & Co., fruit and vegetable packers, Sterling, Ill., and Sec'y and Treas. of Rock River Packing Co. At the burning of the Co.'s building in Jan., 1882, he contracted a cold, which settled on his lungs, and from which he died.

"In his business relations he was always upright and conscientious, and gave his best energies to whatever he undertook.

"His prospects were bright, and his future promising.

"Among his associates he was kind and obliging, a very agreeable companion, and had a kind word for all. During his sickness he never complained, and to the last exhibited a cheerful state of mind, and an indomitable will in bearing his suffering."

2094. iii. ARTHUR DAVIS, b. Jan. 7, 1861; d. Aug. 7.
2095. iv. HATTIE CORNELIA, b. Dec. 30, 1862; d. Apr. 7, 1863.
2096.   v. JENNIE MADELINE, b. Dec. 20, 1864; d. Dec. 25, 1887; m. Sterling, Ill., Oct., 1885, *Andrew C. Warrick* of Chicago, lived in Toledo, Ohio; he is chief clerk, Tol., St. Louis & Kansas City R. R.; child, WARRICK: [1.] *Madeline*, b. Sep. 1, 1887; d. Jan. 22, 1888.
2097. vi. JULIA LOUISA, b. Sep. 22, 1867; d. July 24, 1868.
2098. vii. MAUD ELIZABETH, b. Aug. 14, 1875.

Mr. Sears removed to Chicago, thence to Como, Whiteside co., and later to Sterling, Illinois, where he now lives.

965.

DE WITT CLINTON SEARS[7] [*John*[6], *Alden*[5], *Judah*[4], *Sam'l*[3], *Paul*[2], *Rich.*[1]], b. Bristol, N. Y., July 1, 1824; m.

Dec. 12, 1849, *Carrie A. Smith,* dau. of Rev. Dennison S. of Lima, N. Y., who d. Jan. 2, 1858; 2d, Jan. 5, 1860, *Laura Wilson.*   Children:

By *Carrie:*
2099.   i. ELLA L., b. Bristol, Apr. 10, 1851; m. Mar. 27 1874, *John Shary,* and lives there; has four children.
2100.   ii. ADA BYRON, b. Br., Aug. 21, 1852; m. May 5, 1880, *Wm. Benedict,* and rem. to Omaha, Neb.; no children.

By *Laura:*
2101. iii. HENRY W., b. Br., Feb. 8, 1861; m. Feb. 8, 1887, *Lizzie J. Taylor,* dau. of C. O. T.
2102. iv. CARRIE E., b. Br., June 9, 1864; m. June, 1887, —— ——.

2103.   v. ALICE E., b. Br., Oct. 2, 1866; was killed by light-ning June 24, 1884.   "She had just returned from the academy at Lyons, N. Y., and the future was exceedingly bright before her, when the change came.   She had just arisen from the piano where she had been playing and singing, 'It shall be white as snow,' and stepped to the door to look upon the sublimity of the storm, when the bolt came, and her life was ended.   She was very beau-tiful and accomplished, the pride of indulgent parents, the idol of brother and sisters, and the loved and admired of all that knew her, and when she was thus instantly and violently torn from the arms of those who would gladly have given their own lives to have saved hers, men stood as if with uncovered heads and dumb lips, feeling that they were in the presence of a power too great for them to comprehend."

Mr. Sears lives at Bristol, Ontario co., N. Y., on the farm that was cleared and owned by his grand-father.

971.

HARPER D. SEARS[7] [*Paul[6], Nathan[5], Judah[4], Sam'l[3], Paul[2], Rich.[1]*], b. Montpelier, Vt., Jan. 9, 1774; d. Stowe, Vt., Mar. 3, 1867; m. there, Jan. 23, 1823, *Susan W. Churchill,* dau. of Joseph and Sarah (Cobb) C., she b. Woodstock, Vt., July 17, 1793–4; d. Stowe, Aug. 2, 1865.   Children:
2103. *a.*   i. LUCY H., b. Stowe, Jan. 13, 1824; m. Dec. 20, 1846, *Wm. Morrison*; children, MORRISON: [1.] Fred. S., b. July 31, 1849; d. Mar., 1872.   [2.] Mary C., b. June 30, 1850; d. Nov., 1874.

2103. *a.* ii. ELIZABETH R., b. Stowe, June 16, 1825.
2103.*a.* iii. NATHAN R., b. Stowe, Apr. 1, 1827.
2103.*a.* iv. SYLVESTER C., b. Stowe, Feb. 5, 1829.
2103. *a.* v. JULIA C., b. Stowe, Aug. 27, 1830.
2103. *a.* vi. HARPER D., b. Stowe, Feb. 20, 1832; d. July 3, 1834.
2103.*a.* vii. FRED. M., b. Morristown, Vt., Oct. 4, 1836.
2103. *a.* viii. STEPHEN D., b. Morristown, Vt., May 3, 1838; d. Aug. 29, 1842.

978.

NATHAN SEARS[7] [*Paul[6], Nathan[5], Judah[4], Sam'l[3], Paul[2], Rich.[1]*], b. Montpelier, Vt., Jan. 12, 1811; d. Fairhaven, Mass., June, 1846, of lock-jaw; m. Rochester, Mass., June 25, 1837, by Rev. John M. Leach, to *Laura Mendall,* dau. of David and Jane M., who died while visiting at Roch., Oct. 8, 1884, æ. 74. Children:

2104. i. LUCY JANE, b. Roch., Mar. 25, 1838; m. *James A. Young* of Marion, Mass., and lives 95 Fourth st., New Bedford.
2105. ii. STEPHEN DELANO, d.
2106. iii. CYNTHIA MENDALL, b. Fairhaven, Apr. 17, 1845; m. *Benj. Tripp, Jr.,* of New Bed., and lives in Knoxville, Tenn.

983.

NATHAN SEARS[7] [*Nathan[6], Nathan[5], Judah[4], Sam'l[3], Paul[2], Rich.[1]*], b. Rochester, Mass.. Oct. 28, 1829; m. Tiverton, R. I., *Betsy L. Sisson,* she b. Westport, Mass. Children:
2107. i. JOSEPH WALTER, b. Sep. 13, 1851; m. *Martha Mills* of N. H.
2108. ii. ROBERT P., b. Nov. 19, 1854; d.
2109. iii. IDA J., b. Mar. 20, 1857; m. 1874, *A. G. Eldredge* of New Bedford.
2110. iv. RHODA A., b. Oct. 13, 1859; m. 1878, *Frank R. Guilford* of New Bedford.
2111. v. FLORA, b. June 8, 1861; d.
2112. vi. FRANKLIN, b. Nov. 8, 1864; d.
2113. vii. LILLIAN E., b. July 8, 1866.
2114. viii. NATHAN, b. Oct. 22, 1869.

2115. ix. SUSAN E., b. July 22, 1872.
2116. x. WILLIAM A., b. July 7, 1876 ; d.

Mr. Sears lives in New Bedford, Mass.; address, 168 Union street.

986.

HENRY SEARS[7] [*Lot*[6], *David*[5], *Judah*[4], *Sam'l*[3], *Paul*[2], *Rich.*[1]], b. Newark, N. Y., Feb. 27, 1801 ; d. Troy, N. Y., Apr. 27, 1857, æ. 56 ; m. there, *Lucy Yale* of Lenox, Mass., (sister of John Y. of L. ;) 2d, Schaghticoke, N. Y., *Harriet Russell* of Easton, N. Y., (she was of the Russell and Howland families of New Bed.)　Children:

By *Lucy*:
2117. i. LUCY L., d.
2118. ii. ELIZA, b. ab't 1833 ; lives in Newark, N. Y., unm.
2119. iii. MILES YALE, d. infant.

By *Harriet*:
2120. iv. HARRIET L., b. Troy, Sep. 1, 1839 ; m. there, Jan. 22, 1867, *J. H. Richardson*, and lives in Gloversville, N. Y.; no children.
2121. v. WILLIAM HENRY, b. July 25, 1844 ; d. July, 1866, of a gun-shot wound in the forehead, while in Union Army at White Oaks Road, Va.; " he was a beautiful boy, had dark olive complexion, black eyes, and looked like a Cuban, as did his father ; stood 6 feet in height."

Mr. Sears removed from Newark to Troy, N. Y., at the age of 17, and went into the grocery business there, prospered in business, but lost his property by a destructive fire, and by indorsing for others, who failed, became despondent and never rallied again.

He was a public-spirited, earnest man, a devout Christian, constant in season and out of season.

988.

JAMES COFFIN SEARS[7] [*Lot*[6], *David*[5], *Judah*[4], *Sam'l*[3], *Paul*[2], *Rich.*[1]], b. Feb. 11, 1804 ; d. Troy, N. Y., Aug. 3, 1832 ; m. Feb. 10, 1831, *Lydia Elmira Howland*, she b. Sep. 27, 1806 ; d. Oct. 28, 1861.　Children:
2122. i. ESTHER ELMIRA, b. Nov. 9, 1831 ; m. 1866, Charles H. Sears, No. 2125.

2123. ii. ELLEN ADELAIDE, b. Nov. 11, 1832; m. Nov. 16, 1853, *Asa Doolittle Short* of Richmond, N. Y., he b. Apr. 2, 1827; and lives on the old homestead in Manchester, N. Y.; children, SHORT: [1.] Elmira, b. July 28, 1856; d. Sep. 27, 1871. [2.] Edwin Robinson, b. Oct. 9, 1863. [3.] Joseph Warren, b. Dec. 4, 1865.

Mr. Sears had a collegiate education, and in early life was engaged in teaching; was a man of great intelligence.

After his marriage he lived on the Howland estate in Manchester, N. Y., which belonged to his wife.

He died in Troy, N. Y., after 12 hours' sickness of cholera.

990.

HIRAM SEARS[7] [*Lot*[6], *David*[5], *Judah*[4], *Sam'l*[3], *Paul*[2], *Rich.*[1]], b. June 21, 1808; d. New Haven, Mich., 1880; m. *Elizabeth Bullis;* 2d, *Eliza Howland.* Children:

2124.   i. ANDREW J.
2125.* ii. CHARLES HENRY, b. July 15, 1838.
2126. iii. JAMES NATHAN.
2127. iv. JOSEPH LOT.
2128.   v. CATHARINE.
2129. vi. ADELAIDE.

Mr. Sears was a farmer and lived in Manchester, Ont. co., N. Y.

996.

JONATHAN PRINCE SEARS[7] [*Prince*[6], *David*[5], *Judah*[4], *Sam'l*[3], *Paul*[2], *Rich.*[1]], b. Taunton, Mass., Apr. 23, 1798; d. Raynham, Mass., Sep. 3, 1847, æ. 48; m. Dighton, Mass., Apr. 22, 1822, by Rev. Bartlett Pease, to *Nancy H. Francis* of Mansfield, Mass., dau. of Dea. Peleg and Nancy (Allen) F. of Dighton, she b. Mans., Apr. 9, 1799; d. Lenox, Mass., June 18, 1863, æ. 64; (Dea. Peleg F. was a son of Peleg and Eliz. (Hathaway) F.; his wife was dau. of John Hathaway; Nancy Allen was dau. of Micah and Catherine (Everett) A. of Mans.) Children:

2130.* i. HENRY BEAUFORT, b. May 24, 1825.
2131. ii. FRANCIS EVERETT, b. July, 1826; d. Aug. 17.
2132. iii. ELVIRA FITZALLAN, b. Taunton, Feb. 22, 1828; lives in Brooklyn, N. Y., unm.; has rendered great assistance in collecting material for this work.

Mr. Sears was but six months old when his father died. On attaining his majority he assumed the prefix of Jonathan.

In early life he was a successful merchant in Taunton; removed to Boston, where he entered into business, but his health failing he was obliged to retire, and in Nov., 1846, he went to Savannah, Ga., hoping to benefit by change of climate, but without avail. In June, 1847, he returned and died at the residence of his sister in Raynham, Mass., and was buried in Greenwood Cemetery, N. Y., as is also his wife.

1000.

ALDEN SEARS[7] [*Roland[6], Roland[5], Seth[4], Sam'l[3], Paul[2], Rich.[1]*], b. Harwich, Mass., July 23, 1774; d. West Hawley, Mass., Dec. 28, 1847; m. Hawley, Nov. 19, 1801, *Sarah Crosby*, she b. there, July 2, 1775; d. Dec. 1, 1825; 2d, Haw., Apr. 9, 1826, *Elizabeth Hall,* who d. Mar. 30, 1839.   Children:

By *Sarah :*

2133.   i. ANSEL, b. Haw., May 25, 1803; m. Springfield, Mich., *Betsy Calkins*, and d. s. p., Apr. 11, 1852.
2134.   ii. HIRAM, b. Haw., May 25, 1805; d. Oct. 2, 1848.
2135.   iii. ALDEN, b. Haw., Jan. 22, 1807; d. Feb. 11, 1809.
2136.* iv. JOSHUA, b. Haw., Sep. 18, 1808.
2137.* v. ALDEN, b. Haw., Aug. 17, 1810.
2138.   vi. SARAH, b. Haw., Apr. 29, 1812; m. there, Jan. 10, 1856, *John W. Hyde*, and d. s. p., June 26, 1866.
2139. vii. REBECCA, b. Haw., June 6, 1814; d. Oct. 17, 1841.
2140.*viii. EBENEZER, b. Haw., June 15, 1816.

Alden Sears removed to Hawley in Mar., 1795.

1001.

ALVAN SEARS[7] [*Roland[6], Roland[5], Seth[4], Sam'l[3], Paul[2], Rich.[1]*], b. Harwich, Mass., Sep. 26, 1775; d. West Hawley, Mass., Apr. 15, 1844, æ. 68; m. Hawley, Feb. 27, 1800, *Bethia Howes*, she b. Nov. 5, 1777; d. Oct. 27, 1863, æ. 86. Children:

2141.* i. SETH, b. Haw., July 27, 1801.
2142.* ii. ALVAN, b. Haw., Jan. 8, 1804.
2143. iii. ABIGAIL, b. Haw., Jan. 9, 1806; m. W. Haw., July 4, 1850, *Horace Elmer ;* 2d, Savoy, Mass., Jan. 5, 1858, *Ira Fuller*, and d. Apr. 8, 1883.

2144. iv. EDMUND, b. Haw., Mar. 26, 1808 ; d. Sep. 26.
2145.   v. JOSHUA H., b. Haw., July 19, 1809 ; m. Oct. 20,
1842, *Abigail C. Bangs* of Springfield, Mass., and d.
Oct. 27, 18—.
2146.* vi. URBAN, b. Haw., Aug. 2, 1813.
2147. vii. VIENNA, b. Haw., Apr. 22, 1816 ; d. Aug. 24,
1856.
2148. viii. BETHIA, b. Haw., July 25, 1819 ; lives in West
Hawley.
2149. ix. DESIRE, b. Haw., July 25, 1819, *gemini ;* d. July
26.
2150.   x. EDMUND, b. Haw., May 27, 1822 ; m. Hadley, Mass.,
Mar. 6, 1844, *Catharine Bartlett,* and d. Nov. 27, 1885.

Alvan Sears removed from Harwich with his parents in the
spring of 1795, and settled on West Hill, Hawley.

The History of Hawley, 1887, says they were from Dennis.
Roland Sears lived in Harwich, and all his children were born
and recorded there, but were baptized in Second Church, Yarmouth, to which church their parents belonged, it being more
convenient to their residence, which was near the Yarmouth
(now Dennis) line.

1002.

ROLAND SEARS[7] [*Roland*[6], *Roland*[5], *Seth*[4], *Sam'l*[3],
Paul[2], *Rich.*[1]], b. Harwich, Mass., Apr. 12, 1777 ; d. West
Hawley, Mass., Oct. 1, 1828, æ. 51 ; m. Hawley, *Persis Thayer,*
who d. Sep. 25, 1828, æ. 53.   Children :
2151.   i. THANKFUL, b. Haw., May 31, 1806 ; m. *Jude Tuttle* of Rowe, Mass.; children, TUTTLE : [1.] Cynthia, m.
Martin V. Cressey. [2.] Roland. [3.] Lyman, m. Hattie
Todd. [4.] Jude, m. Lora Bemis.
2152. ii. PERSIS, b. Haw., Mar. 1, 1809 ; m. —— *Seagraves,*
was divorced, and d.
2153. iii. ROLAND, b. Haw., July 20, 1811.
2154. iv. MERCY, b. Haw., May 8, 1813 ; m. *Warren Albee*
of Charlemont, Mass.; children, ALBEE : [1.] Henry, d.
[2.] Persis. [3.] Mercy.
2155.* v. ROLAND, b. Haw., Sep. 16, 1815.
2156.* vi. JOSEPH, b. Haw., May 28, 1818.
2157.* vii. SYLVESTER, b. Haw., May 5, 1821.

Mr. Sears removed to Hawley with his parents in Mar., 1795.

1005.

BENJAMIN SEARS[7] [*Roland[6], Roland[5], Seth[4], Sam'l[3], Paul[2], Rich.[1]*], b. Harwich, Aug. 27, 1783; d. West Hawley, Mass., Apr. 21, 1855, æ. 72; m. *Rebecca Eldridge,* who d. Dec. 25, 1850. Children:

2158.   i. Lydia, b. Haw., Oct. 25, 1813; d. Oct., 1845.
2159.   ii. Rebecca E., b. Haw., Nov. 5, 1815; m. *Fred. H. Sears,* No. 1964.
2160.   iii. Harriet, b. Haw., Jan. 18, 1818; m. Mar. 3, 1836, *Rodolphus Hawkes.*
2161.   iv. Mary, b. Haw., Apr. 19, 1820; m. *Jonathan Sears,* No. 1983.
2162.   v. Benjamin, b. Haw., Apr. 16, 1822; m. there, Oct. 10, 1848, *Louisa Atkins,* dau. of Freeman and Rebecca (Baker) A., she b. Apr. 26, 1828; d. Feb. 14, 1868, æ. 40; he d. s. p., Feb. 11, 1870.
2163.   vi. Elizabeth, b. Haw., Apr. 22, 1824.

1007.

SYLVESTER SEARS[7] [*Roland[6], Roland[5], Seth[4], Sam'l[3], Paul[2], Rich.[1]*], b. Harwich, Mass., Feb. 26, 1788; was drowned just below the bridge in West Hawley, Mass., while bathing, Aug. 26, 1820, æ. 32; m. Hawley, Sep. 17, 1812, *Persis Hall,* who d. Feb. 10, 1871, æ. 79.   Children:

2164.   i. Olive, b. Haw., July 22, 1817; d. Jan., 1821.
2165.   ii. Emily, b. Haw., June 17, 1819; m. Nov. 28, 1831, *H. C. Coates.*

1010.

CHARLES SEARS[7] [*Peter[6], Benj.[5], Benj.[4], Sam'l[3], Paul[2], Rich.[1]*], b. Litchfield, N. Y., Aug. 20, 1803; d. Sardinia, N. Y., June 16, 1885; m. there by Esq. Clark, to *Miranda Powers.* Children:

2166.   i. Louisa, b. Sard., June 4, 1827; m. *A. D. Hedges,* and lives in Rothbury, Mich.; children, Hedges: [1.] Em., m. Eugene Heath, and lives in Shortsville, N. Y. [2.] Charles. [3.] John.
2167.   ii. Susan, b. Sard., Dec. 28, 1830; m. *O. P. Goodspeed,* and lives in Mt. Pleasant, Mich.; children, Good-

speed: [1.] Charles, lives in East Saginaw, Mich. [2.] Frank, lives in Minneapolis, Minn. [3.] Kittie, m. Spencer Hughes of Arcade, N. Y. [4.] Ellen, d.

2168.* iii. FRANKLIN, b. Sard., May 3, 1831.
2169.* iv. SEWARD, b. Sard., Sep. 16, 1838.
2170. v. MARTHA, b. Sard., Aug. 22, 1841; d. 1853.
2171. vi. CRETE, b. Sard., Feb. 9, 1847; m. *J. S. Bushnell,* and lives in Arcade, N. Y.; children, BUSHNELL: [1.] Lillian, and 3 others, who d. inf.

Mr. Sears was a good farmer; he had been in poor health for a year, but only confined to his bed for two weeks previous to his death.

1011.

ALBERT SELIM SEARS[7] [*Peter[6], Benj.[5], Benj.[4], Sam'l[3], Paul[2], Rich.[1]*], b. Richfield, N. Y., Sep. 30, 1810; d. Mar. 22, 1867; m. Springville, N. Y., Sep. 24, 1839, *Margaret A. Graves,* she b. Belchertown, Mass., Mar. 14, 1819. Children:

2172. i. SUSAN ABIGAIL, b. Buffalo, N. Y., Sep. 24, 1848; m. there, Nov. 15, 1871, *Wm. S. Sizer* of B., he b. Mar. 22, 1843; lives 126 Chippewa st., Buffalo; children, SIZER: [1.] Henry Sears, b. July 29, 1872. [2.] William Sears, b. July 13, 1876. [3.] Margaret Sears, b. May 25, 1880. [4.] Grace Sears, b. Feb. 23, 1883.
2173. ii. EMMA URSULA, b. Buff., Feb. 26, 1853.
2174. iii. FRANCES GRAVES, b. Buff., Nov. 25, 1857.

Mr. Sears removed, in early life, to Springville, N. Y., and thence, about 1847, to Buffalo, N. Y., and was engaged in business there until his death. He was a man of culture, and greatly respected.

His widow resides at 132 Chippewa st., Buffalo.

1019.

BRADLEY SEARS[7] [*Isaac[6], Benj.[5], Benj.[4], Sam'l[3], Paul[2], Rich.[1]*], b. South East, N. Y., Apr. 23, 1804; d. Oct. 9, 1884, æ. 80; m. Jan. 17, 1832, *Mary Norris.* Children:

2175. i. ANNIE, b. So. East, Sep. 27, 1833.
2176. ii. GEORGE E., b. So. East, July 19, 1835.
2177. iii. MELISSA, b. So. East, Nov. 10, 1837; m. Apr. 6, 1881, *David Hall* of Brewsters, N. Y., son of John and Harriet (Northrop) H., he b. Dec. 30, 1830.

2178. iv. RACHEL DE FOREST, b. So. East, May 9, 1843; lives at home.

Mr. Sears was a farmer, and lived on part of the old homestead in South East, 4 miles from Brewsters on the Harlem railroad.

"Mr. S. did not seem robust in his early years; a tendency to asthma was with him in his boyhood, but there must have been much vigor in his frame.

"He was ill comparatively little; only two severe illnesses, and they of the shorter duration, and of a nature that might affect the strongest physical manhood.

"In his early married life, in the prosecution of an avocation for a little while followed, he was able to endure readily the fatigue associated with riding horseback even as far as Lake Erie.

"His death was the first break in the family circle; father, mother, and all the children God gave to them, have been permitted to live together till the father's four-score years have been reached.

"During the summer of 1884, when the illness began separating him from more active care, he was disposed to give the reminiscences of his early life; to tell of his father, and of his own wishes and hopes in his young manhood, and the memories of the church service and life in the old church.

"But especially was there always grateful dwelling upon the comforts and the blessings of his own home.

"His children were to him pride and joy, and with that trembling of the lip and moistening of the eye, they who knew him the more readily recall, he would speak of their unfailing kindness; of their anticipation of every want; of how good God had been to him and his.

"He did not seem to be an old man, the years had not so told upon him. The face was unwrinkled, and the frame was vigorous. Till the last summer he was permitted to be actively employed in the concerns of his home.

"When the difficulty of breathing, and the heart trouble abated, some thought him better, and there was the entertainment of hope.

"But especially upon his own spirit as the end drew near, there was the conviction of approaching death.

"He would tell the children of what he desired to have done upon the farm, as soon as he would not be here, while to his pastor, who was often with him, he spoke of his consciousness of himself as a sinner, and of his trust in Christ as a Saviour, and of the absence of the fear of death.

" It had been a growing peace, and as the spirit advanced into the depths of the shadow, the darkness had passed, clinging with tender affection to the beloved with him, yet content to go at the Father's call, so quietly the spirit slipped from earth.

" It was as the morning hour advanced that death came.

"And so for him ' the night passed, and the morning came.' "

1020.

JOSEPH SEARS⁷ [*Isaac⁶*, *Benj.⁵*, *Benj.⁴*, *Sam'l³*, *Paul²*, *Rich.¹*], b. South East, N. Y., April 4, 1806 ; d. in fall of 1885 ; m. May 28, 1834, *Caroline Reed*. Child :

2179. i. DANIEL R., b. June 25, 1836 ; m. Dec. 19, 1872, *Mary Frances Weed*, dau. of Oscar and Ann Eliza (Quintard) W., she b. Danbury, Ct., Oct. 7, 1842, lives in So. E.

1028.

AARON SEARS⁷ [*Sam'l⁶*, *Benj.⁵*, *Benj.⁴*, *Sam'l³*, *Paul²*, *Rich.¹*], b. Sep. 18, 1812 ; m. Feb. 10, 1848, *Maria Spencer*, who d. Nov. 7, 1848 ; 2d, Dec. 11, 1851, *Harriet Bushnell*, dau. of Calvin and Polly (Williams) B., she b. Vernon, N. Y., July 29, 1823. Children :

By *Harriet :*

2180. i. LOTTIE MARIA, b. Sep. 16, 1853 ; d. Mar. 8, 1855.

2181. ii. BENJAMIN CALVIN, b. May 11, 1855.

Mr. Sears removed to Morris, Ill., and engaged in the lumber business.

1032.

BENJAMIN SEARS⁷ [*Steph.⁶*, *Steph.⁵*, *Benj.⁴*, *Sam'l³*, *Paul²*, *Rich.¹*], b. June 2, 1798 ; d. Sharon, Ct., June 10, 1875 ; m. Sep. 11, 1844, *Emeline Crouch* of Canaan, Ct. Children :

2182. i. EMILY CROUCH, b. Sharon, Dec. 30, 1845 ; lives at home.

2183. ii. LOIS, b. Sharon, May 11, 1848 ; m. *John J. Williams* of Rossville, Staten Island ; children, WILLIAMS : [1.] Charles Edward, b. June 5, 1874. [2.] Julia Banker, b. July 30, 1876.

2184. iii. STEPHEN, b. Sharon, May 11, 1848, *gemini;* d. Mar. 27, 1860.
2185. iv. AMELIA, b. Sharon, Jan. 5, 1851; d. Sep. 15.
2186. v. JULIA, b. Sharon, Jan. 5, 1851, *gemini.*

1036.

JOHN SEARS[7] [*Steph.[6], Steph.[5], Benj.[4], Sam'l[3], Paul[2], Rich.[1]*], b. Feb. 18, 1806; m. Feb. 2, 1835, *Abigail W. Noyes* of Edinburgh, N. Y., who d. Oct. 29, 1864. Children:

2187. i. CYNTHIA E., b. Apr. 3, 1836; d. May 6, 1865.
2188. ii. MARY E., b. Feb. 23, 1838; m. Jan. 16, 1873, *Judson S. Bird;* children, BIRD: [1.] John C., b. Nov. 6, 1873; d. Mar. 19, 1882. [2.] Jennie Elizabeth, b. Apr. 1, 1878.
2189.* iii. SEABURY L., b. Apr. 16, 1840.
2190. iv. ELIZABETH L., b. Feb. 10, 1842; m. May 12, 1881, *Albert T. Hoover.*
2191. v. HELEN B., b. Nov. 7, 1843; m. Jan. 25, 1863, *Ransom T. Ford*, and d. June 3, 1866; children, FORD: [1.] George R., b. Nov. 23, 1863. [2.] C. Robert, b. June 22, 1865.
2192.* vi. SAMUEL N., b. Apr. 6, 1846.
2193. vii. JOHN W., b. Dec. 16, 1848; d. June 15, 1868.
2194. viii. ABBIE A., b. Aug. 22, 1851; d. Sep. 18, 1867.
2195. ix. FREDERIC W., b. Aug. 24, 1853; d. Oct. 22, 1872.

Mr. Sears is a farmer in Jackson, Mich.

1038.

STEPHEN H. SEARS[7] [*Steph.[6], Steph.[5], Benj.[4], Sam'l[3], Paul[2], Rich.[1]*], b. Sharon, Ct., Nov. 9, 1811; d. Jackson, Mich., Nov. 18, 1876, æ. 65; m. there, Dec. 6, 1839, *Martha Hale*, she b. Royalton, N. Y., Aug. 22, 1815, dau. of Sol. and Louisa (Smith) H. Children:

2196. i. CHARLES ALBERT, b. Jackson, Nov. 20, 1844, is unm., and of firm Tannar & Sears, Horton, Mich.
2197.* ii. NEWTON H., b. Jackson, Oct. 19, 1854.

Mr. Sears removed from Sharon to Michigan in 1831–32, with a few hundred dollars in his purse, and located on government lands in the township of Spring Arbor in Jackson co., worked hard all his life, improved his farm, and when he died left to his sons two as nice farms as there are in the State of Michigan, besides a round sum in cash.

He was a very liberal and generous man ; especially to the poor.

1041.

SIMEON B. SEARS[7] [*John*[6], *Steph.*[5], *Benj.*[4], *Sam'l*[3], *Paul*[2], *Rich.*[1]], b. Sharon, Ct., Sep. 16, 1816 ; m. there, *Mary Jeanette Roberts* of S., dau. of Sam'l and Pamela (Patchin) R., she b. 1816.   Children :

2198.   i. MARY, b. Sharon, Jan. 18, 1842 ; m. Dr. *Charles C. Eastman* of Binghamton, N. Y., Physician to the Insane Asylum; no children.

2199.   ii. ALBERT ROBERTS, b. Sharon, Aug., 1843 ; lives on the homestead.

2200.   iii. AMANDA GERMOND, b. Sharon, June, 1845 ; m. Dec. 12, 1866, *Henry C. Browne* of West Bloomfield, N. Y., has 3 sons, and lives on the farm formerly of Jasper Peck Sears, No. 798.

2201.   iv. LOUISA MERSENE, b. Sharon, July, 1847 ; m. *George Parmalee* of Canandaigua, N. Y., and has 1 son.

2202.   v. ALMIRA GOULD, b. Sharon, 1849 ; m. July 22, 1871, *Frank A. Ellis* of Canandaigua ; no children.

Mr. Sears removed from Sharon to East Bloomfield, N. Y., where he carried on a large farm.

1042.

JOHN SEARS[7] [*John*[6], *Steph.*[5], *Benj.*[4], *Sam'l*[3], *Paul*[2], *Rich.*[1]], b. May 20, 1818 ; m. Sep. 17, 1856, *Mary Jewitt.* Children :

2203.   i. MARY J., b. July 9, 1857 ; m. Jan. 27, 1880, *E. J. Poster* of Utica, Neb.

2204.   ii. FRANK S., b. Oct. 13, 1860.

2205.   iii. JOHN, b. Nov. 27, 1861.

2206.   iv. SARAH A., b. Feb. 29, 1864.

2207.   v. NELLIE, b. June 30, 1870.

2208.   vi. WILLIAM H., b. Nov. 28, 1875.

2209.   vii. JESSIE S., b. Sep. 9, 1878.

Mr. Sears is a farmer at Cornwall, Ill. Post-office, Atkinson.

1043.

VINCENT G. SEARS[7] [*John*[6], *Steph.*[5], *Benj.*[4], *Sam'l*[3], *Paul*[2], *Rich.*[1]], b. Aug. 24, 1823; m. Oct. 7, 1856, *Julia Jewitt*, (sister of Mary J., who m. his bro. John.)   Children :
2210.   i. William J., b. Cornwall, Ill., July 14, 1857.
2211.   ii. Carrie J., b. Lima, N. Y., Aug. 16, 1863.
2212.   iii. Charles, d. young.

Mr. Sears lives in Batavia, N. Y.

1051.

ISAAC UNDERHILL SEARS[7] [*Ira*[6], *Enoch*[5], *Benj.*[4], *Sam'l*[3], *Paul*[2], *Rich.*[1]], b. Bennington, Vt., Sep. 19, 1803 ; m. Hoosick Falls, N. Y., Aug. 29, 1824, *Sabrina Burrell*, she b. there, July 14, 1806.   Children :
2213.*   i. Thaddeus Patchen, b. Hoosick F., Sep. 2, 1825.
2214.   ii. Samuel Burrell, b. Broadalbin, N. Y., Mar. 29, 1830; m. Oct. 28, 1863, *Mary Phillips* of Dryden, N. Y., and is City Engineer of Kingston, N. Y.
2215.   iii. Charles Cushman, b. B., July 11, 1833; m. Dec. 29, 1854, *Carrie Hard* of Pittsford, N. Y., and lives in Buffalo, N. Y.
2216.   iv. Jennie Pamelia, b. Albion, N. Y., Apr. 27, 1842; m. there, *Edwin O. Swan* of Medina, N. Y., and lives in Chicago, Ill.
2217.   v. William Randall, b. Albion, Jan. 24, 1844; is a Real Estate Agent in Chicago, Ill.

Mr. Sears removed in the Spring of 1821 to Hoosick Falls, N. Y., and in 1835, to Albion, N. Y.
Is a wagon and carriage manufacturer.
Has been a Methodist for 56 years.

1054.

HENRY SEARS[7] [*Ira*[6], *Enoch*[5], *Benj.*[4], *Sam'l*[3], *Paul*[2], *Rich.*[1]], b. Bennington, Vt., Nov. 8, 1810 ; m. Broadalbin, N. Y., Sep. 20, 1832, *Harriet Alvord*, she b. Amsterdam, N. Y., Feb. 15, 1809 ; d. Albion, N. Y., June 28, 1882. Children :
2218.*   i. Alpheus Henry, b. Broadalbin, Mar. 14, 1836.

2219. ii. SARAH HARRIET, b. B., Sep. 3, 1837 ; d. Oct. 4, 1854.
2220. iii. WILLIAM ALVORD, b. B., Sep. 1, 1840 ; lives Albion, N. Y.
2221. iv. ANNA EMMONS, b. Albion, N. Y., Apr. 10, 1846 ; lives there.

Mr. Sears has been an Elder in the Presbyterian Church in Albion since 1853. Has manufactured and dealt in carriages since 1840.

1057.

ROBERT SEARS[7] [*Isaac*[6], *Sunderland*[5], *Benj.*[4], *Sam'l*[3], *Paul*[2], *Rich.*[1]], b. —— ; m. —— ——. Child :
2222. i. CHARLES, d. æ. 21.

Mr. Sears lived in Mechanicsville, near Waterford, N. Y.

1063.

Dr. REUBEN E. SEARS[7] [*Reuben*[6], *Sunderland*[5], *Benj.*[4], *Sam'l*[3], *Paul*[2], *Rich.*[1]], b. Dracut, Mass., July 31, 1824 ; m. Saratoga, N. Y., *Cynthia Ann Guild ;* 2d, *Patience P. Meigs*, she b. Munroe, N. H., June 19, 1835. Children :
2223.* i. REUBEN EDWARD, b. June 6, 1848.
2224. ii. CYNTHIA ANN, b. May 16, 1852 ; m. *Henry D. Churchill* of Vt. ; no children.
2225. iii. FLORENCE MAY, b. May 3, 1854 ; m. *Arthur S. Burnell ;* children, BURNELL : [1.] Helen. [2.] Florence.
2226. iv. AUGUSTUS G.

Mr. Sears was a physician, but relinquished practice to engage in the manufacture of barb-wire for fences.
Resides in Marshalltown, Iowa.

1066.

SUNDERLAND GREGORY SEARS[7] [*Wm.*[6], *Sunderland*[5], *Benj.*[4], *Sam'l*[3], *Paul*[2], *Rich.*[1]], b. Saratoga, N. Y., Sep. 27, 1817 ; d. St. Louis, Mo., May 1, 1880, æ. 63 ; m. N. Y. city, Dec. 25, 18—, by Rev. Mr. Forbes, to *Isabella Wells Bagley*, she b. Blackburn, Eng., Apr. 11, 1819. Children :
2227. i. JANE ANNA, b. Long Island, N. Y. ; m. —— *Miller.*
2228. ii. WILLIAM HENRY, b. Fulton co., Ill.

2229. iii. EDWARD, b. St. Louis, Mo.
2230. iv. ISABELLA MATILDA, b. Barry, Ill.; m. —— *Smith*.
2231. v. HIRAM ST. JOHN, b. St. Louis, Mo.; lives there.
2232. vi. CORA WELLS.
    And 6 others, who d. young.

"Mr. Sears began his business life as a clerk in N. Y. city.

"In 1838 he removed to St. Louis and traveled through some of the Northern States engaged in different pursuits.

"In 1848 he located in St. Louis, and entered into the milling business with Henry Whitmore, in the Old Momantum Mills, on Mill Creek, continuing the business till 1869, built the Laclede Mills, and remodeled and rebuilt the Atlantic and Empire Mills.

"In 1863 the St. Louis Elevator was built, and **Mr.** Sears was one of the first Board of Directors.

"In the fall of 1869 Mr. Sears was elected President of the Board, and from that time the company which had previously had a severe struggle to maintain itself, entered upon an era of success, which has placed it at the present day as one of the largest and most successful enterprises in the West.

"Of late years he has had charge of the Empire and Phœnix Flour Mills.

"Few men have been more intimately connected with the flour and grain interests of St. Louis, and few have contributed as much toward making the city the important grain market it is.

"He eschewed politics, and directed his wonderful energies entirely to business pursuits."

1075.

MILES SEARS[7] [*Wm.*[6], *Seth*[5], *Benj.*[4], *Sam'l*[3], *Paul*[2], *Rich.*[1]], b. Ct., Dec. 1, 1798; d. Rileyville, Pa., Jan. 1, 1872; m. Glenville, N. Y., *Sally Bowers*, who d.; 2d, Oct. 6, 1835, *Catharine Misner*, she b. Mar. 4, 1820. Children:

By *Sally* :
2233.   i. JOHN H., b. Feb. 3, 1823; is a farmer at La Honda, San Mateo co., Cal.

2234.   ii. LEWIS MORTIMER, b. Nov. 24, 1824; is a carpenter in Honesdale, Pa.

2235.   iii. CLARISSA C., b. Sep. 19, 1826; m. *David Riessler*, Damascus, Pa.

2236.   iv. ALFRED W., b. Feb. 11, 1829; lives Middletown, N. Y.

2237.*   v. CHARLES B., b. Aug. 20, 1831.
2238.   vi. GEORGE E.
By *Catharine:*
2239.* vii. OLIVER C., b. Sep. 21, 1839.
2240. viii. ANN AUGUSTA, m. —— *Conklin*, and lives in Cal-
       licoon, N. Y.
2241.   ix. MARY A., m. —— *Curry*, and lives in High Fells,
       N. Y.
2242.   x. HARRIET V., b. July 1, 1848; m. *John B. War-
       wick*, and had Eva.
2243.   xi. HERMAN O., b. Jan. 23, 1852; lives in Cameron
       co., Pa.
2244. xii. HELEN ADELIA, b. Feb. 3, 1855; m. —— *Parmer*
       of Dyberry, Pa.
2245. xiii. CAROLINE OPHELIA, b. Feb. 3, 1855, *gemini;* lives
       in Dyberry.

1093.

DAVID SEARS[7] [*John[6], Paul[5], Eben'r[4], Paul[3], Paul[2],
Rich.[1]*], b. Knox, Me., Aug. 19, 1813; d. Monticello, Wis.,
Sep. 24, 1880, æ. 67; m. Knox, Apr. 2, 1837, by Rev. Ephraim
Emery, to *Sarah Millby Walker*, dau. of Joshua and Maria
(Stover) W., she b. Albion, Me., Apr. 17, 1815 (see No. 484).
Children:

2246.*   i. ALLEN, b. Knox, Dec. 14, 1838.
2247.   ii. ACHSAH, b. Knox, July 11, 1840; d. Aug. 19,
       1841.
2248.* iii. GEORGE WASHINGTON, b. Knox, Mar. 18, 1843.
2249.   iv. VESTA, b. Knox, Nov. 2, 1844; m. Monticello,
       Feb. 8, 1863, *Wm. Edwin Noble*, son of David and
       Asenath (Knight) N., he b. Norway, Me.; rem. to Monti-
       cello at an early age with his parents; taught school and
       engaged in mercantile pursuits; lived for a time in Mon-
       roe, Wis., and in Aug., 1877, rem. to Santa Barbara,
       Cal.; children, NOBLE: [1.] Eldon Edwin, b. Mar. 24,
       1864; d. June 8. [2.] Lona Vesta, b. Oct. 13, 1866.
       [3.] Chris. Marie, b. Oct. 12, 1871. [4.] Clare Adams, b.
       June 23, 1877. [5.] Grover Chester, b. May 31, 1881.
2250.   v. ROSCOE, b. Knox, Jan. 21, 1847; d. July 31, 1866;
       he became a cripple through sickness in infancy, was an
       excellent student, a school teacher, and died at college
       while preparing for the ministry.

2251. vi. Maria, b. Knox, Apr. 17, 1849; also became a cripple, is a school teacher in Hillsdale, Mich.

2252.* vii. Wesley, b. Knox, Oct. 22, 1851.

2253. viii. Frances, b. Knox, Sep. 22, 1853; d. Apr. 21, 1856.

2254. ix. John Franklin, b. Monticello, Wis., Jan. 28, 1857; m. Nora Springs, Iowa, Sep. 19, 1882, *Amelia H. Pickford*, dau. of Benj. and Sarah (Wood) P., she b. Shepley, York, Eng., Jan. 25, 1861; came to Freeport, Ill., May 1866, with her parents, and later to Monticello, Wis., and Nora Springs, Iowa. He is a farmer, dairyman and stock-raiser in Monticello; no children.

2255. x. Theo. Hall, b. Mont., Aug. 28, 1859; m. there, Oct. 8, 1885, *Arthur Pickford*, bro. of Amelia H., he b. Shepley, Eng., July 9, 1855, was in Woolen Mills, Freeport, Ill., now a farmer and stock-raiser; his wife was a school teacher for several years before her marriage.

Mr. Sears lived in Knox till autumn of 1855, when he removed to Wisconsin and settled in Monticello, living for a time at Hillsdale, but returning to M.; has been a teacher and farmer.

He and his wife were good and consistent Christians, and leaders in the Baptist Church.

1094.

JOHN SEARS[7] [*John[6], Paul[5], Eben'r[4], Paul[3], Paul[2], Rich.[1]*], b. Knox, Me., Aug. 22, 1815; d. Monticello, Wis., Jan. 29, 1851, (another account says Jan. 7, 1852;) m. *Louiza Tripp.* Children:

2256. i. John L., lives North Loup, Loup Valley, Neb.

2257. ii. Eaton S., lives North Loup, Loup Valley, Neb.

John Sears grad. Freedom Acad., Freedom, Me., settled there a few years as a millwright, and taught school, then removed to Monticello, Wis., and became a farmer.

1095.

THOMAS SEARS[7] [*John[6], Paul[5], Eben'r[4], Paul[3], Paul[2], Rich.[1]*], b. Knox, Me., Oct. 18, 1819; m. Freedom, Me., Dec. 29, 1847, by Rev. Mr. Gray of Unity, Me., to *Sarah Adeline Holt*, dau. of Isaac and Sophia (Emery) H., she b. Clinton,

Me., Nov. 29, 1827; (her father was a soldier in the war of 1812, and now lives, hale and hearty, on his farm with his second wife Lydia, he æ. 95 and his wife 93.) Children:

2258.* i. WILMER, b. Freedom, Dec. 10, 1848.

2259. ii. SARAH MARIA, b. Mt. Pleasant, Wis., Dec. 8, 1851; was a teacher; m. there, Sep. 30, 1875, *Joshua Hernandez Berkey*, son of Jacob W. and Mary Richards (Moore) B., he b. Post Oak Springs, Tenn., Mar. 11, 1852; ent'd Union Christian Coll., Huron, Ind., rem. 1876, to Monroe, Wis., was a drug clerk, and in 1877, established a drug and grocery business in Monticello; in 1881 rem. to Denver, Col., was sec'y of a mining co., and business manager of "Pomeroy's Great West." In 1882 he settled at Geuda Springs, Kan., on a farm, and is editor and proprietor of a weekly paper called "The Crank;" children, BERKEY: [1.] Ada Almoda, b. Aug. 24, 1876. [2.] Iva Idalia, b. July 25, 1878. [3.] Ena Elvina, b. Apr. 7, 1881. [4.] Ola Olivia, b. Dec. 18, 1884.

2260. iii. CARROLL, b. Mt. Pl., June 12, 1855; d. Mar. 27, 1858.

2261. iv. ELLA AUGUSTA, b. Mt. Pl., May 27, 1857; m. Mont., Apr. 4, 1878, *H. W. Pickford*, son of Benj. and Sarah (Wood) P., he b. Hardingly, York, Eng., Feb. 18, 1854; came to Freeport, Ill., with his parents in 1866, and was employed in woolen mills there, and in Monticello. In 1876, he removed to Nora Springs, Iowa, and engaged in farming and stock-raising, returning in 1877 to Mt. Pleasant, Wis. His wife has been a teacher, and both are Unitarians; children, PICKFORD: [1.] Merle Sears, b. Aug. 10, 1879. [2.] Theo Beatrice, b. Dec. 14, 1880. [3.] Gertrude Cecil, b. Apr. 19, 1886.

2262. v. FREDÉRIC, b. Mt. Pl., Feb. 25, 1859; m. Janesville, Wis., June 14, 1881, *Mary U. Taft*, and lives in Monticello; she was dau. of Daniel B. and Elizabeth (Flagler) T., and b. there, Mar. 12, 1861; he is a farmer and stock-raiser.

Mr. Sears lived on a farm in Knox, Me., until 1836, when he removed to Freedom, Me., and engaged in the lumber and milling business. In 1849 he removed to Mt. Pleasant, Green co., Wis.; P. O. Monticello, where he has since been engaged in farming and stock-raising.

44

1096.

MOSES B. SEARS[7] [*Paul[6], Paul[5], Eben'r[4], Paul[3], Paul[2], Rich.[1]*], b. Winthrop, Me., Dec. 2, 1806; d. Mar. 5, 1872, æ. 65; m. Oxford, Me., 1832, *Deborah Thomas,* she b. Middleboro, Mass.; d. Feb. 13, 1870, æ. 62.   Children:

2263.   i. LIZZIE, b. Winthrop, Sep. 8, 1835; m. Jan. 15, 1868, *George W. Webb,* he b. Farmington, Me., Dec. 18, 1827; child, WEBB: [1.] Francis Everett, b. July 6, 1870.

2264. ii. WILLIAM THOMAS, b. Winth.; owns the old homestead, and lives in Boston.

2265. iii. NELLIE WARREN, b. Winth.; m. —— *Bonney,* and lives Auburn, Me.

2266. iv. MOSES B., b. Winth.; d. at sea, 1862, æ. 20.

  Mr. Sears lived on the old homestead in Winthrop, Me.; was Selectman 1852–53, and Constable 1854.

1101.

FRANCIS B. SEARS[7] [*Paul[6], Paul[5], Eben'r[4], Paul[3], Paul[2], Rich.[1]*], b. Winthrop, Me., Dec. 2, 1822; m. Readfield, Me., Sep. 22, 1848, *Hannah V. Luce,* she b. there, Apr. 4, 1827.   Children:

2267.   i. FRANCIS H., b. June 18, 1849; d. Oct. 18.

2268. ii. CURTIS L., b. Nov. 9, 1855; m. Sep. 2, 1880, —— ——, and lives in Augusta, Me.

  Mr. Sears lives in Augusta, Me.

1113.

WILLIAM SEARS[7] [*Eben'r[6], Wm.[5], Paul[4], Paul[3], Paul[2], Rich.[1]*], b. Dover, Vt., Feb. 29, 1788; d. Carroll, N. Y., Aug. 10, 1827; m. Dover, Apr. 27, 1809, *Ruby Cheney,* dau. of Eben'r and Anna (Nelson) C., she b. Apr. 21, 1787; d. Hartfield, N. Y., (having m. 2d, Apr. 16, 1834, Charles Arnold.) Children:

2269.   i. CALISTA, b. Dover, Feb. 4, 1810; d. Carroll, Feb. 4, 1812.

2270.* ii. NATHAN LAZELLE, b. Car., June 16, 1812.

2271. iii. ANNA NELSON, b. Car., Aug. 29, 1813; m. there, Aug. 25, 1831, *Samuel Bigelow Winsor*, and lives in Jamestown, N. Y.; has descendants in 3d gen.

2272. iv. CALISTA RUBY, b. Car., June 12, 1815; m. Nov. 7, 1833, *Abner O. Hunt*, son of Salmon H. of Reedsburg; and d. Limestone, Pa., Sep. 10, 1848; (he m. 2d, 1850, Marg'y H. Shaw;) children, HUNT: [1.] Charles S., b. June 9, 1834; m. —— ——. [2.] Mary E., b. July 14, 1837; m. Jan. 22, 1863, John F. Macomber of Framingham. [3.] Henry C., b. Jan. 27, 1840. [4.] Albert C., b. June 4, 1842. [5.] Helen A., b. Dec. 3, 1844. [6.] Eunice C., b. Mar. 28, 1848.

2273. v. STATIRA PHILENA, b. Car., Jan. 1, 1817; d. June 16, 1830.

2274. vi. ELLICOTT WILLIAM, b. Car., Dec. 5, 1818; d. Apr. 2, 1820.

2275.* vii. CLINTON WILLIAM, b. Car., Apr. 27, 1820.

2276. viii. ELECTA MARIA, b. Car., July 30, 1823; m. Oct. 24, 1847, Dr. *Daniel Tompkins Brown*, he b. Benton, N. Y., Oct. 28, 1822; lives in Milwaukee, Wis.; children, BROWN: [1.] Clarence S., b. Oct. 27, 1854; lives in Chicago, Ill. [2.] Ella E., b. May 27, 1853; d. Sep. 4, 1856. [3.] Wallace N., b. May 10, 1855; drowned, Sep. 6, 1870. [4.] Edward, b. May 14, 1857; lives Portland, Oregon. [5.] Fred. E., b. Mar. 5, 1861; lives in Buffalo, N. Y. [6.] Clinton H., b. Aug. 8, 1863; lives at home.

Mr. Sears and wife removed from Dover, Vt., in Feb., 1811, and settled on the "Holland Land Purchase," at Carroll, now Kiantone, Chautauqua co., N. Y.

They traveled 500 miles with all their household goods upon a sled drawn by a yoke of oxen; were 29 days on the road, and took up land in the then wild country, surrounded by tribes of Seneca Indians. He was chosen Com. Highways, 1813.

1117.

EBENEZER SEARS[7] [*Eben'r[6]*, *Wm.[5]*, *Paul[4]*, *Paul[3]* *Paul[2]* *Rich.[1]*], b. Dover, Vt., Aug. 11, 1796; d. Wilmington, Vt., Aug. 29, 1859; m. Wardsboro, Vt., Sep. 6, 1817, by Rev. James Tufts, to *Diana Jones*, she b. there; d. Dover, Dec. 22, 1852. Children:

2277. i. *Dau.*, b. and d. Carroll, N. Y., June 7, 1819.

2278. ii. MARY LUCRETIA, b. Car., July 9, 1820 ; m. Apr. 15, 1845, *Oscar L. Lincoln*, and lives in Wilmington, Vt.

2279.* iii. AMOS GOULD, b. Car., Apr. 24, 1823.

2280. iv. HENRY CURTIS, b. Dover, Vt., Sep. 23, 1825 ; d. Oct. 27.

2281. v. *Son*, b. and d. Sep. 1, 1827.

2282. vi. LYDIA MERILLA, b. Dover, Oct. 18, 1828 ; d. Sep. 14, 1847.

2283. vii. JOHN CHANDLER, b. Dover, July 13, 1831; m. Wardsboro, Vt., Mar. 17, 1852, *Sarah M. Nichols*, and d. s. p., Bellows Falls, Vt., Feb. 5, 1876; was Capt. Battery E, 1st Vt. Art'y, during the Civil war.

2284. viii. CAROLINE CALISTA, b. Dover, July 15, 1835; d. Dec. 29, 1842.

2285. ix. ELIZABETH DIANA, b. Dover, June 25, 1838 ; m. May 16, 1863, Rev. *George O. Atkinson*, and lives 375 Washington ave., Albany, N. Y.

2286. x. SUSAN ESTELLE, b. Dover, May 4, 1844; m. Oct. 29, 1868, *Wm. O. Jennison*, and lives So. Windham, Vt.

1120.

OTIS SEARS[7] [*Wm.[6], Wm.[5], Paul[4], Paul[3], Paul[2], Rich.[1]*], b. (perh. at Dover, Vt.,) about 1789 ; d. Dec., 1812; m. Sep., 1812, *Luly Stearns*. Child :

2287. i. DRUSILLA, b. Jan. 3, 1813 ; m. ab't 1830, *Samuel A. Hatch*, Chautauqua, N. Y., and d. ab't 1855.

Otis Sears enlisted in a New York Regt., and died of disease contracted while in camp at Plattsburgh, N. Y., in War of 1812.

1121.

CLARK SEARS[7] [*Wm.[6], Wm.[5], Paul[4], Paul[3], Paul[2], Rich.[1]*], b. (perh. at Dover, Vt.,) about 1794 ; d. Woodstock, Ill., ab't 1865 ; m. Ellicott, N. Y., about 1815, *Lucy Tobey*. Children :

2288. i. ALVAN.

2289. ii. STEARNS.

Mr. Sears removed about 1855 to Woodstock, Ill., and is said to have died there ten years later.

1129.

JOSEPH SEARS[7] [*Silas*[6], *Nath'l*[5], *Paul*[4], *Paul*[3], *Paul*[2], *Rich.*[1]], b. Rochester, Mass., Apr. 11, 1783; d. May 7, 1860, æ. 77; m. Morristown, Vt., Sep. 30, 1810, *Lemira Walker*, she b. there, Sep. 14, 1793; d. there, Dec. 7, 1862, æ. 69.
Children:

2290. i. *Son*, b. Apr. 1, 1812; d. infant.
2291. ii. *Son*, b. Mar. 20, 1813; d. infant.
2292.* iii. ARAD WEST, b. Aug. 15, 1816.
2293. iv. DORMAN DUSTIN, b. Feb. 7, 1819; d. unm., May 29, 1844.
2294. v. LEMIRA MARION, b. July 26, 1821; d. unm., May 3, 1843.
2295. vi. LEONORA ALICE, b. Sep. 25, 1823; m. Feb. 5, 1867, *Julius Shaw*, he b. Mar. 22, 1808; lives at Essex, Vt. I am indebted to her for many items relative to her branch of the Searses.
2296. vii. JOSEPH, b. Feb. 15, 1828; lives in Oregon, Ill.
2297.* viii. SILAS, b. Feb. 13, 1830.
2298. ix. JACOB WALKER, b. Apr. 8, 1832; d. Dec. 20, 1856.
2299. x. SARAH DELIA, b. Jan. 12, 1834; m. Jan. 2, 1854, *Leander W. Lewis*, he b. Georgia, Vt., Feb. 7, 1827; lives in Corning, Iowa; children, LEWIS: [1.] Dustin E., b. Nov. 16, 1854; m. Nov. 16, 1879, Kate Veirs of Fontinell, Iowa; is a telegraph operator at Shanandoa, Iowa, and has, i. Son, b. Apr. 27, 1884. [2.] Joseph Sears, b. Nov. 13, 1856; m. Apr. 25, 1879, Maggie M. Tracy of Richford, Vt.; is a bridge builder at Corning, Iowa, and has, i. Frank W., b. Mar. 7, 1880. ii. Eva A., b. July 27, 1882. [3.] Mortimer L., b. Mar. 17, 1859; d. July 17, 1877. [4.] Albert Bush, b. Aug. 12, 1861. [5.] Fanny L., b. June 17, 1863; lives at home. [6.] Leonora Alice, b. Dec. 20, 1867.
2300. xi. ALVIN FRANKLIN, b. Apr. 28, 1838; lives in Bannock City, Montana, is Probate Judge, and unmarried.

1131.

SILAS SEARS[7] [*Silas*[6], *Nath'l*[5], *Paul*[4], *Paul*[3], *Paul*[2], *Rich.*[1]], b. Weathersfield, Vt., Mar. 30, 1788; d. Coventry

Falls, Vt., Apr. 10, 1873 ; m. Cambridge, Vt., *Abigail Page.*
Children :

2301. i. THOMAS P., b. Cambridge, 1813 ; rem. in 1837 to
Buffalo, N. Y.; is Pres't Western Savings Bank, and
resides 63 Genesee st.

2302. ELIAS G., b. Cambridge, Nov. 12, 1834 ; went to live
with his uncle Alden when a boy, and now lives at
Council Bluffs, Iowa ; unmarried.

1132.

NATHANIEL SEARS[7] [*Silas[6], Nath'l[5], Paul[4], Paul[3], Paul[2], Rich.[1]*], b. Weathersfield, Vt., Sep. 15, 1790 ; d. Richford, Vt., May 16, 1868 ; m. Apr. 3, 1817, *Saloma Alexander Leland,* she b. Chester, Vt., June 26, 1795 ; d. Richford, Dec. 8, 1864.   Children :

2304.* i. SHERMAN WEST, b. Cambridge, Vt., Feb. 24, 1824.

2305. ii. JESSE, b. Camb.

2306. iii. JOSHUA, b. Camb., Aug. 7, 1831 ; m. Jan. 1, 1855,
Mary McKenney ; 2d, Feb. 26, 1873, *Jane Noyes,* and
lives in Richford.

2307. iv. DELIA ALIDA, b. Camb., Jan. 22, 1835 ; m. *Lucius
Noyes ;* 2d, *Amos Noyes,* and lives in Richford.

And seven other children who d. young.

1135.

ALDEN SEARS[7] [*Silas[6], Nath'l[5], Paul[4], Paul[3], Paul[2], Rich.[1]*], b. Weathersfield, Vt., Aug. 6, 1797 ; d. Columbia, Cal., Mar. 8, 1861 ; m. Cambridge, Vt., Mar. 7, 1824, *Caroline Carleton,* she b. there, Nov. 16, 1807 ; d. Salem, Oregon, Jan. 17, 1878, æ. 71.   Children :

2308. i. LOUISE, b. Richford, Vt.; d. æ. 13.

2309. ii. ELVIRA, b. Rich.; d. æ. 4.

2310. iii. LUCY VILA, b. Rich., Mar. 5, 1830 ; m. Dr. *S. H.
Fickett,* and lives in Stockton, Cal.

2311. iv. MALCOLM, b. Rich. ; d. æ. 6 mos.

2312. v. ELLEN AUGUSTA, b. Rich., Apr. 22, 1835 ; m.
Columbia, Cal., June 29, 1856, Rev. *John Henry Brodt,*
he b. Troy, N. Y., June 2, 1827 ; d. Dansville, N. Y.,
Sep. 8, 1875 ; he was a Presb. Min., grad. Williams Coll.
and Union Theo. Sem'y ; went to California in early

days as a missionary, was pastor of a large church in Brooklyn, N. Y., at the time of his illness, which terminated fatally at Dansville, where his widow now lives; children, BRODT: [1.] Carrie, b. Apr. 13, 1857; is an artist of marked ability. [2.] John Ingold, b. Jan. 30, 1859; d. Dec. 30, 1861. [3.] Edwin Elwell, b. Feb. 8, 1861; d. Dec. 28, 1861. [4.] Henry Snowden, b. Feb. 1, 1863; grad. Mass. Agri. Coll., is a civil engineer, Riverside, Wyoming. [5.] Ellen Reese, b. May 17, 1865. [6.] Charles Hawley, b. Oct. 25, 1867. [7.] Daisy Louise, b. Sep. 29, 1869. [8.] Philip Ernest, b. June 21, 1871. [9.] Clifford Randolph, b. Dec. 18, 1873; d. Aug. 23, 1874.

2313.　vi. CHARLES WEST, b. Rich., 1838; lives Salem, Oregon.

2314.* vii. GEORGE CARLETON, b. Rich., 1840.

2315.　viii. HOMER ALDEN, b. Rich., 1843; lives Seattle, Washington Ter.

Mr. Sears was a prominent merchant in Northern Vermont, widely known in political circles, and a member of the State Legislature three terms.

He went to California in 1850, and made an honorable record in connection with the southern mines.

1137.

Hon. LEONARD SEARS[7] [*Silas*[6], *Nath'l*[5], *Paul*[4], *Paul*[3], *Paul*[2], *Rich.*[1]], b. Windsor co., Vt., May 12, 1802; d. Onawa, Iowa, Feb. 20, 1859, æ. 57; m. Canton, N. Y., Sep. 16, 1827, *Delia S. Foote*, she b. there, Nov. 25, 1812; lives with her son Millard in Omaha, Neb. Children:

2316.　i. CAROLINE L., b. St. Law. co., N. Y., May 11, 1835; m. Council Bluffs, Iowa, Dec. 2, 1855, *Andrew J. Poppleton*, he b. Troy, Mich., July 24, 1830; children, POPPLETON: [1.] Ellen Elizabeth, b. Sep. 10, 1856. [2.] Mary Zada, b. Apr. 4, 1859; d. Nov. 17, 1862. [3.] William, b. Apr. 7, 1866. [4.] Mary Delia, b. July 23, 1873.

2317.　ii. CHARLES WEST, b. St. Law. co., N. Y., July 12, 1837; d. Missoula, Montana, Feb. 25, 1870.

2318.* iii. STILLMAN FOOTE, b. St. Law. co., N. Y., June 29, 1842.

2319.　iv. MARY RUST, b. St. Law. co., N. Y., June 29, 1844; m. Onawa, Iowa, Dec. 2, 1860, *Charles Atkins*, he b.

Hallowell, Me., Oct. 20, 1831; child, ATKINS: [1.] Carrie M., b. Nov. 25, 1861.

2320.* v. JOSEPH LEONARD, b. Oswegatchie, N. Y., July 1, 1846.

2321. vi. MILLARD FILLMORE, b. Osweg., Nov. 25, 1848; lives with his mother, No. 1590 18th st., Omaha, Neb.; unm.

2322. vii. DELIA LOUISE, b. Osweg., Jan. 18, 1851; m. Omaha, Apr. 16, 1879, *Arthur N. Ferguson*, he b. Albany, N. Y., 1844; children, FERGUSON: [1.] Alice S., b. Sep. 8, 1880. [2.] ELIZABETH F., b. July, 1884.

Mr. Sears removed to western Iowa, May 1, 1854, arriving Council Bluffs, June 10, and engaged in hotel-keeping; kept the "Pacific House" till 1856, when he removed to a farm in Onawa, Monoma county.

He built the first dwelling-house having a floor, and board roof, rung the first dinner bell, was the first county judge, justice, and coroner, built the first barn, and started the first public school in the county.

During his life he took a deep interest in public business, and every enterprise that promised to result in general good, found in him a warm advocate and liberal supporter.

1140.

Capt. WILLIAM SEARS[7] [*Nath'l[6], Nath'l[5], Paul[4], Paul[3], Paul[2], Rich.[1]*], b. Rochester, Mass., Aug. 31, 1789; d. there, Dec. 9, 1870, æ. 81; m. Charlton, Mass., Aug. 13, 1816, *Susan Fiske Butler* of Oxford, Mass., she b. Rutland, Vt., Oct. 21, 1798; d. Taunton, Mass., Mar. 18, 1883, æ. 84. Children :

2323. i. JAMES BUTLER, b. Roch., Aug. 19, 1817; m. Fairhaven, Mass., Oct. 21, 1842, *Mary C. Thacher*, dau. of Charles F. and Sylvia (Crocker) T., and d. s. p., New Bedford, Mass., Mar. 3, 1885; she d. May 26, 1884, æ. 58.

2324. ii. DANIEL FISKE, b. Roch., July 9, 1819; d. Aug. 6.

2325.* iii. JOHN FISKE, b. Roch., May 26, 1821.

2326.* iv. WILLIAM, b. Roch., July 8, 1823.

2327.* v. NATHANIEL, b. Roch., Oct. 3, 1825.

2328. vi. SUSAN FISKE, b. Roch., Oct. 29, 1828; m. there, Apr. 26, 1855, *Job Deane*, who d. June 9, 1873, æ. 67; she lives in Taunton, Mass.; child, DEANE: [1.] Job Franklin, Nov. 10, 1856; lives Myricks, Mass.

2329.   vii. SALLIE BUTLER, b. Roch., July 14, 1831; unm.,
and lives in New Bedford.

2330.* viii. FRANKLIN KEENE, b. Roch., Mar. 12, 1834.

2331.   ix. HANNAH KEENE, b. Roch., July 21, 1836; m.
June 27, 1867, *Isaac M. Cole*, and lives in New Bedford; no child.

2332.* x. STEPHEN CRANSTON, b. Roch., Dec. 23, 1838.

Mr. Sears was a farmer, Captain in the militia, and Rep. to
State Leg., 1836, 1854; was Selectman 14 years, Assessor,
Overseer of the Poor, etc.

1143.

JESSE SEARS[7] [*Nath'l[6], Nath'l[5], Paul[4], Paul[3], Paul[2],
Rich.[1]*], b. Rochester, Mass., Apr. 3, 1796; d. 1877, æ. 80;
m. Apr., 1820, *Love M. Tobey* of New Bedford, Mass., she b.
Apr. 20, 1801; d. Acushnet, Mass., June 23, 1879. Children:

2333.   i. SILAS TOBEY, b. Roch., Mar. 10, 1821; d. Oct. 27,
1845.

2334. ii. MARIA TOBEY, b. Roch., Mar. 25, 1823; d. Oct. 2,
1855.

2335. iii. ADELIA M., b. Roch., 1825; d. Aug. 29, 1839.

2336. iv. MARY A., b. Roch., Mar. 26, 1834; d. Oct. 6, 1862.

1145.

NATHANIEL SEARS[7] [*Nath'l[6], Nath'l[5], Paul[4], Paul[3],
Paul[2], Rich.[1]*], b. Rochester, Mass., Aug. 15, 1799; d. Long
Plain, Mass., June 23, 1883, æ. 83; m. No. Rochester, Sep.
23, 1821, by Rev. Oliver Cobb, to *Abigail F. Thatcher*, dau.
of Lot and Abigail F. T., she b. there, Apr. 1, 1798; d. July
16, 1878, æ. 80. Children:

2337.   i. SARAH THATCHER, b. Roch., July 3, 1823; m. there,
July 30, 1843, *Stephen Waite* of New Bedford, he b.
Tiverton, R. I., Mar. 30, 1821; lives in New Bed.

2338.* ii. HARRISON GRAY OTIS, b. Roch., Nov. 10, 1825.

2339. iii. EMILY M., b. Roch., Sep. 2, 1827; m. *Charles M.
Blackmer*, and lives in Acushnet, Mass.

2340. iv. ELIZABETH A., b. Roch., May 20, 1831; m. *Elihu
D. Manter*, and lives in Long Plain, Mass.

45

2341.   v. Lot T., b. Roch., Oct. 3, 1834; is a carpenter in Fall River, Mass.
2342.   vi. Abby F., b. Roch., Mar. 4, 1838; m. there, Apr. 12, 1856, *Charles A. Howland*, who d.; 2d, —— *Waterman;* lives in Long Plain.
2343.   vii. James H., b. Roch., Mar. 31, 1839.

1147.

JOSEPH SEARS⁷ [*Nath'l⁶, Nath'l⁵, Paul⁴, Paul₃ Paul², Rich.¹*], b. Rochester, Mass., Mar. 15, 1804; d. New Bedford, Mass., 1885, æ. 81; m. Roch., Apr. 8, 1827, by Rev. Oliver Cobb, to *Susan W. Snow* of Roch. Children:

2345.   i. Abby M., b. Roch., Mar. 21, 1828.
2346.   ii. Sarah E., b. Roch., Apr. 29, 1830.
2347.   iii. George T., b. Roch., July 26, 1832; served in Co. I, 3d Mass. Vols., Apr. 23 to July 22, 1861, 3 mos'. men; is an apothecary in Boston.

1150.

STEPHEN SEARS⁷ [*Nath'l⁶, Nath'l⁵, Paul⁴, Paul³, Paul², Rich.¹*], b. Rochester, Mass., Sep. 18, 1813; d. Abington, Mass., 1880; m. Nov., 1845, *Hannah D. Corthell* of New Bedford. Children:

2349.   i. Adelaide, b. Roch., Dec. 1, 1851.
2350.   ii. *Dau.*

1152.

LEONARD W. SEARS⁷ [*Prince⁶, Nath'l⁵, Paul⁴, Paul³, Paul², Rich.¹*], b. *1777*; m. *Roxana Sanger* of St. Johnsbury, Vt. Child:

2351.   i. Paul, was not adopted by his uncle Paul D. Sears of Ludlow, Vt.

1155.

MARSHALL GIFFORD SEARS⁷ [*John⁶, Nath'l⁵, Paul⁴, Paul³, Paul², Rich.¹*], b. Rochester, Mass., Feb. 15, 1807; m. Middleboro, Mass., May 10, 1829, *Lois S. Alden*, she b. there, Feb. 13, 1809. Children:

2352.   i. Lydia.

2353. ii. ELIZA, m. ——— ———.
And 6 other children who d. young.

Mr. Sears is a builder in New Bedford, Mass.

1164.

THOMAS BARTLETT SEARS[7] [*Thos.*[6], *Thos.*[5], *Thos.*[4], *Paul*[3], *Paul*[2], *Rich.*[1]], b. Plymouth, Mass., July 19, 1808 ; d. June 2, 1883, æ. 74; m. 1831, *Louiza H. Churchill*, dau. of Amaziah and Polly (Harlow) C. of P., she b. Feb. 18, 1809 ; d. Apr. 1, 1881, æ. 72. Children :

2354. i. LOUISA FRANCIS, b. Ply.,¦Dec. 25, 1831; lives there.
2355.* ii. THOMAS BARTLETT, b. Ply., July 2, 1834.
2356.* iii. AMASA CHURCHILL, b. Ply., June 22, 1836.
2357. iv. WALTER HERBERT, b. Ply., Dec. 8, 1847 ; lives there.
2358. v. FRANCIS DANA, b. Ply., Aug. 30, 1851 ; d. May 19, 1878, æ. 26.

Was Selectman and Justice of the Peace.

1170.

WILLIAM SEARS[7] [*Eleazar*[6], *Will'd*[5], *Thos.*[4], *Paul*[3], *Paul*[2], *Rich.*[1]], b. Plymouth, Mass., Jan. 5, 1808; m. 1832, *Mercy B. Churchill*, dau. of Jabez and Nancy (Bartlett) C., who d. Ply., Dec. 15, 1882, æ. 78 yrs. 7 mos. Children :

2359.* i. WILLIAM HENRY, b. Ply., Oct. 7, 1833.
2360. ii. ANDREW CHURCHILL, b. Ply., June 8, 1836; m. *Julia Mason* of Oxford, N. H.; no children; is a carpenter.
2361. iii. EVERETT, b. Ply., July, 1839 ; d. Mar. 21, 1841.
2362. iv. HERBERT, b. Ply., Jan. 29, 1841; d. Mar. 29.
2363.* v. EVERETT H., b. Ply., July 26, 1842.
2364. vi. CHARLOTTE M., b. Ply., Aug. 25, 1846 ; d. Sep. 27.

Mr. Sears was a ship carpenter and farmer, and light-keeper at the Gurnet for 17 years ; lives in Plymouth.

1172.

HIRAM BARTLETT SEARS[7] [*Eleazar*[6], *Will'd*[5], *Thos.*[4], *Paul*[3], *Paul*[2], *Rich.*[1]], b. Plymouth, Mass., May 19, 1816 ; m.

there, Dec. 12, 1842, *Lydia Williams Davie*, dau. of Joseph and Hannah (Faunce) D., she b. there, Jan. 17, 1819. Children :

2365.   i. HARRIET NEWELL, b. Plv., Sep. 9, 1843 ; m. Oct. 16, 1864, *Elkanah Bartlett ;* children, BARTLETT : [1.] Elma H., b. 1865. [2.] Orin T., d. Feb. 12, 1886.

2366.* ii. BARTLETT, b. Ply., Dec. 28, 1845.

2367.* iii. ROBERT DAVIE, b. Ply., Oct. 19, 1849.

2368. iv. EMMA AUGUSTA, b. Ply., Nov. 11, 1859 ; d. Aug. 11, 1860.

1171.

DANIEL H. SEARS[7] [*Eleazar[6], Will'd[5], Thos.[4], Paul[3], Paul[2], Rich.[1]*], b. Plymouth, Mass., Mar. 20, 1811 ; d. there, Sep. 1, 1882, æ. 71 ; m. there, Dec. 22, 1844, Mrs. *Belinda H. Hamilton*, dau. of Eber and Eliz'h (Burgess) Hall, who d. Ply., Oct. 21, 1872, æ. 58 yrs. 2 mos. 15 days. Children :

2369.   i. FREDERIC W., b. Ply., Nov. 14, 1845 ; d. Oct. 23, 1847.

2370. ii. DANIEL F., b. Ply., Oct. 11, 1847 ; d. young.

2371. iii. JULIA F., b. Ply., Sep. 13, 1849 ; m. there, Jan. 12, 1881, *Thaddeus Faunce, Jr.*, son of Thaddeus and Mary Ann (Warner) F., he b. 1838.

2372. iv. ELIZA ANNIE, b. Ply., Sep. 23, 1851.

2373.* v. DANIEL WINSLOW, b. Ply., July 8, 1853.

2374. vi. ANDREW, b. Ply., Dec. 25, 1854.

2375. vii. LUCY JANE, b. Ply., June 9, 1856 ; d. Aug. 17, 1858.

2376. viii. LUCY JANE, b. Ply., 1859.

1175.

WINSLOW SEARS[7] [*Eleazar[6], Will'd[5], Thos.[4], Paul[3], Paul[2], Rich.[1]*], b. Plymouth, Mass.; m. there, May 2, 1858, *Nancy (Methuren) Bryant*, dau. of Seth M., and widow of Homer B. Children :

2377. i. *Son*, b. Ply., July 13, 1868.

2378. ii. EUNICE B., b. Ply., Mar. 29, 1871 ; d. Feb. 29, 1876.

2379. iii. HATTIE E., b. Ply., Mar. 29, 1873 ; d. Mar. 6, 1876.

2380. iv. *Dau.*, b. Ply., Oct. 7, 1876.

1183.

Capt. BENJAMIN WARREN SEARS[7] [*David[6], Will'd[5], Thos.[4], Paul[3], Paul[2], Rich.[1]*], b. Plymouth, Mass., Oct. 4,

1831; m. there, Apr. 4, 1872, *Louiza F. Cornish*, dau. of Thos. E. and Zoraida (Thompson) C., she b. Ply., July 13, 1841; d. Jan. 28, 1885. Child:

2381. i. MARY H., b. Ply., Aug. 7, 1873.

Mr. Sears was a Captain in United States Navy during the last years of the war, and now commands a steamer on the Pacific, with residence in San Francisco, Cal.

1186.

JOSEPH HENRY SEARS[7] [*David[6], Will'd[5], Thos.[4], Paul[3] Paul[2], Rich.[1]*], b. Plymouth, Mass., Oct. 1, 1836; m. Ocala, Florida, Apr., 1871, *Emilie C. Stowe*, she b. New Haven, Ct., Sep. 1, 1836. Child:

2382. i. CARRIE WARREN LEES, b. St. Louis, Mo., Nov. 7, 1875.

Mr. Sears was educated in Phillips Academy, Andover, and entered Yale College; enlisted Aug. 31, 1862, in Co. G, 6th Mass. Vols., for 9 mos., and was discharged June 26, '63, at expiration of service; Supt. Educ'n Dallas co., Ala., 4 years, and member State Board of Educ'n of Ala. 4 years; member 3d Cong. Ch., St. Louis, Mo., and Clerk 1 year.

Is now traveling agent for Deere, Mansur & Co., dealers in farm machinery, St. Louis, Mo.; address, 1824 Grand ave.

1188.

EDMUND LUCAS SEARS[7] [*Edm'd[6], Will'd[5], Thos.[4], Paul[3], Paul[2], Rich.[1]*], b. Carver, Mass., Aug. 20, 1808; d. June 2, 1879; m, July 5, 1840, *Lucetta Jane Thomas* of Middleboro, Mass., who d. July 21, 1884. Children:

2383. i. REBECCA WINSLOW, b. June 2, 1844; m. Plymouth, Mass., Oct. 19, 1866, *Timo. M. Benson;* child, BENSON: [1.] Clara Manter, b. June 19, 1870.
2384.* ii. BENJAMIN LEWIS, b. Feb. 20, 1849.
2385. iii. EUGENE E., b. May 8, 1851; d. Aug. 13, 1852.

Was a carpenter.

1191.

IVORY H. SEARS[7] [*Edm'd[6], Will'd[5], Thos.[4], Paul[3], Paul[2], Rich.[1]*], b. Carver, Mass., Mar. 5, 1810; d. Middleboro,

Mass., Aug. 29, 1880, æ. 70 ; m. there, Sep. 17, 1835, by Rev. E. C. Messenger, to *Eveline Thomas.* Children :

2386. i. BETSY L., m. *Andrew A. Bisbee.*

2387. ii. GARAPHELIA A., m. *Israel T. Bishop.*

The will of Ivory H. Sears, carpenter, dated 1876, was allowed Oct. 11, 1880, Everett Robinson, Exec'r, and names wife Eveline and daus. Betsy L., wife of Andrew A. Bisbee, and Garaphelia A., wife of Israel T. Bishop.

1196.

ALLEN SEARS[7] [*Jos.*[6], *Will'd*[5], *Thos.*[4], *Paul*[3], *Paul*[2], *Rich.*[1]], b. Easton, Mass., Jan. 9, 1812 ; m. Middleboro, Mass., July 29, 1832, (June 12 another account,) by Rev. Nicholas Medbury, to *Matilda Robbins,* she b. there, Jan. 15, 1816, d. Plympton, Mass., Mar. 17, 1868, æ. 52.   Children :

2388.* i. HENRY ALLEN, b. Abington, Mass., Aug. 6, 1833.

2389. ii. SARAH MATILDA, b. Midd., Oct. 21, 1836 ; m. Aug. 15, 1861, *Howard O. Bonney,* and lives in Plympton ; child, BONNEY : [1.] W. Nelson, b. Sep. 1, 1862.

2390. iii. SUSAN S., b. Carver, Feb. 20, 1840 ; m. *Frank Ripley* of Plympton, and has a dau.

1198.

LEANDER SEARS[7] [*Jos.*[6], *Will'd*[5], *Thos.*[4], *Paul*[3], *Paul*[2], *Rich.*[1]], b. Carver, Mass., Mar. 20, 1820 ; d. North Easton, Mass., æ. 35 ; m. *Sarah Wheeler ;* 2d, *Myra Pierce* of No. E. Children :

By *Sarah :*

2391.   i. EDWIN FRANCIS, b. Providence, R. I., Mar., 1847.

By *Myra :*

2392. ii. CHESTER PIERCE, b. No. E., 1852.

2393. iii. FLORA N., b. No. E., 1855.

1199.

JAMES T. SEARS[7] [*Thos.*[6], *Will'd*[5], *Thos.*[4], *Paul*[3], *Paul*[2], *Rich.*[1]], b. Plymouth, Mass.; m. there, Oct. 8, 1838, *Almira W. Hodges,* dau. of Nath'l H., who d. Mar. 11, 1886, æ. 63 yrs. 5 mos. 15 days.   Children :

2394.   i. JULIA ANN, b. Ply., July 19, 1839 ; m. there, Aug. 15, 1870, *Howard K. Swift* of Whateley, Mass.

2395. ii. JAMES F., b. Ply., Oct. 11, 1840 ; m. there, Nov. 24, 1864, *Harriet A. Stickney* of Maine ; he enl'd in Co. B, 3d Reg. Mass. Vols., Sep. 26, 1862; disch'd June 26, 1863, exp'n of service.

2396. iii. GEORGIANNA, b. Ply., Mar. 22, 1848; m. there, Nov. 27, 1866, *Adams Stevens* of Bridgewater, Mass.

2397. iv. MERCY D., b. Ply., July 23, 1849 ; m. *H. K. Nash.*

2398. v. NATHANIEL T., b. Ply., Nov. 25, 1851; d. June 21, 1853.

2399.* vi. NATHANIEL, b. Ply.

2400. vii. ALMIRA WINSOR, b. Ply., Dec. 6, 1854; d. Feb. 21, 1855.

2401. viii. LAURA W., b. Ply., Aug., 1856; d. Mar. 7, 1858.

2402. ix. LAURA ANN, b. Ply., Feb 23, 1859 ; d. Oct. 12.

2403. x. HATTIE A.

2404. xi. MORRILL.

The last two names are given in Davis' History, Plymouth, but are not on town records.

1200.

HORATIO SEARS[7] [*Thos.*[6], *Will'd*[5], *Thos.*[4], *Paul*[3], *Paul*[2], *Rich.*[1]], b. Plymouth, Mass. ; m. *Hannah Lucas*, who d. there, Oct. 19, 1863, æ. 43. Children :

2405.* i. HORATIO N., b. Ply.

2406. ii. ANDREW THOMAS, b. Ply.; m. *Ellen Atwood ;* 2d, July 15, 1865, *Lucinda J. Bumpus*, (?*Burgess;*) 3d, Oct. 15, 1878, *Mary O'Neil ;* he enl'd in Co. E, 23d Regt., Mass. Vols., Oct. 12, 1861, and served till June 25, '65·

2407. iii. ALBERT, b. Ply. ; lost at sea, æ. 17.

2408. iv. WILLIAM H., b. Ply., Dec. 22, 1846 ; lost at sea, æ. 14.

2409. v. SARAH A., b. Ply., Feb. 17, 1850 ; m. there, Mar. 16, 1871, *Pascal White.*

2410. v. ADDIE A., b. Ply., Aug. 29, 1852 ; m. there, Apr. 13, 1871, *Wm. G. Felton.*

2411. vii. LOUISA, b. Ply., Mar. 11, 1855 ; m. there, Sep. 11, 1873, *Chas. H. Powers* of Abington.

2412.* viii. FREDERIC L., b. Ply., Aug. 27, 1861.

2413. ix. HANNAH, b. Ply. ; m. —— *Leach.*

Mr. Sears served in Co. G, 38th Regt., Mass. Vols., Aug. 20, 1862, to June 30, 1865.

1201.

ELBRIDGE G. SEARS[7] [*Thos.*[6], *Will'd*[5], *Thos.*[4], *Paul*[3], *Paul*[2], *Rich.*[1]], b. Plymouth, Mass.; m. there, Oct. 31, 1847, *Lydia Ann Vaughan*, dau. of Elisha V. of Middleboro, Mass., who d. Ply., May 2, 1880, æ. 54. Children:

2414.   i. *Son*, b. Ply., Dec. 20, 1848.
2415.   ii. ANNA R., b. Ply., Mar. 9, 1850; m. there, Nov. 26, 1868, *Freeman Manter*.
2416.   iii. LYDIA FRANCIS, b. Ply., June 19, 1854; m. there, June 22, 1880, *Oliver T. Peters*.
2417.   iv. ELLEN, b. Ply., July 11, 1859.
2418.   v. CARRIE.
2419.   vi. *Son*, b. Ply., Oct. 22, 1861.
2420.   vii. RUFUS A., b. Ply., Apr. 25, 1865; d. same day.
2421.   viii. ANNA C., b. Ply., Jan. 12, 1872.

1202.

OTIS SEARS[7] [*Thos.*[6], *Will'd*[5], *Thos.*[4], *Paul*[3], *Paul*[2], *Rich.*[1]], b. Plymouth, Mass., 1836; d. there, Jan. 5, 1864, æ. 28; m. there, Nov. 18, 1860, *Sarah M. Gibbs*, dau. of George and Esther G., (who m. 2d, Ply., Sep. 6, 1864, Horatio N. Sears, No. 2405.) Children:

2422.   i. OTIS FRANKLIN, b. Ply., Aug. 21, 1861.
2423.   ii. ALBERT N., b. Ply., Jan. 7, 1864.

Otis Sears enlisted in Co. G, 38th Regt., Mass. Vols., Aug. 20, 1862, and died Jan. 5, 1864, while at home on furlough.

1211.

CHAUNCEY SEARS[7] [*Isaac*[6], *Elkanah*[5], *Josh.*[4], *Paul*[3], *Paul*[2], *Rich.*[1]], b. Chatham, Ct., 1787; d. Cascade, Mich., Feb. 28, 1881, æ. 93; m. New Durham, N. Y., *Sally Shufeldt*, she b. there. Children:

2424.* i. HORACE, b. New Dur., May 3, 1819.
2425.   ii. AUSTIN, b. New Dur., 1822; m. *Hannah Johnston;* is a farmer in Grattan Centre, Mich.
2426.   iii. GROSVENOR, b. New Dur.; m. *Julia Hatch*, and has a large farm at Geneva Lake, Mich.
2427.   iv. ADELINE, m. *Jos. Bumpus* of Brushy Prairie, Ind.; a farmer, and preacher of Church of Christ.

2428. v. LANSING, was lost on a Mississippi river steamboat.
Mr. Sears was in war of 1812.

1218.

OGDEN SEARS[7] [*Will'd[6], Elkanah[5], Josh.[4], Paul[3], Paul[2], Rich.[1]*], b. Chatham, Ct., Aug. 19, 1798; d. So. Barre, N. Y., Feb., 1883, æ. 84; m. Dec. 1, 1819, *Betsy Harding*, dau. of Daniel and Betsy (Strong) H. of East Hampton, Ct., she b. July 9, 1803; d. Children:

2429. i. EUNICE D., b. Dec. 28, 1820; m. *John Church;* child, CHURCH: [1.] Daniel.
2430. ii. BETSY A., b. Nov. 28, 1823; m. *Geo. Bachelder,* who d. ab't 1884; children, BACHELDER: [1.] Philena, d. æ. 16. [2.] John; lives So. Barre, N. Y.
2431. iii. MARY A., b. July 7, 1824; d. Jan. 13, 1829.

1219.

WILLARD SEARS[7] [*Will'd[6], Elkanah[5], Josh.[4], Paul[3], Paul[2], Rich.[1]*], b. Chatham, Ct., Oct. 19, 1799; d. Aug. 27, 1866, æ. 66; m. June 7, 1820, *Sally Young* of East Hampton, Ct., who d. Oct. 14, 1838, æ. 36. Children:

2432. i. LYDIA ADELINE, b. Nov. 6, 1821; m. *James Fuller* of Marlboro, and d. Moodus, Ct., Sep. 11, 1867; had a son who d. infant.
2433. ii. BETSY EMELINE, b. Sep. 26, 1822; d. Feb. 23, 1833.
2434. iii. SARAH ANN, b. July 1, 1824; m. May 3, 1852, *John Robinson Bailey,* and lives in Cromwell, Ct.; address box 137; children, BAILEY: [1.] Albert John, b. Mar. 17, 1853. [2.] Edward Clayton, b. Sep. 30, 1858. [3.] Lavinia Arabella, b. Apr. 13, 1866. [4.] Merrick Arnold, b. July 16, 1869; d. Jan. 14, 1870.
2435.* iv. WILLARD SHELDON, b. Jan. 2, 1827.
2436.* v. WILLIAM HENRY, b. Nov. 24, 1831.
2437. vi. ROSETTA CERILLA, b. Jan. 8, 1833; m. *M. V. B. Taylor* of Cromwell, Ct., who d. in U. S. Army; child, TAYLOR: [1.] Frank B.; lives in Lowell, Mass.
2438. vii. MARY MATILDA, b. Oct. 12, 1835; m. —— *Guild* of Ohio; 2d, *John Hanchett* of Glastenbury, Ct., and d. Dec. 22, 1875; she had, by her 1st husband, a son, d. infant; and a dau.

46

1221.

Dea. STEPHEN GRIFFITH SEARS[7] [*Will'd[6]*, *Elkanah[5]*, *Josh.[4]*, *Paul[3]*, *Paul[2]*, *Rich.[1]*], b. Chatham, Ct., Sep. 27, 1803 ; d. East Hampton, Ct., Oct. 12, 1874, æ. 71 ; m. Chatham, May 3, 1831, *Emily Veazey*, dau. of Eleazar and Elizabeth (West) V. of E. Hamp., she b. Feb. 14, 1805 ; d. Apr. 3, 1879, æ. 74.   Children :

2439.   i. MARY ELIZABETH, b. Chat., Jan. 12, 1835 ; m. May 19, 1868, *Bennette Gillette* of Prospect, Ct., he b. Sep. 5, 1826 ; son of Garry and Nancy (Platt) G., and lived in E. Hamp., where she d. Mar. 12, 1875.

2440.* ii. CLARK OSPREY, b. Chat., July 24, 1836.

2441.* iii. CUSHMAN ALLEN, b. Chat., Sep. 26, 1838.

2442. iv. CAROLINE DESIRE, b. Chat., Apr. 24, 1843 ; lives in E. Hamp.

In the life of Dea. Sears there were no striking events, nothing that could be called great or grand, yet the whole life, viewed in its course of seventy years, leaves the impression on the hearts of all who knew him, of completeness, of beauty, of harmony ; his best eulogy is in the hearts of those who knew him best and longest.

One who knew him from youth to old age, testifies that he was never guilty of a mean action, even as a boy ; that even then his conduct was irreproachable.

He was a perfect example of a man whose life was a continuous moral growth, and yet he sought for the deeper life based on faith in Christ.

His whole speech was a witness to the need of the Christ-life in the soul ; but not only in words did his witness consist, it was in the course of his daily life, in the faithful performance of all his duties, that he gave testimony to Him who came to do His Father's work.

Those who loved him well, tell how scrupulously he performed every little duty in the family, and how anxious he was to relieve his family, and make their burdens light.

Like the true Christian, his light threw a cheerful glow around his household hearth, and made his home one of happiness and content.

1222.

ELIJAH CLARK SEARS[7] [*Will'd[6]*, *Elkanah[5]*, *Josh.[4]*, *Paul[3]*, *Paul[2]*, *Rich.[1]*], b. Chatham, Ct., June 23, 1805 ; m.

Dec. 24, 1826, *Ann B. Hills*, she b. 1808 ; d. Crystal Lake, Ill.; 2d, Clinton, Iowa, May 6, 1875, *Mary Price.* Children :

2443.* i. FRANCIS J., b. Sep. 15, 1827.
2444. ii. CAROLINE, b. Sep. 24, 1829 ; m. *Wm. N. Shields.*
2445.* iii. JAMES HENRY, b. N. Y. State, July 23, 1831.
2446. iv. JOHN L., b. Nov. 24, 1834 ; m. *Ellen D. Goodrich.*
2447. v. AMANDA J., b. Jan. 1, 1837; m. *John B. Eaker.*
2448. vi. MARY A., b. June, 1843 ; m. *J. Bannister.*

Mr. Sears settled for a time in Orleans co., N. Y. ; removed thence to Crystal Lake, McHenry co., Ill.; Post-office, Nunda ; lived for a time in Clinton, Iowa, and later in Canton, Lincoln co., Dakota.

1223.

SELDEN PHILO SEARS[7] [*Will'd[6], Elkanah[5], Josh.[4], Paul[3], Paul[2], Rich.[1]*], b. Chatham, Ct., July 21, 1813 ; m. Nov. 29, 1843, *Eveline Dickinson* of Marlboro, Ct., she b. May 6, 1813. Children :

2449.* i. PRESCOTT A., b. E. Hampton, Ct., Oct. 16, 1846.
2450. ii. NEWMAN E., b. E. Hamp., Sep. 16, 1848; m. Oct. 19, 1884, *Florence A. Smith*, dau. of Henry and Helen (Niles) S. of E. Hamp., and lives in Elmwood, Ct.
2451. iii. ALIDA A., b. E. Hamp., June 2, 1852 ; grad. Hartford H. S., 1872; d. Feb. 2, 1877.
2452. iv. DAVID EDWARD, b. E. Hamp., May 23, 1854; d. Feb. 23, 1879.

Mr. Sears lives in Elmwood, West Hartford, Ct.

1224.

ELKANAH SEARS[7] [*Benj.[6], Elkanah[5], Josh.[4], Paul[3], Paul[2], Rich.[1]*], b. New Durham, N. Y., June 22, 1795; d. East Rockport, Ohio, Nov. 15, 1886, æ. 91 ; m. Franklin, N. Y., Mar. 21, 1820, *Desiar Phelps*, dau. of Obadiah and Arminda (Phelps) P., (not related,) she b. Hebron, Ct., Sep. 12, 1794 ; d. Sep. 21, 1872. Children :

2453.* i. JOHN DUDLEY, b. Meredith, N. Y., Feb. 2, 1821.
2454.* ii. BENJAMIN, b. Mere., Oct. 11, 1824.
2455. iii. AMANDA, b. Mere., Feb. 29, 1828 ; m. Sep. 1, 1872, *Lewis Nicholson* of East Rockport, O.
2456.* iv. CYRUS, b. Mere., Mar. 10, 1832.

Mr. Sears removed with his father in 1798 from New Durham, Greene co., to Meredith, Delaware co., N. Y., and was married at Franklin, in the same county, to Desiar Phelps, and settled on a hill farm in Meredith, where all his children were born.

He was bred a farmer, and followed that vocation until prevented by failing health, and the infirmities of old age.

In 1836 he removed with his family to Ohio, and settled on a farm near Bucyrus, removing later to Bucyrus, where he lived many years.

After the death of his wife in 1872, he went to the home of his only daughter, Mrs. Nicholson, with whom he has ever since lived, and under whose roof he died.

His life was quiet and uneventful; he tried to do his duty, and lived and died an honest man.

His death was caused by falling from a verandah to which he went every pleasant day to enjoy the fresh air and sunshine, and the beautiful outlook over Lake Erie and the adjacent shore.

After dinner he was helped from his chair, and made his way to his favorite resort. He had been out but a few minutes when it was noticed that he was not in his usual place.

Search was at once made, and he was found lying on the ground, to which he had fallen over the railing, a distance of about twelve feet. He never spoke and breathed only a few times before death came to his relief.

He was as well as usual, so far as known, and his vital organs were apparently almost unimpaired.

It is probable he slipped or stumbled while leaning over the railing, and was unable to save himself, owing to the crippled condition of his limbs.

1225.

Rev. JOHN SEARS[7] [*Benj.*[6], *Elkanah*[5], *Josh.*[4], *Paul*[3], *Paul*[2], *Rich.*[1]], b. New Durham, N. Y., Apr. 20, 1797; d. Lake Zurich, Ill., Nov. 14, 1856, æ. 59; m. May, 1822, *Mary Ann Slater*, she b. Rhinebeck, N. Y.; d. Detroit, Mich., July 2, 1871, æ. 73. Children:

2457.   i. ELIZA OCTAVIA, b. Sep. 18, 1823; m. Palmyra, N. Y., July 7, 1841, *Marvin McOmber*, he b. Greenfield; d. Galena, Ill., May 30, 1849; 2d, May 31, 1859, *Ambrose Dodd*, he b. Holland Patent, N. Y., Jan. 20,

1803 ; d. Algonquin, Ill., Nov. 2, 1876, where she still
lives; children, McOMBER: [1.] David A., b. Apr. 20,
1842. [2.] John Sears, b. Aug. 7, 1844. [3.] Richard,
b. Jan. 30, 1847. [4.] Marvin, b. Aug. 13, 1849 ; children, DODD: [5.] Cornelia, b. Mar. 23, 1858. [6.] Albert Henry, b. Sep. 4, 1860. [7.] Louis Ambrose, b.
Sep. 24, 1863.

2458. ii. MARY OLIVIA, b. Dec. 17, 1824 ; m. June 10, 1845,
Henry T. West ; lives in Greeley, Col. ; children, WEST:
[1.] Lina. [2.] George. [3.] Henry.

2459. iii. ANN ELIZABETH, b. Sep. 29, 1826 ; m. Dec., 1848,
Luzerne Armstrong, and lives Detroit, Mich. ; children,
ARMSTRONG: [1.] Annie. [2.] Kate.

2460.* iv. JOHN JAMES, b. June 10, 1828.

2461. v. LUCY CAROLINE, b. June 6, 1830; m. Feb. 13,
1851, *J. Howard Nichols,* and lives in Berlin, Wis. ;
children, NICHOLS: [1.] James. [2.] Julia. [3.] MARY.
[4.] Albert. [5.] Charles. [6.] Paul.

2462. vi. SARAH LOUISE, b. Nov. 11, 1833 ; m. July 26,
1866, *A. P. Kennedy,* and lives in Donners Grove, Ill. ;
children, KENNEDY: [1.] Lina. [2.] Asa. [3.] Grace.
[4.] Carl.

2463. vii. HARRIET SLATER, b. May 2, 1836 ; m. Oct. 17,
1859, *Albert Thomas,* and lives in Rockford, Ill. ; children, THOMAS: [1.] Luther. [2.] Gertrude. [3.] Mabel.

2464.* viii. ASA BIGELOW, b. Aug. 25, 1838.

Mr. Sears was educated in N. Y. city ; ordained to the Baptist ministry in 1822, and appointed a missionary to the Indians
by the Baptist B. of M., Jan. 17, 1821, the appointment being
confirmed by Gov. Lewis Cass of Michigan, under army regu-
lations, July 16, 1822, and his salary fixed at $400.

He was appointed to teach the Ottawas, and with his wife
arrived at Fort Wayne, Ind., August 1, 1822, his father, Rev.
Benjamin Sears, and his brother, Benj. Sears, Jr., a lay minister of the Baptist Church, arriving the next day.

Articles of religion were at once drawn up, and on August
3, 1822, the first Baptist Church at Fort Wayne was organized.

The Rev. Corbly Martin of Staunton, Ohio, preached on
the occasion, and the Rev. Elder Benj. Sears gave the right
hand of fellowship.

The members of the first Baptist Church at Fort Wayne,
who signed the articles and thus became the founders of the
church there, were, Isaac McCoy, Christiana McCoy, Giles

Jackson, Mary Jackson, John Sears, Mary Sears, Johnston Lykins, Benjamin Sears, Jr., missionaries; and one woman of the Delaware tribe, one woman of the Miami tribe, and one black man.

Affliction, disappointment and bereavement soon followed Mr. Sears. His father died at Delaware, Ohio, on returning home to New York. His wife was attacked with sickness peculiar to the country and the season.

His brother Benjamin having labored in the mission but twenty-three days, was taken down, and after a protracted spell of typhus fever, died on the third day of November.

Rev. John Sears and his wife left the mission soon afterward — Nov. 26, 1822.

He was settled at Franklin, N. Y., from 1823 to 1827; at Ithaca, N. Y., from 1828 to 1830; Mecklenburg, N. Y., from 1832 to 1842; and at Newfield, N. Y., from 1843 to 1845.

In 1846 he removed to Lake Zurich, Ill., where he settled on a farm, which remained his home till his death in 1856.

1227.

DAVID SEARS[7] [*Benj.[6], Elkanah[5], Josh.[4], Paul[3], Paul[2], Rich.[1]*], b. Meredith, N. Y., July 17, 1803; d. Maquoketa, Iowa, Apr. 15, 1870; m. *Marcia Wheal.* Children:

2465.   i. SUSAN, b. May 3, 1830; unm.
2466.   ii. GEORGE, b. Aug. 7, 1832; unm.
2467.* iii. WILLIAM, b. Aug. 7, 1832, *gemini.*
2468.* iv. BENJAMIN, b. Nov. 23, 1834.

Mr. Sears removed to Franklin, N. Y., and thence to Warren, Pa., and Covington, Ky. For many years previous to his death, he lived at Maquoketa, Jackson co., Iowa.

He was a farmer, merchant and mill-owner.

1228.

Dea. ORIN SEARS[7] [*Benj.[6], Elkanah[5], Josh.[4], Paul[3], Paul[2], Rich.[1]*], b. Meredith, N. Y., Dec. 12, 1805; d. near Mecklenburg, N. Y., Jan. 14, 1886, in his 81 year; m. Feb. 7, 1828, *Jennette Mitchell.* Children:

2469.   i. JANE, b. July 13, 1829; unm.
2470.* ii. ISAAC B., b. Nov. 9, 1831.

2471.* iii. PRESTON, b. Apr. 24, 1834.

2472. iv. ELIZA, b. Aug. 12, 1837; d. Jan. 17, 1839.

2473. v. ANNE, b. June 23, 1841; m. Apr. 26, 1860, *Hiram J. Darling;* child, DARLING: [1.] Andrew S., b. Sep. 15, 1867.

2474. vi. SARAH, b. May 4, 1844; m. Dec. 20, 1865, *Martin O. Sine;* children, SINE: [1.] John J., b. July 29, 1867. [2.] Hiram T., b. Aug. 18, 1869.

2475. vii. RUTH M., b. Mar. 2, 1849; m. Feb. 1, 1871, *Charles L. Duryea.*

Dea. Sears lived for a time in Franklin, and later in Mecklenburg, N. Y., on his own farm, with his children settled near him.

He was converted in 1828, and baptized by Rev. Washington Kingsley.

In 1832, he removed to Mecklenburg, and united with the Baptist church in that place.

He was a faithful and efficient worker in the cause of the Master, though for twenty-five years deafness deprived him of the blessing of the spoken word.

His end was peaceful.

1230.

HIRAM SEARS[7] [*Benj.*[6], *Elkanah*[5], *Josh.*[4], *Paul*[3], *Paul*[2], *Rich.*[1]], b. Meredith, N. Y., May 25, 1811; d. there, Jan. 31, 1864; m. Nov. 13, 1834, *Phidelia Tuttle*, who d. Aug. 12, 1843; 2d, Apr. 26, 1844, *Elizabeth Frisbie.* Children:
By *Phidelia:*

2476. i. ANGELINE, b. Mere., Jan. 13, 1836; m. May 20, 1853, *Peter C. Durham*, and d. Apr. 4, 1864; children, DURHAM: [1.] Charles, d. young. [2.] George P. [3.] Myron R. [4.] Willard S., d. young.

2477.* ii. RUFUS A., b. Mere., Jan. 20, 1838.

By *Elizabeth:*

2478. iii. HIRAM, d. æ. 15.

2479. iv. SARAH ELIZABETH, b. Mere.; m. *De Witt Jacobs;* had Frank.

2480. v. PHIDELIA, b. Mere.; m. *O. C. Sargent*, and lives in Jewett City, Ct.

2481.* vi. MILLARD D., b. Mere., Oct. 27, 1860.

1239.

JASON SEARS[7] [*Dan'l*[6], *Josh.*[5], *Josh.*[4], *Paul*[3], *Paul*[2], *Rich.*[1]], b. Sandisfield, Mass., Feb. 29, 1803 ; m. —— ——. Children :

2482. i. ALBERT.
2483. ii. TIMOTHY.

Mr. Sears was a merchant in Alabama; married a southern lady, by whom he became the owner of several slaves; accumulated considerable property, but lost largely by the Rebellion.

1241.

HENRY MORRIS SEARS[7] [*Dan'l*[6], *Josh.*[5], *Josh.*[4], *Paul*[3], *Paul*[2], *Rich.*[1]], b. Sandisfield, Mass., Mar. 10, 1808; m. —— ——. Children :

2484. i. JAMES AMOS, b. Feb. 22, 1854.
2485. ii. *Dau.*

Mr. Sears removed to New York State.

1242.

Rev. DANIEL SEARS[7] [*Jos.*[6], *Josh.*[5], *Josh.*[4], *Paul*[3], *Paul*[2], *Rich.*[1]], b. Sandisfield, Mass., Apr. 13, 1801; m. *M. Ross.* Children :

2486. i. JOSEPH.
2487. ii. DANIEL.

Mr. Sears was a Methodist clergyman, and removed to Wachita, La.

1244.

JOSHUA MILTON SEARS[7] [*Jos.*[6], *Josh.*[5], *Josh.*[4], *Paul*[3], *Paul*[2], *Rich.*[1]], b. Sandisfield, Mass., Sep. 19, 1808 ; m. *Catharine Bosworth*, dau. of Jabez B. Children :

2488. i. HELEN MARCIA, b. Sand., Oct. 13, 1833; d. Dec. 9, 1844.
2489. ii. CATHARINE BOSWORTH, b. Sand., Aug. 1, 1840.
2490.* iii. EDMUND BACON, b. Sand., 1844.

Mr. Sears was prominent in town affairs, and was Rep. to State Leg. in 1862. He now lives in New Boston, Sandisfield, Mass., with his son.

1245.

Rev. EDMUND HAMILTON SEARS[7] [*Jos.*[6], *Josh.*[5], *Josh.*[4], *Paul*[3], *Paul*[2], *Rich.*[1]], b. Sandisfield, Mass., Apr. 6, 1810; d. Weston, Mass., Sabbath morning, Jan. 16, 1876, æ. 66; m. Barnstable, Mass., Nov. 7, 1839, *Ellen Bacon*, dau. of Hon. Eben'r and Abigail (Crocker) B., she b. there, Apr. 11, 1811; lives in Weston. Children:

2491. i. KATHARINE, b. Lancaster, Mass., Feb. 25, 1843; d. Wayland, Mass., Jan. 12, 1853.
2492.* ii. FRANCIS BACON, b. Jan. 21, 1849.
2493. iii. EDMUND HAMILTON, b. Apr. 20, 1852; grad. Yale, 1874; lives in Weston.
2494. iv. HORACE SCUDDER, b. Feb. 26, 1855.

Rev. Edmund H. Sears was graduated at Union Coll. in 1834, and at Cambridge Theo. School in 1837; began to preach as a missionary at Toledo, Ohio, remaining nearly a year, — was ordained Pastor of 1st Church, Wayland, Mass., 1839, installed at Lancaster, Mass., Dec. 23, 1840, as successor to Rev. Dr. Nath'l Thayer; resettled in Wayland, 1848; installed as colleague of Dr. Field, Pastor of the Unit. Ch. at Weston, Mass., in May, 1865, and succeeded him as Pastor in Nov., 1869.

"He visited Europe in 1873, and was severely injured by the fall of a tree in his orchard in 1874.

"He was a man of singularly modest and retiring nature. His health had long been feeble, and he shrunk from personal display of any sort. But as a writer, as a preacher, and as a man, he has left a memory which will be long and lovingly cherished by all who knew him.

"A saintlier soul has rarely been enshrined in mortal frame.

"But for his early impaired health and enfeebled voice, he would have been deemed eloquent in utterance, no less than in style, for his delivery had every attractive and impressive quality, within the limited spaces in which alone he dared to seek a hearing.

"Those who knew him felt that his place was with the beloved apostle, in closest union and sympathy with his Divine Master.

"There was a sweet serenity of spirit in his whole demeanor,

47

speech and character, which made him in every relation of life unspeakably dear.

"Simple, modest, unassuming, even diffident, he was the last person to make of set purpose any manifestation of piety; but a beauty of holiness so pure and radiant as his could not be kept under cover.

"All who came within its sphere felt profoundly the sanctity, purity and loveliness of its character.

"His style was the transcript of his thought and feeling.

"There was a view of high poetic inspiration, not only in those lyrics which are finding their place in the worship of Christian sanctuaries wherever the English tongue is spoken, but almost equally in his prose, which is never otherwise than rhythmical, glowing and fervent."

Amongst other works of his were: "Regeneration," "Athanasia," "The Fourth Gospel the Heart of Christ," "Sermons and Songs of the Christian Life," "Christian Lyrics," etc., and he edited, with Rev. R. Ellis, "The Monthly Religious Magazine."

In 1857 he published an historical romance entitled "Pictures of the Olden Time," in connection with which he edited the "Sears Genealogy," from papers furnished him by Hon. David Sears of Boston, but which have since been found to contain much erroneous information based upon legends incapable of proof. See *ante*, "English Ancestry."

1247.

ALFRED SEARS⁷ [*Paul⁶, Paul⁵, Josh.⁴, Paul³, Paul², Rich.¹*], b. Sandisfield, Mass., Sep. 25, 1795; d. Rockford, Ill., Oct. 13, 1880; m. *Eliza Daland.* Children:

2495.* i. BARNAS C.
2496.* ii. DELOS AMBROSE, b. Perrysville, N. Y., Aug. 19, 1828.

Mr. Sears served as a musician in the war of 1812; was a farmer and merchant in the interior of New York State for many years, and in 1855 removed to Rockford, Ill., where he continued to reside until his death.

1250.

Rev. BARNAS SEARS⁷ [*Paul⁶, Paul₅ Josh.⁴, Paul³, Paul², Rich.¹*], b. Sandisfield, Mass., Nov. 19, 1802; d. Saratoga, N. Y., July 6, 1880, and was buried at Brookline in his wife's family tomb ; m. *Elizabeth Griggs Corey*, dau. of Timo. and Eliz'h (Griggs) C. of Brookline, Mass., she b. Nov. 21, 1809 ; d. Staunton, Va., Mar. 23, 1883, æ. 73. Children :

2497.* i. WILLIAM BARNAS, b. June 11, 1832.
2498. ii. ELIZABETH COREY, b. Newton Centre, Mass., Oct. 14, 1838; m. May 8, 1862, *Robert B. Chapman* of Prov., R. I.; 2d, Oct. 12, 1874, Dr. *James Hampden Fultz*, he b. May 5, 1840, and lives in Staunton, Va.
2499. iii. EDWARD HENRY, b. New. Cen., Oct. 4, 1840; d. s. p., Aug. 22, 1886; m. Brooklyn, N. Y., Apr. 20, 1869, *Amelia L. Wiley*, she b. Prov., R. I. Mr. Sears was educ. in Brown Univ., left at commencement of senior year to join 2d Regt. R. I. Vols.; app. 1st Lt., June 6, 1861; promoted to Capt. after Bull Run fight, July 22, 1861; transf. by request to Battery G, R. I. Lt. Art'y, Oct. 19, 1861; app. A. A. Paymaster, U. S. Navy, Aug. 27, 1863; taken prisoner Feb. 2, 1864, and held 8 months in Libby Prison; was one of the number placed under fire at Charleston, S. C.; hon. dischg'd June 2, 1868; app. Postmaster, Staunton, Va., by Gen. Grant, May 5, 1869; also Registering Officer of 17th Military Division of Va., by Gen. E. Canby, June 2, 1869; was a member of the City Council of Staunton, Va.; removed to Boston in Jan., 1874, and engaged in insurance business with his bro. Capt. Wm. B. Sears; resided in Roxbury.
2500. iv. ROBERT DAVIS, b. June 28, 1842.
2501. v. EDWARD DWIGHT, b. June 28, 1852; d. Staunton, Va., Nov. 10, 1882.

Rev. Barnas Sears, D. D., LL. D., S. T. D., grad. Brown Univ., 1825, and Newton Theo. Sem'y, 1829; studied several years at Halle, Leipsic and Berlin; was two years Pastor 1st Bapt. Ch., Hartford, Ct.; afterward Prof. Ham. Theo. Sem'y, N. Y., (now Madison Univ.,) and Prof. and Pres. Newton Theo. Sem'y, Newton, Mass.

In 1848, he succeeded Horace Mann as Sec. Mass. Board of Education, and was from Aug. 21, 1855, to Feb., 1867, President of Brown University.

From 1867 until his death, he rendered valuable services as General Agent of the Trustees of the Fund given by the late George Peabody for the benefit of Southern education.

He published "Nohden's Grammar of the English Language," in 1842; "Classical Studies," 1843; "Ciceronia, or the Prussian mode of Instruction in Latin," 1844; "Memoir of Rev. Bela Jacobs," 1847; "Life of Luther," 1850; since republished in England with the title "Mental and Spiritual Life of Luther," 1850; numerous reports on education, occasional addresses, and contributions to reviews and other periodicals, and to "Appleton's American Cyclopedia."

In 1838, and for several years he edited the "Christian Review," and later the "Bibliotheca Sacra."

In 1864, he published a discourse on the "Completion of the first century of Yale College."

Dr. Sears was in public life from the time he returned to this country from Europe in 1837, until the year of his death, 1880.

By many he was considered one of the greatest men of the age, and no doubt he was the foremost educator.

He had made every effort to secure his own scholarship, as his parents were unable to render him much assistance, and what he possessed himself he earnestly wished others to share.

He never was in the company of the young, that on parting, they had not something to remember, which he had imparted in a pleasant manner.

His social and domestic life was not so full of incidents as might be expected, considering his peculiar gifts of wit, conversation and quick repartee, for he was a devoted student, even to the last days of his career.

Each year he was accustomed to take some one of the languages, and renew his intimacy with it.

He spoke and wrote with comparative ease, Greek, Latin, French, German, Spanish and Italian, and had a fair knowledge of Hebrew and Sanscrit.

In English he was a sure authority, and it was an absolute pain to him to hear it badly spoken by those who should use it correctly.

His wife was accustomed to say that she almost wished she was a book, as then she should receive his attention occasionally, and his children sometimes remarked that they wished company would come, so that the sound of his voice would be heard.

Such things rather pained him, while he treated them as jests, and he would lay aside pen and paper, and endeavor to "be sociable," but soon he would be seen in his own familiar place, utterly oblivious to his surroundings.

He had a very warm and affectionate nature, and although separated from all his brothers and sisters for many years, he seldom spoke of them without emotion.

Of his mother he had the tenderest remembrance; he always described her to his children, who never saw her, as one of the best and sweetest Christians.

His father was quick-tempered and uneven in his spirits, but the mother was uniform and mild.

He had an old uncle Simeon, who used to be rather severe with his mischievous nephews.

Although Barnas was his favorite, he was very impatient at his fondness for books, and when he found him stretched under the shade of a tree, or sheltered from sight in any sequestered nook, he would chide him for laziness, and not unfrequently lay his riding whip about the boy's legs.

In spite of his fault-finding, however, he was proud of his talents, and in later life often said, he "always knew that youngster would make his mark."

While religious in the deepest and truest meaning of the word, Dr. Sears was neither sectarian or narrow minded.

He had a broad catholic spirit, and saw good in all men.

When others were sitting in harshest judgment on some unfortunate one, he had a word of exculpation, or a loophole for possible escape.

In a little pocket diary, found in his coat after death, were a few rules for self-government. One was, "Criticise yourself severely, others mildly." Another was, "If not able to say a kind thing of the absent, keep silent."

These maxims were most faithfully observed.

He had inherited a quick temper, but by the time his family were grown, he had it under perfect control.

After he died, an old colored man-servant, who had lived with him many years, told his associates that he had *never* heard his master speak angrily, and a colored girl who waited on Mrs. Sears seventeen years bore the same testimony.

Every one loved him who served him, and while the whole country took sad note of his death, there was no sincerer regret anywhere than amongst the humble poor, who were connected with him in domestic life.

1251.

LYMAN SEARS[7] [*Paul[6], Paul[5], Josh.[4], Paul[3], Paul[2], Rich.[1]*], b. Sandisfield, Mass., Sep. 19, 1804; d. Brooklyn, N. Y., Apr. 10, 1866; m. Mrs. *Samantha (Hubbard) Phelps*, who d.; 2d, Mrs. —— *Savage.* Children:

By *Samantha* :

2502. i. ELLEN A., b. 1836; d. 1848.

2503. ii. Edward L., b. 1847; d.

Mr. Sears lived in Brooklyn, and was of firm Burt, Sears & Co., dealers in leather and hides, and large manufacturers of boots and shoes.

1252.

DAVID G. SEARS[7] [*Paul*[6], *Paul*[5], *Josh.*[4], *Paul*[3], *Paul*[2], *Rich.*[1]], b. Sandisfield, Mass., June 29, 1806; m. there, Feb. 20, 1828, *Olive Deming*, she b. there, Oct. 12, 1806. Children:

2504.* i. Edwin, b. Sand., Oct. 13, 1829.
2505. ii. Rolin(?), b. Sand., Mar. 16, 1832; d. Hartford, Ct., Mar. 22, 1840.
2506. iii. Mary L., b. Sand., Dec. 30, 1834; m. Scott, Ill., Jan. 28, 1864, *Wm. A. McHenry*, he b. Mar. 6, 1841; was in the war till its close, then rem. to Denison, Iowa, and engaged in banking.
2507.* iv. Henry, b. New Boston, Mass., Sep. 14, 1836.
2508. v. George, b. Hartford, Ct., Oct. 11, 1839; m. Scott, Ill., Jan. 1, 1860, *Lovisa J. Brooks*, she b. Oct. 12, 1840; rem. to Rockford, Ill., with his father, and d. Elgin, Ill., Oct. 12, 1866. His widow married again.

Mr. Sears was for many years in the hide and leather business in Hartford, Ct., removed to New York and engaged in the sale of boots and shoes, firm of Sears, Morley & Co., removing thence to Rockford, Ill., where he now resides.

1253.

JOHN R. SEARS[7] [*Paul*[6], *Paul*[5], *Josh.*[4], *Paul*[3], *Paul*[2], *Rich.*[1]], b. Sandisfield, Mass., Jan. 11, 1809; d. Poughkeepsie, N. Y.; m. *Louisa Hyde*, who d.; 2d, *Esther Hyde* of New Marlboro, Mass., who d. Leavenworth, Kan.; 3d, in Leavenworth, ―― ――. Children:

By *Louisa:*
2509. i. Jane, d. Hartford, Ct.
By *Esther:*
2510. ii. James, d. Hartford.

Mr. Sears was in the grocery and real estate business in Hartford, Ct., and in New York city; removed to Illinois and dealt in grain and hogs. He removed thence to Leavenworth, Kan., and engaged in the flour business, failed, and returned to Poughkeepsie, N. Y., where he died.

1254.

HIRAM SEARS[7] [*Paul[6]*, *Paul[5]*, *Josh.[4]*, *Paul[5]* *Paul[2]*, *Rich.[1]*], b. Sandisfield, Mass., July 8, 1811 ; d. Vail, Iowa, Sep., 1878 ; m. *Julia A. Pickett*, dau. of Sam'l P. of Otis, Mass. Children :

2511. i. SAMUEL, b. 1839 ; was in business with his father in New York, and died in a dentist's chair under the influence of chloroform.

2512. ii. LUCIA L., b. 1841 ; m. *James J. Fitch* of N. Y., who was in fancy goods business, and later with his father-in-law in boot and shoe trade; removed to Vail, Iowa, and engaged in lumber and grain business.

Mr. Sears was in boot and shoe business in New York city, residing in Brooklyn ; removed to Vail, Iowa, where he died.

1255.

HENRY SEARS[7] [*Paul[6]*, *Paul[5]*, *Josh.[4]*, *Paul[3]*, *Paul[2]*, *Rich.[1]*], b. Sandisfield, Mass., Aug. 3, 1815 ; m. Norwich, Ct., Sep. 10, 1839, *Lucretia Brewster*, she b. Preston, Ct., July 27, 1811 ; d. Rockford, Ill., Sep. 3, 1854, æ. 43 ; 2d, Norwich, Ct., Sep. 20, 1855, Mrs. *Esther* (*Brewster*) *Statesbury*, she b. Jan. 25, 1818. Children:

By *Lucretia :*

2513. i. FRANCES E., b. Hartford, Sep. 27, 1841 ; m. Rockford, Ill., Aug. 7, 1877, *George A. Seeley*, and lives there ; has 2 children.

2514.* ii. EDMUND B., b. Sandisfield, Dec. 20, 1845.

By *Esther :*

2515. iii. MARIA B., b. Rockford, Ill., July 6, 1856; m. there, May 3, 1881, *Ernest H. Potter*, and lives in San Jose, Cal.; child, POTTER : [1.] Wallace S.

Mr. Sears lived with his brother in Hartford, Ct., for a few years, then returned to Sandisfield, and took care of his parents and grand-mother until their death ; he then removed to Rockford, Ill., and engaged in farming for a few years ; went into trade there, and in 1872, after the fire, moved his business to Chicago ; is a wholesale dealer in cutlery, fire-arms, etc., manf'rs and importers, firm of Henry Sears & Co.

His health failing, he left his business in charge of his son and another partner, and went to San Jose, Cal., still retaining his interest in the business.

1258.

NORMAN SPENCER SEARS[7] [*Sim.*[6], *Paul*[5], *Josh.*[4], *Paul*[3], *Paul*[2], *Rich.*[1]], b. Sandisfield, Mass., Jan. 7, 1805; m. S. Tyringham, (now Monterey,) Mass., 1828, *Abigail Jones*, she b. Sand., 1803; ·d. So. T., 1836, æ. 33; 2d, 1837, *Olive Spear*, she b. Otis, Mass., 1803; d. Mont., 1878, æ. 75. Children:
By *Abigail*:
2516.		i. Harriet Jones, b. New Marlboro, Mass., 1830; was educated in Le Roy, N. Y., and was a school teacher for four years in Rochester, N. Y., and vicinity. She m. 1854, Rev. *Stephen Keyes, Jr.*, a Bapt. min., who d. 1868; had two sons, of whom one lives with his mother in Monterey.
2516. *a.* ii. Mary Louisa, b. New M., 1832; d. So. T., 1834.
2516.*a.* iii. Hiram Porter, b. So. T., 1834.
2516. *a.* iv. Harlow Milton, b. So. T., 1836; d. 1843, of scarlet fever.
By *Olive*:
2516. *a.* v. Barnas Norman, b. Mont., 1840; d. 1849, of scarlet fever.
2516.*a.* vi. John Simeon, b. Mont., May 31, 1842.

Mr. Sears is a farmer in Monterey, Mass., has been Selectman, Assessor and Juryman for many years, and is a member of the Congregational Church.

1259.

JULIUS SEARS[7] [*Sim.*[6], *Paul*[5], *Josh.*[4], *Paul*[5] *Paul*[2], *Rich.*[1]], b. Sandisfield, Mass., Apr. 3, 1807; d. Vinland, N. J., 1889, æ. 82; m. *Mary Barker.* Children:
2516. *b.* i. Edward.
2516. *b.* ii. Milton S.
2516. *b.* iii. *Dau.*
2516. *b.* iv. *Dau.*

Mr. Sears injured himself when a young man in running to a fire, and always after had poor health, but lived to the age of 82.

1261.

SIMEON SEARS[7] [*Sim.*[6], *Paul*[5], *Josh.*[4], *Paul*[3], *Paul*[2], *Rich.*[1]], b. Sandisfield, Mass., July 13, 1811 ; m. there, Nov. 5, 1834, *Ann Eliza Adams*. Children :

2517. i. LAURA ELIZA, b. Sand., May 5, 1837 ; m. *Osmund Huntley*, and lived in Hillsboro, N. H.
2518.* ii. GILBERT N., b. Lempster, N. H., Jan. 1, 1839.
2519. iii. GEORGE, m. and lived in E. Deering, N. H.

Mr. Sears was a carpenter and joiner, removed to Lempster, N. H., and is a member of Baptist Church there.

1262.

Rev. EDWARD G. SEARS[7] [*Sim.*[6], *Paul*[5] *Josh.*[4], *Paul*[3], *Paul*[2], *Rich.*[1]], b. Sandisfield, Mass., Dec. 9, 1813; d. Springfield, Mass., Nov. 13, 1878, æ. 65 ; m. West Scituate, Mass., Aug. 6, 1839, *Betsy Collamore*, she b. there, Nov. 15, 1807 ; d. St. Albans, Vt., May 5, 1880, æ. 72. Children :

2520. i. ELIZABETH C., b. Newton, Mass., July 14, 1841; d. West Scituate, Mass., Oct. 16, 1841.
2521.* ii. EDWARD SHAILER, b. No. Wrentham, Mass., Apr. 23, 1844.
2522. iii. ANDREW FULLER COLLAMORE, b. Franklin, Mass., Jan. 31, 1848; d. Brookline, Mass., Aug. 4, 1849.

Rev. Edward G. Sears was educated at Madison Univ., Hamilton, N. Y., and at Newton Theo. Sem'y, Mass., and ordained minister of the Baptist Church. He was a fine scholar, and early in boyhood showed his love for mathematics by secretly borrowing an advanced arithmetic and entirely mastering its contents, and finishing every example in it before his parents knew any thing about it.

He was settled in Marshfield, Sharon, North Wrentham, Franklin and other places in Mass., and afterward became a Professor in New Hampton Institute, N. H.

He was for a year or two editor of the " Christian Review," in Boston ; afterward engaged in manufacturing business in Nashua, N. H. ; in furniture business in Baltimore, Md., and in farming in Agawam, Mass., from 1857 to 1865.

In the latter year he became editor of the Springfield, Mass., " Daily Union," which position he held until within a year or

48

two of his death, when he retired to a small place he had purchased in the suburbs of Springfield. He had for many years
been in poor health.

1264.

JAMES SEARS[7] [*Sim.*[6], *Sim.*[5], *Josh.*[4], *Paul*[3], *Paul*[2],
Rich.[1]], b. New York State, Nov. 6, 1790; d. Kansas, 1871,
æ. 81; m. 1816, *Elizabeth Gregory*, she b. N. Y., 1788; d.
1862, æ. 73.   Children:

2523.   i. BELINDA, b. 1818; m. *Thomas Bolles*, and lives in
         Michigan.
2524.   ii. SARAH, b. 1820; m. *Nicholas Worthington*, and
         lives in Mich.
2525. iii. HELEN, b. 1822.
2526.   iv. ELIZABETH, b. 1824; lives in Minnesota.
2527.*   v. GREGORY A., b. Ithaca, N. Y., Feb. 27, 1827.
2528.* vi. JAMES DOUGLASS, b. 1829.
2529. vii. WILLIAM R., b. 1834; went to White Plain, Nevada,
         with his bro. James during the mining excitement, and
         later to North Carolina, where he died about 1870.

1271.

DAVID BENTON SEARS[7] [*Jos.*[6], *Sim.*[5], *Josh.*[4], *Paul*[3],
Paul[2], *Rich.*[1]], b. Lima, N. Y., Apr. 28, 1804; d. Sears, Ill.,
Jan. 22, 1884, æ. 80; m. Shawneetown, Ill., 1824, *Melinda
Stokes*, she b. and d. there; 2d, 1835, *Delia Caldwell*, she b.
Ky., 1813; d. Moline, Ill., June 28, 1862, æ. 49; 3d, *Eunice
Sayles*, who d. s. p.; 4th, Mo., Oct. 29, 1875, *Margaret J.
Merchant*, who lives in Sears, Ill.   Children:

By *Melinda:*
2530.   i. MELINDA, b. Shaw.; d. young.
2531.   ii. MARY, b. Shaw.; m. *W. W. Bass*, Platteville, Wis.,
         and d.
2532. iii. ABIGAIL, b. Shaw.; m. *Henry Shall;* both d.
2533.   iv. *Child*, b. Shaw.; d. young.
2534.   v. CAROLINE, b. Shaw.; d. young.
2535.   vi. SARAH, b. Shaw.; m. *L. W. Eastman*, and lives
         in Chicago, Ill.
By *Delia:*
2536. vii. POLLY, m. *Theodore Waterman*, and d.

2537.   viii. MARGARET.
2538.*   ix. DAVID, b. Moline, Ill., Mar. 23, 1839.
2539.*   x. WILLIAM H. H., b. M., Nov. 18, 1840.
2540.*   xi. GEORGE WASHINGTON, b. M., Nov. 23, 1842.
2541.   xii. BARBARA JANE, b. M.; d. young.
2542.   xiii. JANETTE, b. M., Mar. 10, 1848; lives in Sears, unm.
2543.*   xiv. HENRY H., b. M., Oct. 18, 1850.

Mr. Sears was born in Lima, Livingston co., N. Y., in Apr., 1804, and in his seventh year removed with his parents to Sciota Valley, Ohio, where they lived during the war of 1812, enduring great hardships, their lives being frequently imperiled by the attacks of marauding Indians.

They were finally compelled to leave their home, and flee for safety to Fort Erie, their flight taking them across the Sciota river, and in making the passage their rude boat was upset, and two of his sisters and a brother were drowned.

Reaching the fort they availed themselves of its protection until after Perry's famous victory, they being within sound of the guns during the engagement.

They then removed to Cincinnati, and in 1814, ventured still further west, settling in Switzerland co., Ind.

In 1818, they again pulled up stakes, and struck out for the Wabash valley, where they finally located permanently.

Two years after, David, who was then in his seventeenth year, yearning for an education, resolved to return to his native State.

Accordingly, wrapping all his spare clothing in a cotton handkerchief, he started for New Orleans on a flat-boat, where he arrived safely, and went round to New York by sailing vessel, from whence he proceeded to his mother's people, living near Syracuse.

Something seems to have occurred which interfered with his plans for obtaining an education, for in the course of a year we find him on his way back to Illinois. The reason for this sudden move may, perhaps, be read in the record of his first marriage, which occurred in 1824, the woman of his choice being Miss Melinda Stokes of Shawneetown, Ill.

The young people commenced life on a farm of eighty acres near that place, and for a period of fourteen years Mr. Sears made farming his vocation, taking annual trips to New Orleans to dispose of his produce, which he shipped by flat-boat.

On these trips lucrative inducements were frequently held

out to him by southern traders to enter the slave trade, but to accept such a proposition was contrary to the cardinal principles of his life, and he never attempted to better his fortunes in that way.

In 1836, Mr. Sears became possessed of a desire to see the Upper Mississippi valley, of whose wonderful fertility and beauty he had heard so much, and leaving his home, he directed his course to the point now covered by the busy little city of Moline.

Not a building of any kind then stood there, the lovely Rock Island had remained as nature had made it. The swift waters of the mighty river flowed wastefully past it on either side.

Five miles below, old " Black Hawk's watch tower " raised its head in primitive grandeur above the broad valley of the Rock river, whose enchained water power now turns the wheels of numerous industries.

The scene unfolded to the gaze of Mr. Sears was not only one of surpassing loveliness, but it also revealed, as his quick eye discovered, superior advantages for the location and development of large manufacturing interests.

The purpose of making this his permanent abiding place was immediately formed. The building of a habitation and removal of his family and chattels was soon accomplished, and then began the work which has made the name of Sears and the history of Moline's industrial progress inseparable.

In 1837, Mr. Sears, in company with J. W. Spencer, Calvin Ainsworth, and Spencer M. White, commenced building the first dam across the river between Rock Island and the Illinois shore.

In the fall of 1841, they erected a two-story saw-mill, and placed on the upper floor a run of burrs, for the accommodation of the neighboring farmers, the nearest flour-mill at that time being one hundred miles distant.

Thomas Patterson supervised the work as millwright, and Jona. Huntoon dressed and fitted the stones.

In 1843, the company built the " big mill," at a cost of some $30,000; it was a four-run mill, and the machinery the best that could be procured at that period.

Mr. Sears was noted for his readiness to adopt improved appliances for the simplification and lightening of labor.

He brought to Moline the first rotary saw used in the Mississippi valley above St. Louis, thereby incurring the transient displeasure of his employees, who looked upon it as an encroachment on their rights.

By an arrangement with his partners, he completed the new structure with his own funds, his right to the water power being made for a term of years.

He controlled the mill and its business until 1848, shipping its products to St. Louis and lower Mississippi river points.

About 1843, Mr. Sears in company with Charles Atkinson, laid out and plotted the town of Moline and its "Island City" subdivision, which consisted of a tract of thirty-seven acres, on the upper end of Rock Island, then held as a military reserve.

This tract he secured the right from Congress to enter at $1.25 per acre, the privilege being granted him in consideration of the benefits to navigation which had accrued from the building of the dam on the Illinois side.

Mr. Sears established a foundry, erected a store and other buildings in Moline, and thereafter for years had a hand in the advancement of every project which had the material improvement of the town for its aim.

In 1845, he built a saw-mill, and in 1859, a three-run flour-mill on Benham's Island, a narrow strip of land lying contiguous to Rock Island on the north, thereby developing a water power between the two islands.

He constructed a steamboat landing below the mill, erected a house and other buildings on the main land, and when in 1865, the government took possession of the island for the purpose of a National arsenal and armory, the commission awarded him $145,175 for his property and improvements.

In 1855, Mr. Sears purchased one-fourth of the present milling site of Minneapolis, (one-fourth of forty-nine acres, and one-fourth of the water power,) which he sold to the late Gov. C. C. Washburn for $4,000, and in doing so made a great mistake, as he frequently remarked, and as events subsequently proved.

He at the same time built a saw-mill and furniture factory on Lake Minnetonka, which with a bridge contract was the end of his building operations until after the war.

In August, 1861, he enlisted in 22d Illinois Regiment, and served honorably as Quartermaster for three years.

In 1867, he built the fine 300-barrel mill at Sears, now operated by his sons, David, William and George, and in 1870, a flour-mill at Cleveland, Mo., and another at Linden in 1873.

In 1875, he went to Tama City, Iowa, erected a large mill, and two years later dug a canal, put in a dam and otherwise improved the water power at Ottumka.

In 1880, he constructed water-works at Red Oak, Iowa, and the following year performed a like work at Joplin, Mo.

Mr. Sears was a man of sterling principles. Honest in all his dealings, he was respected by all with whom he had business relations. Liberal to an extreme, none ever asked his charity, who did not receive what he could afford to give.

He was a strong advocate of temperance, and practised what he preached.

Up to within a few moments of his death, he seemed to be in the enjoyment of good health, in his 80th year, apparently as hale and hearty as at any period of his life.

The history of his life is a record of good deeds, and worthy of emulation.

1287.

Dr. PAUL SEARS[7] [*Nath.*[6], *Paul*[5] *Dan.*[4], *Paul*[3], *Paul*[2], *Rich.*[1]], b. near Zanesville, Ohio, June 5, 1820 ; m. May 5, 1841, *Eliza J. Gibson* of Cincinnati, O., dau. of Alex. and Martha (Sturges) G. Children :

2544. i. ALFRED ALEXANDER, studied medicine and grad. Jefferson Med. Coll., Phila. ; d. Dec. 13, 1867.

2545. ii. CHARLES NATHAN, read medicine and took one course at same college, and d. Aug. 18, 1864. They were both bright young men, and gave promise of future usefulness, and adornment to the profession.

2546. iii. CLARISSA A., m. Oct. 31, 1865, Hon. *S. J. Landes;* children, LANDES : [1.] Pauline, b. May 24, 1868. [2.] Herbert Sears, b. Sep. 5, 1870. [3.] Bernard Sears, b. July 31, 1877.

Dr. Sears was educated in Elyria High School, and Granville Coll., Ohio ; removed with his parents to Michigan in 1834 ; remaining until the spring of 1840, when he went to Mt. Carmel, Wabash co., Ill., his father having preceded him a year.

He studied medicine with his father, assisting him in his office ; entered Ohio Med. Coll. in 1843, and received his diploma in 1845, when he commenced practice in Mt. Carmel.

Dr. Sears is personally known in almost every household in Wabash and surrounding counties ; has had a large and lucrative practice, and frequently rode 60 miles in 24 hours to visit patients.

He also kept a dry goods store, and engaged in other enterprises not interfering with his profession ; has been successful professionally and financially, and bears the reputation of being an honorable, public-spirited citizen, an honest man, and a kind-hearted, obliging neighbor.

1291.

LEWIS SEARS[7] [*Dan'l[6], Enos[5], Dan'l[4], Paul[3], Paul[2], Rich.[1]*], b. Ashfield, Mass., Dec. 24, 1806; d. Caledonia, Wis., Jan. 7, 1860; m. Ash., May 27, 1842, *Achsah Mills*, she b. there, Apr. 5, 1812. Children:

2547.　i. HELEN M., b. Cale., Apr. 19, 1843; m. Racine, Nov. 26, 1862, *Erastus C. Peck*, and d. Mar. 23, 1879; children, PECK: [1.] Lewis N., b. Sep. 2, 1864. [2.] Lilian A., b. July 21, 1867. [3.] Ella, b. Jan. 30, 1872; d. Aug. 14, 1873. [4.] Charles T., b. Mar. 20, 1875; d. Jan. 23, 1876.

2548.　ii. SARAH A., b. Cale., Jan. 28, 1845; d. Sep. 26, 1846.

2549.* iii. DANIEL M., b. Cale., Dec. 24, 1846.

2550.　iv. LYDIA A., b. Cale., Aug. 19, 1848; lives in Franksville, Wis.

2551.* v. EDGAR L., b. Cale., Mar. 21, 1850.

2552.　vi. ELLA E., b. Cale., Mar. 16, 1852; m. Sep. 18, 1872, *Terry G. Adams;* children, ADAMS: [1.] Jessie M., b. Aug. 26, 1873. [2.] George G., b. Jan. 30, 1875. [3.] Carrie L., b. Nov. 4, 1879.

Mr. Sears removed in 1837, to Caledonia, Racine co., Wis., where his widow still lives.

1292.

WILLIAM SEARS[7] [*Dan'l[6], Enos[5], Dan'l[4], Paul[3], Paul[2], Rich.[1]*], b. Ashfield, Mass., Dec. 17, 1808; d. Mt. Pleasant, Wis., Aug. 12, 1888; m. Ash., Apr. 29, 1833, *Annis Ames*, she b. Conway, Mass., Apr. 19, 1811; d. Mt. Pl., Sep. 17, 1889, and was buried beside her husband in Mound Cemetery. Children:

2553.　i. ALONZO, b. Caledonia, Wis., Jan. 11, 1835; lives Mt. Pleasant, Wis.

2554.　ii. MARTIN LUTHER, b. Caledonia, Aug. 6, 1836; d. Oct. 5, 1839.

2555.　iii. MARY ANN, b. Caledonia, Oct. 12, 1838; d. Apr. 23, 1871.

2556.　iv. ELECTA OLIVIA, b. Caledonia, Oct. 8, 1840; d. 18—; m. Oct. 22, 1863, *Henry Dwelle*, and lived in Lake City, Minn.; (he m. 2d, her sister, Mrs. Eliz'h A. Lambertson); children, DWELLE: [1.] Ruby E. [2.] Myrtle M.

2557.* v. MARTIN LUTHER, b. Caledonia, Oct. 18, 1843.

2558. vi. ELIZABETH ANNIS, b. Caledonia, Apr. 22, 1849;
m. Sep. 13, 1871, *George H. Lambertson*, who d. Feb.
14, 1881; 2d, Oct. 5, 1887, her bro.-in law *Henry
Dwelle*, and lives in Lake City, Minn.; children, LAM-
BERTSON: [1.] George H. [2.] Edward E. [3.] Herbert Sears.

2559. vii. LAURA MELISSA, b. Caledonia, June 18, 1852; m.
Thos. Dwelle, and lives in Lake City, Minn.; child,
DWELLE: [1.] Pearl.

2560. viii. ADELINE, b. Caledonia, Aug. 4, 1854; m. *Chas. K.
Stearns*, and lives in Mt. Pleasant, Wis.; children,
STEARNS: [1.] Mary. [2.] Orin C.

In November, 1836, Mr. Sears removed to Racine county,
Wis., and was followed the next year by his wife. He located
upon the land in what is now the town of Caledonia, in which
town they resided until 1870, when they removed to the house
in Mt. Pleasant, in which they died.

As in their earlier years, Mr. Sears preceded his wife to the
wilderness, she following him after a year's separation, to join
in the trials, hardships and privations attendant upon the life
of pioneers in a new and sparsely-settled territory; so now,
after a year's separation, she has followed him through the
dark valley to "that better country," to enjoy with him an
eternity of peaceful rest. Mr. and Mrs. Sears celebrated their
golden wedding in 1883, a rare ceremony, which will long be
remembered by those who were privileged to be present. Mr.
Sears was a member of the Old Settlers' Society, and was
highly esteemed by all who knew him. His wife was a loving
and devoted mother, a kind friend, and a sincere Christian.
Her children, friends and neighbors, and fellow-members of
the Old Settlers' Society, will ever cherish her memory as fra-
grant of all that is pleasant and lovable. One brother survives
her, Mr. Alvin Ames of Chautauqua, N. Y., and two sons and
three daughters, with thirteen grand-children.

1293.

LUTHER RAWSON SEARS[7] [*Dan'l[6], Enos[5], Dan'l[4],
Paul[3], Paul[2], Rich.[1]*], b. Ashfield, Mass., Dec. 9, 1810; m.
Savoy, Mass., Aug. 26, 1846, *Sophia Hanks* of S.; 2d, *Abby
T. Kirker*. Children:

By *Sophia:*

2561. i. LEANDER SLAWSON, b. Caledonia, Wis., July 13,
1847; lives there.

2562.　ii.　NATHAN WESTERN, b. Cale., Mar. 21, 1849 ; d. Aug. 1, 1870.

2563.　iii.　ELECTA SOPHIA, b. Cale., Nov. 26, 1850 ; d. Feb. 4, 1853.

2564.　iv.　SARAH FRANCELIA, b. Cale., Aug. 27, 1852; m. *Wm. James ;* children, JAMES : [1.] Nathan W., b. Feb. 13, 1873. [2.] Edith A., b. Oct. 19, 1875.

2565.　v.　LUTHER KIRKER, b. Cale., Sep. 28, 1855 ; m. Mt. Pleasant, Dec. 22, 1880, *Minnie Longwell*, and lives in Racine.

2566.　vi.　ROSE SOPHIA, b. Cale., Sep. 9, 1869.

Mr. Sears removed to Caledonia, Racine co., Wis., in 1837. Some of the children were by second wife.

1296.

DANIEL SEARS[7] [*Dan'l[6], Enos[5], Dan'l[4], Paul[3], Paul[2], Rich.[1]*], b. Ashfield, Mass., Mar. 28, 1824 ; d. Charlemont, Mass., July 15, 1880, æ. 56 ; m. Hawley, Mass., Jan. 9, 1854, *Susan A. Mansfield*, she b. there, Sep. 9, 1831. Children :

2567.　i.　SARAH FLORENCE, b. Ash., Dec. 27, 1854; d. Sep. 1, 1870.

2568.　ii.　ESTELLA JANE, b. Ash., Mar. 18, 1857 ; and lives there.

2569.　iii.　LEWIS WILLARD, b. Ash., Aug. 8, 1859 ; m. Charlemont, Jan. 21, 1884, —— ——, and lives there.

2570.　iv.　ERWIN ERASTUS, b. Ash., Jan. 23, 1864; d. Aug. 18, 1870.

2571.　v.　AMELIA SUSANNA, b. Ash., Sep. 4, 1866.

2572.　vi.　ESEK OLIN, b. Charlemont, Aug. 22, 1869 ; d. Sep. 1, 1870.

Mr. Sears lived on the old homestead in Ashfield for some years after his parents' death, and then removed to Charlemont, where his widow still lives.

He was considered a very reliable and respectable man, as were all his brothers.

1298.

NATHAN SEARS[7] [*Wm.[6], Enos[5], Dan'l[4], Paul[3], Paul[2], Rich.[1]*], b. Ashfield, Mass., about 1813 ; m. *Abigail Bates.* Children :

2573.* i.　LEMUEL, b. Ash., Feb. 17, 1835.

2574.　ii.　ELIZA, b. Ash., Mar. 2, 1839 ; m. *Duane Lilly.*

49

1299.

WILLIAM SEARS[7] [*Wm.[6], Enos[5], Dan'l[4], Paul[3], Paul[2], Rich.[1]*], b. Ashfield, Mass., June 20, 1818; m. Albany, N. Y., Oct. 16, 1845, *Judith Adams*, she b. N. Y., Nov. 9, 1824; d. Grand Rapids, Mich., Apr. 28, 1875, æ. 51. Children:

2575.   i. Emma Virginia, b. Brooklyn, N. Y., Dec. 5, 1847; m. Grand Rapids, Aug. 16, 1870, *Charles D. Lyon*.

2576.   ii. William Edward, b. Bedford, Va., Oct. 6, 1850; d. Lynchburg, Va., Apr. 25, 1852.

2577.   iii. Stephen Adams, b. Academia, Tenn., Oct. 3, 1853; m. Nov. 10, 1880, *May Godfrey*, and lives in Grand Rapids.

Mr. Sears is of firm of Wm. Sears & Co., cracker manuf's, Grand Rapids, Mich.   They do a large business, and are called " The Cracker Kings."

1300.

SAMUEL SEARS[7] [*Wm.[6], Enos[5], Dan'l[4], Paul[5] Paul[2], Rich.[1]*], b. Ashfield, Mass., July 28, 1820; m. Winfield, N. Y., Aug. 13, 1850, *Amanda Dodge*, she b. there; d. Sep. 3, 1866, æ. 41; 2d, Grand Rapids, Mich., Mar. 1, 1870, *Mary E. Evans*.   Child:

By *Amanda :*

2578.   i. Edward Merchant, b. Grand Rapids, Oct. 16, 1860; d. Jan. 27, 1887.

Mr. Sears removed to Grand Rapids, Mich., after 1836, and engaged with his brother in manufacture of crackers; firm, Wm. Sears & Co.

1301.

STEPHEN SEARS[7] [*Wm.[6], Enos[5], Dan'l[4], Paul[3], Paul[2], Rich.[1]*], b. Ashfield, Mass., Sep. 11, 1822; m. Nov. 14, 1850, *Minerva Lilly*; she b. Conway, Mass., Mar. 29, 1824.   Children :

2579.   i. Frank E., b. Conway, Aug. 9, 1852; d. Aug. 16, 1867.

2580.   ii. Lucy T., b. Conway, Oct. 27, 1858; d. Aug. 28, 1867.

Mr. Sears was a farmer in Conway, Mass.

1302.

DANIEL SEARS[7] [*Jacob*[6], *Edm'd*[5], *Edm'd*[4], *Paul*[3], *Paul*[2], *Rich.*[1]], b. Dennis, Mass., Oct. 20, 1797; d. East Den., Feb. 18, 1840, æ. 42; m. Jan. 31, 1822, *Lucy Eldridge*, dau. of Dan'l E. of D. Children:

2581. i. JACOB, b. Den., May 5, 1823; m. Apr. 29, 1860, *Olive F. Kelly*, she b. Harwich, Mass., July 18, 1840, lives in E. Den.; he d. Aug. 8, 1871.

2582.* ii. SILAS, b. Den., Nov. 30, 1826.

2583. iii. SALLY E., b. Den., Feb. 2, 1830; m. *David S. Chapman*, and lives in E. Den.

1303.

NATHAN FOSTER SEARS[7] [*Jacob*[6], *Edm'd*[5], *Edm'd*[4], *Paul*[5] *Paul*[2], *Rich.*[1]], b. East Dennis, Mass., Sep. 26, 1800; d. there, Aug. 1, 1848; m. Jan. 30, 1823, *Susanna Howes*, dau. of Judah H., she b. Den., Feb. 2, 1803; d. Newark, N. J. Children:

2584.* i. JUDAH HOWES, b. Den., Dec. 20, 1823.

2585. ii. THANKFUL HOWES, b. Den., June 20, 1829; d. July 18.

2586.* iii. NATHAN NORRIS, b. Den., Jan. 5, 1831.

2587. iv. SUSANNA HOWES, b. Den., July 28, 1834; m. *Jesse S. Hall*, and lives in Peru, Fla.

" Child of Nathan Sears and wife died Sep. 24, 1831, æ. 4 years." (T. Rec.)

1309.

EBEN SEARS[7] [*Judah*[6], *Edm'd*[5], *Edm'd*[4], *Paul*[3], *Paul*[2], *Rich.*[1]], b. July 3, 1802; d. Charleston, S. C., Dec. 26, 1858; m. Sep. 12, 1826, by Rev. Mr. Cogswell to *Joanna Horton*, dau. of Zebina H. of Dennis, Mass. Children:

2588. i. MARY HORTON, b. Den., Apr. 20, 1827; d. July 25, 1889; m. Apr. 20, 1848, *Seth K. Crowell*, son of Isaiah and Abigail K. C. of Yarmouth, Mass.; children, CROW-ELL: [1.] Horace S., b. Boston, June 24, 1849; m. Oct. 14, 1875, Lizzie E. Corey, dau. of Thos. and Eliza J. C. of Marlboro, Mass., and had, i. Marguerite, b.

Marl., Oct. 10, 1877. ii. Fay, 'b. Marl., Sep. 7, 1881 ; residence, Newton, Mass. [2.] Frances Mary, b. Boston, July 29, 1850 ; m. Oct. 27, 1875, Chas. F. Richardson of Boston, son of Chas. and Sarah R., he b. Boston, Mar. 4, 1850; and has, i. Lowell, b. Boston, June 17, 1879. [3.] Charles Seth, b. Boston, July 15, 1857.

2589.* ii. EBEN THAXTER, b. Den., June 3, 1829.
2590. iii. JOANNA, b. Den., May 8, 1832 ; m. Oct. 5, 1855, *John T. Duncan* of Rutland, Vt.; no children.
2591. iv. SARAH, b. Den., Feb. 6, 1834; m. Oct. 21, 1858, *Ellis M. Swift* of Sandwich, Mass.; children, SWIFT : [1.] Charles Sears, b. Boston, Jan. 18, 1866. [2.] Eben Ellis, b. Boston, May 10, 1871.

Removed to Boston.

1310.

JUDAH SEARS[7] [*Judah[6], Edm'd[5], Edm'd[4], Paul[3], Paul[2], Rich.[1]*], b. Dennis, Mass., Nov. 17, 1804 ; d. Boston, Sep. 16, 1878, æ. 73 ; m. Den., Oct. 4, 1827, *Priscilla H. Howes*, dau. of Jabez H., she b. there, 1805.   Children :

2592.* i. JABEZ H., b. Den., Feb. 1, 1829.
2593. ii. JUDAH R., b. Den., Oct. 24, 1830; m. (pub. Den., Dec. 29, 1852,) *Cynthia H. Hall*, lived in Boston, and d. Nov. 15, 1853.
2594.* iii. ZENAS, b. Den., Nov. 23, 1833.
2595. iv. ELIZABETH A., b. Boston, Aug. 7, 1838 ; m. E. James.
2596. v. LORIE H., b. Boston, May 20, 1844 ; m. J. Snow.

Mr. Sears removed to Boston in 1835, and became a well-known builder and contractor, continuing in business till 1870, when he was compelled to retire on account of the distressing complaint, asthma, with which he had been afflicted for fifty years.

He erected some of the best buildings in Boston ; the Chickering Piano Factory, and Gilmore's Coliseum.

He had a peculiar fancy for building high steeples.

He will be remembered by his associates as a man of large and muscular build, and reckless of danger, of which many incidents could be related.

He was one of six to organize the Methodist Society in South Boston, of whom he was the last survivor.

Those who have heard the story of their early struggles, will know how much he loved, by what he gave.

He was a Rep. in Mass. Leg., 1859 and 1860, and died venerable in character and years.

1317.

Capt. DEAN SEARS[7] [*Paul⁶, Edm'd⁵, Edm'd⁴, Paul³, Paul², Rich.¹*], b. East Dennis, Mass., Feb. 22, 1802; d. Mar. 27, 1875, æ. 73; m. Aug. 5, 1827, *Phebe Howes*, who d. Mar. 22, 1828, æ. 20, gr.-st., Br.; 2d, Jan. 5, 1829, *Rosanna Sears*, No. 666, dau. of Reuben S. of Brewster, she b. May 15, 1805; d. E. Den., Jan. 2, 1885, æ. 79. Children :

By *Rosanna :*
2597. i. PHEBE H., b. Den., Aug. 13, 1830; d. Apr. 20, 1834, gr.-st., Br.
2598.* ii. DEAN SMITH, b. Den., Sep. 1, 1832.
2599. iii. CHARLES EDWARD, b. Den., Mar. 8, 1835; m. *Delia Crosby*, and rem. to Council Grove, Kan., where she d. Mar. 8, 1886.
2600. iv. LEWIS H., b. Den., Feb. 2, 1837; d. Sep. 5.
2601. v. RUTH ANN, b. Den., Sep. 6, 1838; m. *Sam'l H. Nye* of East Sandwich, Mass.
2602.* vi. PAUL FREEMAN, b. Den., Apr. 26, 1846.

Was a sea captain and lived in East Dennis.

1320.

Capt. PAUL SEARS[7] [*Paul⁶, Edm'd⁵, Edm'd⁴, Paul³, Paul², Rich.¹*], b. East Dennis, Mass., Dec. 3, 1812; m. West Brewster, Mass., Sep. 29, 1836, *Eunice Thacher Crosby*, she b. there, May 15, 1811. Children :

2603. i. BARNABAS, b. E. Den.; d.
2604.* ii. GEORGE THACHER, b. E. Den., Dec. 27, 1839.
2605. iii. HOWARD, b. Boston, Oct. 12, 1841; m. and lives in Dorchester, Mass.
2606. iv. EDWIN PAUL, b. Boston, June 12, 1843; m.
2607. v. ALBERT WALLACE, b. Boston, May 5, 1845; m.
2608. vi. LEWIS HOWES, b. Boston, July 11, 1851; m. Milton, Mass., Sep. 5, 1889, *Eliz'h A. Woods.*
2609. vii. HATTIE LAVINIA, b. Boston, Apr. 21, 1853; m. Dorchester, Mass., Jan. 21, 1880, *Robert B. Fairbairn.*

Capt. Sears resides in Dorchester, Mass.

1321.

BARNABAS HOWES SEARS[7] [*Paul[6]*, *Edm'd[5]*, *Edm'd[4]*, *Paul[3]*, *Paul[2]*, *Rich.[1]*], b. East Dennis, Mass., June 27, 1815; m. there, Dec. 17, 1840, *Elizabeth Allen Seabury*, she b. there, Dec. 19, 1820; d. June 23, 1878; 2d, Harwich, Mass., July 3, 1879, Mrs. *Lottie Burgess*, she b. Sandwich, Mass., Oct. 1, 1835.   Children:

By *Elizabeth*:

2610.   i. Mary Elizabeth, b. E. Den., Oct. 25, 1842; m. there, Aug. 2, 1866, *Ramon Chapman*, and lives in Brockton, Mass.

2611.   ii. Phebe Howes, b. E. Den., Aug. 17, 1846; m. there, Nov. 23, 1871, *Thomas Baxter Clark* of Spencer, Mass., and lives there.

2612.   iii. Sarah Seabury, b. E. Den., Apr. 14, 1848; m. there, Dec. 17, 1872, *Lot Williams Taylor* of Yarmouth, Mass., who d. Boston, Mar. 19, 1879; she lives in E. Den.

2613.   iv. Emma Josephine, b. E. Den., July 26, 1850; m. there, Nov. 11, 1875, *Josiah Manley Gurney*, and lives in Brockton, Mass.

2614.* v. Barnabas Allen, b. E. Den., Apr. 7, 1853.

2615.   vi. Betsie Emeline, b. E. Den., June 10, 1855; m. there, Apr. 16, 1878, *Ellis Franklin Ames* of Kingston, Mass., who d. Brockton, Jan. 17, 1881; she lives in E. Den.

Lives in East Dennis, Mass.

1324.

NATHAN SEARS[7] [*Edm'd[6]*, *Edm'd[5]*, *Edm'd[4]*, *Paul[3]*, *Paul[2]*, *Rich.[1]*], b. East Dennis, Mass., Aug. 30, 1821; m. there, July 4, 1844, *Sarah Clarke Howes*, dau. of Isaiah H., she b. there, Feb. 20, 1823; d. North Cambridge, Mass., Nov. 5, 1883, æ. 60; 2d, Boston, Sep. 24, 1885, *Julia F. Long* of E. Den.   Children:

2616.*   i. Henry Howes, b. E. Den., July 17, 1845.

2617.   ii. Mary, b. E. Den., Apr. 17, 1848; d. June 9, 1850.

2618.   iii. Myra Howes, b. E. Den., Feb. 26, 1851; m. there, Sep. 19, 1872, *Geo. Nelson Spear*, he b. there, Feb. 25, 1849; d. Feb. 23, 1885, Greely, Col.

2619.   iv. Chloe C., b. E. Den., Aug. 19, 1853 ; m. *Stillman F. Kelly*, son of Stillman and Olive Howes (Sears) K., and lived in No. Cambridge, Mass.

2620.   v. Nathan Crowell, b. E. Den., Jan. 17, 1856 ; m. there, Jan, 17, 1884, *Myra Eliza Howes*, dau. of Levi H., she b. E. Den., July 29, 1856 ; lives in North Bend, Nebraska.

2621.   vi. Seth, b. E. Den., Feb. 7, 1859 ; d. May 16.

2622.   vii. Seth, b. E. Den., Aug. 19, 1860 ; Principal of School, Quincy, Mass. ; m. Brewster, Aug. 17, 1887, Frances B. Winslow.

2623.   viii. Sadie Maud, b. E. Den., Jan. 21, 1869; d. June 30.

Mr. Sears is a prominent and wealthy citizen of East Dennis ; a grocer and farmer.

1326.

SETH SEARS[7] [*Edm'd[6], Edm'd[5], Edm'd[4], Paul[3], Paul[2], Rich.[1]*], b. East Dennis, Mass., Sep. 15, 1829 ; d. Roxbury, Mass., July 12, 1857 ; m. Feb. 9, 1853, *Thankful Homer*, dau. of Stephen H., she b. Den., June 27, 1830. ` Child :

2624.   i. Hannah C., b. Den., Feb. 10, 1855 ; m. *Zebina D. Kelly*, son of Stillman and Olive Howes (Sears) K.

1328.

Capt. JOSHUA SEARS[7] [*Ezra[6], Josh.[5], Edm'd[4], Paul[3], Paul[2], Rich.[1]*], b. East Dennis, Mass., June 10, 1817 ; d. winter of 1884–5 ; m. Harwich, Mass., June 11, 1840, *Minerva Handren* of Har., she b. Attleboro, Mass., Jan. 29, 1819. Child :

2625.   i. Louize Maria, née *Catharine Martin*, July 12, 1852 ; adopted Sep. 11, 1855.

Capt. Sears followed the sea from the age of 10 to 50 years, commencing as cook in a fisherman ; he commanded several ships sailing out of Boston, in the India and China trade, and to most all the ports east of Cape of Good Hope, and west of Cape Horn.
Resided in East Dennis.

1331.

DAVID S. SEARS[7] [*Ezra[6], Josh.[5], Edm'd[4], Paul[3], Paul[2], Rich.[1]*], b. East Dennis, Mass., Jan. 16, 1823 ; d. Dec. 13,

1882, æ. 60 ; m. Oct. 15, 1846, *Harriet A. Mathews* of So. Yarmouth, Mass. Children :

2626.* i. Ezra Freeman, b. Den., Apr., 1852.
2627. ii. David Warren, b. Den., Feb. 16, 1854 ; m. there, Dec. 23, 1884, *Elsie N. Smulley.*
2628. iii. Selek M., b. Den., Oct. 18, 1856 ; d. Aug. 22, 1877.
2629. iv. Edward B., b. Den., Aug. 18, 1868 ; d. Sep. 24, 1869.

Was a seaman.

1333.

⚹ HEMAN G. SEARS⁷ [*Ezra⁶, Josh.⁵, Edm'd⁴, Paul³, Paul², Rich.¹*], b. East Dennis, Mass., Sep. 1, 1829 ; d. Jan. 10, 1878, æ. 49 ; m. there, Dec. 23, 1856, *Hannah Howes* of Den. Child :

2630. i. *Son,* b. Den., Apr. 28, 1872 ; d. Apr. 29.

Was a blacksmith.

1338.

GEORGE OLIVER SEARS⁷ [*Geo.⁶, Josh.⁵, Edm'd⁴, Paul³, Paul², Rich.¹*], b. Boston, Mass., Jan. 31, 1835 ; m. Bentonsport, Iowa, Jan. 10, 1859, *Sarah Gardner Richards,* she b. Enfield, Mass., Nov. 14, 1836. Children :

2631. i. George Gray, b. Boston, Oct. 22, 1859 ; grad. Amherst Coll., and Harvard Med. School ; lives in Boston.
2632. ii. Mary Cornelius, b. Boston, Dec. 15, 1861.
2633. iii. William Richards, b. Boston, Oct. 8, 1869.

Mr. Sears is of firm Manning & Sears, cotton merchants, Boston.

1350.

ISAIAH C. SEARS⁷ [*Thos.⁶, Elkanah⁵, Edm'd⁴, Paul³, Paul², Rich.¹*], b. East Dennis, Mass., Dec. 10, 1833 ; m. there, Jan. 15, 1856, *Myra S. Long,* dau. of Jere. L., she b. Brewster, Mass., Sep. 16, 1837. Children :

2634. i. George, b. Den., Dec. 8, 1856 ; was drowned at Mananzary, Madagascar, Nov. 25, 1885, æ. 29. He was in the employ of George Ropes & Co., merchants of Boston, as their agent; had been with them four years, and had their full confidence. He was an estimable young man, an affectionate son, and a great loss to his parents, who anticipated for him a brilliant future.

2635. ii. NELLIE F., b. Den., Aug. 23, 1858; m. there, Nov. 14, 1884, *Osborn F. Snow*, he b. Brewster, Apr. 22, 1859.

2636. iii. ARTHUR C., b. Den., Oct. 13, 1871.

1352.

WILLIAM G. SEARS⁷ [*Wm.⁶, Elkanah⁵, Edm'd⁴, Paul³, Paul², Rich.¹*], b. Dennis, Mass., Oct. 4, 1838; m. Yarmouth, Mass., Nov. 28, 1872, *Mary H. Thacher*, she b. there, July 12, 1839. Children:

2637. i. SAMUEL THACHER, b. Den., Nov. 26, 1874.
2638. ii. EDMUND HAMBLEN, b. Den., Mar. 19, 1881.

Is a mechanic and lives in East Dennis.

1353.

ISAAC B. SEARS⁷ [*Wm.⁶, Elkanah⁵, Edm'd⁴, Paul³, Paul², Rich.¹*], b. Dennis, Mass., Mar. 25, 1841; m. Harwich, Mass., Feb. 22, 1877, *Caroline P. Snow* of Har., dau. of Isaiah and Rhoda S. of Har., she b. Apr., 1845. Child:

2639. i. RUTH B., b. Har., Sep. 12, 1878.

Lives in E. Dennis.

1354.

ELKANAH H. SEARS⁷ [*Wm.⁶, Elkanah⁵, Edm'd⁴, Paul³, Paul², Rich.¹*], b. Dennis, Mass., Apr. 25, 1349; m. Chatham, Mass., Dec. 22, 1881, *Lelia T. Eldridge* she b. there, Aug. 7, 1850. Children:

2640. i. JAMES W., b. E. Den., Oct. 21, 1882.
2641. ii. LEWIS E., b. E. Den., Feb. 21, 1885.
2642. iii. *Dau.*, b. E. Den., May 13, 1887.

Is a mechanic in East Dennis.

50

1355.

FRANKLIN SEARS[7] [*Elisha*[6], *Elisha*[5], *Elisha*[4], *John*[3], *Paul*[2], *Rich.*[1]], b. Dennis, Mass., Sep. 4, 1826; m. Sandwich, Mass., 1849, *Susan Ann Chadwick.* Children:

2643.* i. Charles Franklin, b. Sand., 1850.
2644.* ii. Edgar Herbert, b. Sand., 1855.
2645. iii. Augustine Chadwick, b. Bowling Green, Ohio, 1857; is a farmer.
2646. iv. Nettie Wing, b. Bow. Gr., 1860.
2647. v. Oscar Ellsworth, b. Bow. Gr., 1863 ; is a farmer.

At the age of sixteen Mr. Sears removed to Sandwich, and learned the trade of wagon and carriage making of Isaac Keith, and worked for him till 1849. In the fall of that year he sailed as passenger in bark " Orion," Capt. Bunker, from Boston to San Francisco, making the passage in 180 days ; helped build the first wharf in San F.; spent one winter on the coast of Peru, another season on Columbia river and in the wilds of Oregon, but did not accumulate much gold, and returned home by way of Panama in 1853.

In 1857, he removed, with his brother and sister, to Wood county, Ohio, and purchased a farm.

In 1864, he enlisted in Ohio National Guard, 100 days' men, but did not go to the war.

He joined the Methodist Episcopal Church in same year, was appointed Trustee and Treasurer of church and parsonage, and has held other minor offices.

About 1882, he withdrew from the church, and now culti-vates an eighty-acre farm in Bowling Green, Ohio.

1356.

ELISHA HARVEY SEARS[7] [*Elisha*[6], *Elisha*[5], *Elisha*[4], *John*[3], *Paul*[2], *Rich.*[1]], b. Dennis, Mass., Jan. 17, 1829; m. Sandwich, Mass., 1854, *Mary Godfrey.* Child:

2648. i. Elisha Harvey.

Resides in Fairhaven, Mass.

1373.

ELIJAH BAILEY SEARS[7] [*Heman*[6], *John*[5], *John*[4], *John*[3], *Paul*[2], *Rich.*[1]], b. East Dennis, Mass., June 7, 1826; m. East

Sandwich, Mass., Nov. 30, 1848, *Harriet N. Fish*, she b. there, Mar. 26, 1828. Children :

2649. i. ARRIETTA F., b. E. Den., Apr. 15, 1850.
2650. ii. HENRY S. F., b. E. Den., Feb. 2, 1852 ; m. West Den., Jan. 6, 1881, *Miranda E. Thacher*, she b. there, Oct. 20, 1854 ; lives in Clinton, Mass.
2651. iii. EDMUND B., b. E. Den., May 2, 1854 ; d. Sep. 4.
2652. iv. FANNIE H., b. E. Den., Dec. 20, 1855 ; d. Nov. 4, 1875.
2653. v. FREDERIC H., b. E. Den., July 18, 1863 ; m. Clinton, Mass., Dec. 17, 1884, —— —— ; lives in West Fitchburg, and has a son.

Is a carpenter in East Dennis.

1374.

Capt. ORIN SEARS[7] [*Heman[6], John[5], John[4], John[3], Paul[2], Rich.[1]*], b. East Dennis, Mass., Aug. 7, 1828 ; m. East Sandwich, Mass., Feb. 6, 1851, *Lydia N. Fish*, she b. there, Aug. 31, 1831 ; d. East Den., June 26, 1880. Children :

2654. i. IDA MAY, b. E. Den., Feb. 18, 1854 ; is a teacher.
2655. ii. ALICE WOODBURY, b. E. Den., Jan. 3, 1856.
2656. iii. ELIZA RHODA, b. E. Den., Jan. 5, 1858 ; d. Jan. 19.
2657. iv. ORIN WILLIS, b. E. Den., Feb. 6, 1860 ; m. Newton Lower Falls, Mass., Dec. 27, 1883, *Anna Louisa Hunt*, she b. Brockton, Mass., Dec. 6, 1858 ; he is a teacher and lives in Milton, Mass.

Lives in East Dennis.

1379.

BARZILLAI SEARS[7] [*Enos[6], John[5], John[4], John[3], Paul[2], Rich.[1]*], b. Dennis, Mass., Oct. 21, 1809 ; m. —— ——. Children :

2658. i. RUSSELL, b. 1842 ; of Rowe, Mass., enlisted Nov. 20, 1861, in Co. C, 31st Mass. Vols.; transferred to Signal Corps, June 22, 1862.
2659. ii. WILSON.
2660. iii. EZRA.
2661. iv. JOSHUA.
2662. v. MILTON R.

1381.

LYMAN SEARS[7] [*Enos[6], John[5], John[4], John[3], Paul[2], Rich.[1]*], b. (perh. Colerain, Mass.); m. —— ——. Children:
2663. i. GEORGE.
2664. ii. HENRY.

1382.

ENOS SEARS[7] [*Enos[6], John[5], John[4], John[3], Paul[2], Rich.[1]*], b. (perh. Colerain, Mass.); m. —— ——. Child:
2665. i. JOHN.

1383.

GILBERT SEARS[7] [*Moody[6], John[5], John[4], John[3], Paul[2], Rich.[1]*], b. Dennis, Mass., Oct. 13, 1813; d. Dec. 23, 1880; m. (pub. Den., Dec. 15, 1849,) *Mary Ann Richardson* of Den. Children :
2666.   i. SARAH J., b. Oct. 12, 1850; m. Brewster, Mass., Nov. 7, 1870, *Charles L. Williams*, son of John and Betsy W. of Den., he b. 1842.
2667. ii. ELINORE, b. Jan. 18, 1862.
2668. iii. FLORENCE K., b. Aug. 14, 1869.

1384.

ENOS SEARS[7] [*Moody[6], John[5], John[4], John[3], Paul[2], Rich.[1]*], b. Dennis, Mass., Nov. 5, 1816; d. East Den., Apr. 4, 1865; m. Apr. 26, 1836, *Thankful Hall*, dau. of Edmund H., she b. Oct. 24, 1815; d. Aug. 2, 1887. Children:
2669.   i. ASA H., b. Brewster, Mass., Oct. 12, 1836; d. Aug. 28, 1844.
2670.   ii. NANCY C., b. Br., July 15, 1838.
2671.* iii. EDMUND H., b. Den., Jan. 28, 1841.
2672. iv. ASA H., b. Den., Nov. 22, 1847; d. Sep. 2, 1849.
2673.   v. EMMA H., b. Den., Jan. 25, 1851.
2674. vi. ELLA, b. Den., Apr. 26, 1856.

1385.

JOHN SEARS[7] [*Moody[6], John[5], John[4], John[3], Paul[2], Rich.[1]*], b. Dennis, Mass., Sep. 19, 1818; m. *Mary* —— ;

[John Sears, *Jr.*, m. Sabra Sears, Nov. 20, 1847.] Children:

2675. i. SARAH E., b. Den., Apr. 10, 1842.
2676. ii. MARY J., b. Den., Nov. 14, 1843; d. Dec. 7, 1845.
2677. iii. MARY D., b. Den., Aug. 11, 1850; d. Mar. 11, 1872.

1391.

Hon. PHILIP HOWES SEARS[7] [*John*[6], *Edw'd*,[5] *Will'd*[4], *John*[3], *Paul*[2], *Rich.*[1]], b. Dennis, Mass., Dec. 30, 1822; [1823] m. Apr. 23, 1861, *Sarah P. Lyman*, dau. of Geo. W. and Anne (Pratt) L., she b. Feb. 4, 1835. Children:

2678. i. ANNIE LYMAN, b. Mar. 10, 1862.
2679. ii. MARY PRATT, b. Aug. 21, 1864.
2680. iii. RICHARD, b. July 19, 1867.
2681. iv. FRANCIS PHILIP, b. Oct. 31, 1869.
2682. v. EVELYN GEORGIANNA, b. Mar. 9, 1875.

Mr. Sears graduated Harvard College 1844, and is a lawyer in Boston; was in Massachusetts Senate 1860–61.

1397.

ELIJAH BAILEY SEARS[7] [*Reuben*[6], *Reuben*[5], *Will'd*[4], *John*[3], *Paul*[2], *Rich.*[1]], b. Brewster, Mass., Nov. 9, 1817; d. North Harwich, Mass., Oct. 3, 1873; m. Har., Nov. 25, 1841, *Almira Crowell*, dau. of Jacob and Hannah C., who d. Br., Apr. 9, 1860; 2d, *Katy E.* ——. Children:

By *Almira:*
2683. i. LYDIA B., b. Br., Mar. 12, 1848.
2684. ii. ALMIRA C., b. Br., May 13, 1852; m. E. Dennis, Dec. 25, 1872, *Samuel S. Ryder*.
2685. iii. HENRY B., b. Br., May 2, 1854.
2686. iv. MELISSA, b. Br., July 19, 1856.
2687. v. AURILLA, b. Br., 1857; d. Sep. 29, 1858.
2688. vi. IDELLA W., b. Br., Apr. 14, 1860; d. July 30, 1877.
By *Katy:*
2689. vii. LOSETTA, b. Br., Dec. 4, 1862.
2690. viii. LEONORA C., b. Br., Dec. 27, 1863; d. Aug. 10, 1864.
2691. ix. FLORA A., b. ——; d. Malden, Mass., Aug. 2, 1887.

Mr. Sears removed to Harwich when a young man, and kept a store there, returning a few years after to Brewster, and commenced trading in the west part of the town.

After the opening of the railroad to North Harwich, he moved to that place, where he engaged in trade up to the time of his last sickness, and was appointed Postmaster in place of Sheldon Crowell, resigned.

Mr. Sears was in feeble health for many years, but the immediate cause of his death was from a fall in alighting from his carriage.

In religions matters Mr. Sears took a deep interest, and in all the moral reforms of his time, and in the advocacy of the principles of prohibition he was firm and consistent.

1399.

REUBEN SEARS[7] [*Reuben[6], Reuben[5], Will'd[4], John[3], Paul[2], Rich.[1]*], b. Brewster, Mass., Aug. 8, 1822; m. there, Mar. 10, 1846, by Rev. Elijah Bailey to *Susanna W. Sears*, No. 3166, dau. of David and Betsy S., she b. June 9, 1828. Children :

2692.*　i. DAVID B., b. Br., Feb. 14, 1847.
2693.　　ii. BETSY W., b. Br., Oct. 27, 1849.
2694.　　iii. SUSAN O., b. Br., Feb. 1, 1852.
2695.　　iv. REUBEN W., b. Br., Sep. 28, 1854.
2696.　　v. WILLIAM W., b. Br., Feb. 26, 1857.
2696. *a.*　vi. MINNIE H., b. ——, June 29, 1860.
2696. *a.* vii. MYRA E., b. ——, Mar. 24, 1863.
2696. *a.* viii. FRANK E., b. ——, Mar. 15, 1869.

After his marriage Mr. Sears lived in the ancient Judah Sears' house at West Brewster, removing later to Chelsea and Malden, Mass.

1403.

HEMAN SEARS[7] [*Reuben[6], Reuben[5], Will'd[4], John[3], Paul[2], Rich.[1]*], b. Brewster, Mass., Feb. 25, 1836; m. Yarmouth, Mass., Jan. 15, 1862, by Rev. J. B. Clark to *Olive Taylor*, dau. of Lot and Eunice T. of Yar., she b. there, Dec. 2, 1837. Children :

2697. i. HEMAN EDDIE, b. E. Dennis, Mass., Dec. 7, 1863.
2698. ii. WILLIAM, b. E. Den., July 27, 1866.

Lives in East Dennis.

1406.

ALDEN SEARS[7] [*Philander*[6], *Reuben*[5], *Will'd*[4], *John*[3], *Paul*[2], *Rich.*[1]], b. ——; m. —— ; 2d, *Hannah* ——. Children:

By *Hannah :*

2699.   i. JOHN.
2700.   ii. FREDERIC.
2701.   iii. WALTER.

1407.

SYLVANUS SEARS[7] [*Philander*[6], *Reuben*[5], *Will'd*[4], *John*[3], *Paul*[2], *Rich.*[1]], b. Oct. 24, 1824; m. Mar. 14, 1850, *Lucy S. Hedge*, dau. of John and Nabby (Sears) H., she b. Jan. 11, 1828.   Children:

2702.   i. ELLA B., b. East Dennis, Mass., Jan. 31, 1851; m. Oct. 16, 1875, *Irving A. Dana*, he b. Rutland, Mass., Aug. 18, 1850; is a milk dealer in Worcester, Mass.; children, DANA: [1.] Luella S., b. July 2, 1876. [2.] Milton J., b. May 18, 1879.
2703.   ii. ABBIE L., b. Worcester, Mass., Apr. 11, 1859; m. Sep. 21, 1880, *John W. Clark*, he b. Oldham, Eng., July 8, 1858; child, CLARK: [1.] George S., b. Feb. 15, 1882.
2704.* iii. MILTON H., b. Wor., June 1, 1854.

Is a farmer in Worcester, Mass.

1415.

CHARLES SEARS[7] [*Thos.*[6], *Reuben*[5], *Will'd*[4], *John*[3], *Paul*[2], *Rich.*[1]], b. Brewster, Mass., Oct. 16, 1832; m. there, Aug. 19, 1854, by Rev. Carlos Marston, to *Susan Hall*, dau. of Edmund and Susan H., she b. June 3, 1831.   Children:

2705.   i. CHARLES H., b. Br., Oct. 8, 1856.
2706.   ii. FRANK L., b. Br., Feb. 8, 1860.
2707.   iii. SUSAN A., b. Br., July 24, 1866.

1416.

DAVID H. SEARS[7] [*Thos.*[6], *Reuben*, *Will'd*[4], *John*[3], *Paul*[2], *Rich.*[1]], b. Brewster, Mass., Mar. 16, 1836; m. there, Jan. 1, 1862, by Rev. Benj. Eastwood, to *Laura A. Crosby*, dau. of Isaiah and Polly C. of Br., she b. Jan. 27, 1839. Children :

2708.   i. MARY E., b. W. Br., Mar. 8, 1863.
2709.   ii. DAVID H., b. W. Br., Oct. 25, 1865.
2710.   iii. THOMAS W., b. E. Dennis, Nov. 23, 1869.
2711.   iv. ISAIAH C., b. E. Den., Mar. 8, 1873.

1418.

Sergt. NATHAN HENRY SEARS[7] [*Orin[6], Reuben[5], Will'd[4], John[3], Paul[2], Rich.[1]*], b. Brewster, Mass., Nov. 28, 1830; m. Millbury, Mass., Sep. 9, 1856, *Anna Elizabeth Moore*, she b. there, Sep. 3, 1836; d. æ. 23; 2d, Petersham, Mass., May 28, 1868, *Luthera B. Wright*, she b. Deerfield, Mass., Jan. 12, 1839. Children :
By *Luthera :*
2712.   i. NATHAN WALTER, b. Mill., Dec. 6, 1870; d. 1887.
2713.   ii. ANNA MOORE, b. Mill., July 27, 1875.

Mr. Sears was educated in Derby Academy, Hingham, Mass.; served 15 months as Quartermaster Sergeant in 10th unattached Co. Mass. Vols. during Civil war, and is now a druggist in Millbury, Mass.

1419.

LORENZO JOHNSON SEARS[7] [*Orin[6], Reuben[5], Will'd[4], John[3], Paul[2], Rich.[1]*], b. Brewster, Mass., Feb. 27, 1832; m. New Bedford, Mass., Apr. 5, 1855, *Ellen Barrows Peckham*, she b. Dartmouth, Mass., July 2, 1832. Children :
2714.   i. EVA VAN EGMOND, b. New Bed., Nov. 22, 1855.
2715.   ii. NELLY LOUISA, b. New Bed., June 16, 1869; grad. Derby Academy, Hingham, 1885.

Mr. Sears was educated in the public schools in Brewster, and Derby Academy, Hingham; went to New Bedford and learned the tanner's trade; served 15 years as Assistant City Marshal; moved back to Hingham, Mass., and now keeps a provision store there.

1422.

ORRIN BREWSTER SEARS[7] [*Orin[6], Reuben[5], Will'd[4], John[3], Paul[2], Rich.[1]*], b. Brewster, Mass., Mar. 8, 1845; m. Hingham, Mass., Mar. 16, 1869, *Mary A. Libby*, she b. Belfast, Maine, Nov. 29, 1841; d. s. p., 1871; 2d, New Bedford, Mass., Nov. 27, 1872, *Ella A. Case*, she b. Mar. 23, 1853. Children :

By *Ella :*

2716. i. MARY AUGUSTA, b. Acushnet, Mass., Sep. 10, 1873.
2717. ii. ARTHUR ALDEN, b. Carver, Mass., May 24, 1875.
2718. iii. HIAL BARNEY, b. Car., Mar. 11, 1879.
2718. *a.* iv. ELLA, b. July 23, 1886.
2718. *a.* v. OLIVER, b. Apr. 13, 1888.
2718. *a.* vi. ORIN, b. Apr. 13, 1888, *gemini.*

Is a machinist.

1425.

CHARLES SEARS[7] [*Chas.*[6], *Eben'r*[5], *Will'd*[4], *John*[3], *Paul*[2], *Rich.*[1]], b. Yarmouth, Mass., Mar. 21, 1819; d. there, Jan. 22, 1884; m. Barnstable, Mass., Oct. 28, 1841, *Zerviah Hamblen*, she b. there, Apr. 18, 1819. Children :

2719. i. ELLEN, b. Yar., Jan. 31, 1843; m. Providence, R. I., Sep. 11, 1863, *Geo. Hallet* of P., and lives in Yarmouthport.
2720. ii. JOSHUA, b. Yar., Oct. 29, 1846; m. Boston, Sep. 30, 1882, *Maude McWilliams*, is a decorator, and lives in Boston.
2721. iii. CHARLES, b. Yar., Oct. 26, 1852; m. Provincetown, Mass., Mar. 11, 1879, *Louise B. Cook* of P., and d. Oct. 30, 1879.
2722. iv. KATE, b. Yar., Aug. 27, 1858.
2723. v. FANNY, b. Yar., Feb. 13, 1861. (1851, T. C.)

Kept "Sears Hotel," Yarmouthport, Mass.

1433.

JOSHUA MONTGOMERY SEARS[7] [*Josh.*[6], *Eben'r*[5], *Will'd*[4], *John*[3], *Paul*[2], *Rich.*[1]], b. Yarmouth, Mass., Dec. 25, 1854; m. Cambridge, Mass., Sep. 18, 1877, *Sarah Carlisle Choate*, dau. of Chas. Francis C., Prest. Old Colony R. R. Child :

2724. i. JOSHUA MONTGOMERY, b. Boston, Dec., 1879.

Mr. Sears graduated Yale Coll., 1877, and resides in Boston, of which city he is the largest tax payer.

51

1440.

WILLARD THOMAS SEARS[7] [*Will'd[6], Eben'r[5], Will'd[4], John[3], Paul[2], Rich.[1]*], b. New Bedford, Mass., Nov. 5, 1837; m. Jan. 1, 1862, *Marian Motte*, dau. of Mellish Irving and Marianne M. of Boston, she b. Aug. 25, 1841. Children:

2725. i. RUTH, b. Oct. 12, 1862; m. Boston, Jan. 8, 1889, *Edw'd Read* of Cambridge, Mass.

2726. ii. MABEL, b. Nov. 23, 1868.

2726. *a*. iii. EDITH HOWLAND, b. Feb. 20, 1873.

2726. *a*. iv. MIRIAM VAN EGMOND, b. July 1, 1874.

Mr. Sears is an architect in Boston, Mass.

1441.

ALEXANDER POMROY SEARS[7] [*Thos.[6], Eben'r[5], Will'd[4], John[3], Paul[2], Rich.[1]*], b. Boston, Mass., Feb. 12, 1836; m. Oct. 20, 1868, *Elizabeth Prescott Jones*. Children:

2727. i. ELLEN WARLAND, b. Boston, Apr. 24, 1870.

2728. ii. MARGARET WARLAND, b. Boston, Apr. 18, 1874.

2729. iii. THOMAS WARREN, b. Boston, Dec. 15, 1880.

Mr. Sears in company with his brother Cyrus, succeeded their uncle Joshua in the wholesale grocery business at the old store on Long Wharf, Boston, under firm name of Sears & Co.

1443.

Lt. CYRUS ALGER SEARS[7] [*Thos.[6], Eben'r[5], Will'd[4], John[3], Paul[2], Rich.[1]*], b. Boston, Mass., June 20, 1841; d. Southampton, L. I., Aug. 4, 1886; m. Feb. 1, 1870, *Lizzie Jean Nelson*. Child:

2730. i. ALINE, b. New York city, Aug. 9, 1875.

Mr. Sears was for some time in the wholesale grocery business in Boston, with his brother, under firm name of Sears & Co., but removed to New York city and engaged in the real estate business.

He served from Sep. 26, 1862, to July 7, 1863, as 2d Lieutenant 45th Regiment, Massachusetts Volunteer Infantry, with much credit, the officers and soldiers associated with him, becoming much attached to him.

He died of apoplexy at his summer residence in Southampton, L. I.

1447.

EBEN SEARS[7] [*Eben*[6], *Will'd*[5], *Will'd*[4], *John*[3], *Paul*[2], *Rich.*[1]], b. Boston, Mass., July 15, 1829 ; m. there, Apr. 15, 1851, *Jane Rebecca Balch*, dau. of Eben Hammett and Sarah Maria (Woods) B., she b. Providence, R. I., Nov. 26, 1832. Children :

2731.   . *Child*, b. and d. Wellington Hill, (now Belmont,) Mass.

2732.* ii. EBEN WARDEN, b. Well. Hill, Aug. 1, 1854.

2733. iii. FLORENCE, b. Watertown, Mass., Dec. 20, 1856 ; m. Boston, Dec. 6, 1877, *Henry Tolman, Jr.* of B.; children, TOLMAN: [1.] Henry, b. Oct. 15, 1879. [2.] Richard Sears, b. Sep. 30, 1881.

2734. iv. MARY CREASE, b. Wat., Aug. 20, 1859.

2735. v. EMMA ELIZABETH, b. Wat., Jan. 12, 1861.

Resides in Boston, formerly of firms Hill, Sears & Co., and E. & R. W. Sears.

1455.

OBED SEARS[7] [*Arnold*[6], *Nath'l*[5], *Nath'l*[4], *John*[3], *Paul*[2], *Rich.*[1]], b. —— ; m. *Emeline Cogswell*, (perh. of Duxbury, Mass.) Children :

2736.* i. JAMES, b. June 17, 1831.

2737. ii. WILLIAM HENRY, d. æ. ab't 10.

2738. iii. ISABELLA WARNER; m. *George Richards* of Arnold's Mill, R. I.; child, RICHARDS: [1.] Mary Emeline, b. July 18, 1875.

2739.* iv. GEORGE.

2740. v. JOSEPHINE, m. *Frank Holbrook ;* children, HOL-BROOK: [1.] Everett, d. young. [2.] Dau., d. infant. [3.] Frederic. [4.] Bertha. [5.] Louis. [6.] Walter King. [7.] Son.

2741. vi. EUGENE.

2742. vii. FREDERIC, d. æ. 1.

Lived in Pawtucket, R. I.

1458.

ARNOLD HOWES SEARS[7] [*Arnold*[6], *Nath'l*[5], *Nath'l*[4], *John*[3], *Paul*[2], *Rich.*[1]], b. —— ; m. —— ——. Children :

2743. i. ALBERT A., b. 1839 ; of Wrentham, Mass. ; served in Co. I, 45th Regt. Mass. Vol. Inf'y, from Oct. 7, 1862, to July 7, 1863, 9 mos'. men.

2744. ii. THEOPHILUS M., b. 1842; of Wrentham; was Corporal in Co. I, 18th Regt. Mass. Vol. Inf'y, Aug. 24, 1861, to Sep. 2, 1864, 3 years' men.

1466.

ALVAN SEARS[7] [*Nath'l[6], Nath'l[5], Nath'l[4], John[3], Paul[2], Rich.[1]*], b. Dennis, Mass., Jan. 10, 1822; m. Harwich, Mass., Oct. 6, 1842, *Eliza Nickerson* of Har.   Child:
2745.* i. ALVAN W., b. Brewster, Mass., Oct. 7, 1848.

1468.

NATHANIEL SEARS[7] [*Nath'l[6], Nath'l[5], Nath'l[4], John[3], Paul[2], Rich.[1]*], b. Brewster, Mass., May 1, 1836; m. there, Dec. 16, 1852, by Rev. Joshua Davis, to *Lydia Ellis*, dau. of Philip and Dorcas E., she b. Har., 1835.   Children:
2746.   i. LYDIA F., b. Br., Sep. 24, 1854; d. 1856.
2747.   ii. LYDIA A., b. Br., 1856; m. there, June 10, 1874, *Judah F. Perry*, son of Judah and Hannah P. of Br., he b. 1856.
2748.   iii. NATHANIEL F., b. Br., 1859; d. Jan. 2, 1861.
2749.   iv. NATHANIEL C., b. Br., Oct. 26, 1861.
2750.   v. CECILLA, (Celia Ella) b. Br., Sep. 19, 1864.
2751.   vi. ISAAC D., b. Br., 1867.
2752.   vii. EVELINE, b. Br., July 4, 1872; d. 1874.
2753.   viii. EVERETT, b. Br., Sep. 18, 1874.
2754.   ix. BENJAMIN W., b. Br., Aug. 17, 1876.
2755.   x. LEONARD, b. Br., Mar. 17, 1878.

1469.

HENRY CLARK SEARS[7] [*Nath'l[6], Nath'l[5], Nath'l[4], John[3], Paul[2], Rich.[1]*], b. Brewster, Mass., Mar. 16, 1845; m. there, July 6, 1863, by Anthony Smalley, J. P., to *Ellen Phillips*, dau. of Nath'l and Lydia P. of Dennis, she b. 1847. Children:
2756.   i. ERNEST L., b. Br., Nov. 18, 1864.
2757.   ii. DAVID H., b. Br., Oct. 25, 1865.
2758.   iii. ELLA N., b. Br., Sep. 15, 1866.
2759.   iv. HENRY B., b. Br., Dec. 26, 1868.
2760.   v. EVERETT W., b. Den., Sep. 29, 1873.
2761.   vi. WILLIAM H., b. Den., Mar. 18, 1877.

1475.

BENJAMIN SEARS[7] [*Lot*[6], *Nath'l*[5], *Nath'l*[4], *John*[3], *Paul*[2], *Rich.*[1]], b. Dennis, Mass., Nov. 20, 1828 ; m. Harwich, Mass., Jan. 21, 1851, *Phebe W. Kendrick,* dau. of Simeon and Pauline (Snow) K., she b. there ; d. June 4, 1857, æ. 27 ; (?2d, *Sarah T——,* who d. Den., Oct. 22, 1879, æ. 46.) Children :
2762.* i. SIMEON K., b. Har., Sep. 7, 1851.
2763. ii. LYDIA N., b. Har., Aug. 10, 1854.

1480.

FREEMAN F. SEARS[7] [*Freeman*[6], *Nath'l*[5], *Nath'l*[4], *John*[3], *Paul*[2], *Rich.*[1]], b. Dennis, Mass., June 28, 1828 ; m. Brewster, Mass., Dec. 8, 1848, *Elizabeth J. Snow,* dau. of Moses and Hannah S., she b. there, Oct. 29, 1829. Children :
2764. i. WARREN F., b. Br., Aug. 25, 1850 ; m. Den., Nov. 18, 1871, *Lizzie B. Chase,* and lives in East Den.
2765.* ii. CLARENCE S., b. Den., Nov. 26, 1851.
2766. iii. WALLACE FOSTER, b. Den., Aug. 12, 1858 ; (Sep. 19, T. Cl'k) m. Brewster, Nov. 13, 1888, *Lydia Churchill Riley* of Den.
2767.* iv. BENJAMIN O., b. Den., Apr. 7, 1860.
2768.* v. HOWARD D., b. Den., Dec. 26, 1861.
2769. vi. EDGAR J., b. Den., Sep. 29, 1863 ; m. Harwich, Apr. 4, 1886, by Rev. Davis Lothrop, to *Anna M. Austin* of Br.
2770. vii. GEORGE C., b. Den., May 25, 1866 ; m. Harwich, Jan. 27, 1889, *Grace Silver* of Br.
2771. viii. FRANKLIN T., b. Den., May 17, 1870.

Lives in East Dennis.

1493.

DAVID SEARS[7] [*David*[6], *David*[5], *Dan'l*[4], *Dan'l*[3], *Paul*[2], *Rich.*[1]], b. 1822 ; d. Mar. 14, 1874 ; m. New York city, May 29, 1849, *Emily Esther Hoyt,* dau. of Gould H., who d. New York, Mar. 27, 1888. Children :
2772. i. EMILY ESTHER.
2773. ii. DAVID, grad. Har., 1874 ; resides in Boston, and at Brigadier's Island, near Bangor, Me.
2774. iii. MIRIAM MASON, b. Nov. 2, 1857 ; d.
2775. iv. HENRY FRANCIS, b. Jan. 8, 1862 ; is a physician.

1494.

FREDERIC RICHARD SEARS[7] [*David[6], David[5], Dan'l[4], Dan'l[3], Paul[2], Rich.[1]*], b. 1824; m. *Marian Shaw,* dau. of Robt. G. and Elizabeth Willard (Parkman) S., she b. Dec. 21, 1828; d. Mar. 9, 1855; 2d, *Albertina H. Shelton,* dau. of Philo Strong and Georgianna Albertina (Homer) S., who derives from Bethia (Sears) Crowell, dau. of Capt. Paul Sears of Yar.   Children:

By *Marian* :
2776.   i. Marian Shaw, m. Nov. 14, 1878, *Charles Taylor Lovering.*
2777.   ii. Frederic Richard, m. June 18, 1879, *Eleonora R. Coolidge,* dau. of T. Jefferson C. of Boston.

By *Albertina* :
2778.   iii. Albertina S., m. Feb. 3, 1881, *Alfred Stackpole Dabney,* grad. Har. Coll., 1871.
2779.   iv. Richard Dudley.
2780.   v. Philip Shelton, }
2781.   vi. Herbert Mason, } *gemini.*

Resides in Boston and Nahant, Mass.

1497.

KNYVET WINTHROP SEARS[7] [*David[6], David[5], Dan'l[4], Dan'l[3], Paul[2], Rich.[1]*], b. 1832; m. June 10, 1858, *Mary C. Peabody,* dau. of Geo. P. of Salem, Mass.   Children:
2782.   i. Mary Peabody, b. Mar. 29, 1859; m. Apr. 19, 1883, *Francis Shaw,* son of Gardiner H. and Cora (Lyman) S., he b. Nov. 27, 1854.
2783.   ii. Clara Payson.

Resides in Boston and Nahant, Mass.

1498.

GRAFTON SEARS[7] [*Edw'd[6], Edw'd[5], Silas[4], Silas[3], Silas[2], Rich.[1]*], b. Dennis, Mass., Feb. 9, 1805; d. Aug. 22, 1871; m. (pub. Den., Feb. 24, 1825,) *Sarah Nickerson* of Den., who d. Sep. 1, 1863.   Children:
2784.*   i. Grafton, b. Den., Jan. 23, 1826.

2785.* ii. Daniel N., b. Den., Aug. 30, 1827.
2786.* iii. Sidney, b. Den., Oct. 5, 1829.
2787.* iv. Edward, b. Den., Feb. 21, 1833.
2788. v. Nehemiah B., b. Den., Feb. 26, 1836 ; drowned, May 24, 1856.
2789. vi. Sarah A., b. Den., Mar. 14, 1840 ; m. Dec. 10, 1857, *Cyrus W. Allen* of Harwich.
2790.* vii. Obed C., b. Den., Feb. 25, 1843.

1499.

EDWARD SEARS[7] [*Edw'd[6], Edw'd[5], Silas[4], Silas[3], Silas[2], Rich.[1]*], b. Dennis, Mass., July 4, 1808; d. Feb. 15, 1877; m. there, July 14, 1833, *Deborah Kelly* of Den. Children :
2791. i. *Child*, b. Den., Feb., 1834; d. Mar. 2.
2792. ii. Lucy Ann, b. Den., Nov. 8, 1835.
2793.* iii. Bartlett, b. Den., Nov. 8, 1837.
2794. iv. Eveline, b. Den., Oct. 17, 1840; m. Apr. 24, 1860, *Joshua Burgess* of Harwich.
2795. v. Alexander B., b. Den., June 14, 1844.
2796. vi. Edward H., b. Den., Sep. 15, 1850.

1500.

SHUBAEL B. SEARS[7] [*Edw'd[6], Edw'd[5], Silas[4], Silas[3], Silas[2], Rich.[1]*], b. Dennis, Mass., July 27, 1810; d. Dec. 16, 1857; m. (pub. Den., Aug. 6, 1830) *Reliance Doane* of Harwich. Children :
2797. i. Susan P., b. Den., Jan. 19, 1832; m. Har., Mar. 10, 1852, *Patrick A. Kelly* of Har.
2798. ii. Shubael, b. Den., Sep. 24, 1834; d. Dec. 4, 1853.
2799. iii. Henry, b. Den., Jan. 30, 1837; d. July 27, 1849.
2800. iv. Laura, b. Den., Oct. 29, 1842.
2801.* v. Isaiah D., b. Den., Mar. 29, 1845.
2802. vi. Joseph H., b. Den., Feb. 1, 1852 ; m. there, July 20, 1876, *Lucy T. Chase* of Har.

1501.

MICHAEL SEARS[7] [*Edw'd[6], Edw'd[5], Silas[4], Silas[3], Silas[2], Rich.[1]*], b. Dennis, Mass., Aug. 30, 1812; d. Mar. 1, 1857; m. Harwich, Jan. 5, 1837, *Anna Doane* of Har., who d. Dec. 24, 1879. Children :
2803. i. Abbie Ann, b. Den., Oct. 28, 1837; m. Oct. 17, 1858, *Ezra Eldredge* of Den.

2804. ii. RUTH D., b. Den., Oct. 9, 1838.
2805. iii. MICHAEL B., b. Den., Apr. 22, 1850.
2806. iv. HANNAH D., b. Den., Nov. 11, 1852.

1502.

SYLVANUS SEARS[7] [*Edw'd[6], Edw'd[5], Silas[4], Silas[3], Silas[2], Rich.[1]*], b. Dennis, Mass., Sep. 4, 1815; d. Feb. 19, 1860; m. there, Feb. 17, 1838, *Phebe Berry* of Pawtucket, R. I. Children :

2807. i. EMELINE, b. Den., Sep. 2, 1842.
2808. ii. HARRIET J., b. Den., Nov. 25, 1844; m. Apr. 14, 1868, *Dennie S. Nickerson* of Harwich.
2809.* iii. SYLVESTER B., b. Den., June 22, 1847.
2810. iv. LOUISA W., b. Den., Nov. 15, 1849; m. Sep. 11, 1873, *Luther H. Chase* of Den.
2811. v. SYLVANUS A., b. Den., Sep. 2, 1852; (Phebe Sears was app. adm'x of estate of Sylvanus A. Sears, Feb. 9, 1886.)
2812. vi. PHEBE, b. Den., Feb. 25, 1855; d. Nov. 22, 1858.

1503.

JEPTHAH B. SEARS[7] [*Edw'd[6], Edw'd[5], Silas[4], Silas[3], Silas[2], Rich.[1]*], b. Dennis, Mass., June 8, 1817; d. Providence, R. I., Jan. 19, 1884; m. Den., Nov. 30, 1839, *Betsy H. Kelly* of Den. Children:

2813. i. ALMIRA H., b. Den., Feb. 20, 1842; m. Nov. 17, 1861, *Samuel K. Berry* of Harwich.
2814.* ii. JEPTHAH B., b. Den., Oct. 15, 1844.
2814. *a.* iii. LATHROP T., b. Den., Oct. 6, 1850; d. Aug. 3, 1851.
2815. iv. ELIHU K., b. Den., Apr. 8, 1853.
2816. v. BETSY K., b. Den., Apr. 8, 1853, *gemini.*
2817. vi. ABIGAIL, b. Den., June 3, 1855.

A dau. m. Capt. Geo. Thacher of Providence, R. I., a son of Constant Sears' 2d wife.

1506.

BENJAMIN P. SEARS[7] [*Edw'd[6], Edw'd[5], Silas[4], Silas[3], Silas[2], Rich.[1]*], b. Dennis, Mass., Sep. 27, 1826; m. South Den., Jan. 22, 1852, *Olive Kelly*, she b. Dennisport, Jan. 6, 1833. Children :

2818. i. BENJAMIN A., b. So. Den., Sep. 22, 1854.

2819.   ii. LAURA BLANCHE, b. So. Den., Mar. 7, 1856 ; m. Mar. 7, 1879, —— ——.

2820.   iii. CHRISTOPHER, b. So. Den., Jan. 6, 1858 ; d. Aug. 20, 1859.

2820. *a*. iv. ROGER W., b. So. Den., Dec. 18, 1859 ; m. *Ada* ——; 2d, Boston, Mar. 28, 1888, *Sadie F. Hall.*

2821.   v. EMERY W., b. So. Den., Sep. 12, 1862 ; m. Dennisport, June 16, 1886, *Kate W. Handren*, dau. of Capt. John S. H.; had dau., b. Feb., 1888; lives Boston Highlands.

Is of firm Rogers & Sears, tug-boats, Boston ; lives in East Boston and Dennisport, Mass.

1511.

JAMES SEARS[7] [*Jas.[6], Moody[5], Silas[4], Silas[3], Silas[2], Rich.[1]*], b. Yarmouth, Mass., Sep. 28, 1799 ; d. Aug. 17, 1865 ; m. Dec. 30, 1823, *Phebe Lewis* of Dennis. Children :

2822.   i. DAVID, b. Yar., Feb. 23, 1825 ; d. Apr. 1, 1826.

2823.* ii. ORIN, b. Yar., Jan. 11, 1828.

2824. iii. LUCY JANE, b. Yar., Mar. 22, 1832 ; m. (pub. Yar., Dec. 24, 1851,) *Amos Farris, Jr.*

2825. iv. JAMES F., b. Den., Oct. 19, 1834 ; m. Dec. 23,1856, *Sophia F. Smalley* of Den., and lived in Yar.

2826.   v. DAVID, b. Den., June 29, 1840 ; d. Apr. 3, 1844.

1518.

Capt. PRINCE SEARS[7] [*Prince[6], Moody[5], Silas[4], Silas[3], Silas[2], Rich.[1]*], b. Dennis, Mass., Aug. 15, 1797 ; d. South Dartmouth, Mass., May 29, 1867, æ. 69 ; m. Dec. 2, 1823, *Sarah Smith Sandford*, she b. So. D., Nov. 5, 1802 ; d. there, Dec. 8, 1839, æ. 37 ; 2d, Oct., 1840, *Nancy Forest Davis*, she b. Long Plain, Mass., Sep. 10, 1815 ; d. there, ab't 1850 ; 3d, Rochester, Mass., May 27, 1855, *Hannah Hathaway Davis*, (elder sister of Nancy,) she b. Long Plain, May 14, 1808. Children :

By *Sarah* :

2827.   i. RICHARD SANDFORD, b. So. Dartmouth, Mass., Mar. 17, 1826 ; d. unm., Feb. 15, 1857.

2828.   ii. CLARA ELIZABETH, b. So. Dart., July 27, 1828 ; d. unm., July 3, 1854.

52

2829. iii. GIDEON SMITH, b. So. Dart., May 24, 1830 ; d. Oct. 19, 1836.
2830. iv. MATILDA McLEAN, b. So. Dart., Apr. 20, 1835; d. unm., Mar. 9, 1863.

Mr. Sears was a shipmaster. His widow resides in New Bedford, Mass.; is a Quakeress, very benevolent, and an active member of many charitable societies.

1527.

MOODY SEARS[7] [*Isaiah[6], Moody[5], Silas[4], Silas[3], Silas[2], Rich.[1]*], b. Yarmouth, Mass., Dec. 13, 1799 ; m. Dennis, Mass., Oct. 5, 1826, by Esq. Stoue to *Hannah Kelly*, dau. of Cyrenius K., she b. there, Dec. 18, 1803.   Children :
2831.   i. EZRA K., b. So. Sandwich, Mass., Mar. 23, 1828 ; m. ——— ———.
2832.   ii. WILLIAM P., b. So. Sand., Sep. 11, 1829 ; d. Sep. 21, 1832.
2833.   iii. ISAIAH, b. Aug. 29, 1832; d. Dec. 25.
2834.   iv. EUNICE K., b. Jan. 10, 1834 ; m. Dec. 30, 1856, *Henry H. Lombard*, and lives Des Moines, Iowa.
2835.   v. WILLIAM P., b. May 22, 1838 ; d. Nov. 12.
2836.   vi. CHARLES H., b. May 5, 1840 ; enlisted in Co. D, 23d Reg. Mass. Vol. Inf'y, Sep. 28, 1861, and was killed Newbern, N. C., Jan. 1, 1863.
2837.   vii. HANNAH W., b. Dec. 9, 1843 ; d. Dec. 11.
2838.   viii. EBEN R., b. Dec. 14, 1844; d. Sep. 1, 1848.

Mr. Sears lives with his daughter Eunice, in Des Moines, Iowa; has had a stroke of paralysis, which affects his mind and speech.

1533.

ISAIAH SEARS[7] [*Isaiah[6], Moody[5], Silas[4], Silas[3], Silas[2], Rich.[1]*], b. Yarmouth, Mass., Oct. 11, 1810 ; m. Mattapoisett, Mass., Sep. 10, 1835, by Rev. Theo. King, to *Sarah Barrows* of Dartmouth, Mass., she b. Oct. 24, 1808 ; d. New Bedford, Mass , Dec. 30, 1880.   Children :
2839.   i. AMELIA BARROWS, b. Rochester, Mass., Aug. 16, 1839.
2840.* ii. PETER COLLINS, b. Roch., Mar. 15, 1842.
2841.   iii. SARAH ANNA, b. Roch., Dec. 28, 1845 ; d. Oct. 1, 1851.

2842. iv. MARY ELIZABETH, b. Roch., Sep. 29, 1850; d. Oct. 4, 1851. (" *Clara* d. Oct. 5, 1851." T. Clk.)

2843. v. SARAH ELIZABETH, b. Roch., Dec. 29, 1852.

Mr. Sears lives in New Bedford, Mass.

1539.

Capt. JONATHAN SEARS[7] [*Lewis*[6], *Eleazar*[5], *Silas*[4], *Silas*[3], *Silas*[2], *Rich.*[1]], b. South Yarmouth, Mass., Dec. 12, 1792; d. Nov. 9, 1825, gr.-st., So. Yar.; m. Brewster, Mass., Feb. 21, 1822, *Tamsen Freeman*, dau. of John, Jr. and Bethia (Crowell) F., she b. there, Mar. 9, 1802; d. May 19, 1885, (having m. 2d, June 11, 1829, Prince Gifford, who d. May 9, 1844.) Children:

2844. i. EMILY, b. Mar. 14, 1824; d. Nov. 23, 1827, gr.-st., So. Yar.

2845.* ii. JONATHAN, b. Mar. 8, 1826.

Was a master mariner. Aug. 8, 1826, the court made an allowance to " Tamsen, wife of Jona. Sears of Yar."

1540.

Capt. LEWIS SEARS[7] [*Lewis*[6], *Eleazar*[5], *Silas*[4], *Silas*[3], *Silas*[2], *Rich.*[1]], b. South Yarmouth, Mass., Sep. 14, 1795; d. Mar. 3, 1829, gr.-st., So. Yar.; m. (pub. Dennis, Nov. 23, 1823) *Polly Nickerson* of Den., who d. Oct. 1, 1845. Children:

2846.* i. THOMAS N., b. Yar., July 5, 1825.

2847.* ii. JONATHAN L., b. Yar., Feb. 26, 1828.

Was a master mariner. The Probate Court made an allowance to his wife, Polly, in 1833.

1543.

HIRAM SEARS[7] [*Lewis*[6], *Eleazar*[5], *Silas*[4], *Silas*[3], *Silas*[2], *Rich.*[1]], b. South Yarmouth, Mass., Oct. 10, 1803; d. there, Mar. 6, 1880, æ. 76; m. Dennis, Mass., Jan. 14, 1841, *Mary Kelly*, she b. there, July 13, 1810; d. New Bedford, Mass., Apr. 12, 1889. Children:

2848. i. DRUSILLA W., b. So. Yar., Dec. 13, 1841; m. July 14, 1885, George Perry Underwood, she was a teacher in New Bedford, Mass.

2849.   ii. MARY K., b. So. Yar., May 6, 1843 ; m. Nov. 30, 1871, Baxter H. Studley of So. Harwich.

2850.   iii. JERUSHA JANE, b. So. Yar., Aug. 7, 1847 ; unm.

2851.   iv. RUTH ELLA, b. New Bedford, Oct. 9, 1854 ; was a teacher, and d. there, Dec. 13, 1887.

Was a ship carpenter.

1551.

Capt. EDWARD SEARS[7] [*Edw'd*[6], *Eleazar*[5], *Silas*[4], *Silas*[3], *Silas*[2], *Rich.*[1]], b. Yarmouth, Mass., May 12, 1800 ; d. So. Yar.; m. Yar., Dec., 1826, *Mary Rider*, she b. Sep. 5, 1801 ; d. Nov. 19, 1871, gr.-st., So. Yar.   Children :

2852.   i. ELIZABETH, b. So. Yar., July 30, 1830 ; m. Jan. 12, 1853, *Richard Smith.*

2853.   ii. ELLERY, b. So. Yar., Oct. 31, 1833 ; m. —— *Allen;* 2d, *Josephine Smith*, keeps "Central House," Providence, R. I.

2854.* iii. EDWARD, b. So. Yar., Nov. 20, 1835.

2855.   iv. MERCY RIDER, b. So. Yar., June 30, 1841 ; (June 23, 1840, T. Clk.) m. Yar., Dec. 12, 1864, *Sears T. Kelly*, and d. Prov., R. I., June 2, 1873.

Was a sea captain.

1552.

SAMUEL SEARS[7] [*Edw'd*[6], *Eleazar*[5], *Silas*[4], *Silas*[3], *Silas*[2], *Rich.*[1]], b. Yarmouth, Mass., 1802 ; m. Yar., June, 1834, *Lavinia Hallet*, who d. Aug. 24, 1851, æ. 44, gr.-st., So. Yar.; 2d, Yar., Oct. 29, 1857, *Keziah P. Baker*, who d. Dec. 15, 1882, æ. 79 yrs., 26 da., gr.-st., So. Yar.   Child :

By *Lavinia :*

2856. i. LUCY HALLET, b. Yar., Sep. 13, 1838 ; d. Aug. 11, 1863, gr.-st., So. Yar.

1553.

EMERY SEARS[7] [*Edw'd*[6], *Eleazar*[5], *Silas*[4], *Silas*[3], *Silas*[2], *Rich.*[1]], b. Yarmouth, Mass., Aug. 25, 1806 ; d. Sep. 25, 1838, gr.-st., S. Yar.; m. (pub. Yar., Jan. 19, 1833,) *Nabby T. Homer*, (who m. 2d, Mar. 2, 1844, Zebina Burgess, and d. Apr. 23, 1846, æ. 38 yrs. 9 mos., gr.-st., So. Yar.)   Children :

2857. i. SUSAN, b. Yar., Dec. 25, 1833 ; d. Oct. 10, 1842, gr.-st., So. Yar.

2858. ii. BENJAMIN H., b. Yar., Mar. 27, 1836 ; d. Feb. 25, 1841, gr.-st., So. Yar.

1565.

ODLIN PAGE SEARS[7] [*Winthrop[6], Eleazar[5], Thos.[4], Silas[3], Silas[2], Rich.[1]*], b. Yarmouth, Mass.; d. Boston, Aug. 20, 1855 ; m. (pub. Yar., May 28, 1831,) *Thankful Lewis,* who d. July 31, 1864. Children :

2859.* i. CYRUS, b. Yar., Nov. 5, 1831.
2860.* ii. RICHARD, b. Yar., Sep. 1, 1833.
2861. iii. EDWARD, b. Yar., Aug. 14, 1841 ; d. Feb. 10, 1865.

1568.

Capt. WINTHROP SEARS[7] [*Winthrop[6], Eleazar[5], Thos.[4], Silas[3], Silas[2], Rich.[1]*], b. Yarmouth, Mass., Jan. 2, 1818 ; d. there, Mar. 7, 1883, æ. 65 ; m. Sep. 6, 1840, *Polly Hallet,* who d. July 31, 1844 ; 2d, Yar., June 8, 1847, *Lucy Ann Sears,* No. 1427, dau. of Charles and Eliz'h (Hallet) S., she b. Yar., May 15, 1823 ; d. May 15, 1867 ; 3d, Yar., Aug. 10, 1869, *Clara Myrick,* dau. of Capt. Isaac and Lucy (Sears) M. Children :

By *Polly :*
2862. i. THOMAS HENRY, b. Yar., June 9, 1841.
By *Lucy :*
2863. ii. MARY ELIZABETH, b. Yar., Mar. 31, 1848 ; m. there, Nov. 2, 1869, *David D. Kelly.*
2864. iii. EBENEZER, b. Yar., Dec. 8, 1849 ; m. —— *Davis,* dau. of Wm. P. D.
2865. iv. ALICE WINTHROP, b. Yar., Nov. 22, 1851.
2866. v. WINTHROP, b. Yar., Jan. 28, 1857.

Capt. Sears was an enterprising and capable shipmaster ; commanded steamer " Saxon," of the Boston and Philadelphia line ; was for several years a Director of the First National Bank of Yarmouth, and filled other important stations in private business enterprises.

1583.

Capt. CHAUNCY SEARS[7] [*Philip[6], David[5], Jas.[4], Silas[3], Silas[2], Rich.[1]*], b. Lenox, Mass., June 30, 1799 ; d. there,

Feb. 10, 1841, æ. 41; m. Pittsfield, Mass., Dec. 28, 1820, *Polly Howland*, she b. Dec. 28, 1800; d. Lenox, Feb. 8, 1869, æ. 68; (she was a dau. of Joseph and Lois (Hamblen) H., and gr.-dau. of Capt. Perry Hamblen, an officer of the Rev'y army.) Children:

2867. i. PHILIP HOWLAND, b. Lenox, Aug. 9, 1823; m· Hinsdale, Mass., Feb. 5, 1849, —— ——; and d. Charlotte, N. C., Feb. 12, 1862, æ. 38.
2868. ii. HORATIO NELSON, b. Lenox, Aug. 29, 1826; d. unm., May 29, 1860; Mem. Leg. 1855–56, and town officer, mail agent, etc.
2869. iii. MARY CORNELIA, b. Lenox, Aug. 22, 1828; m. there, Nov. 25, 1852, *Simeon L. Hobbs* of Northampton, Mass., and d. Aug. 12, 1883.
2870.* iv. HENRY CLINTON, b. Lenox, Feb. 11, 1832.
2871.* v. CHAUNCY, b. Lenox, Nov. 13, 1834.
2872. vi. LOIS HAMBLEN, b. Lenox, Aug. 23, 1837; is a teacher, unm., and lives in New Lenox.

Capt. Sears was a farmer, and lived on the old homestead in Lenox.

1585.

DANIEL SEARS[7] [*David[6], David[5], Jas.[4], Silas[3], Silas[2], Rich.[1]*], b. Lenox, Mass., June 13, 1785; m. Milton, N. Y., 1810, *Clarissa Blinn*, she b. Aug. 20, 1790; d. Feb. 1, 1868. Children :

2873.* i. ORANGE, b. Milton, Aug. 13, 1812.
2874. ii. SOLOMON, b. Milton, Nov. 8, 1815; m. Camillus, N. Y., *Charlotte Wheaton*, and d.
2875. iii. DAVID, b. Fabius, N. Y., Apr. 17, 1817; d. Apr. 18.
2876. iv. HULDAH, b. Fabius, Apr. 17, 1817, *gemini;* d. Apr. 18.
2877. v. BETSY, b. Fabius, Apr. 18, 1818; d. Nov. 18, 1839.
2878. vi. MAJOR, b. Fabius, Sep. 12, 1822; d. Mar. 1, 1855.
2879. vii. DAVID, b. Fabius, Oct. 13, 1826; m. Apulia, N. Y., Jan. 23, 1862, *Fidelia Clark*, and d. May 22, 1883.

1589.

ELEAZAR SEARS[7] [*David[6], David[5], Jas.[4], Silas[3], Silas[2], Rich.[1]*], b. Milton, N. Y., July 31, 1801; d. Lagrange, Ind. ; m. Camillus, N. Y., *Sarah Wheaton*, who d. Lagrange. Child :
2880. i. ISAAC, lives in Lagrange.

1597.

NELSON SEARS[7] [*Luther*[6], *David*[5], *Jas.*[4], *Silas*[3], *Silas*[2], *Rich.*[1]], b. Lenox, Mass., Aug. 12, 1798; d. Oswego, N. Y., 1882, æ. 84; m. Lenox, Jan. 18, 1820, by Rev. Sam'l Shepard, to *Amanda Cole.* Children:

2881. i. JAMES; lives in Oswego, N. Y.
2882. ii. MELISSA, m. —— *Wheeler* of Volney, N. Y.
2883. iii. NANCY, m. —— *Cook* of Volney.
2884. iv. HARRIET.

Mr. Sears removed to Volney, Oswego co., N. Y.

1599.

MARSHALL SEARS[7] [*Luther*[6], *David*[5], *Jas.*[4], *Silas*[3], *Silas*[2], *Rich.*[1]], b. Lenox, Mass., Feb. 24, 1802; d. July 9, 1883, æ. 81; m. there, Aug. 30, 1829, by Rev. Sam'l Shepard, to *Mary Sabin*, she b. there, Feb. 3, 1803; d. Oct. 2, 1879, æ. 76. Children:

2885. i. MARY C., b. Lenox, Aug. 22, 1830; d. Apr. 3, 1844.
2886. ii. SUSAN E., b. Lenox, Feb. 17, 1832; m. there, Dec. 17, 1849, *Gideon N. Smith*, he b. Stockbridge, Mass., Oct. 19, 1825; lives in Lenox.
2887.* iii. CHARLES M., b. Lenox, Sep. 11, 1837.
2888. iv. NANCY B., b. Lenox, Feb. 15, 1842; m. there, Dec. 2, 1863, *Hiram B. Wellington*, he b. Williamstown, Mass., Sep. 12, 1840, and lives in Pittsfield, Mass.; children, WELLINGTON: [1.] Marshall Sears, b. Mar. 11, 1869. [2.] Thomas J., b. May 10, 1870. [3.] Mary E., b. Dec. 17, 1871. [4.] Susan E., b. Feb. 18, 1873. [5.] Fanny A., b. Aug. 22, 1874. [6.] Hiram C., b. Dec. 22, 1876. [7.] Harvey C., b. Aug. 3, 1879. [8.] Charles S., b. Jan. 25, 1884; d. Mar. 19.

1600.

ZACHARIAH P. SEARS[7] [*Luther*[6], *David*[5], *Jas.*[4], *Silas*[3], *Silas*[2], *Rich.*[1]], b. Lenox, Mass., 1804; m. (pub. Mar. 11, 1832,) *Maryette Judd* of L. Child:

2889. i. ANNA· A., b. Lenox; m. there, Apr. 22, 1856, *Chas. H. Lay* of Lee, Mass.

1601.

LUTHER SEARS[7] [*Luther*[6], *David*[5], *Jas.*[4], *Silas*[3], *Silas*[2], *Rich.*[1]], b. Lenox, Mass., Nov. 26, 1806; d. Feb. 16, 1877, æ. 70; m. *Chloe Clark*, she b. Mar. 21, 1807; d. Mar. 18, 1847; 2d, *Emily Howland.* Children:
By *Emily:*
2890. i. EDWARD E., b. Lenox, Aug. 7, 1849; lives in West Lenox.
2891.* ii. MARTIN LUTHER, b. Lenox.
2892. iii. DAVID D., b. Lenox, May, 1854; d. Aug. 5, 1861.

1607.

DIOCLESIAN SEARS[7] [*Jas.*[6], *David*[5], *Jas.*[4], *Silas*[3], *Silas*[2], *Rich.*[1]], b. Lenox, Mass., Nov. 15, 1808; m. Richford, N. Y., Dec. 11, 1830, *Laura L. Holcomb*, she b. Hamilton, N. Y. 1817. Children:
2893. i. JAMES M., b. Rich., Sep. 26, 1837; m. *Jeannette Davis.*
2894. ii. LUCY H., b. Rich., Dec. 11, 1839; m. *Alonzo S. Ostrander.*
2895. iii. LAURA H., b. Rich., Mar. 6, 1841; m. *J. M. Davis.*
2896. iv. MARY D., b. Rich., Mar. 26, 184—.
2897. v. JERUSHA, b. Rich., July 11, 1844; d. Jan. 1, 1847.
2898. vi. EMILY K., b. Rich., July 28, 1848; m. *Burr Marsh.*
2899. vii. SARAH H., b. Rich., July 18, 1850; m. *Frank M. Root.*
2900. viii. FLORA A., b. Rich., July 6, 1856; d. Jan. 5, 1871.
2901. ix. AGNES E., b. Rich., Nov. 12, 1858; m. *Charles Satterley.*

1609.

PHILIP SEARS[7] [*Jas.*[6], *David*[5], *Jas.*[4], *Silas*[3], *Silas*[2], *Rich.*[1]], b. Lenox, Mass., May 21, 1812; m. Richford, N. Y., Aug. 19, 1841, *Sally M. Tyler*, she b. Locke, N. Y., Oct. 31, 1823. Children:
2902. i. GEORGE O., b. Rich., July 17, 1842; d. Oct. 29, 1849.
2903. ii. MARYETTE, b. Rich., June 26, 1844; d. Dec. 29, 1877.
2904. iii. URIAH J., b. Rich., July 7, 1845; d. Jan. 12, 1849.

2905. iv. QUINCY A., b. Rich., Feb. 28, 1851.
2906. v. HARRIET M., b. Rich., Jan. 3, 1853; m. Harford, N.
Y., May 31, 1873, *Tim. M. Holcomb.*
2907. vi. ELLA L., b. Rich., Apr. 29, 1856; m. there, Nov.
29, 1874, *Jesse Talcott,* and d. Sep. 21, 1878.
2908. vii. NELLIE J., b. Rich., Apr. 25, 1864.

1612.

SAMUEL H. SEARS[7] [*Zach.[6], David[5], Jas.[4], Silas[3], Silas[2], Rich.[1]*], b. Lenox, Mass., 1808; d. May 16, 1881, æ. 73; m. *Elizabeth M. Bradley.* Child:
2909. i. DAVID, b. Lenox, Aug. 7, 1843; d. Apr. 11, 1847.

1613.

JOHN SEARS[7] [*Zach.[6], David[5], Jas.[4], Silas[3], Silas[2], Rich.[1]*], b. Lenox, Mass., Dec. 3, 1812; m. Lee, Mass., Feb. 10, 1837, *Martha Thacher,* youngest dau. of Timo. T., she b. there, Feb. 5, 1815. Children :
2910.* i. SAMUEL, b. Lenox, Feb. 22, 1838.
2911. ii. BETSY E., b. Lenox, Feb. 10, 1840 ; d. Feb. 2, 1841.
2912. iii. ADA E., b. Lenox, Nov. 2, 1843 ; m. there, May 10,
1864, *John Radie;* children, RADIE: [1.] John E., b.
Jan. 5, 1869. [2.] Lena T., b. Feb. 5, 1871.
2913. iv. JULIA F., b. Lenox, Jan. 5, 1846; m. Dec. 10,
1867, *Vincent Shanks,* and d. May 2, 1882; children,
SHANKS: [1.] Jennie M., b. Nov. 27, 1868. [2.] Ida
May, b. Mar. 27, 1870.
2914. v. GILBERT J., b. Lenox, Oct. 21, 1848 ; m. Dec. 19,
1875, —— ——.
2915. vi. JOHN G., b. Lenox, Oct. 23, 1848, (?) (perh. *gemini.*)
2916. vii. EDWARD M., b. Litchfield, Ohio, Sep. 27, 1851, m.
Oct. 4, 1876, —— ——.

Mr. Sears removed to Litchfield, Medina county, Ohio, where he had a farm, and was member of Leg., 1860–61.

1614.

ELIJAH SEARS[7] [*Zach.[6], David[5], Jas.[4], Silas[3], Silas[2], Rich.[1]*], b. Lenox, Mass.; d. ——; m. *Matilda French.* Children :
2917. i. ALLEN, b. Lenox, Nov. 5, 1845.

2918. ii. ZILPHA A., b. Lenox ; m. Apr. 4, 1862, *Edmund N. Schofield.*

1616.

JAMES SEARS[7] [*Zach.[6], David[5], Jas.[4], Silas[3], Silas[2], Rich.[1]*], b. Lenox, Mass. ; m. *Lydia Merrills.* Child ::
2919. i. JAMES H., b. Lenox, 1831 ; m. there, Dec. 29, 1868, *Celia M. Parsons* of L. ; he served in Co. K, 8th Regt., Mass. Inf., from July 21 to Nov. 10, 1864, 3-mos.' men.

Resides in Pittsfield, Mass.

1617.

LEVI L. SEARS[7] [*Zach.[6], David[5], Jas.[4], Silas[3], Silas[2], Rich.[1]*], b. Lenox, Mass., Apr. 8, 1825 ; m. Lee, Mass., Nov. 8, 1848, *Sarah W. Schofield,* who d. Lenox, Nov. 18, 1856, æ. 29 ; 2d, Lenox, Jan. 29, 1858, *Charlotte Schofield,* she b. Andover, Mass. Children :
By *Sarah :*
2920. i. JOHN, b. Lenox, Feb. 9, 185—.
2921. ii. GEORGE LEVI, b. Lenox, Mar. 8, 1854 ; m. Oct. 9, 1878, *Emma Bradbury,* and is a florist in Elyria, Ohio ; child : [1.] Albert Leroy, b. 1885.
By *Charlotte:*
2922. iii. LILIAN, b. Litchfield, Ohio, Apr. 16, 1867.

Mr. Sears is a farmer in Elyria, Lorain county, Ohio.

1622.

ALEXANDER SEARS[7] [*Enoch[6], Seth[5], Jas.[4], Silas[3], Silas[2], Rich.[1]*], b. Aug. 9, 1782 ; d. Oct. 6, 1828, æ. 46 ; m. 1802, *Mary Howes,* dau. of David H. of Ballston Spa, N. Y., she b. Oct. 24, 1785 ; d. Apr. 13, 1874, æ. 89. Children :
2923. i. DAVID H., b. Oct. 2, 1803 ; d. May 2, 1806.
2924. ii. RUTH M., b. Nov. 19, 1805 ; d. Oct. 4, 1808.
2925. iii. LEWIS H., b. Feb. 5, 1808 ; m. Nov. 29, 1832, *Hannah Ann Wheeler,* who d. s. p., Oct. 1, 1882 ; he lives in Ballston, N. Y.
2926. iv. HENRY L., b. July 8, 1810 ; m. *Mary Van Vorst,* and d. s. p., Aug. 28, 1861.
2927. v. EPENETUS H., b. May 3, 1815 ; m. *Julia A. Allen* of Chautauqua co., N. Y. ; removed to Sidney, Iowa,

about 1855, and d. s. p., Jan. 20, 1881 ; was a lawyer
and District Judge for several terms ; was an Elder in
the Presbyterian Church ; had a high reputation in the
county, and died much lamented.

2928.* vi. ALEXANDER, b. June 10, 1818.
2929.* vii. ISAAC H., b. Oct. 9, 1821.
2930. viii. MARY, b. Aug. 29, 1825 ; lives in Ballston Centre,
N. Y.

1639.

ODELL M. SEARS[7] [*Eleazar*[6], *Seth*[5], *Jas.*[4], *Silas*[3], *Silas*[2],
Rich.[1]], b. De Ruyter, N. Y., 1815 ; m. there, 1846, *Mary
Gidley*, she b. Devonshire, Eng., 1825. Children :

2931. i. GEORGE ALONZO, b. De Ruy., Dec. 3, 1848; m. 1870,
—— ——, and lives in Syracuse, N. Y.
2932. ii. FRANK, b. De Ruy., Nov. 23, 1860; lives at home.

Resides in Cortland, N. Y.

1641.

ARZA SEARS[7] [*Dan'l*[6], *Knowles*[5], *Jas.*[4], *Silas*[3], *Silas*[2],
Rich.[1]], b. Rensselaerville, N. Y., Oct. 17, 1790; d. near Bald-
winsville, N. Y., July 15, 1859; m. Aug. 3, 1817, *Elizabeth
Betts*, dau. of Josiah and Hannah (Sherman) B., she b. Feb.
12, 1796; d. Dec. 19, 1880, at her son James' house in Van
Buren, N. Y. Children :

2933. i. RUFUS, b. July 1, 1819; m. Sep. 29, 1847, *Jane
Smith*, and d. Nov. 12, 1876 ; she lives in Baldwinsville,
N. Y.
2934.* ii. JAMES, b. Dec. 26, 1822.

1643.

AHIRAM SEARS[7] [*Dan'l*[6], *Knowles*[5], *Jas.*[4], *Silas*[3], *Silas*[2],
Rich.[1]], b. Apr. 5, 1795; d. Baldwinsville, N. Y.; m. *Ann
Bell*. Child :

2935.* i. DANIEL D., b. Bald.

Mr. Sears removed about 1838, to the vicinity of Baldwinsville, N. Y., where he and his wife and children died, and are
buried.

1656.

JAMES SEARS[7] [*Abijah[6], Knowles[5], Jas.[4], Silas[3], Silas[2], Rich.[1]*], b. Eaton, N. Y., May 12, 1797; d. Danby, N. Y., June 29, 1835; m. *Matilda Cartwright*, dau. of Daniel C. of D. Children:

2936.   i. ERASTUS, b. Danby, and lives there.
2937.   ii. DAVID, b. Danby, and lives there.
2938.   iii. WILLIAM, b. Danby, and lives there.
2939.   iv. EGBERT, b. Danby.
2940.   v. JOHN, b. Danby.

Was a farmer in Danby, N. Y.

1657.

CHARLES SEARS[7] [*Abijah[6], Knowles[5], Jas.[4], Silas[3], Silas[2], Rich.[1]*], b. Eaton, N. Y., abt. 1800; d. Allen, Mich.; m. *Clarissa Tabor*, dau. of Ziba T. of Genoa, N. Y. Children:

2941. i. HENRY, b. Newark Valley, N. Y., abt. 1823.
2942. ii. HANNAH, b. Genoa, N. Y.; rem. to Mich. and m.

Mr. Sears was a tailor. In 1821, he settled in Newark Valley, N. Y., where in 1823, he built the house, which since 1827, has been occupied by the Byington family. In the latter year he removed to Genoa, N. Y., and in June, 1836, to Allen, Hinsdale co., Mich., where he died.

1659.

HART BOUGHTON SEARS[7] [*Abijah[6], Knowles[5], Jas.[4], Silas[3], Silas[2], Rich.[1]*], b. Eaton, N. Y., Aug. 15, 1807; d. Newark Valley, N. Y., May 11, 1885; m. *Cynthia Maria Williams*, dau. of Oliver and Freelove (Newell) W., she b. Apr. 10, 1810; was bap. Nov. 1, 1820, and joined the Ch. in New. Vall., Nov. 2, 1834, by letter from the Ch. in Genoa. Children:

2943.*   i. CHARLES WILLIAMS, b. New. Vall., June 13, 1830.
2944.*   ii. ALBERT EDGAR, b. Venice, N. Y., Jan. 10, 1832.
2945.   iii. HENRY WILLIAMS, b. Genoa, N. Y., Dec. 9, 1833; m. abt. 1853, *Angeline Dean*, dau. of Stafford A. and Abigail (Warren) D., she b. New. Vall., Dec. 9, 1829; d. s. p., 1881. He was Capt. Co· E, 10th Mich. Cav., in 1861; was conductor on Ch., Bur. and Q. R. R., and

killed by the cars at the depot in Burlington, Iowa, Feb. 25, 1879.

2946.* iv. MARTIN V. B., b. New. Vall., Apr. 1, 1836.

2947. v. CORYDON BIRCH, b. New. Vall., Dec. 23, 1839; m. *Mary O. Day;* is a tinner in Lisle, N. Y.

2948. vi. DELPHINE AUGUSTA, b. New. Vall., Apr. 9, 1842; was a music teacher, and m. Muskegan, Mich., Feb. 19, 1867, *Charles Pyncheon Lyman,* son of Henry D. and Sophia (Buckman) L. of Caneadea, N. Y., he b. Aug. 12, 1831; was a lumber dealer in Chicago, Ill., where he d. Mar. 4, 1868, having been thrown from his carriage. She m. 2d, Oct. 6, 1881, *Lucius Wells Spalding,* a farmer in New. Vall., son of Moses and Eunice (Johnson) S., he b. Sep. 9, 1832; child, LYMAN: [1.] Charles Pyncheon, b. May 10, 1868; lives in New. Vall.

2949. vii. MARY ANN, b. New Vall., Oct. 28, 1843; d. Apr. 29, 1844.

2950.* viii. OLIVER WILLIAMS, b. New. Vall., June 13, 1845.

2951. ix. CAROLINE MIRANDA, b. New. Vall., Feb. 3, 1848; was a music teacher, and m. Binghamton, N. Y., Nov. 18, 1875, *Charles Gouder Estabrook,* son of Thaddeus and Eliza (Buck) E., he b. Great Valley, Catt. co., N. Y., Oct. 6, 1850; grad. Univ. Penn., 1871; spent a year in European travel and study, and then settled in Binghamton, where he had a fine practice and took high rank as a physician; he d. Aug. 2, 1880; his wid. lives in New. Vall.; children, ESTABROOK: [1.] William Sears, b. Dec. 12, 1877. [2.] Charles Scott, b. June 23, 1879.

2952. x. FREDERIC JEROME, b. New. Vall., May 18, 1851; d. Oct. 5, 1863.

Mr. Sears was a tailor; dwelt in Newark Valley till spring of 1831; at Talcott's Corners, Venice, N. Y., till spring of 1833, and at Northville, Genoa, N. Y., till fall of 1834, when he returned to Newark Valley, where his widow still lives.

In his early days he was a great hunter, and killed many deer on the hills about Newark Valley.

He joined the "Washingtonians" in 1840; was baptized and joined the Cong. Ch. in Newark Valley, Jan. 2, 1859.

1666.

HEMAN SEARS[7] [*Isaac⁶, Knowles⁵, Jas.⁴, Silas³, Silas², Rich.¹*], b. May 23, 1807; m. —— ——. Child:

2953. i. *Dau.,* m. *Charles Shaw,* and lives Maple Street, Niagara co., N. Y.

1667.

HAMAN SEARS[7] [*Isaac*[6], *Knowles*[5], *Jas.*[4], *Silas*[3], *Silas*[2], *Rich.*[1]], b. May 23, 1807 ; m. May 2, 1828, *Eliza Moore*, she b. Apr. 8, 1809. Children :

2954. i. ABIGAIL, b. Sep. 25, 1829.
2955.* ii. ISAAC, b. Sep. 4, 1833.

1669.

EDWIN COLLINS SEARS[7] [*Chas.*[6], *Knowles*[5], *Jas.*[4], *Silas*[3], *Silas*[2], *Rich.*[1]], b. Ridgefield, Ct., Jan. 17, 1808; d. Danbury, Ct., June 7, 1866, æ. 48 ; m. North Salem, N. Y., Feb. 22, 1835, *Marietta Jarvis*, dau. of James and Lucy (Platt) J. of No. S. Children :

2956.   i. CLARA MARIA, b. Ridge., Feb. 4, 1836 ; m. there, Dec. 22, 1852, *John Canfield*, son of Rufus and Polly (Northrop) C. of Dan. ; children, CANFIELD : [1.] Edwin Job, b. Mar. 4, 1854; m. Dec. 31, 1876, Lucy Alice Thomas. [2.] Charles, b. July 5, 1856 ; m. Apr. 21, 1876, Ida Stone. [3.] Caroline Frances, b. May 10, 1861. [4.] Wilfred, b. July 29, 1863. [5.] John Alexander, b. June 18, 1872.
2957. ii. JANE ELIZA, b. Reading, Ct., Apr. 25, 1838 ; m. *Charles E. Butler*, and lives in Mich.
2958. iii. MARY ANN, b. Sharon, Ct., Jan. 15, 1841 ; m. Sep., 1859, *Adoniram Blackman* of Danbury, and d., 1880, New Milford, Ct.

Mr. Sears was a hatter, lived for a time in Ridgefield, Reading and Sharon, and died in Danbury, Ct., and was buried in Wooster Cemetery. His widow lives in Millplain, Ct.

1670.

GEORGE SEARS[7] [*Chas.*[6], *Knowles*[5], *Jas.*[4], *Silas*[3], *Silas*[2], *Rich.*[1]], b. Camillus, N. Y., Mar. 12, 1823 ; d. Danbury, Ct., Nov. 1, 1866, æ. 43 ; m. Ridgefield, Ct., 1844, *Sarah Gregory*. Children :

2959.   i. GEORGE, lives in Bridgeport, Ct.
2960. ii. BETSY, unm.
2961. iii. CHARLES, m. —— *Taylor* of Danbury, and had a dau.

2962. iv. EMMA.
2963. v. SAMUEL.
2964. vi. BENJAMIN, m. and had a dau.
2965. vii. NATHAN.

Mr. Sears was a hatter, died in Danbury, Ct., and was buried in Wooster Cemetery.

1671.

THOMAS BALDWIN SEARS[7] [*Eli*[6], *Thos.*[5], *Jas.*[4], *Silas*[3], *Silas*[2], *Rich.*[1]], b. South East, N. Y., Mar. 2, 1789; d. Searsburg, N. Y., June 28, 1871; m. Covert, N. Y., Mar. 1, 1816, *Maria Boardman*, she b. N. Hamp., Jan. 15, 1800; now lives in Searsburg. Children:

2966.* i. ELI, b. Dec. 7, 1816.
2967.* ii. ALFRED, b. Oct. 19, 1818.
2968.* iii. BALDWIN, b. Hector, N. Y., Apr. 30, 1820.
2969. iv. EMELINE, b. Hector, Apr. 3, 1822; m. there, Sep. 11, 1845, *Woodard S. Wixom*, he b. June 13, 1822; children, WIXOM: [1.] Clermont, b. Sep. 13, 1856; m. Oct. 20, 1880, Frank Olivia Niles, she b. Feb. 4, 1856.
2970. v. EDGAR, b. Hector, Mar. 10, 1824, is a surveyor, and lives in Pine River, Wis., has been twice Mem. of Assembly.
2971. vi. MALAMA, b. Hector, Dec. 24, 1825; m. July 8, 1856, *John R. Buckbee*, he b. Sep. 17, 1827; d. June 29, 1873; was at one time considered the ablest criminal lawyer in California; was elected Mem. of Assembly 4 times, and was strongly talked of for U. S. Senator at the time Cornelius Cole was elected. His family live in San Francisco; children, BUCKBEE: [1.] Alvah, b. May 21, 1857. [2.] Lorna, b. Apr. 19, 1859. [3.] Ossain, b. Jan. 11, 1862. [4.] Harriet, b. Sep. 20, 1863; d. May 25, 1870. [5.] Flora, b. Feb. 19, 1866. [6.] Peace, b. Oct. 16, 1867; d. Nov. 5, 1868.
2972.* vii. SACKETT, b. Hector, Apr. 7, 1827.
2973. viii. HANNA, b. Hector, Aug. 25, 1829; unm.
2974. ix. LORNA, b. Hector, July 6, 1831; m. Searsburg, Jan. 20, 1864, *Arthur M. Mekal*, he b. Dec. 12, 1831; was twice Mem. of Assembly from Lima co., and lives in Fairfax, Iowa; no child.
2975. x. TRUMAN, b. Hector, Oct. 29, 1833; is a surveyor, and lives Pine River, Wis.; unm.

2976.*   xi. David Elbert, b. Hector, Apr. 25, 1836.
2977.* xii. Clermont, b. Hector, Dec. 27, 1838.
2978.* xiii. Ossain, b. Hector, Feb. 18, 1843.

Mr. Sears was a soldier in the war of 1812. He removed to Hector, Schuyler co., N. Y., and the village of Searsburg, his residence, was named for him. He was a Member of the Assembly in 1846, to revise the Constitution of the State of New York, and Supervisor of Hector during many years.

1672.

Capt. DAVID F. SEARS[7] [*Eli*[6], *Thos.*[5], *Jas.*[4], *Silas*[3], *Silas*[2], *Rich.*[1]], b. South East, N. Y., Apr. 17, 1791; d. Searsburg, N. Y., June 29, 1872; m. Colchester, N. Y., Apr. 1, 1812, *Sally Pine*, she b. Sep. 25, 1792; d. Searsburg, Aug. 27, 1859.   Children:

2979.*   i. Almoin Pine, b. Dec. 17, 1812.
2980.* ii. George W., b. Hector, N. Y., Aug. 5, 1814.
2981.   iii. Hannah, b. Hector, June 11, 1816; d. June 15.
2982.   iv. Emeline M., b. Hector, May 30, 1817; d. June 8, 1821.
2983.*   v. Benjamin P., b. Hector, Dec. 7, 1819.
2984.   vi. Adaline E., b. Hector, Jan. 2, 1822; m. Searsburg, Dec. 22, 1842, *John D. M. Woodworth*, he b. Apr. 19, 1818; 2d, *Cyrus Barker :* child, Woodworth : [1.] John De Mott, b. June 8, 1845 ; d. May 13, 1877.
2985.   vii. Caroline C., b. Hector, Nov. 14, 1823; m. Searsburg, Jan. 23, 1849, *Ferry Smith*, he b. Mar. 30, 1820; d. July 27, 1869; children, Smith : [1.] James Hobart, b. Jan. 5, 1850; d. Nov. 30, 1870. [2.] Ellen Douglass, b. Nov. 30, 1850.
2986.* viii. Franklin, b. Hector, Oct. 12, 1826.
2987.* ix. De Witt C., b. Hector, Jan. 21, 1829.
2988.   x. Jane C., b. Hector, Nov. 6, 1830; m. Searsburg, Feb. 15, 1853, *Abraham V. Mekal*, he b. Mar. 30, 1829 ; children, Mekal : [1.] Carrie, b. Sep. 27, 1857 ; m. No. Hector, Oct. 25, 1876, Francis M. Smith, he b. June 27, 1854; and had, i. Lulu, b. May 18, 1879. ii. Eva Maria, b. Dec. 27, 1880. [2.] Arthur Mott, b. Dec. 27, 1860.
2989.   xi. John D., b. Hector, Oct. 1, 1832 ; d. Sep. 29, 1833.

Was styled Captain.

1685.

Hon. BENJAMIN ROBINSON SEARS[7] [*Jared*[6], *Jas.*[5], *Jas.*[4], *Silas*[3], *Silas*[2], *Rich.*[1]], b. Bennington, Vt., Dec. 21, 1807; m. there, Nov. 20, 1831, *Mary Ann Waters*, she b. there, Oct. 28, 1805. Children :

2990.   i. BETSY ROBINSON, b. Benn., May 11, 1833.
2991.   ii. MARTIN, b. Benn., Feb. 26, 1835 ; d. Nov. 16, 1837.
2992.   iii. MARY, b. Benn., Feb. 12, 1837 ; m. there, Jan. 28, 1862, *Edward Walbridge*, he b. there, Aug. 10, 1831 ; lives in No. Benn.; she d. Apr. 27, 1884.
2993.   iv. ESTHER ROBINSON, b. Benn., Feb. 24, 1839; m. there, June 28, 1864, *John P. Harwood*, and d. Sep. 23, 1870.
2994.   v. CHARLES FOLLETT, b. Benn., May 23, 1841 ; m. there, Jan. 15, 1867, *Sarah Metcalf Ammen*, she b. Washington, Miss., Jan. 28, 1845 ; he served 3 years in Union Army during the Civil war, and now lives in Benn. Centre.
2995.   vi. DELIA MARIA, b. Benn., June 5, 1843 ; m. there, Aug. 20, 1872, *Orvin J. Roe*, he b. Shoreham, Vt., Nov. 13, 1848 ; lives in Leola, Dakota.
2996.   vii. GEORGE BENJAMIN, b. Benn., Jan. 1, 1847; m. Momence, Ill., May 11, 18—, *Antoinette Keyes*, and lives in Benn.
2997.   viii. WALTER FOBES, b. Benn., Nov. 12, 1849 ; lives in Palatka, Fla.

Mr. Sears lives in Bennington Centre, Vt. ; was Rep. to State Leg. in 1858, and Judge of County Court, 1862–63.

1689.

JOHN SEARS[7] [*Jas.*[6], *Jas.*[5], *Jas.*[4], *Silas*[3], *Silas*[2], *Rich.*[1]], b. perh. in Canada, about 1810 ; m. Rush co., Ind., *Esther Knox*, who d. 1868. Children :

2998.   i. MARTHA E., m. *H. Snodgrass*, and d. æ. 46.
2999.   ii. WILLIAM K., m. *Sarah Caldwell.*
3000.* iii. JOHN W., b. Knightstown, Ind., Mar. 23, 1841.
3001.   iv. MARIA E., m. *J. W. Tillman*, and lives in Kansas.
3002.   v. GEORGE G., m. *Mary Horner.*
3003.   vi. HICKLEN, d. æ. 7.

Mr. Sears now lives in Kansas with his dau. Maria.

54

1691.

DAVID SEARS[7] [*Jas.*[6], *Jas.*[5], *Jas.*[4], *Silas*[3], *Silas*[2], *Rich.*[1]],
b. N. Y. State; d. 1867–68; m. Brown co., Ohio, *Pauline Lane.* Child:

3004. i. J. W., m., and has a m. dau.; he lives in Spice-
land, Ind.

1692.

JAMES SEARS[7] [*Jas.*[6], *Jas.*[5], *Jas.*[4], *Silas*[3], *Silas*[2], *Rich.*[1]],
b. Canada, Oct. 20, 1812; m. Rush co., Ind., Oct. 30, 1834,
Sarah Ann Cooper, dau. of Moses and Catherine C. Children:

3005.   i. Lydia Ann, b. Jan. 27, 1836; m. 1853, *Isaac Steel,*
(nephew to John Steel, who m. Anna Sears, dau. of
James and Elinor ;) he was a soldier in the Union Army,
and killed at Missionary Ridge, 1863 ; she m. 2d, Joseph
Smith of Crawfordsville, Ind., who d. ; children, Steel :
[1.] Elmer, b. 1863, lives Crawfordsville ; and Smith :
[2.] Emery.

3006. ii.   Ellen Catharine, b. Oct. 18, 1837; m. 1854,
Reuben Moffatt ; children, Moffatt : [1.] Lycurgus, m.
Amanda Anderson, and had i. Mila, b. 1876 ; she m.
2d, *Charles Clauten ;* children, Clauten : [2.] Nora,
m. Frank Galloway ; she m. 3d, *Christopher A. Swaim,*
by whom she had 4 children, and now lives in Ogden,
Ind.

3007. iii. Priscilla Jane, b. Apr. 25, 1834 ; m. Sep. 24,
1859, *James C. Deathe,* and lives in Indianapolis, Ind. ;
children, Deathe : [1.] Sarah Freeman, b. July 9, 1860 ;
m. Apr. 19, 1881, Walter C. Dunham, son of Geo. H.
and Fannie D., and had, i. Clarence Edward, b. May 15,
1882. ii. Elsie Allen, b. Oct. 12, 1883. [2.] Walter
Grant, b. July 23, 1865 ; d. July 25.

3008. iv. Matilda Francis, b. Mar. 3, 1842; d. Aug. 30,
1844.

3009.   v. Elizabeth Caroline, b. Aug. 22, 1844; m. 1862,
Edward Wilson, and had a child who d. ; was divorced,
and m. 2d, 1866, *Henry Wiggins ;* lives in Ogden, Ind. ;
child, Wiggins : [1.] Sarah Ion.

3010.* vi. Josephus Theodore, b. Dec. 3, 1847.

3011. vii. Mary Elinor, b. July 30, 1849 ; d. Sep. 11, 1856.

3012. viii. WILLIAM CRISPIN, b. Oct. 26, 1854; d. unm., May 24, 1883.

3013.* ix. JAMES OTTO, b. June 16, 1857.

Mr. Sears removed with his father to Indiana in 1819, and now lives in Roysville, P. O. Ogden, Henry county, Ind.

1695.

WILSON SEARS⁷ [*Jas.⁶, Jas.⁵, Jas.⁴, Silas³, Silas², Rich.¹*], b. Ohio, Oct. 6, 1815 ; d. Greenfield, Ind., July 10, 1845; m. Roysville, Ind., May 22, 1838, *Louiza Rebecca Tripp*, dau. of Gideon D. and Eve. T., she b. Switzerland, Ind., Dec. 8, 1820; now lives in Indianapolis, Ind. Children :

3014. i. ANN ELIZA, b. Mar. 17, 1839; m. May, 1857, *William Fisk* of Patriot, Ind., who d. 1873; 2d, Oct. 8, 1876, *N. B. Arnold*, and lives in Topeka, Kans.; children, FISK : [1.] Ada May, m. 1877–78, John L. Paine of Topeka, and has 3 children. [2.] Son, d. inf.

3015. ii. OSCAR WILSON, b. Ogden, Ind., Mar. 12, 1841; is a chemist in Indianapolis, Ind.; unm.

3016. iii. JAMES IVON, b. Sep. 13, 1843; "died wearing the blue," on Missionary Ridge, Nov. 25, 1863.

1696.

GEORGE WASHINGTON SEARS⁷ [*Jas.⁶, Jas.⁵, Jas.⁴, Silas³, Silas², Rich.¹*], b. near Hillsboro, Ohio, May 18, 1820 ; m. Roysville, Ind., May 4, 1840, *Catharine Graham*, she b. West Alexandria, Ohio, Aug. 22, 1822. Children:

3017. i. HENRY WILSON, b. Henry co., Ind., Jan. 11, 1841; d. Nov. 20, 1845.

3018.* ii. JOHN A., b. Rush co., Ind., Apr. 27, 1843.

3019. iii. LOUISA R., b. Rush co., Sep. 7, 1845; m. Lapell, Ind., Oct. 4, 1866, *D. E Studley*, and d. Apr. 20, 1880; children, STUDLEY : [1.] Ulysses C., b. July 1, 1867. [2.] Catharine A., b. Dec. 21, 1868. [3.] Orrie S., b. Aug. 22, 1871. [4.] Earl. [5.] Hiram, b. Mar. 5, 1876. [6.] Datus E., b. June 2, 1878.

3020. iv. ELIZABETH E., b. Rush co., Dec. 10, 1848 ; m. Fisherburg, Feb. 2, 1879, *Thomas Cook*, and lives in Lapell, Ind.

3021. v. WILLIAM A., b. Madison co., Ind., Dec. 24, 1851 ; m. Pendleton, Ind., Nov. 30, 1876, *Arminta Povey*, and lives there.

3022.* vi. THEOPHILUS M., b. Mad. co., Mar. 12, 1854.
3023.*vii. JAMES W., b. Mad. co., Mar. 3, 1857.
3024. viii. ALBERT, b. Mad. co., May 5, 1860; lives in Lapell, Ind.
3025. ix. MARY C., b. Mad. co., Nov. 1, 1862; d. Jan. 7, 1870.

Is a farmer.

1702.

GEORGE BELDEN SEARS[7] [*Jas.*[6], *Comfort*[5], *Jas.*[4], *Silas*[3], *Silas*[2], *Rich.*[1]], b. Millplain, Ct., June 25, 1809; d. Newark, N. J., Nov. 17, 1877; m. Sep. 15, 1829, *Marinda B. Rockwell*, she b. Ridgefield, Ct., Jan. 12, 1813; d. s. p., and he m. 2d, Mar. 28, 1832, *Mary Jane Northrop*, dau. of James N., (and sister of Francis B. N.,) she b. South East, N. Y., July 18, 1813.   Children:

By *Mary Jane*:
3026. i. AUGUSTA M., b. Ridge., Aug. 29, 1834; m. Newark, N. J., Sep. 7, 1853, *James J. Dickerson*, he b. Petersburg, N. J., Nov. 25, 1829, is a wholesale leather dealer in N. Y. city, and lives Newark, N. J.; child, DICKERSON: [1.] James Sears, b. Aug. 6, 1854; d. Feb. 26, 1876.
3027. ii. ANN O., b. Ridge., Nov. 7, 1836; d. Aug. 31, 1841.
3028. iii. ANNA A., b. Hopewell, N. Y., Sep. 7, 1842; m. Newark, N. J., Mar. 18, 1863, Rev. *Charles T. Berry*, pastor of Presb. Ch., Caldwell, N. J., he b. Dover, N. J., Mar. 18, 1837; she d. Caldwell Jan. 2, 1880; children, BERRY: [1.] George T., b. May 20, 1865. [2.] Edward P., b. June 29, 1867. [3.] Laura W., b. Sep. 17, 1868; d. Feb. 1, 1869. [4.] Louise, b. Nov. 25, 1869.
3029. iv. MARY LOUISE, b. Sep. 7, 1851; m. Newark, N. J., Sep. 20, 1871, *James A. Coe*, a wholesale iron merchant in N. Y. city, he b. Newark, Feb. 2, 1846, and lives there; children, COE: [1.] Alice Louise, b. Nov. 7, 1872; d. Aug. 7, 1873. [2.] Laura M., b. May 29, 1874. [3.] James D., b. Dec. 29, 1875. [4.] Annie F., b. Dec. 29, 1875, *gemini*. [5.] Fred. Sears, b. Aug. 6, 1877. [6.] Helen A., b. Nov. 29, 1880. [7.] Rowland B., b. July 3, 1883.

Mr. Sears was born in Ridgefield, Ct., and educated in the district school except two terms, when he attended a select school for the study of Latin and the higher mathematics. At the age of fifteen he taught school winters, working upon his father's farm summers, but devoting all his spare time to study.

About 1837-38 he removed to Hopewell, N. Y., and was that year appointed instructor in Genesee Wesleyan School, Lima, N. Y. In March, 1850, he removed to Newark, N. J., to take a position in Newark Wesleyan Academy (now Newark Academy.) In Jan., 1855, he was elected Vice-Principal of the High School there, and in 1859 Superintendent of the Public Schools, and in 1860 Secretary of Board of Education, continuing in these offices till Sep., 1877, "having been, during eighteen years, as honest, faithful and devoted a servant as ever served the city of Newark."

Resigning these positions on account of ill-health, he died Nov. 17, 1877.

1703.

GOULD BOUGHTON SEARS[7] [$Jas.^6$, $Comfort^5$, $Jas.^4$, $Silas^3$, $Silas^2$, $Rich.^1$], b. near Millplain, Ct., Apr. 18, 1811 ; m. Reading, Ct., Oct. 21, 1834, *Betsy A. Sanford*, she b. there, Jan. 22, 1816. Children :

3030.* i. JAMES SANFORD, b. Reading, Ct., Oct. 16, 1836.
3031. ii. DE WITT CLINTON, b. Phelps, N. Y., Sep. 26, 1838; m. 1869, *Clara Van Gelder ;* was in 148th Regt., N. Y. Vol. Inf'y, from summer of 1864 until the close of the war. Is a farmer in Seneca Castle, N. Y.
3032. iii. ANNETTE ELIZA, b. Barre, N. Y., June 4, 1847 ; m. *Charles Van Gelder*, and removed to Quincy, Mich.; has 3 children.

Is a farmer at Seneca Castle, Ontario co., N. Y.

1706.

CLARKE CROSBY SEARS[7] [$Jas.^6$, $Comfort^5$, $Jas.^4$, $Silas^3$, $Silas^2$, $Rich.^1$], b. Millplain, Ct., Oct. 23, 1827 ; m. Orleans, N. Y., Apr. 10, 1851, *Harriet E Warner*, dau. of John and Susan W., she b. Phelps, N. Y., Sep. 13, 1832. Children :

3033.* i. CHARLES SUMNER, b. Seneca, N. Y., Nov. 1, 1853.
3034. ii. FLORENCE MINNIE, b. Clifton Springs, N. Y., Dec. 10, 1855; m. Quincy, Mich., Oct. 18, 1876, *Miles D. Campbell*, a lawyer of that place ; has no children.

3035. iii. Helen D., b. Seneca Castle, N. Y., Dec. 18, 1859 ;
m. Quincy, Mich., June 20, 1883, *Sereno R. Mansell* of
Coldwater, Mich. ; child, Mansell : [1.] Ruth, b. Aug.
6, 1884.
3036. iv. George W., b. Quincy, Mich., Nov. 6, 1863.

Is a farmer at Quincy, Branch county, Mich.

1707.

HERMAN BARNUM SEARS[7] [*Jos.[6], Comfort[5], Jas.[4],
Silas[3], Silas[2], Rich.[1]*], b. South East, N. Y., Nov. 11, 1815 ;
m. Paterson, N. Y., Jan. 1, 1840, *Almira Raymond*, dau. of
John and Betsy (Pickett) R. of Norwalk, Ct., she b. Dutchess
co., N. Y., Oct. 8, 1819. (See *ante*, No. 126.)   Children :
3037.   i. Mary Augusta, b. N. Y. city, Nov. 21, 1840 ; m.
there, Sep. 6, 1871, *John Chester Williams* of Pittsfield, Mass., and lives in Toledo, Ohio ; children, Williams : [1.] Mabel, b. Dec. 16, 1872. [2.] Chester, b.
1877.
3038.   ii. Joseph Raymond, b. N. Y. city, Jan. 26, 1847 ; is
an assayer, and lives in Mohave co., Arizona ; unm.
3039.* iii. Charles Elmore, b. N. Y. city, Jan. 2, 1850.
3040. iv. Carrie Judson, b. N. Y. city, Nov. 5, 1856 ; m.
Oakland, Cal., July 24, 1883, *Theodore J. Fish*, and
lives there ; child, Fish : [1.] Florence M., b. July 15,
1884 ; d. Jan. 29, 1885.
3041.   v. Herman Bourchier, b. N. Y. city, Sep. 6, 1860 ;
lives in Oakland, Cal.

Mr. Sears removed to New York in 1831 ; was a jeweler
and later an assayer, and in 1873, removed to Oakland, Cal.,
where he now lives.

1709.

JACOB BRUSH SEARS[7] [*Jos.[6], Comfort[5], Jas.[4], Silas[3],
Silas[2], Rich.[1]*], b. South East, N. Y., Apr. 9, 1823 ; m. Danbury, Ct., Feb. 4, 1846, *Harriet Northrop*, she b. So. East,
Jan. 24, 1824.   Children :
3042. i. Mary Elizabeth, b. Dan., Mar. 30, 1847 ; m. Vineland, N. J., about 1865, *Robert McMahan*, and rem. to
Troy, N. Y. ; children, McMahan : [1.] Child, d. inf.
[2.] Harriet, b. ab't 1868.   [3.] Sarah, b. ab't 1870.
[4.] Robert, b. ab't 1877.   [5.] Howard, b. ab't 1881.

3043. ii. EMMA FRANCIS, b. Dan., Jan. 5, 1852 ; d. Vineland, Sep. 8, 1874.

Is a carpenter in Vineland, N. J.

1710.

ALONZO ELMORE SEARS[7] [*Jos.*[6], *Comfort*[5], *Jas.*[4], *Silas*[3], *Silas*[2], *Rich.*[1]], b. South East, N. Y., Oct. 3, 1825; d. N. Y. city, July 30, 1862 ; m. North Salem, N. Y., June 23, 1853, *Susan A. Smith*, she b. there, Mar. 10, 1829. Children :

3044. i. MARIAN JOSEPHINE, b. N. Y. city, Feb. 17, 1857 ; m. there, Nov. 28, 1881, *Charles F. Patterson*, he b. Jersey City, Jan. 23, 1854 ; lives there; child, PATTER-SON : [1.] Harold Forman, b. Jan. 17, 1883.

3045. ii. GERTRUDE CAMILLA, b. N. Y. city ; m. there, July 17, 1879, *Wm. Crosby Renwick*, he b. there, May 30, 1845 ; lives in Owego, N. Y., and has a son, b. June 21, 1883.

3046. iii. EDWARD ARTHUR, b. N. Y. city, Aug. 4, 1860 ; d. Dec. 9, 1861.

Was a manufacturing jeweler in New York.

1714.

Hon. THEODORE CROSBY SEARS[7] [*Lewis*[6], *Comfort*[5], *Jas.*[4], *Silas*[3], *Silas*[2], *Rich.*[1]], b. Danbury, Ct., Aug. 4, 1828 ; m. there, Oct. 27, 1851, *Elizabeth Hoyt*, dau. of Starr and Sally Maria H., she b. there, Aug. 8, 1829; d. Elmira, N. Y., Jan. 5, 1886. Children :

3047.* i. THEODORE HOYT, b. Dan., Apr. 1, 1853.

3048. ii. LOUIS STARR, b. Cleveland, Ohio, May 27, 1855.

3049. iii. AUGUSTA HOWARD, b. Dan., Nov. 30, 1861.

3050. iv. ELIZABETH HOYT, b. New York, Nov. 19, 1864 ; d. Dan., Sep. 6, 1866.

3051. v. ALLISON RIDDELL, b. Ottawa, Kan., Sep. 17, 1869.

Mr. Sears was educated at the public school in his native village and at the Academy in Danbury ; entered Amherst College 1848. Failing health compelled him to leave before graduating, but the college gave him his degree in course.

He studied law at Albany, N. Y., and after graduating was admitted to the bar, and practiced there 3 years, at Cleveland a short time, and afterward in New York city till 1864, when

he removed to Kansas.   President Lincoln appointed him Provost Marshal of the Southern District, which office he held until
the close of the war.   Was State Senator for 2 years from 1870.
In 1872 he was appointed Attorney-General for the Missouri,
Kansas and Texas railroad, which position he held till 1881,
when the railroad was sold to another company.   He then went
to New York for a short time, and thence to Washington Ter.,
and is now employed as counsel for the North Pacific railroad,
and resides in Tacoma.

1716.

FRANCIS AUGUSTUS SEARS[7] [*Lewis[6]*, *Comfort[5]*, *Jas.[4]*,
Silas[3], *Silas[2]*, *Rich.[1]*], b. Danbury, Ct., Sep. 18, 1833 ; m. Sep.
15, 1857, *Roxcellana Parish*, dau. of Isaac P. of Canandaigua,
N. Y., she b. Apr. 5, 1838 ; d. Buffalo, N. Y., Sep. 6, 1867, æ.
29 ; 2d, *Agnes Dubois* of B., who d. s. p.; 3d, Buffalo, Feb.
24, 1885, Mrs. —— *Fargo*, widow of Jerome F., who d. Feb.,
1887.   Children :

By *Roxcellana :*
3052.* i. STEPHEN PARISH, b. Buff., Sep. 20, 1860 ; m. Aug.
          17, 1887, *Bessie Watson Fargo*, his step-sister, and lives
          in Tacoma, Wash. Ter., has [1.] Jerome Fargo, b. May
          31, 1889.
3053. ii. ALFRED DAW, b. Buff., Nov. 21, 1863.
3054. iii. LEWIS FRANK, b. Buff., Oct. 26, 1865 ; lives in Ta-
          coma, W. T.
3055. iv. SARAH CROSBY, b. Buff., June 16, 1867 ; d. Mar. 7,
          1875.

Mr. Sears was in the grain business in Buffalo, N. Y., making barley and malt a specialty ; was President of Common
Council several terms, and Police Commissioner.   He removed
to Tacoma, Wash. Ter., in July, 1887.

1721.

JOHN AUGUSTUS SEARS[7] [*John[6]*, *Geo.[5]*, *Seth[4]*, *Rich.[3]*,
Silas[2], *Rich.[1]*], b. Danvers, Mass.; m. June, 1836, *Nettie
Madeline Kent*, she b. Boston ; d. Dan., Dec., 18—, æ. 37.
Children :
3056. i. MADELINE.
3057.* ii. JOHN HENRY, b. Dan., June 18, 1843.

3058. iii. ROBERT, d.
3059. iv. KATE.
3060. v. ROBERT KENT, of firm Sawyer, Eaton & Sears,
Danvers.

Is a farmer in Danvers, Mass.

1726.

RICHARD SEARS[7] [*Jasper*[6], *John*[5], *John*[4], *Rich.*[3], *Silas*[2],
Rich.[1]], b. West Bloomfield, N. Y., Apr. 24, 1800; d. Montclair, N. J., May 29, 1870, æ. 70; m. Dayton, Ohio, June 9, 1834, *Sophia Stone*, she b. Walpole, N. H., Mar. 20, 1808; dau. of David and Hannah (Bellows) S. Children:
3061. i. RICHARD STONE, b. Buffalo, N. Y., May 29, 1840; d. Feb. 28, 1848.
3062. ii. MARIE LOUISE, b. Buff., Apr. 14, 1842; d. Feb. 22, 1848.
3063. iii. SOPHIA STONE, b. Buff., Mar. 7, 1847; m. Montclair, N. J., June 1, 1870, *Fred. Augustus Brantigan*, and lives there; children, BRANTIGAN: [1.] Edith Gertrude, b. Apr. 2, 1871. [2.] Fred Willard, b. Oct. 30, 1877.
3064. iv. WILLIAM HENRY, b. Buff., June 14, 1849; m. Oct., 1884, —— ——; is a stationer in N. Y. city, and lives in Montclair.
3065. v. MARY TUDOR, b. Brooklyn, N. Y., Jan. 19, 1851; d. Aug. 22, 1857.

Mr. Sears was born Apr. 24, 1800; (or May 29, by another account.)

When but a boy, he obtained a clerkship in a dry goods store; removed in 1818 to Sandusky, Ohio, and commenced business on his own account, dealing in furs and trading with the Indians.

In 1826, he moved to Buffalo, N. Y., and became interested in the forwarding business, owned two warehouses, and a number of steamers and sailing vessels plying on the lakes.

He was a strong advocate of temperance, and worked for the cause; he was the first owner to prohibit both the use and carrying of liquors on board of his boats.

He was also largely interested in mining, and at the age of 34 had accumulated what was then considered a large fortune.

55

He was one of the founders of St. John's Episcopal Church, in Buffalo.

In 1851, he retired from business, and removed to Brooklyn, N. Y., and thence, in 1857, to a farm near Paterson, N. J.

In 1867, he removed to Montclair, N. J., where he died in 1870.

1727.

JASPER PECK SEARS⁷ [*Jasper⁶*, *John⁵*, *John⁴*, *Rich.³*, *Silas²*, *Rich.¹*], b. West Bloomfield, N. Y., May 17, 1807; d. Denver, Col., Aug. 27, 1881; m. Marion, Ohio, 1830, Mrs. *Lydia (Holmes) Couch.* Children :

3066.   i. PARSONS, b. Ohio, Mar. 26, 1831; rem. with his father to Janesville, Wis., in 1839, and to Denver, Col., 1860; he rem. to Omaha, Neb., in fall of 1860, and enlisted in 2d Neb. Regt.; was in several battles and promoted to 1st Lt.; he contracted sickness in the army from which he died, Oct. 26, 1862, and was buried in Fremont Cemetery, St. Louis, Mo.; was unm.

3067.   ii. WILLIAM, b. Sep. 1, 1832; d. Sep. 7, 1834.

3068.* iii. JASPER PECK, b. Ohio, Jan. 3, 1835.

Mr. Sears removed to Lower Sandusky, Ohio, in 1826, and engaged in farming and mercantile pursuits until 1839, when he went to Janesville, Wis., continuing in same business. In 1860, he removed to Denver, Col., and in addition to his mercantile business traded largely with the Indians. In 1867, he took a stock of goods to Elizabethtown, New Mexico, but his health failing, he returned to Denver in 1871, where he continued to reside until his death in 1881.

1728.

ISRAEL PARSONS SEARS⁷ [*Jasper⁶*, *John⁵*, *John⁴*, *Rich.³*, *Silas²*, *Rich.¹*], b. West Bloomfield, N. Y., Aug. 6, 1810; d. Lancaster, N. Y., Feb. 9, 1873; m. there, *Alice Green.* Children :

3069.   i. EMILY MARTHA, b. Lanc., July 29, 1849; d. Nov. 12, 1850.

3070.* ii. EDWIN PARSONS, b. Lanc., Jan. 13, 1851.

3071. iii. EMILY JOANNA, b. Lanc., July 14, 1852; m. May 8, 1873, *Lyman Hubbell*, and rem. to Buffalo, N. Y.

3072. iv. IDA LOUISE, b. Lanc., July 14, 1856; m. Dec. 22, 1885, *Chas. Myron McLean*, and lives in Whitehall, Mich.

3073. v. MERCY HUNT, b. Lanc., May 13, 1858; lives in Buff.

Mr. Sears removed to Buffalo, N. Y., in 1827, and was in mercantile business there for about twenty years, removing thence about 1848 to Lancaster, N. Y.

1729.

LORENZO SEARS[7] [*Zach.*[6], *Roland*[5] *Zach.*[4], *Jos.*[3], *Silas*[2], *Rich.*[1]], b. Fabius, N. Y., Dec. 23, 1806; d. Danby, Mich., Nov. 15, 1863; m. Mar. 18, 1840, *Semantha E. King*. Children:

3074. i. MARY JANE, b. Danby, May 30, 1843; m. Nov. 29, 1860, *James Brown*, a farmer in Sebena, Mich.

3075. ii. MILDRED E., b. Danby, Apr. 23, 1845; m. Jan. 1, 1863, *Chas. H. Halliday* of Sebena.

3076. iii. WILMOT H., b. Danby, Apr. 5, 1848; m. Oct. 12, 1871, *Anna Halliday* of Sebena.

3077. iv. AMANDA, b. Danby, Feb. 9, 1852; m. Sep. 11, 1870, *Jasper Bidwell*, a farmer in Danby.

3078. v. BURTON, b. Danby, Jan. 25, 1862; m. Dec. 15, 1885, *Nellie Smith*, and is a farmer in Sebena.

Was a farmer in Danby, Ionia co., Mich.

1730.

ORANGE S. SEARS[7] [*Zach.*[6], *Roland*[5], *Zach.*[4], *Jos.*[3], *Silas*[2], *Rich.*[1]], b. Fabius, N. Y., Feb. 3, 1811; d. Apr. 11, 1842; m. Green Oak, Mich., 1836, *Elvira Tancrey*, she b. Otsego co., N. Y., Oct. 4, 1814–15, (who m. 2d, *Warren C. Sears*, No. 1731.) Children:

3079. i. EDSON C., b. Green Oak, Feb. 13, 1838; m. Brighton, Mich., Apr. 17, 1879, *Susanna E. Holderness*, she b. Lincolnshire, Eng., Oct. 10, 1832; and lives in Hartland, post-office Milford, Mich.

3080. ii. LOUISA E., b. Green Oak, Mar. 11, 1841; m. Brighton, Mich., Dec. 16, 1862, *Orson Tancrey*, he b. Gr. O., Mar. 11, 184— (?), and lives in Hamburg, Mich.

1731.

WARREN C. SEARS[7] [*Zach.*[6], *Roland*[5], *Zach.*[4], *Jos.*[3], *Silas*[2], *Rich.*[1]], b. Fabius, N. Y., Dec. 20, 1812; m. Mar. 19, 1853, *Elvira (Tancrey) Sears* (widow of Orange S.,) who d. July 17, 1878. Child:

3081.   i. PITT, b. Brighton, Mich., Feb. 3, 1854; m. Dec. 11, 1878, *Ada Traverse*, and is a farmer in B.

Mr. Sears removed with his father, who was a farmer, to Ann Arbor, Mich., in 1829; worked for him several years, and at the age of 21, commenced as a carpenter.

In Feb., 1845, he moved to the township of Brighton, Mich., purchased about 200 acres of land, and built a log-house, which is still standing, 12 years later building the house which he now occupies. When he settled in Brighton, the country was yet new, and no improvements had been made on the land which he bought. Deer, wild turkeys and wolves abounded.

He carried his wheat to Detroit, and sold it for 50 cents a bushel, making the trip with his yoke of oxen. At present he cultivates about 100 acres.

1734.

LYSANDER SEARS[7] [*Zach.*[6], *Roland*[5], *Zach.*[4], *Jos.*[3], *Silas*[2], *Rich.*[1]], b. Fabius, N. Y., July 21, 1822; d. May 20, 1881; m. Ann Arbor, Mich., May 19, 1852, *Julia Conover*, who d. Jan. 30, 1856; 2d, Lyons, Mich., Oct. 14, 1862, *Cornelia A. Mead* of that place, who now lives in Rose Center, Mich. Children:

By *Cornelia :*
3082.   i. ORANGE ALMOIN, b. Sep. 4, 1863.
3083.   ii. CHARLES LUTHER, b. Dec. 29, 1864.
3084.   iii. AMOS ULYSSES, b. Oct. 2, 1866.
3085.   iv. CLARA ALVINA, b. Dec. 16, 1870.
3086.   v. EMMA MAY, b. Apr. 25, 1874.
3087.   vi. OTTO CURTICE, b. Jan. 12, 1877.

Mr. Sears was a farmer in Brighton, Livingston co., Mich.

1742.

PETER SEARS[7] [*Peter*[6], *Roland*[5], *Zach.*[4], *Jos.*[3], *Silas*[2], *Rich.*[1]], b. Ashfield, Mass., June 3, 1811; m. Salem, Mich.,

May 25, 1843, *Mary E. Hoisington*, she b. Penfield, N. Y., Apr. 8, 1823. Children:

3088. i. ALONZO E., b. Ann Arbor, Mich., Feb. 2, 1845 ; m. Feb. 26, 1867, *Rowena Strobridge* of Allegany co., N .Y.

3089. ii. ESTHER C., b. Ann A., July 14, 1847 ; m. Charlotte, Mich., July 21, 1866, *Francis Gordon Griffin ;* children, GRIFFIN : [1.] Nettie, b. June 19, 1868. [2.] Clarissa, b. Mar. 26, 1870. [3.] George, b. Oct. 24, 1873.

3090. iii. MILLARD F., b. Ann A., July 24, 1850.

3091. iv. EDNA A., b. Ann A., Nov. 7, 1859; m. Nov. 7, 1878, *Charles Mourer* of Carmel, Mich. ; children, MOURER : [1.] Eunice M., b. July 31, 1879. [2.] Millie Rose, b. Oct., 5, 1881.

Mr. Sears lives in Carlisle, Eaton co., Mich.

1744.

SOLOMON FULLER SEARS[7] [*Peter[6], Roland[5], Zach.[4], Jos.[3], Silas[2], Rich.[1]*], b. Ashfield, Mass., June 22, 1816 ; m. Tecumseh, Mich., Dec. 24, 1845, *Olive Dickinson Fisher*, she b. Charlemont, Mass., Oct. 18, 1820 ; d. Northfield, Mich., abt. 1874; 2d, Ann Arbor, Mich., Aug. 25, 1875, Mrs. *Phebe L. Robinson*, she b. Hartland, N. Y., Jan. 29, 1832. Children : By *Olive :*

3092. i. LUCY ELIZABETH, b. Northfield, Apr. 5, 1847; m. Dec. 3, 1873, Dr. *Lee McFarland.*

3093. ii. DWIGHT BRAINARD, b. Northfield, Nov. 12, 1852; lives Ann Arbor.

3094. iii. HENRY LEWIS, b. Northfield, July 14, 1855 ; lives Ann Arbor.

Mr. Sears lives on the homestead taken up in 1826, by his father, from the government. He has many old family papers and letters.

1745.

SAMUEL D. SEARS[7] [*Peter[6], Roland[5], Zach.[4], Jos.[3], Silas[2], Rich.[1]*], b. Ashfield, Mass., Oct. 9, 1818; d. Michigan City, Ind., Mar. 18, 1855; m. *Hannah Rhodes*, who d. Child :

3095. i. EMMA.

1747.

GEORGE SEARS[7] [*Peter*[6], *Roland*[5], *Zach.*[4], *Jos.*[3], *Silas*[2], *Rich.*[1]], b. Charlemont, Mass., Mar. 13, 1824; m. —— ——.
Children :
3096. i. GEORGE.
3097. ii. GRACE.

Mr. Sears lives in Leadville, Col.

1751.

SILAS C. SEARS[7] [*Roland*[6], *Roland*[5], *Zach.*[4], *Jos.*[3], *Silas*[2], *Rich.*[1]], b. Dec. 20, 1815 ; d. Hannibal, N. Y., Mar. 1, 1859; m. Jan. 31, 1842, *Phebe Clark*, who d. Oct. 11, 1845 ; 2d, Oct. 28, 1848, *Elenor E. Keeney*, she b. Apr. 1, 1826, (m. 2d, —— *Lawrence*.)   Children :
By *Phebe:*
3098. i. ELLEN, b. Jan. 22, 1844; d. Feb. 23.
3099. ii. ORRIE ANN, b. May 6, 1845 ; m. 1871, *E. R. Barrus*, and d. May 13, 1875 ; children, BARRUS : [1.] Frank, b. July, 1872. [2.] Charles, b. July, 1874.
By *Elenor:*
3100. iii. ALICE, b. Sep. 4, 1850 ; m. May 31, 1869, *G. M. Ward*, a farmer, and lives in Volney, N. Y.; child, WARD : [1.] Charles Sears, b. Mar. 9, 1875.
3101. iv. FRANK SILAS, b. Sep. 7, 1854; m. Oct. 17, 1879, *Nellie Harris*, and is a wagon builder in Fulton, N. Y.
3102. v. SILAS C., b. July 26, 1859; d. Feb. 8, 1860.

Was a farmer.

1755.

WARREN J. SEARS[7] [*Roland*[6], *Roland*[5], *Zach.*[4], *Jos.*[3], *Silas*[2], *Rich.*[1]], b. Clay, N. Y., Jan. 14, 1836 ; m. Geddes, N. Y., Feb. 17, 1858, *Eunice Caykendall*, she b. there, Mar. 22, 1834.   Children :
3103. i. ELLA R., b. Mar. 17, 1859; m. Feb. 2, 1882, *Grove Hamlin*, and lives in Euclid, N. Y.
3104. ii. CLARA A., b. Apr. 16, 1867 ; lives in Liverpool, N. Y.
3105. iii. GERTIE M., b. Nov. 16, 1870.

Lives in Liverpool, Onondaga co., N. Y., address Clay P. O.

1757.

Gen. CLAUDIUS WISTAR SEARS[7] [*Thos.*[6], *Roland*[5], *Zach.*[4], *Jos.*[3], *Silas*[2], *Rich.*[1]], b. Peru, Mass., Nov. 8, 1817 ; m. Houston, Texas, Aug. 6, 1853, *Susan Alice Gray*, she b. Fredericksburg, Va., June 12, 1835. Children :

3106.　i. CLAUDE GRAY, b. Chelsea, Mich., July 16, 1855 ; d. Holly Springs, Miss., Apr. 16, 1861.

3107.　ii. ALICE GRAY, b. New Orleans, La., May 2, 1857.

3108.　iii. KATE SAMPSON, b. New O., Aug. 24, 1858 ; d. Holly Sp'gs, Mar. 30, 1861.

3109.　iv. FRANKLIN, b. New O., Nov. 3, 1859 ; d. Holly Sp'gs, Mar. 29, 1861.

3110.　v. WILLIAM GRAY, b. Holly Sp'gs, June 9, 1861 ; is a lawyer in Houston, Tex.

3111.　vi. GEORGE FAIRFAX, b. Shocco Springs, No. Car., Apr. 30, 1863 ; is in City Bank, Houston, Tex.

3112.　vii. PETER GRAY, b. Oxford, Miss., Oct. 11, 1866 ; was in Senior Class, Univ. Miss., 1884.

3113.　viii. THOMAS COURTNEY, b. Oxford, Dec. 14, 1867 ; in Freshman Class, Univ. Miss., 1884.

3114.　ix. EDWARD ABERNETHY, b. Oxford, June 26, 1870.

Mr. Sears graduated West Point Military Academy, in class of 1841 ; 2d Lt., 8th Regt., U. S. Inf. ; was in Florida war till October, 1842 ; resigned ; Prof. University Louisiana, at New Orleans till 1860 ; in Confederate Army as Colonel and Brigadier-General from 1861 to 1865 ; lost a leg at battle of Nashville, December 15, 1864 ; Prof. Mathematics in University of Mississippi, at Oxford, Miss., since 1865. Address P. O. University, Mississippi.

1768.

BARZILLAI SEARS[7] [*Zach.*[6], *Jos.*[5], *Zach.*[4], *Jos.*[3], *Silas*[2], *Rich.*[1]], b. East Dennis, Mass., Nov. 22, 1822 ; d. there, May 23, 1881 ; m. Brewster, Mass., Nov. 6, 1845, by Rev. Jas. L. Stone, to *Elizabeth J. Bangs*, dau. of Elkanah and Sally B., she b. 1826. Children :

3115.　i. BETSY OLIVIA, b. E. Den., Feb. 18, 1847 ; m. there, Aug. 11, 1867, *Paul Freeman Sears*, No. 2602.

3116.　ii. ISADORE M., b. E. Den., Dec. 11, 1849 ; d. Apr. 17, 1851.

3117. iii. ISADORE M., b. E. Den., Oct. 4, 1851; m. Nov. 12, 1872, *Augustus C. Snow* of Harwich.

3118. iv. HENRY BANGS, b. E. Den., Apr. 17, 1855; d. July 27, 1856.

3119. v. SARAH E., b. E. Den., Nov. 29, 1857; m. Harwich, Dec. 10, 1878, *Walter B. Ingraham* of Prov., R. I.; child, INGRAHAM: [1.] Walter S., b. Sep. 25, 1881.

Was a carpenter.

1769.

BENJAMIN SEARS[7] [*Zach.*[6], *Jos.*[5], *Zach.*[4], *Jos.*[3], *Silas*[2], *Rich.*[1]], b. East Dennis, Mass., Oct. 27, 1826; m. Dec. 12, 1850, *Mehitable Hedge*, dau. of John and Nabby (Sears) H. of E. Den., she b. Aug. 22, 1830; d. Worcester, Mass., æ. 39. Children :

3120. i. ISAAC H., b. E. Den., Sep. 12, 1852; d. Worcester, 1872.

3121. ii. SUSAN H., b. E. Den. Oct. 24, 1854; m. Dec. 9, 1879, *Alpheus Howes*, he b. there, May 30, 1854; lives in Harwich, Mass.; child, HOWES: [1.] Olive Sears, b. Mar. 23, 1881.

3122. iii. BENJAMIN LEE, b. E. Den., Apr. 8, 1860; m. New York city, June 20, 1882, *Maggie Lockwood*, she b. Williamsburg, N. Y., Jan. 13, 1862; is a telegraph operator in Rochester, N. Y.

3123. iv. CARLTON PARKE, b. E. Den., May 10, 1868.

Is a tinner in East Dennis, Mass.

1777.

Capt. CHARLES ZEBINA HARRIS SEARS[7] [*Zebina*[6], *Jos.*[5], *Zach.*[4], *Jos.*[3], *Silas*[2], *Rich.*[1]], b. Boston, Mass., May 11, 1813; drowned Nov. 3, 1883; m. South Edgecomb, Me., July 20, 1843, *Mary Ann Williams*, she b. there, Sep. 16, 1821; d. May 20, 1882. Children :

3124. i. CHARLES ARNOLD, b. Boston; served during the Rebellion for 3 years, and was at the capture of New Orleans; died.

3125. ii. ALFRED FRANCIS, b. Charlestown, Mass., Aug. 2, 1846; m. Cambridge, Mass., Dec. 5, 1883, *Sarah Ellen Chittick*, she b. there, Sep. 16, 1860; and lives there.

3126. iii. ELLEN AUGUSTA, b. Newcastle, Me.; lives in Cambridge.

Mr. Sears was a Boston pilot, served in U. S. Navy for 2 years during the Rebellion, and received injuries by the recoil of a gun from which he suffered much in late years, and for which he drew a pension. Was member G. A. R. Post 56.

He was Foreman of Torrent No. 16, located in Purchase st., and afterward of Hook and Ladder No. 2, located in High st., and was a great favorite of Chief Engineers Amory and Barnicoat; was a daring fireman, and when Hollis Street Church steeple was set on fire by lightning, distinguished himself and risked his life in extinguishing the fire.

He was drowned by falling from a yacht in Boston harbor, Nov. 3, 1883, being unable, owing to his crippled condition, to save himself.

1779.

JOSEPH HENRY SEARS⁷ [*Zebina⁶, Jos.⁵, Zach.⁴, Jos.³, Silas², Rich.¹*], b. Boston, Mass., Mar. 13, 1821; m. there, July 27, 1848, by Rev. Baron Stow, to *Eliza Taylor Hook*, she b. there, July 20, 1822; d. there, Aug. 13, 1855; 2d, Mar. 13, 1856, *Rosa Fanny Carney*, she b. Chapel Hill, Lowell, Mass. Children:

By *Eliza:*

3127. i. WILLIAM HENRY, b. Boston, Nov. 5, 1850; lives in Amesbury, Mass.

3128. ii. JOSEPH WARE, b. Boston, July 14, 1855; d. Nov. 17, 1873.

By *Rosa:*

3129. iii. GEORGE WASHINGTON WARREN, b. Jersey City, Apr. 23, 1858; m. Arlington, Mass., Jan. 12, 1887, *Margaret L. Fowle*, dau. of S. A. F. of A., and is head salesman with Coburn & Whitman, Boston.

3130. iv. MARY ELIZABETH, b. Beaufort, S. C., Apr. 7, 1862; is a member of Boston Museum stock company.

3131. v. HENRY CARNEY, b. Roxbury, Mass., July 17, 1864; d. Aug. 5.

3132. vi. FRANK CARNEY, b. West Newton, Mass., Apr. 12, 1863; lives Boston.

Mr. Sears was born in Washington place, Fort Hill, Boston,

56

and was formerly of firm Sears, Johnson & Putnam, whole-sale clothiers, Boston.

In the fall of 1862, he went as government agent in charge of the stores in S. S. "Vanderbilt," and was at the taking of Port Royal, S. C., Nov. 7, 1862. Was shortly after appointed Postmaster for the Army of the South, and South Atlantic squadron.

In March, 1863, and until 1866, he published and edited the "New South," paper, files of which are preserved in the library of Har. Coll.

He is now a commercial traveler for Coburn & Whitman, 73 Summer street, Boston.

Family tradition says he derives from "King" Isaac Sears, in which case it is probably through his mother.

Col. Sears had a dau., Hester, who m. a Smith, connected with the Lloyd family of Boston, and Mr. Sears' mother, Eliz'h *Lloyd* Dexter, perhaps derived through that line.

1780.

Maj. ALFRED FRANCIS SEARS[7] [*Zebina*[6], *Jos.*[5], *Zach.*[4], *Jos.*[3], *Silas*[2], *Rich.*[1]], b. Boston, Mass., Nov. 10, 1826; m. Bridgewater, Mass., Jan. 29, 1850, *Augusta Bassett*, she b. there, May 17, 1825; is a descendant from one of the original "Proprietors" of Bridgewater. Children:

3133. i. AUGUSTA FRANCIS, b. Dec. 18, 1850; d. Jan. 4, 1852.
3134.* ii. ALFRED FRANCIS, b. Concord, N. C., Sep. 4, 1852.
3135. iii. MARY LIZZIE, b. Mar. 22, 1856; d. Oct. 16, 1865.

Is a civil engineer, and connected with Metropolitan Rail-way Co., Portland, Oregon.

" The Peruvian government has decreed an immense conces-sion to our fellow-citizen, Major Alfred F. Sears, and it has been confirmed with great unanimity by the Congress. This concession is to build an irrigation work in the department of Piura, the most northern of that republic, and carries with it the right to 750,000 acres of public lands. The water rents are made obligatory on the people of the district, and are se-cured by their crops.

" The studies and location of this work were made by Major Sears in 1874 and 1875, and the grant is the result of a three years' struggle on his part and that of his friends. Important American and English houses have already offered to raise the capital. The English house is known in this country as bankers and cotton brokers. The concern has a house in Piura, which is a cotton-producing district. The work embraces a dam eighty feet high and 4,000 feet long, by which is formed an artificial lake eighteen miles long and three miles wide. This lake will be navigable and feed navigable canals to a point near the coast." [Oregonian, Nov., 1889.] "It is now an open secret that Maj. Sears is the author of 'THE LOST INCA,' a dazzling tale of adventure in a Peruvian wonderland, containing graphic and accurate descriptions of natural scenery in Peru, fauna and flora, atmospheric phenomena and quaint folk legends."

1787.

HENRY SEARS[7] [*Jos.*[6], *Jos.*[5], *Zach.*[4], *Jos.*[3], *Silas*[2], *Rich.*[1]], b. near Fayette, Mo., Nov. 24, 1825; m. Missouri City, Mo., Oct. 29, 1868, *Tabitha Williams*, she b. Monroe co., Tenn., Nov. 24, 1845, dau. of Benaiah and Nancy (Holloway) W. Children:

3136.   i. AUGUSTUS, b. near Excelsior Sp'gs, Mo., Aug. 16, 1869.
3137.   ii. MARTHA EMELINE, b. near Ex. Sp'gs, Dec. 2, 1870.
3138.   iii. CORA BELLE, b. near Kearney, Mo., July 28, 1872.
3139.   iv. FRANCIS MARION, b. near Kearney, Nov. 22, 1874.
3140.   v. MARGARET ANN, b. near Kearney, May 15, 1876.
3141.   vi. JAMES HENRY, b. near Ex. Sp'gs, Apr. 24, 1879.
3142.   vii. MARY ALICE, b. near Ex. Sp'gs, Mar. 19, 1881.

Mr. Sears lived with his uncle Peter in Kane co., Ill., in 1858–59; is now a farmer near Kearney, Clay co., Mo.

1794.

PETER R. SEARS[7] [*Jos.*[6], *Jos.*[5], *Zach.*[4], *Jos.*[3], *Silas*[2], *Rich.*[1]], b. Howard co., Mo., Jan. 2, 1841; m. Mar. 12, 1859, *Mary Alice Rover*, she b. Fayette co., Mo., June 27, 1847; d. Feb. 3, 1881. Children:

3143.   i. BENNETTA A., b. Glasgow, Mo., Aug. 16, 1861; grad. Pritchett Inst., 1880, and is a teacher in High School in G.
3144.   ii. WILLIAM J., b. Glas., Mar. 24, 1863; lives in Sedalia, Mo.
3145.   iii. JOHN A., b. Glas., Sep. 7, 1865; lives in Moberly, Mo.

3146. iv. Mary Alice, b. Glas., Feb. 20, 1868.
3147. v. Rebecca May, b. Glas., Oct. 4, 1871.
3148. vi. Squire A., b. Glas., July 18, 1873.
3149. vii. Eugene, b. Glas., Feb. 22, 1876.

Is a jeweler in Glasgow, Howard county, Mo.

1795.

JOHN T. SEARS[7] [*Jos.*[6], *Jos.*[5], *Zach.*[4], *Jos.*[3], *Silas*[2], *Rich.*[1]], b. Howard co., Mo., Sep. 18, 1843 ; m. Jefferson City, Mo., Nov. 17, 1869, *Bettie Boone*, she b. Howard cô., Mo., Nov. 17, 1846.   Children :
3150. i. Lucy, b. Jefferson City, May 8, 1875.
3151. ii. John T., b. Jeff. City, Aug. 22, 1877.

Is of firm Fleming & Sears, bankers, Jefferson City, Mo.

1798.

ROBERT C. SEARS[7] [*Jos.*[6], *Jos.*[5], *Zach.*[4], *Jos.*[3], *Silas*[2], *Rich.*[1]], b. Mo., Apr. 27, 1849 ; d. there, Sep. 18, 1882 ; m. *Sarah Smith*, who lives in Rolling Home, Randolph co., Mo. Child :
3152. i. Squire Archibald, b. Randolph co., Mo., ab't 1878.

1803.

Capt. JOSEPH BAINBRIDGE SEARS[7] [*Roland*[6], *Jos.*[5], *Zach.*[4], *Jos.*[3], *Silas*[2], *Rich.*[1]], b. East Dennis, Mass., Apr. 18, 1842 ; m. June 14, 1873, Mrs. *Martha A. Byam* of New York.   Child :
3153. i. Frederic Everett, b. June 12, 1881.

Mr. Sears commands a steamer in Line from N. Y. to Para, South America, and resides in Brooklyn, N. Y.

1805.

GEORGE FULTON SEARS[7] [*Roland*[6], *Jos.*[5], *Zach.*[4], *Jos.*[3], *Silas*[2], *Rich.*[1]], b. East Dennis, Mass., Feb. 20, 1847 ; m. May 2, 1872, *Clara Whiton*, she b. Boston, Aug. 13, 1854. Child :
3154. i. Louis Clifton, b. Boston, Jan. 26, 1873.

Is with Ellis Bros., wholesale dry-goods dealers, Boston.

1809.

MULFORD SEARS[7] [*Isaac*[6], *Steph.*[5], *Jos.*[4], *Jos.*[3], *Silas*[2], *Rich.*[1]], b. Yarmouth, Mass., Nov. 1, 1785 ; d. East Dennis, Aug. 4, 1827; m. (pub. Den., Aug. 31, 1811,) *Patty Crosby*, dau. of Barnabas C. of Den., (who m. 2d, —— ——, and 3d, *John Hopkins*.) Children :

3155. i. SOLOMON, b. Den., July 10, 1812 ; d. May 11, 1821.
3156.* ii. CALVIN, b. Den., Dec. 6, 1813.
3157.* iii. ISAIAH CROSBY, b. Den., Aug. 2, 1816.
3158. iv. MULFORD, b. Den., Sep. 7, 1818 ; d. May 10, 1821.
3159. v. BARNABAS, b. Den., Nov. 1, 1820 ; d. June 20, 1821.
3160. vi. MULFORD, b. Den., Mar. 26, 1823.

1811.

ELDREDGE SEARS[7] [*Isaac*[6], *Steph.*[5], *Jos.*[4], *Jos.*[3], *Silas*[2], *Rich.*[1]], b. Dennis, Mass., Sep. 25, 1790; d. there, July 9, 1875, æ. 84 yrs. 9 mos., gr.-st., Br.; m. Brewster, (pub. Feb. 24, 1815,) *Hannah C. Clark*, dau. of Enoch C., she b. there, Oct. 25, 1792 ; d. ; 2d, Jan. 8, 1855(?), *Ruth Ellis* of Yarmouth ; 3d, May 17, 1855(?), *Hannah Crowell* of Den., who d. Apr. 3, 1868, æ. 76, gr.-st., Br. ; 4th, June 26, 186-, *Betsy Howes* of Den. Children :

By *Hannah :*

3161.* i. ELDREDGE C., b. Den., Sep. 14, 1816.
3162. ii. SALLY, b. Den., Mar. 7, 1819 ; d. May 10, 1876.
3163. iii. JOSHUA, b. Den., Mar. 7, 1819, *gemini ;* d. Sep. 10, 1822.
3164.* iv. JOSHUA, b. Den., June 21, 1829.
3165. v. HANNAH C., b. Den., Apr. 23, 1832; d. Mar. 22, 1834.

" Child Eldred Sears, d. Oct., 1824." " Child Eldred Sears, d. Apr. 2, 1835."

1812.

Capt. DAVID SEARS[7] [*Larned*[6], *Steph.*[5], *Jos.*[4], *Jos.*[3], *Silas*[2], *Rich.*[1]], b. Dennis, Mass., Dec. 7, 1789 ; d. Brewster, Mass., Jan. 3, 1875, æ. 87 yrs. 27 days (?) ; m. *Betsy Wakefield*, who d. Nov. 20, 1848, in 51 yr., gr.-st., Br. Children :

3166. i. SUSANNAH WAKEFIELD, b. Br., June 9, 1828 ; m. there, Nov. 10, 1846, *Reuben Sears*, No. 1399.

3167. ii. BETSY A., b. Br., Oct., 1833; d. Nov. 30, 1833, æ. 6 wks., gr.-st., Br.

Capt. Sears was born in East Dennis. In early life he moved to Connecticut, but soon returned and bought the ancient residence of his grand-father in West Brewster, where he died. He formerly commanded a vessel in the Labrador fisheries, but most of his days were spent in mechanical pursuits. He was an estimable citizen and bore a good, honest reputation.

1815.

LARNED B. SEARS[7] [*Larned*[6], *Steph.*[5], *Jos.*[4], *Jos.*[3], *Silas*[2], *Rich.*[1]], b. Dennis, Mass., Apr. 29, 1795; d. May 8, 1866; m. Oxford, Mass., *Hannah F. Rockwood.*   Children :

3168.* i. GEORGE W., b. Oxford, Mass., Dec. 2, 1821.
3169.* ii. CHARLES WILLIAM, b. Oxford, Mass., Aug. 25, 1823.
3170. iii. DELIA A.
3171. iv. EDWIN L., served under Banks in Red River Exp'n, and d. in service at N. Orleans ; m. —— ——, and had dau. May.
3172. v. FRANKLIN R.
3173.* vi. LORAN A., b. Webster, Mass., Feb. 11, 1832.
3174. vii. HANNAH A.
3175. viii. ELLEN J.
3176. ix. AUGUSTUS.
3177. x. HENRY A., served under Banks in Red River Exp'n, and discharged at end of war.

Was a comb-maker, lived in Oxford, Mass., in that part set off as Webster, in 1832.

1828.

LUTHER SEARS[7] [*Levi*[6], *Steph.*[5], *Jos.*[4], *Jos.*[3], *Silas*[2], *Rich.*[1]], b. ab't 1815; m. (pub. Dennis, Mass., Oct. 19, 1839,) *Margaret Rice* of Springfield, Mass., she b. ab't 1813. Children :

3178. i. LABAN A., b. Den., June 1, 1840 ; d. June 2.
3179.* ii. LUTHER A., b. Den., Jan. 30, 1843.
3180. iii. MARY F., b. Den., Sep. 8, 1844 ; m. *Nath'l Spindle,* and lives Milford, Mass.
3181. iv. LUCY J., b. Den., May 1, 1851 ; m. Harwich, Nov. 24, 1870, *Eben N. Howes* of West Chatham.
3182. v. GEORGE H., b. Den., Dec. 13, 1852 ; d. Sep. 22, 1855.

3183.* vi. LEVI L., b. Den., Sep. 5, 1854.
3184. vii. ABBIE W., b. Den., Apr. 22, 1859; m. Walter S. Chase of W. Den.

Lives in East Dennis.

1830.

JOSIAH F. SEARS⁷ [*Levi*⁶, *Steph.*⁵, *Jos.*⁴, *Jos.*³, *Silas*², *Rich.*¹], b. Dennis, Mass., Dec. 12, 1818; m. May 14, 1848, *Olive Gage*, she b. Jan. 21, 1818. Children:
3185. i. LABAN FOSTER, b. June 19, 1849–50.
3186.* ii. JOHN GAGE, b. Jan. 7, 1852.
3187. iii. *Son*, b. and d. Dec. 27, 1855.
3188. iv. *Son*, b. and d. June 5, 1860.

1833.

BARZILLAI SEARS⁷ [*Steph.*⁶, *Steph.*⁵, *Jos.*⁴, *Jos.*³, *Silas*², *Rich.*¹], b. Sandwich, Mass.; m. Plymouth, Mass., July 24, 1825, *Patty Ellis*, dau. of Francis and Joanna (Briggs) E., she b. 1801. Child:
3189. i. BARZILLAI W.

Lived in Sandwich, Mass.

1834.

STEPHEN SEARS⁷ [*Steph.*⁶, *Steph.*⁵, *Jos.*⁴, *Jos.*³, *Silas*², *Rich.*¹], b. Sandwich, Mass.; m. —— ——. Child:
3190. i. STEPHEN A.

1842.

Rev. FRANKLIN SEARS⁷ [*Jos.*⁶, *Steph.*⁵, *Jos.*⁴, *Jos.*³, *Silas*², *Rich.*¹], b. Brewster, Mass., Aug. 8, 1808; d. Harwich, Mass., May 22, 1875; m. there, Aug. 2, 1832, *Lucy S. Smith* of Har.; 2d, Har., May 20, 1849, *Ruth Ryder*, she b. there, Jan. 28, 1816; d. Harwichport, June 15, 1888. Children:
By *Lucy*:
3191. i. LUCY A., b. Dennis, Dec. 13, 1833; m. Har., Nov 1, 1853, *Franklin S. Parlow*.
3192. ii. LORING, b. Den., Dec. 14, 1835.
3193. iii. SAMUEL S., b. Den., Jan. 28, 1838.
3194. iv. FRANKLIN, b. Har.

By *Ruth :*

3195. v. ADELAIDE F., b. Har., Mar. 29, 1851; m. there, Dec. 14, 1876, *James F. Eldredge,* and d. Orleans, Mass., 1879, æ. 28.

Was a Methodist minister.

1844.

FREDERIC SEARS[7] [*Jos.*[6], *Steph.*[5], *Jos.*[4], *Jos.*[3], *Silas*[2], *Rich.*[1]], b. Brewster, Mass., June 30, 1812; d. Fall River, Mass., July 13, 1880; m. Br., Nov. 26, 1835, *Alcy Reed Baker,* dau. of Obadiah and Nabby B., she b. Yarmouth, Mass., Sep. 22, 1814; lives in Fall River. Children:

3196. i. FREDERIC BAKER, b. F. R., Feb. 22, 1837; d. Jan. 2, 1841.

3197. ii. ALCY REED, b. F. R., May 30, 1839; d. Apr. 24, 1864.

3198. iii. FREDERIC BAKER, b. F. R., Nov. 22, 1841; grad. Phillips Acad., Andover, 1859; Brown Univ., 1863; after at Harvard Law School; adm. Suff. Bar, Feb. 17, 1865; practised law in New York city, and d. Jan. 9, 1871.

3199. iv. LUZETTA AMELIA, b. F. R., Feb. 7, 1844; d. May 10, 1845.

3200. v. LUZETTA AMELIA, b. F. R., Apr. 13, 1846; m. Aug. 3, 1865, *Wm. H. H. Young;* 2d, June 22, 1875, *Wm. H. Swift;* child, YOUNG: [1.] Elsie R. E., b. Sep. 23, 1866.

1845.

JOSEPH ELLERY SEARS[7] [*Jos.*[6], *Steph.*[5], *Jos.*[4], *Jos.*[3], *Silas*[2], *Rich.*[1]], b. Brewster, Mass., Sep. 14, 1814; d. Taunton, Mass., Jan. 20, 1878, æ. 63; m. Harwich, Mass., Apr. 7, 1844, *Eunice Howard Nickerson,* she b. there, July 3, 1821. Children:

3201.* i. LORING, b. West Br., Jan. 16, 1845.

3202. ii. ELISHA BEARSE, b W. Br., July 7, 1846; m. Boston, July 7, 1868, *Martha E. Parsons;* is a fur dealer in Boston.

3203.* iii. JOSEPH EMERY, b. Br., Apr. 4, 1848.

3204. iv. ELLA FLORIN, b. Br., Jan. 25, 1850; d. June 17, 1867.

3205.   v. MARY ELIZABETH, b. Br., Apr. 25, 1852; m. So. Har., Apr. 15, 1879, *Henry Beecher Nickerson*, and lives there.

3206.   vi. ALICE MARY, b. Br., Aug. 24, 1854; m. So. Har., Oct. 17, 1879, *Jas. Munroe Lasselle* of Maine, who d. Nov. 25, 1881; she lives in So. Har.

3207.   vii. BENJAMIN FRANKLIN, b. Br., Apr. 15, 1858; m. Cotuit, Mass., Jan. 12, 1881, *Stella Lucinda Nickerson*, she b. there, Mar. 30, 1857; is of firm Sears Bros., dry-goods and groceries, So. Har.

3208.   viii. WILLIAM FREDERIC, b. Br., June 19, 1862; m. Nov. 24, 1887, *Minnie Harward;* is of firm Sears Bros., So. Har.

1849.

GEORGE SEARS[7] [*Wash.*[6], *Steph.*[5], *Jos.*[4], *Jos.*[3], *Silas*[2], *Rich.*[1]], b. Brewster, Mass., Oct. 2, 1808; m. Boston, Sep. 26, 1841, by Rev. Thos. Driver, to *Abby T. Gale*.   Child:

3209.   i. GEORGE.

1850.

WILLIAM SEARS[7] [*Wash.*[6], *Steph.*[5], *Jos.*[4], *Jos.*[3], *Silas*[2], *Rich.*[1]], b. Brewster, Mass., Sep. 6, 1810; m. —— ——. Children:

3210.   i. HENRY.

3211.   ii. THADDEUS.

1862.

ALPHEUS FREEMAN SEARS[7] [*Roland*[6], *Freeman*[5], *Roland*[4], *Jos.*[3], *Silas*[2], *Rich.*[1]], b. Greenwich, Mass., May 7, 1808; d. Dec. 3, 1844, æ. 36; m. New Salem, Mass., Dec. 18, 1833, *Myrtha A. Andrews*, dau. of Joseph and Anna (Haven) A., she b. there, July 3, 1810.   Children:

3212.   i. MARY JANE, b. New S., Aug. 22, 1836; m. there, Feb. 13, 1859, *George Burt*, he b. Barre, Mass.

3213.   ii. ALPHEUS F., b. New S., Mar. 1, 1840.

3214.* iii. CHARLES M., b. New S., Apr. 4, 1842.

1865.

CALVIN SEARS[7] [*Andrew*[6], *Freeman*[5], *Roland*[4], *Jos.*[3], *Silas*[2], *Rich.*[1]], b. Greenwich, Mass., Oct. 30, 1789; d. Hart.

57

ford, Ct., Oct., 1869, æ. 79 ; m. *Martha Chapman* (or *Chapin*) of Springfield, Mass., who d. Weathersfield, Ct.; 2d, *Relief Sears*, No. 1859, dau. of Roland S., she b. Greenwich, Mar., 1799; d. Hartford, Nov., 1877, æ. 78.   Children:

By *Martha :*

3215. i. Rachel F., m. *Samuel Holt* of Hartford ; child, Holt : [1.] Russell S.; lives in H.

3216. ii. Hezekiah K., m. Windsor, Ct., *Julia O. Halsey*, and d. Hartford, æ. 48.

By *Relief :*

3217. iii. Martha A., b. Nov. 10, 1832 ; grad. Hartford High School, 1849 ; m. Hartford, Nov., 1852, *Benj. Haskell*, he b. New Salem, Mass., Oct., 1828, of firm Haskell & Fowler, Atchison, Kans. ; child, Haskell : [1.] Kate L., b. Sep. 26, 1857 ; m. Sep., 1881, Chas. S. Osborn, he b. St. Louis, Mo., Sep. 6, 1850 ; lives in Atchison.

3218. iv. Calvin F. H., b. Hartford, Jan., 1835 ; m. there, *Eliza A. Johnson*, and lives there.

Kept a hotel in Hartford, Ct.

1868.

TURNER SEARS[7] [*Andrew*[6], *Freeman*[5], *Roland*[4], *Jos.*[3], *Silas*[2], *Rich.*[1]], b. Greenwich, Mass., Apr. 4, 1797; d. there, Sep. 14, 1860, æ. 63 ; m. Woodstock, Ct., Mar. 6, 1822, *Mary Eliza Marcy*, dau. of Asahel and Persis (Burley) M., she b. there, Mar. 9, 1801; d. Nov. 24, 1885.   Children:

3219.   i. Mary E., b. Greenwich, July 22, 1824 ; scalded to death, Feb. 12, 1826.

3220.   ii. Eliza Maria, b. Green., Dec. 10, 1825 ; m. Nov. 17, 1855, *Jas. F. Powers*, and d. Amboy, Ill., Apr. 9, 1860.

3221.* iii. Chauncy D., b. Green., June 4, 1828.

3222.   iv. Hattie F., b. Green., Feb. 2, 1830 ; m. Aug. 23, 1852, *Oliver Keith* of Prescott, Mass., a farmer, and lives in Lansing, Mich.

3223.   v. Caroline P., b. Green., July 19, 1832 ; m. May 20, 1856, *Oscar Clark*, a lumber dealer in No. Lansing, Mich.

3224.* vi. Warren Clark, b. Green., Aug. 1, 1834.

3225. vii. Myra A., b. Green., July 17, 1836 ; m. June 5, 1857, *Charles J. Matthews*, a cabinet maker, and lives in Bayswater, London, Eng.

3226. viii. Mary E., b. Green., Mar. 31, 1838 ; a music teacher; d. Amboy, Ill., May 8, 1863.

3227. ix. HENRY T., b. Green., Feb. 23, 1840; m. May 5, 1863, *Mary A. Parker;* was a farmer, and d. Amboy, Ill., Oct. 3, 1866; his widow returned to Greenwich.
3228.* x. LUCIUS E., b. Green., Mar. 22, 1842.
3229. xi. OPHELIA A., b. Green., May 8, 1844; m. Dec. 2, 1863, *Sylvester S. Cleveland,* a farmer, and lives in Athol, Mass.

Mr. Sears was a farmer, and a very worthy Christian man.

1872.

ANDREW HASKELL SEARS[7] [*Andrew[6], Freeman[5], Roland[4], Jos.[3], Silas[2], Rich.[1]*], b. Greenwich, Mass., Oct. 10, 1806; d. there, Aug. 28, 1854; m. there, Nov. 10, 1827, *Lucinda Bar Edson,* she b. there, 1807.; d. May 15, 1840; 2d, Oct. 20, 1842, *Philena Lyon,* she b. there, 1804; d. July 28, 1867. Children:
By *Lucinda:*
3230. i. VISONIA LUTHER, b. Green., 1829; d. May 22, 1840.
3231. ii. LUCINDA LYDIA, b. Green., Dec. 3, 1838; d. Nov. 10, 1858.
3232.* iii. OSCAR HASKELL, b. Green., Mar. 11, 1840.
By *Philena:*
3233. iv. VISONIA LUTHER, b. Green., Mar. 2, 1843; m. Nov. 20, 1860, *John C. Perry* of New Salem, Mass.; lives in Springfield, Mass.; children, PERRY: [1.] Lillian May, b. Aug. 2, 1862. [2.] William Edward, b. July 26, 1874.

Was a hotel-keeper in Greenwich, Mass.

1879.

ROWLAND SEARS[7] [*Barnabas[6], Barnabas[5], Roland[4], Jos.[3], Silas[2], Rich.[1]*], b. Scipio, N. Y., Mar. 24, 1816; m. Sep., 1837, *Sarah Freeman,* dau. of James and Sarah F., who d. Apr., 1841; 2d, Lockport, N. Y., Feb. 16, 1844, *Annis M. Orr,* she b. Batavia, N. Y., Jan., 1823; (a relative of the late Gov. Jas. Lawrence Orr, and cousin of the late Hon. Zach. Chandler of Mich.) Children:
By *Sarah:*
3234. i. FRANCES MARION, b. Lockport, N. Y., July 5, 1839; d. May 16, 1841.

By *Annis :*
3235. ii. Frances Isabel, b. Lock., May 12, 1849; d. Sep. 13, 1850.
3236. iii. Albert Rowland, b. Lock., Sep. 7, 1851; is a mechanical engineer; was employed by Holly Water-works Co., 1870; Asst. Eng'r Auburn Steam Co., 1878; Eng'r Milwaukee Steam Power Co., 1880; Eng'r Thorington Mining Co., 1882, and constructed Reduction Works at Santa Rita, U. S. Colombia; is now Asst. Gen'l Supt. N. Y., Lake Erie & Western R. R. Co.; office Jersey City, and residence 51 E. 20th street, N. Y. city.
3237. iv. Clara Eloise, b. Lock., May 6, 1854.
3238. v. Anna Florence, b. Lock., Aug. 20, 1860.
3239. vi. Lizzie Gertrude, b. Lock., Nov. 14, 1865.

Mr. Sears removed to Lockport, N. Y., in 1829, and was one of the first settlers there; was for many years a leading hardware merchant, and afterward identified with the development of manufacturing interests; was secretary of a large cutlery works, and also interested in banking.

1881.

SUMNER SEARS[7] [*Barnabas[6], Elisha[5], Roland[4], Jos.[3], Silas[2], Rich.[1]*], b. Barre, Mass., Feb. 9, 1804; d. May 18, 1877; m. there, Sep. 21, 1824, *Asenath Vokes.* Children:
3240.   i. Harriet, b. Barre, Oct. 16, 1825; m. *George Cutler*, and lives in B.
3241.   ii. Sarah Jones, b. Barre, Sep. 10, 1828; m. there, Nov. 24, 1854, *Hiram Hawes*, he b. there, Jan. 2, 1811; d. Mar. 7, 1879, æ. 68; children, Hawes: [1.] George Austin, b. Dec. 14, 1855. [2.] Ella Jane, b. Jan. 14, 1858; d. June 10, 1881. [3.] Flora Lizzie, b. Mar. 7, 1870.
3242. iii. Elizabeth, b. Barre; d. Sep. 6, 1863, æ. 30.
3243.   iv. Mary, b. Barre; m. John Stone, and d. Jan. 9, 1863, æ. 26.
3244.   v. Franklin, b. Barre; d. Jan. 12, 1864; æ. 24.
3245.   vi. Charles Edwin, b. Barre, 1844; d. Oct. 21, 1850, æ. 6.

1886.

BARNABAS SEARS[7] [*Barnabas[6], Elisha[5], Roland[4], Jos.[3], Silas[2], Rich.[1]*], b. Barre, Mass., Aug. 12, 1819; m. —— ——.
Child:
3246.   i. George, b. Barre, 1841; d. Aug. 31, 1843.

1889.

Rev. EDMUND WINSLOW SEARS[7] [*Franklin[6], Elisha[5], Roland[4], Jos.[3], Silas[2], Rich.[1]*], b. Groveland, N. Y., Oct. 9, 1821; m. Moscow, N. Y., June 21, 1842, by Rev. McDonald, to *Sophronia Reed Brush* of M., she b. Rochester, N. Y., June 27, 1824. Children:

3247.   i. ROBERT HENRY, b. Moscow, Oct. 28, 1843; was in U. S. army, and killed at Newtown, Va., Aug. 11, 1864; unm.

3248.   ii. MARTHA EMILY, b. M., Jan. 21, 1845; m. Goshen, Ind., May 18, 1871, *Thos. Mortimer Haviland*, he b. Ridgefield, Ct., Feb. 13, 1844, son of Jacob Thomas and Lucy Ann (Smith) H., and lives Kill Creek, Kans.; child, HAVILAND: [1.] Nelly Sears, b. Dec. 7, 1872; d. Jan. 18, 1874.

3249.   iii. AMELIA E., b. M., Jan. 5, 1847; m. Sturges, Mich., Dec. 24, 1868, *Eli M. Albright*, and lives Goshen, Ind.; children, ALBRIGHT: [1.] Estella Sears, b. July 8, 1872. [2.] Vaulleda White, b. Nov. 26, 1873; d. Oct. 22, 1874.

3250.   iv. FRANCES, b. M., Apr. 4, 1849; m. there, Oct. 15, 1873, *John W. Kellogg*, a teacher, and lives there; child, KELLOGG: [1.] Bessie, b. June 18, 1877.

3251.   v. ESTELLA K., b. M., July 28, 1852; m. Portage, N. Y., Oct. 3, 1875, *Frank M. Tilton*, and lives in M.; children, TILTON: [1.] Susan Alice, b. Feb. 25, 1877. [2.] Eveline, b. May 6, 1880. [3.] Laura, b. Dec. 2, 1884.

3252.* vi. WILLIAM BRUSH, b. M., Feb. 17, 1856.

3253. vii. MARY E., b. M., Dec. 19, 1857; d. Apr. 26, 1860.

3254. viii. HATTIE BELLE, b. M., May 4, 1861; d. July 12, 1863.

3255.   ix. FLORA BURCHARD, b. M., Oct. 20, 1865.

Mr. Sears was a shoemaker by trade; he joined the Methodist Episcopal Church in 1840, and was licensed to preach in 1857, traveled 3 years under presiding elder, and was ordained by Bishop James in 1866. Has been Superintendent of Sunday School 36 years; since 1840 a teetotaler; was appointed Postmaster 1865; resides Moscow, N. Y.

1899.

BARNABAS SEARS[7] [*Steph.[6], Steph.[5], Barnabas[4], Jos.[3], Silas[2], Rich.[1]*], b. Dennis, Mass., July 30, 1790; d. South Yar-

mouth, Mass., July 17, 1875, æ. 85, and was buried in Quaker
Cem'y ; m. Yar., Dec. 12, 1815, *Hannah Crocker*, dau. of
Isaiah C., she b. there, Nov. 13, 1792; d. Jan. 7, 1879, æ. 86
yrs. 2 mos., gr.-st.   Children :

3256.   i. JOHN KELLY, b. So. Yar., Sep. 11, 1816 ; m. Nantucket, Mass., *Sarah Burdette ;* was Rep. 1861–62, and
is a lumber and hardware dealer in So. Yar.

3257.* ii. BARNABAS, b. So. Yar., Sep. 14, 1818.

3258.* iii. STEPHEN, b. So. Yar., July 15, 1822.

3259. iv. SETH, b. So. Yar., Sep. 27, 1825 ; d. July 17, 1847,
gr.-st., Q. Cem'y.

3260.   v. ELIZABETH, b. So. Yar., Nov. 18, 1828 ; m. Nov.
30, 1851, Dr. *John Stetson* of Abington, Mass., he b. 1815.

3261.* vi. DAVID, b. So. Yar., July 6, 1832.

1902.

ALMOND SEARS[7] [*Steph.*[6], *Steph.*[5], *Barnabas*[4], *Jos.*[3],
Silas[2], *Rich.*[1]], b. Dennis, Mass., May 1, 1798 ; d. Georgia,
Aug. 19, 1824 ; m. Den., Jan. 11, 1820, *Olive Seabury* of
Den.   Children :

3262.   i. ELVIRA G., b. Den., Dec. 2, 1820.

3263.   ii. SALLY, b. Den., Aug. 10, 1822 ; d. Oct. 9, 1869.

3264.   iii. OLIVE A., b. Den., Oct. 7, 1824.

The Probate Court made an allowance to Olive Sears, widow
of Almond S., Sep. 15, 1825.

1904.

STEPHEN SEARS[7] [*Steph.*[6], *Steph.*[5], *Barnabas*[4], *Jos.*[3],
Silas[2], *Rich.*[1]], b. Dennis, Mass., July 5, 1804 ; was lost on
Georges Bank, Oct. 3, 1841 ; m. Den., Nov. 17, 1831, *Lydia
Stone*, dau. of Job C. S., who d. Mar. 29, 1856.   Children :

3265.   i. LYDIA, b. Den., Oct. 14, 1832.

3266.   ii. JOHN C., b. Den., May 15, 1835 ; m. No. Yarmouth,
Me., Dec. 30, 1863, *Julia E. York*, dau. of Eliot Y.,
she b. there ; lives in Boston.

3267.   iii. SARAH E., b. Den., Apr. 8, 1841.

Lived in North Dennis.

1909.

HIRAM SEARS[7] [*John*[6], *Rich.*[5], *Silas*[4], *Jos.*[3], *Silas*[2], *Rich.*[1]], b. Hinesburg, Vt.; d. Washington co., N. Y.; m. *Sarah Adams*, who d. ab't 1884. Children:

3268. i. H. PETER, lives in Chicago, Ill.
3269. ii. MARTHA, m. —— *Hay*, who d.; she lives in South Bend, Ind.
3270. iii. GEORGE W., lives in Elgin, Ill.
3271. iv. ELIZABETH, m. —— *Knott*, and lives in Elgin.
3272. v. FRANCES, m. —— *Davenport*, and lives in Elgin.
3273. vi. MARY A., m. —— *Clarke*, and lives in Elgin.

Was a cordwainer.

1917.

HENRY LEE SEARS[7] [*John*[6], *Rich.*[5], *Silas*[4], *Jos.*[3], *Silas*[2], *Rich.*[1]], b. Hinesburg, Vt., Mar. 24, 1820; m. Monkton, Vt., Nov. 7, 1842, *Julia Fidelia Wheaton*, she b. there, Mar. 20, 1824; d. Aug. 24, 1872, æ. 48. Children:

3274.* i. CASSIUS CLAY, b. Monkton, Sep. 8, 1844.
3275. ii. CASPAR HENRY, b. M., Oct. 12, 1845; served 3 years in Co. C, 9th Regt., Vt. Vols., and d. June 19, 1865.
3276.* iii. FRED EUGENE, b. M., Sep. 15, 1850.
3277. iv. MARY JANE, b. M., Aug. 20, 1854; m. there, Aug. 31, 1886, *De Witt Thompson.*
3278. v. HARRY VIDITO, b. M., June 20, 1857; m. Bristol, Vt., Oct. 4, 1883, *Aurelia A. Finney*, she b. M., Oct. 4, 1858; he is a farmer and teacher.

Is a carpenter in Monkton, Vt.

1919.

RICHARD SEARS[7] [*Rich.*[6], *Rich.*[5], *Silas*[4], *Jos.*[3], *Silas*[2], *Rich.*[1]], b. Rome, N. Y., Aug. 21, 1801; d. Dundee, Ill., Jan. 27, 1852; m. Rome, Feb. 2, 1831, *Almira Howard* of R., she b. Oct. 8, 1809; d. near Dundee, June 14, 1848; 2d, Dundee, Jan. 20, 1852, Mrs. *Amy Fuller.* Children:
By *Almira:*
3279. i. CORDELIA M., b. Rome, N. Y., Feb. 11, 1832; m. Elgin, Ill., July 4, 1848, *Smith Tubbs*, removed to near

Dundee, Ill., and thence in 1856 to Rome, Wis., where he d. Jan. 28, 1865, bur. Crowder Cem'y ; was a farmer; his widow lives at Fort Atkinson, Iowa ; children, TUBBS : [1.] Martha Almira, b. Aug. 15, 1850 ; d. Nov. 18. [2.] Martha Ann, b. Oct. 6, 1851 ; m. July 21, 1869, Josiah Goddard, he b. Detroit, Mich., Mar. 22, 1829 ; d. Oct. 8, 1883 ; a farmer near Fort Atkinson, Iowa; had, i. Martha A., b. Jan. 26, 1871. ii. Granger J., b. June 22, 1873. iii. Charles, b. Nov. 26, 1876. [3.] Clara T., b. Sep. 25, 1854 ; d. Jan. 8, 1855. [4.] Lillian Adel, b. Jan. 1, 1856 ; m. Dec. 31, 1874, Wm. F. Bright, he b. Penn., Oct. 10, 1853 ; is a grocer in Rolfe, Iowa ; had, i. Henry F., b. June 10, 1878. [5.] Alice Cordelia, b. June 12, 1859 ; m. Sep. 4, 1878, Ferdinand C. Thomas, a farmer at Ft. Atkinson ; had, i. Harris F., b. Oct. 2, 1882. ii. Ralph, b. July 12, 1885. [6.] Herbert Ellis, b. Oct. 16, 1861 ; is a farmer at Fort A.

3280. ii. MARY CATHERINE, b. Camden, N. Y., July 25, 1834 ; m. Aug. 27, 1857, *Seth B. Tubbs*, bro. of Smith T., he b. Maple Flats, N. Y., Jan. 11, 1830; was in Mexican war, and U. S. Army from 1861 to 1862 ; removed to Marion, Kan., in 1870 ; is a carpenter; children, TUBBS : [1.] Lottie, b. June 3, 1858 ; a teacher ; m. Nov. 12, 1882, Edward R. Clark, he b. Wis., Dec. 12, 1857 ; is a farmer near Marion, Kan. ; had, i. Elsie, b. Jan. 20, 1886. [2.] Ida May, b. Oct. 15, 1860 ; m. Jas. H. Barker, a Canadian, and lives near Marion, Kan. ; had, i. Sam'l Edward, b. Nov. 21, 1879. ii. Mary Louise, b. Aug. 1, 1883. [3.] Fanny Fern, b. Sep. 14, 1863 ; a teacher ; m. Dec. 16, 1885, Ralph H. Hodge, he b. Minn., Nov. 2, 1861 ; a farmer near Marion, Kan. [4.] Vinnie Ream, b. Mar. 15, 1866 ; a teacher; m. June 18, 1885, Rev. Ezra A. Burkholder, a Canadian, he b. 1857 ; is in lumber trade in Hillsboro, Kan., and has, i. William Arthur, b. June 3, 1886. [5.] Nona Adell, b. Apr. 19, 1868 ; a teacher. [6.] Lillian, b. Mar. 18, 1873. [7.] Lois, b. May 20, 1877.

3281. iii. LOIS ANN, b. Camden, Oct. 29, 1836 ; d. near Dundee, Sep. 20, 1846.

3282.* iv. JOHN M., b. Reading, Mich., Mar. 9, 1839.

3283. v. DARIUS MARTIN, b. Reading, July 20, 1842 ; d. Apr. 3, 1843.

3284.* vi. HENRY BELA, b. Reading, Mar. 29' 1844.

3285. vii. GEORGE EVERNETT, b. near Dundee, Ill., May 23, 1848 ; was adopted by Arnold Locke, and took that name ; he lives near Winnecoma, Wis.

After living for a time in Camden, N. Y., Mr. Sears re-moved in fall of 1837 to Reading township, Hillsdale co., Mich., and later to Kane co., Ill., near Dundee, where his wife died in 1848. He then broke up housekeeping and went to Jefferson co., Wis., leaving his children in Illinois provided with good homes in different families. He was married in 1852 to Mrs. Amy Fuller, taken sick the same day, and died seven days after ; was a farmer.

1921.

Rev. SILAS SEARS[7] [*Rich.*[6], *Rich.*[5], *Silas*[4], *Jos.*[3], *Silas*[2], *Rich.*[1]], b. Rome, N. Y., Aug. 8, 1806; d. Rome, Wis., Aug. 20, 1859; m. Westmoreland, N. Y., Feb. 17, 1831, by Rev. Jas. Kelsey, to *Betsy M. Seelye*, dau. of Dan'l and Betsey (Doolittle) S., she b. there, Aug. 31, 1813; lives in Star, Wis. (Her bro. Reuben, b. June 19, 1811; m. Sabrina Sears, No. 1923.) Children :

3286.* i. LOWELL CLARK, b. Camden, N. Y., May 13, 1833.
3287. ii. REUBEN SEELYE, b. C., Apr. 24, 1835 ; d. Rome, Wis., Sep. 9, 1845.
3288. iii. DAVID SANFORD, b. Westmoreland, N. Y., Apr. 21, 1839 ; d. Genesee, Wis., Dec. 18, 1843.
3289. iv. RHODA ANN, b. Camden, Feb. 24, 1842 ; d. Gene-see, Wis., Dec. 17, 1843.
3290. v. GEORGE M. WEBSTER, b. Rome, Wis., Nov. 29, 1846; d. Star, Wis., May 31, 1868.

On the 22d Oct., 1843, Mr. Sears with his wife and four chil-dren removed from Camden, N. Y., to Rome, Jefferson co., Wis. They suffered greatly from the lateness and rigor of the season, and lost two children by small-pox. Settled in their new home they had a severe struggle to maintain themselves for the first two years, until they could get the ground cleared, and crops planted and harvested.

In 1858, at the request of her pastor, Mrs. Sears wrote a long and pathetic account of their trials and tribulations, which was read to the Sunday School in Rome, Wis., and which I much regret not having space to print here.

58

Mr. Sears was for many years an honored local preacher in the Methodist Church.

1925.

WALTER S. SEARS[7] [*Rich.*[6], *Rich.*[5], *Silas*[4], *Jos.*[3], *Silas*[2], *Rich.*[1]], b. Rome, N. Y., Oct. 19, 1823; m. Adrian, Mich., Nov. 13, 1856, *Sarah A. Mills*, she b. Macclesfield, Eng., May 6, 1833; came over in 1841. Children:

3291. i. WALTER E., b. Sep. 20, 1859; d. Oct. 20.
3292. ii. GEORGE A., b. Adrian, Nov. 28, 1862; clerk in freight office, Toledo, O.
3293. iii. MARY L., b. Oct. 7, 1868.

Mr. Sears lives in Adrian, Mich., and has been for many years connected with the railroad there.

Mr. S. has in his possession the powder-horn which was carried by his grand-father at the battle of Bunker Hill, June 17, 1775.

1927.

OSCAR SEARS[7] [*Orange*[6], *Rich.*[5], *Silas*[4], *Jos.*[3], *Silas*[2], *Rich.*[1]], b. Arlington, Vt., June 23, 1812; m. near Valley Falls, N. Y., July 4, 1836, *Mary Moore.* Children:

3294.* i. GEORGE W., b. Rensselaer co., N. Y., Mar. 31, 1838.
3295.* ii. JOHN HENRY, b. Rens. co., Oct. 13, 1839.
3296. iii. MARY ELIZABETH, b. N. Y. State; d. Nov. 22, 1841.
3297. iv. CHARLOTTE ANN, b. N. Y. State; d. Butler, N. Y., July 4, 1845.
3298.* v. WILLIAM O., b. Butler, N. Y., Nov. 22, 1845.
3299. vi. ANDREW J., b. near Wattsburg, Pa., June 7, 1848; m. *E'lla A. Chaffee*, a teacher; he is an intelligent physician and scholar; no children.
3300. vii. MARY ADELL, b. near Watts., Sep. 30, 1856; m. *Augustus J. Grant,* her half cousin, and lives near Lowville, Pa.

Mr. Sears lived for a time in West Butler, N. Y., removing in 1847, to Venango township, Pa., and now lives in vicinity of Lowville ; is a farmer.

1929.

HIRAM SEARS[7] [*Orange*[6], *Rich.*[5], *Silas*[4], *Jos.*[3], *Silas*[2], *Rich.*[1]], b. Valley Falls, N. Y., July 17, 1818; m. Jonesville,

N. Y., June 1, 1842, *Clara M. Davis*, dau. of Elijah and Mary D. Child:

3301. i. CARLIE C., b. West Butler, N. Y., Jan. 24, 1845; m. Shelbyville, Ill., Feb. 18, 1864, *H. W. Hibbard*, gen. freight agt., Vandalia R. R., and lives in St. Louis, Mo.; child, HIBBARD: [1.] May, b. Aug. 1, 1866.

Mr. Sears removed to Illinois in 1845, finally settling in Shelbyville, Shelby county. Is a millwright.

1933.

Dr. ALEXANDER SEARS⁷ [*Abner⁶, Rich.⁵, Silas⁴, Jos.³, Silas², Rich.¹*], b. near Cherry Valley, Otsego co., N. Y., Mar. 16, 1814; d. Marshall, Texas, Feb. 6, 1855; m. Texas, Dec. 15, 1847, *Vesta Cordelia Hawley*, she b. June 6, 1827; d. Marshall, Oct. 1, 1854. Children:

3302. i. VESTA CORDELIA, b. Marshall, Aug. 21, 1848; m. Feb. 15, 1882, *Edwin Vawters*, a native of Texas; child, VAUTERS: [1.] Addison Sears, b. May 15, 1884.
3303. ii. ADDISON HAWLEY, b. Marsh., Sep. 19, 1850; d. July 8, 1856.
3304. iii. MARY ELIZA, b. Marsh., Sep. 23, 1854; m. Apr. 18, 1876, *Charles H. Ray*, he b. Lewisburg, No. Car., Nov. 29, 1852; child, RAY: [1.] Child, b. and d. Feb. 6, 1882.

Dr. Sears removed with his parents to Yankeetown, Madison township, Fayette county, Ohio, in fall of 1818; studied medicine with Dr. Eleazar Martin of Bloomingburg, O.; removed to Leesburg, Ind., and thence to Naples, Ill., practising for a while at Meredocia, Ill.; graduated medicine, Louisville, Ky., and finally settled in Marshall, Texas, where he became eminent as a physician and surgeon.

1934.

WASHINGTON SEARS⁷ [*Abner⁶, Rich.⁵, Silas⁴, Jos.³, Silas², Rich.¹*], b. near Cherry Valley, Otsego co., N. Y., June 3, 1816; m. near Oxville, Ill., Nov. 7, 1841, *Elizabeth J. Morrison*. Children:

3305.* i. ALEXANDER, b. near Naples, Ill., Aug. 20, 1842.
3306. ii. CLARK, b. near Naples, Ill., Apr. 22, 1844; d. Sep. 23, 1845.

3307.   iii. MARY ANGELINE, b. near Naples, Ill., Aug. 29,
       1846 ; m. June 30, 1873, *Eden Moore*, he b. near Pike-
       ton, Ohio, July 12, 1847; is a farmer; children, MOORE :
       [1.] Newton, b. Feb. 21, 1874. [2.] Bessie E., b. Aug.
       1, 1875. [3.] Son, b. and d. July 4, 1877. [4.] Charles
       Augustus, b. Aug. 26, 1878. [5.] Queen, b. Mar. 19,
       1881. [6.] Dellie, b. Sep. 14, 1883.
3308.   iv. WELLINGTON, b. near Naples, Ill., Dec. 15, 1848;
       d. July 25, 1862.
3309.   v. AUGUSTUS W., b. near Naples, Ill., Dec. 16, 1851 ;
       d. Jan. 22, 1870.
3310.* vi. CHARLES WILLARD, b. near Naples, Ill., Dec. 1,
       1854.
3311.   vii. CYRUS, b. near Naples, Ill., Mar. 1, 1857; d.
       Mar. 15.
3312.   viii. CAROLINE, b. near Naples, Ill., Mar. 13, 1858; d.
       Mar. 13, 1864.
3313.   ix. FANNIE, b. near Naples, Ill., Feb. 6, 1861 ; d. Aug.
       24, 1871.
3314.   x. WILLIAM S., b. near Naples, Ill., Feb. 1, 1863 ; d.
       July 27, 1865.
3315.   xi. HARRY, b. near Naples, Ill., Dec. 17, 1865.
3316.   xii. HARVEY, b. near Naples, Ill., Apr. 26, 1869; d.
       Sep. 21, 1874.

Mr. Sears removed with his parents to Yankeetown, Madison township, Fayette county, Ohio, in fall of 1818, and to
vicinity of Naples, Ill., in fall of 1836, where he now lives on
the old homestead.

He is a wealthy and intelligent farmer, has been Justice of
the Peace many years, and is an honored member and officer
of the Methodist Church.

1936.

RICHARD VAN RENSELLAER SEARS[7] [*Abner*[6],
Rich.[5], *Silas*[4], *Jos.*[3], *Silas*[2], *Rich.*[1]], b. Yankeetown, Mad. tp.,
Fay. co., Ohio, Nov. 5, 1819 ; d. Oxville, Ill., Feb. 23, 1884 ;
m. there, Dec. 2, 1841, *Hannah Pike*, dau. of Daniel P., she
b. Exeter, Ill., Oct. 11, 1825 ; lives on the homestead. Children :

3317.   i. DANIEL ABNER, b. Oxville, Nov. 11, 1842 ; was in
       Co. I, 129th Regt., Ill. Vols., and d. Mitchellville, Tenn.,
       Dec. 9, 1862, from exposure with measles, and was
       buried there.

3318. ii. GENNETT, b. Oxville, May 5, 1844; m. Aug. 12, 1862, *Clayton Wills*, he b. Scott co., Ill., Nov. 1, 1840; served in Co. I, 129th Regt., Ill. Vols., during the war and settled as a blacksmith in Alsey, Scott co., Ill.; children, WILLS: [1.] Richard M., b. Aug. 19, 1865. [2.] Fannie G., b. Nov. 20, 1866. [3.] Vesta C., b. Oct. 4, 1868. [4.] Clayton, b. Oct. 3, 1870. [5.] Philander, b. Mar. 7, 1872. [6.] Christopher, b. June 7, 1874; d. Jan. 4, 1880. [7.] Lafayette, b. Mar. 17, 1876. [8.] Joseph H., b. Jan. 17, 1878.

3319. iii. GEORGE WASHINGTON, b. Oxville, Mar. 6, 1846; d. Mar. 7, 1847.

3320. iv. VESTA CORDELIA, b. near Naples, Mar. 7, 1848; d. Mar. 9, 1850.

3321. v. PHILANDER, b. near Naples, June 16, 1850; a farmer.

3322. vi. HIRAM, b. near Naples, Feb. 15, 1852; m. Oct. 2, 1879, *Anna Adella Patterson* of Chapin, Ill.; is a farmer; no children.

Mr. Sears removed with his parents in fall of 1836 to the vicinity of Naples, Ill., settling later at Oxville, Scott co., Ill., as a blacksmith; was of an inventive mind and congenial disposition; he subsequently became a farmer.

1938.

Rev. HIRAM SEARS[7] [*Abner*[6], *Rich.*[5], *Silas*[4], *Jos.*[3], *Silas*[2], *Rich.*[1]], b. Yankeetown, Mad. tp., Fay. co., Ohio, Apr. 10, 1825; m. Whitehall, Green co., Ill., May 25, 1851, *Mary Henderson Prentice*, dau. of Rev. Amos and Hope (Henderson) P., she b. there, July 30, 1832; (she is a niece of Rev. Dr. Wm. S. Prentice of the Ill. Conf., and a relative of Miss Dr. Clara A. Swain, the first lady physician sent out by the Mission Society of the Methodist Episcopal Church to India.) Children:

3323. i. EMILY JANE, b. Benton, Ill., Feb. 14, 1852; d. Sep. 13.

3324. ii. ROSA MARIA, b. near Fairfield, Ill., June 19, 1853; m. Carbondale, Ill., May 25, 1874, by Rev. Wm. Jesse Grant, to Hon. *Erastus N. Rhinehart* of Effingham, Ill., he b. Watson, Ill., Mar. 1, 1847; a lawyer; has been Mem. Leg., for a number of years; no children.

3325. iii. LIZZIE ANN, b. Sullivan, Ill., Sep. 21, 1855; d. unm., Carbondale, Ill., June 22, 1876.
3326. iv. WILLARD PRENTICE, b. near Godfrey P. O., Mad. co., Ill., Nov. 4, 1859; grad. in law McKendren College, 1883, and lives in St. Louis, Mo.
3327. v. CARRIE BELLE, b. Cairo, Ill., Mar. 4, 1866; d. Vandalia, Ill., Apr. 3, 1867.
3328. vi. NELLIE POWERS, b. Effingham, Ill., Nov. 24, 1870.

Mr. Sears emigrated with his parents to the vicinity of Naples, Ill., in the fall of 1836; attended the Illinois College at Jacksonville for some time, and graduated from McKendren College, Lebanon, Ill., in summer of 1849; he united with the Illinois Conference of the Methodist Episcopal Church at Jacksonville in fall of 1851, and by a division of that conference fell into the Southern Illinois Conference, of which he has been a member ever since.

He resided in Effingham, Ill., and since 1886 has been a traveling agent of the Western Seaman's Friend Society, address, Seaman's Bethel Home, Cleveland, Ohio.

Mr. Sears has for years taken much interest in the family history, and has collected much data regarding different branches in the North-west, which he has kindly placed at my disposal for this work.

1940.

Dr. ADDISON SEARS[7] [*Abner[6], Rich.[5], Silas[4], Jos.[3], Silas[2], Rich.[1]*], b. Yankeetown, Mad. tp., Fay co., Ohio, Jan. 1, 1830; m. Marion co., Texas, Feb. 27, 1861, *Adelaide Delphine Warner*, she b. Bradford co., Pa., Apr. 5, 1835. Children:
3329. i. MARY DELPHINE, b. Marshall, Texas, Dec. 25, 1861; d. unm.; a mem. of Cumberland Pres. Ch., a talented and devoted young Christian woman, and greatly lamented.
3330. ii. HARRIET ADDISON, b. Marsh., May 10, 1877.

Mr. Sears removed with his parents in fall of 1836 to the vicinity of Naples, Ill.; studied medicine with his brother, Dr. Alexander Sears, in Marshall, Texas; grad. Louisville, Ky., Mar. 3, 1853, and settled in M., where he has been successful as a physician and druggist.

He has been an honored elder in the Cumberland Presb. Ch. for many years, of which his wife is also a member.

1941.

CHARLES OLIVER SEARS[7] [*Barnabas[6], Barnabas[5], Silas[4], Jos.[3], Silas[2], Rich.[1]*], b. Hadley, Mass., Jan. 29, 1819 ; m. Amherst, Mass., Dec. 12, 1844, *Sophia Foster Ingram*, she b. there, Aug. 31, 1821; d. Dec., 1871; 2d, *Mary Edwards.* Children :

By *Sophia :*

3331.* i. EDWARD BRADFORD, b. New Salem, Mass., Oct. 6, 1845.

3332. ii. GEORGE HENRY, b. Amherst, Dec. 31, 1851; lives in Brattleboro, Vt.

3333. iii. ALLIE FLORENCE, b. A., Mar. 23, 1855 ; d. æ. 4.

3334. iv. FRED. FOSTER, b. A., July 14, 1862, and lives there.

3335. v. ANNIE, b. A.

By *Mary :*

3336. vi. WILLIAM GRAY, b. A., July 10, 1874.

Mr. Sears lives in Amherst, Mass.

1951.

WILLIAM SEARS[7] [*Holmes[6], Edw'd[5], Edw'd[4], Josiah[3], Silas[2], Rich.[1]*], b. Halifax, Mass., Sep. 4, 1796 ; d. there, Mar. 7, 1851; m. Hal., Feb. 2, 1822, *Hannah Richmond*, who d. Aug 31, 1822; 2d, Hal., Jan. 20, 1825, *Mary Hudson Ward*, she b. there, Jan. 17, 1804; d. Dec. 5, 1851. Children :

By *Mary :*

3337. i. WILLIAM HOLMES, b. Hal., Mar. 27, 1826 ; m. there, Nov. 29, 1849, *Caroline Allen ;* is a shoemaker in Brockton, Mass.

3338. ii. HENRY WARD, b. Hal., Apr. 29, 1829; m. No. Hanson, Mass., Jan. 2, 1876, *Josephine M. Luther*, and lives E. Bridgewater, Mass.

3339. iii. MARY MERCY, b. Hal., Apr. 8, 1831 ; m. there, Oct. 13, 1858, *Wm. Gallagher*, and lives in So. Boston.

3340. iv. EBENEZER WARD (perhaps *Eleazar* W.), b. Hal., Aug. 14, 1833 ; m. Plympton, Mass., Mar. 5, 1857, *Arabella T. Robbins*, dau. of Lewis and Betty T. (Backus) R., and lives in Brockton.

3341. v. HANNAH RICHMOND, b. Hal., Oct. 27, 1835 ; m. there, Oct. 18, 1857, *Benj. F. Washburn*, who d. May

17, 1865; she d. E. Bridgewater, Jan. 1, 1885; child,
WASHBURN: [1.] William S., lives E. Bridgewater.
3342. vi. AMANDA, b. Hal., Nov. 2, 1837; m. there, Nov. 8,
1857, *Augustus H. Soule*, and lives in E. Middleboro,
Mass.
3343. vii. ANDREW RICHMOND, b. Hal., Aug. 19, 1839; m.
Campello, Mass., Dec. 15, 1864, *Sarah R. Wild*, and
lives in Brockton.
3344. viii. LUCINDA, b. Hal., Mar. 21, 1842; m. there, Apr. 20,
1862, *Seramus Thompson*, and lives in Brockton.
3345.* ix. JOSIAH EDWARD, b. Hal., Aug. 17, 1844.

The will of Mary H. Sears of Halifax, Mass., dated Nov.
18, 1851, and allowed Jan. 26, 1852, names sons, William H.,
Andrew R., Josiah E., and ~~Eleazar W.~~, (? *Ebenezer*) and daus.
Mary M., Hannah R., Amanda and Lucinda.

1956.

NATHANIEL SEARS[7] [*Rufus[6], Nath'l[5], Sam'l[4], Josiah[3],
Silas[2], Rich.[1]*], b. Hawley, Mass., Aug. 3, 1796; m. Williamsburg, Mass., 1825, *Eliza Hubbard*, she b. there, Apr. 22, 1805;
d. Oct. 29, 1834; 2d, June 18, 1835, *Cordelia Morton*. Children:
By *Eliza:*
3346. i. ELIZA H., m. June 25, 1861, *Enos Parsons;* child,
PARSONS: [1.] Frank Sears, b. abt. 1863; student Med.
Coll., Boston, 1884.
By *Cordelia:*
3347.* ii. LORENZO, b. Apr. 18, 1838.

1960.

RUFUS SEARS[7] [*Rufus[6], Nath'l[5], Sam'l[4], Josiah[3], Silas[2],
Rich.[1]*], b. Hawley, Mass., Dec. 23, 1803; d. 1882; m. Dec. 4,
1825, *Elizabeth Ely*, she b. Middle Haddam, Ct.   Children:
3348.   i. HARRIET M., b. Portland, Ct., Nov. 23, 1826.
3349.   ii. ELIZA A., b. Port., July 20, 1828.
3350.*   iii. WILLIAM H., b. Port., Sep. 1, 1830.
3351.   iv. VIENNA C., b. Port., Aug. 31, 1832.
3351. *a.* v. MARY J., b. Port., July 4, 1834.
3351. *a.* vi. BENJAMIN F., b. Port., Jan. 8, 1837.
3351. *a.* vii. DELPHINE, b. Port., Aug. 4, 1839.
3351. *a.* viii. DANIEL F., b. Port., Oct. 28, 1841.

3351. *a.* ix. MARION H., b. Port., June 12, 1845.
3351. *a.* x. CHARLES A., b. Port., Feb. 20, 1849.

Mr. Sears removed to Portland, Ct.

1961.

ANTHONY SEARS[7] [*Rufus[6], Nath'l[5], Sam'l[4], Josiah[3], Silas[2], Rich.[1]*], b. Hawley, Mass., Aug. 18, 1805 ; d. there, Juiy 16, 1873, æ. 68 ; m. Haw., May 4, 1828, *Lovina Sprague*, dau. of Wm. and Rhoda S., she b. Sep. 26, 1808; d. Apr. 7, 1866. Children :

3352.   i. RUFUS, b. Haw., Mar. 15, 1829 ; d. Farmington, Ct., Dec. 27, 1850, and was buried in West Haw.
3353. ii. JANE M., b. Haw., Jan. 16, 1833 ; m. Joseph Vining, and d. young.
3354.* iii. LEWIS E., b. Haw., June 7, 1838.
3355.* iv. EDWIN W., b. Haw., 1847.

Mr. Sears lived in Fullerville, Hawley, Mass.

1964.

Dea. FREDERIC H. SEARS[7] [*Rufus[6], Nath'l[5], Sam'l[4], Josiah[3], Silas[2], Rich.[1]*], b. Hawley, Mass., June 25, 1811 ; m. there, Mar. 3, 1836, *Rebecca E. Sears*, No. 2159, dau. of Benj. and Rebecca (Eldredge) S., she b. Nov. 5, 1815.   Children:

3356.* i. HENRY F., b. Haw., Dec. 25, 1836.   •
3357. ii. MARY E., b. Haw., May 28, 1839 ; m. there, Jan. 1, 1867, *S. S. Morse*, a teacher.
3358. iii. FREEMAN B., b. Haw., May 10, 1842 ; m. *Caroline Harr,* and is engaged in the sewing machine business in Ohio.
3359. iv. HATTIE M., b. Haw., Apr. 15, 1850 ; d. Apr. 14, 1880 ; grad. Normal School, and taught in Somerville, Mass.
3360. v. AMELIA J., b. Haw., Oct. 7, 1852 ; grad. Westfield Normal School, with her sister, and is a teacher in Somerville, Mass.
3361. vi. CHARLES F., b. Haw., May 4, 1856 ; is a farmer, and lives on the old homestead in Haw.

Mr. Sears is a farmer, and lives on the old homestead in Hawley, Mass. ; is a Deacon, and prominent in town affairs ; Selectman, 1862–1871.

59

1965.

BENJAMIN F. SEARS[7] [*Rufus*[6], *Nath'l*[5], *Sam' l*[4], *Josiah*[3], *Silas*[2], *Rich.*[1]], b. Hawley, Mass., Mar. 15, 1813 ; d. Collinsville, Ct., 1880; m. *Emeline Kelley;* 2d, 1844, *Rosetta Hale,* who lives in Northampton, Mass. Children:

By *Rosetta :*
3362.* i. EDWARD HALE, b. 1846.
3363. ii. FRANK HOWARD, b. 1850.
3364. iii. JULIA E., b. 1856.
3365. iv. CHARLES HOWES, b. 1860.

Mr. Sears learned the blacksmith's trade, and became an expert in the art of tempering edge tools ; lived in Collinsville, Ct.

1967.

EARL SEARS[7] [*Earl*[6], *Zebedee*[5], *David*[4], *Josiah*[3], *Silas*[2], *Rich.*[1]], b. Middleboro, Mass., Dec. 2, 1796; d. Lakeville, Mass., Aug. 8, 1862, æ. 65 ; m. Freetown, Mass., Jan. 1, 1836, *Charity Winslow*, she b. there, Apr. 8, 1802. Children:
3366. i. EARL, b. Free., June 30, 1838 ; d. Lake., May 29, 1855.
3367. ii. JOHN WINSLOW, b. Midd., Dec. 26, 1839 ; d. Aug. 15, 1841.
3368.* iii. JOHN WINSLOW, b. Midd., Jan. 21, 1842.
3369. iv. ABNER JONES, b. Midd., Jan. 20, 1845 ; m. Lakeville, July 9, 1866, —— —— ; and d. there, Apr. 22, 1874 ; enlisted in 22d unattached Co., Mass. Vols., Aug. 18, 1864, and dischg'd exp. service, Nov. 24, 1864.

Was a farmer.

1968.

OLIVER LEONARD SEARS[7] [*Leonard*[6], *Zebedee*[5], *David*[4], *Josiah*[3], *Silas*[2], *Rich.*[1]], b. Middleboro, Mass., Mar. 1, 1795; d. Troy, N. Y., Mar. 28, 1844, æ. 49; m. there, Nov. 1, 1821, *Frances Field*, she b. there, 1795. Children :
3370.* i. LEONARD, b. June 23, 1823.
3371. ii. CALEB, b. Nov. 30, 1825 ; unm.
3372. iii. DANIEL, b. July 21, 1827; d. unm. 1854.
3373. iv. EMELINE, b. July 25, 1829 ; d. Oct. 1, 1830.

3374. v. EDWIN, b. Troy, Sep. 13, 1832; lived for a time in St. Johns, N. B., and is now with his sister in Brooklyn, N. Y.

3375. vi. ELIZA M., b. Mar. 28, 1835; m. June 4, 1856, —— Branshaw, and was divorced; child, BRANSHAW: [1.] Effie F., b. May 22, 1858; m. John Megaw, and d. Dec., 1884.

Settled in Troy, N. Y., when a young man.

1972.

ISAAC SEARS[7] [Peter[6], Peter[5], Jona.[4], Josiah[3], Silas[2], Rich.[1]], b. Boston, Mass., Aug. 9, 1806; d. So. Scituate, Mass., Feb. 5, 1863; m. there, 1828, *Sarah S. Sutton*, she b. there, 1810; d. Dec. 14, 1869, æ. 59.   Children:

3376.* i. JAMES ISAAC, b. So. S., June 29, 1829.

3377. ii. CAROLINE, b. So. S., Apr., 1831; d. Nov. 3, 1855.

3378. iii. GEORGE ALFRED, b. So. S., May, 1836; d. Sep. 17, 1856.

ʻ The will of Isaac Sears of South Scituate, Mass., dated Nov. 11, 1862, was proved Mar. 3, 1863, by wife Sarah, Exec'x, and names son, James, Jr., of South Scituate, and the will of Sarah Sears, widow, of South Scituate, dated June 3, 1869, and proved Jan. 18, 1870, mentions son, James, Jr., of South Scituate, and brother, Seth Sutton of Weymouth, Mass.

1977.

CLARK SEARS[8] [*Jona.[7], Jona.[6], Jona.[5], Jona.[4], Sam'l[3], Paul[2], Rich.[1]*], b. Ashfield, Mass., Jan. 30, 1804; d. West Hawley, Mass., Nov. 29, 1879; m. Ash., Nov. 27, 1828, *Emeline Kelley*, she b. there, Jan. 10, 1809; lives in West H. Children:

3379. i. CLARINDA, b. Ash., June 30, 1830; m. Adams, Mass., Mar. 22, 1851, *Wm. Waite*, and lives in West Haw.; no children.
3380. ii. STILLMAN, b. Tyringham, Mass., Apr. 6, 1832; d. Hawley, July 30, 1855.
3381. iii. BETSY, b. West Haw., July 19, 1833; m. Feb. 14, 1855, *Chas. Rice*, and d. Charlemont, Mass., Sep. 17, 1870; children, RICE: [1.] Alice. [2.] Addie.
3382. iv. EMELINE, b. West Haw., Feb. 12, 1835; m. Jan. 16, 1855, *Fred. Guilford*, and d. Ash., May 4, 1869; children, GUILFORD: [1.] Fred. [2.] Frank, *gemini*.
3383. v. PHILENA, b. West Haw., Mar. (or *Nov.*) 20, 1837; m. Shelburne, Mass., Nov. 28, 1854, *Alonzo F. Turner*, and d. Haw., Sep. 10, 1857; children, TURNER: [1.] Addie, b. Aug. 11, 1855. [2.] Stillman C., b. July 31, 1857.
3384. vi. HANNAH M., b. West Haw., June 22, 1839; m. there, May 18, 1860, *Benj. Wing*, and lives at Salt River, Mich.; children, WING: [1.] Walter. [2.] Wallace. [3.] Lizzie. [4.] Clara.
3385.* vii. AMBROSE, b. West Haw., Nov. 3, 1841.
3386. viii. WALTER, b. West Haw., Dec. 23, 1846; m. Buckland, Mass., May 18, 1881, *Anna King*, she b. Ash., May 4, 1857; is a farmer, and lives on the old homestead in West Hawley; was Selectman, 1875–76.

Mr. Sears removed about 1832 to West Hawley, Mass., and was a farmer and mill-owner. He was for many years prominent in town affairs, often chosen as Moderator of town meetings; was Selectman 10. years, and Representative to State Legislature, 1845, 1852 and 1869. Was on committee to build Town House, Apr. 3, 1848.

"Uncle Clark" was a plain-spoken, good-hearted man, and in every way worthy of confidence and esteem.

1979.

WILLIAM SEARS[8] [*Jona.*[7], *Jona.*[6], *Jona.*[5], *Jona.*[4], *Sam'l*[3], *Paul*[2], *Rich.*[1]], b. Ashfield, Mass., Mar. 28, 1808; d. Nov. 15, 1875, æ. 67; m. *Olive Eldredge.* Children:

3387. i. SARAH W., m. July 4, 1855, *Frank S. Howes,* and d.

3388. ii. LEWIS F., b. 1841; m. *Olive Blood,* who d. June 15, 1885, æ. 41; he lives in Ashfield, and has 2 children.

3389. iii. LEVI, b. 1848; d. Nov. 9, 1867.

1980.

FREEMAN SEARS[8] [*Jona.*[7], *Jona.*[6], *Jona.*[5], *Jona.*[4], *Sam'l*[3], *Paul*[2], *Rich.*[1]], b. Ashfield, Mass., Aug. 30, 1810; m. Goshen, Mass., Nov. 27, 1844, *Eunice Parsons,* she b. there, Mar. 18, 1813; d. Aug. 15, 1850; 2d, Buckland, Mass., May 28, 1851, Mrs. *Angeline Corey,* she b. there, July 2, 1820. Children:

By *Eunice:*

3390. i. ELLEN PHILENA, b. Ash., Dec. 21, 1835; d. Feb. 26, 1854.

3391. ii. MARY ELDREDGE, b. Goshen, Sep. 6, 1837; d. May 27, 1861.

3392. iii. OLIVE SOPHIA, b. G., Jan. 20, 1840; m. Ash., Prof. *Henry C. Howland,* and lives in Eau Claire, Wis.

3393.* iv. FREEMAN WILLIS, b. G., Aug. 21, 1842.

3394.* v. MILTON FOSTER, b. G., Mar. 20, 1845.

3395. vi. CHLOE EDNA, b. G., Nov. 13, 1847; lives in Eau Claire, Wis. Is Librarian of City Library.

By *Angeline:*

3396.*vii. FRANK GRAHAM, b. G., May 13, 1852.

3397. viii. GEORGE HERBERT, b. G., Apr. 16, 1854; d. July 22, 1884.

3398.   ix. JESSIE FREMONT, b. G., May 27, 1856; m. Hartford,
Ct., June 25, 1879, *Frank J. Davis*, he b. Willington,
Ct., Jan. 18, 1856; lives Boston road, Springfield, Mass.;
children, DAVIS: [1.] Roy S., b. June 29, 1881.
[2.] Hazel J., b. May 13, 1884.
3399.* x. CHARLES FREMONT, b. G., June 29, 1859.

Mr. Sears lives in Goshen, Mass., has been Assessor, and
Selectman, 14 years; 12 years Chairman of the Board, and has
held divers other offices of trust.

1982.

STILLMAN SEARS[8] [*Jona.*[7], *Jona.*[6], *Jona.*[5], *Jona.*[4],
Sam'l[3], *Paul*[2], *Rich.*[1]], b. Ashfield, Mass., Sep. 23, 1815; d.
Shelburne, Mass., Oct. 10, 1854; m. Ash., Sep. 27, 1842, *Abigail Eldredge*, who d. Nov. 20, 1854.   Children:
3400.   i. ISABELLA.
3401.   ii. HENRY G., lives in Holyoke, Mass.; is of firm Lemuel Sears & Co.

1983.

JONATHAN SEARS[8] [*Jona.*[7], *Jona.*[6], *Jona.*[5], *Jona.*[4],
Sam'l[3], *Paul*[2], *Rich.*[1]], b. Ashfield, Mass., Oct. 27, 1818; m.
Goshen, Mass., Mar. 20, 1845, *Rhoda Parsons*, who d. July
17, 1850, æ. 30; 2d, Hawley, Mass., May 28, 1851, *Mary
Sears*, No. 2161, dau. of Benj. and Rebecca (Eldredge) S. of
H., she b. there, Apr. 19, 1820.   Children:
3402.   i. JOHN MILTON, b. Ash., Dec. 12, 1854; grad. Mass.
Agri. Coll., 1876.
3403.   ii. FRED. STILLMAN, b. Ash., Oct. 3, 1856; d. Aug. 29,
1857.
3404.   iii. MARY ELLA, b. Ash., Sep. 23, 1858.
3405.   iv. CLARK BENJAMIN, b. Ash., Nov. 15, 1861.

1987.

Rev. OLIVER M. SEARS[8] [*Azarelah*[7], *Jona.*[6], *Jona.*[5],
Jona.[4], *Sam'l*[3], *Paul*[2], *Rich.*[1]], b. Ashfield, Mass., Nov. 29,
1817; d. Dalton, Mass., 1852, æ. 36; m. Dec. 15, 1847, *Maria
Williams*, who d. Westfield, Mass., Sep. 12, 1860.   Children:
3406.   i. SARAH ELDREDGE, b. Oct. 31, 1848; is a missionary
in Turkey.

3407. ii. ABBIE W., b. Aug. 12, 1850; d. May 31, 1852.
3408. iii. LUCY A., b. June 13, 1852; d. June 18, 1862.

Mr. Sears graduated Williams College, and was settled as minister in Dalton, Mass.

1989.

JOSEPH SEARS[8] [*Azarelah*[7], *Jona.*[6], *Jona.*[5], *Jona.*[4], *Sam'l*[3], *Paul*[2], *Rich.*[1]], b. Ashfield, Mass., June 4, 1820; m. Buckland, Mass., Nov. 27, 1849, *Catherine Williams.* Children:

3409. i. JOSEPH WARREN, b. Plainfield, Mass., Aug. 23, 1851; m. there, Mar. 15, 1876, *Julia F. Gurney*, she b. there, May 7, 1857.
3410. ii. S. HERBERT, b. Plain., Aug. 25, 1854.
3411. iii. MARY W., b. Plain., Nov. 24, 1857; m. Northampton, Mass., Feb. 27, 1884, *Wm. W. Parsons*, he b. there, Mar. 19, 1859, and lives in New Haven, Ct.

Mr. Sears lives in Plainfield, Mass.

1992.

WILLIAM HALE SEARS[8] [*Azarelah*[7], *Jona.*[6], *Jona.*[5], *Jona.*[4], *Sam'l*[3], *Paul*[2], *Rich.*[1]], b. Ashfield, Mass., Aug. 8, 1826; d. Dec. 29, 1862, æ. 36; m. *Louiza Eldredge.* Children:

3412. i. AZARELAH.
3413. ii. LOUISE E., b. May 2, 1857; m. Apr. 14, 1882, *W. B. Phelps*, and lives in Chenoa, Ill.

1994.

EDWIN SEARS[8] [*Azarelah*[7], *Jona.*[6], *Jona.*[5], *Jona.*[4], *Sam'l*[3], *Paul*[2], *Rich.*[1]]; b. Ashfield, Mass., Apr. 17, 1832; d. Northampton, Mass., May 20, 1883; m. June 20, 1863, *Laura (Edson) Selden.* Children:

3414. i. EDWIN EWING, b. May 9, 1866.
3415. ii. VINTON AZARELAH, b. Apr. 1, 1868.
3416. iii. HANNAH MAYNARD, b. Apr. 11, 1869.
3417. iv. ARTHUR ELDREDGE, b. Feb. 24, 1872.
3418. v. HERMAN DINGWELL, b. May 2, 1873.
3419. vi. FRED. BLISS, b. Sep. 2, 1876.
3420. vii. LILLIAN BLANCHE, b. Sep. 17, 1879.

2001.

ABRAHAM WINSLOW SEARS[8] [*Nathan*[7], *Jos.*[6], *Prince*[5], *Jona.*[4], *Sam'l*[3], *Paul*[2], *Rich.*[1]], b. Brewster, Mass., Feb. 14, 1835; m. Dorchester, Mass., Aug. 17, 1864, *Anna Atherton Clark*, dau. of Lot and Mary (Barnard) C. of Boston, she b. Roxbury, Mass., Jan. 0, 1842. Children:

3421.   i. HENRY DARRAH, b. Dorchester, Mar. 7, 1866.
3422. ii. MARY CLARK, b. Dor., Apr. 18, 1868.
3423. iii. NATHAN FREDERIC, b. Dubuque, Iowa, Oct. 13, 1870.

Is a wholesale dealer in boots and shoes, Dubuque, Iowa.

2003.

JOSEPH HENRY SEARS[8] [*Jos.*[7], *Jos.*[6], *Prince*[5], *Jona.*[4], *Sam'l*[3], *Paul*[2], *Rich.*[1]], b. Brewster, Mass., June 8, 1829; m. Jamaica Plain, Mass., May 26, 1858, *Emily Crosby Nickerson*, she b. South Boston, Mar. 26, 1834; d. Dorchester, Mass., Mar. 10, 1887, æ. 52. Children:

3424.   i. ALICE MAY, b. Brewster, May 10, 1859; m. Dorchester, Oct. 2, 1883, *Wm. B. Lawrence* of Medford, Mass.
3425. ii. EMILY NICKERSON, b. Br., June 26, 1862; m. Oct. 16, 1888, *Jas. King Hoyt.*
3426. iii. JOSEPH HAMBLEN, b. Dor., Apr. 10, 1865.

Mr. Sears is a shipping merchant in Boston, and lives in Dorchester.

2004.

ELISHA FREEMAN SEARS[8] [*Jos.*[7], *Jos.*[6], *Prince*[5], *Jona.*[4], *Sam'l*[3], *Paul*[2], *Rich.*[1]], b. Brewster, Mass., Mar. 28, 1831; m. *Bethia Mayo*, dau. of J. K. M., who d. at sea, Jan. 24' 1857; 2d, Charlestown, Mass., May 2' 1860, *Ellen Foster*, she b. Medford, Mass., Nov. 16, 1834. Child:

By *Ellen:*
3427. i. ANNIE FOSTER, b. Melrose, Mass., Apr. 14, 1863.

Resides in Jamaica Plain, Mass.

2010.

ISAAC HENRY SEARS[8] [*Isaac*[7], *Josh.*[6], *Josh.*[5], *Josh.*[4], *Sam'l*[3], *Paul*[2], *Rich.*[1]], b. Boston, Mass., Sep. 17, 1833; m.

Chelsea, Mass., Apr. 27, 1859, *Frances A. Todd*, she b. Boston, Aug. 26, 1837. Children :

3428. i. FRANK THOMAS, b. Chelsea, Aug. 27, 1861; d. Oct. 10, 1864.
3429. ii. GRACE BIGELOW, b. Ch., June 27, 1864; m. Longwood, Mass., June 27, 1889, Chas. Henry Mead.
3430. iii. ISAAC H., b. Brookline, Mass., Oct. 10, 1872; d. there, May 27, 1873.
3431. iv. ARTHUR WINTHROP, b. Br., Oct. 8, 1876; d. there, July 13, 1881.

Is of firm Sears & Bean, shoe manuf's goods, Boston, Mass.

2016.

ROBERT SEARS[8] [*Robt.[7], Thatcher[6], Nath'l[5], Josh.[4], Sam'l[3], Paul[2], Rich.[1]*], b. New York city, Dec. 7, 1841; m. St. Louis, Mo., Dec. 6, 1867, *Mary R. Mitchell*, dau. of George and Sarah S. M., she b. Spring Hill, Tenn., June 28, 1844. Children :

3432. i. HARRIET HOWARD, b. St. Louis, Feb. 14, 1869; d. May 17.
3433. ii. FREDERIC HOWARD, b. St. Louis, May 1, 1870.
3434. iii. GEORGE MITCHELL, b. Springfield, Mo., Apr. 21, 1872.
3435. iv. SELIM, b. Toronto, Can., Apr. 26, 1874.
3436. v. WINTHROP, b. T., Apr. 28, 1876.
3437. vi. MIRIAM, b. T., July 26, 1879.
3438. vii. GRACIE, b. Kingston, Can., July 25, 1881.

Mr. Sears enlisted as a private in 2d Mich. Cav. at the commencement of the Rebellion in 1861, and faithfully served his country during the entire conflict, and up to October, 1865, when he was honorably discharged. He now resides in Kingston, Canada.

2022.

GEORGE SEARS[8] [*John[7], Thatcher[6], Nath'l[5], Josh.[4], Sam'l[3], Paul[2], Rich.[1]*], b. St. John, N. B., Jan. 11, 1844; m. Sheffield, Eng., at St. Mark's Ch., *Emily Stayner*, she b. Halifax, Nova Scotia, May 27, 1845. Children :

3439. i. ANNIE MAUDE, b. Toronto, Can., July 31, 1873.
3440. ii. EDWARD STAYNER, b. Kingston, Can., Jan. 27, 1875.

3441. iii. FRANCES EMILY, b. King., Nov. 13, 1876.
3442. iv. JOHN, b. King., June 30, 1879.
3443. v. ROBERT SIDNEY, b. King., Dec. 18, 1881.

Mr. Sears left St. John, N. B., when 17 years of age, and lived in New York city about 12 years; now lives in Kingston, Can., where he resides, about 2 miles out of the city.

2034.

ADELBERT H. SEARS[8] [*Aaron*[7], *Alden*[6], *Alden*[5], *Judah*[4], *Sam'l*[3], *Paul*[2], *Rich.*[1]], b. May 25, 1851; m. *Ettie Matdruff*. Child:
3444. i. ZOE, b. Feb. 10, 1882.

2039.

IRVING COE SEARS[8] [*Leonard*[7], *Alden*[6], *Alden*[5], *Judah*[4], *Sam'l*[3], *Paul*[2], *Rich.*[1]], b. Belvidere, Ill., Aug. 2, 1843; m. Avoca, Iowa, Oct. 7, 1874, *Emma Powell*, she b. Belv., Sep. 24, 1855. Children:
3445. i. HORACE BROWNELL, b. Avoca, Aug. 2, 1875.
3446. ii. HARRY ALDEN, b. Avoca, July 18, 1877.
3447. iii. ARTHUR DEWEY, b. Avoca, Oct. 31, 1878.
3448. iv. FLORA LOUISE, b. Avoca, Oct. 10, 1880.
3449. v. ELECTA LELIA, b. Bruce, Dec. 29, 1882.

Mr. Sears is a farmer in Bruce, Wright co., Iowa.

2044.

HIRAM A. SEARS[8] [*Zeph.*[7], *Alden*[6], *Alden*[5], *Judah*[4], *Sam'l*[3], *Paul*[2], *Rich.*[1]], b. Marengo, Ill., Apr. 19, 1851; m. *Harriet Adelaide Burton*. Children:
3450. i. NINA IDELL, b. Garden Prairie, Ill., Jan. 19, 1878; d. Apr. 29, 1889.
3451. ii. HARRY ELMER, b. Gar. Pra., Nov. 29, 1879; d. Dec. 13, 1889.
3452. iii. ARTHUR AUGUSTUS, b. Gar. Pra., Oct. 16, 1881.
3452.*a.*iv. LOTTIE JANE, b. Gar. Pra., July 26, 1883.
3452.*a.*v. WASHINGTON BURTON, b. Gar. Pra., Mar. 8, 1885.

Mr. Sears was a farmer in Garden Prairie, Ill., and removed to Boulder, Col., in Nov., 1888.

2045.

HENRY W. SEARS[8] [*Zeph.*[7], *Alden*[6], *Alden*[5], *Judah*[4], *Sam'l*[3], *Paul*[2], *Rich.*[1]], b. Sep. 3, 1858; m. *Anna Pringle.* Child:

3453. i. BERTHA C., b. Jan. 25, 1883.

2047.

EDWARD C. SEARS[8] [*Horace*[7], *Alden*[6], *Alden*[5], *Judah*[4], *Sam'l*[3], *Paul*[2], *Rich.*[1]], b. Mar. 27, 1845; m. *Jennie Mc-Glashin.* Children:

3454. i. ROY M., b. Apr. 9, 1870.
3455. ii. GRACIE A., b. Aug. 28, 1877.

Is a farmer, and lives in Garden Prairie, Boone co., Ill.

2049.

THERON M. SEARS[8] [*Horace*[7], *Alden*[6], *Alden*[5], *Judah*[4], *Sam'l*[3], *Paul*[2], *Rich.*[1]], b. Apr. 7, 1849; m. *Sarah Culbertson.* Children :

3456. i. FRANK G., b. Jan. 16, 1872.
3457. ii. NORA M., b. Sep. 1, 1874.
3458. iii. HOWARD O., b. Oct. 26, 1876.
3459. iv. ROY M., b. Nov. 19, 1878.
3460. v. RALPH M., b. Dec. 18, 1880.
3461. vi. MARY, b. Mar. 17, 1882.

2071.

THOMAS MILLVILLE SEARS[8] [*Asahel*[7], *Edw'd*[6], *Alden*[5], *Judah*[4], *Sam'l*[3], *Paul*[2], *Rich.*[1]], b. Sep. 7, 1849; m. *Sarah Greenwood* of Verona, Mo. Child:

3462. i. OTIS.

2072.

OLIVER TRIMBLE SEARS[8] [*Asahel*[7], *Edw'd*[6], *Alden*[5], *Judah*[4], *Sam'l*[3], *Paul*[2], *Rich.*[1]], b. June 25, 1852; m. Monterey, Ill., 1872, *Ellen Richie,* who d. June 17, 1875; 2d, *Jane Powers.* Children:

By *Ellen :*
3463. i. CLARENCE PARKER, b. Dec. 31, 1873.

By *Jane* :
3464. ii. ROSELLA MAY.
3465. iii. OSCAR.

2074.

WILLIE LINCOLN SEARS[8] [*Asahel*[7], *Edw'd*[6], *Alden*[5], *Judah*[4], *Sam'l*[3], *Paul*[2], *Rich.*[1]], b. June 25, 1860; m. Stewardson, Ill., Aug. 12, 1885, *Hattie B. Reed.* Child :
3466. i. BERTHA COE, b. Nov. 20, 1886.

Mr. Sears removed to Brenham, Texas, and now resides No. 1011 N. Evans street, Bloomington, Ill.

2083.

JOSEPH SEARS[8] [*John*[7], *John*[6], *Alden*[5], *Judah*[4], *Sam'l*[3], *Paul*[2], *Rich.*[1]], b. Des Plaines, Ill., Jan. 22, 1841 ; m. Chicago, Ill., June 30, 1868, *Helen Stedman Barry*, dau. of S. S. B. Children :
3467. i. JOHN BARRY, b. Chicago, Aug. 23, 1869.
3468. ii. PHILIP RASSELAS, b. C., July 21, 1874.
3469. iii. HELEN ABIGAIL, b. C., Feb. 9, 1877.
3470. iv. MARIAN LOUISE, b. C., Aug. 22, 1880; d. Apr. 10, 1882.
3471. v. DOROTHY, b. C., 1886.

Is connected with N. K. Fairbank & Co., Chicago, Ill.

2087.

WM. HENRY HOSMER SEARS[8] [*John*[7], *John*[6], *Alden*[5], *Judah*[4], *Sam'l*[3], *Paul*[2], *Rich.*[1]], b. Chicago, Ill., Jan. 17, 1853 ; m. Sep. 21, 1876, *Kate Wilmer.* Children :
3472. i. JOSEPH WILMER, b. Aug. 27, 1877.
3473. ii. JOHN HAROLD, b. May 9, 1881.

Is Supt. " Garden City Dairy," Chicago, and lives in Hyde Park, Ill.

2103. a. iii.

NATHAN R. SEARS[8] [*Harper*[7], *Paul*[6], *Nathan*[5], *Judah*[4], *Sam'l*[3], *Paul*[2], *Rich.*[1]], b. Stowe, Vt., Apr. 1, 1827 ; m. Oct. 17, 1856, *Rosaltha Lathrop.* Child :
3473.* a. i. NED MORILLO, b. Stowe, Vt., Jan. 29, 1858.

2103. a. iv.

SYLVESTER C. SEARS[8] [*Harper[7], Paul[6], Nathan[5], Judah[4], Sam'l[3], Paul[2], Rich.[1]*], b. Stowe, Vt., Feb. 5, 1829; m. Feb. 4, 1860, *Mary J. Morrison.* Children:

3473. *b.* i. EMMA F., b. Feb. 3, 1861.
3473. *b.* ii. FRANK A., b. Aug. 16, 1865.
3473. *b.* iii. FRED. P., b. May 26, 1867.
3473. *b.* iv. JAMES W., b. June 20, 1871.
3473. *b.* v. CHARLES H., b. Mar. 26, 1879.

Mr. Sears lives at Motley, Minn.

2103. a. vii.

FREDERIC M. SEARS[8] [*Harper[7], Paul[6], Nathan[5], Judah[4], Sam'l[3], Paul[2], Rich.[1]*], b. Morristown, Vt., Oct. 4, 1836; m. Mar. 8, 1865, *Susan Thomas.* Children :

3473. *c.* i. HENRY A., b. Dec. 1, 1866.
3473. *c.* ii. FLORA E., b. Dec. 29, 1867.
3473. *c.* iii. WALTER A., b. Sep. 22, 1880.

Mr. Sears lives in Stowe, Vt.

2125.

CHARLES HENRY SEARS[8] [*Hiram[7], Lot[6], David[5], Judah[4], Sam'l[3], Paul[2], Rich.[1]*], b. July 15, 1838; m. Mar. 10, 1866, *Esther Elmira Sears*, No. 2122, dau. of Jas. C. S., she b. Nov. 9, 1831. Children :

3474.   i. GEORGE WELLS, b. Jan. 23, 1867.
3475. ii. CLARENCE HOWLAND, b. Sep. 11, 1869.
3476. iii. ELMIRA ANTOINETTE, b. Oct. 7, 1871.

2130.

Maj. HENRY BEAUFORT SEARS[8] [*Prince[7], Prince[6], David[5], Judah[4], Sam'l[3], Paul[2], Rich.[1]*], b. Taunton, Mass., May 24, 1825; d. Liverpool, Eng., Feb. 12, 1880; m. New York city, Oct. 6, 1846, by Rev. Dr. McVickar, to *Harriet Louiza Clitz*, dau. of Capt. John and Mary (Mellen) C., she b. Sackett's Harbor, N. Y., Oct. 27, 1831; (her mother was dau. of Capt. John and Mary M. of Keene, N. H.) Children:

3477. i. ELLA CLITZ, b. Saugerties, N. Y., Apr. 24, 1849 ; m. Liverpool, Eng., Nov., 1873, by Canon Farrar of Chester Cathedral, assisted by Rev. Francis O'Brien of St. Bride's Church, to *Irvine Stevens Bullock* of Savannah, Ga., who was Lt. of "Alabama" and "Shenandoah," Confederate cruisers, and now a cotton broker in Liverpool.

3478. ii. HARRIET LEILA, b. New Haven, Ct., Jan. 12, 1851; is unm., and lives in Detroit, Mich.

Mr. Sears was "appointed cadet West Point Military Academy, July 1, 1842 ; graduated July 1, 1846; Brevet 2d Lt., July, 1846; served in the garrison Fort Columbus, Governor's Island, N. Y.; was in the war with Mexico, 1846–47, being engaged in the siege of Vera Cruz, Mar. 9–29, 1847; (made 2d Lt. Art'y, Mar. 3, 1847;) defense of Convoy at Pass Ovejas, Aug. 10; National Bridge, Aug. 14 ; Cerro Gordo, Aug. 16, and Los Animas, Aug. 19; also combat of Humantla, Oct. 9, 1847; (he was Division Quartermaster,) and at the action of Allixco, Oct. 12 ; brevetted 1st Lt. Aug. 15, 1847, for gallant and meritorious conduct in several affairs with guerillas at Pass Ovejas, National Bridge and Cerro Gordo, Mexico ; on special duty in the Adjutant-General's office, Washington, D. C., from Dec. 8, 1847, to Mar. 8, 1848; and in command garrison at Fort Macon, No. Car., 1848, (1st Lt., 2d Art'y, Oct., 1847 ;) resigned June 30, 1849." [Army Reg.]

He was twice sent home by Gen. Scott as bearer of dispatches, bringing in charge as prisoner of war Gen. Iturbide, son of the former Emperor of Mexico.

Was engaged in explorations in South America from 1850 to 1853 ; Consulting Engineer of the Phil., Wil. & Balt. R. R. for submarine operations at projected bridge across the Susquehanna river in 1854–55 ; Supt. of Alterations in Victoria Docks, London, Eng., 1858–59; and since a merchant in Liverpool, Eng., until his withdrawal from business in 1878.

While in London he lectured before the Society of Arts and Manufactures, of which Prince Albert was President, and received from the society a medal for the " Invention of the Nautilus Diving Bell."

He married, in 1846, Harriet Louiza Clitz, daughter of Capt. John Clitz, U. S. A., (who died while in command at Fort Mackinaw in 1836,) and sister of Adm. John Clitz, U. S. N., and Gen. Henry B. Clitz, U. S. A.

2136.

JOSHUA SEARS[8] [*Alden[7], Roland[6], Roland[5], Seth[4], Sam'l[3], Paul[2], Rich.[1]*], b. Hawley, Mass., Sep. 18, 1808; d.

Oct. 23, 1842; m. New Haven, Ct., Sep. 6, 1836, *Roxanna Beecher* of that place. Children :

3479.   i. ELIZABETH BEECHER, b. July 2, 1837; m. *Chas. E. Wilcox;* child, WILCOX: [1.] Lille Louise.
3480. ii. CHARLES CROSBY, b. May 8, 1840; d. Jan. 21, 1864.

2137.

ALDEN SEARS[8] [*Alden[7], Roland[6], Roland[5], Seth[4], Sam'l[3], Paul[2], Rich.[1]*], b. Hawley, Mass., Aug. 17, 1810; d. Feb. 25, 1862; m. Michigan, Dec. 10, 1853, *Elizabeth Montraville.* Children :

3481.   i. MARY, b. Aug. 13, 1851.
3482. ii. SARAH E., b. Jan. 25, 1855.
3483. iii. WILLIAM ANSEL, b. Nov. 10, 1858.

2140.

EBENEZER SEARS[8] [*Alden[7], Roland[6], Roland[5], Seth[4], Sam'l[3], Paul[2], Rich.[1]*], b. Hawley, Mass., June 15, 1816; m. there, May 30, 1839, *Cordelia Fales,* she b. Heath, Mass., Dec. 6, 1812.   Children:

3484.* i. ALBERT F., b. Haw., Mar. 10, 1840.
3485. ii. JAMES F., b. Haw., Feb. 9, 1845 ; m. Saratoga Springs, N. Y., *Cora R. Spaulding,* she b. Sheldon, Vt., and is a farmer in H.
3486. iii. *Child,* d. Aug. 11, 1855.

Mr. Sears is a farmer in Hawley.

2141.

SETH SEARS[8] [*Alvan[7], Roland[6], Roland[5], Seth[4], Sam'l[3], Paul[2], Rich.[1]*], b. West Hawley, Mass., July 27, 1801 ; m. Dalton, Mass., May 9, 1827, *Ann Stockwell,* she b. West H., Feb. 7, 1804.   Children :

3487.   i. SARAH ANN, b. Haw., Aug. 13, 1828; m. Jan. 2, 1862, *E F. Harris* of Buckland, Mass.
3488. ii. HENRY, b. Haw., Apr. 16, 1830; m. Jan. 1, 1854, *Louisa Raymond,* she b. Peru, Mass., July 27, 1834, and lives in Dalton, Mass.
3489. iii. SILAS S., b. Haw., Feb. 9, 1833 ; m. Apr. 9, 1856, *Minerva E. Raymond,* she b. Peru, July 29, 1831 ; lives in Dalton.

3490.* iv. ROSWELL, b. Haw., May 7, 1835.
3491.* v. ROYAL, b. Haw., May 7, 1835, *gemini*.
3492. vi. BETHIA H., b. Haw., June 16, 1843; m. Coleraine,
Mass., Feb. 15, 1863, (Feb. 21, 1866, Hist. Haw.) *Henry*
Sayles Barton, and lives in Savoy, Mass.

Mr. Sears is a farmer, and lives on West Hill, West Hawley,
Mass. He was the oldest native living there in 1887.

2142.

ALVAN SEARS[8] [*Alvan*[7], *Roland*[6], *Roland*[5], *Seth*[4],
Sam'l[3], *Paul*[2], *Rich.*[1]], b. Hawley, Mass., Jan. 8, 1804; d.
June 3, 1872; m. West Haw., July 2, 1829, *Ann H. Maxfield*.
Children:
3493. i. DENNIS, is a farmer in Hawley, and a licensed Ad-
vent minister.
3494. ii. *Child*, d. May 1, 1830.
3495. iii. *Child*, d. Feb., 1833.
3496. iv. URBAN, b. 1836; was of Savoy, and in Co. H, 37th
Regt. Mass. Vols., and d. Hagerstown, Md., Nov. 12,
1862.

2146.

URBAN SEARS[8] [*Alvan*[7], *Roland*[6], *Roland*[5], *Seth*[4],
Sam'l[3], *Paul*[2], *Rich.*[1]], b. Hawley, Mass., Aug. 2, 1813; d.
there, Apr. 6, 1875; m. Haw., Apr. 17, 1838, *Tryphosa*
Hawkes, she b. Queensbury, N. Y., May 14, 1819. Children:
3497. i. MARTHA TRYPHOSA, b. W. Haw., May 22, 1839; m.
there, May 27, 1858, *Willis Vincent*, son of John and
Lucretia (Howes) V., he b. Dec. 1, 1829, and lives in
Haw.
3498. ii. EDMUND HOWES, b. W. Haw., Nov. 2, 1841; enlisted
Aug. 14, 1862, in Co. H, 37th Regt. Mass. Vol. Inf.,
and d. Spottsylvania C. H., Va., May 12, 1864, having
been accidentally shot by a comrade while on picket duty,
and was buried in Hawley.
3499. iii. ELLA CYNTHIA, b. W. Haw., Oct. 18, 1849; m. there,
Sep. 12, 1871, *Lewis W. Temple*, and lives on the old
homestead in Haw.; children, TEMPLE: [1.] Eddie S., b.
Apr. 30, 1873. [2.] Bessie E., b. Sep. 4, 1876. [3.] Lizzie
E., b. Nov. 6, 1885. [4.] Lida E., b. Nov. 6, 1885,
gemini.

3500.* iv. GEORGE WILLIAMS, b. W. Haw., May 18, 1855.
3501. v. CLARA BELL, b. W. Haw., Apr. 29, 1857; m. there,
Jan. 15, 1878, *Theodore Childs*, and lives in Deerfield,
Mass.

2155.

ROLAND SEARS[8] [*Roland*[7], *Roland*[6], *Roland*[5], *Seth*[4],
Sam'l[3], *Paul*[2], *Rich.*[1]], b. Hawley, Mass., Sep. 16, 1815; m.
—— ——. Children:
3502. i. MARY.
3503. ii. ROYAL, m.
3504. iii. ROLAND.
3505. iv. MONROE.
"Roland Sears' child d. Oct., 1844." Mr. Sears removed to
Kansas about 1855, and died soon after. His widow removed
with her children to Missouri.

2156.

JOSEPH SEARS[8] [*Roland*[7], *Roland*[6], *Roland*[5], *Seth*[4],
Sam'l[3], *Paul*[2], *Rich.*[1]], b. Hawley, Mass., May 28, 1818; m.
—— *Henry*. Child:
3506. i. JOSEPH HENRY, m.

2157.

SYLVESTER SEARS[8] [*Roland*[7], *Roland*[6], *Roland*[5], *Seth*[4],
Sam'l[3], *Paul*[2], *Rich.*[1]], b. Hawley, Mass., May 5, 1821; m.
Rowe, Mass., about 1844, *Abigail Kenrick*. Children:
3507. i. SARAH E., b. Haw., Jan. 9, 1845; m. *Charles Mas-
chy*, and was divorced; had no children.
3508.* ii. SYLVESTER L., b. Rowe, Mar. 5, 1848.
3509. iii. HERBERT ASA, b. Rowe, Mar. 10, 1859; d. Aug.
23, 1863.
Is a farmer in Hawley, Mass.

2168.

FRANKLIN SEARS[8] [*Chas.*[7], *Peter*[6], *Benj.*[5], *Benj.*[4],
Sam'l[3], *Paul*[2], *Rich.*[1]], b. Sardinia, N. Y., May 3, 1831; d.
East Saginaw, Mich., Oct. 30, 1875; m. —— ——. Children:
3510. i. FRANKLIN.
3511. ii. WILLIAM.

3512. iii. MARION, m. *Clarence Judd.*
3513. iv. GEORTNER.
3514. v. SUSAN.

All living in East Saginaw, Mich.

2169.

SEWARD SEARS[8] [*Chas.*[7], *Peter*[6], *Benj.*[5], *Benj.*[4], *Sam'l*[3], *Paul*[2], *Rich.*[1]], b. Sardinia, N. Y., Sep. 16, 1838; m. ——
——. Children:
3515. i. SADIE.
3516. ii. MAGGIE.
3517. iii. WALTER.
3518. iv. FRANK.

Lives in Sardinia, N. Y.

2189.

SEABURY L. SEARS[8] [*John*[7], *Steph.*[6], *Steph.*[5], *Benj.*[4], *Sam'l*[3], *Paul*[2], *Rich.*[1]], b. Apr. 16, 1840; m. Mar. 17, 1871, *Martha Reasner.* Children:
3519. i. CHARLES EDGAR, b. Feb. 22, 1879.
3520. ii. MABEL LOIS, b. Mar., 1882.

2192.

SAMUEL N. SEARS[8] [*John*[7], *Steph.*[6], *Steph.*[5], *Benj.*[4], *Sam'l*[3], *Paul*[2], *Rich.*[1]], b. Apr. 6, 1846; d. Dec. 18, 1875; m. Sep. 9, 1872, *Rebecca Valentine.* Child:
3521. i. ABBIE MYRTLE, b. Oct. 20, 1874.

2197.

NEWTON H. SEARS[8] [*Steph.*[7], *Steph.*[6], *Steph.*[5], *Benj.*[4], *Sam'l*[3], *Paul*[2], *Rich.*[1]], b. Spring Arbor, Mich., Oct. 19, 1854; m. June 13, 1876, *Eulalie K. Wilson* of Jackson, Mich., she b. Dundee, N. Y. Child:
3522. i. FREDERIC W., b. Spring Arbor, June 24, 1881; d. inf.

Is of firm Tannar & Sears, general merchandise dealers, Horton, Jackson county, Mich.

2213.

THADDEUS PATCHEN SEARS[8] [*Isaac*[7], *Ira*[6], *Enoch*[5], *Benj.*[4], *Sam'l*[3], *Paul*[2], *Rich.*[1]], b. Hoosick Falls, N. Y., Sep. 2, 1825 ; m. June 29, 1848, *Frances C. Peirce*, she b. New York city, 1828. Children :
3523. i. MARK H., is city physician, Leadville, Col.
3524. ii. ROBERT CUSHMAN, b. Chicago, May 28, 1857.

Mr. Sears was one of the " Forty-Niners," arriving in San Francisco, July 19, 1849. Was elected to State Senate in 1850.
Was Secretary Mississippi Constitutional Convention under which the State was reorganized after the war. Is now in the lumber trade in Chicago, Ill.

2218.

ALPHEUS HENRY SEARS[8] [*Henry*[7], *Ira*[6], *Enoch*[5], *Benj.*[4], *Sam'l*[3], *Paul*[2], *Rich.*[1]], b. Broadalbin, N. Y., Mar. 14, 1836 ; m. there, Aug. 25, 1880, *Laura E. McEwen*, she b. Johnstown, N. Y., July 2, 1853. Child :
3525. i. HENRY PAUL, b. Apr. 9, 1886.

Lives in Albion, N. Y.

2223.

REUBEN EDWARD SEARS[8] [*Reuben*[7], *Reuben*[6], *Sunderland*[5], *Benj.*[4], *Sam'l*[3], *Paul*[2], *Rich.*[1]], b. June 6, 1848 ; m. *Agnes Child.* Child :
3526. i. AGNES.

Is an attorney in Marshalltown, Iowa.

2237.

CHARLES B. SEARS[8] [*Miles*[7], *Wm.*[6], *Seth*[5], *Benj.*[4], *Sam'l*[3], *Paul*[2], *Rich.*[1]], b. Sullivan co., N. Y., Aug. 20, 1831 ; m. *Ettie E. Powers*, she b. Ellenville, N. Y., Dec. 2, 1835. Children :
3527. i. PRISCILLA E., b. Glenville, N. Y.; d. Mar. 22, 1858.
3528. ii. SADIE L., b. Sandburgh, N. Y.; m. Jan., 1881, ——.
3529. iii. GRACIE, b. La Honda, Cal., July, 1875.

Is a farmer in La Honda, San Mateo co., Cal.

2239.

OLIVER C. SEARS[8] [*Miles*[7], *Wm.*[6], *Seth*[5], *Benj.*[4], *Sam'l*[3], *Paul*[2], *Rich.*[1]], b. Sullivan co., N. Y., Sep. 21, 1839 ; m. Damascus, N. Y., Nov. 28, 1869, *Sarah D. Wilmarth*, she b. Cold Spring, Pa., July 29, 1850. Children :
3530.   i. THERON, b. ab't 1871.
3531. ii. MINNIE, b. ab't 1872.
3532. iii. OTTO, b. ab't 1874.
3533. iv. EDWARD, b. ab't 1876.
3534.   v. MARTHA, b. ab't 1880.

Lives in Rileysville, Wayne co., Pa.

2246.

ALLEN SEARS[8] [*David*[7], *John*[6], *Paul*[5], *Eben'r*[4], *Paul*[3], *Paul*[2], *Rich.*[1]], b. Knox, Me., Dec. 14, 1838; m. Monticello, Wis., Feb. 20, 1861, by Rev. Wm. Small, to *Abbie J. Corey*, dau. of Nelson Tibbits and Silvia Janet C. of M., she b. Silver Creek, N. Y., May 24, 1842 ; (who m. 2d, Wm. Fred. Crangle of Burns, Ill., and rem. in 1871 to Holmesville, Neb.) Children :
3535.   i. CARRIE LAVANTIA, b. Mont., June 26, 1862 ; m. Dec. 10, 1885, *Geo. H. Davis*, station agent and operator, Holmesville, Neb.
3536. ii. TRELLA PAREPA, b. Mont., June 1, 1866; is a teacher in M.

Allen Sears removed in fall of 1855, to Monticello, Wis., and engaged in farming and stock-raising. He enlisted Aug. 22, 1862, in 22d Regt. Wis. Vols.; was taken prisoner, and confined in Libby prison ; was honorably discharged June, 1865, when he resumed his former occupation in Monticello.
In March, 1867, he left his family, and has not been heard from since. He was a good musician, and taught singing school in winter; his wife was also a music-teacher, and both were Free-Will Baptists.

2248.

GEORGE WASHINGTON SEARS[8] [*David*[7], *John*[6], *Paul*[5], *Eben'r*[4], *Paul*[3], *Paul*[2], *Rich.*[1]], b. Knox, Me., Mar.

18, 1843; m. Monroe, Wis., May 1, 1867, by Rev. J. S. Dins-
more, to *Sylvia Ann Davis*, dau. of Rev. K. R. and S. A. D.,
she b. Candia, N. H. Children:

3537. i. Melva Osborne, b. Monticello, Wis., Mar. 7, 1868.
3538. ii. Ina Vesta, b. Salem, Neb., Nov. 29, 1869.
3539. iii. Olna David, b. S., May 31, 1876.
3540. iv. Orva Kinsman, b. S., May 31, 1876, *gemini*.
3541. v. Wesley Lindel, b. S., Feb. 28, 1878.
3542. vi. Georgia Zella, b. S., Nov. 25, 1881.

Mr. Sears removed from Knox, Me., with his parents in 1855,
and engaged in farming and stock-raising at Monticello, Wis.

He enlisted Aug. 22, 1862, in 22d Regt. Wis. Vols.; was
taken prisoner and confined in Libby prison; was with Sherman in his "March to the Sea;" mustered out June, 1865,
and resumed farming.

In 1869, he removed to Verdon, near Salem, Neb., where he
now resides; is a farmer, stock-raiser and manufacturer of
sorghum syrup.

2252.

WESLEY SEARS[8] [*David[7], John[6], Paul[5], Eben'r[4], Paul[3],
Paul[2], Rich.[1]*], b. Knox, Me., Oct. 22, 1851; m. Lansing,
Mich., Dec. 29, 1880, by Rev. Dr. Fiske, to *Nellie Olivia Law*,
dau. of Rev. Hiram and Sarah Maria L., she b. Birmingham,
Mich., Apr. 1, 1850. Children:

3543. i. Arthur Wesley, b. Mt. Clements, Mich., Sep. 20,
1881.
3544. ii. Clarence Howard, b. Mt. C., Apr. 13, 1883; d
Sep. 24.

Prof. Sears removed with his parents in fall of 1855 to Mon
ticello, Wis., and in June, 1866, to Hillsdale, Mich.; graduated classical course Hillsdale College, 1874; taught school at
Newbury, Mich., during winters of 1871–74; was Superintendent Schools Eaton Rapids, Mich., Sep., 1874, to July, 1876,
and Principal of School at Mt. Clements, Mich., Sep., 1876,
to July, 1885; then Superintendent Schools Flint City to
spring of 1887, and of State Public School at Coldwater till
Aug., 1889, when he was elected Superintendent of Schools
at Hillsdale, Mich.

2258.

WILMER SEARS[8] [*Thos.[7], John[6], Paul[5], Eben'r[4], Paul[3],
Paul[2], Rich.[1]*], b. Freedom, Me., Dec. 10, 1848; m. Exeter,

Wis., Nov. 12, 1876, *Sarah A. Butler*, dau. of John and Ann B., she b. Green co., Wis., Feb. 9, 1855. Children :

3545. i. NORA, b. Monticello, Wis., Nov. 7, 1877.
3546. ii. FRANK, b. Mont., May 30, 1879.
3547. iii. LESTER, b. Mont., Oct. 20, 1880.
3548. iv. FREDERIC, b. West Union, Iowa, June 7, 1882.
3549. v. ROBERTA, b. W. U., Oct. 3, 1883.
3550. vi. ORRIN, b. W. U., Mar. 21, 1885.

Mr. Sears removed with his parents in 1849, to Mt. Pleasant, Green co., Wis. In 1871–74, he had charge of a cattle ranch on the western plains, but resumed farming and stock-raising at Mt. Pleasant till 1881, when he removed to West Union, Fayette co., Iowa, where he now resides, and is engaged in selling agricultural implements and machinery.

2270.

NATHAN LAZELLE SEARS[8] [*Wm.*[7], *Eben'r*[6], *Wm.*[5], *Paul*[4], *Paul*[3], *Paul*[2], *Rich.*[1]], b. Carroll, (now Kiantone,) N. Y., June 16, 1812; m. July 3, 1831, *Deborah Perry Hall*, who d. Aug. 1, 1835 ; 2d, June 21, 1838, Mrs. *Polly (Scudder) Marsh*. Children :

By *Deborah :*
3551. i. STATIRA PHILENA, b. Apr. 18, 1832; m. Aug. 25, 1851, *Henry M. Barr*, and lives in Louisville, Ky.; has 8 children.
3552. ii. SUSAN DEBORAH, b. Sep. 23, 1834; m. *Josiah Davis*, and d. Jamestown, N. Y., Mar., 1866; had 5 sons.
By *Polly:*
3553. iii. WILLIAM SEWARD, b. Oct. 15, 1839; killed, Raymond, Miss., May 12, 1863; was 2d Lt., 20th Regt. Ill. Vols., under Gen. Logan ; had been a school teacher; unm.
3554. iv. NATHAN LEISTER, b. May 10, 1821; d. Aug. 20, 1862, of fever, at Lowand, Ill.; he enlisted July, 1862, and was 1st Sergt. 70th Reg. Ill. Vols.
3555. v. CHARLES CLINTON, b. Randolph, N. Y., June 30, 1844 ; lives Gibson City, Ill.
3556. vi. JOSEPHINA CALISTA, b. Rand., Aug. 5, 1848; m. Nov. 19, 1867, *S. A. Armstrong*, and lives in Bloomington, Ill.; has 6 children.
3557.*vii. ABNER HUNT, b. Rand., Aug. 5, 1851.

3558. viii. LEWIS HALL, b. Rand., Nov. 22, 1853; d. Feb. 4, 1854.
3559. ix. RUBY HANNAH, b. Rand., July 15, 1855 ; m. Jan., 1879, *Wm. H. Flint*, Mem. Traveling Conf. M. E. Ch., and lives in Rutland, Iowa; has 2 sons.

At his father's death, Mr. Sears took his portion of the property, and commenced business at Jamestown, N. Y.; at the age of 18, he experienced religion, and joined the M. E. Ch.; he removed to Randolph, N. Y., after 1838, thence to Limestone, Bradford co., Pa., and 8 years later to McLean co., Ill., and 15 years after to Gibson City, Ill., where he now resides.

2275.

Rev. CLINTON WILLIAM SEARS⁸ [*Wm.*⁷, *Eben'r*⁶, *Wm.*⁵, *Paul*⁴, *Paul*³, *Paul*², *Rich.*¹], b. Carroll, (now Kiantone,) N. Y., Apr. 27, 1820 ; d. Urbana, Ohio, Aug. 29, 1863 ; m. Cincinnati, O., June 1, 1842, *Angeline Brooks*, dau. Moses and Lydia (Ransom) B., she b. Sep. 20, 1817; d. Mt. Auburn, O., Dec. 17, 1848 ; 2d, Sep. 17, 1850, *Helen Catherine Graff*, she b. Feb. 18, 1828 ; d. Oct. 30, 1857 ; 3d, Apr. 7, 1859, Mrs. *Laura Ann (Henshaw) Jones*, she b. Aurora, N. Y., June 13, 1833 ; lives in Delaware, Ohio. Children :
By *Angeline :*
3560. i. *Son*, b. Vienna, N. Y., Feb. 11, 1843 ; d. Feb. 13.
3561.* ii. CLINTON BROOKS, b. Penn Yan, N. Y., June 2, 1844.
By *Helen :*
3562.* iii. JOHN McKNIGHT, b. Chillicothe, O., Aug. 28, 1851.
3563. iv. LEAVITT, b. Bloomington, Ill., Mar. 18, 1853; d. May 19, 1854.
3564.* v. J. MAGOUN, b. Bloom., Sep. 2, 1855.
By *Laura :*
3565. vi. HELEN ANGELINE.

Rev. Clinton William Sears, A. M., graduated July 3, 1841, Wesleyan University, Middletown, Ct., and in 1842, from Lane Theological Seminary, Cincinnati, O. ; was Professor of Ancient Languages and Literature, Illinois Wesleyan University, Bloomington, Ill., and the same in Wesleyan University, Athens, Ohio ; President Illinois Wesleyan University, and for many years an active member of the Ohio and Illinois Conferences of the Methodist Episcopal Church ; was Chaplain of 95th

Regt., Ohio Vol. Inf., and died August 29, 1863, at Urbana, Ohio, of disease contracted during the Vicksburg campaign ; he was buried with military honors in the Wesleyan Cemetery at Cummingsville, near Cincinnati, O.

2279.

Prof. AMOS GOULD SEARS[8] [*Eben'r*[7], *Eben'r*[6], *Wm.*[5], *Paul*[4], *Paul*[3], *Paul*[2], *Rich.*[1]], b. Carroll, N. Y., Apr. 24, 1823 ; m. Rockingham, Vt., June 1, 1847, *Susan Augusta Davis*, she b. there, Nov. 18, 1827. Child :

3566. i. NATHANIEL CLINTON, b. Gallipolis, Ohio, Aug. 23, 1854 ; m. Elgin, Ill., June 22, 1881, *Mattie Lee Barclay*, she b. there, Dec. 10, 1860 ; d. s. p., Chicago, Ill., Nov. 28, 1881, æ. 20 ; 2d, May 26, 1887, *Laura Raymond Davidson* of Elgin ; he studied at Elgin, grad. Amherst Coll., Mass., 1875, and was adm. to the bar in Illinois, 1878 ; is now of firm Nath'l C. Sears and Charles Arnd, lawyers, Chicago, Ill.

Mr. Sears studied at Waterville, Me., and Amherst, Mass. ; was a teacher, and Principal of Gallia Academy, Gallipolis, Ohio, for 11 years, and of Elgin Academy 11 years, when he retired, and now resides in Chicago, Ill., engaged in real estate business.

Prof. and Mrs. Sears took charge of Elgin Academy under unfavorable circumstances. The attendance had been low ; the growing popularity of the public schools interfering with its prosperity ; a debt was hanging over it, and the enthusiasm of its friends had waned.

They brought to the work just the qualities needed ; were quick to perceive what to do, and proceeded to the work in hand with directness and energy.

The debt was paid, the grounds improved, the students came in greater numbers, the school was advertised, the alumni interested, and the students themselves began to help the work of building up.

The school grew to number more than 200 students ; each year something was added to the apparatus and to the grounds ; each year a larger class was graduated, and the school was elevated to a standing among the best in the State.

Prof. and Mrs. Sears won the confidence of the community, and compelled the respect and love of all with whom they were associated.

As teachers, they were eminently successful; and as business managers, they succeeded beyond expectation.

2292.

ARAD WEST SEARS[8] [*Jos.*[7], *Silas*[6], *Nath'l*[5], *Paul*[4], *Paul*[3], *Paul*[2], *Rich.*[1]], b. Morristown, Vt., Aug. 5, 1816; d. Richford, Vt., Aug. 8, 1869, æ. 53; m. there, Sep. 6, 1840, *Elizabeth F. Goff*, she b. Sheldon, Vt., Jan. 8, 1823; now lives in Richford. Children:

3567.* i. WILLIAM GOFF, b. Rich., Feb. 28, 1848.
3568. ii. MARY ELLEN, b. Rich.; m. *Melvin J. Smith*, and lives Schuyler, Neb.
3569. iii. EMMA E., b. Rich.; m. *Fred. W. Hatch*, and lives there.
3570. iv. ABBIE ISABEL, b. Rich.; m. *Wm. J. Walker*, and lives in Boston, Mass.
3571.* v. GEORGE FREDERIC, b. Rich., Jan. 19, 1856.
And 5 children, who died young.

2297.

SILAS SEARS[8] [*Jos.*[7], *Silas*[6], *Nath'l*[5], *Paul*[4], *Paul*[3], *Paul*[2], *Rich.*[1]], b. Morristown, Vt., Feb. 13, 1830; m. Prophetstown, Ill., May 4, 1852, *Sarah C. Warnes*, she b. St. Louis, Mo., Feb. 18, 1829. Children:

3572.* i. FREDERIC WEST, b. Prophetstown, Jan. 28, 1853.
3573. ii. FRANK C., b. Prophetstown, Jan. 13, 1870; d. 1870.

Mr. Sears was for 20 years Deputy and County Surveyor of Whiteside county, and lived in Prophetstown, Ill.

2304.

SHERMAN WEST SEARS[8] [*Nath'l*[7], *Silas*[6], *Nath'l*[5], *Paul*[4], *Paul*[3], *Paul*[2], *Rich.*[1]], b. Cambridge, Vt., Feb. 24, 1824; d. Richford, Vt., Oct. 1, 1876, æ. 52; m. there, *Catharine Cook*, she b. Sutton, Can., Aug. 28, 1825; d. R., Jan. 17, 1877, æ. 51. Children:

3574. i. MARY LEMIRA, b. Rich., May 22, 1844; m. there, Nov. 20, 1862, *Myron Winslow Bailey*, he b. Waterville, Vt., Feb. 9, 1835; grad. Albany Law School, 1858; practised law until 1861, and then went into the
62

army; received an injury a few months later, which caused paralysis of the lower limbs, was discharged in 1862, and renewed practice of the law till 1867, when he was elected Judge of Probate for Franklin co.; was R. R. Com'r in 1872–78; resides in St. Albans, Vt.; children, BAILEY: [1.] Carrie Maria, b. Nov. 14, 1863; m. June 4, 1886, Edw'd W. Thompson, Pass. Agt., C., R. I. & P. R. R. [2.] Kate Sears, b. Feb. 27, 1868. [3.] Richard Myron, b. Oct. 27, 1871; d. Feb. 25, 1875.

3575.* ii. FRANK COOK, b. Duxbury, Vt., May 30, 1846.
3576. iii. LAFAYETTE, b. Rich., Sep. 11, 1848; d. Mar. 2, 1849.
3577. iv. SHERMAN NATHANIEL, b. Rich., July 1, 1850; m. Mar., 1879, *Martha Goff*, who d. July 19, 1883; he is a druggist at East Berkshire, Vt.
3578. v. CARRIE SALOMA, b. Rich., Apr. 6, 1853; lives in St. Albans, Vt.
3579. vi. EDWIN WHITE, b. Rich., Sep. 18, 1860; d. July 16, 1869.
3580. vii. ALIDA LEONORA, b. Rich., Nov. 26, 1862; lives in St. Albans.
3581. viii. DORA LELAND, b. Rich., May 20, 1866; lives in St. A.

Mr. Sears lived 7 years in California, served in the Union army during the Rebellion, and then settled down as a farmer in Richford, Vt.

2314.

Capt. GEORGE CARLTON SEARS[8] [*Alden[7]*, *Silas[6]*, *Nath'l[5]*, *Paul[4]*, *Paul[3]*, *Paul[2]*, *Rich.[1]*], b. Richford, Vt., 1840; m. San Francisco, Cal., May, 1865, *Jenny M. Aldrich.* Children:
3582. i. *Son.*
3583. ii. *Dau.*
3584. iii. *Dau.*
3585. iv. *Dau.*

Mr. Sears emigrated with his father to California in 1850, and was a clerk in Columbia county till 1857, when he entered college at Oakland for 4 years' term.

In 1861, he enlisted in 4th Regt. Cal. Inf'y, and in 1863, in 8th Regt. Cal. Inf'y; served to the close of the war, and mustered out at Fort Point, with rank of 1st Lt.; was on duty at

Fort Point, and on provost duty at San Francisco throughout the war.

He was engaged in mercantile business in Contra Costa county, Cal., under firm name of Penniman & Sears, several years, when he removed to Santa Cruz and erected a saw-mill, which he sold out, and engaged in cattle business. Later he removed to Portland, Oregon; went into the grocery business, and kept the "Dexter Livery-Stable."

He was elected Assessor in 1878, leading his ticket by several hundred votes; and in 1882, Sheriff of Multnomah county by an unprecedented majority, discharging the duties of that office with his characteristic energy and ability, meeting the approbation of all good citizens.

At the time of the last Indian war in Eastern Oregon, Mr. Sears enlisted a company of 100 men, and was chosen captain.

Having many personal friends, he is a strong man in his party, is a good political manager, and an honorable politician.

He is noted for his liberality, and is the personification of good humor and geniality.

Is Great Sachem, Imp. Order Red Men of Oregon; Sec'y Harmony Lodge, F. A. M.; Post Com. "George Wright" Post No. 1, G. A. R.; D. D. Grand Chan. Kts. of Pythias; Treas. No. 11, A. O. O. Foresters; Treas. Portland Fire Dept.; Pres. Tiger Fire Eng. Co.; and member Board Portland Fire Delegates.

2318.

STILLMAN FOOTE SEARS[8] [*Leonard*[7], *Silas*[6], *Nath'l*[5], *Paul*[4], *Paul*[3], *Paul*[2], *Rich.*[1]], b. Canton, N. Y., June 29, 1842; m. Castana, Iowa, Oct. 16, 1864, *Maggie Searle*, she b. Stark co., Ill., 1840. Children:

3586. i. LEONARD C., b. Onowa, Aug. 2, 1865.
3587. ii. MELVIN L., b. O., Sep. 16, 1866.
3588. iii. CHARLES WILBUR, b. O., May 12, 1870.
3589. iv. CARRIE E., b. O., Mar. 14, 1874.

Mr. Sears lives in Onowa, Monona co., Iowa.

2320.

JOSEPH LEONARD SEARS[8] [*Leonard*[7], *Silas*[6], *Nath'l*[5], *Paul*[4], *Paul*[3], *Paul*[2], *Rich.*[1]], b. Oswegatchie, N. Y., July 1,

1846; d. Laramie, Wyo. Ter., May 13, 1883; m. Pioche, Nev.,
Oct. 20, 1877, *Gertrude Zahnan*, b. Germany.　Children:
3590.　i. DELIA Z., b. Pioche, Oct., 1878.
3591.　ii. JOSEPH M., b. Pioche, Feb. 20, 1880.

2325.

JOHN FISKE SEARS[8] [*Wm.*[7], *Nath'l*[6], *Nath'l*[5], *Paul*[4],
Paul[3], *Paul*[2], *Rich.*[1]], b. Rochester, Mass., May 26, 1821; d.
Islip, N. Y., Mar. 22, 1862 (?), æ. 42; m. Sayville, L. I., 1847,
Mary Ann Hulse.　Children:
3592.　i. JOHN FRANKLIN.
3593.　ii. SILAS HULSE.
3594.　iii. MARY ANN.

2326.

WILLIAM SEARS[8] [*Wm.*[7], *Nath'l*[6], *Nath'l*[5], *Paul*[4], *Paul*[3],
Paul[2], *Rich.*[1]], b. Rochester, Mass., July 8, 1823; m. Sayville,
L. I., *Sarah Hulse*, who d. Oct., 1870.　Children:
3595.　i. WILLIAM.
3596.　ii. JAMES, d.
3597.　iii. SARAH.
3598.　iv. SAMUEL.
3599.　v. SUSAN.
3600.　vi. *Child*, d.
Lives in New Bedford, Mass.

2327.

NATHANIEL SEARS[8] [*Wm.*[7], *Nath'l*[6], *Nath'l*[5], *Paul*[4],
Paul[3], *Paul*[2], *Rich.*[1]], b. Rochester, Mass., Oct. 3, 1825; m.
June 27, 1849, *Imogene C. Benson*, dau. of Alonzo and Catharine (Clark) B., she b. Aug. 15, 1831; d. Apr. 20, 1851, æ.
19; 2d, Brockton, Mass., Oct. 24, 1852, *Mary W. Benson*,
(her sister,) she b. Middleboro, Mass., Mar. 24, 1833. Children:
By *Imogene :*
3601.　i. NATHANIEL AUSTIN, b. Wareham, Mass., May 6,
　　　　1850; d. Hyannis, Mass., Oct. 6, 1879.
By *Mary :*
3602.　ii. CHARLES BUTLER, b. Hyannis, Nov. 23, 1863; m.
　　　　Providence, R. I., May 13, 1886, *Nellie G. Hallet*, dau.
　　　　of Capt. Geo. H. H. of H.

Mr. Sears is a conductor, and has been connected with the Old Colony Railroad for some 30 years. Was Representative to Legislature, 1872–73. Resides Hyannis, Mass.

Has many old family papers, including the deed from the Winslows of the old homestead in Rochester.

2330.

FRANKLIN KEENE SEARS[8] [*Wm.*[7], *Nath'l*[6], *Nath'l*[5], *Paul*[4], *Paul*[3], *Paul*[2], *Rich.*[1]], b. Rochester, Mass., Mar. 12, 1834; m. Aug. 10, 1859, *Catherine E. Hunt,* dau. of Elbridge G. and Betsy (Lane) H. of Norton, Mass., she b. Mar. 12, 1835. Children:

3603. i. FRED. LAWRENCE, b. Raynham, Mass., June 4, 1860.
3604. ii. GEORGE FRANKLIN, b. Taunton, Mass., May 10, 1866.

Lives in Long Plain, Mass.

2332.

STEPHEN CRANSTON SEARS[8] [*Wm.*[7], *Nath'l*[6], *Nath'l*[5], *Paul*[4], *Paul*5 *Paul*[2], *Rich.*[1]], b. Rochester, Mass., Dec. 23, 1838; m. there, Dec. 31, 1865, *Sarah L. Eliot,* she b. there, 1845; d. there, June 23, 1868, æ. 22. Child:

3605. i. LOUISA BONNEY, b. Roch., Sep. 1, 1866.

Is a locomotive engineer on B. & M. R. R., and lives in Lawrence, Mass.

Was in Co. I, 3d Regt., Mass. Vol. Inf., from Sep. 23, 1862, to June 26, 1863.

2338.

HARRISON GRAY OTIS SEARS[8] [*Nath'l*[7], *Nath'l*[6], *Nath'l*[5], *Paul*[4], *Paul*5 *Paul*[2], *Rich.*[1]], b. Fairhaven, Mass., Nov. 10, 1825; m. New Bedford, Mass., *Mary Kelly Sherman,* she b. Dartmouth, Mass. Children:

3606. i. HARRISON G. O., b. New Bed., Dec. 6, 1853; and lives there.
3607. ii. LUCY KELLY, b. Hyde Park, Mass., Sep. 15, 1871.

Lives in New Bedford, Mass.

2343.

JAMES H. SEARS[8] [*Nath'l[7], Nath'l[6], Nath'l[5], Paul[4], Paul[3] Paul[2], Rich.[1]*], b. Rochester, Mass., Mar. 31, 1839 ; m. *Helen E. Swift.* Child :

3608. i. Helen Thacher, b. Roch., Nov. 8, 1868.

2355.

Capt. THOMAS BARTLETT SEARS[8] [*Thos.[7], Thos.[6], Thos.[5], Thos.[4], Paul[3], Paul[2], Rich.[1]*], b. Plymouth, Mass., July 2, 1834 ; m. Milton, Mass., May 4, 1863, *Mary C. Wellington.* Children :

3609. i. Fred. C.
3610. ii. Thomas B.

Mr. Sears was commissioned Act'g Master U. S. Navy, Jan. 22, 1862, and honorably discharged, Feb. 18, 1866 ; now lives in Churchill, Kansas.

2356.

Capt. AMASA CHURCHILL SEARS[8] [*Thos.[7], Thos.[6], Thos.[5], Thos.[4], Paul[3], Paul[2], Rich.[1]*], b. Plymouth, Mass., June 22, 1836 ; m. there, Oct. 22, 1861, *Eugenie F. Diman,* dau. of Thomas and Polly (Sylvester) D. Children :

3611. i. Willard T., b. Ply., Nov. 17, 1865 ; with Putnam Machine Co., Fitchburg, Mass.
3612. ii. Eugenie C., b. Ply., Sep. 3, 1870.

Mr. Sears is a ship-master in the East India trade, and resides in Plymouth, Mass. ; was appointed Acting Ensign U. S. N., Aug. 12, 1863 ; Acting Master, Aug. 16, 1864 ; Acting Vol. Lt., July 15, 1865, and honorably discharged, Sep. 27, 1865.

2359.

WILLIAM HENRY SEARS[8] [*Wm.[7], Eleazar[6], Will'd[5], Thos.[4], Paul[3], Paul[2], Rich.[1]*], b. Plymouth, Mass., Oct. 7, 1833 ; m. Yarmouth, Mass., July 22, 1863, *Lucy A. Wood.* Children :

3613. i. *Child,* b. Ply., June 23, 1866 ; d. ⎫ *gemini.*
3614. ii. *Child,* b. Ply., June 23, 1866 ; d. ⎭

3615. iii. EMMA A., b. Ply., June 2, 1867.
3616. iv. *Son*, b. Ply., May 21, 1869 ; d. May 29.
3617. v. ETTA MAY, b. Ply., Aug. 31, 1870.

Is a ship-carpenter in Plymouth, Mass.

2363.

EVERETT H. SEARS[8] [*Wm.*[7], *Eleazar*[6], *Will'd*[5], *Thos.*[4], *Paul*[3] *Paul*[2], *Rich.*[1]], b. Plymouth, Mass., July 26, 1842 ; m. there, Dec. 15, 1869, *Sarah Allen Tripp*, dau. of Ellis and Angeline R. T. Children :
3618. i. ELLA LEE, b. Ply., July 1, 1870.
3619. ii. EVERETT WILLIAM, b. Ply., Oct. 1, 1879.
3620. iii. ALTON ELLIS, by Ply., Sep. 29, 1883.

Is a carpenter, and lives in Plymouth, Mass.

2366.

BARTLETT SEARS[8] [*Hiram*[7], *Eleazar*[6], *Will'd*[5], *Thos.*[4], *Paul*[3], *Paul*[2], *Rich.*[1]], b. Plymouth, Mass., Dec. 28, 1845 ; m. Hyde Park, Mass., June 12, 1871, *Harriet Augusta King*, she b. Ply., July 1, 1841. Children :
3621. i. HATTIE BARTLETT, b. Hyde P., Jan. 23, 1875.
3622. ii. HORACE HOLMES, b. Hyde P., Mar. 23, 1876.
3623. iii. FRANK DANA, b. Hyde P., Sep. 12, 1877.

Is contracting agent for Great Western Dispatch Line, and South Shore Fast Freight Line in Boston, and resides in Hyde Park. In Plymouth record of births, his name is recorded as *Hiram* B.

2367.

ROBERT DAVIE SEARS[8] [*Hiram*[7], *Eleazar*[6], *Will'd*[5], *Thos.*[4], *Paul*[3] *Paul*[2], *Rich.*[1]], b. Plymouth, Mass., Oct. 19, 1849; m. there, July 16, 1874, *Sarah W. Howland*. Children :
3624. i. GEORGE R., b. Ply., Jan. 2, 1875.
3625. ii. LUTHER F., b. Ply., Sep. 17, 1877.
3626. iii. IDA LEWIS, b. Ply., Apr. 23, 1882.

2373.

DANIEL WINSLOW SEARS[8] [*Dan'l*[7], *Eleazar*[6], *Will'd*[5], *Thos.*[4], *Paul*[3], *Paul*[2], *Rich.*[1]], b. Plymouth, Mass., July 8, 1853; m. there, June 26, 1878, *Louisa C. Holsgrove*. Child:
3627. i. JENNIE L., b. Ply., Mar. 12, 1880.

2384.

BENJAMIN LEWIS SEARS[8] [*Edm'd*[7], *Edm'd*[6], *Will'd*[5], *Thos.*[4], *Paul*[3], *Paul*[2], *Rich.*[1]], b. Feb. 20, 1849; m. 1871, *Marantha Miles*. Child:
3628. i. HAROLD BENJAMIN, b. Nov. 27, 1875.

2388.

HENRY ALLEN SEARS[8] [*Allen*[7], *Jos.*[6], *Will'd*[5], *Thos.*[4], *Paul*[3] *Paul*[2], *Rich.*[1]], b. Abington, Mass., Aug. 6, 1833; m. Middleboro, Mass., Sep. 3, 1862, by Rev. J. N. Putnam, to *Catharine Sullivan*, she b. Cloheen, Ireland, Apr. 9, 1838; d. Bridgewater, Mass., Aug. 8, 1882. Child:
3629. i. JULIA ELIZABETH, b. Plympton, Mass., July 6, 1863.
Lives in Titicut, Mass.

2399.

NATHANIEL T. SEARS[8] [*Jas.*[7], *Thos.*[6], *Will'd*[5], *Thos.*[4], *Paul*[3], *Paul*[2], *Rich.*[1]], b. Plymouth, Mass.; m. there, Oct. 31, 1883, *Bessie Mahoney*. Child:
3630. i. WARREN, b. Ply., Aug. 1, 1884.

2405.

HORATIO N. SEARS[8] [*Horatio*[7], *Thos.*[6], *Will'd*[5], *Thos.*[4], *Paul*[3], *Paul*[2], *Rich.*[1]], b. Plymouth, Mass.; m. there, Sep. 6, 1864, *Sarah M. (Gibbs) Sears*, dau. of Geo. H. and E. G., and widow of Otis Sears, No. 1202; she d. June 6, 1868, æ. 23 yrs. 7 mos. 27 days; and he m. 2d, Ply., June 13, 1871, *Margaret Kenny*. Child:
By *Sarah*:
3631. i. HATTIE B., b. Ply., Feb. 5, 1866; m. there, July 31, 1881, *Oliver T. Lapham*.

Mr. Sears served in Co. H, 18th Regt. Mass. Vols., from Aug. 24, 1861, to May 2, 1862, and was discharged for disability; he enlisted in Co. E, 23d Regt. Mass. Vols., Nov. 30, 1863, and was mustered out June 25, 1865.

2412.

FREDERIC LEWIS SEARS[8] [*Horatio*[7], *Thos.*[6], *Will'd*[5], *Thos.*[4], *Paul*[3], *Paul*[2], *Rich.*[1]], b. Plymouth, Mass., Aug. 27, 1861; m. there, July 3, 1878, *Eudora F. King.* Children:

3632. i. FREDERIC LEWIS, b. Ply., May 5, 1879.
3633. ii. MAUD FLORENCE, b. Ply., Jan. 11, 1882.
3634. iii. EFFIE FRANCES, b. Ply., Mar. 18, 1884.

2424.

HORACE SEARS[3] [*Chauncey*[7], *Isaac*[6], *Elkanah*[5], *Josh.*[4], *Paul*[3], *Paul*[2], *Rich.*[1]], b. New Durham, N. Y., May 3, 1819; m. Carryville, N. Y., Nov. 22, 1840, *Jane Warner*, she b. Parma, N. Y., Nov. 26, 1822. Children:

3635. i. OLIVE, b. Aug. 19, 1847; m. *Charles Dunham*, and lives in Caledonia, Mich.; he is a farmer, and breeder of imported stock horses.
3636. ii. LEVANT C., b. Cascade, Mich., Mar. 13, 1853; m. *Julia Hall*, and has 6 children; is a farmer in Codilla, Mich.
3637. iii. WALTER, b. Cascade, Mar. 7, 1856; d. Apr. 7.
3638. iv. WILLIAM W., b. Cascade, Dec. 25, 1857; m. Caledonia, Apr. 10, 1882, *Lizzie McGregor*, she b. New York city, July 15, 1859; is an extensive farmer, and stock-raiser in Alaska, Mich.; has no children.
3639. v. ADDIE, b. Cascade, Aug. 29, 1859; m. *Samuel Snyder*, a farmer, and lives at Mt. Pisgah, Ind.

Lives in Cascade, Alaska, Kent co., Mich.

2435.

WILLARD SHELDON SEARS[8] [*Will'd*[7], *Will'd*[6], *Elkanah*[5], *Josh.*[4], *Paul*[5] *Paul*[2], *Rich.*[1]], b. Jan. 2, 1827; m. Aug. 11, 1850, *Rowena E. Bailey*, she b. Chatham, Ct., Feb. 9, 1825; d. May 7, 1887. Children:

3640. i. ADELA JANE, b. Aug. 22, 1851; m. Sep. 11, 1876, *Austin E. Rouse*, and d. June 23, 1884, æ. 33; children,

ROUSE: [1.] Grace May. [2.] Elmer Ellsworth, and 3 others, who d. inf.
3641. ii. CHARLES EUGENE, b. Mar. 8, 1855 ; d. Dec. 13, 1866.
3642. iii. MARY AMELIA, b. May 5, 1856 ; d. May 17, 1872.
3643. iv. SUSAN ROBINSON, b. May 11, 1859; d. Oct. 17, 1876.

Lives in Cobalt, Middlesex co., Ct.

2436.

WILLIAM HENRY SEARS[8] [*Will'd[7], Will'd[6], Elkanah[5], Josh.[4], Paul[3], Paul[2], Rich.[1]*], b. Chatham, Ct., Nov. 24, 1831 ; d. Glastenbury, Ct., July 7, 1872 ; m. 1853, *Nancy Elizabeth Blythe* of New Marlboro, Ct. Children :
3644. i. ELLEN, b. East Hampton, Ct. ; m. —— *Moody.*
3645. ii. MARION VICTORIA, b. Marlboro, Ct. ; m. No. Manchester, *Leroy M. Cowles.*
3646.* iii. ARZA TREAT, b. E. Hamp.
3647. iv. IDA BELL, b. Moodus, Ct.
3648. v. HESTER ANN, b. Moodus ; m. Waterville, Ct., —— ——.
3649. vi. FLORA, b. Glastenbury.
3650. vii. BERTHA, b. G.
And 5 others who d.

Thomas K. Blythe of California, who died in 1883, left a fortune estimated at $7,000,000, which is claimed by his five brothers and sisters, of whom Mrs. Nancy E. Sears is one.

2440.

CLARKE OSPREY SEARS[8] [*Steph.[7], Will'd[6], Elkanah[5], Josh.[4], Paul[3], Paul[2], Rich.[1]*], b. July 24, 1836 ; m. June 8, 1857, *Charlotte Josephine Fielding*, dau. of Frederic and Mary Buell (Overton) F. Children :
3651. i. ROSA FLORILLA, b. Nov. 4, 1858; d. Jan. 10, 1875.
3652. ii. MARY EMILY, b. Mar. 17, 1860 ; m. *Clayton L. Smith;* child, SMITH : [1.] Annie Emma, b. Jan. 12, 1883.
3653. iii. IDA JOSEPHINE, b. Dec. 10, 1861.
3654. iv. LIZZIE ADELAIDE, b. June 26, 1863.
3655. v. CARRIE VEAZIE, b. Aug. 8, 1865.

Mr. Sears lives in East Hampton, Ct. ; was Rep. to Leg. 1875–76, and appointed Postmaster, 1885.

2441.

Dr. CUSHMAN ALLEN SEARS[8] [*Steph.*[7], *Will' d*[6], *Elka-nah*[5], *Josh.*[4], *Paul*[3], *Paul*[2], *Rich.*[1]], b. Chatham, Ct., Sep. 26, 1838; m. Lyme, Ct., Nov. 11, 1862, *Evelyn Lay.* Children :
3656. i. ANNIE BELLE, b. Glastenbury, Ct., Nov. 25, 1864 ; m. Dec. 9, 1884, *William H. Selden*, son of Wm. H. and Sarah (Loper) S. of Lyme, Ct., and a nephew of Chief Justice Waite. He is largely interested with his father in mines at Stambaugh, Mich., where he resides.
3657. ii. WALTER C., b. Portland, Ct., June 10, 1868.
3658. iii. BERTHA E., b. Port., Feb. 22, 1875.

Is a physician in Portland, Ct.

2443.

FRANCIS J. SEARS[8] [*Elijah*[7], *Will'd*[6], *Elkanah*[5], *Josh.*[4], *Paul*[3], *Paul*[2], *Rich.*[1]], b. Ct., Sep. 15, 1827; m. Algonquin, Ill., Jan. 1, 1848, *Mary I. Dewey*, who d. July 29, 1850 ; 2d, July 3, 1855, *Martha Freeman*, who d. Dec. 3, 1870 ; 3d, Aug. 12, 1872, Mrs. *Arabella (Purcupile) Coats*, widow of John W. Coats, she b. May 10, 1853, Rensselaer, Ind. Children :
By *Mary :*
3659.   i. MARY F. J., b. Algonquin, 1849 ; m. *J. S. Arnold* of Watseka, Ill.
3660.   ii. AUKAH A., b. June, 1850 ; d.
By *Martha :*
3661. iii. W. E., b. Rainsville, Ind., July, 1855 ; m. Animas City, Col., *Lou. Wakefield*, and lives there.
3662. iv. CHARLES G., b. Rains., Apr., 1856 ; m. *F. G. Thompson*, and lives in Rens.
3663. v. HATTIE E., b. Milford, Ill., Jan., 1868 ; d.
3664. vi. SALLIE B., b. Watseka, Ill., Feb., 1870 ; d.
By *Arabella :*
3665. vii. ANNIE E., b. Rens., Feb. 2, 1879 ; d. Aug. 21, 1882.

Mr. Sears was reared and educated in Orleans county, N. Y.
In May, 1846, the family removed to McHenry county, Ill., and in 1850, he went to Indiana, and taught school there several terms ; in 1855, he opened a small grocery store in Rains-

ville, Ind., removed in 1859, to Milford, Ill., and in 1860, started a branch store in Watseka, Ill., doing a good business for 8 years, during which he was Township Trustee, Supervisor and Overseer of the county poor farm.

In 1860, he removed to Chicago, opened a wholesale dry-goods and notions store on Lake street, was burnt out in October, 1871, and lost all the hard earnings of 20 years.

He removed in 1872, to Clinton, Iowa, opened a retail dry-goods store, and in 1874, to Rensselaer, Ind., where he engaged in mercantile business; sold out and took an interest in Commercial Bank of Oxford, Ind., and is now Vice-President, in full charge of the Citizens' Bank of Rensselaer, his present residence.

2445.

JAMES HENRY SEARS[8] [*Elijah*[7], *Will'd*[6], *Elkanah*[5], *Josh.*[4], *Paul*[3], *Paul*[2], *Rich.*[1]], b. Shelby, Orleans co., N. Y., July 23, 1831; m. *Mary E. Freeman,* dau. of Benj. F. and Cynthia A. F., she b. Richmond, O., Mar. 11, 1836. Children:
3665. *a.* i. HATTIE A., b. Crystal Lake, Ill., Dec. 3, 1860.
3665. *a.* ii. FRANK GRANT, b. Crystal Lake, Ill., July 25, 1864, is with Northrup, Braslan & Goodwin Co., Minneapolis, Minn.

Mr. Sears was reared in Orleans county, N. Y., removed with his parents to McHenry county, Ill., lived for a time at Crystal Lake, P. O. Nunda, and now lives in Jamestown, No. Dakota.

2449.

PRESCOTT A. SEARS[8] [*Selden*[7], *Will'd*[6], *Elkanah*[5], *Josh.*[4], *Paul*[3], *Paul*[2], *Rich.*[1]], b. East Hampton, Ct., Oct. 16, 1846; m. Mar. 12, 1878, *Julia Roberts* of South Hadley, Mass. Child:
3666. i. CHARLES E., b. July 16, 1879; d. Jan. 8, 1882.

Lives in Elmwood, Ct.

2453.

JOHN DUDLEY SEARS[8] [*Elkanah*[7], *Benj.*[6], *Elkanah*[5], *Josh.*[4], *Paul*[3], *Paul*[2], *Rich.*[1]], b. Meredith, N. Y., Feb. 2, 1821; m. Aug. 5, 1847, *Frances Eveline Manley.* Child:
3667. i. CLARA, b. Aug. 1, 1848; m. June 11, 1868, *Pliny Watson,* and lives in Toledo, Ohio; children, WATSON:

[1.] Dudley Sears, b. Mar. 21, 1869. [2.] Kate Coe, b. Jan. 8, 1871. [3.] Fanny Adele, b. Apr. 30, 1873.

Mr. Sears removed to Ohio in 1836; was admitted to the bar in 1844, and is an attorney at law, in Upper Sandusky, O.

2454.

BENJAMIN SEARS[8] [*Elkanah*[7], *Benj.*[6], *Elkanah*[5], *Josh.*[4], *Paul*[3], *Paul*[2], *Rich.*[1]], b. Oct. 11, 1824; m. May 15, 1851, *Melissa Merrick.* Children:

3668. i. ANNA BIGELOW, b. Apr. 3, 1852; a missionary to China.
3669. ii. ALICE MELISSA, b. Dec. 28, 1853.
3670. iii. MINDA PHELPS, b. June 6, 1857; a stenographer in Cleveland, O.
3671. iv. RUFUS VICTOR, b. May 8, 1860.
3672. v. FRANCIS OSCAR, b. Apr. 24, 1863.
3673. vi. HIRAM BENJAMIN, b. Oct. 19, 1866.
3674. vii. BERTHA ALMIRA, b. Sep. 13, 1869.
3675. viii. RUBY DESIRE, b. Mar. 22, 1874.

Is a farmer in Bucyrus, Ohio.

2456.

Lt.-Col. CYRUS SEARS[8] [*Elkanah*[7], *Benj.*[6], *Elkanah*[5], *Josh.*[4], *Paul*[3], *Paul*[2], *Rich.*[1]], b. Mar. 10, 1832; m. May 27, 1865, *Sarah A. Harpster.* Children:

3676. i. HORACE HARPSTER, b. Oct. 1, 1866.
3677. ii. EVA RACHEL, b. July 25, 1869.
3678. iii. FANNY EVELINE, b. Feb. 16, 1872.
3679. iv. LAURA JANE, b. Dec. 3, 1882.

Mr. Sears studied law, but abandoned the profession for trade; enlisted in 11th Ohio Battery in 1861; was commissioned 1st Lt., and later Lt.-Col. 11th Louisiana Vols. (colored), and served until mustered out at the end of the war.

Is now in mercantile business at Fowler, Wyandotte co., Ohio.

2460.

Capt. JOHN JAMES SEARS[8] [*John*[7], *Benj.*[6], *Elkanah*[5], *Josh.*[4], *Paul*[3], *Paul*[2], *Rich.*[1]], b. Ithaca, N. Y., June 10, 1828; d. Memphis, Tenn., Sep. 13, 1878; m. Apr. 12, 1857, *Ellen*

Thomas; 2d, 1870, *Florence Bailie;* 3d, Memphis, Aug. 14, 1878, *Mary M. McGazy*, she b. Syracuse, N. Y., Feb. 6, 1838; lives in Rochester, N. Y. Children :

By *Ellen :*

3680.   i. NELLIE, d. inf.

3681.   ii. BENJAMIN BUTLER.

Was a captain in Union army during the war, and afterward settled in Memphis, Tenn., where he died of yellow fever.

2464.

ASA BIGELOW SEARS[8] [*John*[7], *Benj.*[6], *Elkanah*[5], *Josh.*[4], *Paul*[3], *Paul*[2], *Rich.*[1]], b. Aug. 25, 1838; m. Dec. 10, 1863, *Mary Fletcher.* Children :

3682.   i. FLETCHER, b. Sep. 11, 1864.

3683.   ii. FLORENCE EVELINE, b. May 24, 1866.

Is an undertaker in Detroit, Mich.

2467.

WILLIAM SEARS[8] [*David*[7], *Benj.*[6], *Elkanah*[5], *Josh.*[4], *Paul*[3], *Paul*[2], *Rich.*[1]], b. Aug. 7, 1832; m. *Maria Cowles.* Children :

3684.   i. LINDAL B.

3685.   ii. MATTIE.

3686.   iii. CARRIE.

3687.   iv. EFFIE.

Lives in Maquoketa, Jackson co., Iowa.

2468.

BENJAMIN SEARS[8] [*David*[7], *Benj.*[6], *Elkanah*[5], *Josh.*[4], *Paul*[3], *Paul*[2], *Rich.*[1]], b. Nov. 22, 1834; m. *Rhoda F. Blanchard.* Children :

3688.   i. FRANK C.

3689.   ii. GEORGE E.

3690.   iii. JESSE R.

3691.   iv. ALBERT E.

Lives in Maquoketa, Jackson co., Iowa.

2470.

ISAAC BIGELOW SEARS[8] [*Orin*[7], *Benj.*[6], *Elkanah*[5], *Josh.*[4], *Paul*[3], *Paul*[2], *Rich.*[1]], b. Nov. 9, 1831; m. Feb. 27, 1856, *Christina Stannard.* Children:
3692. i. ORIN J.
3693. ii. GEORGE.
3694. iii. MYRON.

Is a farmer near Horseheads, Chemung county, N. Y.

2471.

PRESTON SEARS[8] [*Orin*[7], *Benj.*[6], *Elkanah*[5], *Josh.*[4], *Paul*[3], *Paul*[2], *Rich.*[1]], b. Apr. 22, 1834; m. Feb. 23, 1860, *Hannah Sayler.* Children:
3695. i. LIDA, b. Dec. 25, 1860.
3696. ii. IRA, b. Apr. 11, 1868.
3697. iii. JENNET, b. May 26, 1874.

Is a farmer in Smith's Valley, Randallville, Madison county, N. Y.

2477.

RUFUS A. SEARS[8] [*Hiram*[7], *Benj.*[6], *Elkanah*[5], *Josh.*[4], *Paul*[3], *Paul*[2], *Rich.*[1]], b. Meredith, N. Y., Jan. 20, 1838; m. Feb. 26, 1861, *Agnes M. Thompson.* Children:
3698. i. ELENA PHIDELIA, b. Feb. 10, 1867.
3699. ii. JOHN HIRAM, b. Aug. 21, 1870; d. inf.
3700. iii. ALONZO JAMES, b. Oct. 14, 1872.

Lives in Barnetts, Morgan county, Mo.

2481.

MILLARD D. SEARS[8] [*Hiram*[7], *Benj.*[6], *Elkanah*[5], *Josh.*[4], *Paul*[3], *Paul*[2], *Rich.*[1]], b. Meredith, N. Y., Oct. 27, 1860; m. Aug. 15, 1882, *Lottie Lyon.* Child:
3701. i. MABEL, b. June 26, 1883.

Is in mercantile business in Delhi, N. Y.

2490.

EDMUND BACON SEARS[8] [*Josh.[7], Jos.[6], Josh.[5], Josh.[4], Paul[3], Paul[2], Rich.[1]*], b. Sandisfield, Mass., 1844; m. there, Dec. 13, 1864, *Jane L. Sage.* Children:

3702. i. ELLEN MARIA, b. Sand., Aug. 28, 1866.
3703. ii. MILTON, b. Sand., Dec. 16, 1868.

Lives in Sandisfield, Mass.

2492.

FRANCIS BACON SEARS[8] [*Edm'd[7], Jos.[6], Josh.[5], Josh.[4], Paul[3], Paul[2], Rich.[1]*], b. Wayland, Mass., Jan. 21, 1849; m. Weston, Mass., 1875, *Mary Elizabeth Sparhawk* of Boston, she b. 1847. Children:

3704. i. KATHARINE, b. Weston, 1876.
3705. ii. EDMUND HAMILTON, b. Boston, 1878.
3706. iii. JACKSON KNYVET, b. Boston, 1881.
3707. iv. FRANCIS BACON, b. Boston, 1882.

Is Cashier of Third National Bank, Boston.

2495.

BARNAS C. SEARS[8] [*Alfred[7], Paul[6], Paul[5], Josh.[4], Paul[3], Paul[2], Rich.[1]*], m. *Louiza Fay.* Children:

3708. i. ELIZA, m. *Byron Winslow,* a farmer in Southern Minnesota.
3709. ii. CHARLES, m. —— *Allen* of Rockford, Ill.; is a stock-raiser in Colorado.
3710. iii. NELLIE; lives in Minnesota with her sister.

Mr. Sears removed to Wisconsin, and engaged in farming for a number of years, and now lives on his farm in Rockford, Ill.

2496.

DELOS AMBROSE SEARS[8] [*Alfred[7], Paul[6], Paul[5], Josh.[4], Paul[3], Paul[2], Rich.[1]*], b. Perrysville, N. Y., Aug. 19, 1828; m. Fenner, N. Y., May 15, 1851, by Elder Clark, Bap't, (of Cazenovia, N. Y.,) to *Louisa Aleha Marshall,* dau. of

Thomas and Phebe (Keeler) M., she b. there, Jan. 23, 1828. Children :

3711. i. EMMA DELIGHT, b. Lima, Wis., June 4, 1853 ; m. —— *Humiston* of Rockford, Ill.
3712. ii. MARY, b. Lima ; m. *O. C. Fay*, and lives in Rockford.

Mr. Sears removed to Wisconsin with his brother ; lived with him for a time, and thence to Rockford, Ill., where he now resides. Was a farmer and carpenter, and is now engaged in the manufacture of metallic coffins.

2497.

Capt. WILLIAM BARNAS SEARS[8] [*Barnas*[7], *Paul*[6], *Paul*[5], *Josh.*[4], *Paul*[3], *Paul*[2], *Rich.*[1]], b. Hamilton, N. Y., June 11, 1832 ; m. Roxbury, Mass., Jan., 1863, *Emily A. Faunce*, who d. Brookline, Mass., Apr. 19, 1879, æ. 44 ; 2d, Prov., R. I., Oct. 24, 1881, *Sadie A. Hunt*, she b. Cranston, R. I., Oct. 24, 1849. Children :

By *Emily :*
3713. i. WILLIAM B., b. Roxb'y, July 4, 1864.
3714. ii. LANGLEY B., b. Roxb'y, July 11, 1870.
3715. iii. HARRY BOWERS, b. Roxbury, Dec. 30, 1872.
3716. iv. STEPHEN F., b. Brookline, Aug. 9, 1874.
By *Sadie :*
3717. v. ELIZABETH H., b. Brook., Mar. 5, 1884 ; d. May 11.
3718. vi. EDWARD H., b. Brook., Sep. 25, 1885.

Capt. Sears is in insurance business in Boston, and lives in Brookline, Mass.

2504.

EDWIN SEARS[8] [*David*[7], *Paul*[6], *Paul*[5], *Josh.*[4], *Paul*[3], *Paul*[2], *Rich.*[1]], b. Sandisfield, Mass., Oct. 13, 1829 ; d. Scott, Ill., Sep. 27, 1860 ; m. Jersey City, N. J., Feb. 25, 1852, *Fannie S. Oliver*, she b. England, Dec. 19, 1831 ; lives in Jersey City. Children :

3719. i. ANNIE, d.
3720. ii. OLIVE.
3721. iii. IDA.
3722. iv. EDWIN, is in coal trade.
3723. v. EFFIE.

64

Mr. Sears was in business with his father in New York city, firm of Sears, Morley & Co., and removed with him to Rockford, Ill., and engaged in farming.

2507.

HENRY SEARS[8] [*David[7], Paul[6], Paul[5], Josh.[4], Paul[3], Paul[2], Rich.[1]*], b. New Boston, Mass., Sep. 14, 1836; m. Jersey City, N. J., Feb. 8, 1855, *Carrie S. Van Syckle*, she b. Bordentown, N. J., July 20, 1838. Child:

3724. i. FRANK.

Mr. Sears removed to Rockford, Ill., and engaged in mercantile business.

2514.

EDMUND B. SEARS[8] [*Henry[7], Paul[6], Paul[5], Josh.[4], Paul[3], Paul[2], Rich.[1]*], b. Sandisfield, Mass., Dec. 20, 1845; m. New York city, Jan. 30, 1884, *Edith Wright.* Child:

3724. *a.* i. PAUL HEREWARD, b. Chicago, Ill., July 27, 1886.

Of " The Henry Sears Co.," 77–79 Wabash avenue, Chicago, Ill., manf'rs and imp'rs of cutlery.

2516. a. iii.

HIRAM PORTER SEARS[8] [*Norman[7], Sim.[6], Paul[5], Josh.[4], Paul[3], Paul[2], Rich.[1]*], b. So. Tyringham, (now Monterey,) Mass., 1834; m. Rochester, N. Y., 1856, *Cornelia A. Phelps.* Children:

3725. i. NORMAN PHELPS, b. Aug. 18, 1858; educated in High School, Monterey, and now lives in Lincoln, Neb.
3726. ii. ABBIE LUCY, b. Sand., Mar. 16, 1861; educ. High School, Monterey; m. 1881, *Jason Lampson,* and lives in Wisconsin; has 1 son and 2 daus.
3726. *a.* iii. JENNIE KATIE, b. Sand., Dec. 16, 1867; educ. New Marlboro Institute, and lives at home.
3726. *a.* iv. LIZZIE, b. New Marlboro, Feb. 27, 1874; d. Mont., Jan., 1885.
3726. *a.* v. NELLIE, b. May 16, 1881.

Mr. Sears finished his education at a private school in Monterey; served as corporal from Oct. 28, 1862, to Sep. 1, 1863, in Co. H, 49th Mass. Vol. Inf.; is now a wholesale traveling merchant, and a member of Cong. Ch.; residence, Monterey, Mass.

2516. a. vi.

JOHN SIMEON SEARS[8] [*Norman*[7], *Sim.*[6], *Paul*[5], *Josh.*[4], *Paul*[3], *Paul*[2], *Rich.*[1]], b. So. Tyringham, (now Monterey,) Mass., May 31, 1842; m. Monterey, Jan. 18, 1866, his cousin, *Julia Ann Thompson*, she b. So. Tyringham, Sep. 7, 1841, dau. of Sam'l and Emily (Sears) T. Children :

3726. *b.* i. MARY LOUISE, b. May 14, 1868; student N. E. Cons. Music, Boston, 1889.

3726. *b.* ii. ROSE JULIA, b. Nov. 19, 1869; senior class, Wellesley Coll., 1889.

3726. *b.* iii. ALFRED JOHN, b. May 9, 1871 ; address 1315 S. street, Lincoln, Neb.

3726. *b.* iv. HARRY BARNAS, b. Aug. 14, 1873 ; lives in Stockbridge, Mass.

3726. *b.* v. EDWARD JAMES, b. Nov. 15, 1874.

3726. *b.* vi. GEORGE PERCY, b. June 16, 1883; d. June 19, 1883.

Mr. Sears was educated in New Marlboro Institute and Suffield Academy. He served in Co. K, 49th Mass. Vol. Inf., from Oct. 23, 1862, to Sep. 1, 1863; was at battle of Port Hudson, and contracted disease from which he has never recovered. He removed to Stockbridge in 1872, and went into partnership with M. L. Dresser in mercantile business; dissolved in one year, Mr. Sears retaining the store, which was burned Feb. 1, 1876; he then rented a store for several years, and started a branch in Curtisville, which was burned Dec. 1, 1885. He now keeps a store connected with his dwelling-house in Stockbridge, Mass.

2518.

Rev. GILBERT N. SEARS[8] [*Sim.*[7], *Sim.*[6], *Paul*[5], *Josh.*[4], *Paul*[3], *Paul*[2], *Rich.*[1]], b. Lempster, N. H., Jan. 1, 1839 ; m. Painesville, Ohio, Apr. 15, 1863, *Mary M. Gage*, she b. Madison co., N. Y., Jan. 22, 1838. Children :

3727. i. LOUIS G., b. Rochester, N. Y., Aug. 27, 1864; lives Cleveland, Ohio.

3728. ii. HATTIE E., b. Scipio, N. Y., July 29, 1866; lives Shelby, N. Y.

3729. iii. EDWARD S., b. Manlius, N. Y., Aug. 12, 1868.

3730. iv. LULU A., b. Manlius, June 3, 1870.

3731. v. GEORGE M., b. Redwood, N. Y., Sep. 20, 1872.
3732. vi. GILBERT N., b. Redwood, N. Y., Sep. 20, 1874.
3733. vii. WILLIE, b. Leyden, N. Y., 1876 ; d. 1878.
3734. viii. MAY, b. Walworth, N. Y., 1879.

Lives in Shelby, Orleans county, N. Y.

2521.

Lt. EDWARD SHAILER SEARS[8] [*Edw' d*[7], *Sim.*[6], *Paul*[5], *Josh.*[4], *Paul*[3], *Paul*[2], *Rich.*[1]], b. North Wrentham, (now Norwood,) Mass., Apr. 23, 1844 ; m. Hartford, Ct., June 9, 1869, *Isabel Waggoner*, she b. Albany, N. Y., Apr. 4, 1849. Children :

3735. i. HARRY EDWARD, b. Boston, Apr. 11, 1870.
3736. ii. STANLEY COLLAMORE, b. Boston, Feb. 20, 1877.

In 1861, Mr. Sears became a reporter on the "Springfield Daily Republican," which position he left in July, 1862, to enlist in Co. I, 37th Regt., Mass. Inf., serving as private and Quartermaster-Sergeant from September 2, 1862, to June 21, 1865, when he was mustered out at Readville, Mass., with Brevet 1st Lieutenant.

He re-entered the service of the "Republican" in fall of 1865, resigning in December, to take a position on the "Union," under his father.

Since then he has been engaged in journalism in Hartford, New Haven and Norwich, Ct. ; Boston, Mass. ; St. Albans, Vt., and Philadelphia, Pa.

In December, 1883, he left the "Boston Daily Advertiser," to become Assistant General Manager of the "American Electric & Illuminating Co.," and is now (1889) President and General Manager "American Decorative Co." in Boston.

2527.

GREGORY A. SEARS[8] [*Jas.*[7], *Sim.*[6], *Sim.*[5], *Josh.*[4], *Paul*[3], *Paul*[2], *Rich.*[1]], b. Ithaca, N. Y., Feb. 27, 1837 ; m. Mich., 1853, *Mary A. Witherell*, she b. N. Y., 1833. Children :

3737. i. LILLIE, b. Mich., 1854 ; m. Kansas, 1872, *H. N. Gardner*, Cash'r Exchange Bank, Eldorado, Kan., he b. New Brunswick, 1846.
3738. ii. JENNIE, b. Kan., 1864 ; m. there, 1884, *Charles Teller*, he b. Ill., 1861 ; lives in Oswego, Ill.
3739. iii. HELEN, b. Nevada, 1866.

Mr. Sears was one of the founders of Carson City, Nev., having with his brother James located and bought together one-half of the site, and was one of the original owners of the famous "Comstock Mine," Virginia City, Nev.

He removed to Kansas in 1870, and has held several minor offices in the township and county, and was elected to the Legislature in 1880.

Is of firm Sears, Blackburn & Co., dealers in lumber, doors, sashes, etc., Saratoga, Kan.

2528.

JAMES DOUGLASS SEARS[8] [*Jas.*[7], *Sim.*[6], *Sim.*[5], *Josh.*[4], *Paul*[3], *Paul*[2], *Rich.*[1]], b. Ithaca, N. Y., 1829 ; m. Michigan, 1854, *Mary Etta Cambron*, she b. N. Y., 1830. Children :

3740. i. CHARLES F., b. Carson City, Nev., Oct. 20, 1856 ; of firm Sears Bros., livery, hay, grain, etc., Candelaria, Nev.
3741. ii. FRANK D., b. Iowa, 1860.
3742. iii. FRED. B., b. Nevada, 1862 ; partner with bro. Charles.
3743. iv. JUSTIN C., b. Nev., 1864 ; lives in Sprague, Wash. Ter.
3744. v. JESSE R., b. Montana, 1867 ; lives in Sprague, W. T.
3745. vi. NETTA EDNA, b. Nev., 1869.

Mr. Sears removed from New York to Michigan, and in 1850 to California, where he made a small fortune, and thence to Minnesota, and later to Dubuque, Iowa.

About 1860, he was at Carson City, Nev., and with his brother Gregory located and purchased half the town site ; removed, in 1867, to Helena, Montana, and in 1869–70 to White Pine during the mining excitement ; afterward to Eureka, Nev., and to Inigo county, Cal. ; carried on a farm in Sprague, Washington Territory, and is now resident at Glendive, Damson county, Montana.

2538.

DAVID SEARS[8] [*David*[7], *Jos.*[6], *Sim.*[5], *Josh.*[4], *Paul*[3], *Paul*[2], *Rich*[1].], b. Moline, Ill., Mar. 23, 1839 ; m. Minnetonka, Minn., Mar. 15, 1858, *Marion Stimpson*, she b. New London, Ohio, Apr. 4, 1838. Children :

3746. i. LILAH MAY, b. Moline, May 17, 1859 ; m. Sears, Ill., *S. K. W. Field*, and lives in Medicine Lodge, Kan.
3747. ii. HUGH, b. Moline, Nov. 10, 1862 ; lives Boiling Springs, Neb.

3748. iii. HARRIET, b. Milan, Nov. 28, 1868.
3749. iv. DAVID, b. Milan, Aug. 18, 1870.
3750. v. HELEN VESTA, b. Sears, Jan. 15, 1878.

Is of firm D. B. Sears' Sons, millers, Moline, and resides in
Sears, Ill.

2539.

WILLIAM H. H. SEARS[8] [*David*[7], *Jos.*[6], *Sim.*[5], *Josh.*[4],
Paul[3], *Paul*[2], *Rich.*[1]], b. Moline, Ill., Nov. 18, 1840; m. Jan.
2, 1864, *Catharine M. Stimpson*, she b. New London, Ohio,
July 27, 1845.   Children :
3751.   i. WILLIAM, b. Moline, Nov. 19, 1865; drowned July,
       1869.
3752. ii. EARNEST, b. Moline, Feb. 22, 1867.
3753. iii. CHAUNCY BURTON, b. Sears, May 20, 1868.
3754. iv. BENJAMIN LOVETT, b. Sears, Jan. 1, 1872.

Of firm D. B. Sears' Sons, Moline, Ill.

2540.

GEORGE WASHINGTON SEARS[8] [*David*[7], *Jos.*[6], *Sim.*[5],
Josh.[4], *Paul*[3], *Paul*[2], *Rich.*[1]], b. Moline, Ill., Nov. 23, 1842;
m. Milan, Ill., Apr. 7, 1870, *Elizabeth Grove Huyett*.   Children :
3755.   i. JOSEPH HUYETT, b. Sears, Feb. 22, 1871.
3756. ii. CLARA, b. Sears, July 11, 1873.
3757. iii. GEORGE LUCIEN, b. Feb. 7, 1877.
3758. iv. *Child*, b. Sears, July 24, 1885.

Is of firm D. B. Sears' Sons, Moline, Ill.

2543.

HENRY H. SEARS[8] [*David*[7], *Jos.*[6], *Sim.*[5], *Josh.*[4], *Paul*[3],
Paul[2], *Rich.*[1]], b. Moline, Ill., Oct. 18, 1850; m. Rock Island,
Ill., Sep. 15, 1875, *Kate Marsh Gilmore*, she b. there, June
22, 1854.   Children :
3759.   i. AGENORIA HOLT, b. Sears, July 20, 1876.
3760. ii. CHARLES EDWIN, b. Sears, Sep. 20, 1878.

Is of firm D. B. Sears' Sons, Moline, Ill.

2549.

DANIEL M. SEARS[8] [*Lewis*[7], *Dan'l*[6], *Enos*[5], *Dan'l*[4], *Paul*[3], *Paul*[2], *Rich.*[1]], b. Caledonia, Wis., Dec. 24, 1846; m. there, Oct. 9, 1877, *Nellie Mann*. Children:

3761. i. LEWIS A., b. Cale., June 25, 1878; d. Aug. 28, 1879.
3762. ii. EDGAR A., b. Cale., Jan. 23, 1880.
3763. iii. MABEL E., b. Cale., June 4, 1884.

2551.

EDGAR L. SEARS[8] [*Lewis*[7], *Dan'l*[6], *Enos*[5], *Dan'l*[4], *Paul*[3], *Paul*[2], *Rich.*[1]], b. Caledonia, Wis., Mar. 21, 1850; m. Racine, Wis., Sep. 20, 1877, *Jennie S. Stevens*. Child:
3764. i. FRANK L., b. Fargo, Dak., July 31, 18—.

2557.

MARTIN LUTHER SEARS[8] [*Wm.*[7], *Dan'l*[6], *Enos*[5], *Dan'l*[4], *Paul*[3], *Paul*[2], *Rich.*[1]], b. Caledonia, Wis., Oct. 18, 1843; m. *Julia Burkhaus*. Children:
3765. i. STELLA, b. Cale.
3766. ii. ALONZO, b. Cale.

Lives in Franksville, Racine county, Wis.

2573.

LEMUEL SEARS[8] [*Nathan*[7], *Wm.*[6], *Enos*[5], *Dan'l*[4], *Paul*[3], *Paul*[2], *Rich.*[1]], b. Ashfield, Mass., Feb. 17, 1835; m. Nov. 27, 1860, *Martha M. Ford*. Children:
3766. *a.* i. JENNIE E., b. Holyoke, Mass., Aug. 31, 1871.
3766. *a.* ii. ARTHUR L., b. Holyoke, July 11, 1879; d. Nov. 9, 1880.

Is of firm Lemuel Sears & Co., merchants, Holyoke, Mass.

2582.

SILAS SEARS[8] [*Dan'l*[7], *Jacob*[6], *Edm'd*[5], *Edm'd*[4], *Paul*[3], *Paul*[2], *Rich.*[1]], b. Dennis, Mass., Nov. 30, 1826; m. Brewster, Mass., Jan. 23, 1855, by Rev. W. R. Tisdale, to *Mercy A.*

Doane, dau. of Joseph and Mary D. of Br., she b. 1839; lives in Boston. Children:

3767. i. Lucy E., b. Br., Dec. 16, 185-.
3768. ii. Lizzie D., b. Br., July 2, 1859.
3769. iii. Daniel W., b. Br., Feb. 4, 1861.

2589.

Capt. EBEN THAXTER SEARS[8] [*Eben'r[7], Judah[6], Edm'd[5], Edm'd[4], Paul[3] Paul[2], Rich.[1]*], b. Dennis, Mass., June 3, 1829; d. Hyde Park, Mass., Apr. 17, 1889, æ. 59 yrs. 10 mos.; m. July 13, 1851, *Susan Elizabeth Leaman* of Bristol, Eng. Children:

3769. *a.* i. Ella Grace, b. Boston, June 14, 1852; d. Jan. 10, 1875.
3769. *a.* ii. Eben James, b. Boston, Feb. 5, 1855; m. Oct. 22, 1879, *Rosamond Pauline Makin* of Vt.; no children.
3769. *a.* iii. Susan Alice, b. Boston, June 20, 1856.
3769. *a.* iv. Edith Horton, b. Boston, Dec. 24, 1859; m. June 20, 1887, *George Lewis Ridley* of Dedham, Mass.; child, Ridley : [1.] George Lincoln, b. Hyde Park, Mass., Nov. 23, 1888.
3769. *a.* v. Laura Crichton, b. Boston, Nov. 3, 1861.
3769. *a.* vi. Jennie Brooks, b. Boston, Feb. 27, 1863; m. Aug. 20, 1888, *Henry Bauer Humphrey* of Braintree, Mass.; child, Humphrey : [1.] Evelyn Miller, b. Hyde Park, Oct. 16, 1889.
3769. *a.* vii. Louise Leaman, b. Boston, May 11, 1866; m. July 1, 1889, *Herbert Appleton Newman* of Ipswich, Mass.
3769. *a.* viii. Horace Thaxter, b. Boston, May 10, 1867.
3769. *a.* ix. John Stone Hale, b. Medfield, Mass., Aug. 16, 1869.
3769. *a.* x. Robert Clifton, b. Medfield, Apr. 18, 1871.

2594.

JUDAH HOWES SEARS[8] [*Nathan[7], Jacob[6], Edm'd[5], Edm'd[4], Paul[3], Paul[2], Rich.[1]*], b. Dennis, Mass., Dec. 20, 1823; d. Apr. 11, 1870; m. *Ellen* ——. Children:

3770. i. Judah W., b. Den., July 5, 1847; d. Oct. 17, 1848.
3771.* ii. Samuel D., b. Den., July 5, 1847, *gemini*.

3772. iii. WARREN, b. Den., Sep. 3, 1849.
3773. iv. SUSAN E., b. Den., Oct. 7, 1863.
3774. v. MINNIE E., b. Den., Mar. 24, 1869.

2586.

NATHAN NORRIS SEARS[8] [*Nathan*[7], *Jacob*[6], *Edm'd*[5], *Edm'd*[4], *Paul*[3] *Paul*[2], *Rich.*[1]], b. East Dennis, Mass., Jan. 5, 1831; m. there, Aug. 12, 1863, *Julia Potter*, she b. Dunstable, Eng., July 10, 1834. Children:
3775. i. JAMES FOSTER, b. Newark, N. J., Aug. 24, 1867.
3776. ii. JULIA MABEL, b. Newark, May 20, 1870.

Of firm Sears & Potter, straw goods, New York, and lives in Hempstead, L. I.

2592.

JABEZ H. SEARS[8] [*Judah*[7], *Judah*[6], *Edm'd*[5], *Edm'd*[4], *Paul*[3], *Paul*[2], *Rich.*[1]], b. Dennis, Mass., Feb. 1, 1829; m. Durham, N. H., Feb. 5, 1852, *Deborah A. York*, she b. Lee, N. H., Apr. 12, 1827. Children:
3777. i. ALBERT R., b. So. Boston, May 23, 1854; d. July 19, 1872.
3778. ii. WILLIS H., b. So. B., Aug., 1857; d. Sep. 2, 1858.
3779. iii. MINNIE P., b. So. B., May 14, 1860.

Lives in South Boston, Mass.

2594.

ZENAS SEARS[8] [*Judah*[7], *Judah*[6], *Edm'd*[5], *Edm'd*[4], *Paul*[3], *Paul*[2], *Rich.*[1]], b. Dennis, Mass., Nov. 23, 1833; m. So. Boston, Mass., *Sarah E. Robbins*, she b. Boston, Apr. 22, 1839. Children:
3780. i. WILLIAM A., b. Sep. 28, 1864; d. Mar. 8, 1865.
3781. ii. ZENAS, b. Dec. 22, 1865.
3782. iii. CHARLES M., b. July 13, 1870.
3783. iv. J. HOWES, b. Sep. 12, 1872.

Is a dealer in shoe manufacturing goods in Boston.

2598.

DEAN SMITH SEARS[8] [*Dean*[7], *Paul*[6], *Edm'd*[5], *Edm'd*[4], *Paul*[3] *Paul*[2], *Rich.*[1]], b. East Dennis, Mass., Sep. 1, 1832; m.
65

Brooklyn, N. Y., Mar. 1, 1857, *Alsa Seabury Howes*, dau. of James H. of Den., she b. Dec. 8, 1833. Children:

3784. i. CHARLES DEAN, b. Jan. 13, 1858; d. Dec. 3, 1861.
3785. ii. ELSIE NORA, b. Brooklyn, Apr. 26, 1861; m. *Chas. T. Patterson* of Livermore, Cal.
3786. iii. LEWIS H., b. Hopkinton, Mass., June 17, 1865.
3787. iv. OTIS JAMES, b. Sheboygan, Wis., Mar. 19, 1870; d. Dec. 15, 1871.
3788. v. BESSIE LOUISE, b. Sheboygan, Dec. 15, 1871.

Lives in Oakland, Cal.

2602.

PAUL FREEMAN SEARS[8] [*Dean*[7], *Paul*[6], *Edm'd*[5], *Edm'd*[4], *Paul*[3], *Paul*[2], *Rich.*[1]], b. East Dennis, Mass., Apr. 26, 1846; m. there, Aug. 11, 1867, *Betsy Olivia Sears*, No. 3115, dau. of Barzillai and Elizabeth (Bangs) S., she b. Feb. 18, 1847. Child:

3789. i. MABEL BETSIE, b. Boston, Feb. 29, 1880; adopted by Act of Mass. Leg., Aug. 9, 1881, née *Georgianna M. Voudy.*

Address, E. Dennis, Mass.

2604.

GEORGE THACHER SEARS[8] [*Paul*[7], *Paul*[6], *Edm'd*[5], *Edm'd*[4], *Paul*[3], *Paul*[2], *Rich.*[1]], b. East Dennis, Mass., Dec. 27, 1839; m. Sep. 19, 1865, *Harriet Thomas*, dau. of Wm. and Sarah Clark (Nickerson) T., she b. Duxbury, Mass., June 3, 1844. Children:

3790. i. GEORGE ALBERT, b. July 12, 1868.
3791. ii. EDITH THACHER, b. Mar. 21, 1875.

Is a salt dealer in Boston, and lives in Dorchester, Mass.

2614.

BARNABAS ALLEN SEARS[8] [*Barnabas*[7], *Paul*[6], *Edm'd*[5], *Edm'd*[4], *Paul*[3] *Paul*[2], *Rich.*[1]], b. East Dennis, Mass., Apr. 7, 1853; m. Brockton, Mass., June, 1873, *Harriet Eliot* of Rochester, Mass. Child:

3792. i. CHESTER L., b. Den., Sep. 20, 1873.

Lives in Brockton, Mass.

2616.

HENRY HOWES SEARS[8] [*Nathan[7], Edm'd[6], Edm'd[5], Edm'd[4], Paul₃ Paul[2], Rich[1].*], b. East Dennis, Mass., July 17, 1845; m. there, Feb. 17, 1870, *Mary Caroline Homer*, dau. of Stephen H., she b. there, Oct. 25, 1848. Children:

3793. i. HENRY EDMUND, b. E. Den., Oct. 26, 1870.
3794. ii. JOSEPH H., b. E. Den., Apr. 6, 1873.

Lives in East Dennis, Mass.

2626.

EZRA FREEMAN SEARS[8] [*David[7], Ezra[6], Josh.[5], Edm'd[4], Paul[3], Paul[2], Rich.[1]*], b. Dennis, Mass., Apr., 1852; m. there, Nov. 30, 1873, *Eleanor S. Bartlett* of Den. Children:

3795. i. CHARLES B., b. Den., Sep. 6, 1874.
3796. ii. EDWARD A., b. Den., Mar. 26, 1876.
3797. iii. SELECK M., b. Den., May 11, 1883.
3798. iv. *Dau.*, b. Den., Mar. 29, 1887.
3799. v. *Dau.*, b. Den., June 2, 1888.

2643.

CHARLES FRANKLIN SEARS[8] [*Franklin[7], Elisha[6], Elisha[5], Elisha[4], John[3], Paul[2], Rich.[1]*], b. Sandwich, Mass., 1850; m. Bowling Green, Ohio, 1872, *Harriet Sterner*. Child:

3800. i. CORA ANN, b. 1881.

Is in employ of Toledo and Southern railroad.

2644.

EDGAR HERBERT SEARS[8] [*Franklin[7], Elisha[6], Elisha[5], Elisha[4], John[3], Paul[2], Rich.[1]*], b. Sandwich, Mass., 1855; m. Bowling Green, Ohio, 1878, *Linnie Youker*. Child:

3801. i. FOSTER GARFIELD, b. 1880.

Is a farmer in Bowling Green, Ohio.

2671.

EDMUND H. SEARS[8] [*Enos[7], Moody[6], John[5], John[4], John[2], Paul[2], Rich.[1]*], b. Dennis, Mass., Jan. 28, 1841; m. there, Dec. 8, 1862, *Mary E. Hinds*. Child:

3802. i. MARY E., b. Den., Aug. 7, 1864.

2692.

DAVID B. SEARS[8] [*Reub.*[7], *Reub.*[6], *Reub.*[5], *Will'd*[4], *John*[3], *Paul*[2], *Rich.*[1]], b. West Brewster, Mass., Feb. 14, 1847; m. Feb. 23, 1871, by Rev. Dr. Webb, to *Emma Isadore Wiggin*, dau. of the late Hiram W.   Children:

3802. *a.* i. MAUD ISOLA, b. Nov. 3, 1872.
3802. *a.* ii. BLANCHE BEULAH, b. Mar. 27, 1874.

Mr. Sears is connected with the house of John H. Pray, Sons & Co., wholesale and retail carpet dealers in Boston. Both his daughters are fine musicians, and have played in public since they were eight years of age.

From the " Boston Journal " of June 30, 1885, I clip:

" TUSSLE WITH A BURGLAR. *He enters a south end residence, but is pitched headlong from a window.*

" Mr. David B. Sears, who lives at 58 Chester square, had a lively tussle with a burglar early Friday morning, and succeeded in throwing him from the chamber window.

" The robber fell heavily to the brick yard below, breaking his leg and stunning him.   He was carried off by two confederates who were waiting for him, and all three are still at large.

" Mr. Sears and his wife occupy a room on the first floor, facing Northampton street.   He is usually a heavy sleeper, but Friday morning he awoke suddenly and saw a man creeping stealthily through the window.   He had climbed up from the yard by means of a trellis, and was crawling noiselessly into the room when Mr. Sears saw him.   The latter sprang from his bed, and the burglar arose to defend himself.   Mr. Sears struck out with both fists, and planted them squarely in the burglar's face.   The force of the blow was sufficient to knock him headlong through the open window.

" There was a dull thud, and when Mr. Sears looked out he saw the fellow lying where he fell, groaning as if in great pain. At that moment two confederates looked through the gate, but dodged back when they saw Mr. Sears.   But a moment later, having assured themselves probably that he had no fire-arms, they rushed to where their wounded *pal* lay and dragged him out of the yard.   This was at 2:30 o'clock.   Mr. Sears called for the police, but as no officer came round he went to bed again.

" An hour later an officer saw tracks where some one had been dragged through the street, and following them found a man lying on the sidewalk on Camden street, and asked him what he was doing there. He replied that he had been on a spree, and had fallen and broken his leg. The officer felt of the limb and assured himself that it was really broken. His charitable instinct led him to go for an ambulance.

" Neighbors who had been watching this little episode say that the officer had been gone but a few minutes, when two men drove up hastily with a horse and buggy, and lifting the helpless man into the carriage, drove off at a furious gait. When the officer came back with the ambulance, he hunted in vain for the unfortunate individual whose leg was broken."

The burglars were afterward arrested, and are now serving terms in the State's prison.

2704.

MILTON H. SEARS[8] [*Sylvanus*[7], *Philander*[6], *Reuben*[5], *Will'd*[4], *John*[3], *Paul*[2], *Rich.*[1]], b. Worcester, Mass., June 1, 1854; m. June 12, 1878, *Emma C. Carpenter*, she b. Grafton, Mass., Apr. 6, 1854. Children:

3803. i. MABEL H., b. July 7, 1879.
3804. ii. H. FRANKLIN, b. Sep. 3, 1880.
3805. iii. WINTHROP S., b. Aug. 21, 1882.

Is a farmer and milk dealer ; address, Worcester, Mass.

2732.

EBEN WARDEN SEARS[8] [*Eben*[7], *Eben*[6], *Will'd*[5], *Will'd*[4], *John*[3], *Paul*[2], *Rich.*[1]], b. Wellington Hill, (now Belmont,) Mass., Aug. 1, 1854; m. Boston, July 23, 1879, *Caroline Roos*, she b. there, Dec. 7, 1857. Children:

3806. i. EBEN WARDEN, b. Boston, May 18, 1880.
3807. ii. RICHARD WILLARD, b. Dorchester, Mass., Oct. 11, 1881.
3808. iii. NATHANIEL PHILIP, b. Winthrop, Mass., Oct. 29, 1883.
3809. iv. FLORENCE, b. 1886.

Is a clerk in Boston.

2736.

JAMES SEARS[8] [*Obed*[7], *Arnold*[6], *Nath'l*[5], *Nath'l*[4], *John*[3], *Paul*[2], *Rich.*[1]], b. June 17, 1831 ; m. Pawtucket, R. I., Nov.

24, 1859, *Mary F. Seeley*, she b. Fermanagh co., Ireland, Feb. 22, 1839.   Children:

3810.   i. EMMA FRANCIS, b. Boston, Mar. 17, 1862 ; d. Sep. 30, 1863.

3811.   ii. WALTER KING, b. Boston, July 13, 1863 ; clerk in Boston.

3812.   iii. HENRIETTA ELLSWORTH, b. Boston, Nov. 24, 1864 ; d. Oct. 11, 1866.

3813.   iv. WILLIAM HENRY, b. and d. Boston, July 15, 1866.

3814.   v. WILLIAM FRANCIS, b. Hebronville, Ct., Oct. 23, 1868.

3815.   vi. LOUIZA ELIZABETH, b. Boston, Sep. 21, 1869 ; d. Jan. 22, 1872.

3816.   vii. FLORENCE MABEL, b. Boston, Jan. 25, 1874 ; d. May 6, 1877.

Lives in South Boston, Mass.

2739.

GEORGE SEARS[8] [*Obed*[7], *Arnold*[6], *Nath'l*[5], *Nath'l*[4], *John*[3], *Paul*[2], *Rich.*[1]], m. *Anne Tucker*.   Children :

3817.   i. EDWARD.

3818.   ii. WILLIAM.

3819.   iii. HENRY BARTLETT.

2745.

ALVIN W. SEARS[8] [*Alvin*[7], *Nath'l*[6], *Nath'l*[5], *Nath'l*[4], *John*[3], *Paul*[2], *Rich.*[1]], b. Brewster, Mass., Oct. 7, 1848 ; m. there, Oct. 23, 1873, by Rev. Davis Lothrop, to *Eleonora F. Cahoon*, dau. of Ellery and Gahan C., she b. 1851.   Children :

3820.   i. *Child*, b. Br., Dec. 14, 1872.

3821.   ii. *Child*, b. Br., Jan. 8, 1875.

2762.

SIMEON K. SEARS[8] [*Benj.*[7], *Lot*[6], *Nath'l*[5], *Nath'l*[4], *John*[3], *Paul*[2], *Rich.*[1]], b. Harwich, Mass., Sep. 7, 1851 ; m. Boston, Mass., Nov. 29, 1874, *Clara A. Ellis*, she b. Har., ab't 1853. Children :

3822.   i. BENJAMIN, b. Har., July 3, 1875.

3823.   ii. CLARA P., b. Har., July 9, 1878.

3824.   iii. *Dau.*, b. Har., Aug. 1, 1884 ; d. Aug. 12.

Is a dry goods dealer in Harwichport, Mass.

2765.

CLARENCE S. SEARS[8] [*Freeman[7], Freeman[6], Nath'l[5], Nath'l[4], John[3], Paul[2], Rich.[1]*], b. Dennis, Mass., Nov. 26, 1851; m. Harwich, Mass., Dec. 23, 1875, *Teresa D. Bearse* of Har. Children:

3825. i. WARREN C., b. Den., Aug. 23, 1876.
3826. ii. LUCY H., b. Har., Apr. 10, 1879. (Mar. 21, T. C.)
3827. iii. CALVIN C., b. Den., Nov. 24, 1883.

Lives in Dennis.

2767.

BENJAMIN O. SEARS[8] [*Freeman[7], Freeman[6], Nath'l[5], Nath'l[4], John[3], Paul[2], Rich.[1]*], b. Dennis, Mass., Apr. 7, 1860; m. Harwich, Mass., Jan. 1, 1882, *Bessie M. Bearse.* Child:

3828. i. RACHEL E., b. Dennis, Sep. 3, 1883.

Lives in Dennis.

2768.

HOWARD D. SEARS[8] [*Freeman[7], Freeman[6], Nath'l[5], Nath'l[4], John[3], Paul[2], Rich.[1]*], b. Dennis, Mass., Dec. 26, 1861; m. there, Aug. 31, 1883, *Sarah A. Chase.* Child:

3829. i. BENJAMIN FREEMAN, b. Den., Dec., 1884.

Lives in West Dennis, Mass.

2784.

GRAFTON SEARS[8] [*Grafton[7], Edw'd[6], Edw'd[5], Silas[4], Silas[3], Silas[2], Rich.[1]*], b. Dennis, Mass., Jan. 23, 1826; lost at sea, Feb., 1863; m. (pub. Den., Jan. 3, 1852,) *Martha J. Crowell* of Den., who d. Oct. 23, 1857; 2d, Harwich, Oct. 5, 1858, *Mehitable Burgess* of Har. Children:

By *Martha:*
3830. i. MARTHA H., b. Den., June 19, 1853.
3831. ii. WILLIS A., b. Den., Nov. 14, 1855; d. May 27, 1856.
By *Mehitable:*
3832. iii. WALTER G., b. Den., Dec. 2, 1859; m. Har., Jan. 13, 1883, *Jane L. Snow* of Har.
3833. iv. ELMER C., b. Den., June 18, 1861; d. Apr. 7, 1883.

2785.

DANIEL N. SEARS[8] [*Grafton*[7], *Edw'd*[6], *Edw'd*[5], *Silas*[4], *Silas*[3], *Silas*[2], *Rich.*[1]], b. Dennis, Mass., Aug. 30, 1827; m. (pub. Den., Aug. 25, 1849,) *Clarissa Harlow* of Smithfield, R. I. Children :

3834.   i. Hannah F., b. Den., Sep. 27, 1852 ; d. Dec. 13.
3835.   ii. Clara, b. Den., July 11, 1855.
3836.   iii. Daniel T., b. Den., May 30, 1860.

2786.

SIDNEY SEARS[8] [*Grafton*[7], *Edw'd*[6], *Edw'd*[5], *Silas*[4], *Silas*[3], *Silas*[2], *Rich.*[1]], b. Dennis, Mass., Oct. 5, 1829 ; m. *Mary* ——. Child :

3837.   i. Mary E., b. Den., Nov. 9, 1862.

2787.

EDWARD SEARS[8] [*Grafton*[7], *Edw'd*[6], *Edw'd*[5], *Silas*[4], *Silas*[3], *Silas*[2], *Rich.*[1]], b. Dennis, Mass., Feb. 21, 1833 ; lost at sea, Jan. 1, 1862; m. Harwich, Mass., Jan. 25, 1855, *Tirzah H. Kelley* of Har. Child :

3838.   i. Anna Augusta, b. Den., Aug. 31, 1857; d. Sep. 14, 1859.

Styled " Edward 3d " in records.

2790.

OBED C. SEARS[8] [*Grafton*[7], *Edw'd*[6], *Edw'd*[5], *Silas*[4], *Silas*[3], *Silas*[2], *Rich.*[1]], b. Dennis, Mass., Feb. 25, 1843 ; m. Yarmouth, Mass., Jan. 10, 1869, *Abby E. Turner.* Child :

3839.   i. Ruth, d. Mar. 30, 1876, æ. 5 yrs., gr.-st., So. Yar.

2793.

BARTLETT SEARS[8] [*Edw'd*[7], *Edw'd*[6], *Edw'd*[5], *Silas*[4], *Silas*[3], *Silas*[2], *Rich.*[1]], b. South Dennis, Mass., Nov. 8, 1837; m. Harwich, Mass., Aug. 31, 1857, *Data C. Smith*, she b. there, June 16, 1841. Children :

3840.   i. Ida W., b. Har., May 22, 1858 ; m. Den., Dec. 9, 1878, *Alvin Smith*, 2d, he b. there, July 12, 1852.

3841. ii. *Son,* b. Har., Sep. 24, 1860.
3842. iii. BARTLETT F., b. So. Den., Dec. 10, 1863 ; m. Har.,
     Dec. 7, 1888, Josephine F. Heylinburg of Har.
3843. iv. RHODA, b. So. Den., July 22, 1866.
3844. v. EMELINE B., b. So. Den., Oct. 27, 1868.

Lives in Dennisport, Mass.

2801.

ISAIAH D. SEARS[8] [*Shubael*[7], *Edw'd*[6], *Edw'd*[5], *Silas*[4],
Silas[3], *Silas*[2], *Rich.*[1]], b. Dennis, Mass., Mar. 29, 1845 ; m.
there, Feb. 18, 1869, *Annie F. Baker.* Child :
3845. i. HANNAH S., b. Den., Mar. 18, 1870 ; d. Mar. 6, 1878

2809.

SYLVESTER B. SEARS[8] [*Sylvanus*[7], *Edw'd*[6], *Edw'd*[5],
Silas[4], *Silas*[3], *Silas*[2], *Rich.*[1]], b. Dennis, Mass., June 22, 1847 ;
m. Harwich, Mass., Feb. 7, 1877, *Tabitha C. Kelly* of Har.
Child :
3846. i. GRACE B., b. Har., June 24, 1878.

2814.

JEPTHAH B. SEARS[8] [*Jepthah*[7], *Edw'd*[6], *Edw'd*[5], *Silas*[4],
Silas[3], *Silas*[2], *Rich.*[1]], b. Dennis, Mass., Oct. 15, 1844 ; drowned
Hereford, N. J., Dec. 23, 1870 ; m. Providence, R. I., May
26, 1868, on board three-masted schooner " Charles E. Gibson," by Rev. Chas. M. Winchester, to *Hope D. Ellis,* dau.
of Capt. Lewis P. and Annie K. E. of Harwichport, Mass.,
she b. there, Aug. 27, 1848. Children :
3847. i. JEPTHAH B., b. Harwichport, Apr. 17, 1869.
3848. ii. LILLIAN WINSOR WHITNEY, b. Harwichport, Apr. 7,
     1871.

Mr. Sears was mate of Boston and Philadelphia steamer
" Aries," and was drowned at Hereford, N. J., Dec. 23, 1870,
with four colored deck hands, while engaged in sounding, the
steamer having got aground.
His body was recovered, and buried at Harwichport.
The daughter was named for the owners of the "Aries."

66

2823.

ORIN SEARS[8] [*Jas.*[7], *Jas.*[6], *Moody*[5], *Silas*[4], *Silas*[3], *Silas*[2], *Rich.*[1]], b. Dennis, Mass., Jan. 11, 1828; d. Kansas; m. *Eleanor M. Bowen.* Children:

3849.   i. Charles Bowen, b. Yarmouth, Nov. 3, 1857; m. there, June 13, 1880, *Mary C. Chase* of Den.
3850.   ii. *Child*, b. Yar., Nov. 3, 1857, *gemini;* d. same day.
3851.   iii. Phebe Ann, b. Yar., Apr. 7, 1860.
3852.   iv. Martin Luther, b. Yar., Nov. 12, 1861.
3853.   v. Prince J., b. Yar., June 30, 1863; d. Sep. 3, 1864.
3854.   vi. *Son*, b. Yar., Oct. 6, 1866; d. same day.
3855.   vii. Lucy Maria, b. Yar., Oct. 6, 1866, *gemini.*

2840.

Capt. PETER COLLINS SEARS[8] [*Isaiah*[7], *Isaiah*[6], *Moody*[5], *Silas*[4], *Silas*[3], *Silas*[2], *Rich.*[1]], b. Mattapoisett, Mass., Mar. 15, 1842; m. Biddeford, Me., June 20, 1866, *Rose Anna Roberts.* Children:

3856.   i. Sarah B., b. June 5, 1867.
3857.   ii. Amelia N., b. Aug. 8, 1872.
3858.   iii. Rose Roberts, b. Feb. 18, 1877.

Mr. Sears was educated in State Normal School, Bridgewater, Mass.; enlisted in Co. I, 33d Regt., Mass. Vol. Inf'y, July, 1862; Sergt., Aug. 5, 1862; 2d Lt., July 29, 1863; 1st Lt., Mar. 24, 1864; Capt., Sep. 27, 1864; discharged, June 11, 1865; was with Sherman on his "March to the Sea."

Is of firm P. C. Sears & Co., fruit and produce dealers, Chicago, Ill.

2845.

Capt. JONATHAN SEARS[8] [*Jona.*[7], *Lewis*[6], *Eleazar*[5], *Silas*[4], *Silas*[3], *Silas*[2], *Rich.*[1]], b. South Yarmouth, Mass., Mar. 8, 1826; lost at sea, Mar. 10, 1855, gr.-st., So. Yar.; m. Providence, R. I., Jan. 16, 1850, *Sarah A. Baker*, she b. So. Yar., Oct. 2, 1830; d. there, Nov. 5, 1859, æ. 29, gr.-st. Children:

3859.* i. Jonathan Hatsell, b. So. Yar., Apr. 18, 1851.
3860.   ii. Eloise A., b. So. Yar., Mar. 1, 1854; is an M. D., and lives in Malden, Mass.

Was master of ship "Wm. A. Cooper," and drowned near Scituate, Mass.

2846.

THOMAS N. SEARS[8] [*Lewis[7], Lewis[6], Eleazar[5], Silas[4], Silas[3], Silas[2], Rich.[1]*], b. Yarmouth, Mass., July 5, 1825 ; m. Dennis, July 1, 1855, *Ann Baker* of Harwich.   Child :
3861. i. ELLEN, b. Har., Dec. 30, 1860.

2847.

Capt. JONATHAN L. SEARS[8] [*Lewis[7], Lewis[6], Eleazar[5], Silas[4], Silas[3], Silas[2], Rich.[1]*], b. Yarmouth, Mass., Feb. 26, 1828; m. Jan. 10, 1858, *Ellen M. Smith* of Harwich.   Children :
3862. i. MARY E., b. Har., Aug. 2, 1862.
3863. ii. *Son,* b. Har., Dec. 28, 1879.

Is a sea captain and resides in Milton, Mass.

2854.

EDWARD SEARS[8] [*Edw'd[7], Edw'd[6], Eleazar[5], Silas[4], Silas[3], Silas[2], Rich.[1]*], b. So. Yarmouth, Mass., Nov. 20, 1835 ; m. Long Plain, Mass., July 19, 1860, *Lydia H. Haswell,* she b. New Bedford, Mass., Dec. 21, 1838.   Children :
3864.   i. STEPHEN H., b. Barnstable, Mass., June 2, 1861;
        d. Nov. 5.
3865. ii. LILLIE F., b. Long Pl., Feb. 16, 1865.
3866. iii. MERCY KILLEY, b. Rochester, Mass., Sep. 2, 1867.
3867. iv. EDWARD H., b. Long Pl., Jan. 22, 1869.
3868.   v. GEORGE E., b. New Bedford, Mass., Jan. 17, 1871;
        d. Aug. 25, 1875.
3869. vi. RUTH H., b. New Bed., Feb. 19, 1872; d. Aug.
        25, 1875.
3870. vii. GRACE L., b. New Bed., June 12, 1878.

Is a painter in New Bedford, Mass.

2859.

Lt. CYRUS SEARS[8] [*Odlin[7], Winthrop[6], Eleazar[5], Thos.[4], Silas[3], Silas[2], Rich.[1]*], b. Yarmouth, Mass., Nov. 5, 1831; m. *Martha R. Baker.*   Child:
3871. i. MARTHA ISABEL, b. Yar., Oct. 17, 1858.

Mr. Sears was appointed Acting Ensign, U. S. Navy, Aug. 12, 1863 ; Acting Master, Aug. 16, 1864 ; Acting. Vol. Lt., July 15, 1865 ; and honorably discharged, Sep. 27, 1865.

2860.

RICHARD SEARS[8] [*Odlin*[7], *Winthrop*[6], *Eleazar*[5], *Thos.*[4], *Silas*[3], *Silas*[2], *Rich.*[1]], b. Yarmouth, Mass., Sep. 1, 1833 ; m. Yar., Apr. 11, 1858, *Reliance Chase*, who d. Feb. 15, 1865 ; 2d, Yar., Feb. 6, 1871, *Betsy S. Crowell*.   Child :
By *Reliance :*
3872. i. ODLIN PAGE, b. Yar., Jan. 26, 1859.

2870.

HENRY CLINTON SEARS[8] [*Chauncy*[7], *Philip*[6], *David*[5], *Jas.*[4], *Silas*[3], *Silas*[2], *Rich.*[1]], b. Lenox, Mass., Feb. 11, 1832 ; m. New Bedford, Mass., Dec. 26, 1861, *Fannie Elizabeth Clark*, she b. there, Nov. 2, 1839 ; d. Roxbury, Mass., Jan. 22, 1890.   Children :
3873. i. FLORENCE MAY, b. New Bed., May 30, 1863 ; m. —— *Fuller.*
3874. ii. ETHEL CRAIG, b. Roxbury, Oct. 29, 1869; d. Feb. 11, 1876.

Is with D. P. Nichols & Co., Boston, and lives in Roxbury, Mass.

2871.

CHAUNCY SEARS[8] [*Chauncy*[7], *Philip*[6], *David*[5], *Jas.*[4], *Silas*[3], *Silas*[2], *Rich.*[1]], b. Lenox, Mass., Nov. 13, 1834; m. there, June 1, 1871, *Anna Aurelia Hart*, she b. Pittsfield, Mass., Dec. 13, 1849.   Children :
3875. i. HORATIO HENRY, b. Lenox, Feb. 2, 1873.
3876. ii. CHAUNCY HAROLD, b. Lenox, Nov. 28, 1875.
3877. iii. MARY AGNES, b. Lenox, Feb. 5, 1882.

Lives on the old homestead in Lenox ; is a Justice of the Peace, Assessor, etc., Rep. to Leg., 1884–85.   P. O., New Lenox, Mass.

2873.

ORANGE S. SEARS[8] [*David*[7], *David*[6], *David*[5], *Jas.*[4], *Silas*[3], *Silas*[2], *Rich.*[1]], b. Milton, N. Y., Aug. 13, 1812 ; d. Jan.

13, 1848, æ. 35; m. Apulia, N. Y., Sep. 5, 1833, *Sarah A. Northrop*, she b. Mar. 4, 1813; d.   Children:

3878.   i. CLARISSA E., b. Apulia, June 14, 1838; m. Greenfield, N. Y., Nov. 2, 1869, *Martin V. Ostrander*, he b. Aug. 8, 1841, and d. Apr. 25, 1875, æ. 36.

3879.   ii. WILLIAM G., b. Greenfield, May 14, 1843; m. there, Apr. 18, 1867, *Mary G. Gaige*, she b. Schoharie, N. Y., Mar. 23, 1846; lives in Schenectady, N. Y.

2887.

CHARLES M. SEARS[8] [*Marshall*[7], *Luther*[6], *David*[5], *Jas.*[4], *Silas*[3], *Silas*[2], *Rich.*[1]], b. Lenox, Mass., Sep. 11, 1837; d. there, Jan. 9, 1883, æ. 46; m. Albany, N. Y., Nov. 3, 1863, *Esther Chase*, she b. there, Feb. 10, 1841.   Children:

3880.   i. GRACE, b. Lenox, Aug. 29, 1864.

3881.   ii. CHARLES, b. Lenox, July 30, 1866.

2891.

MARTIN LUTHER SEARS[8] [*Luther*[7], *Luther*[6], *David*[5], *Jas.*[4], *Silas*[3], *Silas*[2], *Rich.*[1]], b. Lenox, Mass.; m. there, Dec., 186—, *Mary Bull* of Springfield, Mass.; 2d, Dec. 25, 1883, *Clara K. Collamore* of Stockbridge, Mass.   Children:

By *Mary:*

3882.   i. MARY, b. Lenox, Sep. 5, 1864; (Jan. 1, 1865, another account.)

3883.   ii. ROBERT L., b. Lenox, Apr. 8, 1871.

3884.   iii. JAMES, b. Lenox, May 2, 1872.

3885.   iv. CLARENCE H., b. Lenox, Mar. 11, 1874.

Lives in New Lenox, Mass.

2910.

SAMUEL SEARS[8] [*John*[7], *Zach.*[6], *David*[5], *Jas.*[4], *Silas*[3], *Silas*[2], *Rich.*[1]], b. Lenox, Mass., Feb. 22, 1838; m. Feb. 12, 1866, *Martha Brooker*.   Child:

3886.   i. WELLS R., b. Jan. 12, 1868.

2928.

ALEXANDER SEARS[8] [*Alex'r*[7], *Enoch*[6], *Seth*[5], *Jas.*[4], *Silas*[3], *Silas*[2], *Rich.*[1]], b. June 10, 1818; m. Feb. 4, 1841, *Juliet Tappan* of Charlton, N. Y.   Children :

3887.   i. CHARLES, m., and lives in Freeman county, Iowa.
3888.   ii. HENRY, m., and lives in Ballston, N. Y.
3889.   iii. PHEBE, m. *John McKnight* of Brooklyn, N. Y., and has 2 children.

2929.

ISAAC H. SEARS[8] [*Alex'r*[7], *Enoch*[6], *Seth*[5], *Jas.*[4], *Silas*[3], *Silas*[2], *Rich.*[1]], b. Oct. 9, 1821; m. Dec. 7, 1843, *Nancie Jennings* of Ballston Centre, N. Y.   Children :

3890.*   i. SAMUEL H., b. Saratoga co., N. Y., Sep. 18, 1844.
3891.*   ii. ALEXANDER, b. Sar. co., N. Y., July 13, 1847.
3892.   iii. MARY, b. Sar. co., N. Y., Feb. 8, 1852.
3893.   iv. JANET, b. Sar. co., N. Y., June 28, 1854; m. *E. S. Bennett*, and d. s. p.
3894.   v. NANCIE, b. Davenport, Iowa, Oct. 24, 1858; m. *John F. Dow;* children, Dow : [1.] George. [2.] Gilbert T.
3895.   vi. BERTHA, b. Dav., Apr. 12, 1861.
3896.   vii. ISAAC L., b. Dav., Mar. 22, 1863.

Mr. Sears removed to Davenport, Iowa, in 1855, and engaged in the saddlery and hardware business, the first store of the kind there.   Is a Director in Davenport National Bank ; Pres't Scott County Savings Bank ; and Chairman Board of Supervisors of Scott co.

2934.

JAMES SEARS[8] [*Arza*[7], *Dan'l*[6], *Knowles*[5], *Jas.*[4], *Silas*[3], *Silas*[2], *Rich.*[1]], b. Van Buren, N. Y., Dec. 26, 1822; m. Feb. 28, 1844, *Hannah Nichols*, dau. of Rev. Browning and Persis (Howe) N., she b. there ; d. there, Mar. 2, 1878.   Children :

3897.   i. VIOLIA, b. Van B., Sep. 22, 1848; d. May 12, 1849.
3898.   ii. FRED. L., b. Van B., Sep. 21, 1850 ; d. Mar. 8, 1889 ; m. Warners, N. Y., Aug. 29, 1878, *Eunice A. Peck*, dau. of Daniel P. and Betsy (Foster) P., she b. Van B., Aug. 30, 1854.   Mr. Sears took great interest in the family history, and in May, 1887, made a pilgrimage to

the homes of his forefathers in Connecticut and Massachusetts, and photographed many objects of interest. His widow resides in Warners.

3899. iii. GRANT, b. Van B., May 24, 1853; d. Feb. 15, 1854.
3900. iv. MARY, b. Van B., Apr. 21, 1855.
3901. v. LIZZIE, b. Van B., June 4, 1861.
3902. vi. LOUIS J., b. Van B., Apr. 14, 1864.

Lives in Van Buren, Onondaga co., N. Y. P. O., Baldwinsville.

2935.

DANIEL D. SEARS^8 [*Ahiram^7*, *Dan'l^6*, *Knowles^5*, *Jas.^{4}*, *Silas^3*, *Silas^2*, *Rich.^{1}*], b. Baldwinsville, N. Y.; m. —— ——. Children :

3903. i. ANNA BELLE, b. Bald.
3904. ii. FRED ALLISON, b. Bald., July 23, 1854.
3905. iii. ARTHUR, b. Bald.

2943.

CHARLES WILLIAM SEARS^8 [*Hart^7*, *Abijah^6*, *Knowles^5*, *Jas.^{4}*, *Silas^3*, *Silas^2*, *Rich.^{1}*], b. Newark Valley, N. Y., June 13, 1830; m. *Augusta R. Howe*, she b. Delhi, N. Y.; d. July 26, 1880. Children :

3906. i. JAMES HAMILTON, b. Binghamton, N. Y., Jan. 6, 1855; app. Mid. U. S. Navy, Sep. 20, 1871; grad. June 20, 1876, Ensign.
3907. ii. FRANK W., b. Bing., 1858; m. 1878, *Fannie Gordon Clark;* of firm Cox & Sears, cigars, Binghamton, N. Y.
3908. iii. MARY H., b. Bing., 1865.

Is a bookseller in Binghamton, N. Y.

2944.

ALBERT EDGAR SEARS^8 [*Hart^7*, *Abijah^6*, *Knowles^5*, *Jas.^{4}*, *Silas^3*, *Silas^2*, *Rich.^{1}*], b. Venice, N. Y., Jan. 10, 1832; m. Grimsby, Can., May 20, 1857, *Mary Ann Allison*, she b. Nelson, Can., Oct. 24, 1833. Children :

3909. i. LOUISA A., b. New. Vall., Feb. 20, 1858.
3910. ii. CHARLES A., b. New. Vall., Oct. 13, 1860.
3911. iii. JOHN W., b. Grimsby, Nov. 1, 1864.

3912. iv. CARRIE M., b. Sand Creek, Mich., Aug. 6, 1867.
3913. v. FRANK W., b. Grimsby, Sep. 20, 1870.

Is a blacksmith in Duluth, Minn.

2946.

MARTIN W. SEARS[8] [*Hart*[7], *Abijah*[6], *Knowles*[5], *Jas.*[4], *Silas*[3], *Silas*[2], *Rich.*[1]], b. Newark Valley, N. Y., Apr. 1, 1836 ; m. Mar., 1861, *Sophronia Moore*, dau. of Dan'l and Electa (Porter) M. of that place, she b. Aug. 12, 1838.   Children :
3914. i. ELIZABETH MOORE, b. New. Vall., Nov. 18, 1864.
3915. ii. FREDERIC JEROME, b. New. Vall., Feb. 17, 1870.

Is an upholsterer, carpenter and joiner in Newark Valley, Tioga county, N. Y.; name originally Martin *Van Buren* S.

2950.

OLIVER WILLIAMS SEARS[8] [*Hart*[7], *Abijah*[6], *Knowles*[5], *Jas.*[4], *Silas*[3], *Silas*[2], *Rich.*[1]], b. Newark Valley, N. Y., June 13, 1845 ; m. *Georgianna Bartlett*, dau. of Robert and —— (Bartlett) B. of Binghamton, N. Y.   Children :
3916. i. SARAH KINGSLAND, b. Bing., Nov. 11, 1875.
3917. ii. ROBERT BARTLETT, b. Bing., May, 1879.

Is a coal dealer in Binghamton, N. Y.

2955.

ISAAC SEARS[8] [*Haman*[7], *Isaac*[6], *Knowles*[5], *Jas.*[4], *Silas*[3], *Silas*[2], *Rich.*[1]], b. Newfane, N. Y., Sep. 4, 1833 ; m. there, Dec. 21, 1858, *Hannah Sweet*, she b. there, Oct. 5, 1835. Children :
3918.   i. ELIZA.
3919. ii. ETTA, m. 1883.
3920. iii. HEMAN.
3921. iv. JENNIE.
3922.   v. JOHN.
3923. vi. BURT.
3924. vii. CARRIE.
3925. viii. EVA.
3926. ix. WILSON.
3927.   x. FRANK.

Is a farmer and lives on the old homestead in Newfane, Niagara county, N. Y.

2966.

ELI SEARS⁸ [*Thos.⁷*, *Eli⁶*, *Thos.⁵*, *Jas.⁴*, *Silas³*, *Silas²*, *Rich.¹*], b. Ovid, N. Y., Dec. 7, 1816; d. Apr. 11, 1872; m. Trumansburg, N. Y., Oct. 24, 1839, *Mary Anna Morris*, she b. July 31, 1818; d. Mar. 7, 1884.   Children:

3928.* i. DEMETRIUS, b. Searsburg, N. Y., Oct. 9, 1841.
3929. ii. ANN ELIZABETH, b. Sears., July 21, 1848; m. Covert, N. Y., Oct. 28, 1868, Dr. *Wm. W. Holmes*, he b.
Mar. 4, 1848; lives in Waldo, Ohio; children, HOLMES ::
[1.] Nina Pearl, b. Feb. 15, 1870.   [2.] Inez May, b.
Nov. 30, 1879.
3930.* iii. MORRIS BALDWIN, b. Sears., July 2, 1850.
3931. iv. OSCAR, b. Sears., Apr. 17, 1854; is a doctor in California.
3932. v. CLEON, b. Sears., Oct. 17, 1858; m. Farmersville,
N. Y., Apr., 1884, *Bertha Farrington*.
3933. vi. RICHARD, b. Sears., Nov. 18, 1860.

Was an auctioneer.

2967.

Dr. ALFRED SEARS⁸ [*Thos.⁷*, *Eli⁶*, *Thos.⁵*, *Jas.⁴*, *Silas³*, *Silas²*, *Rich.¹*], b. Hector, N. Y., Oct. 19, 1818; m. Farmersville, N. Y., Sep. 30, 1846, *Harriet Woodworth*, she b. Apr.
1, 1824.   Children :

3934. i. IDA, b. July 31, 1847; m. Townsendville, N. Y.,
June 10, 1868, *Francis Colgate Townsend;* children,
TOWNSEND: [1.] Chauney, b. Nov. 20, 1869.   [2.] Cora
Allen, b. Dec. 28, 1874.
3935. ii. EDLA, b. May 31, 1850; m. Towns., Jan. 15, 1880,
Archibald Knight; children, KNIGHT: [1.] Alfred S., b.
Nov. 27, 1880; d. Sep. 7, 1881.   [2.] Edith, b. Oct. 21,
1883.
3936. iii. LUELLA, b. July 30, 1854.

Is a physician.

2968.

BALDWIN SEARS⁸ [*Thos.⁷*, *Eli⁶*, *Thos.⁵*, *Jas.⁴*, *Silas³*, *Silas²*, *Rich.¹*], b. Hector, N. Y., Apr. 30, 1820; m. Covert,

N. Y., Jan. 27, 1848, *Mary M. Whiting*, she b. Winsted, Ct., Feb. 19, 1826. Children :

3937.   i. CLARA, b. Winsted, Nov. 5, 1848.
3938. ii. ALIDA, b. Winsted, Jan. 1, 1850 ; m. Pine River, Wis., Sep. 26, 1875, *Gilbert L. Hart*, he b. Sep. 23, 1854 ; children, HART : [1.] Raymond, b. Aug. 6, 1876 ; d. Sep. 2, 1883. [2.] Llewellyn, b. Nov. 24, 1878. [3.] Stanley Douglass, b. Dec. 21, 1881.
3939.* iii. THOMAS SELMA, b. Pine River, Wis., Aug. 20, 1853.
3940. iv. EMILY BOARDMAN, b. Pine R., Sep. 21, 1857.
3941.   v. TRUMAN, b. Pine R., Apr. 6, 1859.
3942. vi. LORRIN, b. Pine R., Mar. 21, 1864.
3943. vii. MARY, b. Pine R., Dec. 16, 1865.
3944. viii. MAY, b. Pine R., Dec. 16, 1865, *gemini.*
3945. ix. MYRON E., b. Pine R., Mar. 7, 1869.

2972.

SACKET SEARS[8] [*Thos.*[7], *Eli*[6], *Thos.*[5], *Jas.*[4], *Silas*[3], *Silas*[2], *Rich.*[1]], b. Searsburg, N. Y., Apr. 7, 1827 ; m. Sacramento, Wis., Nov. 7, 1852, *Kate Langworthy*, she b. Feb. 6, 1835. Children :

3946.   i. MARIA, b. Oct. 16, 1853 ; m. Princeton, Ill., Dec. 31, 1876, *James W. Thompson ;* has no children.
3947. ii. ALLA, b. Jan. 10, 1855 ; m. Mar. 26, 1876, *Jacob Beisser ;* children, BEISSER : [1.] John Sacket. [2.] Katie May, b. June 20, 1879.
3948. iii. VILA, b. Aug. 20, 1858 ; m. Mar. 7, 1877, *Alphonse Riley ;* child, RILEY : [1.] Golda Emeline, b. May 20, 1879.
3949. iv. LUCIA, b. July 23, 1863 ; d. June 2, 1865.
3950.   v. LILIAN, b. Aug. 20, 1864 (? 1861 ;) m. Oct. 20, 1881, *Wm. Thompson*, he b. July 9, 1857.
3951. vi. LENA, b. Dec. 22, 1871.

Served during the war in Illinois volunteers.

2976.

DAVID ELBERT SEARS[8] [*Thos.*[7], *Eli*[6], *Thos.*[5], *Jas.*[4], *Silas*[3], *Silas*[2], *Rich.*[1]], b. Searsburg, N. Y., Apr. 25, 1836 ; m. Trumansburg, N. Y., Jan. 27, 1869, *Phebe Eliza Wright*, she b. Feb. 12, 1841. Children :

3952.   i. BLAKE, b. Apr. 18, 1873.
3953. ii. ANNA M., b. Oct. 21, 1877.

2977.

CLERMONT SEARS[8] [*Thos.*[7], *Eli*[6], *Thos.*[5], *Jas.*[4], *Silas*[3], *Silas*[2], *Rich.*[1]], b. Searsburg, N. Y., Dec. 27, 1838 ; m. Covert, N. Y., Feb. 18, 1864, *Mary E. Brown*, she b. Aug. 5, 1838. Children :

3954. i. PURLIE FONDA, b. Mar. 27, 1866.
3955. ii. ART, b. Aug. 20, 1867.

Lives in Trumansburg, N. Y.

2978.

OSSAIN SEARS[8] [*Thos.*[7], *Eli*[6], *Thos.*[5], *Jas.*[4], *Silas*[3], *Silas*[2], *Rich.*[1]], b. Searsburg, N. Y., Feb. 18, 1843 ; m. Hector, N. Y., Feb. 18, 1874, *Kate Stillwell*, she b. Peoria City, Iowa, Apr. 20, 1852.   Children :

3956. i. KEITH, b. Jan. 6, 1875.
3957. ii. WOODARD, b. Aug. 18, 1878.
3958. iii. WINNIE BUDD, b. Feb. 17, 1881.

Is a farmer in Searsburg, Schuyler county, N. Y.

2979.

ALMOIN PINE SEARS[8] [*David*[7], *Eli*[6], *Thos.*[5], *Jas.*[4], *Silas*[3], *Silas*[2], *Rich.*[1]], b. Dec. 17, 1812 ; d. Aug. 5, 1883 ; m. Covert, N. Y., Nov. 21, 1836, *Lucinda Smith*, she b. May 7, 1813 ; d. Nov. 19, 1867.   Child :

3959.* i. EUGENE B., b. Aug. 29, 1841.

2980.

GEORGE W. SEARS[8] [*David*[7], *Eli*[6], *Thos.*[5], *Jas.*[4], *Silas*[3], *Silas*[2], *Rich.*[1]], b. Hector, N. Y., Aug. 5, 1814 ; d. Mar. 14, 1883 ; m. Lodi, N. Y., Oct. 3, 1836, *Maria Townsend*, she b. July 19, 1819 ; d. Mar. 22, 1869.   Children :

3960.* i. GILBERT T., b. Townsendville, N. Y., July 17, 1840.
3961.* ii. WALLACE, b. Andover, N. Y., Oct. 22, 1844.
3962. iii. LAURA A., b. And., Apr. 18, 1847 ; m. Searsburg, N. Y., June 13, 1866, *Robert M. Bunda ;* child, BUNDA : [1.] Lorna Maria, b. May 7, 1873 ; d. June 16, 1876.

3963. iv. DELOS T., b. And., Nov. 31, 1852; d. July 20, 1858.

2983.

BENJAMIN P. SEARS[8] [*David[7], Eli[6], Thos.[5], Jas.[4], Silas[3], Silas[2], Rich.[1]*], b. Tompkins county, N. Y., Dec. 7, 1819; m. Lodi, N. Y., May 5, 1848, *Elvira Shannon*, she b. there, Jan. 15, 1827. Children :

3964. i. WILLIAM S., b. No. Hector, N. Y., Oct. 5, 1852; m. Tomp. co., N. Y., Apr. 5, 1876, *Esther Brewer*, she b. Trumansburg, N. Y.

3965. ii. FREDERIC T., b. No. Hector, May 23, 1859; d. Sep. 5, 1864.

Lives in Bowling Green, Ohio.

2986.

FRANKLIN SEARS[8] [*David[7], Eli[6], Thos.[5], Jas.[4], Silas[3], Silas[2], Rich.[1]*], b. Oct. 12, 1826; m. Hector, N. Y., Jan. 16, 1855, *Calphurnia Crissey*, she b. Dec. 17, 1834. Child :

3966. i. CLAUDE C., b. Nov. 8, 1855; m. Oswego, N. Y., Aug. 31, 1881, *Emma C. Timson*.

2987.

DE WITT C. SEARS[8] [*David[7], Eli[6], Thos.[5], Jas.[4], Silas[3], Silas[2], Rich.[1]*], b. Jan. 21, 1829; m. Mecklenburg, N. Y., Nov. 13, 1855, *Cornelia Garrison*, she b. Apr. 26, 1834. Children :

3967. i. GEORGE DEWITT, b. Nov. 21, 1858.

3968. ii. BELL CARRIE, b. July 14, 1868.

3000.

JOHN W. SEARS[8] [*John[7], Jas.[6], Jas.[5], Jas.[4], Silas[3], Silas[2], Rich.[1]*], b. Knightstown, Ind., Mar. 23, 1841; m. West Newton, Ind., Dec. 24, 1867, *Julia A. Glessner*, she b. Martinsville, Ind., Sep. 21, 1844. Children :

3969. i. WILLIE G., b. Mattoon, Ill., Oct. 22, 1868; d. Feb. 23, 1870.

3970. ii. WALTER C., b. West Newton, Ind., Oct. 19, 1870.

3971. iii. Ross G., b. Indianapolis, Ind., Nov. 15, 1872.

3972. iv. GEORGE W., b. Brightwood, Ind., Jan. 30, 1878; d.

Mr. Sears served in the Union army, during the war; is a blacksmith, and lives in Brightwood, Marion co., Ind.

3010.

JOSEPHUS THEODORE SEARS[8] [*Jas.*[7], *Jus.*[6], *Jas.*[5], *Jas.*[4], *Silas*[3], *Silas*[2], *Rich.*[1]], b. Dec. 3, 1847; m. 1867, *Melissa Breckenridge.* Children:

3973. i. HERBERT GAIL.
3974. ii. HANLEY.
3975. iii. ETHEL.
3976. iv. FRANK.

Lives in Ogden, Henry co., Ind.

3013.

JAMES OTTO SEARS[8] [*Jas.*[7], *Jas.*[6], *Jas.*[5], *Jas.*[4], *Silas*[3], *Silas*[2], *Rich.*[1]], b. June 16, 1857; m. 1876, *Ellen Ballenger.* Children:

3977. i. EARL.
3978. ii. CLAUDE.
3979. iii. ARTHUR, d. inf.

Lives in Carthage, Rush co., Ind.

3018.

JOHN A. SEARS[8] [*Geo.*[7], *Jas.*[6], *Jas.*[5], *Jas.*[4], *Silas*[3], *Silas*[2], *Rich.*[1]], b. Rush co., Ind., Apr. 27, 1843; m. Lapell, Ind., Aug. 12, 1866, *Mary L. Studley*, she b. there. Child:

3980. i. OLIVE R., b. near Lapell, Sep. 29, 1867.

Mr. Sears is a wagon-maker; was a private in 89th Regiment Indiana Volunteers during the war, and now lives in Lapell, Ind.

3022.

THEOPHILUS M. SEARS[8] [*Geo.*[7], *Jas.*[6], *Jas.*[5], *Jas.*[4], *Silas*[3], *Silas*[2], *Rich.*[1]], b. Madison co., Ind., Mar. 12, 1854; m. Lapell, Ind., May 12, 1880, *Alice Hersberger*, she b. Frederic co., Md., Oct. 11, 1852. Children:

3981. i. ARNA, b. Lapell, Sep. 15, 1881.
3982. ii. *Dau.*, b. Lapell, Feb. 19, 1886.

Is a farmer in Lapell, Ind.

3023.

JAMES W. SEARS[8] [*Geo.*[7], *Jas.*[6], *Jas.*[5], *Jas.*[4], *Silas*[3], *Silas*[2], *Rich.*[1]], b. Madison co., Ind., Mar. 3, 1857; m. Lapell, Ind., Mar. 3, 1885, *Ellen Hersberger*, she b. Pendleton, Ind., Feb. 5, 1860.   Child:

3983. i. *Child*, b. Lapell, Nov. 27, 1885.

Is a blacksmith, and lives in Lapell, Ind.

3030.

JAMES SANFORD SEARS[8] [*Gould*[7], *Jas.*[6], *Comfort*[5], *Jas.*[4], *Silas*[3], *Silas*[2], *Rich.*[1]], b. Reading, Ct., Oct. 16, 1836; m. Benton Centre, N. Y., June 15, 1870, *Mary L. Collin*, she b. there, June 7, 1848.   Child:

3984. i. EMMA COLLIN, b. Aug. 2, 1871.

Mr. Sears enlisted as a private in 14th N. Y. Heavy Arty., Aug. 1, 1863; was soon made quartermaster-sergeant, and held such position during the war, and until discharged, Sep., 1865; was stationed at Port Richmond, Staten Island, during winter of 1863–64; was in Army of Potomac, during battle of the Wilderness, and until close of war.   Is now of firm Sears, Henry & Co., Nurserymen, Geneva, N. Y.

3033.

Dr. CHARLES SUMNER SEARS[8] [*Clarke*[7], *Jas.*[6], *Comfort*[5], *Jas.*[4], *Silas*[3], *Silas*[2], *Rich.*[1]], b. Seneca, N. Y., Nov. 1, 1853; m. Auburn, Ind., Sep. 14, 1880, *Nettie Schaffer·*   Child:

3985. i. CARL C., b. Auburn, Nov. 6, 1881.

Is a physician in Auburn, Ind.

3039.

CHARLES ELMORE SEARS[8] [*Herman*[7], *Jos.*[6], *Comfort*[5], *Jas.*[4], *Silas*[3], *Silas*[2], *Rich.*[1]], b. New York city, Jan. 2, 1850; m. Dalles, Oregon, Apr. 17, 1881, *Carrie Randall*, dau. of Matthew and Hester (Parker) R. of Swansea, Wales, she b. Aurora, Ind., Aug. 12, 1861; (her father was Orderly Sergt. Grenadier Guards in Household troop, Windsor Castle, and

stands 6 ft. 4 in. in height; her mother was born in Ind.)
Children:

3986. i. HERMAN RAYMOND, b. Portland, Oregon, Jan. 31,
1882.
3987. ii. HESTER A., b. Olympia, Wash. Ter., Jan. 23, 1884.

Is U. S. Surveyor, Olympia, Wash. Ter.

3047.

THEODORE HOYT SEARS[8] [*Theo.*[7], *Lewis*[6], *Comfort*[5],
Jas.[4], *Silas*[3], *Silas*[2], *Rich.*[1]], b. Danbury, Ct., Apr. 1, 1853;
m. Tioga, Kans., July 7, 1872, *Virginia Louise Jones*, she b.
Mt. Pleasant, Iowa, July 15, 1852. Children:

3988. i. HOWARD FIELDING, b. Ottawa, Kans., Aug. 11, 1873;
d. Oct. 2, 1874.
3989. ii. LOUIS THEODORE, b. Ottawa, Oct. 5, 1874.
3990. iii. AUGUSTA LOUISE, b. Ottawa, Nov. 22, 1876.
3991. iv. ELIZABETH, b. Ottawa, Dec. 10, 1879.
3992. v. WARREN CLINTON, b. Ottawa, July 4, 1881.
3993. vi. GORDON RAYMOND, b. Ottawa, Jan. 31, 1885.

3052.

STEPHEN PARISH SEARS[8] [*Fran.*[7], *Lewis*[6], *Comfort*[5],
Jas.[4], *Silas*[3], *Silas*[2], *Rich.*[1]], b. Buffalo, N. Y., Sep. 20, 1860;
m. Aug. 17, 1887, *Bessie Watson Fargo*, dau. of Jerome F.
Child:

3993. *a.* i. JEROME FARGO, b. May 31, 1889.

Is of firm Sears & Co., dealers in grain, hops and wool,
Tacoma, Washington.

3057.

Prof. JOHN HENRY SEARS[8] [*John*[7], *John*[6], *Geo.*[5], *Seth*[4],
Rich.[3], *Silas*[2], *Rich.*[1]], b. Danvers, Mass., June 18, 1843; m.
Boston, Nov. 23, 1868, *Lucinda Cutting Wallace*, she b. Sand-
wich, N. H., Oct. 16, 1851. Children:

3994. i. NETTIE MADELINE, b. May 16, 1869.
3995. ii. WALLACE PALMER, b. Dec. 6, 1871.
3996. iii. ANNIE RUSSELL, b. Jan. 26, 1874.
3997. iv. JOHN, b. Feb. 14, 1876.

Mr. Sears served in Co. K, 8th Mass. Vol. Inf'y, from Oct. 1, 1862, to Aug. 7, 1863, and was honorably discharged at expiration of term of service ; is now Professor and Curator in Peabody Academy, Salem, Mass.

3068.

JASPER PECK SEARS[8] [*Jasper*[7], *Jasper*[6], *John*[5], *John*[4], *Rich.*[3], *Silas*[2], *Rich.*[1]], b. Ohio, Jan. 3, 1835; m. Canon City, Col., Mar. 4, 1866, *Annie Love George.* Children:

3998.   i. CHARLES J., b. Denver, Col., Dec. 10, 1866 ; d. Jan. 15, 1867.
3999.   ii. MAGGIE WILSON, b. Denver, Col., Sep. 25, 1868.
4000.   iii. LAURA, b. Denver, Col., Mar. 10, 1870.
4001.   iv. GEORGIANNA, b. Denver, Col., May 15, 1872.
4002.   v. CLARA C., b. Denver, Col., Oct. 2, 1876.
4003.   vi. LYDIA HOLMES, b. Denver, Col., Mar. 13, 1879.
4004.   vii. JASPER PARSONS, b. Denver, Col., Apr. 28, 1883 ; d. May 30.

Mr. Sears removed with his father to Janesville, Wis., in 1839; went to Denver, Col., in 1859, crossing the plains with eleven wagons, each drawn by five yoke of oxen, and loaded with groceries, with which he opened the first grocery store in Denver. In 1863, in company with C. A. Cook he opened the first bank in Denver, under firm name of C. A. Cook & Co. He was for a number of years a government contractor, and of late interested in real estate operations.

3070.

EDWIN PARSONS SEARS[8] [*Israel*[7], *Jasper*[6], *John*[5], *John*[4], *Rich.*[3], *Silas*[2], *Rich.*[1]], b. Lancaster, N. Y., Jan. 13, 1851 ; m. Buffalo, N. Y., Sep. 3, 1874, *Francis Eliza Demarest.* Children :

4005.   i. GEORGE DEMAREST, b. June 9, 1876.
4006.   ii. ELIZA BROWN, b. May 15, 1881.
4006. *a.* iii. ALICE PARSONS, b. Sept. 4, 1885.
4006. *a.* iv. RICHARD PARSONS, b. July 31, 1887.

Mr. Sears removed to Buffalo, N. Y., in 1865, and now represents the firm of Pratt & Letchworth, saddlery, hardware, etc.

3134.

ALFRED FRANCIS SEARS, Jr.^{8} [*Alfred^7, Zebina^6, Jos.^{5}, Zach.^{4}, Jos.^{3}, Silas^2, Rich.^{1}*], b. Concord, No. Car., Sep. 4, 1852; m. *Ellen Carver*, dau. of Joseph C. of Bridgewater, Mass. Children :

4007.   i.   ALFRED FRANCIS, b. Nov. 22, 1877.
4008.   ii.   RICHARD, b. Apr. 7, 1880.
4009.   iii.   MINNIE, b. Aug. 22, 1882.
4010.   iv.   ROBERT, b. Nov. 30, 1884.

Mr. Sears prepared at Phillips Academy, Exeter, N. H., and graduated from Dartmouth College; studied law in Boston University, during which time he sat in office of Brown & Alger, Boston.

In the spring of 1880, he began the practice of law in Portland, Oregon, where he has acquired a good practice, and enjoys the confidence of the community. In 1883, he was nominated to the Board of Aldermen by the Democrats in a ward overwhelmingly Republican, and was elected by two-thirds of the votes cast in a severe struggle.

3156.

CALVIN SEARS^8 [*Mulford^7, Isaac^6, Steph.^{5}, Jos.^{4}, Jos.^{3}, Silas^2, Rich.^{1}*], b. Dennis, Mass., Dec. 6, 1813; m. there, Jan. 7, 1835, *Laura Ann Spindleow*. Children :

4011.   i.   MARY L., b. Den., Sep. 4, 1837; m. Nov. 17, 1858, *Richard L. Baker* of Harwich.
4012.   ii.   JEDIDAH, b. Den., Oct. 16, 1838; m. Brewster, Nov. 26, 1857, *Daniel H. Robbins*, son of John and Rhoda R., he b. Br., 1836.
4013.* iii.   DAVID W., b. Den., June 23, 1841.
4014.   iv.   BETHIA R., b. Den., Mar. 4, 1844; m. Br., *Jesse Eldredge, Jr.*, son of Jesse and Lydia E. of Br., he b. 1840.
4015.   v.   CALVIN C., b. Den., July 4, 1846; d. Feb. 28, 1872.
4016.   vi.   MARTHA A., b. Den., Aug. 14, 1849.
4017.   vii.   MERCY F., b. Den., Sep. 30, 1852; d. Oct. 20, 1879; m. Br., Jan. 16, 1876, *Clarence L. Parker*, son of Wm. C. and Mary W. P. of Br., he b. 1855.

68 .

4018. viii. JUDITH O., b. Den., Nov. 12, 1854; d. July 9,
1880; m. Br., July 14, 1874, *Augustus Parker*, son of
Chas. and Lucinda P. of Br., he b. 1856.

Lived in East Dennis.

3157.

ISAIAH CROSBY SEARS[8] [*Mulford*[7], *Isaac*[6], *Steph.*[5],
Jos.[4], *Jos.*[3], *Silas*[2], *Rich.*[1]], b. Dennis, Mass., Aug. 2, 1816;
d. E. Den., Mar. 19, 1882, æ. 66; m. Brewster, Mass., Nov.
15, 1838, *Jedidah Snow Baker*, dau. of Obadiah B., she b.
Yarmouth, Sep. 14, 1810; d. 1888. Children:

4019. i. OBADIAH BAKER, b. Den., Aug. 20, 1839; d. Apr.
10, 1841.
4020.* ii. OBADIAH BAKER, b. Den., July 25, 1842.
4021.* iii. ISAIAH FRANCIS, b. Den., Jan. 20, 1844.
4022. iv. HERBERT WALLACE, b. Den., July 31, 1848; lives
E. Den.
4023.* v. HORACE AUGUSTUS, b. Den., Nov. 1, 1851.
4024. vi. CHAUNCY HOWE, b. Den., Dec. 5, 1853; m. Fall
River, Mass., June 14, 1883, *Georgianna Teresa Newell*,
she b. there, Sep. 3, 1863; is a grocer in Fall R.

Lived in East Dennis.

3161.

ELDREDGE C. SEARS[8] [*Eldredge*[7], *Isaac*[6], *Steph.*[5], *Jos.*[4],
Jos.[3], *Silas*[2], *Rich.*[1]], b. East Dennis, Mass., Sep. 14, 1816; m.
Mar. 16, 1839, *Achsah H. Bray*, dau. of Thos. B., she b. Yar-
mouth, May 19, 1814; 2d, Den., June 10, 1886, by Rev. Mr.
Dodge, to Mrs. *Rosanna Carlow* of Wood's Hole, Mass.
Children:

By *Achsah:*
4025.* i. EDWIN, b. Den., Jan. 16, 1840.
4026. ii. HANNAH C., b. Den., Aug. 24, 1841.
4027. iii. HENRY B., b. Den., Feb. 16, 1843; m. there, Mar.
25, 1869, *Cynthia Howes* of D., and lives Centreville,
Mass.

Lives in Dennis, Mass.

3164.

JOSHUA SEARS[8] [*Eldredge*[7], *Isaac*[6], *Steph.*[5], *Jos.*[4], *Jos.*[3], *Silas*[2], *Rich.*[1]], b. East Dennis, Mass., June 21, 1829; m. there, Apr. 6, 1852, *Rosanna McCabe*, she b. Ireland, Aug. 15, 1828. Children:

4028.* i. JAMES F., b. E. Den., Jan. 6, 1853.
4029. ii. JOSHUA A., b. E. Den., Apr. 6, 1855; lives in Taunton, Mass.
4030. iii. ROSIE B., b. E. Den., July 17, 1857; m. *Fred. E Goff* of Attleboro, Mass.
4031. iv. EDWIN L., b. E. Den., July 4, 1859; d. Oct. 1, 1864.
4032. v. WILLIAM L., b. E. Den., Aug. 24, 1861; lives in Boston; m. No. Den., Dec. 25, 1888, *Olive C. Howes*.
4033. vi. FLORA L., b. E. Den., Dec. 22, 1863; m. *Wm. Hathaway*.
4034. vii. GERTIE MARGET, b. E. Den., Dec. 14, 1870; lives in Taunton, Mass.

Lives in East Dennis.

3168.

GEORGE W. SEARS[8] [*Larned*[7], *Larned*[6], *Steph.*[5], *Jos.*[4], *Jos.*[3], *Silas*[2], *Rich.*[1]], b. Oxford, Mass., Dec. 2, 1821; m. Chatham, Pa., Aug. 13, 1857, *Marietta Butler*, she b. Delmar, Pa. Children:

4035. i. JENNY B., b. Wellsboro, Pa., Sep. 16, 1858; m. *W. W. Madison*, and lives Pike's Mills, Potter co., Pa.
4036. ii. CHARLES R., b. Wells., Jan. 30, 1860, and lives there.
4037. iii. MAGGIE A., b. Wells., Feb. 6, 1864; m. *Arthur Anderson*, and lives in Balltown, Forest co., Pa.

Mr. Sears was born in the "South Gore," now known as Webster, Mass., on the border of Douglass Woods, and near the Nipmuck Indian reservation.

Before he was five years old he formed an abiding friendship for a young Indian named "Nessmuk," (wood duck,) from whom he imbibed his love for woodcraft, and became a devotee of nature in her wildest and roughest of aspects; a lover of field sports; a hunter, angler, trapper and canoeist;

an uneducated man withal, save the education that comes of long and close communion with nature, and a perusal of the best English authors.

Endowed by nature with an instinctive love of poetry, Mr. Sears early dropped into the habit of rhyming, jotting down his thoughts on paper, or as often happened, when in the woods, on birch bark.

Under the pseudonym of "Nessmuk," he has written much for the "Spirit of the Times," and "Forest and Stream," and has published a work entitled "Woodcraft," and a volume of poetry called "Forest Runes."

During the Civil war, Mr. Sears served in the "Bucktail" Regt. Pa. Vols., and was discharged for physical disability at Camp Curtin, Harrisburg, Pa. Now resides in Wellsboro, Pa.

3169.

CHARLES WILLIAM SEARS[8] [*Larned*[7], *Larned*[6], *Steph.*[5], *Jos.*[4], *Jos.*[3], *Silas*[2], *Rich.*[1]], b. Oxford, Mass., Aug. 25, 1823; d. Wellsboro, Pa., June 11, 1887; m. ―― ――. Children:

4038. i. *Son.*
4039. ii. *Dau.*

Mr. Sears was a mere lad when he began, as he expressed it, to shift for himself. He worked for several years on a farm, and learned the shoemaker's trade before he was fifteen. In the spring of 1851, he removed to Wellsboro, Tioga co., Pa., and was for many years a partner with his brother George in the shoe business. His career of thirty-six years was marked with several reverses, but he kept up good courage, and energetically labored to surmount all difficulties.

Mr. Sears was a quiet, unassuming man, and possessed many excellent qualities of mind and heart. He was a good citizen, and a steady, faithful Christian worker. For more than twenty years he was a member of the Meth. Epis. Church, and Supt. of Sunday School in the country district for years He was a kind and indulgent husband and father, a faithful, helpful son, and brother.

3173.

LORAN A. SEARS[8] [*Larned*[7], *Larned*[6], *Steph.*[5], *Jos.*[4], *Jos.*[3], *Silas*[2], *Rich.*[1]], b. Oxford, Mass., Feb. 11, 1832; m.

Wellsboro, Pa., 1852, *Fannie M. Locke,* she b. Cortland, N. Y., 1836. Children:

4040. i. FRANKLIN A., b. Wells., Mar. 15, 1854; m. Weston, N. Y., 1881, *Cora Heald,* who d. there, Apr., 1886; is in mercantile business.
4041. ii. WALTER JESSE, b. Wells., Mar. 10, 1856; app'd Mid. U. S. Navy, June 24, 1875; Ensign, Naval Training Station, Newport, R. I.
4042. iii. WILLIAM G., b. Wells., Aug. 16, 1858; m. Gaines, Pa., 1884, *Minnie Lewis,* and is in mercantile business in G.
4043. iv. LORA A., b. Wells., Mar. 7, 1862; d. Aug. 28, 1863.
4044. v. EDWIN L., b. Wells., Apr. 20, 1864.
4045. vi. LE ROY, b. Wells., June 26, 1866.
4046. vii. LOVISA GERTRUDE, b. Wells., Apr. 11, 1869.

Lives in Wellsboro, Tioga co., Penn.

3179.

LUTHER A. SEARS[8] [*Luther*[7], *Levi*[6], *Steph.*[5], *Jos.*[4], *Jos.*[3], *Silas*[2], *Rich.*[1]], b. Dennis, Mass., Jan. 30, 1843; m. *Annie* ——. Children:

4047. i. ANNIE J., b. Den., Nov. 8, 1869; d. Mar. 3, 1870.
4048. ii. HATTIE R., m. Chatham, Nov. 20, 1887, *Alonzo F. Eldridge.*
4049. iii. *Son.*

3183.

LEVI L. SEARS[8] [*Luther*[7], *Levi*[6], *Steph.*[5], *Jos.*[4], *Jos.*[3], *Silas*[2], *Rich.*[1]], b. Dennis, Mass., Sep. 5, 1854; m. Harwich, Mass., July 2, 1876, *Idella B. Chase* of Har. Child:

4050. i. BERTIE G., b. Har., Apr. 25, 1877.

3186.

JOHN GAGE SEARS[8] [*Josiah*[7], *Levi*[6], *Steph.*[5], *Jos.*[4], *Jos.*[3], *Silas*[2], *Rich.*[1]], b. Dennis, Mass., Jan. 7, 1852; m. Harwich, Mass., Aug. 5, 1875, *Sallie J. Bearse* of Har. Children:

4051. i. OLIVE MAY, b. Den., Jan. 23, 1876.
4052. ii. NETTIE A., b. Den., Dec. 2, 1877.
4053. iii. *Child,* b. Den., Sep. 12, 1883.

3201.

LORING SEARS[8] [*Jos.*[7], *Jos.*[6], *Steph.*[5], *Jos.*[4], *Jos.*[3], *Silas*[2], *Rich.*[1]], b. West Brewster, Mass., Jan. 16, 1845 ; m. Fitchburg, Mass., Oct. 18, 1871, *Hattie Elizabeth Putnam*, she b. there, May 5, 1848. Children :

4054. i. LORING PUTNAM, b. Jan. 2, 1874.
4055. ii. MILDRED GERALDINE, b. June 7, 1883.

Is in dry goods business in Fitchburg, Mass.

3203.

JOSEPH EMERY SEARS[8] [*Jos.*[7], *Jos.*[6], *Steph.*[5], *Jos.*[4], *Jos.*[3], *Silas*[2], *Rich.*[1]], b. Brewster, Mass., Apr. 4, 1848; m. Dighton, Mass., June 17, 1874, *Sarah Rebecca Walker*, she b. there, Nov. 8, 1850; (grad. Bridgewater Normal School, and taught in Dighton and Fall River.) Child :

4056. i. WINIFRED WALKER, b. Dighton, Feb. 27, 1876.

Mr. Sears was educated in public schools in Brewster, studied four years in Greenwich, R. I.; grad. Prov. Conf. Sem., and finished at Boston Univ., 1877.

Resides on the old Walker homestead in Dighton, Mass., and carries on the farm.

3214.

CHARLES M. SEARS[8] [*Alpheus*[7], *Roland*[6], *Freeman*[5], *Roland*[4], *Jos.*[3], *Silas*[2], *Rich.*[1]], b. New Salem, Mass., Apr. 4, 1842 ; d. Athol, Mass., Sep. 28, 1885, æ. 43; m. Hartford, Ct., Sep. 15, 1863, *Annie F. Chapin*, who d. Apr. 9, 1868, æ. 23; 2d, Athol, Nov. 10, 1870, *Annis J. Smith*, she b. Watertown, N. Y. Children :

4057. i. *Son*, b. Athol; is a book-keeper in wholesale grocery, Chicago, Ill.
4058. ii. *Son*.
4059. iii. *Dau*.

Was of firm Brooks & Sears, grocers, Athol, Mass.

3221.

CHAUNCY D. SEARS[8] [*Turner*[7], *Andrew*[6], *Freeman*[5], *Roland*[4], *Jos.*[3], *Silas*[2], *Rich.*[1]], b. Greenwich, Mass., June 4,

1828; m. Moline, Ill., Oct. 16, 1853, *Julia A. Mason*, she b. Palmer, Mass., Oct. 16, 1825. Children:

4060. i. LIZZIE M., b. Amboy, Ill., Aug. 6, 1861; m. Jan. 30, 1883, *T. C. Cowley*, and lives in Princeton, Ill.
4061. ii. JENNIE M., b. Amboy, Mar. 22, 1865.

Is a mechanic in Amboy, Ill.

3224.

Dea. WARREN CLARK SEARS[8] [*Turner*[7], *Andrew*[6], *Freeman*[5], *Roland*[4], *Jos.*[3], *Silas*[2], *Rich.*[1]], b. Greenwich, Mass., Aug. 1, 1834; m. Amboy, Ill., May 5, 1857, *Nancy Ives* of A., she b. Pavillion, Ill., June 15, 1838. Children:

4062. i. CLARA O., b. June 2, 1858; m. Mar. 26, 1878, Rev. *Henry Wilson*, and d. Dec. 15, 1880.
4063. ii. FRANK W. b. June 1, 1863; m. Kansas city, Mo., Nov. 25, 1883, *Mary E. English* and lives there.

Is of firm Sears & Wattles, Druggists, Burlington, Kansas, and has been for several years Deacon in the church there.

3228.

LUCIUS EDWARD SEARS[8] [*Turner*[7], *Andrew*[6], *Freeman*[5], *Roland*[4], *Jos.*[3], *Silas*[2], *Rich.*[1]], b. Greenwich, Mass., Mar. 22, 1842; m. there, Jan. 10, 1865, *Sarah E. King*, she b. Dana, Mass., Jan. 10, 1848. Children:

4064. i. LILLY E., b. Green., Apr. 15, 1867.
4065. ii. MINNIE E., b. Green., Jan. 26, 18—.
4066. iii. MABEL E., b. Dana, Aug. 12, 1871.

Is in Post-office, North Lansing, Mich.

3232.

OSCAR HASKELL SEARS[8] [*Andrew*[7], *Andrew*[6], *Freeman*[5], *Roland*[4], *Jos.*[3], *Silas*[2], *Rich.*[1]], b. Greenwich, Mass., Mar. 11, 1840; m. Belchertown, Mass., Apr. 8, 1867, *Abbie Rosetta Walker*, she b. there, Apr. 26, 1845. Child:

4067. i. CHARLES CALVIN, b. Oct. 20, 1867; d. Mar. 25, 1869.

Mr. Sears served in Co. K, 6th Vermont Regiment, 6th Corps, under Gen. Phil. Sheridan, and was wounded at Winchester, Va., Sep. 19, 1864, by a shell, necessitating amputation of left leg below the knee, and loss of great toe of right foot.

Is a silver plater in Greenwich, Mass.

3252.

WILLIAM BRUSH SEARS[8] [*Edm'd*[7], *Franklin*[6], *Elisha*[5], *Roland*[4], *Jos.*[3], *Silas*[2], *Rich.*[1]], b. Moscow, N. Y., Feb. 17, 1856; m. Cuylersville, N. Y., Nov. 13, 1878, *Nellie Daily*. Children :

4068. i. LINA, b. Aug. 19, 1881.
4069. ii. ROBERT.

Is a farmer in Moscow, N. Y.

3257.

BARNABAS SEARS[8] [*Barnabas*[7], *Steph.*[6], *Steph.*[5], *Barnabas*[4], *Jos.*[3], *Silas*[2], *Rich.*[1]], b. South Yarmouth, Mass., Sep. 14, 1818; m. Yar., Nov. 26, 1840, *Ruth H. Crowell*, dau. of Rev. Simeon and Charlotte C., she b. Jan. 28, 1806; d. Oct. 31, 1851, gr.-st., So. Yar.; 2d, Brewster, Mass., Oct. 18, 1852, by Rev. F. R. Newell, to *Deborah Manter Clark*, dau. of William and Lydia C. of Br., she b. Oct. 9, 1832; d. Apr. 28, 1885, gr.-st., So. Yar.; 3d, So. Yar., May 2, 1886, by Rev. J. H. George, to Mrs. *Susan H. Doane* of Somerville, Mass. Children :

By *Ruth :*
4070.   i. HENRY, b. Yar., June 24, 1842; d. Feb. 8, 1843.
4071.   ii. JOHN, b. Yar., May 29, 1845; d. Sep. 12.
4072. iii. JOHN K., b. Yar., Sep. 16, 1846; d. July 29, 1847.
4073. iv. SIMEON CROWELL, b. Yar., Oct. 16, 1847; d. Mar. 29, 1864, of injuries, having fallen from aloft, off Cape Horn, Mar. 17, while on passage from Rio Janeiro to San Francisco in ship "Fleetwing."
By *Deborah :*
4074.   v. ISAIAH CLARK, b. Brewster, Sep. 11, 1853.
4075. vi. HENRY WILLIAM, b. So. Yar., Apr. 24, 1859; m. Middleboro, Mass., Dec. 5, 1883, by Rev. H. M. Grant, to *Martha S. Pickens* of M.
4076. vii. ETTA FRANCES, b. Yar., Feb. 26, 1866.

Is a dealer in lumber and hardware, Middleboro, Mass. Summer residence, old Crowell homestead, South Yarmouth.

3258.

STEPHEN SEARS[8] [*Barnabas[7], Steph.[6], Steph.[5], Barnabas[4], Jos.[3], Silas[2], Rich.[1]*], b. South Yarmouth, Mass., July 15, 1822; m. Clarence, N. Y., Apr. 16, 1846, *Henrietta A. Hall*, she b. Wellington, Ct., Apr. 13, 1828. Children :

4077. i. LAURA HELEN, b. So. Yar., Apr. 18, 1848 ; m. Yar., Dec. 6, 1871, *James G. Hallett*, he b. there.

4078. ii. HANNAH E., b. So. Yar., Oct. 11, 1852 ; d. May 29, 1862, gr.-st.

4079. iii. STEPHEN HALL, b. So. Yar., July 31, 1854 ; m. Barnstable, Aug. 23, 1881, *Marianna C. Parker*, she b. there ; he graduated Bellevue Hospital, practised as a physician in Newport, R. I., and was connected with Marine Hospital there ; now lives in So. Yar.

4080. iv. HENRIETTA A. H., b. So. Yar., Sep. 26, 1855 ; d. Jan. 17, 1856, gr.-st.

4081. v. SARAH LEONARD, b. So. Yar., Apr. 26, 1857 ; d. Apr. 4, 1858, gr.-st.

4082. vi. MARY P., b. So. Yar., June 5, 1860; d. June 20, gr.-st.

Mr. Sears was a teacher for many years ; has held various town offices — Selectman, Assessor, School Committee, etc.

3261.

DAVID SEARS[8] [*Barnabas[7], Steph.[6], Steph.[5], Barnabas[4], Jos.[3], Silas[2], Rich.[1]*], b. South Yarmouth, Mass., July 6, 1832 ; m. Dec. 9, 1855, *Lucy Goodwin Howes* of Dennis, Mass., she b. Dec. 21, 1830. Children :

4083.* i. URIAH H., b. So. Yar., Mar. 6, 1857.

4084. ii. SARAH ELIZABETH, b. So. Yar., July 3, 1859 ; m. July 6, 1881, *William Henry Hurst* of So. Yar.; child, HURST : [1.] Florence Sears, b. Nov. 22, 1886.

4085. iii. DAVID FRANKLIN, b. So. Yar., Aug. 15, 1866.

4086. iv. JOHN GORHAM, b. So. Yar., Mar. 6, 1870.

4087. v. GEORGE BRAYTON, b. So. Yar., Sep. 20, 1872.

4088. vi. WILLIS BARNABAS, b. So. Yar., July 27, 1875; d. Nov. 18, 1879.

Is a farmer in South Yarmouth, Mass.; has been Selectman, etc.

3274.

CASSIUS CLAY SEARS[8] [*Henry*[7], *John* , *Rich.*[5], *Silas*[4], *Jos.*[3], *Silas*[2], *Rich.*[1]], b. Monkton, Vt., Sep. 8, 1844 ; m. there, Mar. 10, 1852, *Eliza Jane Kellogg*, dau. of Rev. J. P. K., she b. Minerva, N. Y., Mar. 10, 1852. Child :

4089. i. CASPER H., b. Mar. 20, 1879.

Served in Co. C, 9th Regt. Vt. Vols., during the war ; is a carpenter, and lives in Monkton ; post-office, Vergennes, Vt.

3276.

FRED. EUGENE SEARS[8] [*Henry*[7], *John*[6], *Rich.*[5], *Silas*[4], *Jos.*[3], *Silas*[2], *Rich.*[1]], b. Monkton, Vt., Sep. 15, 1850 ; m. Panton, Vt., May 29, 1876, *Augusta J. Carter*, she b. M., Nov. 28, 1853. Child :

4090. i. Fannie F., b. Panton Springs, Vt., June 3, 1881.

Is a farmer and proprietor of Elgin Springs ; address, Vergennes, Vt. ; Rep. 1884–86.

3282.

JOHN M. SEARS[8] [*Rich.*[7], *Rich.*[6], *Rich.*[5], *Silas*[4], *Jos.*[3], *Silas*[2], *Rich.*[1]], b. Reading tp., Mich., Mar. 9, 1839 ; m. Rome, Wis., July 3, 1863, *Mary E. Crowder*, she b. there, Jan. 7, 1843 ; d. July 19, 1883. Children :

4091.   i. ALMA L., b. Rome, Wis., May 13, 1864 ; m. Dec. 30, 1884, *Alfred R. Ames*, he b. Nov. 24, 1861, and lives near Schaller, Sac co., Iowa.

4092.   ii. MARY ANN, b. Rome, Mar. 30, 1866.

4093.   iii. JESSIE MAY, b. Rome, Dec. 5, 1867.

4094.   iv. MATTIE MAUD, b. Grundy co., Iowa, July 15, 1871 ; d. Aug. 28, 1873.

4095.   v. JOHN LEWIS, b. Grundy co., Mar. 21, 1875.

4096.   vi. FRANK HENRY, b. near Schaller, Iowa, July 24, 1877.

4097.   vii. WALTER SCOTT, b. near Schaller, Oct. 28, 1879.

4098.   viii. ELMER EVERETT, b. near Schaller, Oct. 24, 1881.

4099.   ix. VIVIA ELLEN, b. near Schaller, June 18, 1883.

Mr. Sears emigrated with his parents to vicinity of Dundee, Ill., in 1845, and removed to Rome, Wis., in 1856.

He enlisted in 1861, in Co. F, 15th Regiment Illinois Volunteers, and served three years ; removed to Iowa in 1868, finally settling in vicinity of Schaller, in Sac co.; is a dealer in leather and harness goods.

3284.

HENRY BELA SEARS[8] [*Rich.*[7], *Rich.*[6], *Rich.*[5], *Silas*[4], *Jos.*[3], *Silas*[2], *Rich.*[1]], b. Reading tp., Mich., Mar. 29, 1844 ; m. Maumee City, Ohio, Sep. 28, 1869, *Louisa Hunter*, she b. there, Feb. 20, 1849. Children :

4100. i. WALTER H., b. Toledo, Ohio, June 3, 1873; d. Sep. 4.
4101. ii. HESSIE L., b. Toledo, Feb. 13, 1877 ; d. Mar. 12, 1881.
4102. iii. LUCIUS J., b. Toledo, Oct. 30, 1878.

Lives in Toledo, Ohio.

3286.

LOWELL CLARK SEARS[8] [*Silas*[7], *Rich.*[6], *Rich.*[5], *Silas*[4], *Jos.*[3], *Silas*[2], *Rich.*[1]], b. Camden, N. Y., May 13, 1833 ; m. Rome, Wis., Feb. 5, 1857, by Rev. S. T. Malthrop, to *Catherine Bornheimer*, she b. Hesse-Darmstadt, Germany, Aug. 4, 1833; came to America with her father in 1840. Children :

4103. i. RHODA A., b. Rome, Wis., Aug. 2, 1858; m. Jan. 12, 1882, *Theodore J. Foljahn*, of Tomah, Wis.; child, FOLJAHN: [1.] Lola, b. May 27, 1885.
4104. ii. LOTTIE M., b. Rome, Sep. 10, 1860 ; is a teacher.
4105. iii. EMMA KATIE, b. Rome, July 24, 1862 ; d. Apr. 18, 1870.
4106. iv. NELLIE M., b. Rome, May 3, 1866 ; is a teacher.
4107. v. CLARA A., b. Rome, Sep. 4, 1870.
4108. vi. BERTHA ELLA, b. Rome, June 2, 1873.

Mr. Sears is a farmer in Rome, Wis., to which place he removed with his parents from Rome, N. Y., in Nov., 1843.

3294.

GEORGE W. SEARS[8] [*Oscar*[7], *Orange*[6], *Rich.*[5], *Silas*[4], *Jos.*[3], *Silas*[2], *Rich.*[1]], b. Pittstown, N. Y., Mar. 31, 1838 ; m. Mar. 30, 1862, *Melissa Whitford*. Children :

4109. i. NETTIE M., b. near Wattsburg, Pa., June 20, 1864 ; m. Posy Hill, Dec. 26, 1882, *Dewitt Wallace*, he b.

Greenfield tp., Erie co., Pa., 1860; and lives in Venango tp., Pa.; child, Wallace : [1.] Josie May, b. Oct. 20, 1883.

4110. ii. Clarissa, b. near Watts., Oct. 5, 1865 ; m. Sep. 25, 1884, *Emmett G. Ploss,* he b. Chautauqua co., N. Y., 1862 ; lives in Venango tp., Pa.; child, Ploss : [1.] Dau., b. Nov. 5, 1886.

4111. iii. Gilbert Andrew, b. near Watts., July 14, 1869 ; d. Dec. 31.

Is a farmer near Wattsburg.   P. O., Lowville, Pa.

3295.

JOHN HENRY SEARS[8] [*Oscar*[7], *Orange*[6], *Rich.*[5], *Silas*[4], *Jos.*[3], *Silas*[2], *Rich.*[1]], b. Rensselaer co., N. Y., Oct. 13, 1839 ; m. Wattsburg, Pa., Mar. 8, 1864, *Harriet M. Faulkner,* she b. Chautauqua co., N. Y., Mar. 25, 1846 ; d. Watts., May 8, 1875, æ. 29 ; 2d, Watts., Nov. 27, 1876, Mrs. *Rhoda A. Austin* of Buffalo, N.Y., she b. Chaut. co., Mar. 11, 1844. Children :

By *Harriet :*

4112. i. Hattie Estelle, b. Feb. 15, 1866; d. Sep. 6, 1869.

4113. ii. Mary Grace, b. Nov. 8, 1869 ; d. Sep. 10, 1872.

4114. iii. Sarah Elizabeth, b. Mar. 25, 1872.

4115. iv. Ernest Oscar, b. Feb. 28, 1874.

By *Rhoda :*

4116. v. Maude Mabel, b. Nov. 1, 1878; d. Mar. 27, 1881.

4117. vi. Edith Emily, b. June 16, 1882.

Mr. Sears removed with his parents to Erie co., Pa. ; received an academical education, and became a teacher; served two years in 111th Regt. Pa. Vols. from 1861. Is a farmer and an honored official of the Meth. Epis. Ch. near Wattsburg, Pa.

3298.

WILLIAM O. SEARS[8] [*Oscar*[7], *Orange*[6], *Rich.*[5], *Silas*[4], *Jos.*[3], *Silas*[2], *Rich.*[1]], b. Butler, N. Y., Nov. 22, 1845 ; m. Union City, Pa., 1874, *Libbie Barnes,* she b. there, Sep. 4, 1857. Children :

4118. i. Edward Wilbur, b. July 1, 1875.

4119. ii. Mary Ellen, b. June 23, 1878.

4120. iii. Velma Adell, b. Mar. 11, 1883.

Is a farmer near Wattsburg, Pa.

3305.

ALEXANDER SEARS[8] [*Wash.*[7], *Abner*[6], *Rich.*[5], *Silas*[4], *Jos.*[3], *Silas*[2], *Rich.*[1]], b. near Naples, Ill., Aug. 20, 1842; m. there, Feb. 28, 1866, *Mary Francis Oakes*, she b. Metropolis, Ill., Nov. 8, 1846. Children:

4121. i. WILLIAM EDWARD, b. near Naples, Ill., Dec. 14, 1866.
4122. ii. HATTIE O., b. near Naples, Aug. 16, 1869; d. Jan. 22, 1871.
4123. iii. ESTELLA O., b. near Naples, Dec. 19, 1871.
4124. iv. AGNES LILLIAN, b. near Naples, Dec. 5, 1875.
4125. v. DUKE PERCIVILLE, b. Eureka, Kans., Mar. 14, 1881.

Mr. Sears served during the Rebellion in Co. I, 129th Regt. Ill. Vols.; part of the time served detail in quarter-master's department; he now lives in Eureka, Kans., and is connected with the railroad.

3310.

CHARLES WILLARD SEARS[8] [*Wash.*[7], *Abner*[6], *Rich.*[5], *Silas*[4], *Jos.*[3], *Silas*[2], *Rich.*[1]], b. near Naples, Ill., Dec. 1, 1854; m. near Winchester, Ill., 1878, *Mary Penton*, dau. of James C. and Elizabeth P., she b. there, Dec. 3, 1859. Children:

4126. i. DAISY MAY, b. near Naples, Ill., Dec. 7, 1878.
4127. ii. ELMER CLARENCE, b. near Naples, May 30, 1880.
4128. iii. MABEL OLIVE, b. near Naples, Mar. 3, 1882.

3331.

EDWARD BRADFORD SEARS[8] [*Chas.*[7], *Barnabas*[6], *Barnabas*[5], *Silas*[4], *Jos.*[3], *Silas*[2], *Rich.*[1]], b. New Salem, Mass., Oct. 6, 1845; m. Amherst, Mass., Oct. 29, 1872, *Hattie Amelia Hawley*, she b. there, Dec. 1, 1852. Children:

4129. i. ALLIE FOSTER, b. Norwich, Ct., Nov. 6, 1873.
4130. ii. BESSIE SOPHIA, b. Amherst, Mass., Sep. 3, 1874.
4131. iii. HARRISON HAWLEY, b. Amherst, Apr. 28, 1877.
4132. iv. FLORENCE LUCINA, b. Amherst, Dec. 24, 1881.
4133. v. MAUD DICKINSON, b. Amherst, May 10, 1884.

Is railroad station-master, Amherst, Mass.

3345.

JOSIAH EDWARD SEARS[8] [*Wm.[7], Holmes[6], Edw'd[5], Edw'd[4], Josiah[3], Silas[2], Rich.[1]*], b. Halifax, Mass., Aug. 17, 1844; m. Hanson, Mass., June 1, 1873, *Lucy Chamberlain Phillips*, she b. there, Sep. 25, 1848; d. Mar. 26, 1875; 2d, Brockton, Mass., May 13, 1879, *Emma Josephine Marshall*, she b. North Bridgewater, Mass., July 12, 1848. Child ::
By *Emma :*
4134. i. WILLIAM MARSHALL, b. Brockton, Jan. 8, 1882.

Served in 20th unattached Co., Mass. Vols., Aug. 11, 1864, to Nov. 18, 1864, and in 24th unattached Co., Dec. 16, 1864, to May 12, 1865; is a stationary engineer, and lives in Brockton, Mass.

3347.

Rev. LORENZO SEARS[8] [*Nath'l[7], Rufus[6], Nath'l[5], Sam'l[4], Josiah[3], Silas[2], Rich.[1]*], b. Hawley, Mass., Apr. 18, 1838; m. —— ——. Child :
4135. i. SOPHY HARRIS.

Was Rector of Grace Church, Manchester, N. H., till 1885, when he was appointed Professor of Rhetoric and English Literature in Burlington University, Vermont.

3350.

WILLIAM H. SEARS[8] [*Rufus[7], Rufus[6], Nath'l,[5] Sam'l[4], Josiah[3], Silas[2], Rich.[1]*], b. Portland, Ct., Sep. 1, 1830; m. Nov. 10, 1856, *Sophia W. Stephens*, who d. soon ; 2d, by Rev. Thos. Starr King, at San Francisco, Cal., Apr. 29, 1863, to *Hattie A. Sinclair*. Children :
By *Sophia :*
4135. *a.* i. LIZZIE J., b. North San Juan, Nev. co., Cal., Sep. 23, 1857; m. 1878, *M. A. Bates ;* children, BATES : [1.] Harry S. [2.] Albert M.
By *Hattie :*
4135. *a.* ii. STELLA M., b. San Fran., Cal., Oct. 8, 1866.

Before he became of age, Mr. Sears removed to California; was elected a Member of the Assembly from Nevada county in 1861, and again in 1862, and appointed Chairman of Committee of Ways and Means; was re-elected in 1863, and chosen Speaker of the House, after which he removed to San Francisco, and was admitted to the Bar in 1865; in 1880, after the adoption of the New Constitution, he was elected to the Senate, and in April, 1884, was appointed Collector of Customs, San Francisco. Is now of firm Whittemore & Sears, Attorneys, San Francisco, Cal.

3354.

LEWIS E. SEARS[8] [*Anth'y*[7], *Rufus*[6], *Nath'l*[5], *Sam'l*[4], *Josiah*[3], *Silas*[2], *Rich.*[1]], b. Hawley, Mass., 1838; m. 1859, *Lucy A. Starks.* Children:

4136. i. *Child*, d. Haw., Jan. 19, 1862.
4137. ii. FRANK LAWTON, b. 1864.
4138. iii. FREDERIC GRANT, b. 1869; lives in Plainfield.

Is a farmer in Plainfield, Mass.

3355.

EDWIN W. SEARS[8] [*Anth'y*[7], *Rufus*[6], *Nath'l*[5], *Sam'l*[4], *Josiah*[3], *Silas*[2], *Rich.*[1]], b. Hawley, Mass., 1847; m. *Mary J. Russell.* Children:

4139. i. RUFUS, b. 1867.
4140. ii. HERBERT R., b. 1873.
4141. iii. GEORGE E., b. 1875.

Is a farmer and lives on the old homestead in Hawley, Mass.

3356.

HENRY F. SEARS[8] [*Fred.*[7], *Rufus*[6], *Nath'l*[5], *Sam'l*[4], *Josiah*[3], *Silas*[2], *Rich.*[1]], b. Hawley, Mass., Dec. 25, 1836; m. Aug. 21, 1866, *Sarah J. Walker*, dau. of Edmund and Justina L. W., she b. Mar. 27, 1837. Children:

4142. i. FREDERIC E., b. May 22, 1871.
4143. ii. HARRY FRANKLIN, b. Aug. 17, 1874.

Mr. Sears graduated Amherst College, 1864; taught school in various places, and the Bunker Hill School, Charlestown, Mass., for many years, and resides in Somerville, Mass.

3362.

EDWARD HALE SEARS[8] [*Benj.*[7], *Rufus*[6], *Nath'l*[5], *Sam'l*[4], *Josiah*[3], *Silas*[2], *Rich.*[1]], b. Williamsburg, Mass., Feb.

23, 1846 ; m. June 18, 1868, *Lillie P. Ames,* dau. of John A., she b. July 3, 1845. Children :

4143. *a.* i. EDWARD HALE, b. June 11, 1873 ; d. same day.
4144. ii. DAVID L., b. Aug. 14, 1875.
4145. iii. ROBERT AMES, b. Feb. 10, 1878 ; d. Apr. 24, 1879.

Has been for many years Agent of the Collins Co., Collins-ville, Ct.

3368.

JOHN WINSLOW SEARS[8] [*Earl[7], Earl[6], Zebedee[5], David[4], Josiah[3], Silas[2], Rich.[1]*], b. Middleboro, Mass., Jan. 21, 1842 ; m. New Bedford, Mass., July 25, 1864, *Mary L. Washburn,* she b. Midd., July 12, 1848. Child :

4146. i. CORA L., b. Taunton, Mass., Aug. 21, 1871.

Is of firm Sears & Keith, Taunton, Mass.
In 1886, he invented a machine for feeding horses by clock-work, by which arrangement 100 horses can be fed at exactly the same time, and two kinds of grain may be fed at once.

3370.

LEONARD SEARS[8] [*Oliver[7], Leonard[6], Zebedee[5], David[4], Josiah[3], Silas[2], Rich.[1]*], b. June 23, 1823; d. —— ; m. *Eliza Carpenter,* (who m. 2d, —— *Whitbeck.*) Child :

4147. i. HELEN JANE, b. Apr. 18, 1856 ; m. *John Carnes.*

3376.

JAMES ISAAC SEARS[8] [*Isaac[7], Peter[6], Peter[5], Jona.[4], Josiah[3], Silas[2], Rich.[1]*], b. South Scituate, Mass., June 29, 1829 ; m. there, Sep. 24, 1854, *Lucinda Wilder Gross,* she b. there, Sep. 2, 1829. Children :

4148.   i. CAROLINE, b. So. S., Mar. 6, 1856 ; m. there, Dec. 7, 1881, *James Henri Farrar,* he b. there, Sep. 14, 1856; lives Mt. Blue, Mass. (?)
4149.   ii. ALFRED JAMES, b. So. S., Jan. 18, 1858 ; m. there, Feb. 9, 1879, *Mary Emma Wheelwright,* she b. Cohas-sett, Mass., Mar. 18, 1860 ; lives in Rockland, Mass.
4150.   iii. HERBERT WILBUR, b. So. S., Dec. 31, 1859 ; m. So. Weymouth, Mass., Apr. 30, 1882, *Flora M. Sprague,* she b. So. S., July, 1864 ; and lives in So. Weymouth.

4151. iv. SARAH ANNA, b. So. S., June 22, 1862; m. So. Weymouth, Sep. 5, 1886, *Alvin Turner Baker*, he b. Marshfield, Mass., Nov. 28, 1858, and lives in So. S.

4152. v. HORACE LINCOLN, b. So. S., Sep. 5, 1864.

4153. vi. CORA AMELIA, b. So. S., Sep. 15, 1866.

4154. vii. OSCAR, b. So. S., Nov. 6, 1867.

4155. viii. MARTIN WILDER, b. So. S., Aug. 4, 1869.

Lives in South Scituate, Mass.

70

NINTH GENERATION.

3385.

AMBROSE SEARS[9] [*Clark*[8], *Jona.*[7], *Jona.*[6], *Jona.*[5], *Jona.*[4], *Sam'l*[3], *Paul*[2], *Rich.*[1]], b. West Hawley, Mass., Nov. 3, 1841; m. Shelburne Falls, Mass., Nov. 28, 1866, *Sarah Lovina Nims.* Child:

4156. i. FRANK H., b. Nov. 13, 1868.

Lives in West Hawley, Mass.; has held local offices, and appointed Postmaster, 1882.

3393.

FREEMAN WILLIS SEARS[9] [*Freeman*[8], *Jona.*[7], *Jona.*[6], *Jona.*[5], *Jona.*[4], *Sam'l*[3], *Paul*[2], *Rich.*[1]], b. Goshen, Mass., Aug. 21, 1842; m. Thompsonville, Ct., Dec. 19, 1868, *Kate S. Sydell*, she b. Northampton, Mass., Sep. 29, 1853. Children:

4157. i. HENRIETTA F., b. Goshen, Aug. 10, 1878; d. Apr. 26, 1880.
4158. ii. CLARENCE W., b. G., Mar. 25, 1881.

Is a successful farmer and dairyman in Goshen, Mass.

3394.

MILTON FOSTER SEARS[9] [*Freeman*[8], *Jona.*[7], *Jona.*[6], *Jona.*[5], *Jona.*[4], *Sam'l*[3], *Paul*[2], *Rich.*[1]], b. Goshen, Mass., Mar. 20, 1845; m. Buckland, Mass., Jan. 1, 1873, *Lizzie Shaw*, she b. there. Child:

4159. i. WINIFRED B., b. Buckland, Nov. 27, 1873.

Lives in Buckland, Mass.

3396.

FRANK GRAHAM SEARS[9] [*Freeman*[8], *Jona.*[7], *Jona.*[6], *Jona.*[5], *Jona.*[4], *Sam'l*[3], *Paul*[2], *Rich.*[1]], b. Goshen, Mass., May 13, 1852; m. Chesterfield, Mass., Apr. 21, 1878, *Etta Wildman*, she b. Quincy, Mass., Mar. 1, 1860; d. Sep. 12, 1879; 2d, Goshen, Feb. 22, 1883, *Sarah White*, she b. Cummington, Mass., Oct., 1850. Children:

By *Etta* :
4160. i. ERNEST F., b. Goshen, Sep. 11, 1879.
By *Sarah* :
4161. ii. WARD G., b. West Cummington, Nov. 17, 1883 ; d. Feb. 5, 1885.

Lives in West Cummington, Mass.

3399.

CHARLES FREMONT SEARS[9] [*Freeman*[8], *Jona.*[7], *Jona.*[6], *Jona.*[5], *Jona.*[4], *Sam'l*[3], *Paul*[2], *Rich.*[1]], b. Goshen, Mass., June 29, 1859 ; m. Hartford, Ct., Oct. 29, 1883, *Myra F. Packard*, she b. Goshen, July 9, 1865. Child:
4162. i. MARION E., b. Goshen, Oct. 6, 1884.

Lives in Goshen, Mass.

3473. a. i.

NED MORILLO SEARS[9] [*Nath.*[8], *Harper*[7], *Paul*[6], *Nath.*[5], *Judah*[4], *Sam'l*[3], *Paul*[2], *Rich.*[1]], b. Stowe, Vt., Jan. 29, 1858 ; m. June 6, 1886, *Maud B. Snow* of Mankato, Minn. Child:
4162. *a.* i. *Son*, b. St. Paul, Minn., Sep. 26, 1889.

Mr. Sears is with Gordon & Ferguson, St. Paul, Minn.

3484.

ALBERT F. SEARS[9] [*Eben'r*[8], *Alden*[7], *Roland*[6], *Roland*[5], *Seth*[4], *Sam'l*[3], *Paul*[2], *Rich.*[1]], b. Hawley, Mass., Mar. 10, 1840; m. Williamsburgh, Mass., June 16, 1870, *Sarah A. Williams*, she b. there, Jan. 16, 1846. Children:
4163. i. EDITH, b. Sep. 16, 1875.

Mr. Sears served in Co. E, 52d Regiment, Massachusetts Volunteers, from Oct. 11, 1862, to Aug. 14, 1863 ; is a farmer in Charlemont, Mass.

3490.

ROSWELL SEARS[9] [*Seth*[8], *Alvan*[7], *Roland*[6], *Roland*[5], *Seth*[4], *Sam'l*[3], *Paul*[2], *Rich.*[1]], b. Hawley, Mass., May 7, 1835; m. Pittsfield, Mass., Jan. 2, 1861, *Mary E. Pierce*, she b. Plattsburgh, N. Y., Aug. 6, 1838. Children :
4164. i. ANNIE, b. July 9, 1863; m. *John T. Carrington.*
4165. ii. SETH W., b. June 21, 1874.

Is a farmer in Hawley, Mass.

3491.

ROYAL SEARS[9] [*Seth*[8], *Alvan*[7], *Roland*[6], *Roland*[5], *Seth*[4], *Sam'l*[3], *Paul*[2], *Rich.*[1]], b. Hawley, Mass., May 7, 1835; m. Savoy, Mass., May 15, 1867, *Roselmah Sturtevant*, she b. Aug. 8, 1845. Children :
4166. i. ERNEST R., b. Aug. 4, 1868.
4167. ii. HERMAN E., b. Mar. 27, 1870.
4168. iii. CORA A., b. Jan. 30, 1872.
4169. iv. WESLEY E., b. Apr. 9, 1874.

Is a farmer in Hawley, Mass.

3500.

GEORGE WILLIAM SEARS[9] [*Urban*[8], *Alvan*[7], *Roland*[6], *Roland*[5], *Seth*[4], *Sam'l*[3], *Paul*[2], *Rich.*[1]], b. West Hawley, Mass., May 18, 1855; m. Hawley, Oct. 29, 1879, (Dec. 28, another account,) *Jennie H. Houston*, she b. Meriden, Ct., Sep. 26, 1856. Children :
4170. i. CLARA BELLE, b. Hawley, May 30, 1881; d. June 5.
4171. ii. MARTHA LOUISE, b. Haw., May 30, 1884.

Is a farmer, and lives with his mother on the old homestead in Hawley, Mass.

3508.

SYLVESTER L. SEARS[9] [*Sylvester*[8], *Roland*[7], *Roland*[6], *Roland*[5], *Seth*[4], *Sam'l*[3], *Paul*[2], *Rich.*[1]], b. Rowe, Mass., Mar. 5, 1848; m. June 22, 1875, *Hattie M. Stiles* of Temple, N. H., she b. Lyndeborough, N. H., July 9, 1852. Children :
4172. i. HARRY ELMER, b. Fitchburg, Mass., July 22, 1876.

4173. ii. ARTHUR EUGENE, b. Akron, Ohio, Mar. 29, 1878.
4174. iii. RALPH ALBRO, b. Akron, Nov. 15, 1884.

Mr. Sears removed to Akron, Ohio, in fall of 1876, and is foreman of " Whitman & Barnes Mf'g Co."

3557.

ABNER HUNT SEARS[9] [*Nathan*[8], *Wm.*[7], *Eben'r*[6], *Wm.*[5], *Paul*[4], *Paul*[3], *Paul*[2], *Rich.*[1]], b. Carrollton, N. Y., Aug. 5, 1851; m. Dec. 23, 1872, *Laura Elizabeth Strickler*, dau. of Wm. A. and Mary E. S. Children:
4175. i. WILLIAM.
4176. ii. *Dau.*

Is a farmer in Quincy, Adams county, Ill.

3561.

Capt. CLINTON BROOKS SEARS[9] [*Clinton*[8], *Wm.*[7], *Eben'r*[6], *Wm.*[5], *Paul*[4], *Paul*[3], *Paul*[2], *Rich.*[1]], b. Penn Yan, N. Y., June 2, 1844; m. at Church of Incarnation, N. Y., by Rev. Dr. Montgomery, Oct. 22, 1873, to *Lydia Evelyn Smith*, dau. of Isaac H. and Phebe S. of N. Y. Children:
4177. i. CLINTON B., b. Los Angeles, Cal., Aug. 31, 1874.
4178. ii. BERTRAM, b. New York city, Oct. 13, 1875.
4179. iii. PAUL EUGENE, b. West Point, N. Y., June 30, 1877; d. Sep. 19, 1878.
4180. iv. MARION SIMS, b. New York city, Dec. 15, 1884.

Capt. Sears left college to enlist as a private in Co. G, 95th Regt. Ohio Vol. Inf'y, July 24, 1862; Corporal, Aug. 19, 1862; Acting Color Sergeant of the Regiment through the Vicksburg Campaign, and as Color Sergeant participated in both assaults at Vicksburg, and both attacks on Jackson, Miss.; before that was in battle of Richmond, Ky.; Buell's campaign after Bragg in Ky.; the battle of Perrysville, Ky.; and in Rosencrans' Stone River Campaign, being on detached duty from his Regiment with Brig.-Gen. Cruft of Ind.; discharged Sep. 20, 1863, to accept a cadetship at West Point, to which he had been appointed by Prest. Lincoln, on recommendation of Gens. Grant and Sherman; graduated U. S. Mil. Acad., June 17, 1867; commissioned same day as 2d Lt. Corps of Engineers U. S. A.; Capt. Eng'rs, Apr. 9, 1880; served detail as Asst. Prof. U. S. M. A., West Point, N. Y., for five and a half years; relieved from duty there, Apr. 20, 1882, and appointed Exec. and Disb'g Officer of the Miss. River Com'n stationed in St. Louis, Mo.; in fall of 1886, ordered to Bismarck, Dakota; now (1890) in office of Chief Engineer, Washington, D. C.

Capt. Sears is F. Nat. Acad. Design; mem. Am. Soc. Civil Eng.; mem. Mil. Order Loyal Legion, U. S.; mem. St. Nicholas, and Univ. Clubs, N. Y., and University Club, St. Louis, Mo.; received Hon. Deg. A. B., from Wesleyan Univ., Ohio, 1881, degree of A. M. to follow in 3 years.

Pub. "Ransom Gen'y in 1882, and made extensive collection for Sears Gen'y," especially the Rochester branch, of which he has kindly given me the use for this work.

3562.

JOHN McKNIGHT SEARS[9] [*Clinton*[8], *Wm.*[7], *Eben'r*[6]. *Wm.*[5], *Paul*[4], *Paul*[3], *Paul*[2], *Rich.*[1]], b. Chillicothe, Ohio, Aug. 28, 1851; m. Cincinnati, O., Feb. 13, 1873, *Mollie Belle Hall.* Children:

4181. i. HARRY CLINTON, b. Cin., O., Dec. 17, 1873.
4182. ii. HELEN CORNELIA, b. Cin., Jan. 12, 1876.

Address, 106 Madison ave., Memphis, Tenn.

3564.

J. MAGOUN SEARS[9] [*Clinton*[8], *Wm.*[7], *Eben'r*[6], *Wm.*[5], *Paul*[4], *Paul*[3], *Paul*[2], *Rich.*[1]], b. Bloomington, Ill., Sep. 2, 1855; m. Cincinnati, O., June 26, 1879, *Clara Bell Baldwin.* Children:

4183. i. MABEL, b. near Covington, Ky., Feb. 10, 1881; d. Feb. 23.
4184. ii. ISABELLA, b. Cin., O., Feb. 10, 1882.

Lives in Cincinnati, Ohio.

3567.

WILLIAM GOFF SEARS[9] [*Arad*[8], *Jos.*[7], *Silas*[6], *Nath'l*[5], *Paul*[4], *Paul*[3], *Paul*[2], *Rich.*[1]], b. Richford, Vt., Feb. 28, 1848; m. Elkada, Iowa, Feb. 15, 1872, *Stella Bigelow*, she b. McGregor, Iowa, May 12, 1854. Children:

4185. i. JULIA WINIFRED, b. Elkada, Aug. 1, 1874.
4186. ii. LISLE TURNER, b. Milwaukee, Wis., Mar. 28, 1878.

Mr. Sears lives in Chattanooga, Tenn., and has recently invented and patented a cotton picker, favorably mentioned in local papers.

3571.

GEORGE FREDERIC SEARS[9] [*Arad*[8], *Jos.*[7], *Silas*[6], *Nath'l*[5], *Paul*[4], *Paul*[3], *Paul*[2], *Rich.*[1]], b. Richford, Vt., Jan. 19, 1856; m. Chicago, Ill., Jan. 16, 1879, *Emma C. Hayman*, she b. there, Apr. 13, 1861. Child:
4187.　i. FREDERIC G., b. Albia, Iowa, ab't 1879.

Mr. Sears is agent C., B. & Q. R. R. at Albia, Iowa; is a prominent temperance man, and in Order of Good Templars; twice delegate to Grand Lodge of the World, and eight times to Grand Lodge.

3572.

FREDERIC WEST SEARS[9] [*Silas*[8], *Jos.*[7], *Silas*[6], *Nath'l*[5], *Paul*[4], *Paul*[3], *Paul*[2], *Rich.*[1]], b. Prophetstown, Ill., Jan. 28, 1853; m. there, Sep. 6, 1874, *Louiza Baldwin*. Child:
4188.　i. PEARL, b. 1877.

3575.

FRANK COOK SEARS[9] [*Sherman*[8], *Nath'l*[7], *Silas*[6], *Nath'l*[5], *Paul*[4], *Paul*[3], *Paul*[2], *Rich.*[1]], b. Richford, Vt., May 30, 1846; m. Apr. 6, 1868, *Addie C. Powell*. Children:
4189.　i. BLANCHE JENNIE, b. Rich., Dec. 14, 1874.
4190.　ii. BELLE FRANCES, b. Rich., July 22, 1878; d. Oct. 21, 1881.

Is in mercantile business in Richford, Vt.

3646.

ARZA TREAT SEARS[9] [*Wm.*[8], *Will'd*[7], *Will'd*[6], *Elkanah*[5], *Josh.*[4], *Paul*[3], *Paul*[2], *Rich.*[1]], b. East Hampton, Ct.; m. ——— ———. Children:
4191.　i. LILLY JANE, b. Glastenbury, Ct., 1878.
4192.　ii. DAISY IDEL, b. Waterbury, Ct., 1884.

Lives in Waterbury, Ct.

3771.

SAMUEL D. SEARS[9] [*Judah*[8], *Nathan*[7], *Jacob*[6], *Edm'd*[5], *Edm'd*[4], *Paul*[3], *Paul*[2], *Rich.*[1]], b. Dennis, Mass., July 5, 1847; d. Apr. 1, 1878; m. —— ——. Children:

4193. i. RUSSELL ADAMS.
4194. ii. JUDAH PERRY.

3859.

JONATHAN HATSELL SEARS[9] [*Jona.*[8], *Jona.*[7], *Lewis*[6], *Eleazar*[5], *Silas*[4], *Silas*[3], *Silas*[2], *Rich.*[1]], b. South Yarmouth, Mass., Apr. 18, 1851; m. Sandwich, Mass., Jan. 27, 1876, *Lucy J. Nye*, she b. there. Children:

4195. i. ANNIE LEE, b. Melrose, Mass., Jan. 12, 1878.
4196. ii. JONATHAN THACHER, b. Melrose, July 4, 1881.
4197. iii. LUCY NYE, b. Melrose, Apr. 9, 1883.

Is connected with Boston Rubber Shoe Co., Malden, Mass.

3890.

SAMUEL H. SEARS[9] [*Isaac,*[8] *Alex'r*[7], *Enoch*[6], *Seth*[5], *Jas.*[4], *Silas*[3], *Silas*[2], *Rich.*[1]], b. Saratoga co., N. Y., Sep. 18, 1844; m. *Nellie Geddes*. Children:

4198. i. HARRY.
4199. ii. WILLIAM.
4200. iii. EARNEST.

Is a book-binder in Davenport, Iowa.

3891.

ALEXANDER SEARS[9] [*Isaac*[8], *Alex'r*[7], *Enoch*[6], *Seth*[5], *Jas.*[4], *Silas*[3], *Silas*[2], *Rich.*[1]], b. Saratoga co., N. Y., July 13, 1847; m. *Ida Perrin*. Children:

4201. i. LEWIS.
4202. ii. NANCIE.

Lives in Davenport, Iowa.

3904.

FRED. ALLISON SEARS[9] [*Dan'l*[8], *Ahiram*[7], *Dan'l*[6], *Knowles*[5], *Jas.*[4], *Silas*[3], *Silas*[2], *Rich.*[1]], b. Baldwinsville, N. Y.,

July 23, 1854 ; m. Grand Island, Neb., June 5, 1877, *Carrie C. Jordan*, she b. Omaha, Neb., May 10, 1858. Children :
4203. i. FRED. JORDAN, b. Apr. 4, 1878 ; d. 1884.
4204. ii. MARY ELIZABETH, b. Apr. 10, 1882.
4205. iii. ROBERT JORDAN, b. Sep. 15, 1884.

Lives in Grand Island, Neb.; has been in drug, grain and stock business, and is now Agent for the C., B. & Q. R. R. Was Representative to State Legislature, 1880–1 (the youngest member, then aged 26.)

3928.

DEMETRIUS SEARS[9] [*Eli*[8], *Thos.*[7], *Eli*[6], *Thos.*[5], *Jas.*[4], *Silas* [3], *Silas*[2], *Rich.*[1]], b. Searsburg, N. Y., Oct. 9, 1841 ; m. Steamburg, N. Y., Jan. 24, 1866, *Mary Yates*, she. b. Jan. 3, 1846. Child :
4206. i. ROSCOE DEWITT, b. July 14, 1867.

3930.

MORRIS BALDWIN SEARS[9] [*Eli*[8], *Thos.*[7], *Eli*[6], *Thos.*[5], *Jas.*[4], *Silas*[3], *Silas*[2], *Rich.*[1]], b. Searsburg, N. Y., July 2, 1850; m. Trumansburg, N. Y., Sep. 20, 1877, *Emma L. Smith*, she b. Feb. 22, 1856. Child :
4207. i. GUY, b. Sep. 25, 1878.

3939.

THOMAS SELMA SEARS[9] [*Baldwin*[8], *Thos.*[7], *Eli*[6], *Thos.*[5], *Jas.*[4], *Silas*[3], *Silas*[2], *Rich.*[1]] b. Pine River, Wis., Aug. 20, 1853 ; m. Winsted, Ct., Sep. 5, 1882, *Hattie A. Burbank*. Child :
4208. i. LENA B., b. Winsted, Aug. 2, 1884.

3959.

EUGENE B. SEARS[9] [*Almoin*[8], *David*[7], *Eli*[6], *Thos.*[5], *Jas.*[4], *Silas*[3], *Silas*[2], *Rich.*[1]], b. Aug. 29, 1841 ; m. Ulysses, N. Y., Feb. 14, 1860, *Maggie A. Smith*, she b. Jan. 25, 1840 ; d. Nov. 23, 1860 ; 2d, Trumansburg, N. Y., Aug. 29, 1862, *Mary L. Dickerson*, she b. Aug. 1, 1845. Children :
By *Maggie :*
4209. i. FANNY, b. Oct. 23, 1860.

71

By MARY:
4210. ii. CORA, b. June 27, 1863.
4211. iii. MAGGIE, b. July 15, 1867.
4212. iv. LUCINDA, b. July 1, 1870.

3960.

GILBERT T. SEARS[9] [*George[8], David[7], Eli[6], Thos.[5], Jas.[4], Silas[3], Silas[2], Rich.[1]*], b. Townsendville, N. Y., July 17, 1840; m. Addison, N. Y., July 13, 1862, *Alice Wilbur*, she b. Feb. 28, 1842. Children:
4213. i. BERTHA, b. Nov. 22, 1863.
4214. ii. LAURA, b. Oct. 8, 1866; m. Feb. 4, 1885, ——
——.
4215. iii. MARIA, b. May 31, 1869; d. July 17.
4216. iv. PEARL, b. Mar. 22, 1878.

3961.

WALLACE W. SEARS[9] [*George[8], David[7], Eli[6], Thos.[5], Jas.[4], Silas[3], Silas[2], Rich.[1]*], b. Andover, N. Y., Oct. 22, 1844; m. Lodi, N. Y., Oct. 22, 1868, *Anna Wycoff*, she b. Apr. 27, 1850. Children:
4217. i. CHARLES W., b. Feb. 25, 1872.
4218. ii. LLEWELLYN, b. Apr. 17, 1880.

Lives in Ellendale, Dakota.

4013.

DAVID W. SEARS[9] [*Calvin[8], Mulford[7], Isaac[6], Steph.[5], Jos.[4], Jos.[3], Silas[2], Rich.[1]*], b. Dennis, Mass., June 23, 1841; m. there, June 25, 1863, *Mehitable Parker* of Brewster, Mass. Children:
4219. i. CORA W., b. Jan. 15, 1864; d. July 12, 1865.
4220. ii. DAVID ERNEST, b. July 18, 1869.

Lives in the old Edward Sears house in East Dennis, near the Sears Cemetery, West Brewster, Mass.

4020.

OBADIAH BAKER SEARS[9] [*Isaiah[8], Mulford[7], Isaac[6], Steph.[5], Jos.[4], Jos.[3], Silas[2], Rich.[1]*], b. Dennis, Mass., July 25,

1842; m. San Francisco, Cal., Oct. 4, 1870, Mrs. *Elizabeth Atchison.* Child:

4221. i. HERBERT.

Lives in Oakland, Cal.

4021.

ISAIAH FRANCIS SEARS[9] [*Isaiah*[8], *Mulford*[7], *Isaac*[6], *Steph.*[5], *Jos.*[4], *Jos.*[3], *Silas*[2], *Rich.*[1]], b. East Dennis, Mass., Jan. 20, 1844; m. Westport, Mass., Nov. 30, 1871, *Sarah A. Little,* she b. Dartmouth, Mass., Aug. 12, 1845. Children:

4222. i. ELENOR S., b. Fall River, Mar. 13, 1874.
4223. ii. NELLIE L., b. F. R., June 7, 1879.

Of firm Sears & Hall, boots and shoes, Fall River, Mass.

4023.

HORACE AUGUSTUS SEARS[9] [*Isaiah*[8], *Mulford*[7], *Isaac*[6], *Steph.*[5], *Jos.*[4], *Jos.*[3], *Silas*[2], *Rich.*[1]], b. Dennis, Mass., Nov. 1, 1853; m. E. Bridgewater, Mass., Mar. 2, 1873, *Carrie F. Robinson.* Child:

4224. i. FREDERIC A.

Is a mason in Fall River, Mass.

4025.

EDWIN SEARS[9] [*Eldredge*[8], *Eldredge*[7], *Isaac*[6], *Steph.*[5], *Jos.*[4], *Jos.*[3], *Silas*[2], *Rich.*[1]], b. Dennis, Mass., Jan. 16, 1840; d. Provincetown, Mass., Feb. 17, 1887; m. Yarmouth, Mass., Nov. 8, 1866, *Elizabeth D. Crocker.* Child:

4225. i. FRANK.

Lived in Provincetown, Mass.

4028.

JAMES F. SEARS[9] [*Josh.*[8], *Eldredge*[7], *Isaac*[6], *Steph.*[5], *Jos.*[4], *Jos.*[3], *Silas*[2], *Rich.*[1]], b. East Dennis, Mass., Jan. 6, 1853; m. Taunton, Mass., July 24, 1876, *Thankful Musick,* she b. Charlottetown, P. E. I., Nov. 16, 1855. Children:

4226. i. ORA MAY, b. Taunton, July 28, 1879; d. Mar. 14, 1881.

4227. ii. ORA FRANCIS, b. Taunton, Mar. 8, 1882.

Is a burnisher and silver-plater.

4083.

URIAH H. SEARS[9] [*David*[8], *Barnabas*[7], *Steph.*[6], *Steph.*[5], *Barnabas*[4], *Jos.*[3], *Silas*[2], *Rich.*[1]], b. South Yarmouth, Mass., Mar. 6, 1857; m. Oct. 24, 1883, *Eldora F. Landers* of Cotuit, Mass. Child:

4228. i. ALBERT ELWELL, b. So. Yar., Sep. 14, 1885.

Is a farmer in South Yarmouth, Mass.

APPENDIX.

OTHER FAMILIES OF SEARS.

In the course of my searches for members of the Yarmouth family, I have accumulated much data relative to divers other families, some perhaps deriving from Richard Sares of Yarmouth, but so far not certainly identified, and others perhaps distantly connected with him, though not in lineal descent.

For the benefit of future genealogists, I will briefly notice them.

1.

ALEXANDER SEARS[1] (Seers, Seares,) of Salem, Mass., Inv'y filed by Hilliard Veren and Thos. Rootes, Salem, June 7, 1667, £61 8 6. Wife Mary, Exec'x, mentions sons Robert and Alexander. He m. Salem, before 1665, *Mary Lemmon*, dau. of Robt. L., (who made his will Aug. 2, 1665, proved June 25, 1667, in which he names dau. Mary Sears,) she bap. Salem, Apr. 7, 1639; m. 2d, Steph. Searle, before Nov. 26, 1667. Sep. 23, 1670, Stephen Haskett of Salem, brought suit against "Stephen Searle and wife Mary, adm'x, estate of her late husband, Alex. Sears, for £40, paid for her to several men of debts due them from said estate." "Mary Searle, sometime y° wife of Alex. Seers," was witness in a case against Allester Greime and Sarah Lambert, Nov. 26, 1667.

Alex. Sears was probably not many years the senior of his wife, (she born about 1639,) and most likely had not long been in this country at the date of his marriage, which took place about 1656. His son Alex'r is sometimes called "Sandy" in the records. Does this indicate Scotch descent? Children:

2.* i. ROBERT, b. 1656.
3.* ii. ALEXANDER.

2.

ROBERT SEARS[2] [*Alex'r*[1]], b. 1656; was in Capt. Wm. Turner's Co., at Indian fight Northampton and Deerfield, Feb. 22, 1675–76; was taxed in Boston, 1687–88, on 2 heads, and is found, 1691–95, an inhabitant of Ward I. Nov. 18, 1696, he signed petition for repeal of law relating to building with brick, and died Dec. 29, 1732, æ. 76, gr.-st., Copp's Hill. He m. *Abigail* ——. I find no adm. on either in Suff. Reg. Prob. Children, all b. Boston :

4.   i. MARY, b. Mar. 23, 1682; bap. Mar. 4, 1694–95; m. Sep. 24, 1708, *Thos. Jenkins ;* ["dau. of *Wm.* and Abigail," T. Rec.]

5. ii. ABIGAIL, b. July 24, 1685 ; d. inf.

6. iii. ABIGAIL, b. July 12, 1687; d. July 3, 1690.

7. iv. ROBERT, b. Oct. 7, 1689; bap. Mar. 4, 1694–95; owned covenant July 11, 1714; m. *Hannah* ——, who d. June 25, 1769, æ. 73, gr.-st., Copp's Hill, (so b. 1696.) He is styled "Captain," but I find no further mention of him, or record of any children. He may have removed, and possibly some of the Penn. and Va. Sears may be his descendants.

8.   v. SARAH, b. Aug. 11, 1692 ; bap. Mar. 4, 1694–95.

9.* vi. ALEXANDER, b. May 23, 1698 ; bap. May 29.

3.

ALEXANDER SEARS[2] [*Alex'r*[1]], was taxed in Boston in 1688, and in 1695 was an inhabitant of Ward I; m. *Rebecca Staines*, dau. of Rich. and Joyse S., she b. Boston, Dec. 26, 1662 ; (her mother m. 2d, —— *Hall*). Alex. and Rebecca Sears were adm. members of Old South Ch., Jan. 11, 1712–13, and were soon dismissed to New North Ch. At the ordination of Rev. John Webb, first minister of that church, in 1714, "the members of the sister churches were entertained at Mr. Sears." Alex. Sears was one of the founders, and of the building Com. of the New North, or "Cockerill church," on Hanover street, in 1721, and his name appears first on the list of members, after the minister, May 23, 1722. He was a shipwright, and had a yard opposite the end of Prince street, on Fish (now Ann) street. Rev. E. H. Sears says, " Alexander Sears and his wife Rebecca were two most worthy people, who lived all their lives on Charter street."

The will of Alex. Sears, dated 1732, gives £50 to dau. Sarah Sears, spinster, with bed, bedding and furniture to make her equal to the rest; residue to his children, Rebecca Hill, Sarah Sears, Mary Treat, Joyce Marble, Ann Phillips, Hannah Snelling and Deliverance Atkins. Children, all b. Boston:

10. i. REBECCA, b. Aug. 12, 1686; m. June 27, 1706, *Joseph Gray;* 2d, *Arthur Hill* "of Gt. Britain"; by the latter she had a son, Alex. Hill, who m. Thankful Allen, and had a son, Alex. Sears Hill, grad. Har., 1764, who m. Mary Richey of Phila.; their dau., Lucy Hill, m. Nov. 6, 1787, Rev. Oliver Everett of Boston, (he b. June 11, 1752; grad. Har., 1779, d. Nov. 19, 1802;) father of Hon. Edward Everett.

11. ii. SARAH, b. Aug. 11, 1688; d. unm., estate settled by Hannah Snelling.

12. iii. MARY, b. Sep. 27, 1690; m. July 20, 1713, *Benj. Treat.*

13. iv. JOYCE, b. Nov. 26, 1692; m. June 26, 1720, *Robt. Marble.*

14. v. ANN, b. Dec. 13, 1694; m. by Rev. John Webb, Dec. 9, 1714, *Wm. Phillips;* (Capt.) son of Wm. and Deborah (Long) P., he b. Nov. 17, 1690; children, PHILLIPS: [1] Nath'l, b. Aug. 11, 1721; d. Oct. 16, 1811; m. Oct. 21, 1747, Ann Maverick, dau. of John and Eliz'h (Mattocks) M., she b. Dec. 6, 1721; d. Jan. 21, 1811; had, i. Eliz'h, m. John Parker. ii. James, m. Ann Tucker. iii. Polly, m. Wm. Lovering. iv. Ann, b. Jan. 6, 1760; d. Feb. 25, 1829; m. Jan. 13, 1789, Joseph Lovering, son of Joseph and Sarah (Ellis) L., he b. Sep. 19, 1758; d. June 13, 1848. From this line descends Fred L. Gay of Boston, who through his mother, Eliz'h Greenough Lewis, dau. of Dr. Winslow L., of Boston, derives also from Richard Sears of Yarmouth. v. Sarah. vi. Samuel. vii. Nathaniel. viii. William. [2.] Alexander. [3] John. [4.] Samuel.

15. vi. HANNAH, b. Jan. 14, 1696–7; m. Apr. 30, 1719, *Abraham Snelling.*

16. vii. ELINOR, b. May 7, 1699; } not ment'd in father's will, 1732, and
17. viii. ALEXANDER, b. June 28, 1701; } prob. d. young and unm'd.

18.   ix. DELIVERANCE, b. Oct. 23, 1703; m. Dec. 11, 1722, *Henry Atkins* of Truro, by Rev. Wm. Waldron.

9.

Capt. ALEXANDER SEARS[3] [*Robt.*[2], *Alex.*[1]], b. Boston, May 23, 1698, bap. May 29; d. Mar. 17, 1758, æ. 60, gr.-st., Copps Hill; m. May 24, 1732, by Rev. John Webb to *Hannah Grant.*

The will of Alexander Sears gives " out of personal estate to wife Hannah, £160, being part of what she received from her father; also, negro woman, Hester; all my household goods, plate, household linen, except one silver tankard and two silver porringers, which I give to my dau. Sarah Lord.   To wife Hannah, improvement of all my real estate, and one-half my real estate to her heirs and assigns, to do with as she thinks proper; also my wearing apparell.   To my dau. Sarah Lord, all those things I purchased for her housekeeping, and all other things necessary to be provided out of my personal estate, and the other half of my real estate after my wife's decease.

" All else to be divided between them."

The will of Hannah Sears, widow of Alexander Sears, gives " all to my dau. Sarah Lord and grand-son Jonathan, except negro woman Hester, who is given her bed and bedding, and £15, and if she chooses not to be free, and to live with her (my) daughter, is to be secured from being a charge, and is not to be sold to any one she don't like, but to choose for herself."

A fire broke out at widow Sears' house and barn on Charter street, April, 1759.   Children :

19.   i. HANNAH, b. Boston, Feb. 22, 1732–3.
20. ii. SARAH, b. Boston, Aug. 17, 1734 ; pub. Sep. 14, 1757, to *Jonathan Lord.*

DEBORAH SIERS was bap. in Old South Ch., Boston, Nov. 20, 1686 ; and a GEORGE SIERS was a petitioner for a license as retailer in Boston, 1732.   I find no further mention of either.

Letters of adm'n were granted Feb. 9, 1651-2, to John Sunderland on estate of *Mary Sears* of Boston, "her husband, DANIEL SEARS, being at sea." There is no mention of children, or other heirs. May 17, 1626, license to marry was granted Dan'l Sears, (Seeres in margin,) of Stepney, Midd., Eng., sailor, and Elizabeth Herring of same, and they were married in the parish church next day, he being called " of Ratcliffe, sailor, and she of Ratcliff Highway, maiden." It has been suggested that he may be the Daniel Sears of Boston, 1651; if so, he apparently married again. John Sunderland was a parchment maker in Boston, and agent for John Scottoway; he removed to Eastham, and m. 1665, Tamsen Mayo, widow, whose dau. by 1st husband, Tamsen Mayo, m. Sam'l Sears. What connection, if any, between Jno. Sunderland and Mary Sears, I know not.

Soon after 1700, we find several of the name of Sears in Boston, some of whom were almost surely brothers, and there is some reason to think that one or more were descended from Edmund Seare, Notary Public, who m. Eliz'h Sewell, dau. of Rich'd S., of Nuneaton, co. Warwick, Eng., she b. 1618; was living in 1648. Her uncle, Henry Sewell, settled in Rowley, Mass., and d. there in 1657; from him derive the Boston family of Sewells. (See Sears of Ulster co., N. Y., *post.*)

About 1800 several families of Sears appear in Boston, but owing to the imperfect state of the town records I have been unable to trace them back or determine their relationship.

ANTHONY SEARS m. Boston, Mar. 30, 1704, *Grace Kenney*, who d. Sep. 13, 1712; 2d, Nov. 30, 1712, *Eliz'h Needham*. (An Eliz'h Sears m. Jan. 21, 1722, Wm. Maycock.) Child:

i. JOHN, b. Boston, Aug 29, 1713.

WILLIAM SEERS, m. Boston, Mar. 12, 1710-11, *Eliz'h White*, who owned covenant in 2d Ch., Feb. 20, 1714-15. Children:

i. JOSEPH, b. Boston, Nov. 29, 1711; perhaps settled in Morrisania, N. Y.; see Sears of Sackville, N. B., *post.*

72

ii. WILLIAM, b. Boston, Dec. 16, 1713 ; is believed to have removed to Whiteplains, N. Y., and about 1760 to Montgomery, N. Y.; see Sears of Ulster and Orange cos., *post*.
iii. JOHN, b. Boston, Feb. 8, 1715–16.
iv. ANTHONY, b. Boston, June 16, 1718. This name suggests a family connection with preceding Ant. Sears.

JOHN SEARS, m. Boston, May 21, 1717, *Elizabeth* ——. Children :

i. ELIZABETH, b. Boston, Mar. 3, 1717–18.
ii. WILLIAM, b. Boston, Apr. 28, 1720.

1.

BARTHOLOMEW SEARS[1] was appointed viewer and sealer of wood for South End Wharves, Boston, 1726, and dismissed 1728. He m. *Elizabeth* ——, and perhaps removed to Stratford, Ct., as I find the will of Bart. Sears of Monroe, formerly Stratford, filed Jan. 2, 1772; but this may have been a son. He was perhaps a Huguenot emigré. Children, all b. Boston :

2. i. *Child*, d. Sep. 21, 1718.
3. ii. HANNAH, d. Nov. 26, 1721, æ. 7 years.
4. iii. BARTHOLOMEW GOZIER, b. Jan. 26, 1720 ; d. inf.
5.* iv. JOHN, b. Mar. 4, 1723.
6. v. BENJAMIN, b. July 11, 1725.
7. vi. BARTHOLOMEW, b. Sep. 6, 1727 ; prob. settled in Monroe, Ct., see *post*.
8. vii. HANNAH, b. June 9, 1729.

5.

JOHN SEARS[2] [*Bart.*[1]], b. Boston, Mar. 4, 1723; m. Stratford, Ct., Mar. 2, 1740–41, by Rev. Sam'l Johnson, Missionary of Ch. Eng., to *Frances Plummer*, or as another account says, *Dec.* 4, 1741, to *Frances Plumb*. Children :

9. i. JOHN, b. Aug. 22, 1742.
10. ii. HANNAH, b. May 2, 1744.
11. iii. BENJAMIN, b. Mar. 15, 1746–47.
12. iv. MARY, b. Mar. 29, 1749.
13. v. FRANCES, b. Oct. 30, 1750.
14. vi. ELIZABETH, b. Aug. 30, 1753.

THOMAS SEERS of Newbury, Mass., m. Dec. 11, 1656, *Mary Hilton,* and d. May 16, 1661. Inv'y filed Nov. 26, 1661, by Wm. Moody, £93. He is thought to have been a bro. of Alex. Sears of Salem. His widow m. 2d, May 25, 1663, Abel Huse, (by whom she had John, who m. Sarah Toppan). Children:

i. MARY, b. Oct. 30, 1657; m. Nov. 14, 1677, *Jas. Carr.*
ii. REBECCA, b. Nov. 5, 1661; m. June 17, 1682, *Jacob Garland.*

JOHN SEIRS, (Seers, Sears,) b. 1613; was at Charlestown, Mass., 1639–40; subscribed town orders, Woburn, Dec. 1640; adm. 1st Ch., Charlestown, Mar. 28, 1641, and freeman, June 2, 1641; Selectman, Woburn, 1667, 1669; drafted in Narraganset war, 1675–76, and com'd Lt. He m. Susanna ——, who was adm. Ch., Charlestown, Feb. 2, 1639–40, and d. Woburn, Aug. 29, 1677; and 2d, Nov. 20, 1677, Esther Mason, who d. Aug. 14, 1680, leaving a will which caused some litigation; and 3d, Nov. 2, 1680, Ann Farrar, widow of Jacob F. He is said to have had no children.

In 1654, Lt. John Sears engaged in the East Settlement, (Falmouth), and next year sold Long Island, in Casco Bay, to Isaac Walker of Boston. "Thos. Kimball's heirs claim * * * a tract of land bott of John Sears att Casco, about Mare's point, with the marsh and an island adjoining, which land Sears bott of Thos. Rideing, deed dated Aug. 26, 1670."

He died Oct. 5, 1697.

1.

"—— SEARS[1], m. *Sarah Simonton* of Camden, Me.; went away and was never heard of again." She m. 2d, Jas. Lawrence of Pepperill, Mass., and had 3 children. (Hist. Thomaston.)

2.

Capt. JAMES SEARS[2] [——[1]], an only child, b. Camden, ab't 1780; m. ab't 1804, *Sophia Barnard,* dau of Dr. Isaac B.

of Thomaston, Me., she b. there, 1788; d. there, Dec. 2, 1845, æ. 57. Capt. Sears lived in what is now Rockland, Me., and was lost at sea on "Cold Friday," Jan. 19, 1810.

3.

Dr. JOHN B. SEARS[3] [*Jas.*[2], ——[1]], an only child, b. Thomaston, Me., Mar. 26, 1807; m. Mar. 11, 1830, *Priscilla F. McIntyre* of Warren, Me., she b. Nov. 19, 1803; d. Rockland, Nov. 26, 1851, æ. 47. Dr. Sears lived in R.; manf'd "Sears Blood Root Pills," etc.; did an extensive business; removed to Stockton, Cal., and d. there ab't 1865-75. Children :

4. i. MARY KIMBALL, b. Nov. 30, 1830; m. Rock., Dec. 21, 1852, *Sam'l M. Veazie*, a hardware merchant, he b. Camden, Mar. 17, 1827; lives in Rock., and had Maurice Clifford, b. Jan. 24, 1859.
5. ii. PRISCILLA F., b. Mar. 26, 1833; m. Jan. 14, 1850, *Chas. A. Harrington,* and d. Rock., Oct. 6, 1854.
6.*iii. JOHN B., b. Mar. 25, 1834.
7. iv. RICHARD W. B., b. Nov. 5, 1836; rem. to Stockton, Cal.
8. v. JAMES F. B., b. Jan. 30, 1839; killed by a falling chimney at burning of Rockland House, Dec. 30, 1859.
9. vi. BENJAMIN F., b. Apr. 3, 1842; m. and lives Rio Dell Cal.; is a farmer.

6.

Capt. JOHN B. SEARS[4] [*John*[3], *Jas.*[2], ——[1]], b. Mar. 25, 1834; rem. to Cal., and commands a steamer on the Pacific; m. Cal., Apr. 8, 1858, *Margaret Reese*, she b. Mo.; d. Cal., 1865; 2d, *Lydia Paine*, dau. of Prof. Henry P. of West Waterville, Me., she b. 1832. Children :

10. i. JAMES, b. Jan. 23, 1859.
11. ii. M. BRADFORD, b. June 24, 1861.
12. iii. Maggie, b. Mar. 20, 1864.
13. iv. JASPER M., b. Apr. 8, 1865.

There is good reason to believe that this family is a branch of that of Yarmouth, but owing to destruction of town, church and family records by fire, the fact cannot now be proved.

JACOB SEARS[1] is said to have lived in Lancaster, Mass. Children :

2.* i. JACOB.
3. ii. ARTEMAS.
4. iii. DAVID.

2.

JACOB SEARS[2] [*Jacob*[1]], b. Lancaster, Mass.; m. Shirley, Mass., *Frances St. John Adams* of S., who d. Brooklyn, N. Y., æ. 94; he d. Hoosick Four Corners, N. Y., æ. 78. Children :

5. i. FRANCIS, b. Lanc.; d. æ. 58.
6. ii. ROLAND PARKER, b. Lanc.; d. æ. 22.
7. iii. MARY ANNE, b. Lanc.; m. *Waterman Freeman*, Troy, N. Y., and d. æ. 61.
8. iv. JACOB, b. Shirley ; d. æ. 54.
9.* v. WARREN ADSON, b. Hoosick F. C., July 25, 1813.
10. vi. WILLIAM HENRY, b. Troy, N. Y.; d. æ. 52.
11. vii. THEODORE, } b. Troy ; *gemini.*
12. viii. ADOLPHUS, }
13. ix. SUSAN, d. æ. 28; } *gemini.*
14. x. HARRIET M., d. æ. 26 ; }
15. xi. ANNA, } *gemini.*
16. vii. SOPHIA, d. æ. 1 week; }

9.

WARREN ADSON SEARS[3] [*Jacob*[2], *Jacob*[1]], b. Hoosick Four Corners, N. Y., July 25, 1813 ; m. Troy, N. Y., July 4, 1847, *Mary Babcock*, she b. East Poestenkill, N. Y., Jan. 19, 1824 ; he is a sailmaker in Troy.   Children :

17. i. JAMES RAWSON, b. Troy, June 20, 1848 ; m. there, June 21, 1869, *Kate Lucretia Bigelow*, she b. Shushan, N. Y., Dec. 4, 1850 ; he is a dry-goods clerk in Troy.
18. ii. ELLA MORE, b. Troy, June 1, 1861; m. East Poesten-kill, N. Y., Mar. 14, 1886, *Wm. O. Ives.*

1.

—— SEARS[1] removed from Cape Cod to Nova Scotia; possibly Freeman Sears, No. 243, see *ante.* Children :

2.* i. FREEMAN, b. Cape Cod.

3.* ii. John, b. Lacadie, Can.
4. iii. Jacob. Query, did he settle in Lancaster, Mass.? see preceding family.
5. iv. Peter.

2.

FREEMAN SEARS[2] [——[1]], b. on Cape Cod, removed to Nova Scotia with his father, and thence to a place near Grand Ligne, Can., (perhaps Lacadie, St. Johns' tp.), after 1814; m. *Rosanna Hoyt.* Children: (Prob. not in order of birth).

6. i. Frederic, d. Port Byron, N. Y., ab't 1874.
7. ii. Nicholas.
8. iii. Freeman.
9. iv. John.
10. v. Nicholas.
11. vi. Josette.
12. vii. Francisca.
13. viii. Julia.
14. ix. Mary.
15.* x. Luke, b. Nova Scotia, June 22, 1814.

3.

JOHN SEARS[2] [——[1]], b. Lacadie, Can.; m. there *Mary Ann Peva*, and d. æ. 50. Children:

16. i. John, b. Lacadie; m. St. Mary, Can., *Ellen Benjamin*, and d. æ. 45.
17. ii. David, m. *Mary Short*, and d. æ. 85.
18. iii. Peter, b. St. Mary, Can., m. *Josephine Peckit*, and d. æ. 85.
19. iv. Augusta, b. St. Mary; m. 1821, *Clemon Sorce*, and d. æ. 80.
20. v. Alexander, b. St. Mary, Oct. 28, 18—; m. there 1828, *Mary L. Shambeau*, lives in Cohoes, N. Y., and has a large family.

15.

LUKE SEARS[3] [*Freeman*[2], ——[1]], b. Nova Scotia, June 22, 1814; m. Auburn, N. Y., 1840, *Mary Tefft,* she b. Greenfield, N. Y; and rem'd to Mentz, N. Y., where he lived till 1851, and thence to Rockford, Kent co., Mich. Children:

21. i. Charles F., b. May, 1841; lives in R.
22. ii. Mary J., b. June, 1844.

23. iii. HARVEY F., b. Apr., 1846; m. and lives in Hamilton, Mich.
24. iv. SARAH A., b. Nov., 1853.

1.

DAVID SHERMAN SEARS[1], b. July 19, 1780, near Bridgeport, Ct., (perhaps in Monroe or Stratford); d. Sennett, N. Y., Jan. 30, 1850, æ. 69; m. Fleming, N. Y., Oct. 30, 1803, *Thankful Irish*, dau. of David I., (who preached the first gospel at Scipio, N. Y., in 1794), she b. Dutchess co., N. Y., Oct. 28, 1789; d. Sennett, N. Y., Jan. 11, 1859, æ. 70. Mr. Sears had sisters, Hannah and Betsy, one of whom m. a Plumb; his parents died when he was quite young. Children:

2. i. ELIDA, b. Nov. 10, 1804; d. Jan 30, 1805.
3. ii. LYDIA, b. Jan. 10, 1806; d. July 7, 1828.
4.* iii. MYRON, b. July 5, 1809.
5. iv. BETSY, b. Oct. 26, 1807; d. Oct. 3, 1817.
6. v. HANNAH, b. Nov. 13, 1811; d. Oct. 27, 1821.
7. vi. PENINAH, b. Sennett, Sep. 24, 1814; m. *Nelson Payne*, he b. Hamilton, N. Y., Oct. 15, 1804; d. Nov. 3, 1883, æ. 79; children, PAYNE: [1.] Robert F., b. Aug. 19, 1834; m.; and d. Mar. 31, 1876. [2.] Myron Sears, b. Apr. 9, 1836; d. Feb. 7, 1837. [3.] Francis W., b. Nov. 19, 1837; m. and lives in Auburn, N. Y. [4.] Lydia E., b. Oct. 3, 1839; m. Nov. 17, 1880, Thos. Luce of New Bedford, Mass. [5.] Henrietta, b. Oct. 20, 1843; d. Nov. 30, 1843. [6.] Lena A., b. Aug. 8, 1847.

4.

MYRON SEARS[2] [*David*[1]], b. July 5, 1809; m. Elbridge, N. Y., 1830, *Amanda Clements*, she b. Jordans, N. Y., Feb. 17, 1809; d. Auburn, N. Y., May 16, 1857; he lives in Cayuga, N. Y. Children:

8.* i. GEORGE E., b. Auburn, Feb. 23, 1831.
9. ii. DAVID SHERMAN, b. Auburn, 1835; m. and lives in San Francisco, Cal.
10. iii. LEE C., b. Auburn, 1839; d. Jan. 11, 1863.

11. iv. SARAH M., b. Auburn, May 1, 1842; m. 1866, *Fred. A. Westlake.*
12.* v. MYRON E., b. Auburn, May 31, 1844.
13. vi. HATTIE E., b. Auburn, July 6, 1846; and lives there.
14. vii. CHARLES H., b. Auburn, Sep. 20, 1848; lives at Grand Rapids, Mich.

8.

GEORGE E. SEARS[3] [*Myron[2], David[1]*], b. Auburn, N. Y., Feb. 23, 1831; m. New Orleans, La., *Emma* ———; is of firm Sears & Pardoe, N. O. Children :
15. i. GEORGE E., b. Oct. 3, 1866; lives in New Orleans.
16. ii. EMMA C., b. June 12, 1868; d. Oct. 12, 1871.
17. iii. STELLA W., b. Feb. 25, 1871.
18. iv. MAUD C., b. Jan. 25, 1873.
19. v. PEARL W., b. Nov. 24, 1874.

12.

MYRON E. SEARS[3] [*Myron[2], David[1]*], b. Auburn, N. Y., May 31, 1844; m. Lafayette, Ind., Apr. 5, 1872, *Lydia M. Skinner*, she b. there, Aug. 11, 1843, resides in L. Children :
20. i. MINNIE E., b. May 14, 1873.
21. ii. JAMES H., b. Sep. 20, 1875.
22. iii. ROBERT L., b. Aug. 14, 1877.
23. iv. MARY A., b. Sep. 1, 1879.
24. v. MYRON E., b. Mar. 1, 1883.

1.

GERSHOM SEARS[1], (perhaps a son of Bartholomew), b. Monroe, Ct., Aug. 21, 1757; d. there, Sep. 12, 1823; m. *Dolly Osborn*, she b. there, Mar. 2, 1761; d. there, Oct. 7, 1819. Children :
2.* i. AARON, b. Monroe, Feb. 18, 1783.
3. ii. MARY, b. Mon., 1788; m. *Isaac Sherman*, and d. Trumbull, Ct., Dec. 12, 1852.
4.* iii. WILLIAM, b. Mon., 1791.
5.* iv. LYMAN, b. Mon., 1796.

2.

AARON SEARS² [*Gershom¹*], b. Monroe, Ct., Feb. 18, 1783; d. there, Oct. 11, 1868; m. *Anna Hayes*, she b. there, Oct. 29, 1788; d. there, Jan. 10, 1826. Children :

6. i. HANNAH, b. Monroe, May 21, 1810; d. June 21, 1855.
7. ii. EUNICE, b. Mon., Apr. 21, 1812; d. Mar. 8, 1827.
8. iii. STEPHEN, b. Mon., Sep. 5, 1815; is a carriage painter in New Haven, Ct., and has a married son, a Dr. in Danbury, Ct.
9. iv. CHARLES, b. Mon., Sep. 9, 1817; d. Ind., Oct. 31, 1880; had 6 children.
10. v. DAVID, b. Mon., Mar. 15, 1821; m. *Jane Lyon*, and is a shoemaker in Monroe.
11. vi. ELIZA, b. Mon., Sep. 18, 1824; d. Jan. 16, 1827.
12.*vii. HENRY E., b. Mon., Aug. 3, 1826.
13. viii. HARRIET, b. Mon., Aug. 3, 1826, *gemini;* m. *John Tomlinson.*

4.

WILLIAM SEARS² [*Gershom¹*], b. Monroe, Ct., 1791; d. there, 1862; m. *Polly Dunning,* she b. 1796. Children:

14. i. MARIAH, b. 1814; m. *John Tomlinson,* " out West."
15. ii. JANE, b. 1816; d. Monroe, æ. 48; m. *Granville Lattin.*
16. iii. JULIA A., b. 1819; m. *Chas. Plumb,* and lives in Botsford, Ct.
17. iv. JOHN, b. 1827; d. 1869, æ. 42; m. *Sylvia Lamphere.*

5.

LYMAN SEARS² [*Gershom¹*], b. Monroe, Ct., 1796; d. there, 1867; m. *Polly B. Winton,* she b. there, 1796; d. 1829. Children :

18.* i. HARVEY, b. June 28, 1820.
19. ii. REBECCA, b. Dec. 29, 1824; m. Jan. 21, 1849, *Burton Sherman.*

12.

HENRY E. SEARS³ [*Aaron², Gershom¹*], b. Monroe, Ct., Aug. 3, 1826; m. *Julia A. French,* she b. there, Aug. 23, 1831; d. Naugatuck, Ct., Jan. 29, 1852; 2d, *Cornelia Downs,* she b. Bethany, Ct., Mar. 15, 1832; d. Naugatuck, July 10,

73

1859 ; 3d, *Mary A. Downs*, she b. Oxford, Ct., May 15, 1838. He served in Union Army till close of the war, and now lives in Naugatuck.   Children :

By *Julia :*

20.   i. Julia E., b. Naug., Jan. 26, 1852 ; m. *Benj. Turney*, he b. Aug. 10, 1859.

By *Cornelia :*

21.   ii. Imogene C., b. Naug., Dec. 5, 1858.

By *Mary :*

22.   iii. Ellsworth H., b. Oxford, Nov. 1, 1863.

23.   iv. Frank A., b. Naug., Feb. 17, 1870.

24.   v. Clarence F., b. Trumbull, Feb. 8, 1875 ; d. Feb. 23, 1876.

18.

HARVEY SEARS[3] [*Lyman[2], Gershom[1]*], b. June 28, 1820 ; d. Jan. 19, 1860 ; m. *Esther M. Knapp*, she b. Mar. 27, 1818 ; d. Sep. 26, 1886.   Children :

25.   i. George W., b. July 12, 1843 ; lives at Long Hill, Ct.

26.   ii. Mary E., b. Feb. 7, 1845.

27.   iii. Frances J., b. Dec. 19, 1847.

28.   iv. Marshall H., b. Oct. 3, 1849.

29.   v. Laura E. M., b. Sep. 5, 1852.

30.   vi. Frances E., b. Mar. 13, 1855.

1.

WILLARD LEONARD SEARS[1], b. Glastonbury, Ct., Sep. 16, 1816; [Sep. 17, 1814, Hall Gen.] d. Sonora, Cal., Nov. 30, 1885, æ. 69; m. Apr. 29, 1836, *Eliza M. Hall*, dau. of Amos H., she b. Aug. 6, 1820 ; d. Mar. 6, 1843 ; 2d, June 9, 1844, *Jane S. Hall*, her sister, (who m. 2d, Sep. 19, 1864, Wm. B. Meigs of Guilford, Ct., having separated from her 1st husband). Dr. Sears went to California in 1852, and successfully followed placer-mining in vicinity of Sonora; he returned to the States in 1857, leaving again for Sonora early in 1862, where he devoted the remainder of his life to the practice of medicine, having graduated at Yale many years previous.   Ever ready to attend a call of distress, without distinction of person, possessing a kind heart, and warm sympathy, he acquired a constant practice; moderate in his charges, with either rich or poor, he was called "the poor man's doctor;" he was an estimable man, and a good citizen. Dr. Sears was one of the oldest Odd Fellows in California, having united with the Order in Connecticut, in 1840, was at the time of his death Dep. Grand Patriarch, and was buried in Odd Fellows Cemetery, Sonora, with the usual ceremonies. Children:

By *Eliza :*

  i. ELLEN MARIA, b. July 27, 1841; m. *Henry Tuttle*, who d. in army.

  ii. ELIZA W., b. Feb. 25, 1843; d. Oct. 2, 1845.

By *Jane ;*

  iii. BENJAMIN WILLARD, b. Guilford, Ct., May 26, 1846; lives in Sonora, Cal.

  iv. MARY ANN, b. Aug. 2, 1847.

  v. CHARLES LEONARD, b. Guil., May 25, 1849; m. San Francisco, Cal., Mar. 19, 1881, *Louise M. Effinger*, she b. Phila., Pa., Dec. 23, 1860. He is a photographer in San Bernardino, Cal.

  vi. JOHN FRANKLIN, b. Guil., Dec. 5, 1851.

1.

DANIEL SEARS[1], of New York city; m. *Hannah Morrison*, and was drowned, leaving it is said, an only child.

2.

DANIEL SEARS[2] [*Dan'l*], a farmer who was killed by a falling tree, while cutting timber for a large barn in Holmes co., Ohio, Feb. 17, 1848. He m. Mercer co., Pa., *Elizabeth Magee*, she b. 1796; d. near Upper Sandusky, O., leaving an infant, an only child.

3.

WILLIAM SEARS[3] [*Dan'l²*, *Dan'l¹*], b. Mercer co., Pa., in spring of 1819; m. June 3, 1845, Holmes co., O., *Mary Henry*, she b. Pa., May 16, 1826. He carried on the farm some years

after his father's death, then sold out, and is now engaged with
all his sons, except David, in shingle business near Galloway,
Ark.   Children :

    i. MARY JANE, b. Holmes co., O., Mar. 10, 1846; m. Onro,
       Wis., July 28, 1874, *Jas. Martin*, a saddle and harness
       maker in Little Rock, Ark., he b. Montreal, Can., May 26,
       1846.

    ii. DAVID H., b. Bucyrus, O., Mar. 9, 1848; m. Oshkosh,
       Wis., Mar. 24, 1874, *Naomi Everett*, she b. Tobigue, N.
       B., June 17, 1854 ; he rem. to Winamee, Ind., with his
       parents, thence to Three Oaks, Mich., and to Oshkosh,
       Wis., in 1868, and is now Supt. R. I. Lumber and Mf'g
       Co., Rock Island, Ill.; has 1 son and 2 daus.

  iii. WILLIAM ANSON, b. Crawford co., O., Nov. 23, 1850.

  iv. JAMES MORRISON, b. Crawford co., Jan. 20, 1853.

   v. JOSEPH, b. Crawford co., Sep. 3, 1855.

  vi. SEVENNA, b. Crawford co., June 23, 1857; m. Little Rock,
       Ark., Mar. 14, 1877, *Henry Gustavus*, and lives in Osh-
       kosh, Wis.; children, [1.] Harry, b. Dec., 1877. [2.] Della,
       b. July, 1879.   [3.] Annette, b. Aug. 1881.

 vii. BURR MORRISON, b. June 3, 1860.

viii. FRANKLIN, b. Three Oaks, Mich., Dec. 30, 1865.

  ix. EDWIN FOWLER, b. Oshkosh, Wis., Aug. 21, 1868.

* * *

1.

WATERMAN SEARS[1] of Boston, Mass.; m. *Phebe
Meyers*, she b. Minetto, N. Y.; d. July 28, 1882, æ. 69.   Children :

2.* i. DARIUS LINDLEY, b. Fulton, N. Y., Feb. 22, 1839.

3. ii. ALICE A., b. Fulton, m. *Ed. Lewis*, at San Bernardino,
Cal., in 1880, and lives in Onondaga Valley, N. Y.

2.

DARIUS LINDLEY SEARS[2] [*Waterman*[1]], b. Fulton,
N. Y., Feb. 22, 1839; m. Syracuse, N. Y., *Eleanor Edgar*,
she b. London, Eng., Dec. 9, 1840; lives in S.; he d. Apr. 4,
1873, æ. 34.   Children :

  4.   i. CLERIN WM., b. Syracuse, Mar. 29, 1860 ; lives in Colo-
      rado Springs, Col.

5. ii. LEWIS LINDLEY, b. Syracuse, Nov. 4, 1863; m. there, Nov. 4, 1885, *Florence L. Reed*, she b. Ithaca, N. Y., Sep. 12, 1864; he is a clerk in post-office, Syracuse, and has 1 son.

6. iii. ELBERT LEONE, b. So. Granby, N. Y., Apr. 18, 1865; lives in Brooklyn, N. Y.

1.

BARTHOLOMEW SEARS[1], m. *Margaret Phillom;* is said to have had a bro. Samuel, and is perhaps descended from Bart. Sears of Monroe, Ct.; see *ante.* Children:

2. i. MATILDA, m. —— *Beeman* of Lapell, Ind.
3. ii. CATHARINE, m. —— *Beeman* of Parkinsville, Ind.
4. iii. SUSAN, m. —— *Redick* of Fisherville, Ind.
5. iv. WILLIAM, m., and lives in Loveland, Ohio.
6. v. CORTLAND, lives with his sister Matilda.
7.* vi. JOHN, b. Apr. 18, 1835.
    And 7 other children, all now dead.

7.

JOHN SEARS[2] [*Bart.*[1]], b. near Loveland, Ohio, Apr. 18, 1835; m. Noblesville, Ind., Oct. 1, 1857, *Sarah Freeman*, she b. Strawville, Ind., Mar. 7, 1843; lived in Lapell, Ind., where he d. Dec. 12, 1877. Children:

8. i. MINOR, b. Hamilton, Ind., Jan. 11, 1859.
9. ii. ISAAC, b. Hamilton, Sep. 29, 1861.
10. iii. ALICE, b. Hamilton, Oct. 17, 1864.
11. iv. WESLEY, b. Hamilton, Mar. 4, 1867.
12. v. WILLIAM, b. Madison county, Ind., Nov. 15, 1873.

1.

WILLIAM SEARS[1], b. New Jersey; removed in 1820 to Indiana, and d. July 9, 1878. He had two bros., Samuel and John, and three sisters, the eldest, Elizabeth, d. a young lady; Sarah and Martha. Children:

2. i. ELIZABETH, b. Apr. 24, 1818.

3.   ii. LEVI, b. Aug. 12, 1819.
4. iii. HANNAH, b. Aug. 20, 1820; d. Oct. 11, 1820.
5.   iv. SARAH JANE, b. Dec. 19, 1821.
6.   v. STEVEN, b. and d. Feb. 24, 1824.
7.* vi. WILLIAM MINTZ, b. Dec. 29, 1824.
8. vii. SAMUEL W., b. May 19, 1827; m. and has a dau.
9. viii. HEZEKIAH, d. Sep. 30, 1832.
10.   ix. JOHN, b. Nov. 23, 1830; d. July 19, 1832.
11.   x. EDITH, b. Apr. 30, 1833; d. Oct. 1, 1866.
12.   xi. MARTHA ANN, b. Oct. 20, 1835; d. 1838.
13. xii. AMY, b. Mar. 5, 1838.
14. xiii. JOSEPH, b. July 5, 1840; unm'd.

7.

WILLIAM MINTZ SEARS² [*Wm.*¹], b. Dec. 29, 1824; m. —— ; and lives one-half mile east of South Gate, Ind. Children:

15.   i. JOSEPH, b. Nov. 22, 1862.
16. ii. FRANCIS, b. July 30, 1866.
17. iii. ELLA C., b. Aug. 7, 1868.
18. iv. SARAH J., b. Jan. 23, 1870.
19.   v. CORA L., b. Feb. 22, 1872.

1.

JOHN SEARS¹, of Granville co., No. Car.   Children:

2.   i. ELIZABETH, b. Granville co., No. Car., 1808; d. unm'd, Homersville, Mo., July, 1883, æ. 75.
3.* ii. THOMAS RALPH, b. Granville co., No. Ca., Mar. 23, 1810.

3.

THOMAS RALPH SEARS² [*John*¹], b. Granville co., No. Car., Mar. 23, 1810; m. there July 30, 1833, *Elizabeth R. White*, she b. there, Nov. 9, 1814; d. May 2, 1879; he. d. Oct. 10, 1881.   Children:

4.   i. JOHN AUGUSTUS, b. Gran. co., No. Car., July 1, 1834; lives in Galveston, Texas.
5.   ii. HENRY MARK, b. Williamson co., Tenn., Sep. 16, 1836 ; m. Laurenceburg, Tenn., Feb. 9, 1857, *Jennie Wooten*, she b. Columbia, Tenn., July 14, 1839; he is Pastor of St. James M. E. Ch., Galveston, Tex.

6. iii. Lucy Adeline, b. Maury co., Tenn., Oct. 5, 1838; m. Laurenceburg, *Wm. F. Davidson;* both d.

7. iv. William Thomas, b. 1840; d. unm'd, Oct., 1861.

8. v. Alfred Nickerson, b. 1842; m. Scott's Hill, Tenn., *Emma McKenzie,* she b. Henderson co.; he is an itinerant minister of M. E. Ch., South, now lives in Louisville, Ky.

9. vi. George Washington, b. 1844; lives in McKenzie, Tenn.

10. vii. Benjamin Franklin, b. 1846; m. Scott's Hill, Tenn., *Annie McKenzie,* she b. Henderson co.; he is a farmer and school teacher in McKenzie, and is said to have family records.

11. viii. Joseph Browne, b. near Laurenceburgh, Tenn., Sep. 6, 1856; m. Scott's Hill, Tenn., May 7, 1878, *Sallie Tatema Cobb,* she b. Sulphur Springs, Texas, July 3, 1857; he is an itinerant minister M. E. Ch., South, and in charge of Flatonia Station, Am. Conf.

About the year 1750, several families of Sears are found settled in various counties of Virginia.

I do not learn that their descendants trace any connection between the different families, but they have a general tradition that they are of English origin, except perhaps the Sears of Prince George co., who claim that their ancestor was from France. While they may be correct as to the fact, I think they were of English origin, though a branch may have settled in France.

Some of the Fauquier co. family think their ancestor had resided for a time in Rhode Island.

PAUL SEARS[1] was probably an Englishman, or of English descent, and perhaps resident in France. The family tradition is clear that four sons came from France to Virginia early in the eighteenth century. Children:

2.* i. Paul.

3. ii. Reeder, went to the Indian war; was gone a long time; ret'd to Va., and stayed a while; went west again, and was not heard of after.

4.* iii. Richard.

5. iv. Daniel, bought 280 acres of land in Prince George co., Va., June 16, 1744; served in the Rev'y army, and was not heard of after.

2.

PAUL SEARS[2] [*Paul*[1]], emigrated with his bros. Reeder, Richard and Daniel from France to Virginia in early life; bought 180 acres of land in Prince George co., Sep. 28, 1730; 400 acres, Feb. 8, 1733; and 285 acres north side of Stoney Creek in Aug., 1745. In the early land records he is called *Junior*, but in 1745 the affix is dropped, from which I infer that his father had d. about that time. He m. *Elizabeth Butler* (who had bros. Jas. and Wm.) Children:

6. i. MARY, b. Prince George co., Va., 19, 4 mo., 1736; m. *Simmons Fowler*, and had an only dau., Martha, m. Peter Binford.

7. ii. MARTHA, b. Prince George co., 19, 4 mo., 1736; *gemini;* d. unm'd.

8. iii. ELIZABETH, b. Prince George co., 5, 4 mo., 1738; m. *Wm. Fowler*, and had: [1.] Wm., m. Sarah Oliver and had dau. Eliz'h. [2.] Simmons, m. Mary Staunton, and d. s. p.; and [3.] Paul; d. young.

9.* iv. JOHN, b. Prince George co., 25, 5 mo., 1741.

10. v. GADITHA, b. Prince George co., 14, 5 mo., 1743; d. 7 mo., 1777, of cancer; unm.

11. vi. TABITHA, b. Prince George co., 4, 9 mo., 1745; m. *Wm. Batt*, and d. s. p.

12. vii. SARAH, b. Prince George co., 23, 12 mo., 1747; m. *Abidon Bailey*, and had, Rebecca, David, Daniel, Josiah, Martha and Michael.

13. viii. ANN, b. Prince George co., 4, 6 mo., 1750; m. *Wm. Hunnicutt*, and d. s. p.

14. ix. MARGARET, b. Prince George co., 13, 10 mo., 1752; d. in Va., unm.

15. x. JEMIMA, b. Prince George co., 29, 7 mo., 1756; when aged, m. *Wm. Walthall*, and had no issue.

Gaditha, Tabitha, Sarah, Margaret, and Jemima were mentioned in the will of their brother John, as living with him in 1799.

There is mention of a Tabithy Irby as born Jan. 4, 1752, who is thought to have been an adopted dau. of Paul, Jr.

4.

RICHARD SEARS[2] [*Paul[1]*], m. —— ——. Children :
16.* i. WILLIAM.
17. ii. POLLY.

9.

JOHN SEARS[3] [*Paul[2], Paul[1]*], b. Prince George co., Va., 25, 5 mo., 1741; d. 1800, æ. 59 ; will dated 1799, calls him of Dinwiddie, Va.; m. *Sarah Peebles* or *Peoples,* she b. 24, 9 mo., 1741; when of a suitable age, he was put to the blacksmith business, and his relations in France being advised of the fact, sent him a complete set of tools, still preserved in the family ; he worked at his trade until middle life, then turned his attention to wheelwrighting, also doing most of his wants at other mechanical trades, as carpenter, silversmith, tanner, shoemaker, etc. ; his general health was good, although afflicted for a time with cancer of the nose, which was operated on successfully. He removed to Dinwiddie co., Va., and d. there, but all his children are said to have been born in Prince George co. Children :
18.* i. PAUL, b. Prince George co., Va., 14, 12 mo., 1768.
19. ii. ELIZABETH, b. Prince George co., 31, 8 mo., 1770 ; d. æ. ab't 40, and bur. Prince George co.; m. *John Mattocs,* and had 1 child ; d. inf.
20. iii. HULDAH, b. Prince George co., 22, 11 mo., 1772; d. unm., æ. ab't 66, having been afflicted with rheumatism most of her life, and was buried in Montgomery co., Ohio, whither she removed ab't 1834.
21.* iv. JOHN, b. Prince George co., 4, 2 mo., 1775.
22. v. SARAH, b. Prince George co., 21, 9 mo., 1777 ; m. *Francis Walthall ;* rem. in 1828, to Springborough, Ohio, and d. s. p.
23. vi. MARTHA, b. Prince George co., 4, 5 mo., 1780; m. *Jas. Brock,* and had, [1.] Robert, m. Penina Dawson, and d. æ. 45 ; had, i. Joel, m. —— ——. ii. Wm., m. Mary R. Hagen, and lives Sewellsville, O. iii. Martha, d. young. iv. Mary, m. John Warrick, and had 3 children; d. young. v. James, d. young. vi. Rebecca, d. young, and 4 other children. [2.] James, d. young and unm. [3.] Sarah, m. 1st, Nathan Dawson, and had Martha ; d. æ.
74

ab't 23, unm.; 2d, Luke Vanosdillen, and had James, who lives in western Ohio. She outlived all her family, and d. æ. 70, of consumption.

24.   vii. SAMUEL, b. Prince George co.; 13, 8 mo., 1783 ; d. 6, 10 mo., 1785.

25.* viii. PETER, b. Prince George co., 5, 4 mo., 1787.

26.   ix. HANNAH, b. Prince George co., 5, 4 mo., 1787, *gemini ;* d. young, unm.

16.

WILLIAM SEARS[3] [*Rich.[2], Paul[1]*], d. young ; m. *Miriam Smith.* Children :

  i. POLLY.

 ii. LUCY.

18.

PAUL SEARS[4] [*John[3], Paul[2], Paul[1]*], b. Prince George co., Va., 14, 12 mo., 1768; d. Centreville, Ohio, 14, 4 mo., 1841, æ. 71 ; m. Dinwiddie co., Va., 5 mo., 1794, *Huldah* (*Ladd*) *Simmons,* (a young widow with one child, Deborah, b. 7, 10 mo., 1792), she d. 1827.   Children :

27.   i. MIRIAM, b. Dinwiddie co., Va., 7, 8 mo., 1795.

28.* ii. SAMUEL, b. Dinwiddie co., 13, 11 mo., 1796.

29. iii. LYDIA LADD, b. Dinwiddie co., 24, 12 mo., 1798.

30. iv. MARIAH, b. Dinwiddie co., 9, 7 mo., 1800.

31.   v. BENJAMIN, b. Dinwiddie co., 26, 5 mo., 1802.

32.* vi. JOHN GILLAM, b. Dinwiddie co., 11, 1 mo., 1809.

" A testimony concerning Paul Sears deceast, by his daughter Maria Sears.   The scripture saith, when the Lords Judgements are in the erth the inhabetants shall learn righteousness.

" The awfull and suden maner in which an all wise Providence saw meet to brake the shekles of mortality to remove from workes to rewards this my beloved Parent, lays with weight on my mind that I showld make it publick for the good of others.   He was born in Dinwidia county state of Virginia the 14th day of the 12th month 1768.   His parents names were John and Sarah Sears who educated him in the Principles of the Christian religion profest by friends in which he was concurned to walk with circumspection.   In 1794 he was married to Huldah Simmons a young widow with one child, to whome he was as affectionate a Father as he was to his own if any ods he rather exceeded.

"In 1797 my Mother came forth in worke of the Ministry and in 1810 when their youngest child was not tow years old she first received a surtificate to travel in the exercise of her gift to which he freely gave her up, not withstanding the double care that devolved upon him, six small children and no care-taker but himself within dores and without. . His exercise and concurn for the upright walking of his family was great, endeavoring to restrain them from every rong thing, all his restraints however positive and puncktal ware sesoned with love.

"He had many triales to encounter in my Mothers absence from home yet he all ways gave her up with a willing heart and encoraging language telling her that his Spirit was at times permited to accompeny hers not only in her tride and proveing sesons but also in her rejoysings.

"Her reply would be, my dear maintain thy noble courage.

"For 17 years of their lives she was the most part of the time from home on religious service, several times visited North Carolina, Philadelphia, Pensylvania, Baltimore and Merilan, twice in Ohio and Indiana, once to Inglant, Ireland, Scotland and Walles, was near 2 years at diferent times engaged in visiting the slave holders of the State of Verginia in a part of which visit he bore her Compeny and they had to remark the tenderness of spirit and openess of most that was found amongst this tyranical part of the human family, he was firm in the beleaf there was no beter way to worke with the oppressor for the releaf of the opprest than by the spirit of Him who worketh by love. He bore her company in her last visit to the meetings of there own quarter which was finished a few weekes before her death. On there return home she told him her worke was done, and that he might prepare for a final seperation, the which he bore with Christian fortitude, and shortly after her death in the year 1827 he removed with his children to the state of Ohio and settled within the verge of Springborough monthly meeting, he had been for some years before this removal in the stasion of an elder, and tho not in that stasion after he came to this country yet his concurn and exercise for the supporte of the discipline was unabated, discoraging the aperance of evil whare ever he saw it, truly a peace maker with all with whome he had to do. His death was occashioned by a fall on the 9th day of 4th month, in the evening the family all from home but he and I, he went to pay attenshion to the Creatures, was on an uper flower in the barn when it gave way and he come down with it head for most, I herd the alarm and ran, when I got to him he said I am killed, I said, no Father, he continued, I am killed, all dead now from here down, laying his hand on the pitt of his stummack, which was indeed true for he never had any more fealing in them parts afterward & he continued saying, Lord have mercy on my Soul, he said his back and breast was broke all to peasces, the dearest object of my life, a destressing a sean beyond descripsion. I had to leave him a few minites to get assistance, when I returned I found him quite composed and engaged in fervent prayer, saying my time is come to leave the world all in an instant, Lord be pleased to have mercy on my Soul, thou has been with me through the many trials of my life, be pleasd to be with me now, be pleasd to preserve my children there Souls, Lord this world is nothing. On this came his son to whome he said, my dear child my time is come to leave you to brave the world all in an instant, he queried how he felt, he answered, nothing to depend upon but the Mercyes of the dear Saviour. I have been scufling along all my life trying to do that which was right, I have no dependence but the Mercyes of the dear Saviour. After he was taken in the house he had considerable to say to his children earnestly entreeting them in all things to do that which is wright. He sufered violent pain in his breast, head and back, and great presure of water in his pipes, no power to cough, all which he bore with remarkable patiance, never making the least complaint, often praying for patiance that he might hold out to the end. He several times gave council and advice to those about him, seting forth the certainty of a never endeing eternity, and of the uncerterty of all the changeable things of time that we should above all things be concurned to do that which is right in the Devine sight, that will bring Peace at the solem close. Forth day the 14 he semd sensable his close was at hand, said to one of his daughters, when I expire I want thee to be quiet, and all of you, thee in particular. A while after he requested to sit up in the bed whare he sit about 3 hours unto the last. Soon after he was sit up he said, my breath gets shorter and shorter, soon after said, I am worrying along with death, I don't expect to see the light of another day. He continued to draw his breath shorter and shorter, and remarkable easy considering the pressure in his pipes. A few minutes before his close, he said, I was killed all but this little part, the ceat of life, that I might speak to you and now I tell you all farewell to geather. He departed this the 14 of the 4th month of 1841, aged 72 years and 4 months."

21.

JOHN SEARS[4] [*John*[3], *Paul*[2], *Paul*[1]], b. Prince George co., Va., 4, 2 mo., 1775; d. Highland co., O., 10, 7 mo., 1817; m. *Penelope Johnson*, she b. Va., 24, 2 mo., 1790; d. Grant co., Ind., 15, 6 mo., 1869. He rem'd in 1808 to Eastern Ohio, and settled on a farm. Children:

33.   i. MARY, b. Highland co., O., 22, 12 mo., 1809; m. Green co., *Moses Bond*, and lives in Marion, Ind.
34.   ii. PLEASANT, b. Highland co., O., 29, 1 mo., 1812; m. Fayette co., *Nancy Pearson*, and d. 1886.
35.* iii. CHRISTOPHER, b. Highland co., O., 3, 8 mo., 1814.
36.* iv. JOHN, b. Highland co., O., 12, 2 mo., 1817.

25.

PETER SEARS[4] [*John*[3], *Paul*[2], *Paul*[1]], b. Prince George co., Va., 5, 4 mo., 1787; d. Barnesville, O., 12, 7 mo., 1863, æ. 76½, of inflammation of stomach and erysipelas; m. 14, 3 mo., 1810, *Anna Doudua*. He was a farmer and miller in Belmont co., O., and the early history of the family is mostly from an account written by him and his sister Sarah, 8 mo., 1847. Children:

37.   i. SARAH, b. Somerton, Belmont co., Ohio, 14, 12 mo., 1812; d. Barnesville, Ohio, 24, 2 mo., 1815, of consumption; m. 29, 3 mo., 1843, *John Hartley*, and had: [1.] Elizabeth, b. Quaker City, O., 20, 2 mo., 1844; m. 20, 5 mo., 1875, Joshua Young, and lives Ochiltree, Kans., and has, i. Osmond H., b. 17, 5 mo., 1876. ii. Joshua D., b. 20, 11 mo., 1878. iii. Mary E., b. 21, 10 mo., 1880.
38.   ii. MARTHA, b. Somerton, Belmont co., 9, 1 mo., 1812; d. Pennsville, Ohio, of Erysipelas, 7, 4 mo., 1845; m. 9, 3 mo., 1836, *Robert Milhous*, (who m. 2d, Rachel Stubbs); children, MILHOUS: [1.] Ruth, b. 1, 12 mo., 1836; d. 31, 1 mo., 1884; m. 1, 5 mo., 1867, Jas. R. Kite, and had, i. Lydia B., b. 9, 5 mo., 1868. ii. Mary M., b. 11, 1 mo., 1874. iii. Anna S., b. 12, 6 mo., 1877, all born Pennsville, O., and now living in Phila. [2.] Anna, b. 9, 11 mo., 1838; d. Smyrna, Ohio, 26, 7 mo., 1880; m. 5, 5 mo., 1871, David Stephen, and had, i. Eliza M., b. 3, 5 mo., 1872, at Smyrna, O., now lives Pennsville, O. [3.] Lydia, b. 23,

7 mo., 1840; d. 14, 2 mo., 1889. [4.] Sarah Ann, b. 27, 7 mo., 1842; d. 10, 6 mo., 1845.

39. iii. ZILLAH, b. Somerton, Belmont co., 30, 7 mo., 1813; d. Barnesville, O., 8, 3 mo., 1839, of consumption.

40.* iv. JOHN, b. Somerton, Belmont co., 10, 11 mo., 1814.

41.* v. PETER, b. Somerton, Belmont co., 20, 5 mo., 1816.

42.* vi. PAUL, b. Somerton, Belmont co., 1, 2 mo., 1818.

43.*vii. DAVID, b. Somerton, Belmont co., 14, 3 mo., 1819.

44. viii. HULDAH, b. Somerton, Belmont co., 3, 9 mo., 1821; d. Barns., 24, 3 mo., 1840, of consumption.

45. ix. ANN, b. Somerton, Belmont co., 30, 8 mo., 1823; d Barns., 27, 10 mo., 1844, of consumption.

46.* x. BENJAMIN, b. Somerton, Belmont co., 23, 6 mo., 1825.

47. xi. JOSEPH, b. Somerton, Belmont co., 10, 5 mo., 1827; d. Barns., 8, 7 mo., 1833.

48. xii. ELIZABETH, b. Barns., 29, 3 mo., 1830; d. there, 3, 8 mo., 1832.

28.

SAMUEL SEARS[5] [*Paul[4]*, *Paul[3]*, *Paul[2]*, *Paul[1]*], b. Prince George co., Va., 13, 11 mo., 1796; m. 1821, *Mary Ann Wilson*, and rem. to Belmont co., Ohio, settling first near Springsboro, in Warren co., afterward permanently on the farm on the Spring Valley pike, now owned and occupied by his son Charles. Children:

49. i. HENRY, b. Prince George co., Va., 1, 3 mo., 1821; m. twice, and has 4 chil. by his present wife.

50. ii. MARIA WILSON, b. Pr. Geo. co., Va., 3, 10 mo., 1822; m. *Morgan Hatfield*, and has 2 children.

51. iii. GEORGE, b. Pr. Geo. co., 28, 3 mo., 1824; m. 14, 3 mo., 1847, *Lavina Hatfield;* 2d, 14, 3 mo., 1856, *Sarah Young;* 3d, 25, 6 mo., 1859, *Lucinda Cramer;* and had Aaron F., Samuel, Mary Jane, George William, and Sarah Ann.

52. iv. JOHN PAUL, b. Pr. Geo. co., Va., 16, 11 mo., 1825; m. 1847, *Rosanna Reeder;* 2d, 1851, *Deborah Anderson,* and had 8 children.

53. v. HULDAH ANN, d. inf.

54. vi. BENJAMIN, b. Warren co., Ohio, 1, 1 mo., 1829; m. 1851, *Hannah Davis,* and had 7 children.

55. vii. ISABELLA, b. Warren co., O., 6, 2 mo., 1831; d. inf.

56. viii. ROBERT G., b. Warren co., O., 4, 2 mo., 1833; m. 1857, *Eunice Ann Anderson,* and had 1 son and 7 daus.

57.   ix. SAMUEL, b. 1834; d. young.
58.   x. JOSEPH STAFFORD, b. Montgomery co., O., 8, 6 mo., 1836; m. *Jane Weller*, and had 1 son.
59.   xi. WILLIAM PENN, b. Mont. co., O., d. inf.
60.   xii. MARY ANN, b. Mont. co., O., 22, 2 mo., 1840; m. 1863, *Wm. Creighton*, and had 6 children.
61. xiii. CHARLES W., b. Mont. co., O., 21, 10 mo., 1842; m. 15, 3 mo., 1865, *Zelinda Peebles;* no children.
61.*a.* xiv. MARTHA, b. 19, 10 mo., 1844; d. young.

This is a race of Anaks, most of the sons and many of their children exceeding six feet in stature.

At a family gathering on Charles Sears' farm, Sep. 30, 1886, eighty guests of the family were present, and a "Sears Society" was organized by the choice of George Sears, President; Samuel Sears of Dayton, Ohio, Vice-President; Martha Sears, Cor. Sec'y; Charles W. Sears, Isaac Hatfield, John Sears, Selma Sears, Mattie Davis and Nora Sears, Exec. Com.; and Charles Sears, Treasurer.

Let the Cape Cod Sears follow their example.

32.

JOHN GILLAM SEARS⁵ [*Paul⁴, John³, Paul², Paul¹*], b. Va., 11, 1 mo., 1809; m. Champaign co., Ohio, 19, 3 mo., 1838, *Elizabeth Winder*, she b. Ross. co., 19, 6 mo., 1819. Children:

62.   i. ABNER W., b. Montgomery co., O., 15, 10 mo., 1839; m. Clark co., 21, 10 mo., 1860, *Julia A. Negley.*
63.   ii. SARAH JANE, b. Montgomery co., 17, 7 mo., 1841; m. Champaign co., O., 3, 6 mo., 1866, *Isaac W. Reams*, and had: [1.] Emma, b. 9, 3 mo., 1868; d. 27, 2 mo., 1877. [2.] Mary, b. 2, 3 mo., 1870. [3.] John S., b. 17, 7 mo., 1872. [4.] Arthur W., b. 5, 10 mo., 1878. [5.] Frederic S., b. 26, 8 mo., 1881.
64.   iii. HULDAH, b. Champaign co., O., 5, 6 mo., 1843; m. Madison co., 25, 7 mo., 1868, *Thos. W. Gaskill;* has several children, and lives 48 William st., Cleveland, O.
65.* iv. SAMUEL, b. Montgomery co., 9, 4 mo., 1845.
66.   v. MOSES W., b. Montgomery co., 18, 7 mo., 1847; m. Green co., 3, 1 mo., 1872, *Emma Stewart.*
67.   vi. MARY E., b. Montgomery co., 3, 2 mo., 1849; m. Cleveland, O., 1875, *Fred. Seager*, he b. Germany, 1837, and lives 240 Dunham st., Cleveland.

35.

CHRISTOPHER SEARS[5] [*John*[4], *John*[3], *Paul*[2], *Paul*[1]],
b. Highland co., Ohio, 3, 8 mo., 1814; m. Clinton co., 24, 8
mo., 1837, *Lydia J. Crane*, she b. there, 15, 11 mo., 1815;
and lives in Hanfield, Ind. Children:

68.   i. Amos W., b. Montgomery co., O., 15, 6 mo., 1838;
     d. Grant co., Ind., 12, 3 mo., 1857.
69.   ii. Isabella C., b. Grant co., Ind., 7, 10 mo., 1840; d.
     2, 4 mo., 1848; m. there, 14, 3 mo., 1861, *Phineas How-*
     ard, he b. there, 1840.
70.   iii. Caroline, b. Grant co., 21, 10 mo., 1842; m. there,
     30, 9 mo., 1866, *Jesse Wright*, and lives in Marion, Ind.
71.   iv. Mary, b. Grant co., 1, 7 mo., 1845; m. there, 30, 9
     mo., 1866, *Joseph Kein*, and lives in Marion, Ind.
72.* v. John C., b. Grant co., 18, 8 mo., 1847.
73.   vi. Mariah, b. Grant co., 3, 6 mo., 1849; m. there, 21,
     11 mo., 1872, *Green A. Campbell*, and lives in Banquo,
     Ind.
74.   vii. George A., b. Grant co., 29, 12 mo., 1851; d. 27, 1
     mo., 1845.
75.   viii. Alice J., b. Grant co., 18, 1 mo., 1855; m. there,
     14, 10 mo., 1877, *John J. Brown* of Ohio, and lives in
     Hanfield, Ind.

36.

JOHN SEARS[5] [*John*[4], *John*[3], *Paul*[2], *Paul*[1]], b. Highland
co., Ohio, 12, 2 mo., 1817; d. 20, 5 mo., 1884; m. 17, 8 mo.,
1837, *Elizabeth Hisey*, who d. 3, 10 mo., 1864, æ. 52 yrs. 11
mos. 8 dys.; 2d, 20, 5 mo., 1866, *Mary Ridge*. Children:

76.   i. Mary J., b. 8, 7 mo., 1838; m. 15, 4 mo., 1863,
     Wm. Cleaver, and had: [1.] Martha E., b. 11, 10 mo.,
     1864; m. 24, 7 mo., 1884, Geo. W. Davis, and had, i. Jos.
     W., b. 3, 8 mo., 1885. ii. Glenn C., b. 27, 6 mo., 1887.
     [2.] Anna L., b. 2, 12 mo., 1866; m. 24, 12 mo., 1884,
     Wm. E. Warwick. [3.] Lutie A., b. 18, 11 mo., 1868;
     d. 30, 8 mo., 1870. [4.] Willie E., b. 22, 7 mo., 1871; d.
     24, 7 mo., 1871. [5.] Warren M., b. 3, 8 mo., 1872.
77.* ii. Joseph M., b. Highland co., 2, 5 mo., 1840.
78.* iii. Jacob C., b. Higbland co., 16, 6 mo., 1841.
79.* iv. J. William, b. Highland co., 16, 6 mo., 1843.
80.   v. Amelia E., b. Highland co., 25, 7 mo., 1847; d. 25,
     11 mo., 1849.

40.

JOHN SEARS[5] [*Peter*[4], *John*[3], *Paul*[2], *Paul*[1]], b. Somerton, Ohio, 10, 11 mo., 1814; d. Barnesville, O., 20, 9 mo., 1844, of consumption; m. 20, 8 mo., 1844, *Phebe Grimshaw*, (who m. 2d, Nathan Hall of Spencer's Station; both d.) Was a farmer. Children:

81.   i. JANE H., b. Barnesville, O., 31, 10 mo., 1837; lives Chester Hill, Ohio.
82.   ii. MARGARET, b. Barnesville, O., 16, 11 mo., 1842; d. Chester Hill, 10, 8 mo., 1859.
83.   iii. JOHN G., b. Barnesville, O., 15, 1 mo., 1844; m. 25, 12 mo., 1872, *Lucinda Walters*, and lives at Chester Hill, Ohio.

41.

PETER SEARS[5] [*Peter*[4], *John*[3], *Paul*[2], *Paul*[1]], b. Somerton, Ohio, 20, 5 mo., 1816; m. 1, 1 mo., 1851, *Phariba Bundy*, who d. 16, 1 mo., 1879; he is a farmer at Barnesville, Ohio. Children:

84.   i. MARY B., b. Barnes., 11, 10 mo., 1852; and lives there.
85.   ii. SARAH D., b. Barnes., 11, 8 mo., 1854; and lives there.
86.* iii. BENJAMIN STANTON, b. Barnes., 22, 1 mo., 1857.
87.   iv. EDWIN WILSON, b. Barnes., 29, 11 mo., 1858; is a farmer in Barnes.

42.

PAUL SEARS[5] [*Peter*[4], *John*[3], *Paul*[2], *Paul*[1]], b. Somerton, Ohio, 1, 2 mo., 1818; d. Smyrna, O., 20, 9 mo., 1864; m. there, 7, 6 mo., 1843, *Abigail Holloway*, who still lives there. He was a farmer. Children:

88.   i. REBECCA, b. Barnes., 1, 1 mo., 1845; is a teacher in Indian School at Tunesassa, N. Y. (?)
89.   ii. ANNA, b. Smyrna, 9, 9 mo., 1846; lives there.
90.   iii. ROBERT S., b. Smyrna, 4, 3 mo., 1851; lives there on a farm with his mother and sister.
90.   iv. RACHEL T., b. Smyrna, 4, 3 mo., 1851, *gemini;* d. 28, 8 mo., 1875; she was almost helpless with rheumatism for 11 years previous.

75

43.

DAVID SEARS[5] [*Peter*[4], *John*[3], *Paul*[2], *Paul*[1]], b. Somerton, Ohio, 14, 3 mo., 1819 ; m. Pennsville, O., 20, 3 mo., 1846, *Rachel Patton,* who d. 8, 12 mo., 1863.   He is a farmer and apiarist in Thornburgh, Iowa.   He m. 2d, 24, 3 mo., 1870 *Sarah W. Briggs.*   Children :

91. i. REBECCA, b. Centreville, O., 3, 3 mo., 1845; m. 16, 2 mo., 1867, *Robert Henry Drake*, and lives Douglass, Wyoming Ter.; children, [1.] Rachel Catharine, b. 17, 3 mo., 1868; m. 9, 7 mo., 1887, John Curtis Denison, and has Ira Curtis, b. 21, 2 mo., 1889. [2.] Robert McKendrie, b. 28, 5 mo.,1869; d. 21, 2 mo., 1876. [3.] Mary Elizabeth, b. 7, 4 mo.,1872 ; d. 23, 9 mo., 1873. [4.] Thos. Henry, b. 19, 10 mo., 1874. [5.] Harry Edward, b. 4, 12 mo., 1876. [6.] Jesse Albert, b. 15, 1 mo., 1879. [7.] Levi Blythedale, b. 11, 11 mo., 1880. [8.] Philip William, b. 4, 3 mo., 1883. [9.] Eva Mabel, b. 30, 11 mo., 1884. [10.] David Curtis, b. 20, 10 mo., 1886.

92. ii. TABITHA, b. Centreville, O., 14, 5 mo., 1846 ; m. 15, 2 mo., 1866, *Jacob Zumwalt*, and lives at Douglass, Wyo. Ter.; children, [1.] Irena A., b. 17, 11 mo., 1866; m. 26, 9 mo., 1883, John W. Conway, and had, i. Chas. J., b. 27, 7 mo., 1884 ; d. 14, 8 mo., 1884. ii. George W., b. 26, 6 mo., 1885 ; d. 22, 7 mo., 1885. iii. William, b. 30, 9 mo.,1886. iv. Elmer, b. 16, 6 mo., 1888. [2.] Armenia M., b. 17, 11 mo., 1866, *gemini ;* m. 23, 4 mo., 1885, Enos Beals, and had, i. Harry E., b. 14, 1 mo., 1886. ii. John W., b. 12, 7 mo., 1887. iii. Lydia A., b. 17, 7 mo., 1889. [3.] Chas. Franklin, b. 24, 5 mo., 1868. [4.] David Frederic, b. 4, 6 mo., 1870 ; d. 17, 4 mo., 1871. [5.] Richard W., b. 24, 6 mo.,1872. [6.] Mary Alice, b. 21, 9 mo., 1873. [7.] Altie Ann, b. 17, 3 mo., 1878. [8.] Cora Ethel, b. 8, 3 mo., 1880; d. 25, 10 mo., 1881. [9.] Della Mabel, b. 12, 2 mo., 1884. [10.] Ernest Arcell, b. 25, 3 mo., 1889.

93. iii. ELVIRA, b. Centreville, O., 4, 9 mo., 1848 ; d. near Thornburgh, Iowa, of consumption, 30, 12 mo., 1870.

94.* iv. TILMAN, b. Centreville, O., 7, 7 mo., 1853.

95. v. ROSELLA, b. Springville, Iowa, 23, 4 mo., 1837; m. 13, 2 mo., 1881, *John Dickerson*, a farmer, and lives in Mo.; children, [1.] Ida May, b. 25, 1 mo., 1882. [2.] David J., b. 28, 4 mo., 1884. [3.] Marion W., b. 4, 9 mo., 1885. [4.] Wilford Earl, b. 19, 11 mo., 1888.

96.* vi. SCHUYLER J., b. Springville, Iowa, 10, 2 mo., 1859.
97.*vii. HARRY CLEMENT, b. Springville, Iowa, 13, 4 mo., 1862.

46.

BENJAMIN SEARS[5] [*Peter*[4], *John*[3], *Paul*[2], *Paul*[1]], b. Somerton, Ohio, 23, 6 mo., 1825; d. near Barnesville, O., 30, 8 mo., 1857; m. 28, 11 mo., 1849, *Esther S. Briggs.* He was a farmer. Children :
  98. i. MARY ANN, b. Barnes., O., 23, 3 mo., 1851; d. 26, 10 mo., 1862, of diphtheria.
  99.* ii. JOSEPH JOHN, b. Barnes., O., 24, 2 mo., 1853.
100. iii. WILLIAM HENRY, b. Barnes., O., 31, 3 mo., 1856.

65.

SAMUEL SEARS[6] [*John*[5] *Paul*[4], *John*[3], *Paul*[2], *Paul*[1]], b. North Lewisburgh, Ohio, 9, 4 mo., 1845; m. Xenia, O., 18, 8 mo., 1870, *Leonora A. Martin,* she b. there, 5, 2 mo., 1849; and lives in Dayton, Ohio. He enlisted in the Union Army and was expelled from the Quaker Church in consequence, and joined the Methodists. He has many old family documents, and the bulls-eye watch presented to his grand-mother in England. Children :
101. i. COURTLAND M., b. Xenia, O., 2, 12 mo., 1871; d. there, 19, 4 mo., 1877.
102. ii. FREDERIC H., b. Xenia, 5, 2 mo., 1873.
103. iii. WALTER E., b. Dayton, O., 15, 10 mo., 1881.

72.

JOHN C. SEARS[6] [*Chris.*[5], *John*[4], *John*[3], *Paul*[2], *Paul*[1]], b. Grant co., Ind., 18, 8 mo., 1847; m. —— ——, and lives in Hanfield, Ind. Children :
104. i. CLAYTON, b. about 1860.
105. ii. MARY JEANNETTE, b. about 1862.
106. iii. ANNIE, b. about 1867.

77.

JOSEPH M. SEARS[6] [*John*[5], *John*[4], *John*[3], *Paul*[2], *Paul*[1]], b. 2, 5 mo , 1840; m. 24, 10 mo., 1860, *Mary E. Jordan.* Children :
107. i. IDA A., b. 4, 10 mo., 1861; d. 18, 6 mo., 1862.

108. ii. LIDA S., b. 1, 8 mo., 1863 ; m. 24, 9 mo., 1884, *Elias Oglesbee*, and had : [1.] Mary, b. 5, 10 mo., 1885 ; d. 12, 3 mo., 1886. [2.] Helen A., b. 20, 7 mo., 1887.
109. iii. CHARLES J., b. 16, 11 mo., 1866.

78.

JACOB C. SEARS[6] [*John[5], John[4], John[3], Paul[2], Paul[1]*], b. 16, 6 mo., 1841 ; m. 18, 10 mo., 1860, *Margaret C. Rich.* Children :
110.* i. ELMER E., b. 14, 7 mo., 1861.
111.* ii. LEWIS M., b. 27, 10 mo., 1862.
112. iii. LIZZIE C., b. 9, 5 mo., 1868.
113. iv. ROSA L., b. 5, 2 mo., 1870.

79.

J. WILLIAM SEARS[6] [*John[5], John[4], John[3], Paul[2], Paul[1]*], b. 16, 6 mo., 1843 ; m. 21, 4 mo., 1874, *Alice M. Harper*, who d. 7, 5 mo., 1875 ; 2d, 22, 2 mo., 1882, *Eleanor Howard.*

86.

BENJAMIN STANTON SEARS[6] [*Peter[5], Peter[4], John[3], Paul[2], Paul[1]*], b. Barnesville, Ohio, 22, 1 mo., 1857 ; m. 28, 12 mo., 1882, *Ellen Patterson ;* is a farmer in Manhattan, Kan. Children :
114. i. HALLECK STANLEY, b. Barnes., 4, 12 mo., 1886.
115. ii. CLARA B., *adopted.*

94.

TILMAN SEARS[6] [*David[5], Peter[4], John[3], Paul[2], Paul[1]*], b. Centreville, Ohio, 7, 7 mo., 1853 ; m. 26, 8 mo., 1876, *Ellen Bigelow*, and is a farmer in Missouri. Children :
116. i. CLEMENTINE, b. 15, 9 mo., 1877 ; d. 20, 9 mo., 1880.
117. ii. CLEMENT, b. 15, 9 mo., 1877, *gemini.*
118. iii. CALVERT, b. 21, 1 mo., 1880.
119. iv. CLYDEY, b. 12, 10 mo., 1881 ; d. 15, 8 mo., 1882.
120. v. ZADA ELLEN, b. 8, 7 mo., 1883.
121. vi. MARY ROSELLA, b. 6, 4 mo., 1885.
122. vii. MAGGIE LULA JANE, b. 18, 3 mo., 1888.

96.

SCHUYLER J. SEARS⁶ [*David⁵, Peter⁴, John³, Paul²,
Paul¹*], b. Springville, Iowa, 10, 2 mo., 1859; m. 23, 2 mo.,
1887, *S. Retta M. Clark*, and is a farmer near Thornburg,
Iowa. Child:
123. i. DAVID J., b. 13, 6 mo., 1888; d. 13, 6 mo., 1888.

97.

HARRY CLEMENT SEARS⁶ [*David₅ Peter⁴, John³,
Paul², Paul¹*], b. 13, 4 mo., 1862; m. 27, 9 mo., 1886, *Rachel
Elizabeth Shaw*, and is a farmer and apiarist near Thornburgh,
Iowa. Child:
124. i. MABEL ELVIRA, b. 4, 8 mo., 1887.

99.

JOSEPH JOHN SEARS⁶ [*Benj.⁵, Peter⁴, John³, Paul²,
Paul¹*], b. Barnesville, Ohio, 24, 2 mo., 1853; m. 21, 10 mo.,
18—, *Ruth Ellen Shry*, and is a master-builder in Piedmont, O.
Children:
125. i. CORA ALICE, b. Barnes., 20, 12 mo., 1876.
126. ii. LILLIE E., b. Barnes., 3, 4 mo., 1878.
127. iii. ROSCOE P., b. Piedmont, 15, 9 mo., 1880.
128. iv. NORA D., b. Piedmont, 17, 8 mo., 1882.

100.

WILLIAM HENRY SEARS⁶ [*Benj.₅ Peter⁴, John³, Paul²,
Paul¹*], b. Barnesville, Ohio, 31, 3 mo., 1856; m. 27, 3 mo.,
1878, *Mary K. Naylor*, and is a farmer and berry-grower in
B. Children:
129. i. FREDERIC L., b. Barnes., 19, 8 mo., 1879.
130. ii. WALTER B., b. Barnes., 3, 4 mo., 1881.
131. iii. ALICE E., b. Barnes., 27, 10 mo., 1886.

110.

ELMER E. SEARS⁷ [*Jacob⁶, John⁵, John⁴, John³, Paul²,
Paul¹*], b. 14, 7 mo., 1861; m. 31, 10 mo., 1883, *Della S.
Moore*. Child:
132. i. MARY E., b. 31, 3 mo., 1885.

111.

LEWIS M. SEARS[7] [*Jacob[6], John[5], John[4], John[3], Paul[2], Paul[1]*], b. 27, 10 mo., 1862; m. 27, 8 mo., 1885, *Leah Belle Howe*. Child:

133. i. HERMAN H., b. 27, 7 mo., 1888.

1.

ROBERT SEARS[1] of Fauquier and Loudon cos., Va., was a soldier in the Revolutionary Army, serving 7 years; emigrated to Belmont co., Ohio, about 1812; m. *Eleanor Dallas,* said to be a connection of Vice-Pres. Dallas.   He had a brother THOMAS who settled in Penn.   Children, all b. in Loudon co., Va.

2.* i. JOHN, b. Loudon co., Va., Sep. 27, 1764.
3.   ii. ROBERT, said to have had lands in Maryland from his father.
4. iii. SARAH, m. *Presby Harding* of Maysville, Ky.
5. iv. ELIZABETH, m. *John Luke.*
6.   v. MARGARET, m. *Henry Harding.*
7.* vi. THOMAS.
8. vii. SAMUEL, removed to Ky.
9. viii. MILDRED, d. in Ohio.

2.

JOHN SEARS[2] [*Robt.[1]*], b. London co., Va., Sep. 27, 1764; m. *Annie McNabb*, and removed to Belmont co., Ohio, and d. Jan. 3, 1859.   Children:

10.* i. ROBERT HARRISON, b. Loudon co., Va., Dec. 1, 1798.
11.* ii. WILLIAM ALFRED, b. Loudon co., Feb. 20, 1800.
12. iii. CATHARINE, b. London co., June 22, 1801; m. Woodgrove, O., *John Dye*, and lived in Morgan co., O.
13. iv. JOHN MANLY, b. Loudon co., Dec. 25, 1803; m. Woodgrove, O., *Patty Sellick.*
14.   v. CALEB JEFFERSON, (Rev.) b. Loudon co., Oct. 26, 1805; m. Woodgrove, O., *Matilda Sears*, dau. of Thos. and Mary (Daniels) S., and d. about 1880; he was a Min'r in Prot. Epis. Ch.; his widow lives near Malta, O.
15. vi. ANN M., b. Belmont co., O., Sep. 17, 1807; m. Woodgrove, O., *Thos. Blackburn*, who d. Mar. 21, 1854; she d. Sep. 29, 1855.

7.

THOMAS SEARS[2] [*Robt.*[1]], b. Loudon co., Va.; m. *Mary Daniels.* Children:

16. i. JAMES.
17. ii. JOHN.
18. iii. MATILDA, m. Rev. *Caleb J. Sears.*

10.

ROBERT HARRISON SEARS[3], M. D. [*John*[2], *Robt.*[1]], b. Loudon co., Va., Dec. 1, 1798; m. Va., Nov. 13, 1827, *Mary Ann Allen,* she b. Loudon co., July 17, 1807; (her mother was a Roberson, descended from Sir Arthur R., Bart., of Eng., by a younger son who sailed for England to inherit the estate, but the vessel was never heard of after. The Robersons lived in Maryland.)

Dr. Sears was an eminent physician, with a large practice; made a fortune, which he lost during the war, and by indorsing since. He was a Union man. He m. 2d, *Jennie E.* ——, and lives at Flint Hill, Va. Children:

By *Mary Ann:*
19. i. JOHN WILLIAM, M. D., b. Sandy Hook, Va., Jan. 21, 1830; m. Abingdon, Va., Apr. 10, 1854, *Theodosia Findley,* she b. Washington co., Va., Feb. 26, 1824; lives in Birmingham, Ala.
20. ii. ROBERTA A., b. Loudon co., Va., May 8, 1832.
21. iii. VIRGINIA A., b. Loudon co., Va., May 8, 1832, *gemini.*
22. iv. MELISSA H., b. Sandy Hook, Va., July 8, 1834; m. Flint Hill, Va., Dec. 13, 1856, *Wm. D. Lovett,* he b. Loudon co., Oct. 30, 1824.
23. v. HATTIE L., b. Flint Hill, Va., Nov. 8, 18——.
By *Jennie:*
24. vi. KATE, m. 1882, and d. next year.

11.

WILLIAM ALFRED SEARS[3] [*John*[2], *Robt.*[1]], b. Loudon co., Va., Feb. 20, 1800; m. Muskingum co., Ohio, 1825, *Mar-*

garet Blackburn, she b. Penn., 1808; he was a farmer, and d. Dec. 31, 1884. Children:

25.   i. Elizabeth A., b. Bristol, O., Sep. 21, 1827; m. *Butler Lyle.*
26.   ii. Elvira J., b. Bristol, O., Mar. 25, 1830; m. *Thomas Harding.*
27.* iii. John W., b. Bristol, O., Aug. 10, 1832.
28.   iv. Thomas B., b. Bristol, O., Mar. 11, 1835; m. Brookfield, O., 1860, *Josephine Coombs*, she b. Renrock, O., 1842; d. 1883; he d. 1869.
29.   v. Mary E., b. Bristol, O., July 3, 1837; m. *Thos. Jameson.*
30.   vi. Anley or Ansley B., b. Bristol, O., May 20, 1840; was a Union soldier, wounded and taken prisoner in the Wilderness; was 8 months in Andersonville prison, and d. June 9, 1865.
31.   vii. Minnie, b. Bristol, O., June 6, 1843; m. *David M. Boy.*
32. viii. Elbridge W., b. Bristol, O., July 20, 1848; d. May 27, 1884.

27.

JOHN W. SEARS[4] [*Wm.*[3], *John*[2], *Robt.*[1]], b. Bristol, Ohio, Aug. 10, 1832; m. there, Apr. 25, 1855, *Louisa Felton*, she b. Wood Grove, O., Dec. 9, 1832; they live in Young Hickory, O. Children:

33.   i. Mary Alma, b. Bristol, O., Apr. 3, 1856; m. Oct. 4, 1874, Rev. *Robt. A. Louther*, he b. Richie co., O.; lives in Gilmore, O.
34.   ii. Ella E., b. Bristol, O., June 24, 18—; m. McConnelsville, June 22, 1880, Rev. *Wm. H. Dye*, he b. Muskingum co., O.; lives in McC.
35.   iii. William A., b. Bristol, O., Feb. 21, 1862; is a teacher in Marietta, O.
36.   iv. Robert F., b. Bristol, O., May 2, 1864; is a teacher in Marietta, O.
37.   v. Blanche, b. Bristol, O., May 23, 1867.
38.   vi. Estella M., b. Bristol, O., Aug. 31, 1869.
39.   vii. Minnie, b. Bristol, O., Nov. 28, 1871.
40. viii. Gertrude, b. Bristol, O., Nov. 15, 1876.

1.

EDWARD SEARS[1], an Englishman, settled in Essex co., Va.; m. —— *Barbee;* (who m. 2d, —— *Spindle,* and had issue.) Children:

2. i. WILLIAM, d. unm.
3. ii. MORDECAI.
4. iii. JEREMIAH, d. unm.
5.* iv. JOHN, b. Essex co., Va., May 15, 1762.
6. v. JANE, m. *John Golding,* and had: Phil, Jack, James and another.
7. vi. MOLLIE, m. *Menus Pilkington,* in Essex co.; a dau. m.; and lived Houston, Tex.

5.

JOHN SEARS[2] [*Edw'd[1]*], b. Essex co., Va., May 15, 1762; m. below Richmond, *Betsy Pritchett,* dau. of John P. of Buckingham co., Va., and d. about 1818. Children :

8. i. NANCY B., b. 1790; m. *Fred. Bagley.*
9. ii. HENRY, b. May, 1792; m. and d. s. p. in Logan co., Ky.
10. iii. MARY, b. Feb., 1794; m. *Henry Coleman.*
11. iv. ARVILLA, b. Feb., 1796; m. *John Dillon.*
12.* v. JOHN, b. Appomattox C. H., Va., Oct. 17, 1798.
13.* vi. JEREMIAH, b. Appomattox C. H., Oct., 1800.
14. vii. MORDECAI, b. Appomattox C. H., Aug., 1802; lived in Orange co., No. Car.; m. 1852, and had several children.
15. viii. ELIZABETH, b. Sep. 18, 1804; m. *Chas. Coleman.*
16. ix. LUCY FOWLER, b. May 12, 1807; d. in Georgia, leaving issue.
17.* x. EDWARD, b. Aug. 20, 1808.
18. xi. ALBERT, b. June 20, 1810; d. young and unm.
19. xii. RHODY, b. Oct. 20, 1812; m. *Pleasant Franklin;* 2d, *Robert Wilkins.*

12.

JOHN SEARS[3] [*John[2], Edw'd[1]*], b. Appomattox C. H., Va., Oct. 17, 1798; m. Charlotte co., Va., *Susan W. Legrand,* she b. there; d. 1845. Children :

20.* i. JOSIAH LEGRAND, b. 1824.
21.* ii. JOHN HENRY, b. Oct. 9, 1826.

76

22. iii. MARCUS, d. æ. 14.
23. iv. BETTIE ANDERSON, b. 1828; m. —— *Colwell;* lives at App. C. H., and has John and James.
24.* v. ALBERT WALKER, b. 1830.
25. vi. SUSAN CANDIER, b. 1832.
26.* vii. JAMES EDWARD, b. 1834.

Family tradition says that "three brothers, Jeremiah, Mordecai and John, emigrated to this country from England, one of whom, Mordecai, is said to have been with the Indians in disguise who threw the tea overboard, and thereafter spelled his name Sayre, and it is so recorded in the family Bible; his descendants live on Long Island. One of them, Chas. D. Sayre, had a plantation in Brazonia co., Texas, and died of yellow fever at Galveston; also his wife, Catharine."

Possibly the family derives from the Sayres of Southampton, L. I. See Howell's Hist. South., ed. 1887.

"The last battle of the war was fought on John Sears' farm, and the last ball fired lodged in his house."

13.

JEREMIAH SEARS³ [*John²*, *Edw'd¹*], b. Oct., 1800; m. *Ann Tweedy.* Children:

27. i. JOHN ALLEN.
28. ii. JEREMIAH.
29. iii. ALICE.
30. iv. ELIZABETH.

17.

EDWARD SEARS³ [*John²*, *Edw'd¹*], b. Aug. 20, 1808; d. young; m. *Sarah Matthews*, in Prince Edward co., Va.; he was a Capt. in Mil. Children:

31. i. SAMUEL C.
32. ii. EDWARD.
33. iii. JOHN.
34. iv. JAMES.
35. v. ALICE.
36. vi. FANNIE.

20.

JOSIAH LEGRAND SEARS⁴ [*John³*, *John²*, *Edw'd¹*], b. 1824; rem. to Texas in 1846; m.Va., 1855, *Mary W. Legrand;* address, Valley Mills, Bosque co., Tex. Children:

37. i. JOHN ARCHER, d. 1885, æ. 29.

38. ii. Charles David, } *gemini*, æ. 28 in 1885.
39. iii. Josiah Legrand,
40. iv. Robert Emil Lee, æ. 20 in 1885.
41. v. James Edward, æ. 17 in 1885.

21.

JOHN HENRY SEARS[4] [*John*[3], *John*[2], *Edw'd*[1]], b. Oct. 9, 1826; m. Waco, Tex., Oct. 9, 1854, *Angie A. Gurley*, she b. Leighton, Ala.; he is a Dr. in Waco. Children :
42. i. Sadie M., b. Aug. 10, 1855; m. 1878, *J. W. Taylor*.
43. ii. Mary D., b. Nov. 1, 1860.
44. iii. John H., b. Aug. 27, 1866.

24.

ALBERT WALKER SEARS[4] [*John*[3], *John*[2], *Edw'd*[1]], b. 1830; m. *Fannie J. Bloodworth*, and lives at Valley Mills, Texas. Children :
45. i. Thomas A.
46. ii. Walker.
47. iii. Finley.
48. iv. Hardy.
49. v. Edward.
50. vi. Joseph.
51. vii. Minnie Lee.
52. viii. Clara.

26.

JAMES EDWARD SEARS[4] [*John*[3], *John*[2], *Edw'd*[1]], b. 1834; m. *Clara Brown*, and lives in Texas. Children :
53. i. Edward.
54. ii. M. E.
55. iii. Brown.

1.

EDWARD SEARS, b. Va. ; d. Balt., Md., 1874; m. Gloucester co., Va., June 11, 1839, *Fannie C. Wiett*, she b. there ; d. Baltimore, 1869. Children :
i. Charles Edward, b. Gloucester co., Va., Nov. 10, 1842, m. Middlesex co., Va., July 6, 1876, *Sallie E. Fauntleroy*;

she b. there; has no children ; he enlisted in Southern
Army in 1861, and served until the surrender; was
wounded ; removed to Ky.; was educated in Univ. Va. ;
practised law a year; entered journalism; was 3 years
leading editor of "Courier Journal;" started "The
Age;" sold out, and bought the "Louisville Post," and
is now Pres. "Evening Post Co."

ii. WILBUR M., d. in Texas.

iii. VIRGIL C., d. in Baltimore.

1.

WILLIAM BERNARD SEARS[1], b. London, Eng., 1732 ;
d. Apr. 27, 1818; he came to this country when a young man,
being engaged in some business connection with Lord Fairfax's
Land Grant, and settled near Centreville, once known as New-
gate, Fairfax co., Va.   He was an architect and surveyor, and
superintended the erection of many public and private edifices
in Virginia.   He m. *Elizabeth Whaley*, dau. of James and
Ann (Talbott) W. of Fairfax co., she b. 1751 ; d. 1823. (Jas.
Whaley, b. 1727; d. July 19, 1786 ; Ann, his wife, d. July
14, 1784.)   He is said, by Rev. A. D. Sears, to have been a
cousin of Gen. Chas. Lee through his maternal ancestress and
Gen. Lee's mother.   He was a Federalist, and opposed to the
War of 1812.

Miss Mary R. Lanphier says she "always heard that five
brothers came with Wm. B. Sears to America, and settled in
various parts of the country ; some of them in New England
and some in the South."   Children :

2. i. FANNY, b. Fairfax co., Va., Mar. 25, 1770 ; m. *Geo.
Peakes*, and removed to Ohio ; children, PEAKES:
[1.] Alexander, removed to Ohio. [2.] Son, removed to
So. Car. [3.] Son, removed to So. Car. [4.] Patsie, m.
—— Wren. [5.] Bettie, m. —— Harman. [6.] Mary,
m. —— ——.   All the daus. removed to Ohio.

3. ii. PATTY, b. Fair. co., Mar. 12, 1772 ; d. unm., from injuries received by her gown taking fire at a ball.

4. iii. ELIZABETH, b. Fair. co., Mar. 8, 1774; m. *Robt. Goin Lanphier*, he b. 1776 ; and lived in Alexandria, Va.; children,

LANPHIER: [1.] Harriet, a twin, b. Mar. 13, 1795; d. Nov., 1886; m. Thos. L. Martin, a hatter of Accomac co., Va., and had: i. Rev. Dr. John Satchell, b. Sep. 7, 1815; d. Balt., July 8, 1888; m. Susan P. Ruff of Lexington, Va.; was a distinguished member of the M. E. Church, South. ii. Robt. Lanphier, b. Aug., 1817; d. Chester, Pa., 1877 or '78; m. Adelaide W. Nevins; 2d, Maria Buckwalter; was a cotton and woolen man'fr. iii. Eliz'h Parmer, unm., lives 1055 W. Fayette st., Balt., Md. iv. Thos. Littleton, d. v. Martha U., unm. vi. Wm. Satchell, m. M. Winchester; 2d, Carrie Winchester; was a merchant. vii. Hattie W., unm. viii. James P., d. [2.] Robert G., d. unm., Nashville, Tenn.; he was an excellent engraver, and engraved the seals for the U. S. Senate and House of Representatives. [3.] William Bernard, d. unm., Springfield, Ill.; was a civil engineer. [4.] Eliza Sears, m. Albert J. K. Baker of Me., a printer. [5.] Martha R., m. Sam'l Ditty, a merchant tailor, in Washington. [6.] Ann J., m. Wm. Walters, a distinguished journalist, in Springfield, Ill. [7.] Mary R., unm. [8.] Charles H., succeeded Wm. Walters, and for twenty years edited the democratic organ at the Illinois capital; lives in Springfield, Ill.; m. Margaret Crenshaw, who d. Oct. 24, 1889, and had a large family. There were 6 more Lanphier children, of whom I have no account, and they probably died young.

5.* iv. CHARLES LEE, b. Fair. co., Feb. 20, 1776.

6. v. GEORGE WASHINGTON, b. Fair. co., Dec. 10, 1777; d. inf.

7. vi. HORATIO GATES, b. Fair. co., Aug. 10, 1779; d. May 7, 1780.

8. vii. MARGARET, b. Fair. co., July 10, 1781; m. *John Ross*, had a large family, and d. in Baltimore.

9. viii. ANN, b. Fair. co., Sep. 5, 1783; d. Lincoln, Ill., May 25, 1873; unm.

10. ix. WILLIAM BERNARD, b. Fair. co., Dec. 6, 1786; d. s. p. in Ohio, about 1870; m. *Sophia Buckley* of Fair. co.

11.* x. JAMES WHALEY, b. Fair. co., Mar. 20, 1789.

12. xi. HECTOR, b. Fair. co., Aug. 9, 1791; d. ab't 1831.

13. xii. JANE, b. Fair. co., July, 1794; m. *Robt. Evans* (bro. to Mrs. James W. Sears,) rem. to Ky., neighborhood of Henderson, many years ago, and had a large family.

2.

CHARLES LEE SEARS[2] [*Wm.*[1]], b. near Centreville, Fairfax co., Va., Feb. 8, 1775; d. Occoquan, Va., 1862; m. *Bittie Worster;* 2d, *Susan Wells* of Colchester, Va. Children:

14.   i. ACHILLES DE GRASSE, D. D., b. near Centreville, Jan. 1, 1804; (and named for a favorite pedagogue, a connection of Count De Grasse of the Rev'n); at the age of 19, settled in Bourbon co., Ky., and studied law.

"Being a young man of graceful form, handsome features, gallant bearing and bright intellect, he was at once admitted to the front rank in the best society, and succeeded in winning for his companion through life, Miss Annie B. Bowie, one of the first ladies of the country, whose force of character impressed itself on every one. Her ancestors were from Maryland, but she was born near Millswood, Clark co., Va.; they were married March 25, 1828, and had four children, two sons and two daughters. They all died in childhood, except one, Mrs. Marietta Major, who now resides in Clarksville, Tenn.

"Dr. Sears was raised under deistical influences; his ambition to defend the doctrine successfully led him to investigate the subject, and the investigation interested him in religion. He and his wife were baptized at the same time by Rev. Ryland T. Dillard, at Bryants' station, in Elkhorn river, on the 19th July, 1838.

"Dr. Sears was solemnly impressed with the beautiful figure in emersion given as an ordinance to teach the resurrection, and from that moment felt impressed with the duty of preaching the Gospel, and determined to prepare himself for the ministry. He was soon called upon to pray in public, and licensed by the church to preach, and in a few months was ordained by a presbytery composed of Revs. R. T. Dillard, Edward Darnaby, and Josiah Leake.

"The ordination took place at David's Fork at a called meeting on Saturday before the third Sunday in February, 1840, according to Baptist forms.

"Thus he was pushed into the ministry before he was ready, according to his own thinking, and forced to combine practice with study, applying himself diligently.

" For days after the ordination, he engaged with Rev. Jas. M. Frost in a protracted meeting at the Forks of Elkhorn in Franklin county, Ky. He continued seven months, giving his time to protracted meetings at Frankfort, Georgetown, and Flemingsburg, and preaching once a month at Stamping Grounds, and once a month at the Forks of Elkhorn. He was not the pastor of either church, but the people liked his preaching, and even those out of the church joined in a pressing invitation for him to preach once a month, and sustained him liberally for the service.

" At this time the Missionary Board of Bracken Association at Maystick, appointed him missionary with a salary sufficient to support his family.

" It is wonderful how God blessed his work.

" While his family remained located at Flemingsburg, his home, he itinerated through three or four counties destitute of the Gospel, and holding protracted meetings with various churches soliciting his services.

" The first year he preached three hundred and sixty-six sermons, baptizing a great many converts.

" He held a meeting with Elder Curry, pastor at Shelbyville, Ky., in April, 1840, preaching twice a day for two weeks, which resulted in the baptism of one hundred and forty-nine persons.

" This was followed by a meeting at South Benson, where quite a number united with the church, then at Burk's branch, where he preached two weeks, and baptized sixty-six persons.

" His success and fame as a minister was spreading among the Baptist people throughout the State. The First Baptist Church sent a pressing invitation for his help, to which he acceded, beginning with a protracted meeting the last week in July, 1842, which continued eight weeks, resulting in his baptizing one hundred and twenty-five converts. He was then called to the pastoral care of the Louisville church, which he accepted on the 1st Sep., 1842, and this ended his evangelical and missionary labors for a time. He continued as pastor seven years, and during the time baptized over three hundred persons. He resigned the care of his church in July, 1849, to accept the appointment as General Agent of the General Association of Kentucky. He spent a year in this work, traveling and preaching.

"He held four protracted meetings at Silvesa, Mercer county, Henderson and Hopkinsville, Ky., and one in Indiana, in which over two hundred and fifty people were converted. He was called from this work to the care of the Hopkinsville church in July, 1850, which was then one of the strongest Baptist congregations in Kentucky. He continued as pastor of this church twelve years, during which time he baptized about three hundred converts.

"The war came up, and Dr. Sears, being intensely southern in sentiment, excited the prejudice of the Federal authorities, and had to surrender the care of the Hopkinsville church, abandon his home, and seek freedom and safety in the South, where he remained four years, preaching one year at Macon, and one at Columbus, Miss., as a mere supply to these churches, and the balance of his exile was spent as a missionary of the Southern Board of Missions in preaching to the Confederate army.

"Mrs. Sears remained in Hopkinsville to take care of their home and effects, surrounded by warm-hearted, influential friends, who notwithstanding the excitement then prevailing, never permitted her to be disturbed.

"Dr. Sears was not permitted to return to Kentucky until 1865, when he decided to locate in Clarksville, Tenn. There were then twenty-five Baptists in the city. Dr. Sears called them together and reorganized the church, and commenced a protracted meeting in the old church on what is now part of the Court-House square, which was successful, and he was chosen pastor in January, 1866, which relation has never been changed, and in no probability will be until he is called to that blissful reward which awaits God's faithful servants. Dr. Sears set on foot at once a move to build a good church house to cost about $25,000. Notwithstanding the congregation was weak, and the membership poor, the work was prosecuted with untiring zeal and energy, and by degrees the work was accomplished, and paid for as it progressed, and the cause prospered greatly in his hands during the time, the membership soon increasing over two hundred. The old saying, and generally a true one, that new churches always change pastors, was not verified in his case.

"He had become so engrafted in the affections of his congregation, that nothing could separate him from the love of the church, and the ties have continued to grow stronger with each succeeding year.

" Dr. Sears is now (1886) in his eighty-third year. His face is a little furrowed, and his hair slightly gray, but his eyes are bright, and he stands erect in the pulpit and preaches two sermons every Sunday with more power of eloquence and Gospel sweetness than ever. His meetings are well attended, and good attention paid to his ministry. He rarely ever preaches over forty minutes, and never reads a sermon. He is a student, prepares his sermons well, and often, when enthused with his subject, takes lofty flights, thrilling the hearts of his hearers by his Gospel eloquence.

" Dr. Sears and his wife celebrated their golden wedding eight years past, and every year since the ladies of his congregation pay some attention to the anniversary.

" Mrs. Sears was born July 25, 1797, and is now in her ninetieth year ; still active, able to attend service regularly, visit, etc. ; attends to her own housekeeping, cultivates her flowers, of which she is very fond, etc. She is a lady of superior intellect, and has given her husband great assistance in his studies, and much comfort through life, always looking at the bright side, possessed of a cheerful spirit and a hearty good will. Pleasing in manners, interesting in conversation, bright in repartee, sparkling in wit and humor, and keen in sarcasm when sarcasm best suits the demand, and at her present ripe old age few people are so charming in conversation.

" Dr. Sears figured conspicuously in the establishment of Bethel College at Russellville, and Bethel Female College at Hopkinsville. During his ministry of forty-seven years, he has, perhaps, baptized over two thousand persons, but has served in that time as pastor of but three churches. Few ministers have been called upon oftener to solemnize the rites of matrimony, and preach Commencement and introductory sermons.

" Dr. Sears has been a most zealous and active Free Mason through life ; was elected Grand Master in Tennessee in 1870, and served the usual term of Right Eminent Grand Commander of Knights Templar of Tennessee. He is now Past Grand Commander, and a prominent member of the Grand Encampment of the United States.

" His days are full of love's labor, his years bright with honors worthily won, and his life blessed by the approving spirit of a loving and All-wise Providence." [" Chronicle," Clarksville, Tenn., 1886.]

14.* ii. Presby W.

15. iii. Cordelia, m. *Wm. Holmead* of Washington, D. C.

16. iv. Charlotte, m. —— *Clark* of Wash., D. C., who d.;
has 3 daus.

11.

JAMES WHALEY SEARS² [*Wm.¹*], b. near Centreville,
Fair. co., Va., Mar. 20, 1789 ; d. June 27, 1853 ; m. *Rebecca
Evans* of Md., she b. 1802 ; d. Washington, D. C., June 28,
1878. He was a successful business man, and lived in Alexandria, Va. Children :

17.* i. James Whaley, b. Alex., Va., Sep. 23, 1822.

18. ii. Mary Elizabeth, b. Alex., Va.; d. Wash., D. C., May
26, 1879.

19. iii. Virginia, b. Alex., Va.; m. —— *Crozier ;* 2d, Capt.
Dabney, U. S. N., and lives in Pittsburg, Pa.; children,
Crozier : [1.] Kate, d. Oct., 1887. Dabney : [2.] Ma-
bel, b. about 1872. [3.] Richard, b. about 1874.

20. iv. Douglass, b. Alex., Va. ; m., and had 2 children.

21. v. Oscar, b. Alex., Va. ; was educated at Gonzaga Coll.,
Georgetown, D. C. ; was a Catholic Priest of wonderful ability, and d. Lynchburg, Va., 1868.

22.* vi. Bernard, b. Alex., Va.

23.* vii. Charles Augustus, b. Alex., Va.

24.* viii. William Leslie, b. Alex., Va.

25. ix. Clinton M., b. Alex., Va. ; was educated at Gonzaga
Coll. m. *Mary Furtney* of Washington, D. C., in 1867,
and died a few months after ; was a Physician and a
Catholic.

26. x. Julian, b. Alex., Va. ; lives in Washington, D. C. ;
unm.

14.

PRESBY W. SEARS³ [*Chas.²*, *Wm.¹*], m. —— *Clayton ;*
and lives in Appanoon co., Iowa. Children :

27. i. William Bernard, m., and lives in Flint, Mich.; is a
man of ability, a civil engineer and R. R. contractor.

28. ii. John, lives in Nevada.

29. iii. Charles Lee, lives in Jersey City.

17.

JAMES WHALEY SEARS³ [*Jas.²*, *Wm.¹*], b. Alexandria
Va., Sep. 23, 1822 ; d. Washington, D. C., Nov. 3, 1887 ; m.

Nov. 25, 1857, *Sophia Freeman* of Chestertown, Kent co., Md., she b. Mar. 20, 1834; dau. of Jacob Theodore and Sophia Ann (Hynson) F., and gr.-dau. of Col. Nathaniel and Sophia (Ringgold) Hynson, and a descendant of the Rodneys and Roberts of Md. He removed to Washington when very young; was for many years a successful business man, and for ten years before his death a land attorney and speculator in real estate and mines. He was an active member of St. Andrew's Epis. Church, Treasurer and Vestryman. Children:

30. i. EMMA SNOWDON, b. Dec. 10, 1866; is unm., and lives with her mother in Washington, D. C.
31. ii. SOPHIA FREEMAN, b. Sep. 26, 1868; d. Jan. 24, 1869.

22.

BERNARD SEARS[3] [*Jas.*[2], *Wm.*[1]], b. Alexandria, Va.; m. —— *Miller* of Wash., D. C., and died there in 1886. Children:

32. i. MARGARET.
33. ii. LAURA.
34. iii. HENRY.

23.

CHARLES AUGUSTUS SEARS[3] [*Jas.*[2], *Wm.*[1]], b. Alexandria, Va.; m. *Eliza Sterrett Mathews*, (cousin to Mrs. Jas. W. Sears, Jr., and a descendant of the Ringgolds,) and lives in Brooklyn, N. Y. Children:

35. i. SALLIE, m. —— *Gentry* of Brooklyn, and has dau. Hattie.
36. ii. RINGGOLD.
37. iii. ELLA.

24.

WILLIAM LESLIE SEARS[3] [*Jas.*[2], *Wm.*[1]], b. Alexandria, Va.; m. *Alice Ogden* of Alex., and is a druggist in Washington, D. C. Children:

38. i. BERTHA ALICE, b. 1875; d. 1883.
39. ii. WILLIAM LESLIE, b. 1879; d. 1889.

An Englishman named Sears, believed to have been a brother of Wm. Bernard Sears, settled on Poplar island, Chesapeake bay, about the same period, and is supposed to have been the progenitor of the Maryland Sears.

1.

JOHN SEARS[1], b. King and Queen co., Va., ab't 1750; was a Rev'y soldier, settled in Orange co., No. Car., ab't 1785, where he lived on his farm till ab't 1810, when he rem. to near Bowling Green, Ky. Soon after the death of his bro. Joseph, in 1820, he rem. to Randolph co., Mo., where he died in 1831. He m. in K. and Q. co., Va., *Matilda Hobson*, who d. several years before him. Children :

2.   i. HARDY, b. Warren co., Ky., 1792; rem. to Mo., in 1819; was a man of more than ordinary intelligence and piety, a deacon in the Bapt. Ch., 30 years, and d. ab't 1850. He was twice married and reared a large family of children, three of them became ministers.

3.*   ii. IVISON, b. Warren co., Ky., Jan. 13, 1796.

4.   iii. HENRY, b. Warren co., Ky., 1798; rem. to Montgomery, Ill., ab't 1820, and located on a farm in the S. W. corner, where he lived till his death in 1860. Was a minister in Bapt. Ch., 35 years, of good ability, and remarkably fine standing and influence, both as a citizen and minister of the gospel, and was well known among the Baptists in southern and central Illinois. He m. in Warren co., Ky., *Priscilla Prather*, but left no children.

5.   iv. WILLIAM, b. Warren co., Ky., 1806; m. Randolph co., Mo., *Sophia Kirby*, who d. several years after marriage, and he m. thrice afterward, and had 19 children. He became a Bapt. min., ab't 1830, and was a very zealous and popular preacher. He d. at his residence in Callao, Mo., beloved by all who knew him. Rev. Henry Sears of Lincoln, Ill., Bazzle M. Sears of Callao, Mo., Walker Sears of La Plata, Mo., Willis, Morton, Jackson and James Sears of Callao, Mo., and Jas. Ivison Sears of La Plata, Mo., are perhaps of this family.

6.   v. MARY, m. *Thos. Hendricks.*

7.   vi. CANDACE, d. unm.

      And other daus.

JOSEPH SEARS[1], bro. of John, b. King and Queen co., Va., ab't 1750–60; was a Baptist minister, and like his bro. a Rev'y soldier.

He settled on a farm in No. Car., ab't 1785, and some years later rem. to Warren co., Ky., where he d. ab't 1820.

HENRY SEARS[1], bro. of John, was a man of bright intellect and fine business tact, an auctioneer, and several times sheriff of Orange co., No. Car., and d. in Mo. in 1850.

3.

IVISON SEARS[2] [*John*[1]], b. Warren co., Ky., Jan. 13, 1796; m. there, 1818, *Sarah Ryal* of No. Car. Children:

8.   i. MATILDA, b. 1819; m. 1838, *John Roan,* and lives at Love Lake, Mo.
9.   ii. MARTHA, b. 1821; m. 1840, *Caswell Courtney* of Keytesville, Mo.
10.   iii. MARY, d.
11.   iv. THEOPHILUS, b. 1823; m. 1849, *Mary Jane Cavins,* and lives in Saulsbury, Mo.
12.   v. GREEN, b. 1825; d. young.
13.   vi. ELIZABETH, b. 1827; m. 1850, *John T. Cavins* of Huntsville, Mo.
14.* vii. JOHN MILTON, b. Jan. 13, 1830.
15. viii. OLIVER PETTIS, b. 1832; m. 1851, *Martha Bradsher,* and lives in Success, Mo.
16.   ix. SALLY ANN, b. 1834; m. 1850, *Sam'l Skinner.*
17.   x. MALINDA JANE, b. 1836; m. 1854, *Calvin Smith* of Huntsville, Mo.
18.   xi. LEWIS, b. 1838; m. *Nancy Bradley,* and lives in Success, Mo.
19.   xii. ALBERT FRANKLIN, b. 1840; m. *Hannah Holman,* and lives in Thomas Hill, Mo.
20. xiii. WOODSON DILLARD, d.
21. xiv. WILLIAM BENNETT, b. 1844; d.

14.

Rev. JOHN MILTON SEARS[3] [*Ivison*[2], *John*[1]], b. Jan. 13, 1830, near Huntsville, Mo.; m. there, July 24, 1851, *Cynthia A. Oliver,* she b. Clark co., Ky., Aug. 10, 1833. Children:

22.   i. MADISON L., b. Mar. 4, 1853; lives in Kansas City, Mo.
23.   ii. VICTORIA ADELAIDE, b. Nov. 15, 1855; m. *Felix Aubochon,* and lives in Grenola, Kan.
24. iii. HENRY LOUTHAN, b. Jan. 13, 1858.
25. iv. EVELINE CORNELIA, b. Oct. 28, 1860; m. *Benj. F. McCrary,* and lives in Prairie Hill, Mo.
26.   v. ANNA MILTON, b. July 4, 1863.

27. vi. MINNIE, b. Sep. 8, 1867; m. Dr. *W. P. Terrill*, and lives in Darksville, Mo.
28. vii. STELLA AUGUSTA, b. Dec. 3, 1872.

1.

JOHN B. SEARS[1], said to have been of English descent. Children :
2.* i. SAMUEL.
3. ii. PETER; was a teacher in Missouri; m., and had 2 sons.
4.* iii. ABRAM.
5. iv. FRANCIS, d.
6. v. SOPHIA, d.
7.* vi. BARTHOLOMEW.

2.

SAMUEL SEARS[2] [*John[1]*]. Children :
8. i. DANIEL.
9. ii. EMANUEL.
10. iii. JOSEPHUS.
11. iv. ROSE ANN.
12. v. SAMUEL, of Kirksville, Iowa.

4.

ABRAM SEARS[2] [*John[1]*], m. *Matilda Buckhannon*, who survived him, and lives in Muscatine, Iowa. Children :
13. i. ELIZABETH, a widow.
14. ii. CATHARINE, m.
15. iii. DELIA, a widow in Muscatine, Iowa.
16. iv. MAHALA, m. and lives Council Bluffs, Iowa.
17. v. REBECCA ANN, m. and d.
18. vi. JOHN B., lives in Conesville, Iowa.
19. vii. GEORGE W., m. and lives in Logans, Ind.

7.

BARTHOLOMEW SEARS[2] [*John[1]*]. This name possibly indicates descent from Bart. Sears of Monroe, Ct., and affiliation with the Sears of Lapell, Ind. ; see *ante*. Children :
20. i. ELIZA JANE, m. *John Pebornot*, and lives Blankester, Ohio.

21. ii. MARGARET JANE.
22. iii. WILLIAM.
23. iv. ISAAC.
24. v. CATHARINE.

1.

JOSEPH SEARS[1], b. about 1746, on Long Island, or in Morrisania, N. Y., (accounts differ,) was probably a grand-son of Wm. and Eliz. Sears of Boston, who were m. there, Mar. 12, 1710–11; he was a farmer in Morrisania; served in the British Army during the Revolution; was wounded in the shoulder, and carried the bullet to his grave.

His farm was confiscated and he exiled to New Brunswick, where he had granted him a large tract of land in Sackville.

He was a hard-working and successful farmer, and d. 1846, æ. 99 yrs. 7 mos. License for Joseph Sears and *Hester Wheaton* to marry was granted N. Y., Apr. 20, 1780. Children:

2.   i. DANIEL, b. N. Y. State; m. —— *Hicks* of Dorchester, N. B., and d. Sackville about 1847.
3.   ii. DAVID, b. N. Y. State; m. *Mary Ward;* both d. Sackville.
4.* iii. JEREMIAH, b. Sackville.
5.   iv. FREDERIC, b. Sackville; m. *Eunice Ward*, and both d. there.
6.* v. WILLIAM, b. Sackville.
7.   vi. THOMAS, b. Sackville; m. *Amy Babcock* of Dorchester, N. B., and d. Maine.
8.   vii. JOSEPH, b. Sackville; m. Sep., 1818, *Mary Geldert*, she b. Moncton, 1798; had 14 children, and d. Eastport, Me., 1865; his widow was living in Boston in 1885.
9.* viii. REUBEN, b. Sackville, 1797.
10.   ix. ESTHER, m. —— *Finney.*
11.   x. CHARLOTTE, m. *Wm. Barnes.*
12.   xi. ELIZABETH, m. *Geo. Crowder*, and a dau. m. —— *McGowan* of Sackville.
13. xii. *Dau.*, m. —— *Bannister.*

4.

JEREMIAH SEARS[2] [*Jos.*[1]], b. Sackville, N. B.; m. —— ——; 2d, —— *McFee*, and d. in S. Children:

14. i. DAVID.

15.   ii. Daniel.
16. iii. William.
17. iv. Joseph.
18.   v. Thomas.
19. vi. Reuben.
20. vii. Frederic.
21. viii. Titus, m. in Sackville, and removed to Pembroke,
        Me., after the birth of his first child; he had a son living
        in Somerset, Mass., in 1886.
22. ix. Esther.
23.   x. Charlotte.
24. xi. Elizabeth.

6.

WILLIAM SEARS[2] [*Jos.*[1]], b. Sep., 1796; was a minister,
and m. Sackville, N. B., about 1818, *Elizabeth Babcock*, she
b. Shediac, N. S.; d. St. John, N. B., 1849; (her mother's
maiden name was Dorcas Bennet;) they lived in Dorchester,
N. B., till about 1853, when they removed to Hillsborough,
where he d. Mar., 1857.   Children:

25.* i. Frederic, b. Sackville, Dec. 10, 1820.
26.   ii. Adoniram, b. Sackville, Dec. 27, 1822; m. Hopewell,
        N. B., Nov., 1845, *Mary Palais*, and was drowned 1853.
27. iii. Dorcas B., b. Sackville, 1825; d. Dorchester, unm.,
        æ. 18.
28. iv. Eunice, b. Dorchester; m. *Thos. McCloskey*, about
        1848.
29.   v. Mary, b. Dorchester; m. —— *Barrett*, at Hillsboro.
30. vi. Ann Jane, b. Dorchester; m. Hillsboro, *John Robert-
        son*.
31. vii. William, b. Dorchester; m. about 1856, —— *Barrett*.
        3 or 4 other children d. inf.

9.

REUBEN SEARS[2] [*Jos.*[1]], b. Sackville, N. B., 1797; m.
Eliz. McCormick, in 1836, she b. there, 1805.   Children:

32.   i. Edward, b. Sackville; m. Boston, 1860, *Nellie Fox*.
33.   ii. Mark, b. Sackville; m. there, *Annie Estabrook*.
34. iii. Cyrus, lives in Sackville.
35. iv. Chauncy, b. Sackville, 1843; m. there, 1865, *Mary
        J. Wheaton*, she b. 1840.
36.   v. Rebecca.
37. vi. Mary.
38. vii. Mahala.

25.

FREDERIC SEARS[3] [*Wm.*[2], *Jos.*[1]], b. Sackville, N. B., Dec. 10, 1820 ; was a teacher in Dorchester, N. B.; m. Botsford, N. B., Nov. 4, 1847, *Catharine Keough* of Ireland, she b. 1819 ; d. Boston, Sep., 1883. Another account says, he m. —— *Wright.* He lives South Side Basin, River Dennis, N. S. Children :

39.   i. AMELIA JANE, b. Botsford, Sep. 24, 1849 ; m. Stoneham, Mass., 1872, *Llewellyn B. Wass,* he b. Addison, Me., ab't 1842.

40.   ii. JOHN WRIGHT, b. Botsford, Sep. 1, 1848.

41.   iii. ELIZABETH, b. Botsford, Feb. 27, 1851 ; m. ab't 1878, *Oliver Hadlock* of Portland, Me.

42.   iv. ALICE WRIGHT, b. Botsford, Jan. 1, 1853; d. unm., 1879.

43.   v. FREDERIC WILLIAM, b. Botsford, Apr. 4, 1854; drowned on Grand Banks, ab't 1870.

44.   vi. JUDSON A., b. Botsford, Apr. 26, 1856 ; m. Boston, Jan. 19, 1884, *Eugenié C. Hagar* of France, and is a clerk in P. O. there.

45.   vii. SOPHIA, b. Botsford, Jan. 24, 1857.

46.   viii. KATE, b. Port Elgin, N. B., June 15, 1859.

47.   ix. LAURA G., b. Arichat, N. S., Dec. 3, 1863.

1.

WILLIAM SEARS[1], sometimes called Wm. *Sewall* Sears, is said to have been one of four brothers born in Boston, Mass., their mother being a *Sewall* of that place. I do not find such marriage recorded there, or mentioned in the Sewall Genealogies, but going back to an earlier generation, I find that Richard Sewall of Nuneaton, co. Warwick, Eng., by his wife Mary, sister of Sir Wm. Dugdale, Garter King of Arms, had a dau., Elizabeth, born 1618, who m. Edmund Seare, Notary Public, and was living in 1648. Henry Sewall, the elder bro. of Richard, came to this country, and died in Rowley, Mass., in 1657, æ. 81. From him descended the Boston Sewalls, and here, I think, we find the basis of the traditionary Sears and Sewall alliance. Probably Wm. Sears was born in Boston,

78

Dec. 16, 1713, son to Wm. and Eliz'h (White) Seers, who were married there, Mar. 12, 1710–11. Elizabeth owned covenant in 2d Ch., Feb. 20, 1714–-15. Their children as recorded were, i. Joseph, b. Nov. 29, 1711. ii. William, ·b. Dec. 16, 1713. iii. John, b. Feb. 8, 1715–16. iv. Anthony, b. June 16, 1718. Which agrees with the tradition of "four brothers." Very likely an examination of the registers of Nuneaton, and wills of Sears of that place, might show a connection with the Bos. ton Sears, and perhaps other branches of the family.

William Sears removed to White Plains, Westchester co., N. Y., (the family having lost their property in Boston by fire,) and thence, about 1760, to Montgomery, Orange co., N. Y., where he died, and was buried in the old brick church at Wal. kill. He m. —— *Hart.* Children:

2.* i. JAMES, b. about 1740.
3.* ii. BENJAMIN.
4.* iii. ELNATHAN, b. 1756.
5.* iv. JOHN, b. May 22, 1758.
6. v. SEWALL.
7.* vi. SAMUEL, b. about 1758.
8. vii. *Dau.*

2.

JAMES SEARS[2] [*Wm.*[1]], b. about 1740; m. —— *Barclay,* and d. 1805.   Children :

9.* i. JOHN.
10. ii. JAMES.
11.* iii. WILLIAM, b. 1782.
12. iv. SAMUEL.
13. v. ELIZABETH.

3.

BENJAMIN SEARS[2] [*Wm.*[1]].   Settled in Montgomery, N. Y.; m. *Mary Crist;* 2d, *Eliza Shaffer,* who d. July 28, 1820.   He was appointed sheriff by Gov. Geo. Clinton, Feb. 18, 1793, and, in 1799, Vendue Master for the county by Gov. John Jay.   He was well known throughout the county as a business man ; was a public-spirited man ; one of the originators, and helped build the Newburgh and Cochecton turnpike, reaching from the Hudson to the Delaware river, etc. ; was at one time a man of large means, but, in the end, left little property, which the sons gave to their sisters who assisted them through college. He d. June 1, 1817. Children:

14.　　i. ANN, b. Oct. 2, 1779.
15.　　ii. SOPHIA, b. July 15, 1781.
16.　　iii. HANNAH, b. Aug. 21, 1784.
17.　　iv. MARY, b. May 1, 1788; d. Oct. 2, 1862.
18.　　v. JANE, b. Mar. 20, 1791.
19.　　vi. NANCY, b. Oct. 23, 1793; d. May 2, 1878.
20.* vii. WILLIAM, b. Sep. 23, 1795.
21.* viii. JACOB CRIST, b. Feb. 9, 1798.
22.* ix. MARCUS, b. June 30, 1802.

4.

ELNATHAN SEARS[2] [*Wm.*[1]], b. 1756; m. —— *Haight*, and d. 1840. He was a Revolutionary soldier, Sheriff, Representative, etc. Children:

23.* i. ELNATHAN HAIGHT, b. 1785.
24. ii. BARKELEY, d. unm.
25. iii. MARY, m. *Peter Miller*, and d. s. p.
26. iv. SARAH, d. unm.

5.

JOHN SEARS[2] [*Wm.*[1]], b. May 22, 1758; was a Revolutionary soldier and pensioner, (called in Census of 1840, æ. 89, which would make him born 1751;) m. —— *Bodine;* 2d, widow —— *White.* Children:

27.　　i. FANNY, m. —— *McElhane.*
28.* ii. JACOB.
29.* iii. PETER.

7.

SAMUEL SEARS[2] [*Wm.*[1]], called 82 in Census of 1840; so born about 1758; was a Revolutionary soldier and pensioner; m. —— *Felter.* Children:

30.* i. SAMUEL.

9.

JOHN SEARS[3] [*Jas.*[2], *Wm.*[1]], was P. M. of Montgomery, N. Y., about 1820. Children:

31. i. JAMES.
32. ii. MARY.

33. iii. HANNAH, m. —— *Preston*, and has a son in N. Y. P. O.
34. iv. ISABELLA, m. —— *Faunce* of Middletown, N. Y., and had : Sarah, who m. —— *Elmer*, 2d Ass't P. M., U. S.
35. v. SARAH, m. *Chas. Cromwell* of Middletown, N. Y.

11.

WILLIAM SEARS³ [*Jas.²*, *Wm.¹*], b. 1782; m. —— *Conger*. Children :
36.   i. WILLIAM E.
37.* ii. SAMUEL J.
38. iii. JOSHUA.
39.   iv. JOHN P., m. —— *Ward*, and lives in Montgomery.
40.   v. CHARLES P., m. —— *Ostrand*.
41.   vi. MELINDA.
42. vii. ELIZA.
43. viii. MARGARET, m. —— *Perkins*.
44.   ix. CORDELIA.
45.   x. PERMILLA.

20.

WILLIAM SEWALL SEARS³ [*Benj.²*, *Wm.¹*], b. Sep. 20, 1795 ; d. Feb. 15, 1875 ; grad. Union Coll. ab't 1822, was a lawyer in New York city, and resided at Fort Hamilton. Children :
46.   i. CHARLES, a very promising young man, who graduated with high honors at Columbia Coll., and studied law with his father.
      At the time yellow fever raged so fearfully at Fort Hamilton, and all the well ones fled the place, he, a boy of only about 17 years, stayed and nursed the sick, going from house to house, giving all his time and strength to caring for the suffering, and strange to say, escaped the fever. He was given a medal by the city of New York, and mentioned with high commendation. He d. ab't 1864.
47. ii. *Dau.*, m. —— *Pender*.
48. iii. *Dau.*, m. —— *Hopkins*, and had a dau., Sallie Sears.
49. iv. *Dau.*

21.

JACOB CRIST SEARS³ [*Benj.²*, *Wm.¹*], b. Feb. 9, 1798; m. *Achsah Halberstadt* of Phila., Pa., and d. ab't 1881. He grad. Union Coll. and New Brunswick Theo. Sem.; was settled at Phila., as a clergyman, and at Franklin Park, N. J., 45 years, and made Emeritus. Children :

50.* i. GEORGE H.
51. ii. BENJAMIN, d.
52. iii. FERDINAND, d.
53. iv. ANNIE H., d.
54.* v. WILLIAM.
55. vi. JACOB C., lives in Franklin Park, N. J.
56. vii. HARRIET, m. *G. W. Reed* of the "Brooklyn Eagle.',

22.

MARCUS SEARS³ [*Benj.²*, *Wm.¹*], b. June 30, 1802; m. May 20, 1834, *Mary C. Caldwell*, who d. 1841; 2d, *Eliz'h Moffatt*, who d. July 9, 1866. At the age of 15, his father dying, he was placed for a time in the store of his cousin, John Sears; afterward studied medicine with Dr. Eager of Montgomery, and was for a time in the office of Dr. Mott of New York; grad. Med. Coll. there, and practiced for a time in Montgomery; held office under Hector Craig, (Surveyor of N. Y. under Gen. Jackson,) his wife's uncle; returned to Blooming Grove, N. Y., and resumed practice, resigning ab't 1860, in favor of his nephew, Geo. H. Sears. He was well known throughout the county as an able physician. Was an elder in Presb. Ch. for a long time, taking a prominent part ; was twice chosen delegate from the Synod to the Gen. Assembly of the church at Washington, and again later to Pittsburg. Children :

57.* i. BENJAMIN C.
58. ii. MARY A., b. Nov. 13, 1839; m. *Jesse Woodhull*, (a descendant of Gen. W. of the Rev'n,) who d. Oct. 10, 1881 ; had [1.] Benj. Sears, b. 1864. [2.] Mary Caldwell, b. 1878.

23.

ELNATHAN HAIGHT SEARS³ [*Elnathan²*, *Wm.¹*], b. 1785; m. *Susan Felter*, and d. Searsville, Ulster co., N. Y., 1845. Children :

59. i. MARY ESTHER, unm.
60. ii. KATHARINE WELLER, unm.
61. iii. JOHN NEWTON, d. inf.
62.* iv. JOHN NEWTON, b. 1830.

63.   v. MARTHA MATILDA, m. *Edward Jarvis Knapp*, a N. Y. merchant, and had, [1.] Edward Jarvis. [2.] Susan Trevor. [3.] Newton Sears, d. inf. [4.] Arthur Haight, d. inf.

64.   vi. EMMA HAIGHT, d. æ. 17.

65.   vii. ANNIE LOUISE, m. *Thos. Ash Bronson*, a Phila. broker, and d. s. p., 1876.

66.   viii. JULIA FRANCES, unm.

67.   ix. SUSAN EUPHEMIA, m. *Geo. Erwin Palmer*, a merchant of Stonington, Ct., and had, [1.] Florida, d. inf. [2.] Mabel. [3.] Geo. Erwin.

28.

JACOB SEARS[3] [*John*[2], *Wm.*[1]], b. Jan. 6, 1786; m. —— *Weller*. Children:

68.   i. DANIEL.

69.   ii. JOHN.

70.   iii. WILLIAM SEWALL, lives in Montgomery, N. Y.

71.   iv. SAMUEL.

72.   v. ALANSON.

73.   vi. BENJAMIN.

74.   vii. RACHEL ANN.

75.   viii. MARY.

76.   ix. EMMA.

77.   x. AUGUSTA.

29.

PETER SEARS[3] [*John*[2], *Wm.*[1]], m. —— *Patterson*; 2d, widow —— *Hunter*; 3d, widow —— *Ward*. Children:

78.   i. HECTOR, m. —— ~~West~~; 2d, ~~Jane~~ *Brown*.

79.   ii. HENRY P., m. —— *McCurdy*.

80.   iii. FRANCIS, m. —— *Giles*.

81.   iv. MARIA, m. —— *Hunter*.

82.   v. RACHEL, m. —— *Mylcraine*.

83.   vi. SARAH, m. —— *White*.

84.   vii. CLARA GERTRUDE, m. Dr. *Sam'l J. Sears*.

30.

SAMUEL SEARS[3] [*Sam'l*[2], *Wm.*[1]], m. —— ——. Children:

85.   i. HECTOR, lives in Walden, N. Y.

86.   ii. JUSTINE, m. —— *Gillespie*, and lives in Walden, N. Y., had, [1.] Arlington Sears, m. Sarah Francis Sears, and lives in Inkster, Dak.

37.

SAMUEL J. SEARS[4], M. D. [*Wm.[3]*, *Jas.[2]*, *Wm.[1]*], m. *Clara Gertrude Sears*, dau. of Peter S.   Children :

87.   i. HECTOR, m. —— *Collins*, is a lawyer in Gardiner, N. Y., and editor of " Gardiner Weekly."

88.   ii. WILLIAM P.

89.   iii. HENRIETTA, m. —— *Hunter*.

90.   iv. LINDA, m. —— *Radcliffe*, and had Samuel and Thomas.

91.   v. SARAH.

92.   vi. SARAH FRANCIS, m. —— *Gillespie*, and has Jesse, Clara and Frederic.

93.   vii. ALICE, m. —— *Petheridge*, and has Ida.

94.   viii. PHEBE P.

95.   ix. SARAH PATTERSON, m. —— *Valet*.

96.   x. CARRIE M., Asst. Editor " Gardiner Weekly."

50.

GEORGE H. SEARS[4], M. D. [*Jacob[3]*, *Benj.[2]*, *Wm.[1]*], m. *Carrie A. Howell*, and lived in Blooming Grove, N. Y., where he d. Feb., 1872.   Child :

97.   i. F. WILLIS.

54.

WILLIAM SEARS[4] [*Jacob[3]*, *Benj.[2]*, *Wm.[1]*], m. *Cynthia Hageman*.   Child :

98.   i. MARY, b. Cranberry Station, N. J., 1865.

57.

BENJAMIN C. SEARS[4] [*Marcus[3]*, *Benj.[2]*, *Wm.[1]*], b. Feb. 9, 1836 ; m. 1866, *Phebe E. Howell*, and is a farmer at Blooming Grove, N. Y. ; he grad. Rutgers Coll., 1857, but took his grandmother's farm, where he now lives ; was chosen to the position his father held in the church ; is Director Orange Co. M. Ins. Co., and Orange Co. Agri. Soc.   Children :

99.   i. MARCUS CALDWELL, b. Oct., 1867.

100.   ii. MARCIA HOWELL, b. Feb. 1, 1879.

101.   iii. *Son*, b. Feb. 4, 1882.

62.

JOHN NEWTON SEARS[4] [*Elnathan[3], Elnathan[2], Wm.[1]*], b. 1830; m. *Virginia Caroline Tupper ;* 2d, *Milicent Fanny Lewis;* is a merchant in London, and resides at Bayswater, Eng.   Children :

By *Virginia :*
102.   i. ALICE PEARSALL.
By *Milicent :*
103.   ii. JOIE MILICENT.
104.   iii. JOHN NEWTON.

1.

TEUSA SEARS[1], m. *Victoria Le Course;* came from France to this country about 1829, and settled in a small town near Three Rivers, Canada; his son

2.

JOSEPH LEWIS SEARS[2] [*Teusa[1]*], b. Paris, France, Nov. 28, 1824; came to this country with his parents; left his home in Canada when still a child, and has not heard from his parents since.   He m. Weld, Me., Jan. 22, 1852, *Jane Phillips*, she b. Avon, Me., Feb., 1824, who d. s. p., about 1859, æ. 35; 2d, Wellesley, Mass., Sep. 29, 1861, *Catharine Stanley*, she b. Belfast, Ireland, Oct. 29, 1840.   He served in Co. K, 24th Mass. Vol. Inf'y, from Dec. 3, 1861, to Dec. 3, 1864; is an officer of G. A. R.; now lives at Newton Lower Falls, Mass.   Children :
   i. JESSE, b. Mar. 16, 1866.
   ii. NETTIE ARVILLA, b. Jan. 25, 1869.
   iii. ELLA GERTRUDE, b. Jan. 27, 1871.
   iv. ALMA LIZZIE, b. Dec. 30, 1872.
   v. MAY FRANCIS, b. Apr. 2, 1876.
   vi. ETHEL BLANCHE, b. Aug. 14, 1879.
   vii. EVA KATHLEEN, b. Sep. 2, 1883.

1.

JOHN SEARS[1], b. 1786; son of Richard and Mary S. ; m. Boston, Jan. 1, 1816, by Rev. Francis A. Matignon, to

Catharine O. Brien, she b. Boston, Aug. 21, 1800; d. Rochester, N. Y., Feb. 15, 1872. In the City Clerk's office his name is given "John Voyez alias Siers."

He soon after removed to N. Y. city, and later to Rochester, N. Y., where he manufactured "Sears' Genuine Bears' Grease," frequently having 6 bears in his pens, and d. there, Feb. 15, 1840. Children:

 i. (?) CATRINA, d. Boston, May, 1818.
 ii. JOANNA, b. N. Y. city, Nov. 28, 1816; m. Roch., *Geo. Gates,* and d. Dec. 28, 1859.
 iii. MARY, b. N. Y. city, Jan. 20, 1818; m. Roch., *Edw'd Ange,* and d. Utica, 1878.
 iv. JOHN, b. N. Y. city, Nov. 24, 1819; m. Roch., *Rachel Girdlestone,* and d. Dec. 20, 1864.
 v. MARGARET, b. N. Y. city, 1821; m. Roch., *Mich. Wackerman.*
 vi. JOSEPH, b. N. Y. city, Nov. 11, 1824; d. Roch., Jan. 26, 1858.
 vii. RICHARD, b. N. Y. city, Jan. 21, 1826; d. Chicago, Nov. 23, 1853.
 viii. CHARLOTTE, b. N. Y. city, Apr. 30, 1829; m. Roch., 1846, *Theo. C. Wilbur;* 2d, 1860, *Lewis V. Griffin,* and lives in Roch.
 ix. SARAH, b. Roch., Dec. 18, 1831; m. there, 1850, *Morris Servey,* and d. Utica, Nov. 8, 1884.
 x. CAROLINE, b. Roch., June 25, 1833; d. unm., Sep. 27, 1848.
 xi. JOSEPHINE, b. Roch., Mar. 17, 1834; m. *Kahn Wilkins,* and d. Dec. 22, 1866.

1.

WILLIAM DE PRATT SEARS[1], born San Domingo, 1783; m. Balt., Md., *Sophia Johnson* of Md., and d. Newark, N. J., Mar., 1858, æ. 75.

His father, Benj. *De Pratt,* was a native of France, and a merchant in San Domingo, visiting this country frequently and educating his children here. I do not learn why his son assumed the name of Sears; but as a son of Col. Isaac Sears of N. Y. city was at that period in business in Dominica with

79

his brother-in-law, Peregrine Bourdieu, there may have been some connection between the families, or in a business way. Children :

2.* i. WILLIAM DE PRATT, b. Balt., Feb., 1815.
3. ii. MARY DE PRATT, b. Balt., 1818 ; d. Newark, N. J., 1868, æ. 50.
4.* iii. EDWARD DE PRATT, b. Balt.

2.

WILLIAM DE PRATT SEARS[2] [*Wm.*[1]], b. Balt., Md., 1815; m. Newark, N. J., May 10, 1849, *Malvina Ray*, she b. there, Dec. 31, 1819. He was a tobacconist and cigar-maker. Children :

5. i. WILLIAM HENRY, b. Newark, Feb. 10, 1850; d. May 17, 1855.
6. ii. ROSANNA SOPHIA, b. Newark ; m. there, July 2, 1873, *D. H. Scudder* of N. Y.
7. iii. MARY A., b. Newark, July 31, 1853.
8. iv. LOUIS ADAM, b. Newark, Apr. 19, 1856 ; was Steward U. S. S. "Minnesota," and now a letter-carrier in Newark.
9. v. MALVINA DE PRATT, b. Elizabeth City, N. J., Dec. 22, 1857.
10. vi. JOSEPH MURRAY, b. Elizabeth City, Aug. 31, 1859 ; d. Feb. 29, 1860.
11. vii. JULIA ANN, b. Elizabeth City, Mar. 21, 1861.
12. viii. ESTELLA, b. Elizabeth City, June 25, 1864 ; d. Aug. 14, 1865.

4.

EDWARD DE PRATT SEARS[2] [*Wm.*[1]], b. Balt., Md.; m. New York city, 1845, *Virginia Smith*, (dau. of Col. S. of Revolutionary Army,) of Ohio, and is a tobacconist in Cincinnati, O. Children :

13. i. EMMA B., b. N. Y. city, about 1845–50 ; lives in Springfield, O.
14. ii. WILLIAM G., b. N. Y. city, 1850–51 ; is a teacher in "Lincoln Institute," Jefferson City, Mo.
15. iii. IDA, b. N. Y. city, about 1854 ; d. æ. 1 year.
16. iv. ADA, b. N. Y. city, about 1854 ; d. Cincinnati, O., æ. 7 yrs.

1.

—— SEARS[1], a comfortable, well-to-do farmer in Fritten-den, Kent, Eng.; m. —— *May.* Children :

2.* i. HENRY.
3. ii. ROBERT.
4. iii. ANN.
5. iv. SARAH.

2.

HENRY SEARS[2] [——[1]], b. Frittenden, Kent, Eng., about 1800–1 ; d. 1849 ; his wife died in Eng., at a good old age, in 1879. Children :

6.* i. HENRY.
7. ii. JAMES, d.
8. iii. JOSEPH, d.
9. iv. JOHN.
10.* v. WILLIAM.
11. vi. FREDERIC, d.
12. vii. ROBERT.
13. viii. GEORGE, d.
14. ix. JESSE.
15. x. SARAH.
16. xi. MARGARET.
    And 4 other daus.

6.

HENRY SEARS[3] [*Henry*[2], ——[1]], b. Frittenden, Kent, Eng., Apr. 5, 1830 ;(?) m. Fabius, N. Y., *Mary J. Hatch.* Children:

17. i. GEORGE H., b. Homer, N. Y., Oct. 8, 1858 ; lived upon a farm till 20 ; graduated Cazenovia Seminary, N. Y., spring of 1882 ; studied law in Syracuse, and admitted to bar, Jan. 14, 1886 ; now of firm Kellogg, Wells & Sears, Syracuse, N. Y.
18. ii. FREDERIC W., b. Homer, Dec. 19, 1859 ; m. Pompey Hill, N. Y., June, 1882, *Jessie Pratt,* and is a Physician in Syracuse.
19. iii. ANNETTE M., b. Homer, Aug. 22, 1861.
20. iv. JESSIE F., b. Preble, N. Y., Jan. 27, 1863 ; m. Delphi, N. Y., Oct., 1883, *Geo. H. Savage,* and d. Mar. 6, 1886.

21.   v. ALBERT BACON, b. Preble, Nov. 8, 1865 ; is a Minister at Evans' Mills, N. Y.
22.   vi. IRVING S., b. Preble, May 30, 18—.
23.   vii. CHARLES M., b. Preble.
24.   viii. WILLIAM H., b. Preble, Mar. 29, 1875.

10.

WILLIAM SEARS[3] [*Henry*[2], ——[1]], b. Frittenden, Kent,
Eng., July 8, 1836. He came over in 1854 ; received a partial academic education at Homer, N. Y., 1858–61, at which
time he entered the Union Army, and served till 1865 ; then
settled in Syracuse, N. Y., and is now in employ of " Central
City Wheel Works." Has been Superintendent Sabbath School;
Deacon and Trustee in Baptist Church. He m. Homer, N. Y.,
Oct. 8, 1867, *Rhoda Minor*, she b. there, July 27, 1842. Children :
25.   i. FRANK M., b. Syracuse, Nov. 26, 1868.(?)
26.   ii. MAY L., b. Syracuse, May 16, 1869.(?)
27.   iii. WILLIAM H., b. Syracuse, Feb. 4, 1871.
28.   iv. LURA M., b. Syracuse, May 20, 1880.

3.

NATHAN SAYRE[3] [*Dan'l*[2], *Thos.*[1]], yeoman of Southampton, L. I., (see Howell's Hist. Southampton,) made his first
purchase of land in Middletown, Ct., of Wm. ——, Nov. 25,
1720, in the district, now town of Maromas, ⸜consisting of a
house and 150 acres of land, and soon after took up his residence
there. His wife was *Mary* ——. This branch of the family
in a few years appear to have changed their name to *Sears*, for
reasons unknown to me. Children :
4.*   i. NATHAN.
5.*   ii. ELISHA.
6.*   iii. MATTHEW.
7.   iv. MARY, m. Feb. 28, 1740, *Wm. Roberts*, Jr., and d.
May 11, 1747, æ. 27; children, ROBERTS: [1.] Esther, b.
May 20, 1741. [2.] Abiah, b. Mar. 10, 1743. [3.] Susanna,
b. Mar. 31, 1745. [4.] William, b. May 9, 1747.

8.   v. DANIEL, bap. Midd., Sep. 29, 1723.
9.* vi. STEPHEN, b. Midd., Feb. 29, 1724–5.
10.* vii. JOHN, b. Midd., Oct. 4, 1726.
11.*viii. CHARLES, b. Midd., Feb. 8, 1729–30.
12.   ix. HANNAH, b. Midd., July 8, 1733.
13.   x. SARAH, b. Midd., Feb. 7, 1734–5.

4.

NATHAN SAYRE[4] [*Nathan*[3], *Dan'l*[2], *Thos.*[1]], m. Feb. 12, 1735–6, *Deborah Prout*, dau. of Dr. Eben'r P., who d. Nov. 9, 1736, æ. 32; had a son, b. Oct. 29, 1736; d. same day.

5.

ELISHA SAYRE[4] [*Nathan*[3], *Dan'l*[2], *Thos.*[1]], d. June 23, 1801, æ. 91; m. Dec. 8, 1735, *Tabitha Miller*, dau. of Joseph and Rebecca (Johnson) M., she b. Jan. 21, 1709–10; d. Jan. 3, 1774; 2d, June 12, 1775, *Martha Gilbert*, who d. Dec. 26, 1789, æ. 71. Children:

By *Tabitha:*
14.   i. HANNAH, b. Midd., Jan. 23, 1735–6; d. Apr. 1, 1736.
15. ii. HANNAH, b. Midd., Sep. 12, 1737; m. Feb. 9, 1764, *Collins Samuel Roberts*, his 2d wife, and perhaps had William, who d. young.
16. iii. ELISHA, b. Midd., July 20, 1739; d. June 12, 1761.
17. iv. REBECCA, b. Midd., Aug. 6, 1742; m. Dec. 16, 1765, *Samuel Caner* (? *Carrier*.)
18.   v. HULDAH, b. Midd., Aug. 6, 1742, *gem.;* d. Aug. 31, 1743.
19. vi. HULDAH, b. Midd., July 31, 1744; m. Nov. 19, 1767, *Oliver Hubbard;* children, HUBBARD: [1.] Huldah, bap. Nov. 13, 1768; d. Aug. 20, 1776. [2.] Enoch, bap. Mar. 18, 1770. [3.] Oliver, bap. Sep. 20, 1778; d. Sep. 9, 1782.
20.*vii. NATHAN, b. Midd., Mar. 10, 1746.
21. viii. MARY, b. Midd., Feb. 3, 1747–8; m. Apr. 9, 1775, *John Colton*, 3d; children, COLTON: [1.] Mary, b. Oct. 30, 1776; d. Jan. 20, 1777. [2.] John, b. Mar. 2, 1778. [3.] George, b. Aug. 25, 1780; d. Sep. 8, 1780.
22.   ix. AARON, b. Midd., Sep. 15, 1749.
23.* x. ELIAS, b. Midd., Apr. 16, 1751.

6.

MATTHEW SAYRE[4] [*Nathan*[3], *Dan'l*[2], *Thos.*[1]], d. Feb. 25, 1796, æ. 79; rem. to Bashan, in East Haddam, Ct.; m.

Mar. 13, 1746, *Martha Warner*, dau. of Dan'l W., who d. Jan. 1, 1770, æ. 80. He built a grist-mill, and afterward settled near the landing, where he had a grist-mill and cloth-works; was a cloth dresser. Children :

24.   i. Mary, b. July 5, 1747.
25. ii. Elizabeth, b. Feb. 12, 1748–9; d. Mar. 10, 1756.
26. iii. Lucy, b. Oct. 5, [1] 1752; d. Sep. 15, 1829; m. Nov. 21, 1776, *John Wright* of Colchester, Ct., son of Timo. and Mehitabel (Brainard) W., he b. May 27, 1745; d. June 6, 1826 in 82 yr.; children, Wright: [1.] Lucy, b. Sep. 4, 1777; d. Mar. 22, 1803. [2.] Timothy, b. Nov. 18, 1779; d. Apr. 3, 1846. [3.] Ann S., b. Feb. 15, 1782; d. Sep. 14, 1814. [4.] John, b. Nov. 25, 1783; d. Chicago, Ill., Sep. 20, 1840. [5.] Amasa, b. Jan. 6, 1787; d. Apr. 30, 1861; m. Nancy Curtis, she b. Jan. 16, 1796; and had, i. Lucy Ann, d. Feb., 1816. ii. Lucy Ann, b. Nov. 25, 1816; d. Apr. 20, 1843; m. Rollin Sanford of Brooklyn, N.Y. Of this family is Mrs. Carolyn Foster, wife of Henry F. F., of 145 Montague street, Brooklyn, N. Y.
27. iv. Matthew, b. Nov. 25, 1754; d. May 8, 1777; was one of the largest land-owners in East Haddam; a dau., Asenath, m. Wm. Gelston.
28.   v. Elizabeth, b. Oct. 27, 1757.
29. vi. Jennie, b. July 11, 1760.
30. vii. Annie, b. Mar. 10, 1763.
31. viii. Martha, b. Oct. 13, 1765.

9.

STEPHEN SAYRE[4] [*Nathan[3], Dan'l[2], Thos.[1]*], b. Middletown, Ct., Feb. 29, 1724–5; m. July 10, 1766, *Mary Chapman* of E. Haddam, Ct. They lived on the old homestead which extended on the Connecticut river from Maromas to Higganum. Children:

32.   i. Mary, b. July 13, 1767; m. Oct. 7, 1788, *Elias Hubbard*, and rem. to Springfield, Mass.; children, Hubbard: [1.] Elias. [2.] Stephen. [3.] Mary.
33.* ii. Stephen, b. Dec. 11, 1768.
34. iii. Dolly, bap. June 6, 1773; m. Nov. 24, 1788, *John Wright;* children, Wright: [1.] John Sears, bap. June 14, 1789. [2.] Harvey. [3.] Henry. [4.] Susanna. [5.] Edward. All bap. Sep. 7, 1800.
35. iv. Esther, bap. July 12, 1776; m. Aug. 31, 1794, *Thos. Spencer* of Haddam, and rem. to Suffield, Ct.

10.

JOHN SAYRE[4] [*Nathan*[3], *Dan'l*[2], *Thos.*[1]], b. Middletown, Ct., Oct. 4, 1726; d. May 26, 1817; m. Dec. 14, 1770, *Lydia Hubbard*, who d. Jan. 3, 1823, æ. 87. (Was he the John Sears who m. Apr. 5, 1753, Elizabeth Freeman, widow of Sam'l F.?) Children:

36. i. LYDIA, b. Feb. 17, 1773.
37. ii. SUSANNAH, b. Aug. 11, 1775; m. *James Thomas.*
38. iii. LYDIA, b. Feb. 29, 1778.
39.* iv. JOHN, b. Aug. 31, 1781.

11.

CHARLES SAYRE[4] [*Nathan*[3], *Dan'l*[2], *Thos.*[1]], b. Middletown, Ct., Feb. 8, 1729-30; rem. to Haddam, Ct. Children:
40. i. SARAH, m. *Nath'l Brooks.*
41. ii. LUCRETIA, m. *David Brooks.*
42. iii. DANIEL.
43. iv. CHARLES.

20.

NATHAN SAYRE[5] or *Sears* [*Elisha*[4], *Nathan*[3], *Dan'l*[2], *Thos.*[1]], b. Middletown, Ct., Mar. 10, 1746; m. Nov. 29, 1772, *Rachel Clark*, dau. of Aaron and Mary (White) C., of Chatham, Ct., she b. Jan. 9, 1750-1; d. Aug. 4, 1789; 2d, Mar. 18, 1790, *Diana Roberts*, dau. of Hinkman and Anna (Wickham) R., she b. Dec. 1, 1761; 3d, Mrs. *Elizabeth Redfield*, dau. of Jona. and Mary (Latham) Pratt, and widow of Peleg R. of Midd.; and rem. to Trumbull, Ohio, before 1808. Children: By *Rachel;*
44. i. SALLY, b. June 27, 1774; d. Sep. 17, 1861; m. Feb. 7, 1796, *Asa Hubbard*, son of Geo. and Mary (Stocking) H., he b. Jan. 13, 1769; d. Jan. 26, 1837; children, HUBBARD: [1.] Hannah Clark, b. May 20, 1797. [2.] Asa, b. May 10, 1800. [3.] Mehitabel Brown, b. Mar. 25, 1803. [4.] Elisha Sears, b. Apr. 13, 1805. [5.] Sally, b. Apr. 4, 1807. [6.] Charles, b. Feb. 5, 1809. [7.] Jacob, b. Feb. 18, 1811. [8.] George Stocking, b. Mar. 21, 1813. [9.] Mary, b. Mar. 21, 1813, *gem.* [10.] Lucy M., b. July 28, 1817.

45.* ii. DANIEL, b. Jan. 27, 1777.
46.* iii. AARON CLARK, b. July 27, 1779.
47. iv. POLLY, bap. June 23, 1783; m. *Sam'l Paddock, Jr.*, of Meriden, Ct.
48.* v. ELISHA, b. Jan. 24, 1784; bap. Aug. 21, 1785.
49. vi. ? NANCY, m. *John Sabin.*
50. vii. ANNA WHITE, bap. June 24, 1787.
By *Diana:*
51. viii. RACHEL, b. Dec. 22, 1792; d. Oct. 5, 1874, æ. 82; m. Dec. 20, 1807, Judge *Joseph Harris* of Randolph, Ohio, he b. Midd., Ct., Feb. 9, 1782; d. Lodi, Ohio, Oct. 2, 1863; children, HARRIS: [1.] Albert, b. Randolph, Sep. 20, 1808; m. Lodi, Feb. 18, 1830, Adaline De Witt, she b. Westminster, Vt., Sep. 15, 1805; d. Lodi, Feb. 21, 1872. [2.] Elvira, b. Lodi, Apr. 25, 1819; m. there, Jan. 1, 1839, Henry Ainsworth, he b. Cape Vincent, N. Y., Sep. 14, 1812; had, i. Henry Harris, b. Ruggles, Ohio, Feb. 13, 1843; d. Sep. 8, 1843.
52. ix. WILLIAM, m. *Margaret Stanley.*
53. x. (?)NATHAN.
54. xi. SAMUEL C., m. *Leodicea Leach.*
55. xii. CHARLES, m. *E'liza Leach.*
56. xiii. ELIAS, m. —— *Cutler.*
57. xiv. HANNAH, m. *Alpheus Dickinson.*

23.

ELIAS SEARS[5] [*Elisha[4], Nathan[3], Dan'l[2], Thos.[1]*], b. Middletown, Ct., Apr. 16, 1751; d. Sep. 18, 1829; m. Dec. 16, 1777, *Patience King*, she b. Sep. 15, 1753; d. May 20, 1784; 2d, May 31, 1790, *Lucy Gilbert*, dau. of Eleazar and Martha (Johnson) G., she b. Oct. 1, 1746; d. Dec. 29, 1833. Children:

58. i. HANNAH, b. Sep. 15, 1779; d. Sep. 18, 1866; m. Oct. 24, 1798, *Elijah Paddock*, son of Seth and Phebe (Johnson) P., he b. Apr. 28, 1779; d. Sep. 2, 1858; children, PADDOCK: [1.] Lucy, b. Aug. 2, 1799. [2.] Nancy, b. Jan. 13, 1801. [3.] Elias, b. Sep. 10, 1803. [4.] Elijah Johnson, b. Sep. 4, 1809. [5.] Hannah Maria, b. Sep. 19, 1812.
59. ii. HULDAH, b. July 16, 1781; d. Dec. 11, 1782.

33.

STEPHEN SEARS⁵ [*Steph.*⁴, *Nathan*³, *Dan'l*², *Thos.*¹], b. Dec. 11, 1768; d. Nov. 16, 1807; m. *Phebe Knowles*, who d. Mar., 1807, æ. 32.   Children:

60.   i. DOROTHY, m. *Jas. Smith;* children, SMITH: [1.] Irving. [2.] Edwin. [3.] Stephen; lives in San Fran. [4.] Frances, m. Sam'l J. Hubbard of Maromas, Ct.
61.* ii. JAMES, b. Apr. 1, 1795.
62. iii. CLARISSA, b. Mar. 23, 1797; m. Mar. 22, 1813, *Elias Selden*, son of Elias and Ruth (Kirby) S., he b. Nov. 4, 1791; d. ; she lives at Rock Landing, Haddam Neck, Ct.; children, SELDEN: [1.] Lavator Kirby, b. Oct. 1, 1815. [2.] James Sears, b. Mar. 30, 1818.   [3.] Esther Louisa, b. Feb. 24, 1824. [4.] Clarissa Serena, b. July 27, 1826. [5.] Joseph Ellis, b. July 21, 1832.
63.* iv. ELISHA, b. Jan. 26, 1801.
64. v. STEPHEN, d. æ. 8.

39.

JOHN SAYRE⁵ [*John*⁴, *Nathan*³, *Dan'l*², *Thos.*¹], b. Aug. 31, 1781; d. Oct. 19, 1820; m. *Polly McNary*.   Children:
65. i. JOHN.
66. ii. MARGARET MARIA, m. *Wm. Tooley* of Haddam, Ct.
67. iii. LUCY ANN, m. *Julius Scovil* of Maromas, Ct.

45.

DANIEL SEARS⁶ [*Nathan*⁵, *Elisha*⁴, *Nathan*³, *Dan'l*², *Thos.*¹], b. Middletown, Ct., Jan. 27, 1772; d. Port Leyden, N. Y., Nov. 7, 1836, æ. 64; m. Midd., Dec. 8, 1796, *Betsy Thomas*, she b. Haddam, Ct., May 23, 1768; d. 1857, æ. 84.(?) Children :
68.* i. DANIEL THOMAS, b. Midd., May 23, 1797.
69.* ii. ELIPHALET CLARK, b. Midd., Feb. 20, 1799.
70.* iii. EZRA, b. Midd., Feb. 25, 1801.
71.* iv. NELSON, b. Midd., Oct. 23, 1802.
72.* v. CHAUNCY, b. Midd., Oct. 23, 1802, *gem.*
73.* vi. ELISHA, b. Midd., Jan. 11, 1805.
74.* vii. ELIAS, b. Nov. 2, 1807.

75. viii. JULIA, b. Port Leyden, N. Y., Jan. 2, 1809; m. Leyden, N. Y., *Jona. Douglass;* children, DOUGLASS:
[1.] Alvin. [2.] Ansel. [3.] Huldah. [4.] Lewis.
[5.] Walter.
76. ix. BETSEY, b. Midd., Jan. 27, 1811; m. Leyden, *Walter
Higley;* children, HIGLEY: [1.] Martin. [2.] Ann.
[3.] Marion.
77.* x. SAMUEL PADDOCK, b. Midd., Feb. 17, 1815.
78. xi. TIMOTHY RANNEY, b. Midd., Feb. 12, 1817.

46.

AARON CLARK SEARS[6] [*Nathan[5], Elisha[4], Nathan[3],
Dan'l[2], Thos.[1]*], b. Middletown, Ct., July 23, 1779; d. Aug.
14, 1828, æ. 49; m. June 30, 1803, *Huldah Tryon*, dau. of
Caleb and Lydia (Hubbard) T., she b. June 5, 1780; d. Oct.
14, 1854, æ. 74; before leaving Connecticut he was a seaman,
and removed, in 1834, to Ohio, settling in Trumbull (?Coits-
ville.) Child:
79.* i. ALFRED CLARK, b. Ct., Mar. 12, 1804.

48.

ELISHA SEARS[6] [*Nathan[5], Elisha[4], Nathan[3], Dan'l[2],
Thos.[1]*], b. Middletown, Ct., Jan. 24, 1784; d. Jan. 25, 1856;
m. Hudson, Ohio, June 15, 1809, *Aurilla Oviatt*, she b. Apr.
3, 1794; d. Mar. 5, 1855. He was drafted in War of 1812,
but sent a substitute. Children:
80.* i. CHAUNCY M., b. Randolph, Ohio, Aug. 27, 1810.
81.* ii. MARVIN O., b. Randolph, June 18, 1813.
82. iii. LUCY ANN, b. Randolph, Oct. 16, 1818; m. *Jason
Moreland*, and lives in Wadesburg, Mo.
83.* iv. NATHAN CLARK, b. Randolph, Sep. 26, 1822.
84. v. BETSY M., b. Randolph, Sep. 26, 1822, *gemini;* m.
Zophar A. Davis, and d. Aug. 21, 1852.
85. vi. HANNAH LOUISA, b. Randolph, Jan. 18, 1824; m. *Sol.
Glass*, and lives in Randolph.

61.

JAMES SEARS[6] [*Steph.[5], Steph.[4], Nathan[3], Dan'l[2], Thos.[1]*],
b. Haddam, Ct., Apr. 1, 1795; d. Brooklyn Village, O., æ.
85; m. Medina, Ohio, Aug. 18, 1823, *Catherine Phelps*, she

b. Feb. 7, 1807; was living in 1886. He removed to Cleveland, Ohio, then called Ohio City, and kept a general store corner of Pearl street and Franklin avenue. After his marriage he built next his store, and lived there five years; the house is still standing, but moved down the hill a little. He then bought near the Public square in Cleveland and manufactured cloth, and kept the first clothing store in Northern Ohio. In March, 1835, he bought 135 acres of land 3 miles from Cleveland, at $10 per acre, the present value being $1,000 per acre. There he built, and a portion of the house remains; he cleared over 100 acres of his land. In June, 1834, he became a member of the Congregational Church of Brooklyn Village, and was chosen Deacon. He always did his duty toward supporting the church, and died a good Christian.

When the new church was built, his profile in stone was placed over the church entrance. Children:

86.* i. SAMUEL, b. Cleveland, O., Oct. 16, 1826.
87. ii. MARY, m. *Joseph Brainard* of Newburgh, O.
88. iii. CLARA, m. *Dan'l Hoyt* of Lindel, O.
89. iv. HATTIE, m. *Chas. Prouty* of Kent, O.
    And six daughters who died in infancy.

63.

ELISHA SEARS[6] [*Steph.[5], Steph.[4], Nathan[3], Dan'l[2], Thos.[1]*], b. Jan. 26, 1801; d. Apr. 29, 1877; m. Nov. 28, 1822, *Esther Southmayd Hendley*, dau. of Henry and Esther H., she b. Aug. 4, 18—. Children:

90. i. JOSEPH BADGER, b. Aug. 16, 1823; lives in Middletown, Ct.
91. ii. ANN ELIZA, b. Oct. 7, 1825; m. *Eben'r Arnold.*
92. iii. DANIEL WHITMAN, b. Aug. 23, 1827; lives in Midd., Ct.
93. iv. HARRIET ESTHER, b. Apr. 15, 1830; m. *John Townsend* of New Haven.
94. v. WILLIAM HENDLEY, b. Apr. 12, 1833; lives in New Haven, Ct.
95. vi. HENRY HENDLEY, b. July 29, 1835; removed to Galveston, Texas.
96. vii. STEPHEN EDGAR, b. Oct. 29, 1838; d. Nov. 7, 1844.

97. viii. Jane Delancy, b. Jan. 12, 1842; m. *H. H. Boardman.*
98. ix. Ellen Maria, b. Mar. 15, 1844; m. Sep. 13, 1866,
George S. Lewis, Jr., of Springfield, Mass.
99. x. Mary Hendley, b. Sep. 5, 1846; m. *Edwin F. Hubbard.*

68.

DANIEL THOMAS SEARS[7] [*Dan'l[6], Nathan[5], Elisha[4],
Nathan[3], Dan'l[2], Thos.[1]*], b. Middletown, Ct., May 23, 1797;
m. Denmark, N. Y., *Abigail Purinton.* Children:
100.* i. Daniel.
101. ii. Ezra.
102. iii. Miranda.
103. iv. Eliza, m. *Harrison Smith.*
104. v. Harriet, m. *Hiram Hemstreet.*
105. vi. Jane, m. *Wm. Viles.*
106. vii. Clarence.

69.

ELIPHALET CLARK SEARS[7] [*Dan'l[6], Nathan[5], Elisha[4],
Nathan[3], Dan'l[2], Thos.[1]*], b. Middletown, Ct., Feb. 20, 1799;
d. 1876, æ. 77; m. Leyden, N. Y., *Sarah J. Talcott.* Children:
107. i. Elmira.
108. ii. Henrietta, m. *George Sweet.*
109. iii. Lois.
110. iv. Sarah, m. *Henry Alger.*
111. v. Emma.

70.

EZRA SEARS[7] [*Dan'l[6], Nathan[5], Elisha[4], Nathan[3],
Dan'l[2], Thos.[1]*], b. Middletown, Ct., Feb. 25, 1801; m. *Belinda* ——. Children:
112. i. Sarah.
113. ii. Harriet.

71.

NELSON SEARS[7] [*Dan'l[6], Nathan[5], Elisha[4], Nathan[3],
Dan'l[2], Thos.[1]*], b. Middletown, Ct., Oct. 23, 1802; d. 1883,
æ. 80; m. there, Jan. 17, 1828, *Lucy Roberts.* Children:
114.* i. Robert.
115. ii. Angeline, m. *Benj. Brickley.*

116. iii. JULIA.
117. iv. HARRIS.
118. v. ELLEN.
119. vi. HORACE.

72.

CHAUNCY SEARS[7] [*Dan'l*[6], *Nathan*[5], *Elisha*[4], *Nathan*[3], *Dan'l*[2], *Thos.*[1]], b. Middletown, Ct., Oct. 23, 1802; d. Oct. 26, 1881, æ. 79; m. Bennington, Vt., *Emily Hollister*. Children:
120.   i. FLORINDA, b. Woodford, Vt., Apr. 6, 1825.
121.   ii. EMMA LOUISE, b. Woodford, Sep. 10, 1826; m. *Rich. Woodrow*, and d. Clarksburg, N. J., July, 1857, æ. 31.
122. iii. FRANCES, b. Woodford, July 22, 1828.
123.* iv. CHARLES MAY, b. Port Leyden, N. Y., Nov. 26, 1829.
124.   v. ADALINE, b. Port Leyden, Aug. 2, 1831.
125. vi. CHAUNCY EDWARD, b. Port Leyden, Apr. 27, 1833; m. Columbus, Ohio, June 7, 1873, *Polly Ann Smith*, she b. Van Buren, N. Y., Nov. 13, 1826. Of firm C. E. Sears & Co., canners, Chillicothe, Ohio.
126. vii. JULIA LOUISE, b. Port Leyden, Sep. 7, 1835; m. *Sam'l Sherman Ray*, had [1.] Edward. [2.] Franklin.
127. viii. ELIZABETH ANN, b. Port Leyden, Aug. 31, 1837.

73.

ELISHA SEARS[7] [*Dan'l*[6], *Nathan*[5], *Elisha*[4], *Nathan*[3], *Dan'l*[2], *Thos.*[1]], b. Middletown, Ct., Jan. 11, 1805; m. Leyden, N. Y., *Theodosia Talcott*. Children:
128.   i. LOIS.
129.   ii. MARY A., m. *Lewis Rodes*.
130. iii. FRANCES.
131. iv. RUCELIA.
132.   v. MILTON A.
133. vi. MARY A.

74.

ELIAS SEARS[7] [*Dan'l*[6], *Nathan*[5], *Elisha*[4], *Nathan*[3], *Dan'l*[2], *Thos.*[1]], b. Middletown, Ct., Nov. 2, 1807; m. Rome, N. Y., *Polly* ——. Children:
135.* i. GEORGE.
136.* ii. ELIPHALET.
137. iii. LOIS, m. *Benj. Parmenter*.
138.* iv. EDGAR.

77.

Rev. SAMUEL PADDOCK SEARS[7] [*Dan'l[6], Nathan[5], Elisha[4], Nathan[3], Dan'l[2], Thos.[1]*], b. Leyden, N. Y., Feb. 17, 1815; m. Russia, N. Y., 1838, *Rosetta Andrews,* she b. there, 1813; lives in Lowville, N. Y.   Children:

139.* i.   SAMUEL A., b. Russia, N. Y., Oct. 3, 1839.
140.   ii.   ROSETTA M., b. Russia, Aug. 17, 1841; d. 1862, æ. 21; m. Montague, 1861, *Benj. F. Freeman,* he b. Adams, N. Y.
141.* iii.   NELSON B., b. Russia, Apr. 24, 1843.
142.   iv.   JULIA E., b. Russia, Apr. 19, 1845; lives in Lowville, N. Y.
143.   v.   LAURA A., b. Russia, Aug. 10, 1847; m. Lowville, 1881, *John R. Lewis,* he b. Lyonsdale, N. Y., 1845; lives in Lowville, and has Emma and Emmett.
144.   vi.   NATHAN W., b. Montague, N. Y., June 11, 1851; d. 1853.

79.

ALFRED CLARK SEARS[7] [*Aaron[6], Nathan[5], Elisha[4], Nathan[3], Dan'l[2], Thos.[1]*], b. Ct., Mar. 12, 1804; d. May 9, 1877, æ. 73; m. Apr. 5, 1827, *Emily Harris,* she b. Apr. 25, 1803; d. June 28, 1876, æ. 73; he was a farmer, and in 1834 moved to Ohio with his mother and family and bought a farm in Coitsville, Mahoning co.   P. O. address, New Bedford, Penn. Children:

144. *a.** i.   AARON CLARK, b. Ct., Jan. 21, 1829.
144. *a.* ii.   EMILY ANN, b. Ct., Aug. 20, 1830; d. Feb. 13, 1875, m. *Robt. Black;* 2d, *John Green;* by her 1st husband she had 4 children, two of whom are living and have families; by 2d, she had 2 children.
144. *a.* iii.   MARY ELLEN, b. Ct., Apr. 5, 1833; m. *Amos Hudson* of Hubbard, Ohio.
144. *a.* iv.   JULIA MARIA, b. Coitsville, Ohio, Sep. 7, 1835; d. Dec. 15, 1860, æ. 25.
144. *a.**v.   DAVID SELDEN, b. Coitsville, July 27, 1837.

80.

CHAUNCY M. SEARS[7] [*Elisha[6], Nathan[5], Elisha[4], Nathan[3], Dan'l[2], Thos.[1]*], b. Aug. 27, 1810; d. Aug. 27, 1883; m. Sep. 19, 1838, *Magdalene Gorby.*   Children:
145.   i.   *Son,* killed in U. S. Army.

146. ii. *Son*, lives in Missouri.
147.* iii. David H., b. Portage, Ohio, Mar. 19, 1848.
   And 2 daus.

81.

MARVIN OVIATT SEARS[7] [*Elisha*[6], *Nathan*[5], *Elisha*[4], *Nathan*[3], *Dan'l*[2], *Thos.*[1]], b. June 18, 1813; m. Hudson, Ohio, Nov. 21, 1833, *Mary Ann Bishop*, she b. there, Oct. 15, 1814; d. Charlestown, Ohio, Sep. 13, 1884. Children :

148. i. Martha Jane, b. Twinsburg, O., Nov. 3, 1834; m. Randolph, O., Apr. 6, 1856, *Leman Brockett*, he b. there, Nov. 25, 1830; d. Apr. 16, 1865; 2d, Charlestown, O., Aug. 15, 1868, *Howard Collins* of C.
149. ii. Clarissa Aurilla, b. Twinsburg, July 15, 1837; m. Charles., May 16, 1865, *David Collins*, he b. there, May 16, 1833.
150. iii. William Henry, b. Brimfield, O., Dec. 24, 1840; m. Charles., Dec. 20, 1869, *Sophia Porter*, she b. Deerfield. He enlisted in U. S. Army on first call for 75,000 men, and was sent home sick; enlisted in Battery A, Light Art'y, for 3 years; was taken prisoner at battle of Stone River; was 4 months in prison pens; then sent to Annapolis on parole and exchanged, and was discharged at end of war, disabled.
151. iv. Francis Sobieska, b. Stow, O., May 16, 1849 ; m. Ravenna, O., *Maria Cope* of R., and lives in Willoughby, Ohio.

83.

NATHAN CLARK SEARS[7] [*Elisha*[6], *Nathan*[5], *Elisha*[4], *Nathan*[3], *Dan'l*[2], *Thos.*[1]], b. Aug. 25, 1822; d. Aug. 22, 1882; m. Randolph, O., Apr. 16, 1845, *Jane E. Siminson*, she b. New Garden, O., Mar. 29, 1826. Children :

152. i. Ginevra L., b. Randolph, O., Dec. 28, 1847; m. there, Feb. 16, 1867, *Jas. M. B. Carothers*, he b. Frankfort Springs, Pa., July 18, 1834 ; lives in Brooklyn, O.
153. ii. Ella, b. Randolph, Aug. 25, 1852 ; d. Dec. 11, 1852.
154.* iii. Howard E., b. Randolph, Jan. 6, 1856.

86.

SAMUEL SEARS[7] [*Jas.*[6], *Steph.*[5], *Steph.*[4], *Nathan*[3], *Dan'l*[2], *Thos.*[1]], b. Cleveland, O., Oct. 16, 1826; m. Brooklyn, O.,

Dec. 18, 1855, *Ellen S. Pelton*, she b. Portland, Ct., Mar. 13, 1831.   Children :

155. i. PAMELIA, b. Jan. 21, 1858.
156. ii. ROSAMOND M., b. Nov. 21, 1859 ; m. Apr. 17, 1878, *Paul Fitzstrimer*, he b. Cleveland, O., Jan. 17, 1853.
157. iii. FRED. W., b. Dec. 27, 1863.

100.

DANIEL SEARS[8] [*Dan'l⁷, Dan'l⁶, Nathan⁵, Elisha⁴, Nathan³, Dan'l², Thos.¹*], m. *Sarah C——*.   Children :

158. i. ELIZABETH.
159. ii. EUGENE.

114.

ROBERT SEARS[8] [*Nelson⁷, Dan'l⁶, Nathan⁵, Elisha⁴, Nathan³, Dan'l², Thos.¹*], m. *Elsie ——*.   Children :

160. i. LEON N.
161. ii. BENJAMIN B.
162. iii. MANLY F.
163. iv. HOWARD M.

123.

CHARLES MAY SEARS[8] [*Chauncy⁷, Dan'l⁶, Nathan⁵, Elisha⁴, Nathan³, Dan'l², Thos.¹*], b. Port Leyden, N. Y., Nov. 26, 1829 ; m. Lebanon Springs, N. Y., Apr. 4, 1854, *Mary Ann Smith*, she b. Catskill, N. Y., May 14, 1835.   Children :

164.   i. EMMA LOUISE, b. Phila., Pa., Mar. 8, 1855 ; m. Mar. 13, 1879, *Francis M. Nichols*, and has Ada, May and Anna.
165.   ii. WILLIAM HENRY, b. Shellsburg, Iowa, Mar. 7, 1858; m. June 25, 1884, *Alice Hubbard Peabody*.
166.   iii. LEWIS ALONZO, b. Lawrence, Kans., Aug. 15, 1860 ; m. Mar. 26, 1884, *Eleonora Taber*.
167.   iv. GEORGE FRANCIS, b. Eudora, Kans., June 10, 1863 ; d. May 2, 1865.
168.   v. CLARENCE HOWDER, b. Eudora, July 26, 1865.
169.   vi. WALTER JAMES, b. Eudora, July 10, 1869.
170.   vii. EUGENE ALFRED, b. Eudora, July 10, 1869, *gemini ;* d. same day.
171. viii. ALVIN FLORENCE, b. Eudora, Dec. 24, 1870 ; d. Oct. 31, 1871·
172.   ix. LORIN BEECHER, b. Eudora, Mar. 10, 1872.

135.

GEORGE SEARS[8] [*Elias*[7], *Dan'l*[6], *Nathan*[5], *Elisha*[4], *Nathan*[3], *Dan'l*[2], *Thos.*[1]], m. *Arminda* ——. Children:

173. i. ELMER.
174. ii. CHARLES.

136.

ELIPHALET SEARS[8] [*Elias*[7], *Dan'l*[6], *Nathan*[5], *Elisha*[4], *Nathan*[3], *Dan'l*[2], *Thos.*[1]], m. *Sarah* ——. Children:

175. i. EMMA.
176. ii. NETTIE.

138.

EDGAR SEARS[8] [*Elias*[7], *Dan'l*[6], *Nathan*[5], *Elisha*[4], *Nathan*[3], *Dan'l*[2], *Thos.*[1]], m. *Esther* ——. Children:

177. i. ALFORD.
178. ii. CHARLES.
179. iii. EGBERT.
180. iv. GEORGE.

139.

SAMUEL A. SEARS[8] [*Sam'l*[7], *Dan'l*[6], *Nathan*[5], *Elisha*[4], *Nathan*[3], *Dan'l*[2], *Thos.*[1]], b. Russia, N. Y., Oct. 3, 1839; m. Montague, N. Y., 1867, *Sarah Fairman*, she b. 1848; d. 1882, æ. 34. Children:

181. i. BERTON A.
182. ii. WILFORD A.
183. iii. JOHN A.
184. iv. HERMAN C.
185. v. IDA.
186. vi. GEORGE E.

141.

NELSON B. SEARS[8] [*Sam'l*[7], *Dan'l*[6], *Nathan*[5], *Elisha*[4], *Nathan*[3], *Dan'l*[2], *Thos.*[1]], b. Russia, N. Y., Apr. 24, 1843; m. Montague, N. Y., 1869, *Elizabeth Moffatt*, she b. Dexter, N. Y.; live in Montague. Children:

187. i. JENNA.
188. ii. LEONA.

144. a. i.

AARON CLARK SEARS[8] [*Alfred*[7], *Aaron*[6], *Nathan*[5], *Elisha*[4], *Nathan*[3], *Dan'l*[2], *Thos.*[1]], b. Ct., (perhaps Middle-

81

town or Haddam,) Jan. 21, 1829; m. Mar. 2, 1870, *Eliza Margaret Frew* of Lawrence co., Pa.; he is a farmer in Coitsville, Ohio; address, New Bedford, Pa.   Children:

188. *a.*   i. JOHN CALVIN, b. Dec. 22, 1870.
188. *a.*   ii. ELIZABETH JANE, b. Aug. 9, 1873.
188. *a.*   iii. SILAS CLARK, b. Jan. 16, 1877.

144. a. v.

DAVID SELDEN SEARS[8] [*Alfred*[7], *Aaron*[6], *Nathan*[5], *Elisha*[4], *Nathan*[3], *Dan'l*[2], *Thos.*[1]], b. Coitsville, Ohio, July 27, 1837; m. *Mary Eliot* of Pittsburgh, Pa., and is a farmer in C.; address, New Bedford, Pa.   Children :

188. *b.*   i. FRANCIS.
188. *b.*   ii. HENRY.
188. *b.*   iii. NELLIE.

147.

DAVID H. SEARS[8] [*Chauncy*[7], *Elisha*[6], *Nathan*[5], *Elisha*[4], *Nathan*[3], *Dan'l*[2], *Thos.*[1]], b. Portage, Ohio, Mar. 19, 1848; m. Oct. 19, 1869, *Amanda Shook;* is a grain dealer in Marion, Ohio.   Children :

189.   i. NELLIE, b. Aug. 27, 1871.
190.   ii. ETHEL, b. May 1, 1876; d. Feb. 2, 1885.
191.   iii. GLADYS, b. Dec. 2, 1886.

154.

HOWARD E. SEARS[8] [*Nathan*[7], *Elisha*[6], *Nathan*[5], *Elisha*[4], *Nathan*[3], *Dan'l*[2], *Thos.*[1]], b. Randolph, Ohio, Jan. 6, 1856; m. there, June 25, 1884, *Nettie M. Redfield*, she b. there, Sep. 29, 1860; lives in Akron, Ohio.   Child :

192.   i. PAUL HOWARD, b. Akron, Ohio, May 23, 1885.

MARTIN SEARS[2], son of MOSES SEARS[1] of Ashford, Ct.   Children :

i. PHILANDER.
ii. JABEZ, m. Vernon, Ct., Oct. 17, 1832, *Reuby Freeman*, dau. of Azariah and Clarissa (Thompson) F., she b. Mansfield, Ct., July 16, 1812; d. Oct. 23, 1848.

iii. HOMER or HIRAM.
iv. HANNAH.
v. MARGARET.
vi. MARTHA.

PHILIP SEARS, d. in hospital N. Y. city. Children:
i. SARAH A., m. —— *Glove*, and lives in N. Y. city.
ii. WILLIAM.
iii. GEORGE.
iv. ALONZO.
v. JANE.
vi. MARY.

EDMUND SEARS[2], son of ISAAC SEARS[1] of Mass.; m. Great Valley, N. Y., ab't 1834, *Ellen Whitehead*, and lived in Salamanca, N. Y. Child: .
3.* i. JAMES H., b. Gt. Vall., Nov. 16, 1840.

3.

JAMES H. SEARS[3] [*Edm'd*[2], *Isaac*[1]], b. Great Valley, N. Y., Nov. 16, 1840; m. Dec. 24, 1863, *Colin Gillis*, and lives in Decatur, Ill. Children:
  4. i. MINNIE E., b. Cochranton, Pa., Mar. 1, 1865; m. Decatur, Ill., Sep. 17, 1884, *Jas. B. King*, and has 1 child.
  5. ii. MAGGIE MAUDE, b. Randolph, N. Y., Dec. 30, 1866.
  6. iii. KITTIE MARY, b. Randolph, Dec. 30, 1866, *gemini*.

1.

BENJAMIN SEARS[1] of Maryland. Children:
2.* i. RICHARD B., b. Calvert co., Md., 1835.
3. ii. MARGARET E., m. 1875, *Geo. W. Robinson* of Washington, D. C.

2.

RICHARD B. SEARS[2] [*Benj.*[1]], b. Calvert co., Md., 1835; m. 1859, *A. P. Harmer;* enlisted in Marine Corps, 1864; served 4 years, and d. 1883. Children:

4. i. JOSEPH C., b. Calvert co., Md., 1861.
5. ii. HATTIE M., b. Calvert co., 1863.
6. iii. SUSAN, b. Prince George's co., Md., 1865.
7. iv. LULIE W., b. Prince George's co., 1873.
8. v. CHARLES W., b. Prince George's co., 1875.
9. vi. EMELINE, b. Prince George's co., 1876.

1.

—— SEARS[1], lived at Culpepper C. H., Va.; "went out hunting one Sunday morning when the children were small, and never returned." His widow m. 2d, —— *Scribner;* 3d, —— *McAfee.* Children:

2. i. POLLY, m. —— *Scribner*, son of her mother's 2d husband.
3. ii. WILLIAM.
4.* iii. JOHN.

4.

JOHN SEARS[2] [——[1]], b. Culpepper C. H., Va.; m. Somerset, Ohio, *Elizabeth Elder*, and d. 1862. Children:

5.* i. HENRY, b. Somerset, O., June 7, 1828.
6. ii. JOHN, b. Somerset, June 21, 1830; m. *Anna Mahoney.*
7. iii. ELIZABETH, b. Somerset, Aug. 3, 1835; m. *Chas. Swineheart.*
8. iv. SAMUEL, b. 1842; d.
9. v. HIRAM, m. *Nora Liddy*, and lives in Cincinnati, O.
10. vi. SARAH, m. *Dan'l Kelly.*

5.

HENRY SEARS[3] [*John*[2], ——[1]], b. Somerset, Ohio, June 7, 1828; m. Lancaster, O., Apr. 12, 1853, *Elizabeth Mooney* and lives in L. Children:

11. i. JAMES H., b. Lancaster, O., Mar. 12, 1854.
12. ii. MARY E., b. Lancaster, Feb. 22, 1856.

13. iii. WILLIAM T., b. Lancaster, Aug. 2, 1859.
14. iv. CHARLES E., b. Lancaster, Sep. 12, 1861.
15. v. GEORGE F., b. Lancaster, Nov. 1, 1864.

1.

WILLIAM SEARS[1], m. Old Warder, Beds., Eng., *Sarah Watts*. Children :

2.   i. JOSEPH, m. *Eliz'h Cutter*.
3.   ii. WILLIAM.
4.   iii. SAMUEL.
5.   iv. GEORGE.
6.   v. DAVID.
7.   vi. ROBERT.
8.   vii. MARY.
9.* viii. JOHN, b. Southell, Beds., Eng., Sep. 2, 1824.

9.

JOHN SEARS[2] [*Wm.*[1]], b. Southell, Beds., Eng., Oct. 13, 1822; m. Northell, Beds., Eng., Dec. 26, 1842, *Sarah Magstaff*, she b. Caldecott, Beds., Sep. 2, 1824. He is a prominent Mormon, styled Captain, and Supt. Zion's Co-operative Mercantile Institution, Salt Lake City, Utah. Children :

10.   i. SEPTIMUS W., b. Caldecott, Beds., Eng., Mar. 8, 1844.
11.   ii. ISAAC, b. Caldecott, Dec. 2, 1845.
12.   iii. NATHAN, b. Caldecott, Aug. 17, 1851.
13.   iv. MARIA ANN, b. Caldecott, Jan. 23, 1854; m. —— *Liddle*.
14.   v. HEBE JOHN, b. Kimbolton, Hants, Eng., Sep. 13, 1861.
15.   vi. ANNA E., b. Santy, Hants, Dec. 22, 1863.
16.   vii. JOHN JOSEPH, b. Pleasant Grove, Utah, Feb. 8, 1869.

1.

JOHN SEARS[1], from N. Y. State, settled in Southern Ohio, near the line of Hamilton and Clermont cos., supposed about 1800. Children :

   i. JOHN.
   ii. BENJAMIN.
   iii. GIDEON, gr.-father of Mrs. P. A. Hall of Goshen, Ohio.

1.

ADAM SEARS[1] of Ohio, m. —— ——.   Children :
2.   i. RILEY.
3.* ii. JEDIDIAH.

3.

JEDIDIAH SEARS[2] [*Adam*[1]], a farmer ; m. *Rachel Hopley* in Ohio, and was killed in Union Army, at Winchester, Va.   Children :
4.   i. MARGARET JANE, b. Delaware co., Ohio, and d. æ. 16.
5. ii. GEORGE WASHINGTON, b. Delaware co., June 22, 1857 ; m. Marion co., O., 1875, *Melissa Ellen Keeler*, she b. Union co., O., May, 1854 ; he is a farmer in Royal Center, Ind., and has 5 children.
6. iii. JAMES PHILO, d. æ. 4 years.
7. iv. CHARLES WESLEY.

———

JOHN SEARS of Bedminster, N. J., m. Dec. 25, 1799, *Margaret Taylor* of Morristown, N. J.

MOSES SEARS, a communicant in 1st Presb. Ch., Morristown, N. J., Aug. 18, 1808, was dismissed Nov. 2, 1825, to Succasunna.   Children :
  i. KEZIA, b. Apr. 27, 1799. ⎫
 ii. MOSES, b. Mar. 1, 1801.   ⎪
iii. OLIVER, b. Dec. 23, 1803. ⎬ bap. Mar. 24, 1809.
 iv. JOSEPH, b. Sep. 4, 1805.   ⎪
  v. BENJAMIN, b. Dec. 18, 1807. ⎭
 vi. MARGARET ELIZABETH, b. Nov. 12, 1810; bap. Jan. 9, 1811.

INDEX.

All of the name of SEARS by birth or marriage, are indexed under their Christian names; all who married Sears, and all other persons, are indexed by their surnames.

Where a name occurs more than once upon a page it is indexed once only.

SEARS.

INDEX II.

OTHER FAMILIES AND PERSONS.

Lightning Source UK Ltd.
Milton Keynes UK
UKHW010241070119
334855UK00011B/1912/P